THE AMERICAN GI IN EUROPE IN WORLD WAR II

THE AMERICAN GI IN EUROPE IN WORLD WAR II

D-DAY: STORMING ASHORE

J. E. KAUFMANN
AND H. W. KAUFMANN

STACKPOLE
BOOKS

INTRODUCTION

The second volume—*D-Day: Storming Ashore*—of this three-volume series on the American GI in Europe in World War II covers the preparations for Operation Overlord and the landings in Normandy on June 6, 1944. The preceding volume provides the background for the United States' entry into the war, the training of the troops, and their shipment to Europe; it also details the North African and Mediterranean campaigns through the first half of 1944. The third and final volume continues with operations in Normandy after D-Day, the Brittany campaign, and the invasion of southern France.

The objective of this work is not to compile a history of individual units of the American armed forces or to thoroughly examine the campaigns in which they took part during the war in Europe, but rather to present the reader with a perspective of the war from the point of view of those who participated. We included only enough historical information to provide a backdrop for the veterans' accounts. We thought it would be of value for the reader to follow some of these American soldiers from the time of their induction and training to their participation in the invasions of Normandy and the French Riviera during the summer of 1944. We also believe it is important to shine the spotlight not only on combat veterans, but also on the men who made it all possible by operating the rear echelons and supporting the men in the front lines.

This book presents a very small sampling of the experiences of American veterans in World War II and makes no claim of being a comprehensive compendium of the war. The reader will notice that sometimes the veterans' accounts contradict not only one another, but also the chronicled versions of the events. These contradictions should come as no surprise since each veteran had his own perspective of events and because the soldiers' memories were distorted either by conditions on the battlefield or by the passage of time. It must also be pointed out that some of the veterans might have been in a position to see what others never did. It must be remembered, too, that there are as many sides to a story as there are witnesses. This does not mean that any of the witnesses intentionally lied or distorted their accounts, but it does demonstrate the difficulty—if not the impossibility—of coming up with an exact and true picture of any historical event from every point of view. This is a problem faced by most historians. It must be hoped, however, that the more witnesses and accounts there are, the greater the chance of achieving accuracy. It is our hope that the veterans' accounts in these volumes will enrich the body of data concerning these momentous events in world history.

The complete introduction, found in the first volume, includes a brief discussion of some of the problems we encountered while we interviewed the veterans decades after the fact. This work is dedicated to all those who contributed their accounts and to their comrades-in-arms.

CHAPTER 1

Amphibious Exercises

Invasion Exercises Duck, Fox, and Beaver

Six thousand inhabitants of eight villages on the southern coast of England around Slapton Sands were evacuated so the area could be used for training, according to Alfred Beck et al. in *Corps of Engineers*. This coastal region was selected because of its scarce population and resemblance to Normandy. The Duck exercises in the area were mainly for the 29th Division, the first division to perform a large-scale practice-landing operation in England. The first was divided into two phases and began on December 27, 1943, continuing through January 1944. The others took place in February.

After the exercise, on January 7, 1944, Col. James H. Hagan, the chief of staff for the 29th Division, submitted a memorandum titled "Comments on Exercise Duck" to the assistant chief of staff, G-3. His report pointed out the deficiencies in transportation and wire communications in the staging area, communications between the chief of staff and the assault elements, traffic control (MPs were needed in the invasion area), and a few other support problems. Lt. Col. Norman C. Atwood, the assistant chief of staff, G-2, of 29th Division, submitted another report to General Gerhardt, titled "Comments, Exercise Duck," in which he expressed his concern about security.

Apparently, the troops were stunned to hear the details of the exercise broadcast over the BBC and described in *Stars and Stripes*. Atwood suggested that instead of canceling leaves and passes before an operation and closing camps a day prior to movement, which alerted the civilian population to the move, it would be better to make several alerts prior to the actual operation. This would prevent German agents from signaling that the real invasion was about to begin. In addition, the troops had to be instructed in convoy discipline during an alert, and a greater number of MPs were required to guard the bivouac area.[1] Finally, Atwood pointed out, light security at night and radio security needed improvement.

Allowing the Germans to have some information about these exercises was an advantage rather than a problem, because it kept them in a state of uncertainty. Since they did not have effective agents in England, they could never be sure whether the troop movements on the coast were the harbinger of an actual attack or a mere training exercise.

In a memorandum dated January 10, 1944, the assistant division commander, Brig. Gen. Norman Cota, advised the assistant chief of staff, G-3, that the flamethrower should be removed from the assault team whose equipment should be reduced. These suggestions were ignored, however. Cota also suggested allowing more time—about thirty minutes—between assault waves because "obstacles cannot be breached by wishful thinking."

In another memorandum, submitted on January 11, 1944, and titled "Notes on Exercise Duck," Col. R. Henriques of Combined Operations Headquarters observed that the exercise did not represent a feasible "Operation of War." Such an operation, he advised, should be undertaken either under cover of darkness or with overwhelming fire support. He also pointed out that tanks with, or even preceding, the leading infantry were essential. The hills that rose steeply from the beaches would have to be "drenched" with air and naval bombardment, rockets, and anything that could be used until the leading infantry got through the wire. Cota also had misgivings about the hedgerows, which he felt could be of great defensive value for the enemy. Henriques believed that a single beach exit, as used in the exercise, would not be enough to allow the troops to get off the beaches. In light of later events on Omaha Beach, it seems that Cota's observations had not received the attention they deserved, or the Allied troops would not have been hung up on Omaha Beach and in the hedgerows of Normandy.

In his memorandum, Cota also made some positive points. During Duck, he had been impressed by the use of the D-8 bulldozer, which Colonel Caffey, commander of the 1st Engineer Special Battalion (ESB), used to create a gap through the steel scaffolding that formed Element C, the "Belgian Gates," by pushing and pulling. As for the 175th Infantry, which had taken part in this phase of Duck, he wrote, "It was most refreshing to see the enthusiasm and keenness with which everyone went ashore—soaking wet—under the make-believe conditions of the Exercise." The unit was "a keen, well-disciplined and well-trained body of troops."

The 116th Infantry, 29th Division, which eventually led the assault for the division on Omaha Beach, took part in Duck II in early February. Not long after these 29ers stormed ashore, more reports came out. Capt. Richard B. Thrift from the Office of the Inspector General of the 29th Division sent his comments to the G-3. He pointed out, too, the lack of adequate fire support and said the smoke had delayed the assault waves. In a detailed report that covered the landing in detail, 1st Lt. T. D. Neal also noted the inadequacy

1. By the time of the assembly for the invasion, the 5th Armored Division was performing mostly MP duty to make up for the lack of such personnel needed to keep the invasion troops isolated.

of naval fire support. In addition, he wrote, there was a problem with getting the air force involved in the action, and communication was poor. In many ways, Duck II was a repeat of Duck I. Other problems also surfaced. Capt. James Porter Jr., with the Planning Group, reported difficulties in unloading towed 105-millimeter guns from LCTs (landing craft, tank) and smoke once again obscured observation.

A final report from the director pointed out the problems caused by the smoke and suggested that careful consideration be given to artillery carried in amphibious trucks called DUKWs (pronounced "ducks"). The chief umpire noted problems with communications and unsatisfactory arrangements for collecting casualties. Nonetheless, both reports proclaimed the overall success of the operation, commended the performance of the airborne units, and censured the 116th Infantry for failing to coordinate operations with the paratroopers properly. The Reconnaissance Troop was lauded for landing a platoon in rubber boats and scaling the cliffs with ropes north of White Beach even though its radio failed to work and it was unable to report back.

The supporting naval gunfire had come from a cruiser, two destroyers, three landing craft armed with 4.7-inch guns, and two LCRs (landing craft, rocket). The fire from two 105-millimeter howitzers on LCTs and the smoke screen were judged to be 80 percent effective. The chief umpire also noted some minor problems in panel identification for liaison aircraft and reported that the tanks that had participated in the exercise, though effective, had been hindered again by the smoke.

The Duck series of exercises was followed by Exercise Fox in March 1944, the most important rehearsal for the 29th Division. The 116th Infantry and 16th Infantry 1st Division, and the supporting 5th and 6th ESBs also joined in.[2] On March 13, 1944, after the exercise was completed, Maj. Clarence L. Benjamin, 743rd Tank Battalion, submitted a report to the 116th Infantry's commanding officer (CO), whose regiment his tank battalion was slated to support in Normandy. Major Benjamin pointed out that more detailed planning was needed if tanks were to be involved in the upcoming operation. Among other things, Benjamin advised against keeping tanks in the water any longer than necessary, because the waterproofing was effective for only about seven minutes. In addition, prolonged submersion could lead to carbon monoxide poisoning of the crews. During Fox, two men had been nearly overcome by the fumes while in their partially submerged tank in hull defilade with the engine running. The crews of two other tanks had also detected exhaust fumes inside their vehicles. While engaged in the exercise, the tanks had been in the water for about two hours before they traveled 4.4 miles, consuming about eighty gallons of gasoline each. Major Benjamin deduced from this that provisions for supplying the tanks with fuel and ammunition had to be made as early as possible. The 743rd Tank Battalion would be equipped with Sherman DD (duplex drive) tanks, which were to "swim" in on D-Day.

In a long report submitted on March 13, Maj. Thornton Mullins, CO of the 111th Field Artillery Battalion, listed the problems that had cropped up during the exercise. On the second day, the several-hour absence of buckets in the latrines caused quite a mess in the staging area. More important, Mullins's battalion experienced serious difficulties getting ashore. Because of poor communications, the three firing batteries carried in DUKWs and LSTs (landing ships, tank) did not come ashore for hours. When the battalion finally landed, the men had trouble getting the howitzers out of some of vessels. Major Mullins

2. The 1st ESB no longer took part because it was slated to land with the 4th Division on Utah Beach.

concluded that DUKWs were less effective than LCTs at transporting artillery to an invasion beach.

Major Putnam, the 29th Division quartermaster who observed the unloading procedure, noted that that ship-to-shore communication was unsatisfactory, and the drivers needed more training, except those of the 116th Infantry who were well trained. He also strongly advised the swift unloading of vessels on a rising tide.

In a report to General Gerhardt dated March 13, 1944, General Cota summarized the problems Fox had laid bare. The difficulties involving loads on landing craft and communications remained unresolved, but a way of reducing the threat from potential enemy air raids after the troops embarked for the real invasion had finally been worked out: The troops would not board their vessels until the last moment before departure time. Many of the soldiers prone to seasickness were thankful for this decision on June 5 when the invasion was delayed, but it is doubtful that they ever realized why the loading schedules had been altered since their rehearsals.

Capt. J. Elmore Swenson of the 29th Division's artillery, who was in charge of preparing a performance critique of the Ninth Air Force, also exposed many problems in coordination and communication. The medium bombers were not allowed to drop below 8,500 feet, and as in a previous exercise, the ceiling was too low for effective bombing. Swenson concluded that the problems stemmed mainly from a lack of time for coordination and stated that Army Air Forces (AAF) personnel were taking the necessary corrective measures. The 29th Division had about two months left to work out its problems before the invasion.

The 16th Infantry, 1st Division, also took part in Exercise Fox, but many of its veterans showed little enthusiasm. In a report sent to the regimental commanding officer, Lt. Col. Charles T. Horner Jr., CO of the 3rd Battalion, attributed his men's lackluster performance in part to the fact that the services of supply (SOS) failed to handle the movement of troops properly. The troops had boarded their trucks at 3 A.M. for a trip of only twenty miles but had to wait until 7 A.M. before the LCVPs (landing craft, vehicle, personnel) were available. It was another hour and a half before the first troops even reached the APA. When the grumbling veterans boarded the ships, the surprised crews had been unaware of their scheduled arrival and had made no arrangements for quartering them. It was not until about 10:30 P.M. that the troops received blankets. In addition, complained Lieutenant Colonel Horner, no one had properly planned the messing arrangements. Only the distribution of sandwiches and coffee before embarkation had gone smoothly. There had been too few men to feed the troops, and some of the soldiers had had to go through the mess line twice to get a complete meal.

To add insult to injury, the 16th Infantry faced even greater problems. In a post–D-Day report dated June 30, 1944, in which he also evaluated Exercise Fox and other operations, Maj. Carl W. Plitt, S-3 of the 16th Infantry, wrote that on February 23, the commander of the 16th Infantry and his S-3 had not had the time to participate in the planning for Fox because they been ordered to the headquarters of the 1st Division at Blandford to study the Overlord plan. The supporting 5th ESB, which was a "green" outfit, still experienced difficulties in planning and carrying out operations efficiently. Since the plans for Operation Overlord were already in the final stages of completion, the lessons from Fox would not apply.

After Fox ended in early March, the newly arrived 4th Division and battle-hardened 1st ESB took part in a series of exercises known as Exercise Beaver in late March 1944. The operation was a rehearsal for the actual landing, securing of causeways, and moving on Cherbourg. The 101st Airborne (A/B) Division jumped from the backs of trucks at 4 A.M. on March 29 to secure its

The following training exercises took place in preparation for the cross-Channel invasion. These exercises were conducted in southern England–Slapton Sands for the Americans and farther east for the Commonwealth forces. This information is compiled from Clifford Jones's *The Administrative and Logistical History of the ETO*, Albert Norman's *Operation Overlord*, and David Chandler and James Collins's *D-Day Encyclopedia*.*

Preinvasion Amphibious Maneuvers

Date	Exercise	Units	Notes
October 1943	Pirate	Canadian 7th Inf Brigade	
January 3–4, 1944	Duck I	175th Inf (29th Div), 1st ESB, 741st Tank Bn	10,200 men, 1,100 vehicles. Commo and traffic problems—need for MPs ashore. G-3 (29th Div) reported operation as well executed.
February 13–15	Duck II	116th Inf (29th Div), 1st ESB, paratroop units	First use of Rhino ferry. L-4 liaison aircraft. Naval fire support from a cruiser, destroyers, and landing craft with rockets, 4.7-inch guns. LCTs with tanks and artillery aboard firing support. Insufficient fire support and no air support.
February 29	Duck III	115th Inf (29th Div), 1st ESB, tank and tank destroyer units	First practice with tanks and tank destroyer units. Same problems as Duck II.
(?)	Savvy	Canadian 8th Inf Brigade	
March 9–10	Fox	37th Eng (Cmbt) Battalion, 5th ESB, 16th Inf (1st Div), 149th Eng Beach Group (6th ESB), 116th Inf (29th Div), 743rd Tank Bn, Ninth AF	17,000 men. Experimenting with other uses for DUKWs and various methods of waterproofing. Gen. Norman D. Cota, assistant division commander of the 29th Division, observed that there were problems in loading, the transport quartermasters needed more training, and the coordination among naval beach battalions, army shore brigade, and force commanders was not satisfactory. He pointed out that all plans that were not simple and flexible failed. DUKWs were determined not to be an effective means of landing artillery. Problems with air support.
March 13–26	Beaver I–VI	Engineer Detachments (1st ESB), 4th Division Battalion landing teams	See table on next page.
March 27–30	Beaver VII	8th and 22nd Inf (4th Div), 1st ESB, 1106th Eng Grp, 502nd PIR, Ninth AF	Simulated A/B drops. Use of 5th Division as relief force for A/B. Confused operation.
April	Tiger	4th Division, 1st ESB, A/B divisions	25,000 men, 2,750 vehicles, DD tanks. DD used for first time, and only two gave effective support. German E-boat attack.
April 1	Fabius I	1st Division, Naval Assault Force O (Omaha Beach)	25,000 men.
May	Fabius II	British 50th Division, Naval Assault Force G (Gold Beach)	
May	Fabius III	Canadian 3rd Division, Naval Assault Force J (Juno Beach)	
May	Fabius IV	British 3rd Division, Naval Assault Force S (Sword Beach)	
May	Fabius V	Staff familiarization	

Note: This is not a complete listing of all the minor units that took part. The British also conducted an exercise called Harlequin in 1943 in the Dover area, and the Canadians performed Spartan before Pirate.

* For complete bibliographical references, see *The American GI in Europe in World War II: The Battle in France.*

Other Exercises

Dates	Exercise	Units	Notes
December 5, 1943	Excelsior I	1st and 29th Division Artillery	Artillery planning Exercises.
December 19	Excelsior II	1st and 29th Division Artillery	Artillery planning Exercises.
January 5–9, 1944	Excelsior III	1st and 29th Division Artillery	Artillery planning Exercises.
January, 19–23	Excelsior IV	1st and 29th Division Artillery	Artillery planning Exercises.
February 2–6	Excelsior V	1st and 29th Division Artillery	Artillery planning Exercises.
February 16–20	Excelsior VI	1st and 29th Division Artillery	Artillery planning Exercises.
February 25– March 1	Chevrolet	5th ESB	Port Talbot and Port Eynon area. Training of troops & supply staffs for loading and CWS* troops in screening harbors & beaches with smoke.
February 27–29	Snipe	1st ESB	A loading and engineering exercise.
March 5–31	Jeep	XV Corps and Northern Ireland Base Section 38th Inf (2nd Division)	Northern Ireland corps troop exercise. Marshaling and embarking.
March 13–23,	Muskrat I (Beaver I)	12th Inf (4th Division)	Firth of Clyde, Scotland
March 24–26,	Muskrat II (Beaver II)	12th Inf , 1st ESB	Battalion-level operations.
March 15–18	Otter I (Beaver III)	3rd Bn, 8th Inf (4th Division)	Slapton Sands.
March 19–22	Otter II (Beaver IV)	1st Bn, 8th Inf (4th Division)	Slapton Sands.
March 15–18	Mink I (Beaver V)	1st Bn, 22nd Inf (4th Division)	Slapton Sands.
March 15–18	Gull	1st ESB	Loading and landing men and vehicles from LSTs.
March 19–22	Mink II (Beaver VI)	2nd Bn, 22nd Inf (4th Division)	Slapton Sands.
March 19–20	Crimson II	Artillery, AA and Tank Destroyers of V Corps	Merrival Range (Slapton Sands).
April	Jalopy	10th Inf and 121st Inf	Northern Ireland. Marshaling and embarking exercise like Jeep.
April 19–30	Boomerang	Ninth Air Force rehearsal, XVIII District of Southern Base Section, 1317th Eng General Service Regt.	5,000 ground troops set up installations on "hostile" shore.
April 28	Cellophane	Service of Supply	Orwigh Bay. Demonstrating of skid loading techniques and off loading for coasters, LCIs and DUKWs and beach transfer to dumps.
April 27–May 6	Curveball I & II	82nd A/B Division	101st A/B Div conducted smaller exercises at same time.
May 11	Eagle	82nd & 101st A/B Divisions, IX Troop Carrier Command, with 28th Division acting as enemy	Hungerford-Newbury area. Parachute and glider landings.
May 14–18	Hawk I & II	VIII Corps Artillery	Sennybridge Range (S.Wales)

The 1st, 5th, and 6th Engineer Special Battalions (ESBs) had numerous similar exercises. In addition to these exercises, others took place. Crackshot (February 19–25) and Splint (April 12) were medical exercises involving processing the wounded in Southern England, and casualty evacuation at Pentewan Beach using the 2nd Naval Beach Battalion and 1st ESB medical personnel. Two Signal Corps exercises took place: Spandu (April 4) for forces under Twenty-First Army Group (U.S. First Army, British Second Army and Canadian First Army); and Pigeon (May 7–10), with 4th Division, 50th Signal Battalion, 1st ESB, 90th Division, Ninth Air Force, and 11th Amphibious Force.

objectives. The 502nd Parachute Infantry Regiment (PIR), the 377th Parachute Artillery Battalion, and Company C of the 326th Engineers moved toward their objectives. The 4th Division landed at 9 A.M. According to Rapport and Northwood's *Rendezvous with Destiny*, the 502nd PIR moved to capture a simulated coastal battery, while the 506th PIR in a command post exercise (CPX) secured the opposite flank on the south side. Like Exercise Fox, this operation used live naval bombardment. The communications problems persisted among and within army, air, and naval units.

After Exercise Beaver, the 4th Division and associated units that were to land on Utah Beach prepared for their final full-scale rehearsal in Exercise Tiger. At the same time, the 1st Division and related units prepared for their own concluding exercise, Fabius I.

Sgt. Vincent Angeloni, 2nd Battalion HQ, 8th Infantry, 4th Division, who served in the Communications Platoon and took part in several exercises from Beaver through Tiger, recalls his experiences.*

> Being in commo, we pulled a lot more CP [command post] problems. We would go into a place, like Ipachrome. One day it was pretty cold, and we got on top of this little knob and there was a hotel there. We were changing socks when this old English fellow came down and raised holy hell with us for being on his property. I thought one of our guys, Martin Landau, was going to knock him down. We didn't want to be there, and this old guy comes down and gives us a lot of trouble.
>
> We did a lot more training than the others, because it was all technical stuff. Every time we pulled a problem—each company had two runners—my job was to get these guys together and find out where their companies were. If any messages had to go, I had to make sure that one runner went and one stayed. Two guys from each company—medics, mortars, etc.—for runners.

Exercise Tiger

Exercise Tiger, like the previous practice assaults, took place on the Devon coast where much of the local population had been removed from the beach area between Blackpool and Torcross, as well as several inland towns. A problem already mentioned in one of the pre-Tiger reports was that the landing area had only one exit. The beach in this area was somewhat similar to the projected invasion beaches in Normandy, but the seawall was closer to the bluffs in France than in England. During Tiger, the engineers had to blast this wall to allow passage for the tanks. They also built a double line of concrete tetrahedrons, placed steel piles in the seabed, and added barbed wire and minefields for a more realistic exercise. As described in Nigel Lewis's *Exercise Tiger*, roadblocks covered the beach exits. Behind the beach area and farther inland were fields enclosed by hedgerows, but the English hedgerows were not as large as those in Normandy.

On the day Exercise Tiger began, the Allied supreme commander and his entourage boarded *LCI(L) 495* at six in the morning. H-Hour had been set for 7:30 A.M. Before that, at 7:15 A.M., the preliminary naval bombardment began, and the Sherman DDs prepared for launching. But then things went downhill. The landing was postponed for one hour, the air support failed to appear, and when the DDs finally waded in, one of them sank and its crew barely escaped drowning by taking to its raft. Furthermore, the LCRs launched their rockets before the landing, creating breaches in the wire obstacles. After this disastrous

* Unless otherwise noted, firsthand accounts come from interviews with veterans or their written or taped accounts.

Dragon's teeth and wire entanglements at the Assault Training Center at Ilfracombe in southwest England.

performance, British Air Marshal Arthur Tedder and Gen. Dwight D. Eisenhower decided that a heavy aerial bombardment was needed. After the landings of the first day, tragedy struck when German E-boats broke into a convoy and sank two LSTs, killing 300 to 400 men. According to *My Three Years with Eisenhower* by Harry Butcher, Eisenhower was informed that the loss of these craft had eliminated all the reserves of LSTs, which were in short supply. In addition, up to ten Bigots were not accounted for.[3] Supreme Headquarters Allied Expeditionary Force (SHAEF) was concerned about the possibility that the Germans could have fished one of these men out of the sea that night and taken him for interrogation.

The 101st A/B Division was the only airborne unit to take part in this exercise, because its 502nd and 506th PIRs were slated to land near the exits on Utah Beach. As in Exercise Beaver, no actual airdrop took place. The 501st conducted a CPX. The Ninth Air Force took part, providing tactical air support.

On April 22, 1944, the trucks loaded up at the various 4th Division camps and rolled out to the marshaling areas, where the men would become familiar with the procedure intended for Operation Overlord. As the men and their equipment moved off, Gen. Raymond O. Barton, the division commander, assembled the commanders of his division's various elements and attached units at South Brent to go over the invasion plan for Exercise Tiger. Personnel from Gen. J. Lawton Collins's VII Corps observed the activities, hoping that things would unfold correctly during this full-dress rehearsal.[4] Troops carried the same ration load, and units the same two-day supply of food that would be used in Normandy, as described by Edwin P. Hoyt in *The Invasion before Normandy*.

3. Bigot was the term used for men with top-secret clearance who were allowed to work with or see the plans for the invasion. The term was also used for men preparing earlier invasion operations.

4. Collins was a veteran of the campaign in the Pacific, leading the 25th Division on Guadalcanal and New Georgia from 1942 to 1943.

Once again, naval fire and air support for the operation used live ammunition during the landings. All types of units demonstrated their skills. The Graves Registration units simulated burials, medical units took care of make-believe casualties, and intelligence units and MPs handled prisoners of war.

The first unit of the 101st A/B was "truck-borne" on April 23 heading for Torquay. The advance details arrived Sunday evening, the main body departed at midnight, other elements boarded trains on the morning of April 24, and the last unit reached the staging area in the early evening of April 25. The glider regiment departed on April 23, and additional elements followed it to five widely dispersed embarkation areas to move by sea, making it impossible for the regimental commander to control the situation.

On April 24, the naval personnel were briefed at Plymouth. Adm. Alan G. Kirk, the commander of the Western Task Force, boarded his flagship, the heavy cruiser *Augusta*, and Adm. Don Pardee Moon, the commander of Force U of the Western Task Force, boarded the headquarters ship *Bayfield*, according to Edwin Hoyt. Units of the 4th Division boarded their assorted transports, LSTs, LCIs, and other vessels. The 327th Glider Regiment embarked at Plymouth and Dartmouth on sixteen LSTs and LCIs, with some of its companies split up onto as many as three different vessels. The 327th Regimental Communication Platoon was split up, and the antitank (AT) gun crews, except the drivers, were separated from their guns, reminiscent of problems with the North African landings. The recon platoon leader was separated from his men before boarding and was unable to find them on the ship. The massive force was not ready to go until late afternoon on April 26, about two days after the first boat was loaded. That morning, the Germans sent aircraft over Plymouth on a reconnaissance. The enemy aviators must have been surprised and concerned to behold the huge buildup.

That same day, the parachute elements of the 101st A/B Division drove from Torquay to their dispersal areas at Kingsbridge, Loddiswell, and Churchstow. At H-5 hours, about 2:30 A.M., the 101st A/B made its "drop," with its paratroopers jumping out of moving trucks, and proceeded to seize the high ground west of Slapton Sands and the crossroad at Mounts. Except for the 3rd Battalion of the 506th PIR, the men encountered no opposition in the drop zone (DZ). By 6:45 A.M., the glider echelon, assigned to fly to Normandy, began "landing" from its trucks; it completed the operation in thirty-five minutes. The amphibious phase began at 7:30. The preliminary naval fire support had begun, but the Ninth Air Force failed to show up. The landing operation was delayed an hour.

At 8 A.M., the 502nd PIR was supposed to move against the strongpoint of Merrifield and secure the beach exits at Slapton-Strete, but it failed to take the strongpoint. The 506th PIR, minus the 3rd Battalion, moved southeast on the right flank of the 502nd PIR to secure the beach exits at Slapton-Stokenham, but it too was held up. The 3rd Battalion of the 506th and Company C of the 326th Engineer Battalion moved southwest to seize the coastline between Salcombe and Thurlestone. The 501st PIR, minus its 3rd Battalion, moved northwest and seized the crossroad at Mounts and the bridges at New Bridge and Aveton Gifford on the Avon.[5] The 3rd Battalion of the 501st PIR was in division reserve and assigned to securing glider landing zones (LZs) north of Kingsbridge.

The landings were finally under way. The Sherman DD tanks of the 70th Tank Battalion and the first elements of the 4th Division and 1st ESB were ashore. The troops advanced past the beach, destroying "enemy" positions on the way.

5. Sometimes called the Lower Avon, it is not to be confused with other Avon River of Shakespeare.

At 11 A.M., however, the tanks were still waiting at Red Beach for the engineers to breach the seawall. By the time the 22nd Infantry Regiment landed, it became apparent that the soldiers were not taking the operation seriously and were lax and sloppy in executing their mission, according to Edwin Hoyt.

At 11:15 A.M., the 506th PIR accomplished its mission. At 11:39, the 502nd PIR finally took Merrifield and proceeded to secure the beach exits. At 1:50 P.M., contact between the 101st A/B and 4th Divisions was established, and in the next hour, the 502nd and 506th PIR were relieved by elements of the 4th Division.

Securing the beachhead, the first phase of the operation, was over, and now the second phase, clearing the enemy, began. The 506th PIR secured the left flank of the 4th Division while the 502nd PIR became division reserve in the vicinity of Churchstow. The 501st PIR was to take St. Ann's Chapel and carry on the attack toward Kingston. The artillery battalions of the 101st A/B Division were assembled. In the meantime, the "German" 916th Regiment, supported by tanks, launched a counterattack from the Dart River. The "German" 338th Division, also with a tank battalion, moved in the direction of Plymouth. The main objective of the landings was to secure the beach and advance across the Dartmoor moors on Okehampton, which, unknown to the troops, served as Cherbourg.

Admiral Moon's amphibious units had unloaded and waited off the beach during the first night for their return to port the next day. One large transport, twenty-one LSTs, twenty-eight LCIs, sixty-five LCTs, ninety-two landing craft, and fourteen other vessels waited for first light to depart. On the morning of April 27, a follow-up convoy, designated T-4, consisting of eight LSTs carrying mainly units of the 1st ESB, departed Plymouth. It was supposed to meet up with the destroyer HMS *Scimitar* and the corvette *Azalea*. The *Scimitar* failed to show up on the evening of April 27, however, because it had sustained some damaged in a collision with an American LCI and had returned to port. The convoy continued toward its destination with the corvette *Azalea* in the lead.

The next day, rumors began to filter among the soldiers that a German submarine had attacked the ships off the coast during the night. Some thought they had heard firing or something like thunder, but most of the men on shore never really understood what happened.

Pvt. William E. Finnigan, 4th Signal Company, 4th Division, gives the following version of the events.

> Although we didn't have any weapons training, we went on a practice assault to Slapton Sands. We left Torquay on an LST. This was the exercise where a number of GIs were lost to German torpedo boats, but I saw none of the LSTs sinking. After we returned to Tiverton, there were rumors of the event.
>
> The practice lasted about ten days. Almost nightly, Plymouth was bombed, and that was my first sight of war—searchlights, antiaircraft fire, and a German bomber that crashed a couple of fields away. We returned to Tiverton, reworked the waterproofing of the vehicles, and later near the end of May, I went to an old British camp at South Brent.

Sgt. Irving Bradbury of Company D, 1st Battalion, 8th Infantry, 4th Division, took part in a practice maneuver.

> We were bushwhacked near a town called Ilfracombe. We used to make these early-morning, before-dawn runs on the beach by engineers under live fire and go up on the moors. There was actually shelling. I believe we made two of those training trips. We were always told that whenever we left Seaton, we left it as if we were going to

France. Nobody was allowed into town or to tell anyone we were going on a maneuver.

I learned forty years later what happened with the E-boats. At the time, we were only told in a company formation back in Seaton that a German U-boat had sunk a couple of LSTs with some six-by-sixes and kitchen gear aboard, and that is all we ever heard.

We did stay on the practice landings and actually went into bivouac. We spent several days in bivouac and ran communications lines and reconnoitered the whole area after we captured those hills [during Exercise Tiger].

Pvt. Howard G. DeVoe, a 57-millimeter antitank gunner with the Defense Platoon, HQ Company, 3rd Battalion, 531st Engineer Shore Regiment of the 1st ESB, was originally drafted in June 1943 at the age of twenty-five. That December, after seventeen weeks of engineering training, he left for Britain as a replacement on the *Edmund T. Alexander* with Pvt. Sam Burns.[6] Most of his regiment arrived at Slapton Sands by truck. The brigade attempted to establish a working beachhead with the dumps and supply bases necessary to maintain the combat divisions. Crews from units of the 1st ESB handled the unloading of supplies on the beach and also operated DUKW units, some of which were on the LSTs that were sunk. That loss affected the 1st ESB's ability to adequately run the beachhead at Slapton Sands, which, according to DeVoe, earned the battalion a critical review from the corps commander, General Collins.

During Operation Tiger, I was sitting out there with half a dozen guys for three days having a good time smoking, eating K rations, shooting the breeze. Our situation was to provide the defense. We just stayed there for three days and no one came around except our platoon sergeant. Just six guys sitting out there about a mile and a half on the south flank of Slapton Sands. We saw a plane bombing Plymouth, the searchlights go on, and they got him. This plane crash happened a couple of miles away from us; the pilot was the only one not killed or injured. He bailed out, landed within a half mile of us, and he was picked up by some of the men of our unit.

As dawn broke on the second day, the troops onshore continued with their problem as if nothing had happened, and hardly anyone noticed the missing men and units. The 502nd PIR moved forward against resistance during the morning. The 501st was directed to establish contact after 11 A.M. with the 82nd A/B Division, which had made its simulated jump on D+1 at Sequers Bridge, south of Ivybridge near Ermington. The 4th Division broke up the thinly spread "German" 715th Division, and the "German" 338th and 242nd Divisions became the center of resistance. The 4th Division moved against its assigned objectives. The 501st and 502nd PIRs pushed the "enemy" back across the Erme River between 6:30 and 10 P.M. and made contact with the 82nd A/B Division at Sequers Bridge at 11 P.M.

April 30 marked the last day of the exercise. Final positions were secured, and the Ninth Air Force established a temporary base in the expanded beachhead. After that, it was time for evaluation of the exercise. In the meantime, units destined for Omaha Beach assembled for an even larger exercise called Fabius I.

Convoy T-4

What happened to Convoy T-4 became the subject of debate for decades. The total number of

6. Burns gives the date of December 27, 1943, for boarding and January 7, 1944, for arrival.

men lost is still questioned. Some of the survivors still argue about how many ships were actually hit and what units were present. The body count has fluctuated from a few hundred to a thousand men. How the burials of the victims were handled has been a long-kept secret, and some civilians claim to have witnessed clandestine mass burials. Several of the survivors have attempted to clear the record. Late in the twentieth century, the leader in this effort was Dr. Eugene Eckstam.[7] His information will be used to summarize the events.

Although the first public release of the military records did not take place until forty years after the event, news of the tragedy appeared in English newspapers the day after the incident. One of the articles was titled "Germans Claim: 3 Sunk, 1 Expected, 1 Assumed." The source of these articles was German and did not specify the types of ships sunk. The first SHAEF press release came on August 7, 1944, and gave casualties for the army and navy: "SUPREME HEADQUARTERS, Allied Expeditionary Force, Aug 7.—AP—The only effective German action against numerous invasion rehearsals was made in April when swift E-Boats sank two Allied landing craft on the British coast, killing 442 U.S. troops, it was disclosed tonight . . . the figures do not include the sailors lost."

The next day, SHAEF issued press release no.77, which listed Allied casualties since June 6, 1944. At the bottom of the statement, mention was made of the E-boat attack, which resulted in losses of 41 wounded in action, 130 killed in action, and 312 missing in action. It is apparent, therefore, that the military did not cover up the incident for decades, as was implied, but that there was some difficulty in obtaining the actual numbers because of sloppy record keeping and because one of the LSTs that went down carried all the personnel records.[8]

It turns out that two LSTs were sunk, and not three. The units came primarily from the 1st ESB. The bodies that were recovered were not placed in a mass grave. The misconception about a mass burial can be attributed to one woman who claimed she witnessed the event, other publicity seekers, and one poorly informed American media source. On January 5, 1990, Emmett N. Bailey Jr., who had served in a Graves Registration unit, sent Dr. Eckstam a list of ten other men who could attest to the fact that those men who died that night were not buried in a mass grave. His unit handled their interment.

As best as the events can be reconstructed, on the morning of April 28, six German E-boats from the 5th Flotilla and three from the 9th Flotilla departed from Cherbourg, arriving in Lyme Bay about 1 A.M. Soon after that, they launched their assault on the eight unescorted LSTs that were traveling in line. The German vessels left the area within the hour, leaving behind two sinking LSTs and a third heavily damaged. Of the German E-boats involved, all three from the 9th Flotilla inflicted the damage, one of them sinking *LST 531*, two others sinking *LST 507*, and one damaging *LST 289*. By the time a British escort reached the scene, the Germans were gone, and the convoy did not stop to pick up survivors. Many of the men on the sinking LSTs made it into the water but did not have rafts. Bobbing in the freezing waters, the survivors of the shipwreck succumbed to hypothermia as they waited for hours to be rescued. The next morning, the survivors were taken to hospitals and ordered not to reveal what had happened.

---

7. Charles MacDonald, a noted military historian who also contributed to the official histories of the U.S. Army, wrote in the 1980s that there was no coverup. British hotel owner Kenneth Small, who wrote *Forgotten Dead*, devoted much of his life to uncovering anything related to the disaster.

8. Some smaller units carried all their personnel records during these operations. The memorial in England lists 749 dead and missing, whereas Small came up with a total of 946 men.

Lt(jg). Eugene Eckstam, the medical officer on *LST 507*, described what happened in a postwar paper titled "Facts about Exercise Tiger, English Channel LST Sinking."

> On April 28, 1944, between 649 and 750 soldiers and sailor were lost during a preinvasion "practice" exercise Tiger.
>
> Five LSTs (*515,496*, *511*, *531*, and *53*) had loaded army troops and equipment at Plymouth, and three (*499*, *289*, and *507*) at Torquay and Brixham. These three LSTs joined the convoy of five LSTs as they sailed northeast past Torquay. As the single-file convoy was making a slow circle and heading almost south, the LSTs were attacked by nine German E-boats that came out of Cherbourg, France. The location was thirty miles due east of Torquay and about fifteen miles west and south of Weymouth.
>
> *LST 507* was hit by one torpedo at 0203. All had to abandon ship by 0230 because of fires and heat. *LST 507* partially floated till dawn, and then was sunk by fire from a British destroyer. About half of the approximately 500 army and navy men died. The army units were: 478th Amphibious Truck Company, 557th Quartermaster Railhead Company, 33rd Chemical Company, 1st Platoon of the 440th Engineer Company and 3891st Quartermaster Truck Company There were two ½-ton trucks, one ¾-ton truck, thirteen 2½-ton trucks, and twenty-two DUKWs.
>
> *LST 531* was hit by two torpedoes at 0218. It rolled over and, except for the bow, sank in seven minutes. After the men that were on the bow were taken off, a British destroyer sank it. About 80 percent of approximately 500 army and navy men died. The army units were 462nd Amphibious Truck Company, 3206th Quartermaster Service Company, 4th Medical Battalion, and the same mix of vehicles.
>
> *LST 289* was hit in the stern by a torpedo, killing about fifteen men. Her own small boats towed her to port. There were some nonfatal casualties on this and other ships due to crossfire by the LSTs and the E-boats.
>
> The survivors were taken to various army hospital units across Southern England for examination, and then to army and navy bases for reassignment, if able. Most of us were told not to talk about the disaster on penalty of court-martial.

Eckstam was asleep at the time of the attack. He awakened to the sound of the general quarters alarm and hurried to his battle station. His LST was the first to be hit.

> After fully dressing, as always, with helmet, foul-weather gear, and gas mask, I reported to the wardroom, which was my battle station as medical officer. The medical supplies were adequate for a small number of people being hurt onboard ship but certainly terribly inadequate for a mass type of disaster.
>
> Since all was quiet for about twenty minutes, I decided I would go topside. The passageway to the hatch on the starboard side led past captain's quarters, which I was passing by when the torpedo hit on the starboard side of the ship amidships in the auxiliary engine room. The explosion was followed rapidly by the sound of crunching metal, a painful landing on both of my knees on the steel deck, falling dust and rust—then darkness and silence—and aching knees, and wondering, "My God, what happened?"
>
> The explosion completely knocked out all electricity and power with which to

Mock-up of Belgian Gates at the Assault Training Center at Ilfracombe. Originally designed by the French and used by the Belgians primarily as antitank obstacles, they were used in large numbers in the Atlantic Wall on possible landing beaches.

fight the fire. I was able to find a lantern. Casualties started to come into the wardroom, but they were very minor. The only major casualty was one sailor with a broken thigh. He was splinted and lowered over the side into a life raft. Because of the small number of casualties and the large number of corpsmen there, I went belowdecks to make sure our casualties could be accounted for. I was stopped in my forward progress by a huge fire in the tank deck. It was necessary to close the hatches on the screaming men inside, because it was a raging inferno and none could enter or get out. One of the most difficult decisions I have ever made, and one that gave me nightmares for years—and still does—was to close the hatches leading to the tank deck. I had tried to call and go into the tank deck, but it was like a huge, roaring furnace fire. The trucks were burning, gasoline was burning, and small-arms ammunition was exploding. Worst of all were the agonizing screams for help from the army men trapped in there. I can still hear them. But knowing that there was absolutely no way anyone could help them, and that the smoke inhalation would end their miseries soon, I dogged [closed] the hatches—hatches can be opened or closed from either side.

After checking all the compartments possible, I returned to the wardroom. After only about three minutes, it was necessary to abandon ship, because the intense heat from the fire was causing our combat boots to heat up. The order was given to abandon ship, but it was really not necessary. The force of the explosion had raised the small boats on their davits, and they came down and jammed the metal bars that held them in place when the ship was under way. Only two small boats were able to get off, and those were in the bow. One of the cables stuck and had to be shot away by a soldier named Stanley Stout. Those small boats were completely filled with soldiers and sailors, few of whom ever got wet in the water.

However, on the aft part of the ship, men were swimming in the water or on life rafts. Many life rafts could not be launched because their pinions were rusted in place, and the ropes that were attached around the rafts had shrunk in the salt water and could not be unrolled for the men to hang on to the rafts. This situation probably caused a lot of additional casualties. Some of the soldiers and sailors jumped off footfirst and headfirst, some in full gear, some partially dressed. Those that dove headfirst with their inner-tube-type lifesavers left the tubes on the surface of the water and kept plunging deeper into the water, their fate unknown, but probably not good. The water was reported to be between 42 and 44 degrees Fahrenheit that day, and normally hypothermia would cause death in a half hour or so. But they were completely dressed with winter underwear, warm socks, pants, shirts, and other gear, and those that survived did so because of the insulation value of these clothes.

As I was coming down the cargo net, I inflated my life belt. There were two tubes about two inches in diameter, and the belt folded and snapped to take the slack out until needed. Squeezing two handles together punctured two CO_2 cartridges, and these inflated the two tubes. I forgot to unsnap it and loosen it and this caused a great deal of constriction around my waistline. I finally realized I must unsnap it and allow it to obtain its full diameter. The water was very cold, so I entered slowly.

As I swam quickly away from the ship to avoid the suction in case it did sink, I felt someone or something tugging on my neck, and I kept hitting something with my left arm. I had become entangled with my gas mask, which I had dangling over my shoulder. Dr. Edward G. Panter, the other physician on the LST, happened to be swimming about twenty yards to my left, and he asked what was wrong. He told me to toss it. I seemed not to want to part with it, because I had to account for it, but I did.

About 300 yards from *LST 507*, now burning with flames shooting high in the sky and lighting up the whole area, I found a life raft. When I reached the raft, there were about five or six rings of people hanging on. As the ones in front of me kept losing consciousness, I had to leave them drift off or drift with them. The last thing I remember is that I was able to get my hand around one of the ropes lining the raft. The next thing I remember is being helped up the ladder of the rescue ship. It seems I have varying memories of someone helping me out of the water onto a small boat and being very, very cold sitting on the deck of the small boat.

We were torpedoed at 0205, and we were picked up by another LST at about 0600. Somewhere in between, I was hauled out of the water. I doubt if I was on the small boat for three hours. I don't know when the captain of the rescue LST returned to pick us up. These are very vague recollections.

Once aboard ship, we were put to bed and given a blanket, and we rested up. After an hour or so, one of the pharmacist's mates awoke me, gave me a shot of whiskey and some coffee, and asked if I could help take care of the injured. Alcohol was not supposed to be carried on a navy ship, but I think every sailor on that ship had a bottle of booze.

They told me *LST 515*, which picked us up with small boats, launched at 4:30 or

4:45 in the morning. We arrived at a port, which I found out later was Portland, south of Weymouth. We passed through a red building on the square, where we were given showers and issued dry survivor clothing. We then were examined by army physicians at an army base hospital someplace, and then sent to Plymouth to a survivor camp for a month's time.

I was in a group of officers, and we didn't have to be reminded not to broadcast the disaster. We were rather noise shy at the time and billeted in Quonset huts. Repeated air raids and diving into the slit trenches at odd hours of the night helped us to recover our normal composure. In about four weeks, we were issued new uniforms and assigned to new stations.

Sgt. Stanley Stout with the 557th QM Railhead Depot Company was also on *LST 507*. The men of his company, more than 200 strong, were busy preparing the equipment and cleaning their weapons after the ship left port. According to a manuscript Stout later wrote, titled *Operation Tiger*, the mission of his unit was to help clear paths through the minefields the day after the landing.

Around midnight, most of the men had moved from the deck down into the hold to bed down and get some sleep, as we would make our run to the beachhead about five o'clock the next morning. I had bedded down in the back of a DUKW with several members of my unit and soon it was quiet.

I hadn't lain down but a short time when I felt and heard a heavy thump in the bottom or side of the ship. At first I thought we had touched bottom and were docking on the beach. Maybe five minutes later, another heavy dull "thud" was felt.

This time I got up and decided to go on deck to report. I started for the stairs that led up to the forward deck and soon arrived at the door that opened to the outside. As I opened the door, all hell broke loose—shell fire, machine-gun fire, and blue tracer shells exploding on our forward deck. The din was terrific. The men in the hold were now running up the steps to get out on deck. I had to keep them back, and then finally let them out, but crawling to keep from being slaughtered.

The men now on deck were immediately in panic, and many were dropping with hits from incoming fire. I went on deck when a tremendous explosion shook the ship. It felt like an earthquake with the deck jumping up and down. This torpedo found its mark, and fires were breaking out all over the ship. The first two thuds I had heard were actual torpedoes that hit the ship bottom and skipped under—it was confirmed later by the German naval officer in command of the attacking E-boats. The oil lines, gas tanks, fuel storage, ammunition, and explosives now all started to explode, burn, and create panic on our ship. Many men were jumping into the sea, and yet the flames were already around the ship in the water.

I looked over the entire forward deck for our officers or senior NCO, but there were none anywhere, so I checked the stairway to see if any more men were left downstairs. By now the smoke was so thick we couldn't get anyone else out from below and more men in panic went over the side into flaming water. In searching, I could find no navy officers or any of my unit officers. Next day, I learned that all five of my officers were killed.

I noticed in the crowds on the rear deck that efforts were being made to lower a lifeboat. The fires, smoke, and explosions were now growing and it was obvious that we had to abandon ship. The major fires seemed to be near the ridge or center of the ship; however, the explosions were still getting more frequent.

I saw one lifeboat being lowered full of men, but halfway down, it capsized, spilling all the men into the water, and the boat just hung there in a vertical position. It is possible that one boat was lowered safely at this time, but the next were all damaged and useless. All the gasoline tanks on the vehicles were now exploding from the heat, and thick, black smoke was billowing above the ship.

The forward deck was now getting hot, and you could feel it through your boots. Men were trying to get several of the large life rafts loose from the deck so they could get them over the side. They soon gave up because they could not get them loose from the deck.

I then went to the lifeboat left on the forward deck, and we started working to lower it into the water. In spite of the heat and exploding ammo, we were able to get it down into the water. Several navy men then threw a net over the side so the men could climb down into the boat. Many of the men now seemed confused and in shock. We guided them to the net, and they climbed down into the boat. It was certain now that it was impossible to stay with the ship.

It was obvious that the ship might blow completely apart soon, and later it did, but after filling our lifeboat with about forty men, we could not get the cables that ran from each end up to the davits loose. They appeared rusted solid and would not unhinge. The navy men worked on them also, but to no avail. I asked the navy men to get the motor going on our boat, and I would go back to the deck and see what I could do to release the cables. I then went back up the net to the deck and started working with the cables, but to no avail. Most of the men had now cleared the deck and gone overboard; however, I recognized a member of my unit lying on deck with his face badly burnt and one pant leg burned off. He was unconscious and very bloody. I grabbed him by the shoulders, pulled him to the rail, and pushed him over the side. I then took my rifle and fired three shots into each cable, and they split and fell away into the sea, thus releasing our lifeboat. I went back down the net and into the boat, and we moved away from the LST.

We stopped to pick up men for the next thirty minutes, until we had close to sixty onboard. I continued to give orders to stop and pick up men until the navy men told me we were so overloaded than any addition may capsize us.

We pulled out about a half to three-quarters of a mile from the burning LSTs and sat there. We could hear the cries of "Help" all over the sea. This was the hardest part: to watch men die and not be able to do anything to help them. It was a horrible experience to watch. Their cries gradually became weaker and you could hear the last words of dying men: "God," "Mother," and "Help" . . .

At dawn, the men on Stout's lifeboat, an LCVP, were picked up by a British ship, and a medic treated him for a gunshot wound above his right knee. He remembers passing numerous bodies floating in the water. When the men finally arrived at Weymouth, an escort of armed guards took them to a hospital under tight security.

Ens. Thomas F. Clark served aboard *LST 507* on the fateful night of April 27–28.

I had the deck watch from 4 to 8 on the evening of April 27 as we left Brixham to join up with the convoy. Somewhere

557th Quartermaster (RHD) Company

According to Stanley Stout, the 557th Quartermaster (RHD, or Railhead) Company was activated at Camp Breckenridge, Kentucky, in January 1943. Most of its personnel came from Camp Lee, Virginia, and Fort Warren, Wyoming, and completed basic training at the Quartermaster School at Fort Lee. The four officers were products of Fort Lee's Officer Candidate School (OCS) program. The company numbered 280 enlisted men, some of whom attended demolition school at Fort Campbell and specialized in mine detection and pillbox destruction.

In August 1943, the company moved to Camp Shanks and departed for England on HMS *Monarch* of Bermuda. The company set up camp at Wem, England, about fifteen miles from Shrewsbury. In January, it moved to southwest England, where it set up a tent camp on an estate near Falmouth.

When the company was assigned to the 1st ESB, which was just returning from the Mediterranean, its men were issued the prized paratrooper boots and special amphibious force shoulder patch. Training continued.

On April 26, 1944, the company traveled by truck to one of the special camps outside Brixham in preparation for embarkation. The 557th Quartermaster Company boarded *LST 507* on April 27. The next morning, many of its men, most of its equipment, and many of its records were in the English Channel as a result of the torpedo attack. The company was removed from the 1st ESB and rebuilt with replacements and survivors.

LST 507 after Exercise Tiger.

around 10:30 that night, I was asleep in my bunk when an officer came to wake me up and told me I had the night watch. I said, "No, I just came off the 4 to 8, and the question was resolved in my favor, so I didn't have to go back on watch at midnight. Somewhere around 0100 hours, I felt an enormous explosion and didn't pay much attention to it. I turned over and went back to sleep because I was still dog tired.

At 0130, we went to general quarters [GQ]. I put a pair of trousers over my pajamas, put some shoes on and a life belt, and went up to my station, which was in the super conn. The super conn was a huge platform that went up about twenty to twenty-five feet on the ship and used to see over the LCT, which was sometimes placed on the deck for transporting over long distances. At the GQ station in the super conn, protocol required that I be there with the captain and communications officer. So we had the captain on the phones, the communications officer, Ensign Beattie, on the phones, and myself, the gunnery officer. We were confused by the sounds and noises about us. We were getting radar reports about these objects, and we didn't know if they were friend or foe. However, when we went to general quarters, there had been some firing, and I recall seeing someone huddled against the deck. Not knowing who it was or what it was, I went to my station up in the conn. I still don't know what the firing was, whether it was the enemy E-boats, small craft that blundered into the area, or what. We stayed at general quarters. We were getting radar reports piped up to us; we all had our headsets on our earphones. I had the guns trained amidships because the reports of activity came all around us, and we really didn't know what was there. We had no information from anybody as to what happened.

We were hit at 2:04. The other ships had heard that loud noise and had gone to GQ and secured. So we were at GQ when we got hit. The *507* was the first ship that got hit. The captain told me, "Look for them in the loon [*sic*] of the moon." I wondered why I would look for them in the loon of the moon, since I wouldn't think they would want to be in a place that would be visible. It was quite a dark night; there was a silver ribbon on our starboard quarter coming right down the ship. It was at this silver ribbon I was looking when the torpedo hit with this fearful noise. The torpedo blast was tremendous. The super conn shook and rattled, and we were kicked and knocked around and about in it. The blast would have been about thirty feet ahead of us in the starboard auxiliary engine room, and it was a fatal blast. What it immediately did was that it ruined or incapacitated the four LCVPs that were in that area, and it broke the ship in half.

Actually, from the onset of the blast till the "abandon ship," we were two ships. We had no communication with the forward part. In layman terms, the aft third of the ship was where we were, and that was separated from the forward two-thirds of the ship. We were dazed. I remember saying to Captain Swarts, who died later, "Captain, we better get the hell out of here!" and we did. We crawled down the ladder. As we went down, the flames had already started, and there was an eerie silence. Captain Swarts went below to the bridge; Ensign Beattie went to the communications shack to try to get communications going. I, having come down off the super conn, was on the deck giving hand orders to the men in the gun turrets. By now I realized I was

LITTLE MAN, YOU'LL HAVE A BUSY DAY.

A cartoon from the June 25, 1943, issue of *Yank* magazine pokes fun at the Germans' defenses in Europe.

barefoot. The blast had blown off one of my shoes. For some reason, I determined I needed to have that shoe, so I crawled back up the ladder, scared stiff, reached up into the super conn, got hold of a shoe, and came back down. I went to put it on, and it was another shoe, the wrong shoe—I later found out it belonged to Beattie.

We made efforts to fight the fire, but we had no water. Our biggest effort was to get the four LCVPs down. We could not get those craft down, because the safety bar for heavy weather on them had ruptured and made it impossible to get any one of those davits to work. So the time we had on the ship was spent on those efforts to get them down. I couldn't fight the fire, because I was working with the gun crew. We had a couple of gun crews there, and I was yelling back and forth. Meanwhile, the flames were up very high, and we couldn't see anything. I understand that shortly after, in this time frame, the *531* went up. She was ahead of us and had a very heavy loss.

I started to get down below to find out what was going on and also because my foot was burning now because the deck was so hot. My foot was still bare. The captain said to go back and stand by and I did. A little bit later, some men started moving out of the gun tubs, but I told them to stay there. Shortly thereafter, the word came up for me to report down belowdeck and to assist Ensign Beattie and Ensign Brown in abandoning the ship.

The abandoning of the ship was very orderly. Men were fearful, but they went bravely. We did have the problem that some of the men would get frozen on the rail as we put them in the water. That is to say, they would hang down by their hands and just push out. We got them out. Sometimes we had to tap them on the nails and pray with them and say, "Sorry, you got to go, it's best for you; it is your biggest chance, you got to go." Beattie and I did that, and so did Jerry Brown. Finally it came time for us to go. We had also been assisting the soldiers with their CO_2 cartridges, blowing them up for them. I had given away my life belt and so did Brown, and I don't know if Beattie had one on. We saw to it that no one went into the water without a belt. When it finally came time for us, I wanted to go back for my wallet. I went back to my cabin. On the way, I had to get down on my knees because of the smoke. I noticed a light in the wardroom and saw the medical officers, who had not got the word, as far as I could tell, about abandoning the ship. So I told them we were abandoning ship and to get out. I proceeded now on my hands and knees to my stateroom, reached in, trying to find my wallet, and thank God, I found a Mae West, which is a large jacket that saved my life. After that, I came back out.

Beattie and I looked at each other. By this time, we had the men over the side, and there was nobody left. On the starboard side, one could walk off the ship into the water. It was going that far; it was sinking by the starboard, and the stern was rising up on the port side. The last position I saw the ship in, later from the water, it was like a huge jackknife.

In any event, Beattie and I jumped in at about the same time. I was carried away by a swell and came up; Jerry did too. Ensigns Brown and Beattie came up and said, "Tom, I see a raft; I can't hack it here, and I'm going back for it." Well, he went back. He saw a raft in the flames and somehow he got it. I didn't see any of this; I was carried away. I had determined now that I wouldn't go near any of the rafts where all the men were congregated. They were just exhausting themselves trying to get on the rafts. People were trying to help them, but the rafts were swamped. Two small boats—LCVPs that got off the forward part—could be heard in the dark, but they held all the men they could and stood off. That was all they could do; they were in danger of being swamped.

As far as my personal chronicle is concerned, I went in and out of consciousness and don't know how long I was in the water, maybe two or two and a half hours. Somewhere in the middle of this night, I awoke and heard a noise. There, out in the distance, was the raft with Ensign Beattie in it. Ensign Brown was there and Captain Swarts was there—he was to die on it a little bit later. Lieutenant Murdoch was on it, but he was out of his mind; he was dazed. Lt. Bruce Hoffmann was on the raft with some army soldiers and navy fellas. I could hear the raft, but I couldn't get to it; my legs were frozen. Somehow or another I did eventually get to the raft. I wound up trying to hold on to Lieutenant Hoffmann, who had no life belt. He was delirious and kept trying to shove off from the raft, and I lost him at the last moment. He got knocked off the raft by an army soldier, pinwheeled around underneath the water, and came up. This was just as we were being rescued. Lieutenant Hoffmann died.

Those who went into the water and had to stay in the water would experience hypothermia in the 42-degree temperature. In this state, one comes in and out of reality as one freezes. Dr. Eugene Eckstam said that none of us should have survived more than one hour. I have also found some studies done by the University of Minnesota that discuss how swift and painless hypothermia is. My thesis is that most of the men who died did not drown, but froze to death.

Ensign Clark did not see any men panicking on his side of the ship. He, Beattie, and Brown helped the men explode the cartridges in their belts and, if they were defective, blew them up by mouth. It took about twenty minutes to get the men off. Clark and the other ensigns followed fifteen minutes later. Clark remembers only two rafts coming off the aft section of the ship. To the relief of the men in the rafts, Capt. John Doyle of *LST 515* returned at 4:45 A.M. to rescue survivors when no other ship did. The British destroyer *Saladin*, which had left Plymouth to replace the convoy's escorts at about the time of the attack, spent most of the time unsuccessfully trying to chase the E-boats across the Channel.

The day prior to the E-boat attack, Pvt. John A. Perry, 462nd Amphibian Truck Company, boarded *LST 531*. "This was the first time we saw the LSTs. They were all lined up at the docks with their doors open and the ramps down. We were instructed to put twenty-two DUKWs in the bottom deck—three across and two men to a DUKW. It was *LST 531*. I drove the twenty-second DUKW in with my buddy T/5 Lawrence R. Flynt, a Texan. We had one officer with us—we were forty-four men."

Perry's LST was fourth in line as the convoy moved along Lyme Bay. Late in the evening, the column made a turn to starboard and began to circle back to Slapton Sands.

> Flynt and I were in the front seat of our DUKW when the first explosion was heard. All we saw was a ball of fire. The center of the truck deck was hit. My buddy got out the right side and called for me to get my gas mask on, because you couldn't breathe. I got my gas mask on and made it to the escape hatch. I climbed to the top side. When I got to the top deck, I was hit in the legs and thrown overboard. I can't quite describe it, but I saw my whole life flash in front of me. I prayed to God as I never prayed before. I said I was too young to die.
>
> I was popping up and down in the water when I saw another LST on fire and bodies floating all around me. Then I saw the bow of my ship sticking out of the water about ten feet. I began to try to swim to it. It was a struggle, but I made it and climbed on it. There were about six or eight other men hanging on to it also. I didn't recognize any of them. To tell the truth, I was too scared. The only sound was "Oh my God, help me!" Then we heard voices and thought this was the end. As the voices came closer, they identified themselves as British. They put the bow of their ship up close to us and took us onboard their ship. I don't remember much more about that. When I came to, I was in a hospital. I was told to immediately send word home to my folks, but not to tell them anything about what happened or that I was in the hospital. I was told I would be court-martialed if I talked to anybody about what happened.
>
> After about two weeks in the hospital and my wounds were taken care of a bit, I was put on a truck. I can't remember how long we were on the road before we pulled into a camp. After looking around, I think it was the same camp I had left from before the accident. I never did see Flynt again.

Private Perry had clung to the bow of the LST for several hours before he was rescued. After returning to his unit, he prepared for the invasion of Normandy. The remainder of his company, the 462nd, which was on *LST 511*, landed at Slapton Sands on April 28 and continued with the exercise. The next day, the men were unloading coasters off the beach.

Capt. David D. Moore, who commanded the 478th Amphibian Company, was the senior army officer on *LST 289* and responsible for all the other units onboard, including a quartermaster company of about 200 men, personnel of the 4th Division medical battalion, and other miscellaneous groups. The 1st Platoon of his com-

Troops loading onto LCVPs from a Coast Guard–manned troop transport.

pany, 2 officers and 47 men, were on *LST 507*, which meant that the remaining 170 men were with him.

For my operational plan in case of an emergency, I set up my CP [command post] in the officers' wardroom. Officers were placed fore and aft, at the top and bottom of the gangways in order to control the evacuation of troops, if such a course of action became necessary. The captain of the Quartermaster Company was assigned to one of the bottom aft gangways, and Lieutenant Damuck was assigned to the other. Lieutenant Burgess was in charge of the CP when I was not present. My enlisted men were bunked in their DUKWs, and other army personnel were in the transient quarters on each side of the tank deck. Navy quarters were in the stern section of the ship.

At about 1 A.M. on April 28, 1944, general quarters sounded and we assumed our stations. Our feeling was that this was just another dry run. However, several minutes later, there was an explosion that jarred the ship. Shortly after, Lieutenant Logan burst into the CP and stated that the LST to our stern had been hit and was on fire. At dusk, the ship to our stern was *LST 507*, and we presumed it still was.

Word was received from the bridge that the convoy was under attack and that the orders were to scatter and run for cover. Shortly, there was another explosion that jarred our LST, and word was received that another LST had been hit and exploded.

I decided that I should go to the bridge in order to minimize any delay in the execution of orders from the ship's captain, Lt. Harry Mettler. I was on the gangway leading to the bridge when our LST was hit. I was holding on to the chain on each side of the gangway and was able to hang on, landing back on my feet. I returned to the bottom of the gangway and checked the aft passages, both of which were blocked in the galley area.

One of the contingencies that I had discussed with the skipper was the possibility of taking the troops off of the LST in the DUKWs in case it became necessary to abandon ship. At this time, the ship's executive officer joined us in the COP, and informed me that the ship was without power and on fire, but not listing appreciably, and that they would undog the front and let down the ramp if I wanted to take the army troops off the LST. Before making a decision, I wanted to know our location and if there were defense craft in the area.[9]

The executive officer and I went to the chart room and scanned the radar screen, which by some miracle was still working. As best we could tell, there were only four blips, which we assumed were LSTs. In plotting our position, the executive officer could only mark where we had been at the time of the alert because of the evasive action that had been taken.

Before I had to make a decision, word was received from the skipper that the fire had been put out, and that we had regained power and would try to make port. I was requested to join the skipper on the bridge so that any needed coordinated actions could be taken as promptly as possible.

The torpedo that struck *LST 289* hit aft of the tank deck at, or close to, the waterline and had carried away the rudder, but both screws were intact and power was regained. The ship's crew quarters were destroyed, and the aft gun deck was blown to a vertical position with some debris dangling over the bridge. Naval personnel who had remained in their quarters because of illness or were stationed at the aft gun position account for most of the killed, missing, and wounded on *LST 289*. I did not keep any records of the incident, but as I recall, there were seven naval personnel killed, eight missing, and about twenty wounded, including the gunnery officer, who had both legs broken, as he had been thrown over the bridge from the force of the explosion. No [army] personnel on *LST 289* were killed, and very few received even minor wounds. The most severely injured was Lieutenant Damuck, who was on duty at the rear of the tank deck when the torpedo struck. A piece of metal was blown through the bulkhead, striking him in the groin. The captain commanding the Quartermaster Company was stationed on the opposite side of the rear of the tank deck and was thrown to the tank deck, breaking a collarbone.[10]

I would be remiss if I did not commend the 4th Division medical team for the fine job they did in locating and helping to treat the injured on *LST 289*.

Upon joining the skipper on the bridge, I observed two separate oil slicks on fire. The skipper had dropped two LCVPs off of the bow and attached them with towlines to provide steerage. The channel was smooth, the moon had set, but it was a bright, starlit night, so we guided on the North Star and limped back toward England at about five knots with a slight list to starboard.

Because of the number of naval casualties, they did not have sufficient crew to man all the remaining guns, and I was asked to furnish a crew for the forward position.

Tracers were observed on the horizon once or twice during the night. However, our first sighting of any craft was about dawn, when we met a British corvette escorting several LCTs along the coast. Shortly afterwards, a U.S. destroyer came alongside and offered to give us a tow. A line was attached but snapped. By then we were making very little headway against the tide. Some time later, a tug arrived. We were taken to Dartmouth Harbor where we docked in the early afternoon.

9. Several DUKWs were slated to mount .50-caliber machine guns, but none had received them yet.

10. He recovered in time to take part in the Normandy invasion.

> After a preliminary investigation of my company, and I presume the other units, we were ordered to an army camp in that vicinity, where we were again interrogated by the G-2s of the First Army, ETOUSA [European Theater of Operation, U.S. Army], and SHAEF. Their primary concern was whether the enemy could have taken any prisoners. We, of course, told them that there was nothing to stop the Germans taking any prisoners they wanted.

The situation for the rest of Moore's platoon on *LST 507* was much more dire. Of the forty-nine men onboard, only one officer and sixteen men survived—one reportedly without a life preserver. The officer who survived was Lt. Lawrence D. McDaniel, who, Moore recalls, had just attended a Survival School in London.

The 478th Amphibian Truck Company disembarked at Dartmouth on April 28, at 4:30 P.M. and moved to Camp Stover. Captain Moore sent Lieutenants Burgess and Logan to identify the bodies of the dead. The two officers brought back the men's personal effects. The captain collected their remaining property in the camp and had it sent to their next of kin with letters of condolence. He was not allowed to inform the families of the circumstances of their deaths, however.

Ens. Walter Treanor was on *LST 58*, behind the doomed *LST 531*. It was the first landing exercise for his ship and its green crew.

> I was underway officer of the deck during the 2000–2400 watch period. We had left Plymouth earlier on the evening of April 27. During my watch, the seas were calm and the air was extremely still and clear. It was a very bright night; all was very quiet as we steamed in very close-order single file, awaiting the dawn, when we would land on the beach. At dusk, as I recall, we were number five in the convoy, and we were towing a barge for a causeway. We were directly behind *LST 531*. When I was relieved at midnight by Lt(jg). Albert Salento, the ship's gunnery officer, he said, "Can you believe it? We were hounded by the U-boats all the way across the Atlantic, and here we are in Hitler's backyard and nothing is happening!" Given what was soon to transpire, the remembrance of our very brief conversation has never left me.
>
> I was asleep when general quarters sounded and I knew at the time it was not a drill, since the night orderly had called for a drill at dawn. As was the custom, I went to sleep fully dressed and was at my battle station in a few seconds on the stern in charge of the aft damage control party. Salento was there, having been relieved by the captain, checking the readiness of the gun crew. He and I looked aft, where the *507* had suddenly burst into flames. I do not remember today being aware of the explosion. Salento and I exchanged what must have been nervous laughs, and he said, "Buddy, we are going to lose our virginity tonight," meaning we could expect to be bloodied and salt watered in this one. He moved on to continue his check of the gun crew, and I joined the damage control crew of my command in the galley area. One of my damage control crew noted that the troops confined below were in a very strange environment for them and were unsettled and nervous. I moved toward the troop compartment passageway to appraise the situation, and several young troopers tried to push their way on deck, where they would clearly be in danger. I ordered them to return to quarters, which they did after some momentary hesitation. I never forgot how tough it must be for the troopers when the battle raged and they had to sit down below and do nothing.

> I barely returned to my battle station near the galley when a tremendous explosion lifted us out of the water. I was certain we had taken a torpedo. When I stepped out of the port-side hatch, I saw a huge sheet of bright orange flame on the bow. Believing that the forward repair party must have been killed, I ordered our group forward to undertake anticipated damage control measures. After moving ahead of the superstructure, I saw that we had not been hit; it was *LST 531*, immediately ahead of us. As we were turning to port, we could see that the *531* was a ball of tremendous fire from bow to stern, waterline to well above the main deck. It burned deep into my immediate memory that there would be few survivors. Suddenly our port batteries fired as E-boats came roaring down from the bow end. I started to prepare to launch our LCVPs for rescue operations involving the *531* but was ordered to discontinue, since all ships had been instructed to take immediate individual evasive action.
>
> I recall the orders to cast the Rhino barge adrift, doing it with reluctance as I had seen E-boats were confused by the Rhino and couldn't line up to launch torpedoes on our ship. One that barely missed our bow ended up in the stern of the *LST 289*. However, we did cast the Rhino adrift and, after sporadic firing for what seemed forever but was only a few minutes, found that we were moving towards refuge at the nearby port of Dartmouth.

Ensign Treanor went ashore the next morning on business. On his return, he ran into a British Wren (female naval personnel of the Women's Royal Naval Service, or WRNS) who had already found out about what happened in the Channel. The next day, Treanor's LST returned to Slapton Sands to continue the exercise. He has no memory of orders to keep the sinkings in the Channel secret.

Pvt. James Ousley of Hamden, Ohio, had been drafted on June 30, 1943, and was in Company B, the 261st Medical Battalion. He was seasick during the entire ten or eleven days of the trans-Atlantic crossing in January 1944. On the night of April 27–28, he was at sea again on *LST 511*.

> My buddy and I were sleeping down in the bottom of the ship that night, when a torpedo hit one of the ships close by us. It bounced me up off the floor. I had been sleeping underneath where two DUKWs came together. I ran for the door to get out of the bottom of the ship but saw the lock turn, trapping me below before I could get to the door.
>
> During this, we could hear bullets hitting the ship. At first I thought we had been hit with a torpedo. I ran for the door without my life jacket and then had to go back after it. My buddy and I then waited at the door. Finally the door was opened, and they came in and got litters to get the wounded off the deck. Everyone was scared.
>
> We had our hospital outfit onboard the ship. There were twenty-two DUKWs down in the bottom of the ship that night. On top of the ship, there were trucks, ambulances, and jeeps all marked with red crosses. This may have been what saved us from being torpedoed.
>
> The next day, I helped take off the wounded. I don't know where we were at that time, only that we were in a cove about a quarter of a mile from shore. After that, we went ahead, made our beachhead landing at Slapton Sands, and set up our hospital as planned.

Pvt. William Montgomery, a litter bearer in Company A, 4th Medical Battalion, 4th Infantry

DUKWs during maneuvers at Slapton Sands.

Division, was on one of the LSTs that came through that night unscathed.

> Gunfire broke out as we sailed during the night. A sailor ran through our compartment locking the bulkhead doors. I tried to escape by climbing up an inside ladder and through a hatch to the deck. As I poked my head up at deck level, I saw what looked like a fourteen-year-old kid in a sailor suit firing a 20-millimeter gun. At that moment, the sight on the gun was shot away. The sailor was unhurt, but I was inspired to drop below quickly.
>
> At the time, we had no idea of the extent of the tragedy. I only learned in recent years that more than 700 men were lost that April night. If I'm not mistaken, we went ahead with the landing exercise after the event.
>
> The next day, I saw one of our LSTs with its stern bent straight up in the air, like the toe of a caliph's slipper. One of our guys was later whisked away from Widworthy Court and given a medal for something he and a ward boy on one of the LSTs had done that night. We were never told what, and he was sworn to silence.

During Montgomery's night onshore, a German aircraft flew over Slapton Sands. He thought he heard the whine of a bomb falling and dived for his foxhole, missed it, and scraped his stomach crashing on the gravel of the beach. The plane, as it turned out, was shot down.

Rear Adm. Don Moon, who commanded the task force to which the T-4 Convoy belonged, sent a cable to the other units concerned, including SHAEF, ETOUSA, VII Corps, First Army, and other naval units. The message, sent at 2:08 P.M.

The 605th Graves Registration Company

Emmett Bailey Jr. was assigned to a special unit with an unenviable assignment that, in some armies, was reserved for miscreants and troublemakers. It is not clear how one received such an assignment. Bailey reported for induction to Fort Bragg on May 22, 1943, and shortly after entered active service there. With a group of other inductees, he boarded a troop train bound for Portland, Oregon. From there, they proceeded to Vancouver Barracks, Washington, where a group of officers and NCOs went through the columns of men, picking out the numbers they needed to fill their companies. Most of the recruits ended up in one of several Graves Registration companies without ever knowing how they landed the assignment. After technical training, they were sent to New York, where they boarded the *Queen Elizabeth* for their trip across the Atlantic on November 3.

Tech 5 Bailey was assigned as a platoon topographic draftsman in the 605th Graves Registration QM Company, located near Plymouth in Southern England at the time of Exercise Tiger.

> While we were there, we were training to open graves and to fill out the forms necessary. This was done using some of our own personnel. We would open graves in a cow pasture or any assigned place, use our buddies as casualties, strip them of their ID such as dog tags, and record all the details as if they were actual casualties. While we were in the process of doing this, the combat troops were holding exercises at Slapton Sands.
>
> One time we were opening some graves in the area of the 4th Infantry Division. Some of their units were walking by on a field march, and despite the fact that we had some tarpaulins to screen what we were doing, one of the men of that unit asked over the barrier what we were doing. Unfortunately, one of our personnel answered that we were digging a grave for him—a most regrettable incident. He was reprimanded severely by all of us and our officer for having made this statement. Graves Registration had no special ID for our unit, other than the ones for the unit we were assigned to, like the 1st Infantry Division. We did not go around advertising what our mission was, particularly to combat troops, because it would have been injurious to their morale.
>
> On April 28, 1944, several German torpedo boats came out of Cherbourg and attacked a troop convoy. We collected the casualties—several hundred of them—and transported them to the old World War I cemetery that was at Brookwood, England, southwest of London. They were given full military honor burials. There were contracted morticians there. They placed the deceased on embalming tables and did what was necessary. We went through the ID process and put some new clothing on them. We took them out into a cemetery and they were interred. These casualties were consolidated at the American Cemetery at Kennekridge [?].[12] To my best memory,

continued

The 605th Graves Registration Company *continued*

we did not participate in any burial of bodies other than from Exercise Tiger while we were in England. Shortly after Exercise Tiger was concluded in May 1944, some other low-level NCOs and I were transferred as cadre to form other Graves Registration units.

Emmett Bailey also gives testimony to the fact that no mass burials took place for the men who died during Exercise Tiger: "The claim that these casualties were buried in a mass grave was an insult to the integrity of our Graves Registration unit, because there was no mass burial in England."

12. There is no "Kennekridge," and it is not clear in Bailey's oral account if he is referring to Brookwood, which is one of two American cemeteries in England, along with Cambridge.

on April 29 and received at 4:05 A.M. on April 30, 1944, stated:

> Convoy of 7 United States LST's in command of Commander B. J. SCAHILL, USN, in force "U" Training exercise TIGER attacked by hostile E-boats April 280220B, 252 degrees, Portland Bill 15 miles.[11]
>
> Regret to report *LSTs 507, 531* loaded with estimated 744 Army and 282 Navy personnel sunk by torpedoes. Total known ambulatory survivors 257, litter cases 33.
>
> *LST 289* received following torpedo damage, wrecked steering gear and crew's quarters. Crack appearing amidships. 4 of crew dead, 9 missing, 18 wounded, 1 critically. 4 Army personnel wounded. *LST 289* towed to Dartmouth.
>
> *LST 511*, no damage, some Naval personnel wounded by gunfire. Number not yet reported.

The next cable, sent at 3:08 P.M. on April 30, 1944, and received at 11:15 A.M. on May 1, imparted additional information.

> Amplifying my 291408B, (see immediately preceding message) convoy T-4 was proceeding independently as a follow up convoy for exercise TIGER to arrive at SLAPTON BEACH, latitude 50 degrees 17 North longitude 3 degrees 38.5 West at 0730B, 28 April. At the time of the attack it was approximately 33 miles from this destination.
>
> Force "U" after landing 4th Division of VII Corps in assault during 27th April at nightfall, had under protection in transport area SLAPTON BEACH, 1 APA, 21 LSTs, 28 LCIs, 65 LCTs, 14 miscellaneous and 92 small landing craft or total of 221 awaiting unloading and sailing empty at daylight.

If the destroyer and corvette had both been present, it is doubtful they could have stopped the attack of nine E-boats, but they might have disrupted the attack and rescued more survivors.

Exercise Tiger revealed the same persistent problems as the earlier exercises, particularly in coordination and communication. But the victims of the E-boat attack had not suffered or died in vain. When Exercise Fabius began shortly after-

11. Commander B. J. Skahill was in charge of Convoy T-4. The attack was marked at 280220B, which means 0220 on April 28. The convoy consisted of eight, not seven, LSTs.

ward, precautions were taken on the ships to prevent the problems involving the rafts and LCVPs. In addition, steps were taken to ensure that the lifebelts were properly used to avoid unnecessary drowning. After Exercise Duck months earlier, a report dated January 9, 1944, had indicated a problem in the use of life preservers: "It was evident that no provision had been made for life preserver discipline. Several men were questioned as to the operation of their preservers but none knew. Many soldiers had managed, through curiosity or accident, to inflate their life preservers while carrying them, unaware that no more than one charge was available for inflation."

In the aftermath of Tiger, Training Memorandum No. 26, from Headquarters, U.S. First Army, dated May 10, 1944, gave proper instructions for the inflation and wearing of lifebelts, accompanying them with clear illustrations.

Exercise Fabius

Exercise Fabius was the last set of amphibious training exercises before D-Day. Only Fabius I involved American assault troops. It was the full-dress rehearsal for the landing on Omaha Beach. The 1st Division veterans still showed a lack of enthusiasm for the field exercises. On June 30, long after the actual invasion, Maj. Carl W. Plitt, S-3 for the 16th Regiment, 1st Division, described the problems in a report in which he pointed out that the exercise had come too soon after Fox. The 16th and 116th Infantry landed in the same formation as in Normandy. Security was so tight for this operation that some unit commanders were incommunicado and didn't even know the unit to which they were attached.

The Engineer Special Brigades took part in Exercise Fabius. The 6th Naval Beach Battalion, one of the numerous units that made up the 5th ESB, also participated. PhM3/C (Pharmacist's Mate 3rd Class) Vincent A. Kordack, Platoon B-6, Company B, 6th Naval Beach Battalion, recorded the events in his diary.

> April 24: After sleeping a few restless hours, we were awakened at 0405 to shoulder our gear and board the trucks. It was still dark when we arrived at Swansea, for it was only 0515 and dawn doesn't break till 0600. We had to wait for the train till 0620 and I was glad to get going for it was a misty morning and I started to get cold.
>
> After sleeping a few hours aboard train, we arrived at Dorchester. It was early afternoon, the time being 1410. We did not see anyone around the station even at this hour. But you could not expect to see many people in this part of England for everybody was north. From there, we went by truck convoy to our marshalling area. All the shelter we had here was a tent, cot, and three blankets; this was what we were expected to keep warm with. . . .
>
> May 1: After we received a few points on the beach we were to hit and studied maps of all types, they gave us the name of the town. It wasn't such a hot name, but everything over here is screwy. The name of the beach was Slapping [Slapton] Sands. The beach was composed of seashells and under this was sand, which was tough as nails to work on.
>
> We left the marshalling area at 0500 by truck convoy. We had all of our gear with us, including one litter for each corpsman. We arrived at Weymouth at 0715 and found a beautiful sight in front of us. This place would be heaven for any liberty hound for there were plenty of service girls and civilians. We had a long walk along the beach before we boarded our ship. On the journey, we were given doughnuts and coffee for a pick up.

When we arrived at the pier, they had an LCVP waiting to take us to our ship. When we arrived at the ship, they had nets for us to climb up on. It was an Army transport APA 45 and the name of the ship was USS *Henrico*. We boarded ship at 1042 and lay below.

They did not have room for thirty of us so they put us in a hold below the water line. We had one advantage though, and that was for chow for we were right below the chow hall. The chow was really delicious for it was the first Navy chow we had eaten for some time. They sold ice cream on board and that went like hot cakes since many had not tasted any for some time. It was the first for me since my arrival in the United Kingdom. All that day we did nothing but stow our gear; we left port at 2000.

May 3: This was the big day of our problem; it was supposed to be the largest scale maneuver ever to have taken place. For us it is good experience for it is the first time under actual fire. H hour was 0800 and I was topside early to see the beginning of the bombardment. They started to blast the beach at H-0730 and it lasted half an hour. It was really a sight to see, the guns working over that little piece of beach, especially the first time you see the real McCoy.

I had no worries for I did not have to go in till H+220 and by that time, most of the action would have cleared away from the beach. We finally lowered away in a Limey LCVP and started away from our ship. But as we started towards shore, we had an accident. An LCT rammed us and the aft of our craft was destroyed. At first, we all thought we would have to go swimming but Turner told the coxswain to go back. Then we transferred to another Limey craft with very little difficulty. But that did not keep us from getting wet. We saw some other craft get hit as it was hard holding the landing formation since the water was rough. Our craft tossed around as though it were a piece of driftwood.

As we kept going in and arrived at the halfway mark, the darn thing went dead. If this had been the real thing with the Germans shelling us, I'm sure we would not have come back. But, after all the misfortune that befell us, we finally hit the beach at H+4.

I threw my litter down and ducked for cover on the beach. After staying under cover for forty-five minutes, I started for the evacuation center, which I found out was in an abandoned hotel. There I remained till I dried out. While there, I saw a "casualty" argue with an umpire about whether he was dead or not. If this had been the real thing, he would probably be arguing with St. Peter and not an Army captain.

Later, I returned to the beach to pitch our pup tent. Jerry and I volunteered to take duty there. Our job was to watch the beach for anything that may turn up. This continued all day and part of the following day.

The early part of May 4, we started bivouacking back in, over the hill. Here we stayed the rest of the day and until 2200 of May 5. Then we took a truck convoy for Weymouth, which is only fifteen miles away. Then we took a train and started back for Dorchester; we arrived at 0700. After which, we took trucks back to our marshalling area. This time, we returned with our sea bags. Now we could go on liberty if we cared to do so.

The problem with the landing craft that Kordack mentioned should not have happened, because the men operating those vessels had had plenty of time to sharpen their skills in what was their only job.

Capt. Harry C. Butcher, Eisenhower's naval aide, wrote on May 1 that he expected to meet enemy opposition since the convoys would sail farther out into the Channel than during Tiger. He observed the movements of the 1st Division from the operations room of the USS *Ancon* until May 6. The exercise did not go without hitches. Enemy aircraft circled overhead, trying to observe the operation; a heavy gale blew in during the maneuvers; a minesweeper ahead of his convoy hit one of the mines the Germans had laid in the area; and German aircraft launched glider bombs at shipping in Plymouth. But no significant damage was reported, and the training was finally over.

CHAPTER 2

Ships, Tanks, and Harbors

The U.S. Navy Prepares

In 1943, the U.S. Navy opened a number of training bases and supply depots in England to prepare for the massive invasion. The majority of the facilities were located in southwest England, mainly in Cornwall and Devon, where most of the assault divisions of the U.S. First Army were posted and trained. The U.S. Navy, along with the Royal Navy, also had to use bases in Great Britain to escort troops and convoys crossing the Atlantic and en route to and from the Mediterranean, since the main U-boat bases were in western France. Between the summer of 1943 and May 1944, the navy made possible the buildup of U.S. troops in Great Britain from about 240,000 to about 1,500,000 with all their associated equipment—jeeps, aircraft, and all types of munitions. Even after the invasion, troops and materiel continued to flow across the Atlantic to sustain the war effort.

Although the U.S. Navy was responsible for the American beachheads, it also had heavy commitments in the Pacific; therefore, the British provided a number of warships to help. According to Samuel Eliot Morison in *The Invasion of France and Germany*, by the end of May 1944, Admiral Ramsay of the Royal Navy, in charge of the naval phase of Neptune/Overlord, had 229 LSTs (61 British manned), 245 LCIs (121 British manned), and 911 LCTs (664 British manned).[1] There were 481 LCMs (landing craft, mechanized), 265 of which were British. The Americans provided 1,089 LCVPs and the Royal Navy 646 LCAs for the invasion force.[2] This would be the largest assemblage of landing craft in the ETO.

For Operation Neptune, the U.S. Navy was organized as follows, according to Morison:

- Task Force 122, the Western Naval Task Force, commanded by Rear Adm. Alan G. Kirk aboard his flagship the heavy cruiser *Augusta*.
- Task Force 125, Assault Force U (Utah Beach), under Rear Adm. Don P. Moon, with his flagship attack transport *Bayfield*. This force included the following:
  - A minesweeper group, including a number of British ships
  - Two assault groups with transports and landing craft
  - An escort group with destroyers and smaller escorts
  - A bombardment group with cruisers, including Allied units, and smaller warships
  - A shore party—the 2nd Naval Beach Battalion, part of the 1st ESB—and a service group
- Task Force 124, Assault Force O (Omaha Beach), under Rear Adm. John L. Hall on his flagship, the HQ ship *Ancon*. This force included the following:
  - A minesweeper group with Allied units
  - Four assault groups
  - An escort group of cruisers and other warships
  - A close gunfire support group of specially equipped landing craft (guns, rockets, and so on)
  - A bombardment group of warships
  - A shore party—the 6th and 7th Naval Beach Battalions from the 5th and 6th ESBs—and a service group
- Task Force 126, known as Follow-Up Force B, commanded by Commodore C. D. Edgar aboard the destroyer escort *Edgar*. This force included the following:
  - Convoy B-1, B-2, B-3, and B-4
  - Mulberry A, under Capt. A. Dayton Clark
  - A salvage and fire-fighting group
  - An area screen of destroyers and escorts

In April 1944, the battleship *Nevada* and the vintage *Texas* and *Arkansas* arrived to provide big-gun fire support for the American Western Task Force of the invasion fleet. They were assigned to the bombardment groups.

The life of a sailor on sea duty varied. Some men spent most of their time in engine rooms belowdecks, rarely knowing where their ship was, while others had duties that kept them topside and remained abreast of the unfolding events. The men who served with gun crews or in the combat information and fire control centers generally had a better idea of what was going on, but they represented a minority of the crew. When a ship was in port, opportunities for contact with the outside world abounded, since many of the sailors' more mundane duties took them off their

1. Neptune was the naval phase and Overlord the ground phase of the invasion of Normandy. Often the terms are used interchangeably. The LSTs, LCIs, and LCTs were built in the United States, and some were transferred to the Royal Navy.
2. The British LCA (landing craft, assault) was slightly heavier than the American LCVP (landing craft, vehicle, personnel). Unlike the American vessel, it had armored doors behind the ramp, and its machine gunners were in the bow instead of the rear. Some British-manned landing craft, including LCAs, were used at Omaha Beach.

ships. Shore leave, which was greatly anticipated, also gave the sailors an opportunity to interact with the outside world. The men who served on smaller ships, such as tugs and landing craft, had a better grasp of the situation, even though their assignments were not considered as glamorous as serving on a warship.

Seaman 2/C Theodore Gaydos of Berwick, Pennsylvania, had joined the navy in 1944 at age seventeen. After only about six weeks of training at Sampson Naval Training Station on Seneca Lake, New York, he was assigned to a tug before he set off across the Atlantic.

> My duties aboard ship were mess cook for three months. I helped the cook in the kitchen by peeling potatoes, scrubbing pots, and serving food to the other crewmembers. For another three months, I ran the ship's laundry, where I washed all the clothes for everybody aboard. I spent three months as a deckhand working on deck chipping paint, scrubbing the deck, painting, and splicing line [rope] and cable.
>
> The worst job of all was "flaking" the chain that the anchor was tied to. As the anchor was hoisted aboard the ship, I had to go into a very small space in the bow of the ship, enter into it from the crew's quarters, and stow the chain neatly, moving it back and forth as it came in from the sea. A hoist would bring up the anchor, and the chain would come down a pipe to this chain locker (very small) and I would have to fix it. Near the end, you would lay on the deck at a manhole and work down into the hole. It was a nightmare—no light, wet, cold, and muddy. If your finger got stuck in the chain, you could lose it. It was bad duty and the seamen took turns doing it.

Larger ships needed a greater number of specialized personnel. For example, a tug had one or two radiomen, whereas a cruiser had several. In addition, larger vessels had men for the turrets, radar, and other equipment not found on most of the smaller craft. Radioman 1/C Carl Hummel served on the cruiser *Augusta*.

> Aboard the *Augusta*, we had approximately forty to forty-five radiomen. All had different jobs. We had four shifts, with each shift having about nine men. All third-class men sat on circuits to copy messages from various sources. One second-class man was the supervisor. Any incoming messages concerning us were typed and routed to the officers that were concerned. These messages were delivered to the officers by radio striker (one who was not fortunate enough to go to a school but wanted to learn radio). His duties were to sit on a circuit and try to learn. Keep the radio shack clean, keep the coffeepot going, and deliver messages. The duties of the first-class radioman were more or less to see that things ran smoothly. One repairman had to be on duty at all times. I recall one buddy that started out making coffee. I kind of took him under my wing and saw him advance to second-class supervisor before he was discharged.
>
> Now as to each man during general quarters, that was a different story. Everyone was scattered throughout the ship, and everyone had different duties. My battle station was in the plotting room. We had radiomen in Radio 1 (main communications), Radio 2, Radio 3, the chart house, navigation bridge, and radar room.
>
> As to what a radioman does in the plot room—to understand this, one must know what a shore fire control party is. Usually army personnel composed the fire control parties, four men in a party. If they made it ashore with their radio transmitters, their

duty was to contact the ship and give us a target to fire at.

Jack Hudgins and I were in the plotting room. He worked a key with fire control parties, and I worked voice with the British and American planes. The plotting room usually had two officers and half a dozen enlisted men. As I recall, the officer in charge was Lieutenant Rowan. All firing of 8-inch guns was controlled in this room. In most cases, the planes worked in pairs, one above the other to protect the plane that was doing the spotting.

Our task force was assigned to a British task force. We took on a couple of radiomen and coders from a British ship as they operated a little differently than we did. They had what they called "Tiddly characters." Instead of sending one letter at a time, they would run two or three letters together (like a word).

Anyway, they changed the name of the USS *Augusta* to the HMS *Lapwing* and changed our call sign from NIDF to something else and we took our orders from the Admiralty. The ships we joined up with in the British Fleet outnumbered us two to one so we had one big task force. We went north off the coast of Norway after the German Fleet. How many planes and ships did not come back I do not know, but I do know that the carrier *Ranger* suffered many losses, and had it not been for the HMS *Glasgow* shooting down a plane that was diving on us, I probably would not be writing this today.[3] I cannot say enough or praise enough when speaking of the British air force and navy. They were great.

The *Augusta* moved to Plymouth in the spring of 1944 shortly before the invasion and served as the flagship for Admiral Kirk's Western Task Force. The crew had shore leave in Plymouth. Radioman Hummel was staggered by the damage inflicted on the city by the German bombs.

Lt(jg). John L. Evans was the disbursing officer on the *Augusta*. His battle station was in the coding room, and one of his main duties was paying the men. While the *Augusta* was in Portsmouth before the invasion, King George came to inspect the ship.

> The only time in my life to talk to a king occurred when I talked with King George when I conducted him on his inspection of the Supply Division of the USS *Augusta*. Admiral Kirk commanded the Normandy invasion fleet from the USS *Augusta*. Prior to the invasion, Admiral Kirk would go to London at times for meetings with General Eisenhower, and both General Eisenhower and General Bradley came aboard the *Augusta* for meetings with Admiral Kirk.
>
> The USS *Augusta* was a command ship equipped with headquarters space and communication equipment necessary for commanding such operations as the Normandy invasion and the southern France invasion.

Lt. William McDaniel of the U.S. Marines served on the *Augusta* in an antiaircraft battery:

> The ship was anchored most of the time in rather narrow waters at Devonport, just beyond Plymouth, and we had very few exercises. I think we did participate in the

3. This refers to a raid against German shipping off the Norwegian coast near Bodo in October 1943. According to some sources, several German ships were sunk, and only three aircraft were lost; however, Gerald W. Thomas, torpedo-bomber pilot, wrote in his diary that seventeen aircraft were lost between September and the end of November 1943. Although Hummel's comments are confusing, he may be referring to an attack on his ship near Scapa Flow in November, since no evidence indicates that the *Augusta* was on the Norwegian raid, and the *Ranger* did not join it until November.

The heavy cruiser *Augusta*, on which marine lieutenant William H. McDaniel served. COURTESY OF WILLIAM H. MCDANIEL

landing at Slapton Sands, but I have little memory of that. We did a lot of training.

I was an officer in the AA battery, and our AA crews practiced loading drills and tracking drills when friendly aircraft would fly over. The main drill that I remember as an officer is that myself and other officers of the AA battery participated in aircraft identification. We did have to know the identification of American, British, and German aircraft that might be operating in the invasion area. We practiced with photographs of aircraft and we had slides. We started off with a second exposure, then cut it down to a half of a second, a tenth of a second, and eventually to a fiftieth of a second. The purpose was to identify the aircraft immediately on sight.

The most common problem we suffered from was that there was little opportunity for liberty, very limited liberty. One thing that bothered the crew very much was the fact that we did not receive any mail for some weeks before the invasion, and just why it was held up I am not sure. Mail continued to arrive from the U.S., but it was not delivered to the ship. This was apparently part of the security arrangement, although it was never quite fully explained to me. It certainly did have a demoralizing effect, because mail from home was very important.

The weather in England was bad; it was wet and cold. I have one odd memory of English girls called Wrens who on occasion came aboard our ship and we were sometimes invited to their affairs ashore. The girls were very attractive except for their teeth. It seemed to me they all had bad teeth.

Lieutenant McDaniel was lucky enough to have leave in London in late 1943, but in the spring of 1944, opportunities for leave dwindled for the crew. According to McDaniel and Evans, it was always difficult to keep an adequate food supply at sea, especially such items as vegetables, which were considered too risky to take on in foreign ports.

Ens. Walt Treanor's assignment on *LST 58* was less glamorous than those of McDaniel and Evans, but no less demanding.

> My job was to supervise what we called the housekeeping of the ship, which was keeping it in good order. That involved a lot of paint scraping. We talked about what happened waiting for the invasion. There was a degree of boredom, which we attempted to ease up on by keeping the crew scraping the paint, and red-lettering the scraped areas, and repainting with the gray paint that was in the standard uniform of the LSTs in our area of action. I will not forget the day I had some bored sailors over the side, facing away from the port of Plymouth, doing some scraping. They got terribly bored as they scraped. They red-lettered in huge letters obscenities on the side of the ship. They forgot that when the tide turned, we were moored to an anchor buoy; the side away from the port would be facing port. I was thoroughly chastised by the captain of the ship when he received messages from the shore that our ship was displaying some very, very foul language to the good people of Plymouth. Needless to say, I had scrapers over the side in great numbers with a lot of gray paint. Anybody who was a deck division sailor learned to loathe that assignment of painting and scraping.
>
> As we were preparing for landing in Normandy, and not knowing what we would encounter, we were issued armbands in the shape and coloring of the American flags, and we were required to wear them on our left arms to identify us as Americans.

The LST

Ens. Walt Treanor's *LST 58* was about as long as a football field and close to fifty feet wide. The tank deck, where all the loading and unloading operations took place through the bow doors, was on the lower deck. The ship's elevators carried equipment and vehicles to the upper deck. On some of the newer LSTs, a ramp replaced the elevators, making movement between decks much faster. After D-Day, when Ensign Treanor served on *LST 311*, railroad tracks were welded on the floor of the tank deck to load locomotives and boxcars from the hards—concrete ramps built by the engineers for loading—in England and unload them at Cherbourg where they rolled right off the ship onto tracks at the pier. The LSTs were able to carry just about everything the army needed. Treanor, impressed by the LSTs' capability, marveled "that a bunch of weenies, as we called ourselves, would get to operate these ships."

LST 58, whose armament was standard, carried seven 40-millimeter antiaircraft guns, twelve 20-millimeter antiaircraft guns, and a few .50-caliber machine guns mounted on the boat deck. Each of its LCVPs carried on davits also sported a .30-caliber machine gun. Reportedly, the very first LSTs carried a 3-inch gun in a concrete-lined gun tub. Treanor was told that this gun severely rocked the entire ship when fired.

As on most LSTs, the crew of *LST 58* was relatively young. The oldest person onboard was a ship fitter named Cook, who was all of twenty-eight years old. Everyone else in the crew was under twenty-five and soon took to calling him Pop instead of by his usual nickname, Cookie.

The LCT

The LCT was about 120 feet long and 32 feet wide, with a ramp in the bow that dropped for loading and unloading. It carried some armor protection and reached a maximum speed of 8 knots. Crew size on an LCT varied, but two officers and ten men seems to have been the maximum. Its weapons consisted of two 20-millimeter guns amidships. Its ability to carry four medium tanks or other vehicles made it quite valuable in a landing operation, but its slow speed limited the range of duties it could handle.

Ens. Thomas Clark served as a gunnery officer on *LST 507* and was given the additional duty of small stores officer.

> We had just about everything a man needed. The way the navy works is the ship's stores keeps the small items like razor blades, etc., that the men purchase, and we have to keep them in stock. We had a lot of materials on credit from the New Orleans Crescent Tobacco Company—a bunch of cigarettes that went down with the ship. Years later, in civilian life, I got a letter from the Crescent Supply Company trying to get about $1,500 out of me. I never acknowledged the letter.

Before the invasion, during the brief time the ship was in port, Clark drilled his men in the proper use of gas masks, as the risk that the Germans would resort to gas was high. The crew of *LST 507* practiced landings on the hards. When *LST 507* was sunk during Exercise Tiger, Clark was reassigned to Admiral Moon's staff, where he served as a courier. Whereas in his previous assignment he had seldom gone ashore, now he traveled frequently between Plymouth and London and experienced firsthand the traffic and congestion caused by the buildup of forces in May. "I know the ships were notified within probably a week in most cases," he recalls, "because I carried to Southampton and other places the top-secret documents that I later found out were for the invasion. I went out in a jeep at night, and I couldn't pick up anyone. I had a .45 strapped to my side."

Ens. Donald E. Irwin was assigned to *LCT 614* in Flotilla 12 after he arrived in Londonderry, Northern Ireland, aboard *LST 291*, which carried his LCT. Irwin and his crew continued their journey to Plymouth, England, where they arrived on May 10, 1944.

> Here, my new LCT with all new equipment aboard was launched from the deck of the LST. This was quite an engineering feat. The *LCT 614* was secured on a wooden weight on the deck of the LST, so that when the large securing chains were unfastened, the LST placed at a list and a steel cable cut, it would slide off the LST deck into the sea. To do this, the inboard ballast tanks of the LST were filled with water to develop the proper list so the LCT would slide off. Then the inboard ballast tanks of the LCT were filled with the proper amount of water so the LCT righted itself when it hit the sea instead of turning over.

The U.S. Coast Guard contributed a rather impressive contingent to the invasion fleet. In addition to the Coast Guard captains who commanded the attack transports *Samuel Chase*, *Joseph T. Dickman*, and *Bayfield*, coast guardsmen also served alongside navy crews on other ships. Moreover, ten Coast Guard LSTs participated in Overlord. A late but important addition was the Coast Guard rescue flotilla of sixty cutters, the LCI(L) Flotilla, under the command of Capt. Miles H. Imlay, which arrived from the Mediterranean in late 1943, ahead of the armada that would assemble off Britain in May 1944. The LCI(L) Flotilla, which included the twenty-four LCIs operated by the Coast Guard, set up its headquarters near Dartmouth at Greenway House, Agatha Christie's summer home.

Lt(jg). Ed Fabian from Los Angeles had joined the Coast Guard in 1941 and served in the Pacific on antisubmarine patrols for almost a year before joining the LCI(L) Flotilla. He was skipper of *LCI 89* and had an engineer officer and two other officers in his crew.

> During our time in England, we made practice runs to various small ports on the south coast of England between Southampton and Falmouth. Many of these ports would dry out at low tide, so we had to go in at high tide just to familiarize ourselves in case the main embarkation points had been damaged and were untenable and we had to pick up troops from the smaller ports.
>
> We constantly were on exercises. We were based temporarily in various ports for training, making landings on beaches or conducting an exercise with other ships to beaches as if we were going to make a landing, but we wouldn't put troops ashore. Other times we would embark troops and actually make the landings, where they would simulate or actually bombard certain beaches in England.
>
> We saw the results of it [Exercise Tiger] afterwards. The whole stern [of the LST] was lifted up over the bridge. It was not salvageable. I think we were in Dartmouth when it happened.

SC1/C Leon C. Rodriguez served as cook on *LCI 323*, but during combat, he operated the winch that lowered the landing ramps and was the captain of a 20-millimeter gun crew.[4] Since he spent most of his time inside, he rarely saw what was happening around his ship unless it was in combat. When his vessel reached England with the flotilla, it put into Plymouth, where the barnacles were scraped off its hull and it underwent repairs. One of few events that broke up the routine of the crew was a visit from the famous boxer Jack Dempsey, who came aboard to referee a boxing match. *LCI 323* also took part in training exercises.

> We carried British and American troops. Any time you took British troops aboard, they would have food in cans with a little lighter on it that would heat up the food. I don't remember them having C rations like the Americans. Some of the British troops had bicycles and some did not. Some paratroopers came on the dock with bicycles. When they brought them on board, their shoes had some type of spikes they made them sound like a bunch of chickens.
>
> We had a new fellow come aboard, a young guy. I was told to train him for firing the gun. We had a British aircraft towing the target. I told him the aircraft would come by at about 100 feet high and 200 feet away and to be sure not to fire at the aircraft. OK, here comes the target. As soon as he started firing, I had to grab him and the gun and tell him I had warned him not to do that. He missed the aircraft because I pushed him away. That was his first training firing a weapon. We both got reprimanded for that.

4. Naval and Coast Guard ranks and titles can be confusing. The men who received NCO stripes were petty officers (PO), but they also were referred to by their specialties, which included an insignia worn inside their stripes. Thus a gunnery PO third class would also be known as a gunner's mate 3/C. An SC1/C was a PO first class, also known as a cook first class. Seamen were not POs and had no specialty in their title. Among the numerous specialties were steward cook (SC), motor machinist mate (MMM), signal man (SM), and yeoman (Y). Almost every position on landing craft were for POs. The largest, the LST, had more than 100 enlisted men, and every position was for a PO, but during the war, seamen had to fill some of these positions.

The LCI

The LCI(L) (landing craft, infantry [large]) was 158 feet long and 22 feet beam (width) and had a 3.5-foot draft. It usually carried a crew of 4 officers, about 25 men, and 150 to 200 passengers. It was equipped with two winch motors that moved the cables of the personnel landing ramps and had to be cranked out manually. Small gasoline engines that had been designed for the purpose were not installed because they were too noisy.

The LCI was armed with 20-millimeter guns in the forecastle, on the conning tower, and on the cockpit. The guns stood in open turrets and could swivel 360 degrees. The gunner was assisted by a loader and an aide who helped him cock the gun by pulling cables on either side of the gun. The three men were supervised by a gun captain. BM2/C Elmer Carmichael of *LCI 85* describes the operation of the LCI.[5]

LCI 326 landing troops.

The way that you beach an LCI is always to go into the beach on an incoming tide, drop your stern anchor, usually about 1,000 feet offshore, and ram the ship hard on the beach. It is a flat-bottom and shallow-draft vessel, so you ram in and hope you put it where a soldier won't have to wade in deep water, but it doesn't always work that way. When you ground the ship, you have twin ramps forward, and you run them down and out with a winch. You have a check line on it. The normal procedure is to send one of your crewmembers ashore and he has a rope line and a small fluke anchor lashed to a buoy. He goes ashore, plants this fluke anchor, and sets on it. This gives the soldiers something to hang on to, because they have their packs and guns and they are pretty vulnerable to stepping into a deep hole.

Once unloaded, you take in your lifeline, you retract your ramps, you back down on your engines, and you winch in on your stern anchor. That anchor keeps you from broaching and keeps you backing straight off. Your engines have to back you off, but the fact that you have lessened your load by taking all your soldiers off helps your buoyancy, and normally, you can retract and come off all right. It doesn't always work that way.

Normally, one of your crewmembers is the first man off. He takes one line, it is yoked, and you secure it to both ramps. He is not armed, just a helmet and a life jacket. You have soldiers going down both sides.

5. A boatswains mate second class, or BM2/C, was equivalent to a technical sergant in the army and was also known as a petty officer (PO) second class in the navy. A PO3/C was equal to an army staff sergeant and a PO1/C to a first sergeant, while a chief petty officer was equal to a master sergeant (the master sergeant was higher than a first sergeant in World War II).

Rodriguez went to London shortly after he arrived in England, only to get caught in an air raid after having just a couple of drinks. "I went into the side of a bomb crater, and it knocked me out. I was taken to a first-aid station," he recalled.

GM3/C Frances L. Enlow from Fort Worth, Texas, joined the Coast Guard in 1942 at age nineteen. By the time he reached the age of twenty, he was a veteran of North Africa, Sicily, and Salerno, serving on *LCI 326*. For him, the best thing about returning to Britain was "seeing some white girls. We had been in North Africa so long that we were looking for anything familiar that looked like American girls." Shortly after the LCI's return, its crew got antiaircraft target practice at the insistence of the British navy. "We had been in North Africa and been in quite a few shooting events. They brought out a chute and wanted us to get good at hitting it. We shot down that thing on the first run, so they went back and got another one. We shot it down again, so they said we were good enough and we went back in. That was the end of the British giving lessons on how to shoot."

Nineteen-year-old S1/C Robert McCrory of Hobort, Louisiana, was on the way to the Mediterranean aboard *LCI 93* with the LCI(L) Flotilla six months after he had joined the navy in 1942.[6] The training, he felt, was for the benefit of the army, since "we had our own training." Enlow agreed with him, adding that they had done a number of practice landings in Africa on the Moroccan coast, some in rough water, where "it is hard to land these things." Several of the LCIs were at Slapton Sands for Exercise Tiger the night of the E-boat attack. Chief Quartermaster John Gatton, on *LCI 96*, was aware that "half the flotilla was involved that night, including all the 80s and 90s—twelve ships.[7] We could see all the firing and hear the sounds of it, but we didn't know what was going on at the time. We all went to general quarters and manned our guns." BM2/C Carmichael, on *LCI 85*, heard the general quarters, and although his vessel was not involved, he recalls, "We saw a lot of shooting and heard the noise in the background, but didn't realize what was going on." Enlow's *LCI 326* had already left the area because it had onboard "the high brass, who went over to observe it, and we did beach, but pulled out and brought them back."

Y2/C George L. Gray worked out of Greenway House with Captain Imlay's flotilla staff. On April 28, 1944, he moved to Weymouth to join the crew of *LCI 87*, which had been converted to a communications headquarters ship and was crammed with radio equipment manned by navy and Coast Guard personnel. The time for the invasion was close at hand.

Many sailors served in naval beach battalions assigned to the army's engineer special brigades. No U.S. Marine units would take part in the landings on the Normandy coast, the largest invasion in the European theater. The beach battalions would represent the navy.

In January 1944, PhM3/C Vincent Kordack arrived with the 6th Beach Battalion, which settled in at Salcombe at first. Aware that he was participating in momentous events, Kordack meticulously recorded his experiences in his diary.

> Thursday 20 (January): Our new base was a hellhole for we arrived two weeks ahead of schedule and we had to help the Seabees finish up the place. For at least a week we had no place to really wash or take a shower except when it rained which was usually all the time. . . .
>
> A few weeks of lectures and not doing much of anything. . . .

6. A seamen first class (S1/C) was equivalent to a sergeant in the army, a seaman second class (S2/C) to a corporal, and a seamen third class (S3/C) to a private first class.

7. Gatton is referring to the LCIs with numbers in the 80s and 90s.

February 17: We left Salcombe with our battle gear and we drove to Paignton, which was around 35 miles. It would not have taken very long but we got lost on the way.

The maneuvers there were very easy for all we did was lay around the beach while the Army unloaded the ships. . . .

March 1: We packed up all our gear, for we were ordered to leave Salcombe. We left camp at 0800 by truck to Kingsbridge where we boarded the train for Swansea, Wales. We arrived here at 1730, then they had a convoy of trucks to take us to our camp, which at first looked like another hellhole after living in a Quonset hut.

They had no kind of hot water here to speak of and the closest drinking water facility was a quarter of a mile away from our tent. If [*sic*] I was told when I first entered the Navy I would live on a bucket of water a day. Then I would have called him a damned liar, but now I take it all back for I use a helmet to heat water and wash and shave from it.

When we first arrived here at Scurlage Castle they said we would be here for a couple of weeks . . . the closest liberty town was 20 miles away.

I went to town a few times and found it very interesting for at first the girls fell all over us and it was a lot of fun talking to them. But you got tired of it for there is something which they lack. Then this stuff they call beer, it is really terrible—we call it D-38. . . .

The navy also contributed special underwater demolition teams, known as Naval Combat Demolition Units (NCDU), to the invasion of Normandy. Many of the men in these units had served in the Seabees, and all of them were skilled at their job. Although they were experienced swimmers, they went ashore dressed in the same uniforms as the soldiers because they had to perform the demolitions during low tide at the same time that the army came ashore. Ten teams reported for duty in February, and more joined them in March. They worked in three different groups, at Fowey, Swansea, and Salcombe. The teams consisted of one officer and five enlisted men, who could operate from a small rubber raft. According to Fane and Moore in *The Naked Warriors*, they trained with the 2nd, 6th, and 7th Beach Battalions, which were attached to the 1st, 5th, and 6th ESBs, respectively.

One of the members of these teams was Shipfitter 2/C Angelos T. Chatas from Chicago, who had enlisted in April 1943 and undergone six months of training. He departed from New York City on the SS *Del Norte* in early November 1943. He was a frogman in NCDU 25.

We did encounter a couple of problems on the way over. Somewhere in the middle of the Atlantic Ocean, our convoy was attacked, or it encountered a German submarine wolf pack. We were a protected merchant marine ship carrying primarily frogmen and a hold full of bangalores. I could tell there was a lot of shooting and depth charges used, but as far as I could tell, none of the ships in our convoy was hit by torpedoes.

On the way over, we celebrated Thanksgiving aboard ship. Except for that meal, we were inadequately fed. It was so bad that a bunch of us guys broke into the storeroom of the ship and foraged some food, which we hid and nibbled. We got a big round of cheese and some dried fruit. One of the meals we had consisted of powdered potatoes, macaroni, and some biscuits, which were moldy. I called down the U.S. Navy medical officer. He looked at this and said it was a bit of an unbalanced meal!

From Plymouth, we were taken to Northern Scotland, then found out we should have been back in Cornwall. Came back down by train. This train took a day—best part of a day—twelve hours or more from Northern Scotland to Southwest England. We stopped at a train station, and there was the Salvation Army. When they found out our plight, they fed us. Let me tell you, since then, my contributions to the Salvation Army must have been the equivalent of gold for every morsel they fed us. Eventually we got down and settled in at a naval station in Salcombe, England.

We did engage in a lot of practice, and this was late December 1943. I remember Exeter, Ilfracombe on the Sea, and Willacombe. We used to say, "If I Combe, Will I Combe." But we operated out of Salcombe. We knew we were going into Europe somewhere, most likely France. We were aware the beaches there had mines, and we were more concerned with obstacles. There were three primarily. Tetrahedra, made of steel and intended to stop vehicles, even tanks. A tetrahedron was a four-sided solid made of equilateral triangles, and no matter what turned them over, they were always right side up. Also, hedgehogs, which were things made of steel, but a lot of diagonal steel. And there were these things that were concrete with a pointed rail sticking up. The biggest obstacle of all we worked on was the Belgian Gate. This thing was about 10 x 10 feet in the front and about 14 feet deep, went to a point in the back, and made with 6 x 6 x ¾-inch angle iron and they locked one against the other so nothing could go through them. It would take hundreds of pounds of explosives just to explode these things.

One of our officers, Lieutenant Commander Hagensen, invented the Hagensen Pack. This was a canvas sack that looked like a sausage, maybe 18 inches long and filled with composition explosives. Back then, it was C-2. It had prima cord coming out of it so each of these little sacks could connect with one another. Then there was a lanyard and a hook. The idea was to wrap it around the angle iron and hook it—you didn't have to tie it—and tie it to the next one with prima cord. There were strategic places where you had to put this.

A tug boat used to support the invasion.
COURTESY OF THEODORE GAYDOS

Back then, we had this naval organization called Naval Combat Demolition Units, which were five men and an officer. We got to where we could put all the necessary charges, I think there were nineteen places, and each one weighed a couple pounds, so we were talking of less than forty pounds. Get them all on—we wouldn't explode them in practice—just get them ready to explode in less than one minute. We got to be pretty good at this.

The Bangalore Farce: Bangalores came in crates that were about 6 to 8 feet long. There were 12 bangalores in a box, and these came wrapped up in bale wire, 12 boxes. So the unit had one gross of bangalores, 144 of them. Somewhere in navy ordnance, there was a big foul-up. We ordered so many bangalores and instead of sending us single bangalores by count, they sent us these big grosses. We had this hold of the *Del Norte* filled with bangalores, and everybody wondered what would happen if we got hit. We would be a big hole in the ocean! When we got to England, the authorities there, both American and English, didn't know what the hell to do with it. We did find an abandoned quarry, and during the winter of 1943–44, we were quartered at the little town of Fowey, Cornwall. Somewhere outside this town, there was an abandoned quarry, and we had to store our bangalores there. There were hundreds of these flat cases, and they were piled high to where we would have to lift them in steps, and every once in a while we would have to change them around. This was a constant chore with us. The comical thing about this is that we never used one in combat, although we did train with them.

In 1943, there were virtually no obstacles on the coast of Normandy, but that changed in January 1944, which necessitated the intervention of the naval teams. These teams arrived early in the year, while the army was preparing a plan for the demolition of beach obstacles by its own special teams. Finally, in April 1944, army and navy planners concurred that the paths through the obstacles would have to be cleared at low tide.[8] Both services combined their troops to create gap assault teams, which would have to clear the obstacles on the American beaches, create 50-yard-wide gaps, and breach several lines of obstacles spanning 300 yards of beach.

Naval officers led the naval teams, composed of five naval frogmen, three seamen, and five army combat engineers, on Omaha Beach. An army lieutenant would command a twenty-six-man team of combat engineers. The army and navy units would combine to form a gap assault team. The army unit was to clear the landward obstacles, while the naval team took the seaward ones. Eight gap assault teams would land on Utah Beach and sixteen on Omaha Beach. They were to be followed by support teams, including tankdozers. According to Beck et al. in *Corps of Engineers*, in the month of May, the men hastily assembled 10,000 Hagensen Packs of explosives. There was little time left to prepare.

Army Tank Battalions Join the Navy

The army's 70th, 741st, and 743rd Tank Battalions received special training after arriving in England. The 70th had already acquired combat experience in North Africa, where it had been equipped with light tanks. It landed in Britain without its vehicles, like the 741st and 743rd coming from the States. The 741st arrived in early in November 1943 and the other two battalions disembarked at the end of the month. The

8. Most German leaders expected that the landings must take place near high tide. The obstacles they emplaced between the high- and low-tide marks would do little to deter a landing at low tide.

An M-4 Sherman duplex-drive tank in a training area with Coast Guard commander Ed Fabian. COURTESY OF ED FABIAN

70th still maintained one company of light Stuart tanks. In 1943, the unit was issued Shermans, which were later taken away. The new Shermans were equipped with special gear, including propellers. Until the men were ready, they trained on specially equipped British Valentine tanks.

About six weeks before D-Day, Lt. Ed Fabian of the Coast Guard received orders temporarily assigning him to an army tank unit on a restricted beach area.

> They didn't tell me what I was going to do. Here was the beach with about twenty of these tanks—General Sherman tanks with inflatable canvas bags. When I got there and saw the commanding officer, he said, "We have been having trouble with these tanks, because they are an army unit and not sailors. We would go out to practice, and it would be conditions that are not right: too foggy, current, etc. We need somebody to help and that is your job."
>
> I stayed there a week and went out with them. They had two LCTs, as I remember, maybe three. They would run these LCTs up to the beach. They would carry three tanks. The bow ramps would go down, and then they would back these tanks up onto the LCTs, three in a row. The first one I saw, I thought I was going to ride on one of those. We went out on the first LCT about two miles. The English Channel has a strong current, sometimes two or three knots, and that is about as fast as one of these tanks could go. They had propellers on the rear end that were actually attached to the cogs on the treads. The tank operator could steer the tank by stopping one tread. The tank commander would sit on top of the conning tower. They were going to launch these

> tanks, and they inflated them, this big bag way up above the conning tower. To look over the bag, you had to stand over the turret and look over the top hoop, which the tank commander and I did.
>
> They launched them off of this LST right down the ramp into the water, which I thought was deep. I expected it would go right on down, but it didn't; it floated very well, and they traveled very well. I was leery about going aboard a 16-ton tank with a canvas bag, and of course, with these hoops, there would be bulges in the canvas. I would say maybe there was three feet of freeboard above the water. The tank was down in the bottom, like a paper bag with a rock in it.
>
> Anyway, that is what we did. I was with that outfit for three weeks. They wanted me to stay with them and be their navigator to the beach, but I said no way! It was a great idea, to go into shallow water with the turret just out of the water. They would have been a great success if we had had fairly smooth water.

Before Lieutenant Fabian got his special assignment, the three battalions had begun their training in February. Lt. Col. Jacob Moon informed his battalion, the 741st, that it had been selected to train on the secret floating tanks. The battalion proceeded to Great Yarmouth for instruction with the Royal Tank Corps, where it took up quarters in the evacuated homes of the town. The tankers had a few days to get acquainted with the British Valentine tanks. Each morning, trucks carried them down to the training area, where they prepared for their water ride. At the end of the battalion's training period, a British general came to announce to the men that they had been chosen to lead the invasion, at which point, Moon recalls, "a man collapsed and fell facefirst into a mud puddle. The shock evidently had been too much for him." As it turned out, it was not the shock of the announcement, but a hangover from the previous night's carousing that brought the trooper down, as described in *The Story of Vitamin Baker* by Lanier et al.

Cpl. Wardell Hopper, a member of a tank crew of Company B of the 741st Tank Battalion, found some problems with the Valentine tanks.

> They were small and hard to maneuver. Our mediums were like a living room compared to them. The driver had the most trouble because they were hard to maneuver. At Fort Monckton, we finished with the Valentines and started working with our M-4s. It was basically the same tank we used [the Sherman], but it had a propeller in the back and the sides went up. We just wondered what they would do in the water. We unpacked our own tanks and cleaned the guns with Cosmoline. I found a note from some gal in Ohio wishing us the best of luck. I wrote her and we corresponded for a while. The tanks were already fully rigged.
>
> We went to Torcross, England; it was beautiful. It was just about like the beaches of Omaha. We trained there and took the M-4s out into the water. Our equipment and training were supposed to be top secret. The training was totally on the coast. We had some classroom instruction, but not much.
>
> They took us out in an LCT, and then we went back in. We trained in the water in the swimming pool in case something happened to the tank. We trained in the pools on what to do if our tanks went down. They threw us into the water, and we inflated our Mae Wests with capsules.
>
> We put the skirt up a couple of times to test it, but not many times. You had it up before you launched it from the LCTs. All four tanks had the skirts up and motors on

The old battleship *Arkansas*, completed in 1912, mounted 12-inch guns. Here it is seen refueling the destroyer *Thompson* (#627) during a rehearsal for the Normandy invasion in April 1944.

before launching. We didn't make many practices using the skirts up. I was the driver of the tank when we were in the water, because the driver could not see when the skirts were up. We had a big rudder. The tank commander and I were on the roof of the tank and exposed. I had the rudder, and he stood up to see where we were going. The rudder was a big, long stick connected to the propellers in the back. It was up to me until we hit the beach and dropped the skirts. The assistant gunner was in the turret and in the gunner's seat. He was supposed to start shooting when the skirt came down, and then I would come down and take his place. We never did get to see if it worked!

According to Hopper, after less than three weeks, the battalion moved from Great Yarmouth to Barton Stacey, and later to Fort Monckton outside of Portsmouth, where it took up residence in antiquated barracks. This was where it traded the Valentines for the Shermans. The 741st continued its training at different points in England and took part in Exercise Fabius.

The 70th Tank Battalion also trained with the medium tanks at Barton Stacey and took its tanks to Cardiff, Wales, to zero in their weapons. This was the first time the men of the 70th handled the 75-millimeter guns of the Shermans, having been a light tank unit in Africa. Companies A and B trained with amphibious tanks on a lake at Great Yarmouth. Company C was equipped with rocket launchers, because it was slated to use them to blast the seawall at Utah Beach. A rack for fifteen rockets was welded to the turrets of the tanks. One of Company C's platoons was given dozer blades to help the gap assault teams.

T/4 Charles J. Myers, a gunner and radio operator in the battalion commander's tank, watched the testing of the rocket launchers at Slapton Sands. Some of the rockets hit the seawall, causing no damage; others went over or fell short of the wall. The gunners found it impossible to aim the rockets. After a couple of armor-piercing shells were fired at the wall, the observers from SHAEF decided to have the rocket launchers removed. The battalion's DD Sherman tanks participated in Exercise Tiger.

S.Sgt. Glenn E. Gibson of Company A, 70th Tank Battalion, was the platoon sergeant for the 4th Platoon. After the battalion arrived in England, it moved to Swindon.

> There we were issued medium M-4 tanks. We trained on them for several months. Trained at Swindon and Castle Martin Range in Wales. Then we moved to Portsmouth, where we trained on the British Valentine DD (duplex drive) tank. This training was on a completely camouflaged freshwater lake. After this, we moved to Torcross, England, on the Channel shore, and here we were issued M-4 DD tanks. These had to be completely waterproofed. All tanks had to be camouflaged with shrimp nets during the day. Torcross was completely off-limits to anyone except Companies A and B of the 70th Tank Battalion.
>
> Our mess supplies were brought to a designated point, where they were picked up by our mess sergeants. No one could leave the Torcross Beach area while here training on DD tanks, but we had excellent food.
>
> We had many night-training missions, where we were loaded on LCTs at night and taken five to ten miles out in the Channel and given a compass bearing (we had a compass on the tank) from the LCT skipper so as to head back to the beach at Torcross.
>
> The DD tank was a regular M-4, except it had a canvas screen that was raised by pneumatic pillars located around a false deck, which had been welded around the tank. These pillars were raised by two compressed-air cylinders, which the driver controlled in his compartment. To raise the screen, the command was "Driver inflate." The screen was then inflated by pillars located around the tank. After the screen was inflated, there were "struts" located fore and aft and around the sides that had to be locked in place to keep the canvas screen from collapsing when the tank was launched. The tank was propelled by two three-bladed propellers that were geared to rear idlers attached to the tracks in the rear. Commands to move the tank forward in the water were "Driver lower propellers and advance in third gear." This turned the tracks, which in turn rotated the propellers, moving the tank forward. After arrival on the beach, the commands were "Driver raise propellers," which was done hydraulically, then the driver "Break struts," which was also done hydraulically. Then the driver deflated the screen by a mushroom valve located in the bottom of the pillars. At this time, the screen had fallen, and we had an M-4 medium tank on the beach ready to fight.

Three battalions of amphibious tanks were ready for the invasion early in May.

The Secret of Success

The British, with assistance from the Americans, developed an important piece of technology that went undetected by the Germans. The code name for this project was Mulberry. The Allies realized in mid-1943 that the success or failure of an invasion would depend upon supplying the forces involved. A large buildup required port facilities to unload ships rapidly. The Dieppe raid had shown that the important ports on the continent would be fortified and that the Germans would concentrate troops around them. It was unreasonable to hope to capture a port quickly, and building up and supplying troops across a beach for an extended period was equally impractical, because it required lighters and was a slow process.[9] Winston Churchill and his officers conceived the idea of building an artificial port. The idea was simple: extend piers and causeways from the shallow beaches into deep water so ships could unload and to form breakwaters to protect them against the forces of nature. Creating the components for such a project was not as simple. Artificial harbors would reduce the value of the German defensive effort that concentrated on turning the French ports into "fortresses," since they would no longer be focal points of the upcoming invasion.[10]

As early as 1941, the British created Directorate Transportation (Tn) 5, under Maj. Gen. Sir Bruce White, to work on the artificial harbor project. In the last half of 1943, General White determined that the Americans would need a Mulberry capable of taking 5,000 tons a day, and the British would need one with a daily capacity of 7,000 tons. On September 3, 1943, the Combined Chiefs of Staff approved the proposal, according to Guy Hartcup's *Code Name Mulberry*.

The British had already begun work on floating piers and causeways early in 1943 and tested them in a secure area in Scotland. They designed the floating roadway or causeway so they could move to and fro with the waves. The piers were designed to adjust to high and low tides.

Capt. A. Dayton Clark, of the U.S. Navy, was placed in charge of Task Force 128, which was to install and operate the American Mulberry. Three U.S. Navy construction regiments arrived in England. The 25th Seabee Regiment was to handle Mulberry A.[11] The regiment's 108th Construction Battalion was to operate it, and the other three battalions were to man the Rhino ferries, pontoons powered by outboard motors that could carry thirty to forty vehicles, as well as pontoon causeways, according to Hartcup. The Rhino ferry pontoon, developed by the U.S. Navy, played a key role in delivering equipment during the invasion and operated in conjunction with the Mulberries after they went into operation.

The planners decided that five small landing shelters called Gooseberries would protect an estimated 4,000 small craft. The Gooseberries were to be built with 70 old ships sunk as blockships. In addition to merchant ships, the vessels to be sunk

Project Mulberry

The components of a Mulberry were as follows:

- Pontoon causeways
- Whale: adjustable floating pier heads, known as Lobnitz after their designer, and roadways
- Bombardons: floating steel tanks used as breakwaters
- Gooseberry: breakwater made by sinking a number of unserviceable ships (Corncobs) to create a sheltered area
- Phoenixes: huge concrete caissons that were towed to the site and then had valves that would flood them so they could be used as part of the breakwaters

9. Lighters are small ships that can negotiate shallow water. They usually had a larger cargo capacity than most landing craft.
10. The Germans assumed that the Allies had to quickly seize a port for any major landing. Until they realized that the Allies were creating artificial ports, the lack of a major port in the invasion area may have contributed to many in the German High Command believing Normandy was only a diversionary invasion.
11. The term Seabee was derived from CB for construction battalions.

General Eisenhower giving his first press conference in June 1944 after the invasion.

included the old British battleship *Centurion*, the French battleship *Courbet*, the British cruiser *Durban*, and the Dutch cruiser *Sumatra*. All the blockships assembled off the west coast of Scotland in late May 1944, as described by Guy Hartcup.

The British employed 45,000 men for the construction of Mulberry components. In January 1944, they decided that they would need twenty-three pier heads, including eight spares; ten miles of floating roadway, including three miles of spares; and 670 floats for the floating roadway. By mid-May, fourteen pier heads were assembled or on the way to Southampton, and all but one was completed by the time of the invasion. Shortly before D-Day, the navy discovered that the LSTs had to be modified to berth at the pier heads, and the changes were made just in time. The huge five-story caissons for the Phoenix breakwaters were still under construction in the spring. One hundred were completed by May, and all those needed for the invasion were ready by the twenty-third. All the caissons were completed by October 1944. These huge caissons actually floated, and tugboats towed them along the coast of England.

The Allies initially estimated that for Operation Overlord, they would need 130 tugboats, 90 of which would be handling the Mulberries. By the end of 1943, however, they realized that they would need an additional 70 tugs, because 164 were needed for the artificial harbors. On D-Day, according to Samuel Eliot Morison's *The Invasion of France and Germany*, 132 tugboats were available, including 51 from the U.S. Army and 19 from the U.S. Navy; 108 were assigned to the Mulberries. They completion of the artificial harbors was delayed from the projected D+14 to D+21.

No invasion could take place without the Mulberries, which were barely ready by early June. Since the Germans were unaware of Project Mulberry, they did not recognize the significance of the components or attempt to destroy them during construction and transportation. By the time they finally realized that the Allies did not have to strike directly at a major seaport, the buildup on the beachhead was well under way. In addition, the Allies came to accept the fact that even if they managed to capture a major port, the Germans might demolish its facilities, rendering it unusable. Therefore, they made preparations to keep the artificial harbors in action until the end of 1944.

Floyd H. Matthews served on a salvage tug that moved the huge Phoenix caissons.

> The USS *Diver*, ARS-5, operating out of the British ports during the spring of 1944, was engaged in the buildup and support of the Normandy invasion. Her primary task during this period was towing components of the portable breakwater [Phoenix] to be used on the landing beaches down the Thames River, into the English Channel, through the Straits of Dover to assembly sites off the British coast. The run through the straits was made at night to lessen the danger from German torpedo boat attacks.
>
> On one such assignment, after reaching the pickup point up the river, the *Diver* received emergency orders to disregard the tow, return to Portsmouth, and report to Captain Elsburg (of salvage fame in the Mediterranean) for a salvage job.
>
> A large Dutch tug of the *Rota Zee* class was ordered to pick up the tow, a Phoenix unit. After sailing down the river into the dark night, she was never heard from again. She disappeared without a trace.
>
> A few days later, the *Diver* pulled into the naval base at Portsmouth to pick up a crane. As she approached the dock, a grisly old sailor, typically British, yelled out, "Aye! It's the bloody *Diver*, back from hell!"
>
> The report had filtered down that it was the *Diver* that was lost. To this day, I have never learned what happened to the Dutch tug. We of the *Diver* felt that some divine being, not the Lords of London, had spared us.

S2/C Theodore Gaydos served on the auxiliary tug *ATA-125* (formerly *ATR-47*), operating out of Portsmouth, before the invasion and towed the large Phoenix units from the vicinity of Dover to other ports on the southern coast of England. The tugs were in high demand, however, and were called upon for other operations including rescue.

> We went out to the North Atlantic and bounced around the sea until a Liberty ship would get hit, and then we would tow it back into an English port. We stayed out for thirty days at a time. Once we were called to tow a Liberty ship to England, for it had been hit by a mine.
>
> The seas were very rough in the North Atlantic, and it was very cold. We wore "foul weather" gear with face masks and rain gear on top of that. We never changed clothes while out at sea, and the rain gear had to be cut off of us when we came into port. I stood four hours on and four hours off lookout duty or watches. It was so rough the cook couldn't light the oil stove and we ate K rations or sandwiches.[12]

Protecting the invasion beaches was the most dangerous mission. The German heavy artillery position at Pointe du Hoc had to be eliminated before the American Mulberry could be built at Omaha Beach and the troops could safely land on Omaha and Utah Beaches, because it could put both beach areas under fire. The battery

12. Gaydos's expressions are a partial mixture of army and navy slang, because he left the navy and eventually retired as a colonel in the army.

occupied partially casemated positions, and farther behind it was another German battery at Caisny, which could also pose difficulties on both beaches. The 2nd Ranger Battalion was assigned the mission of taking out the battery position on top of Pointe du Hoc. The Germans had heavily fortified the position against an attack from the rear or air landing. They did not anticipate, however, an assault from the small beaches at the base of the cliffs, which were covered only by the artillery on the east coast of the Cotentin Peninsula and other batteries near the point. In addition, the German troops at the top of the cliff could simply rain grenades down upon assailants coming from that direction.

The Rangers Arrive and Prepare

Lt. James Eikner, the 2nd Rangers' communications officer, sailed with his battalion aboard the *Queen Elizabeth* in late November 1943. The Rangers were assigned as MPs on the ship, a new experience for them. At the end of the month, the ship anchored at Greenoch, Scotland.

> We arrived at night; on the following morning, I was awakened by some pretty singing—some ladies, singing in unison one of the latest American tunes. When I looked out from my stateroom, there were these ladies down on their knees with buckets swabbing down the deck manually. I looked out the porthole; the sun was out and I could see the snow on the hills.
>
> They took us ashore in lighters; we picked up buses, and we were taken to an armory in Glasgow. From there we boarded a train that wound its way to the seaside resort of Bude in Cornwall on December 2. We took over the Hotel Links as our headquarters. An advance party had been sent to take care of billeting, and we were all put in private homes since there was no camp.
>
> The first night, I was trying to find my way and everything was blacked out. I just couldn't get used to that and I got lost. It took a couple of hours to find the building.
>
> We immediately went into a training situation. Our first assignments were to raid positions on the French coast and Jersey Islands. We had several groups of Rangers around England training for these missions. I spent my time visiting the various camps, making sure my boys were doing their job.
>
> There were two types of raids: One was aggressive to pick up intelligence information, and the other you went in to blow up and shoot up things. I spent most of my time with a larger force that was going to raid in a "Rece" [reconnaissance] situation to get samples of barbed wire and stuff and locate the minefields. If we ran into the enemy, we were going to turn it into an attack and then double-time by compass cross-country to where our boats were. I was on the other craft, and we used little dories to take in these fellows. You could only make these raids on certain times of the month—no moon, good weather, and no phosphorescence on the water so the wake could not be seen. There were only about three days a month you could make these raids.
>
> The headquarters of the British commandos that we worked under was in Dover. They had a way of signaling as to whether the weather was right or not—they used a flag to signal if the conditions were right. The weather was never suitable for us, and before we could make that raid, it was called off and we were to train for the big one—D-Day. The raid was canceled

The Big Ranger Raids

Company A of the 2nd Ranger Battalion, led by Capt. Cleveland Lytle, and several members of the HQ Company's commo section, led by Lt. James Eikner, reported at Folkstone, where they trained for a raid on the French coast near Calais. The mission of this ninety-four-man Ranger force was to bring a prisoner back from France.

A British commando, General Sturgess, came to review the unit to determine whether it was ready for the operation. By sheer coincidence, the *Luftwaffe* had decided to mount a raid on the very night of the general's visit. The review went on with the staccato sound of the AA guns and the beams of the searchlights in the background. Finally, General Sturgess told Eikner to pull over into a pub for some refreshment and wait out the rest of the raid.

The Rangers were ready to depart from Dover before the end of January 1944. All they needed now was the proper weather conditions. The plan was for the company—divided into four groups, with two groups to an LCI—to travel across the Channel from Dover and land in LCAs. Once the first group landed, it was to secure a prisoner, signal the ships, and conclude the operation. If it failed to take a prisoner, it was to clear a path through the wire and minefields so the remaining three groups could pass through. These three groups would then move toward a well-fortified strongpoint of about seven bunkers, believed to be virtually abandoned because this section of the coast had been flooded by Channel storms. The second group was to breach the defenses of this position, and if no prisoner were caught, the other two groups, which would be covering the second, would proceed to a cluster of buildings thought to contain a command post. The third group would then attempt to take these positions, and if successful, both groups would withdraw toward the other two and evacuate. Time was of the essence, since the heaviest weapons the men carried were 60-millimeter mortars and light machine guns.

Lieutenant Eikner, with a British Radio 46, traveled in one of the LCIs. His job was to use this radio to find direction. The landing party would carry a similar piece of equipment to guide it back to the evacuation point. Everyone was ready during January, but the weather did not cooperate, and the mission was canceled.

Meanwhile, Company D under Captain Slater practiced scaling cliffs with No. 4 Commando. Company D had a very special mission: It was to land on the German-occupied British Channel Island of Herm, try to take a prisoner, and reconnoiter the enemy positions. To achieve this, the men would have to scale a cliff as soon as they landed. This ambitious raid, like the preceding one, was secret—so secret that the troopers would have to clean up and don their dress uniforms before they made their way back to camp and pretend the raid never happened. Ultimately, the Rangers did not have to worry about letting the cat out of the bag, because the British also canceled this mission because of poor weather at the end of January, according to *Rudder's Rangers* by Ronald Lane.

> on February 15, and the whole battalion reassembled.

The 2nd Rangers re-formed at Bude in February and began intensive training, which included cliff scaling from the beaches adjacent to the town.

After several weeks of training, Lt. Col. James E. Rudder allowed his men to go on leave, and they scattered across the island. During his furlough, Lieutenant Eikner came to grief.

> In Southampton, we were having a party and got hold of some of the British navy's rum. For some reason, it tasted like it had garlic in it. One gal asked me to drive her home. She didn't tell me it was on the outskirts of London. We drove for miles and miles, and the taxi driver had to go into black market locations to get gasoline. It taught me a lesson. She was silly enough to drop her calling card in my pocket. Several days later, I called and her husband answered. I said, "Wrong number."

The planners of Overlord concluded that the six 155-millimeter gun battery at Pointe du Hoc had to be taken out, and the task fell to the 2nd Rangers. The 5th Ranger Battalion, which had just arrived in Britain, was assigned a support task.

> When Colonel Rudder was called in, he took a small staff with him to London. When he was first shown Pointe du Hoc, he thought they were kidding. When he found out for sure this was going to be a Ranger mission, they formed both battalions into a provisional Ranger force, with him as the senior commander. There were a number of plans worked out before they settled on one.
>
> The most ridiculous plan considered simply bombing or shelling the position. General Bradley knew there was no way to guarantee bombing it out, and you would have to dig them out. We made the plans along with his staff. We planned to go in at Omaha Beach, pass through the lines, and hightail it down about five miles. That was ruled out because those big guns would be shelling the beaches in the meantime.
>
> Then Rudder worked out his own plan with his staff. Originally, we would land three companies. They would establish a beachhead. Then the 5th Rangers, with Companies A and B of the 2nd Battalion, the reserve Ranger force, would come in and clean up the Germans there and stand by for the 116th Infantry to come up from the main beach. Later on, we added an addendum to the order approved by General Huebner of 1st Division and on up to Gerow. If the escalade up the cliff didn't go well or it was delayed longer than thirty minutes, then Schneider's [5th] Ranger force would land at Omaha Beach.
>
> There was a Captain Eickner in the 5th Battalion who enlisted Colonel Rudder's help to get rid of their incompetent commander. We got rid of the 5th Battalion commanding officer and had our executive officer, Max Schneider, a veteran of North Africa, take over on March 26.

The Rangers practiced all types of cliff climbing: hand, mortar rocket-launched ropes, ladders, and steel tubular section ladders that could reach up to 100 feet in height. Someone proposed placing 100-foot extension ladders borrowed from the London Fire Brigade on a couple of DUKWs. The vessels would get onshore, drive across the beach, and place the ladders up against a cliff. A light machine gun on top of the ladder would keep the enemy at bay as the Rangers scrambled up. Experiments proved it could work, according to Ronald Lane.

During Exercise Fabius, the final dress rehearsal at the beginning of May, the Rangers boarded three transports. Companies E, D, and F, on two of the vessels, moved on the right flank of the 116th Infantry, the way they were slated to do on D-Day, and assaulted the cliffs successfully. When the exercise was over, the Rangers completed a twelve-mile march before they shipped for Swanage on May 7. There they continued to scale cliffs, until they moved to their staging area on May 19 in preparation for the invasion.

CHAPTER 3

The Air Element

Airborne Exercises

The 101st Airborne (A/B) Division, in Great Britain, had time to prepare from the fall of 1943, whereas the 82nd A/B Division, which returned from the Italian campaign, had only a few months to reorganize and train replacements. During the spring of 1944, both divisions trained intensively and participated in some major amphibious exercises. Some battalions of the 101st A/B even played the "Germans." Neither unit, however, was airdropped in these exercises that supported the training of the amphibious elements.

The British exercises had a slightly different character than the American. In March 1944, elements of the 101st A/B Division played the role of the enemy for the British 6th A/B Division during Exercises Bizz I and II. The objective of Bizz I was to seize and hold a bridge over the Thames and destroy several "enemy" batteries before 5:30 A.M. These exercises served as the rehearsal for taking key bridges in the British sector, the Merville Battery, and other positions on the morning of D-Day.

The enemy units in Bizz I played by the Americans included the "German" 288th and 799th Infantry Divisions.[1] The British, unlike the Americans, did not want to fake actual units on the Western Front, because that might give clues as to where the real invasion might take place in their training orders.

One of the largest practice drops took place on March 23, when—as recounted in Rapport and Northwood's *Rendezvous with Destiny*—a regimental-size force of the 101st A/B Division put on a demonstration jump for Winston Churchill; Generals Eisenhower, Bradley, and Brereton; and the media. Sgt. H. G. "Bud" Houser of the 502nd PIR took part in this jump.

> We made the jump for all the bigwigs there. We went out over the west coast and came back for that one. This is when that lieutenant came down in a streamer, but he made it safely. I hit the ground and I heard somebody holler; I looked up, and here was this chute coming down in a streamer, with the lines wrapped around him. Just before he hit the ground, he pulled his reserve. He hit the ground kind of hard, and he jumped up and said: "Ddddddaaaa ddddddaaaa yaaa seeee daa daat streaaamer I had?" He was white as a ghost, but he made it down all right. The bigwigs were up the airfield where we jumped.

During the months before the invasion, the glider pilots trained as well, but they usually carried no passengers. The glider pilots preferred the American CG-4A glider to the less maneuverable and larger British Horsa. CWO William Hart was with the ground crew of the 437th Troop Carrier Group and prepared C-47s and gliders for the invasion.

> The pilots and glider pilots were always in training. They would drop the gliders and usually return to our base. They towed a big nylon rope attached to the tail of the C-47; the pilot had control of the release at one end, and the glider pilot had control at the other. It was held by a steel fitting. The pilot would come back with the rope after dropping the glider and drop the rope on the base to save it because they were expensive. That big long rope with its big steel anchor would come whistling in when he dropped it. During combat, they didn't bring the ropes back because they would return at low levels, flying full speed.
>
> One time we had bad weather and a blackout, and the birds were landing all over England. We were waiting until morning for the crews to call in. Basically our losses in gliders resulted from the wind. They were made of tubular steel and plywood floor. They were very light, and many airframes got bent—not much damage in practice, it was all minor. We did some repairs. In the glider section, we had a glider pilot in charge of the glider mechanics. The glider is like a kit you get and put together. They uncrated them, put them together, and checked the rigging.
>
> The gliders were kept separate from the aircraft, and when the aircraft went out to the runway, they met their gliders out there.

The last large-scale American air drop, Exercise Eagle, took place on May 9–12. For this full-scale rehearsal, the paratroopers departed from the same airfields they would be using in less than a month, and the objectives were the same as they would be in Normandy. The movement from garrison area to assembly sites at the air-

1. In this case, these two divisions were fictitious. Some of the regiments of these fictitious divisions, such as the 474th and 483rd, were actually on the Eastern Front in April–May 1944.

fields began on May 9. When the 28th Infantry Division, which was not slated for D-Day, took up positions on the night of May 10–11 to support the airborne exercise, the movement and assembly problems that had beset the previous amphibious exercises resurfaced. On the night of May 11–12, 850 C-47s with 110 CG-4A gliders carried the assault battalions of the airborne division over the Bristol Channel, turned back toward England with the help of preset markers, dropped their troops, and headed back to base.[2] According to Frank Guild's *Action of the Tiger*, flying a similar return route was an attempt to duplicate the conditions of the actual invasion.

The pathfinders flew from North Witham first, and they were followed by the main body of paratroopers in the early hours of the morning. Problems soon developed during the airdrop. Twenty-eight planes went the wrong way and returned to base without dropping their paratroopers. One company of the 502nd dropped on Ramsbury by mistake. More than 400 men in the division suffered broken bones or other injuries during the exercise. After the gliders landed in the morning, it was deemed that the 101st had successfully completed its mission, according to Rapport and Northwood.

Pvt. Ray B. Hood of the 502nd PIR had an opportunity to observe Exercise Eagle from the ground in the vicinity of Newbury, where the operation took place.

> Because I had a wrenched knee from a previous training jump, I was excused from the jump itself and assigned as a jeep driver for an officer (name forgotten) whose job was to observe the jump from the ground. It was a night operation.
>
> I drove the officer into Newbury, seven miles from our base near Hungerford, then perhaps three or four miles northwest to the DZ [drop zone]. As is usual in such cases, we were several hours too early—a typical matter of hurry-up-and-wait.
>
> A middle-aged British farmer walked up to our jeep and invited the officer and me to come to his home, a thatch-roofed stone house, for tea. We did accompany him back to his home. The man and his wife were most hospitable, offering us, along with the tea, scones and cake. By then we were all well aware of the rigorous system of rationing such things as sugar and flour, and we accepted the tea but refused the snack, with the excuse that we had just eaten.
>
> As I remember, the 2nd Battalion of the 502nd PIR was scheduled to jump almost exactly at midnight. This was my unit. The officer and I heard and saw the planes two or three miles away (distance was difficult to judge), but the 2nd Battalion did not jump. No explanation was given other than "pilot error." I have forgotten the exact figures, but you can bet your hat I'm close: More than twenty-five planes brought back more than 500 men (the entire battalion) to Greenham Common.
>
> Most of Company H, 3rd Battalion, was given the green light and jumped directly over a village called Ramsbury, more than five miles from the drop zone. I knew some of the men involved—knew them very well. They landed on houses and barns and on or in all the other odd places that you might expect. There were quite a few injuries—I have no idea how many. We were told that this monumental error (a considerably more harsh term was used) was caused by an Air Corps error with an Aldis lamp--the strong light used to signal between planes.

2. About 1,200 transports were used on D-Day for the two American and one British A/B divisions. The 82nd A/B did not take part in Exercise Eagle, but its assigned aircraft did, each carrying a single paratrooper from the 82nd.

The failure of the 2nd Battalion to jump was an obvious Air Corps blunder. The pilots simply couldn't find the DZ. It was a clear night, no cloud cover.

That night, after everyone had returned to our hut at 3 A.M., a loud bull session was taking place because the men didn't know what had happened—why they hadn't jumped. I heard one wiseacre in my company make the remark that the troop carrier pilots' idea of formation flying was two airplanes going in the same direction on the same day without a map.

The training was over and the men were ready, but those who had been injured during the exercise would remain behind. Others, such as Sergeant Houser, missed Normandy for different reasons.

I was over at a friend's place, and I was on the way back. I was walking on the left-hand side of the road, although I should have been on the right, but I was clear off the road a good four feet. All of a sudden, I heard this car. As I started to look around to see if I could get a ride, I was knocked further to the side of the road. The car stopped; it happened to be a command car with a lieutenant colonel in the backseat. The lieutenant colonel said, "Are you all right?" and I said, "Sure." He asked where I was going and said he would take me there, and when we got there he told me to go to the dispensary. It was late and I felt all right, so I went to bed, but later that night my arm started hurting. I went to the dispensary first thing in the morning and found that my arm was broken in two places. This was a couple of weeks before the invasion. I was a staff sergeant and then relieved of my duty as first sergeant of Company A and sent up to the 1st Battalion HQ.

The Troop Carrier Command

The bad feelings that developed between the paratroopers and the C-47 pilots after Exercise Eagle were exacerbated after Normandy.

Many paratroopers accused the pilots of being Air Corps rejects and not as good as combat pilots. Although it is easy to sympathize with the disgruntled paratroopers who dropped over an English village or, later, into inundated areas in Normandy, it is important to keep the incidents in perspective. Pilots in those days were hampered by the technological limitations. Even the bomber pilots, who performed virtually all their operations in daylight, had to rely on special navigational equipment on cloudy days and were not always accurate in locating their objectives. The C-47 pilots, on the other hand, were asked to fly at night, relying on their navigational equipment. In addition, they had to depend on the pathfinders who marked the drop zones, an operation that required as much luck as skill when executed on a large scale. Failure to find the correct DZ was not necessarily a sign of incompetence. Furthermore, transport pilots, unlike bomber pilots, did not fly combat missions over enemy territory regularly; they did so only during airdrops, which were relatively rare occurrences. Flying over enemy territory required fortitude and experience; the bomber pilots who were unable to tolerate the pressure of combat flying were transferred to other, less demanding units. In the case of the transport pilots, it will never be known how many actually lost their nerve in a combat situation. Although a fair number of pilots, though not the majority, already had acquired some experience in Sicily and Italy and knew their business, for many it was their first time in enemy airspace. One nervous pilot or one aircraft hit by flak could cause several other ships to drop their sticks at the wrong place. The problems were magnified during night missions.

Because the skills of the C-47 pilots were no better or worse than those of the bomber pilots,

Axis Sally Welcomes the 437th Troop Carrier Group

In January 1944, Lieutenant Thompson traveled by train with other pilots and aircrews from Pope Field, North Carolina, to Fort Wayne, Indiana, to pick up C-47s fresh from the factory. They took the planes on one test flight before they loaded up for their trip across the Atlantic. The group of forty-eight aircraft landed at Homestead Airbase, Florida, in early January 1944.

CWO William Hart, on the other hand, traveled by sea on the liner *Mauritania* with the ground crew. They sailed from New York.

> No escort across the Atlantic and only our ship. They would run out the gun crews. They probably had three or four antiaircraft stations. We had a hell of a storm just outside of Liverpool. We landed at Liverpool, unloaded in the late afternoon, and boarded a train when it was dark. We ran into a blackout—enemy bombers. Nothing happened, but we thought we were in a hell of a pickle. When they put four or five people in each compartment with all our gear, you were kind of stuck.
>
> We were picked up by trucks and hauled out to our air base. Our air echelon was already there. We didn't have lights; it was a new base called Ramsbury, to the northwest of London, and it was all going on in the dark. At daylight, we got more coordinated and established. It was winter; the weather was icy, and it got pretty chilly. Our group was at this one base. We all had a common mess hall. Our squadrons were in different parts of the base. Each squadron had its own engineering and operation sections on the base. A day or two after we got there, we were welcomed to the theater by Axis Sally. She named a few of us by name and said she would visit us one of these days. In a few days, we had an air raid. The bomb shelter was just a trench with piles of dirt. Sally said she would be over to see us, and this sort of spooked us. The next alert, we could see the light in the bomb bay and the antiaircraft fire; it looked like a Christmas tree at nighttime. Maybe a couple of times a week they came. They never dropped anything on our base, though. They were on the way to London, yet we were west of London.

it would not be fair to blame them for problems that developed during training and in Normandy. Unlike the bomber pilots, they had to live with the fact that if they made an error, a stick of paratroopers may have jumped to their death. The bomber pilot never knew whether his bombs had hit the target, but he did know that he had not caused the death of his comrades if he missed the objective.

The 47th Squadron of the 313th Troop Carrier (TC) Group was a veteran unit that had served in the Mediterranean campaign and flown paratroopers into Sicily. During the winter, the squadron spent most of its time evacuating wounded from Italy to Sicily and North Africa. Sometime in March, the group packed up and flew from Sicily to England. Its route took it to Folkington, England, via Oran and Gibraltar. Lt.

Lyle Foutz, one of the officers in the squadron, recounted the trip back to England.

> At Gibraltar, there was a lot of space. We had several squadrons there at the same time and the British were flying as well. It was quite an experience. We were weathered in and spent several days there. They had a little town, but all the civilian employees came from Spain and crossed into Gibraltar. The runway sat between two huge rocks and was built over the water. It was good and wide, but it had a hump to it.
>
> When we landed at our base in England, we found it had no facilities on it. The unit that had moved off had not cleaned up, so they gave the whole squadron a blanket pass. When we came back, the base was in operation.

While the squadron was setting up in England, 2nd Lt. Paul Cody of Oak Park, Illinois, crossed the Atlantic. He had been drafted in April 1941 at age twenty-three and had been stationed at Howard Field, Panama, with the 108th Observation Squadron. On his return to the United States, he became a pilot after completing flying school in late 1943.

> I came from the States on a transport, a C-47, via the southern way, since it was wintertime, which meant Florida to Puerto Rico, to British Guiana, to Belem at the mouth of the Amazon River, to Natal on the eastern tip of South America, to Ascension Island in the South Atlantic, to Liberia, to Dakar, to Marrakech. We spent another day in the Sahara Desert because we had an engine problem. After Dakar, we flew out off the coast of Portugal and Spain, because they were neutral, and on up to England, but way out in the Atlantic, well off the coast of France, because the German fighter sweeps came out that way and we had no protection against fighters. I think there were five on the aircraft: pilot, copilot, navigator, crew chief, and radio operator. It was carrying mail and I was the copilot. We were flying alone. There were other aircraft ahead of us and behind us spaced maybe ten minutes apart. We were ferrying aircraft over to Europe—this was routine with these brand new aircraft. When we arrived in England, we left them with Troop Carrier Command and we were assigned to an outfit. The navigators went back to the States and flew with somebody else because they were in short supply.

Lieutenant Cody joined the 47th Squadron as it was going back into training, which did not lack excitement on occasion.

> We made a drop in Southern England in the middle of the night. We had the whole group, and we were following. The other two squadrons were ahead of us, and then German fighters got mixed up in the formation. The German fighters just scattered the squadron when they came down over the formation. They just accidentally came in, and they were not really fighters but Ju 88s, which were bombers occasionally used as fighters. We never lost a plane, but it sure confused you. One group of the squadron broke radio silence, which was against regulations, and they were confined to the base for six weeks or something like that. They really got rough on them.

Lieutenant Foutz dropped British paratroopers at least once during a war exercise, perhaps Exercise Bizz. The event resulted in a great deal of confusion.

Planning for an airborne exercise, February 1944.

> We took a week's training with the RAF in night flying. They were experts, and that was a good course. We admired the RAF. One of the things they taught us was that you don't smoke, because when you light up that cigarette and it flares up, the retina of your eye will close down for about half an hour and will slowly open up again. You don't dare light a match, so we couldn't smoke; of course, the flare could be seen too.

The 47th Squadron flew many practice night formation missions, but it made no more than three or four practice airdrops. According to Lieutenant Foutz, the practice in quick landing and takeoff—one plane every ten seconds—had little value in combat. In Italy, the squadron had had plenty of experience with mud, gravel, concrete, and steel-matting airfields.

Lt. William M. Thompson arrived in Britain in early 1944. During the few months before the invasion, his group participated in a considerable number of nighttime navigational problems, including locating drop zones, and even dropped paratroopers during daylight on a couple of missions.

> The one mission that sticks in mind was in May, when we flew with another group. Our group was forty-five airplanes, and there were forty-five airplanes ahead of us, but I don't know how many aircraft there were on this night mission. We didn't have troops at this time, but it was a preparation for D-Day. We had to fly a triangular course, and so we were briefed to fly at a certain altitude into this drop zone. England being so small, we had to fly three different

legs to make an equal distance to what we would fly on D-Day to a designated drop zone. We were to fly north from Ramsbury, then west toward Ireland; then, off the west coast of England, we turned back towards the drop zone over Land's End.

Going in, we had all lights out for blackout except for the little formation lights on top of the wings when all of a sudden, up in front, I saw lights coming on. To make a long story short, what happened was our leader or the leader of the other forty-five ships was coming back, and we all met head-on at the same altitude at night. Would you believe that no airplanes got knocked out? I remember looking up there when the navigational lights started coming on. When that happened, everybody started turning his lights on. The only vacant place where I couldn't see lights was right straight under me. So I just pulled the throttle back, stuck the nose down, and dived down to what was minimum altitude to get out of the way. Of my two wingmen, one stayed with me, but I lost the other. I leveled off at what I thought was minimum altitude with 500 feet indicated, not knowing for sure where I was. That busted up the formation. Almost everybody got home, but some had to land at other bases.

When I got back to my home field, I found out it was the one time I had taken off with the altimeter set at 1,000 feet off, and this was in my favor.

This incident took place on May 15, 1944, when seventy-two aircraft of the 437th TC took part in a maneuver with all the groups of the wing. It was never discovered which group ran into them. To complicate matters, at the time of the exercise, there was an alert about a *Luftwaffe* raid. According to Guild's *Action of the Tiger*, British night fighters added to the confusion, but they found and challenged nothing but C-47s; the Germans had gone.

As the airplanes scattered and returned to their bases, they had to be careful not to land on dummy airfields with runway lights and no landing strips designed to deceive the Germans. Surprisingly, no planes were lost that night, even though several accidents had happened earlier on more routine missions.

According to Lieutenant Thompson, the 47th also flew some intelligence personnel from London when they made four drops to get qualified. His unit never took part in any mass drops such as Exercise Eagle, however.

Although most of the glider pilots had acquired combat experience in the Mediterranean, some, like Lt. William D. Knickerbocker, had plenty of training but no combat. Surprisingly, Knickerbocker got little practice with gliders at Fort Benning because, he claimed, the power pilots were too busy dropping paratroopers. He arrived in North Africa before the German surrender and underwent additional training.

We had those dirt fields, and when the planes took off, we couldn't see the tow plane because of the dust. We got in extremely valuable training in North Africa, which probably kept most of us alive through the war. We also spent several weeks in night training. It was not my first night training, but the most intensive I had. We hung around Kairouan, Tunisia, until after the invasion of Sicily. We were scheduled to go on that mission, but when the navy shot down some of our ships, we had no tow planes, so the mission was called off.

We moved to the western plain of Sicily, where we stayed and trained for quite a while, and then they started transferring us. I got a lot of C-47 time flying supplies to British forces as a copilot. After eight months in Sicily, we were put on boats and shipped to Scotland in early 1944. After landing in Scotland, we went down to the Midlands, to Saltby just outside Crampton between Leicester and Nottingham.[3]

My original outfit was the 52nd Wing, but they did not tow gliders in combat, although we had a full complement of gliders and glider pilots. So any time a mission or training came up, we had to transfer to a wing that carried gliders. The only time they ever did tow us in was at Wessel, Germany, in 1945.

While I was with the 50th Squadron, the head glider officer, Captain Spring, had to go into the hospital for some reason, and I was left in charge. He said D-Day was coming up and that I was more valuable to the squadron, so I would have to transfer about twenty men but not myself. As soon as he left, I put my name at the head of the list, asked for volunteers, and assigned nineteen others to the squadron. We went down and joined the 435th Group's 76th Squadron for D-Day. When we got to Welford Park, we received a hell of a lot of training and flew mainly Horsa gliders.

Somewhere down the line, we got back to the 50th Squadron. I was sent to the Horsa factory, which was named Airspeed and was located at Christchurch. I stayed there two weeks watching them build the Horsa glider, which is much bigger than the American Waco. It carried twenty-six men, was all plywood, and had flaps instead of spoilers (spoilers are a little flap on the top wing, while flaps can drop and slow the plane). I got tired of hanging around the factory, so I spent all my time riding with the test pilots. They took the gliders when they came off the line for a test flight. I was supposed to learn about Horsa gliders, come back, and teach my fellow pilots all about the Horsa, but it never happened. The CG-4A had spoilers that disrupted the airflow to let you drop. I probably had as much time in Horsas as any other American glider pilot, or more. A large number of pilots never flew a Horsa, and I never flew one in combat. It was a good experience for me but never helped anybody else.

Flight Off. Charles V. Gauntt was injured during one of the training exercises.

On the last training exercises, troops carried live ammunition. I suppose they were carrying it on the glider, but I am not sure.

In April, we were given live ammunition, and they told us not to load our rifles until we went out to the rifle range. One of the guys loaded it in the barracks and got it jammed. He was messing with the bolt and somehow or another set off the gun. I got hit in the leg with a piece of shrapnel.

The Bigots

The operational plan known as Overlord had an additional code name for the naval phase: Neptune. All the information was top secret, and great care was taken to keep it that way. The select few who knew of the operation probably numbered in the hundreds. These included officers and NCOs from every higher headquarters and representatives of divisional and regimental headquarters of the units that were to take part in the

3. Saltby was an RAF airfield used by the U.S. Army Air Force 314th TC Group to carry the 508th Parachute Infantry Regiment to Normandy on D-Day. There is no town called Crampton; he may be referring to Grantham, where the AAF had a headquarters.

Green Glider Pilots to England

Flight Off. Charles V. Gauntt and Lt. Lambert G. Wilder left the United States for England on the liner *Aquitaine* in late 1943. They did not know each other and were destined for different squadrons of the 435th Group. Before boarding, Flight Officer Gauntt's group "marched something like three or five miles from the train to the ship, since the trucks did not arrive." He recalls, "I had to carry all that equipment, flight gear, and I had an extra radio and personal clothing—I was like a pack mule." Somehow he managed to stagger up the gangplank. Lieutenant Wilder was in the same group.

> We were assigned a place to sleep. I was a second lieutenant at that time, and lieutenants were supposed to have staterooms. There being so many officers aboard, you had to be a captain to have a stateroom, and some of them didn't get one. There just was not enough room for everybody. Some of the people would sleep during the night and then change with others. There was plenty of seasickness. I didn't get seasick. Half the equipment the enlisted men brought on went overboard, such as gas masks and things like that. They would use their helmets for urinating because they couldn't get to a latrine.

During the trip, Gauntt was once assigned as the officer of the day:

> I went down into the hold of the enlisted men, and you had to pick your way going down the steps or you would step in a pile of it. It almost made me sick. I stayed down there five minutes and had to get out. The whole squadron was on the ship except for the C-47 pilots.
>
> The battleship *Texas* escorted us, and there must have been about 240 ships. On the day I was officer of the day, I went to the forward part of the ship where these big waves would come over, the ship would go down under, and I would duck under the bulkhead. The water would go flying over, and I would come up and wait a few minutes until we went into another big trough. When we got on top of that wave, I could see the battleship.
>
> We had too many people on for abandon-ship drills. It was a British ship, and they fed their officers like kings. I was lucky; about three days before we shipped out, I missed one of my buddies and couldn't find him anywhere. I was laying there on the deck, and one of them tapped me on the shoulder and told me to come with him. He had a stateroom and he was an FO. I asked how he managed this. He said he and three others in our squadron got on the crew that helped load the ship, and they picked themselves out a stateroom. How they got by, I don't know, because there were only captains up in the crow's nest. One day, I was coming out of that room when a captain was coming down the hall. He looked at me and said, "Hey there, is that your room?" and I said, "Oh no, I am looking for somebody." I lied.

continued

Green Glider Pilots to England *continued*

> We arrived in England on November 1, 1943.

The trip was equally memorable for Lieutenant Wilder.

> There was a tanker in the forward part of the convoy, and one of its crewmembers fell overboard. The convoy wasn't going to stop, but he was fortunate because an armed ship following the convoy picked him up. We also ran into a lot of fog, and I wondered how the ships kept their station, because radar was still new.

After an uneventful berthing at Liverpool, Wilder and Gauntt went to Nottingham, where they were assigned Nissen huts, which were so frigid that the men called them "refrigerators." Wilder and Gauntt were some of the first flight officers to make it to Britain, and most of the British soldiers didn't know what to make of them.

> When we were trying to get a truck to load our baggage to go to our base, we couldn't get one, because every time we did, some major would come along and bump us. Finally one of these FOs went in there and told them his rank, and they asked what it was. They asked if it was like a flight lieutenant, and he said yes—a flight lieutenant for the British is like a captain. They immediately got him a truck, and we all piled on there. About this time, a captain came out yelling to hold that truck. We yelled, "Go on, go on!" and the driver did.

Wilder and Gauntt's group was made of the 75th, 76th, 77th, and 78th TC Squadrons, which took part in maneuvers that included night training with gliders. A few times, they carried troops on the gliders. Flight Officer Gauntt had a midair collision during a demonstration.

> I was the copilot, and the guy I was flying with didn't cut off when he was supposed to. Here we were, already past our turning point, so we had to circle back, and all of a sudden we felt a lurch. We sat down on a glider that tried to come in under us. We went one way, he went the other, and we tore off part of his wing. Fortunately, no one was hurt. We rotated as pilot and copilot.

For a combat mission, Lieutenant Wilder flipped a coin to decide who the pilot would be. Rank did not matter; the lieutenants usually had less flight time, since they spent more time on paperwork.

landings. The men who knew about Overlord also carried the identification code of "Bigot."[4] The sinking of the two LSTs during Exercise Tiger caused a great deal of consternation among the planners, who feared that some Bigots on the sunken vessels might have been captured. These men carried in their heads some of the most important secrets of the European campaign.

CWO-2 Larry Knecht, assistant adjutant, 8th Infantry, 4th Division, was one of the Bigots.

> I was cleared for top secret and was also cleared for "Bigot." My job was working with a Capt. Walter Hollis. What we did was alternated going down to Huntington from Sidley, where division headquarters was. We would pick up the plans for the invasion and bring them back. As I remember, we would always use two jeeps. One of us would be in the lead jeep with the driver, and two guards in the back jeep with machine guns would follow us at a safe distance. We would go down to the division headquarters and pick up the plans. They were always sealed in a container, and we would bring them back to the adjutant, John Galvin.

Capt. John Galvin, the Adjutant for the 8th Infantry, was involved in the planning for Overlord.

> My participation in preparation for the invasion was at the headquarters, knowing what was going to happen, working on the logistics of what we needed, personnel we needed, how we were going to get personnel. We had other fellows doing S-3 and S-2 work. My job with Larry [Knecht] and Walter Hollis, a captain in personnel, was working out a plan for our replacements. I knew maybe four months in advance what was going to happen, although I was not informed when the forces would land in France. I guess the biggest problem with my situation at the time was knowing all of this in advance and trying not to relate it to anyone else. I remember a couple of instances where you would avoid going to pubs, you would avoid going out, you would be scared to death you might make a mistake, a slip. It had to be top secret. It was rather scary, too, because on this relief map we had in the regiment, you could see the hills. But at the time, if you had never been in combat, it didn't bother you.
>
> Aside from that, I guess there were three memorable things that happened. One was having the little, tiny General Roosevelt arrive at headquarters. Strangely, he was so small and his father was so big. This brought a lot of joy to me, and then of course I met General Eisenhower. As he walked in, I saluted him and said, "Captain Galvin, adjutant of the 8th Infantry Regiment." He said, "Galvin, is this old SOB bothering you too much?"—referring to Colonel Van Fleet. And then later, meeting General Montgomery.

First Lt. Peter P. Triolo served in the S-2 section, 1st Battalion, 12th Infantry, 4th Division.

> I found out about D-Day early in April when I was called in from the field and told to report to regimental headquarters. Upon arriving at regimental headquarters, I found my stuff there with the other two battalion S-2s. After questioning and talking to the

4. The term "Bigot" was stamped on the ID cards of those given access to top-secret documents in September 1943, according to the BBC press pack titled *D-Day on the BBC*. Supposedly, no one would brag about being a bigot.

A stick of paratroopers of the 82nd Airborne Division take a group photo before departing from England on the evening of June 5, 1944.

regimental S-2, I was informed that my gear was being sent up to regiment because I was being assigned to a special detail as a liaison officer.

Shortly after that, my driver, Shanks, brought my gear up from battalion. I was issued a brown-bag lunch. I was then escorted outside and loaded into an army 2½ truck with all the canvases down and a guard in there with us. We picked up two other men, as I recall. I assume they were the battalion S-2s from the 8th and 22nd. We traveled together for a number of hours and finally came to a farmhouse. There we were detrucked and escorted into the office area. We talked to an officer from the 82nd

A/B Division. At that time, I was assigned a sergeant as a bodyguard. I was asked questions about my loyalty to my country and asked how I felt about retaining information and keeping my mouth shut if I was questioned by anyone. Upon satisfaction of my answers, I was escorted to a big barn and taken to an attic. There on the wall were the D-Day landings for June 5 to D+26, showing the units, where they were landing, the phase lines showing what they planned to reach.

During the final days before the invasion, thousands of troops of the assaulting divisions were "Bigoted." After arriving at the old British camp at South Brent, William Finnigan, 4th Signal Company, 4th Division, was able to leave camp only once.

Our division commander, Maj. Gen. R. Barton, was here, and I often saw Brig. Gen. Teddy Roosevelt, the assistant division commander, in his jeep named the "Rough Rider." This camp had a varied group of army branches, but nearly all 4th Division people. One day, in small groups of eight to ten, we went to a small building, and we were shown maps of Normandy beach areas. One was a black silhouette as though taken from a submarine. "If lost, go to St. Martin-de-Vareville; there will be directors on the beach"—of course, there weren't. As we left, the sign beside the door said, "You now know the greatest secret in the world."

A few days later, navy personnel arrived. We exchanged our British money for French money. It was printed by the U.S., and it didn't look French.

CHAPTER 4

The Air Campaign

"Bombs Away"

As the troops and naval units made their final preparations for the invasion during May, the AAF continued to carry out its mission. The Eighth and Ninth Air Forces and the RAF maintained their bombing campaign, but on Eisenhower's orders, they shifted their focus to the transportation plan. The Ninth Air Force and elements of the RAF also kept up their attacks on V-weapons sites and coastal fortifications. They could not concentrate solely on Normandy, however, for fear of revealing the objective of the invasion.

In May 1944, the Eighth and Ninth Air Forces began to concentrate on targets in northern France and the Low Countries. On most fair-weather days, waves of B-17s, B-24s, and medium bombers of the Ninth Air Force struck Operation Crossbow targets—V-weapons sites—and transportation targets such as marshaling areas, bridges, and airfields. P-38 and P-47 fighters took on bombing missions, blasting away at similar targets. The Allies did not exclude coastal defense sites, but they were careful to seek out fortified spots from Normandy to Belgium to prevent the Germans from pinpointing the actual locale for the long-awaited invasion. On May 9, the preinvasion aerial assault on German airfields began in earnest. During the last week of May, the Fifteenth Air Force, operating out of Italy, began striking at targets in southern France. By this time, the transportation lines in France had been seriously impaired, virtually isolating the invasion zone.

The 379th Squadron bombs Germany. COURTESY OF ALVIN ANDERSON

The Allies could not unleash the full fury of their air forces against Normandy until they launched the invasion, however. Allied air units had to hit every selected target equally hard in order to keep the enemy guessing. The Bigot planners were especially careful not to single out the coastal defenses in the invasion area for fear of alerting the Germans. Thus the Ninth Air Force attacked the key battery position at Pointe du Hoc only a few times, in late May and on June 4. By June 5, the position was so badly cratered that it looked like a surreal lunar landscape. In May, the Ninth Air Force medium bomber missions against coastal gun positions all along the coastline had a greater impact than the heavy bombers of the Eighth. The RAF also targeted several coastal positions, including Merville in Normandy.

Sgt. Herbert Beatty of New York City joined the 702nd Squadron, 445th Bomb Group, in England in April 1944 after a ten-day ocean voyage. He was just in time to take his place as a gunner in a B-24 of the 2nd Bombardment Division on bombing missions in preparation for Operation Overlord. On his fifth mission, his badly shot-up bomber cracked up on landing, but the crew survived with no major injuries.

On May 15, 1944, Lt. Graydon Eubank flew the last of his fifty missions. He had flown on May 9, 11, 12, 13, and 15, with the first four missions against gun positions including one near Cherbourg on May 9 and another near Bayeux on May 13.[1] After flying his last mission against an airfield at Beaumont on May 15, Eubank boarded the *Queen Elizabeth* with other men rotating or

1. There were several large coastal gun positions on either side of Cherbourg, several smaller coastal gun positions north of Bayeux, the Longues Battery to the east of Omaha Beach and Pointe-du-Hoc, and the Caisny batteries on the west.

going home on leave on May 16. Eubank's career as a bomber pilot was not yet over, however. At the end of July, he boarded the *Mauritania*, once again filled to the rafters with soldiers and airmen, as he returned to combat flying.

On May 26, Lt. William Denham's group flew on a memorable Crossbow mission against Cherbourg.

> Another guy in this group, Smedley, was leading the squadron, and I was flying off his left wing. At a low altitude, they figured it should be a smooth run, no flak or anything. Until we come along and, boy, they start sending those shells up like they are shooting at you—not the airplanes, you! That stuff was so accurate. Old Smedley was coming ahead, and there was a boom here, a boom there, and the next one had to be right on him, but he just pulls out of its path and then sucked back in time for the target. Boy, did he get chewed out! But he figured that third round was his. We found out later on what caused the accurate flak. It was an R and R camp for antiaircraft artillery, and the people that went down there to get a little time off were crack crews. When anything came along, they would man the batteries that happened to be there. That is why they were so accurate.

On one hair-raising mission in the late spring against a coastal target, Lieutenant Denham's crew took off late at night.

> We were forming up. We would come back, start looking for flares—fly around looking for a formation firing your color flares—and hook onto it. At this time, I was the second ship in the formation, and we just circled to the left until everybody joined up.
>
> There was another group circling the same way. I was watching this guy to make sure we didn't run into him, and we were just about to pass when I decided to take one more look. He was just clear, and that lead ship—it was the first time he saw him. The tail gunner—they always put the copilot in the tail-gun position in the lead ship and usually have some wheel [VIP] in the front seat—says, "You know, I saw right underneath us and I figured I was gone, I was dead." I looked back, and all I could see was the bottom of a B-17. I took that stick and jammed it forward. The copilot didn't have his belt on, and he got scrunched up in the window, about three feet off his seat. Everybody else was pretty well messed up. When we were taking off, McRielly, the bombardier, was supposed to go back and pull the pin so the bombs were ready to go. He had about half of them out when he said that they were probably going to scrub this mission, and if they didn't, he would pull them off [to arm them]. So I said, "Mac, you will have to go back to the bomb bay. I heard some noise." He went back there and said, "I guess you heard some noise; we got three bombs missing, and there are two hanging by one shackle." Well, the bomb-bay doors were bent open, and they went right through the doors they bent open.
>
> They told us to go up the Wash to get rid of these bombs. We went up there, and the navigator tripped the bomb release. McRielly said that was the hairiest thing he had ever seen; all those bombs went down, and as they did, they hit this one that hung up and bounced off. Five-hundred-pounders banging away! We had to pry it away because it was jammed up.
>
> We tried to tell them where they might find those two or three that went out through the doors, gave them our estimated location, and returned to base.

Long-Range B-17 Mission: One Engine and a Prayer

Lieutenant Denham's long-distance mission against oil targets in Brux, Czechoslovakia, on May 12, 1944, gives an idea of the airmen's experience.

> We were about halfway in and started picking up German fighters in all directions, ten here, fifteen there, and so forth. Their procedure was to fly a gaggle of fighters, all fifteen aircraft, or whatever, up until they were in front of the formation they were going to hit, then they would turn and come in head-on, and in many cases, they flew their airplanes between ours. On one of these passes, the copilot said he could count the rivets on the plane as it went right over the top of our left wing. At the same time, he put an explosive 20-millimeter cannon round into the leading edge of the wing between the two engines, and it cut the fuel line. I lost the number 1 engine. We were scheduled to go in at 16,000 feet and climb to 18,000 but I lost this engine. I could not keep up with the group or climb, so I dropped behind. I had hoped to cut the corner and catch up with the group after the bomb run but lost another engine, and they just disappeared into the distance. Alone, we finally made it back, but as we crossed the French coastline, we lost the number 3 engine—it ran out of gas—and we had one engine left. I did not know the actual condition of the fuel line in the left wing from the damage, but with nothing to lose, I transferred some gas from the number 4 engine across to the other side of the wing, so the gas tank of the number 4 went to the number 2 engine tank and then transferred to the number 3, which I was able to start up. I had to find a field to land on and came in on a fighter base. We went through the twenty-foot hedgerow at the end of the runway, where we came to a stop.

The plane was badly damaged, and although it was repaired, it seemed to "never fly right" again. According to the gunners, they shot down thirteen enemy fighters but received credit for only four. Denham's 452nd Bomb Group lost fourteen B-17s, and another group lost seven. A few days later, Lieutenant Denham and his crew were on their way to Berlin. They flew one mission every other day until they completed their final one on May 31 over the Ruhr. His crew was one of the lucky ones, as they never lost a man.

One May 7, 8, 19, and 24, in addition to other missions that month, Lieutenant Denham flew against Berlin. During the same month, his squadron also bombed a variety of targets, ranging from Orleans in France to Brux in Czechoslovakia. He flew his last B-17 mission for the 730th Squadron, 452nd Bomb Group, at the end of the month against the marshaling yards at Schwerte.

> They had flak all over the place in the Ruhr Valley. We went around from the east side, where we didn't have to go through the flak, and entered from the open end of the flak area. It was the longest run under flak conditions I had been on. Once we hit the target and turned left, it stopped, and

> they turned on the other guys coming in. From there on, it was smooth sailing.[2]

T.Sgt. William F. French, who was also in the 452nd Bomb Group, served as a radio operator on a B-17 in the 729th Squadron and participated in bombing missions between January and mid-June 1944. On his first combat mission in early January, his squadron sought out a target at Romilly, France, where it ran into intense and accurate flak fire. By the time he completed his fourth mission, his badly shot-up aircraft had to be replaced. "I had a little radio compartment, which was a little room right behind the bomb-bay compartment and just over the edge of the wing," he recalls. "It was about six by six, enough for one man and the radio equipment. I had one flexible .50-caliber machine gun out of the hatch. I used it, especially on Poznan, several times. It had a limited arc of fire compared to the waist guns. I could get it out quite a ways and up of course."

French's squadron flew the mission to Poznan, Poland, on April 11, 1944, after several rough missions over Germany. On this fourteen-hour mission, the squadron's fighter escort, whose range was shorter, turned back over Denmark. It ran into strong opposition from German fighters and had to fight its way over the target, which turned out to be shrouded in clouds. The squadron was forced to turn away and find a secondary target in northern Germany. The 3rd Bombardment Division lost thirty-three B-17s that day.

Sergeant French flew only three missions in May. During the first, a No Ball (V-weapons site) mission on May 1, the targets turned out to be heavily protected and the flak gunners unusually accurate. At the end of the month, French flew the same mission to Schwerte as Lieutenant Denham, where the antiaircraft fire was thick but losses were minimal.

Lt. Robert Walsh, a bombardier on a B-17 of the 524th Squadron, 379th Bomb Group, had been flying missions since early December 1943, including one over Berlin at the end of April. On one of the missions, his crew was on a B-17F—instead of the G model like the other crews—when his aircraft ran out of fuel looking for the clouded-over airfield. A Spitfire guided his pilot safely to an airstrip, where they landed just as the third engine shut down as its fuel supply ran out. In May, Walsh's crew moved south to Italy for practice bombing.

> They [the Allies] were making the push on Rome and the pilots wanted to get another citation and help, but they decided against it because we could be hit. There were about seven aircraft from the Eighth Air Force attached to the Fifteenth Air Force. The little blue powder bombs were used. Apparently they were getting us ready for D-Day and we didn't know it.
>
> We went down through the Mediterranean, landed in Africa, and then on to Foggia, Italy, where we were stationed for about three weeks. On the way back, we went through Gibraltar. As we were trying to come in on its narrow strip, the Spaniards sent a couple of cannonballs our way! It may be they didn't realize we were American air force. They fired as we got within one or two miles of Gibraltar over the water. There was nothing we could do; we only had .50-caliber, and we didn't fire back.

Lt. Jack R. Sargeant arrived in Great Britain in April 1944 as a replacement, after leaving the plane he had flown over the Atlantic in Northern Ireland. He was sent to Stone, England, where he received orders after two weeks to report with his crew to the 326th Squadron, 92nd Bomb Group,

2. Although the flak was heavy, 3rd Bombardment Group lost only a single B-17 on this and other targets that day.

at Podington, England, Station 109.

> The aircraft I flew was a B-17G. They had all the people's names that made it under what you could call a horn button, a centerpiece of the control. My first mission was on May 9 in the aircraft named *Devil Make Hair*. They told me I was to fly with an experienced crew to get the feel for combat. My experienced crew happened to be Jim Shanks, and it was his third mission. As luck would have it, we saw no flak, no enemy fighters, nothing. We flew in, dropped our bombs, and flew back. I thought if combat were going to be like this, it would be a piece of cake. The whole mission lasted about six and a half hours. Little did I know my next mission was to Stettin [May 13].
>
> Although the mission report does not say this, we were caught by roughly 125 German fighters, and that was my first experience with fighters. Believe me, I did everything possible to avoid German fighters. One fighter made a head-on pass from twelve o'clock high and dove down, and at about 500 yards, started blinking lights on his wings. I soon realized the blinking lights were guns firing at me. The rate of closure was so fast, he flipped over, turned over on his back, and split us out before my bombardier could reach the controls for the chin turret to bring it down into the firing position. As luck would have it, they left us alone after that one pass and hit the group behind us—hit them pretty heavy.
>
> I distinctly remember one humorous incident on the mission. It was the plane piloted by Lieutenant Williams in our squadron. Williams thought he was transmitting on interphone, but he was actually transmitting over the air. One of the fighters got mixed up with our formation, and he was flying alongside Williams while he was instructing his crew to "shoot the son of a bitch! Shoot him! Shoot him! Shoot him!" Little did he know he was broadcasting over the air. Finally somebody mashed the button and said, "Let him alone; maybe he will go away." That was our introduction to enemy action.

Although Lieutenant Sargeant flew few missions during May, most were pretty rough.

T.Sgt. Alvin J. Anderson of the 525th Squadron, 379th Bomb Group, who was a veteran by May 1944, enjoyed life on base.

> We carried three dextrose cubes to eat during the missions. They would sure give you a lot of energy, but when you got on the ground, you were hungry. There were a lot of times that we ate mutton stew, and I thought it was pretty good. When we flew on Sunday, we had fried chicken. It seemed like on the Sundays that we flew, they didn't have any chicken left from Saturday night. Well, the pilot complained to the CO, and the CO said, "You eat with your boys next time, and if they don't have chicken, you call me, and they will have chicken if it takes those cooks until midnight to prepare it." Well, the cooks must have got the idea, because we had chicken every Sunday night.
>
> I think the air force probably was fed better than the other branches. You had a permanent base, a place that was dry, and a place to sleep with decent food. If you didn't get back, it really didn't make much difference then. On Sundays, you always had a good meal at noon, and in the evenings, it was leftovers and cold cuts. I have eaten a lot of cold cuts in my life, but some way or other those were the best you ever ate: cheese and bologna, and so forth like that; it was doggone good.

Lieutenant Sargeant on Flying a B-17

Jack Sargeant's description of flying a B-17 was typical for flyers in Europe.

You could look down and see the muzzle flash of the gun shooting at you, and it took twenty seconds for that shell to get to our altitude, and in that time we could be long gone. The flak that got us was the barrage-type, where they blocked a certain area altitude and made a box out of it, and to get to the target you had to fly through that. Berlin was a good example of block-type flak, because the city was like a black cloud. That mission lasted about eleven hours and twenty minutes, a long time to sit and hope.

At 10,000 feet, we went on oxygen with our masks on and started to climb. At about 5,000 feet, we took off our oxygen masks and had a cigarette.

One piece of gear we used was a harness for a chest pack. My dress usually amounted to putting on long underwear, flying pants, my GI OD [olive drab] shirt, and over that my flying suit, the Mae West, and over that the parachute harness. The parachute had a couple of quick-release clips you snapped into the harness. The parachute you kept along the seat of the aircraft. There was armor plate right behind the pilot's seat. We wore a flak suit, which was mail. The gunners that didn't have armor plate had a complete suit, front and back. The pilots only wore the front part.

The chest-pack parachute—I remember one fellow in our squadron took a direct hit and blew up over Pas de Calais; we reported him as dead. This was a Noball target—V-1 or V-2 sites. We reported them as lost. About six months later, there he was in the squadron, in a hut. We questioned him and said, "Hey, you're dead!" It seemed he had a backpack on. When the aircraft blew, it blew him out the top. When he came to, he was falling through space; he pulled the ripcord on the parachute and saved his life. Immediately I went down and turned in my chest pack for a backpack, which I flew with the rest of the war.

I flew most of my missions in an aircraft called *Cooking with Gas*. It was an old-timer and left-wing-heavy. I liked left-wing-heavy aircraft, because you can trim it up to fly real tight formation. I really liked this airplane, because it was the last one in the squadron that had glass all the way around. This aircraft was eventually lost in a midair collision while I was in London on a forty-eight-hour pass, but everybody got out all right.

We had a lot of fun when we could. We got a pass and went to London once or twice. I never did quite like it. London was getting bombed quite regularly at that time in 1944. They had their underground transportation systems, and you would be surprised how many people had to live in the tubes, as they called them, because their homes were damaged or just from fear. Whole families went down to live there. You couldn't help but feel sorry for the English people. We took a lot of things for

B-17s in flight. COURTESY OF WILLIAM FRENCH

granted, like oranges and apples, which they hadn't had for years. Lipstick and silk hose for the women were nonexistent; they had done without lots of things.

When we were down in London, we saw Big Ben, Westminster Abbey, the changing of the guard, and Piccadilly Circus. You name it, and we sure toured it when we could. Usually, the place we liked to go was Bedford, England. It was a smaller town, and we sure kept the pubs a-popping. We never drank them dry; we tried! They just put a night shift on and manufactured more. Up there at Bedford, they had a stream—a small river, I would call it—and I took many a boat ride down it and watched the swans. It was enjoyable and we were treated well. At times, the American soldiers were a little overbearing. Of course, you want to understand too that I was a tech sergeant with flight pay and overseas pay. That was at the time $110 a month, which was more than a British major made. When an American ordered, they would never question you, but when a British soldier ordered, they would tell him what the cost was. If you went into a restaurant and ordered a meal, like the one in Bedford, they served a steak that was like shoe leather. It was meat of some kind, probably horse.

Our officers and enlisted men were very close in the bomber command. I know one day in Norfolk [where they had been sent for a couple weeks of rest], Lieutenant Smith came into the room I was in and asked if I had seen his blouse. I said, "Yeah, Sergeant Levy had it on when I saw him leave." "I wonder where the devil he went," he replied. He then asked where his jacket was. So Lieutenant Smith put on Sergeant

Levy's jacket with stripes on it, and he finally found him and they traded jackets in the middle of nowhere. You did not see that with other branches of service.

When we went to town, it was not unusual for an officer and three or four enlisted men, or vice versa, to go together. On base, or wherever an officer told you anything, he was the boss. I think this said a lot, with ten men there and each dependent on the other to do his duty.

On May 7, Sergeant Anderson returned to Berlin, and on May 12, he went to Merzburg. His next day off happened to be his twenty-first birthday. A week later, he and his crewmates were back on their way to Berlin for another memorable mission.

About the worst hit on our own plane was due to flak. It took about a third of the vertical stabilizer and the rudder off, broke both ammunition belts of the tail gunner, and knocked out both guns. He had his flak jacket over his shoulders, and he was wearing a flak vest underneath it. It looked like rats made a nest in his jacket. He had one little piece of flak in his leg. When we got back and landed, he went to the hospital. They took the flak out, gave him a shot of scotch, and told him to come back and get a good night's sleep because we were flying combat tomorrow.

One of Anderson's later missions in May almost ended in disaster for the target.

One day, we took off, got up above the overcast, and once again we couldn't find our formation. There was another there that needed a plane, so we slid in, which was normal procedure. We got over the English Channel. Normally, while crossing, you are climbing for altitude, but we weren't. In fact, we got over France, and instead of climbing, the lead plane dropped down lower and lower. We got down to near 1,000 feet; he opened his bomb-bay door and dropped his landing gear. The pilot broke radio silence and said, "We got bombs on here, and for Christ's sake don't drop them." About that time, we were over a large wooded area somewhere in France and they dropped whatever they were carrying—supplies or material, I presume. I never saw so many men come running out of a wooded area, gathering up this material and fading back into the woods. It would have been a terrible catastrophe if we had dropped our bombs, for we probably would have wiped out several of the resistance fighters in France. The only thing we could do was bring our bombs back over the Channel and drop them in the water.

During the May missions, Anderson's copilot's twin brother was shot down. Several years later, Anderson learned that he was one of the few survivors of the entire crew. "Our copilot almost came unglued, and he didn't fly a few missions, but he was always out there waiting for us to come back." At the end of the month, Anderson's squadron flew a special mission.

Our outfit was practicing with a glide bomb, which was nothing but a bomb with a couple of two-by-fours, stubby wings, and a gyro on it. We flew several practice missions with it in England to get used to it. In fact, there were two of them strapped on underneath the plane. You were supposed to raise the nose of the plane when you released, and they were supposed to glide to the target. Well, the day came when we were going to go out with them—the twenty-eighth of May—to Cologne, Germany, and

> we had a camera in the ball turret. He [the ball turret gunner] was to take pictures of what happened, because they were not quite sure what would happen when you released those bombs. We got over there within about fifty miles of Cologne. They raised the nose of the plane at a certain speed, and by golly, those things dropped, and pretty soon, they glided right off for the target at Cologne. We had turned around, and when we could see back, there was a burst of flak over Cologne, but we were on the way home. Man, we thought that was great. To my knowledge, that was the only time they were actually used.

Despite Anderson's optimistic account, the glide bombs turned out to be ineffective against the marshaling yards of Cologne, but according to Roger Freeman in *The Mighty Eighth*, they were possibly a better terror weapon, since they landed within the city.[3]

Sgt. Byron Cook, who had been wounded, left the hospital to fly a nine-hour mission to Berlin—his eleventh—on May 7. The following excerpts from his diary cover his eleventh, fourteenth, and sixteenth missions.

> May 11—Eleventh Mission—Berlin . . . run was undertaken in poor weather. . . . PFF [radar] was used for navigation and for the strike on the target. No fighter opposition was encountered but flak was intense and severely accurate in the target zone. We lost four heavies out of our Division over Berlin and two more went down over the troublesome Dummer Lake region.
>
> . . . Some of the new B-17s were being sent to us without the usual olive-drab camouflaging paint which slowed the forts up to five to ten miles an hour. Jerry air raids had slackened considerably, by this time and camouflage was felt no longer necessary. The bright silver ships certainly looked conspicuous in the formation though!
>
> May 12—Fourteenth Mission—Brux (9½ hours)
>
> We took off in clear weather over England but had to climb high to pass over thick undercast of billowy clouds obscuring the whole of France and western Germany. Our escort of Thunderbolts and Mustangs proved to be quite good; we were seldom left alone. We passed through only moderate barrages of flak, skirting the worst of it. We did lose one ship, however, as the result of a direct hit, which blew her tail off—no chutes seen. When the Third Division was just south of Coblenz trouble arrived in the form of a pack of fifty or sixty ME-109s and FW-190s!
>
> About twenty of them immediately engaged our escorting fighters in fierce dogfights. Our fighters were forced to drop their auxiliary fuel tanks and fought as long as their fuel held out, then turned for home. In the meantime, the rest of the Krauts were ganging up for passes at the bombers. They came in at us from all angles, singly and in groups. After passing through our Wing, they reformed and reverted almost entirely to head-on attacks, pressing them very closely. The interior of our plane was a bedlam of sound as the fighters closed from the front. Our nose guns opened up first, then the engineer's turret and the ball turret took up the chorus, swinging around as our attackers flashed past. Next, the waist guns

3. Fifty-eight B-17s from the 303rd, 379th, and 384th Bomb Groups each carried two of these 2,000-pound glide bombs, known as grapefruits, on external racks and launched them at 20,000 feet. They were launched at twenty miles, not fifty, from the city. On May 31, the 458th Bomb Group used radio-controlled, 1,000-pound Azon guided bombs against bridges in France without success, although the Azon did better in Burma later, according to Freeman.

opened up while the twin-fifties in the tail spewed out their lethal streams. The air was full of zooming fighters and falling planes. Everywhere could be seen the twinkling flashes of the German's time-fused cannon fire and the stream of smoke puffs from the bomber's stuttering fifty's. In between bursts from my own gun, I could see Hay crouched over his, firing in short bursts to prevent the barrel from burning out. Galson was up on the step in the Radio Room, the barrel of his flexible fifty, smoking hot. Blue-white puffs of smoke from the nose guns were whipping past my waist window. A fort with one wing shot off, pitched down out of the high squadron, and spun down through the low, narrowly missing another fortress. Two more forts went down and Bleem and Babicky's excited voices came over the intercom, claiming two Focke-Wulfes. Carney was sure that he had one too. The Jerries tried several more attacks, bagging a couple of fortresses each time. Then they dove for the deck, with the appearance of more of our P-51s and twin boomed P-38s. I had the satisfaction of seeing two of the large Lightnings shoot a couple of ME-109s to pieces.

We continued on, with escort . . . across Germany. Passing over the trailing edge of the cloud blanket, we could plainly see the brilliant greens and browns of the country far below. The air was clear: no blanket of haze over the heart of the Reich. Winking flashes of light from the ground were enemy flak guns shooting at us, but we were mostly out of range.

We reached a point directly north of Frankfurt when I saw a Thunderbolt falling past me in flames. On its tail were two Focke-Wulfes. I immediately called out "Bandits at eight o'clock, high!" A swarm of them swept in and saturated our escort and again the air was filled with battling planes. The fighter engagements gradually drifted away from the bomber stream leaving approximately sixty Focke-Wulfes and Messerschmidts for attacks on the bombers. They singled out our 45th Combat Wing for their attention, concentrating mainly on the 452nd and 96th Groups. They were flying high and low group respectively, the 388th in the middle.

Again the Germans resorted to head-on attacks, sweeping in against the formations in waves, then reforming for more mass saturation assaults. They really hit the high and low groups damaging them badly. Three doomed fortresses fell down out of the 452nd and several others dropped back behind the formation, too crippled to keep up. These were picked off by the enemy scavengers at leisure. Ships out of the 96th Group were spinning down or blowing up. The air was crisscrossed with gun smoke and tracer. The enemy was opening up with cannon fire, and then closing with machine-gun bursts. The bombers too were getting in their deadly licks for long plumes of smoke marked the final downward plunge of many single seaters. A group of twenty, lined up abreast, swept in on our Group, shooting down the ship in front of us and damaging several others. A long blue flame trailed out of the fort to our left, growing in volume. Their waist door was released, then one after the other five of the crew leaped clear. Another jumped from the nose door. Then the whole ship blew up before any of the others could get out.

Expended shells were falling at my feet and rolling around the floor making it difficult to keep my footing while firing. . . .

Hervatine called out three fighters coming in from two o'clock level. I swung my gun around to the eight o'clock position in order to pick them up as they went past. The first one flashed under our tail as I put my sights on him. They were evidently flying "in trail," for the second went past in the same place. I gave him a long burst but he was out of range before it took effect. The third cut right over into my gunfire and pieces of metal flew off his fuselage like feathers off a wounded pheasant. Then flame burst out of the engine cowl and engulfed the whole plane as it dropped straight down like a stone. I tried to report it on the intercom but my mike was out. Babicky saw it and confirmed it for me later.

Bleem had his reticules set perfectly for an FW-190, which was attacking the High Group. He cut the wing right off it and she dropped behind us.

Another fort went down past my waist window; I didn't know whether it came out of the 452nd or our own high squadron. The 452nd was really taking a pasting; her elements were ragged and empty positions were everywhere evident. The 96th was almost as badly decimated—most of their ships had feathered props or gaping holes in wings and tails.

At least six fortresses were strung out behind the Wing formation unable to keep up. These were being worked over by individual fighter attack.

Gradually the fury of the battle died down. . . . Our own ship . . . sustained some damage in wing and tail. No one had been wounded and our plane was still in good shape. . . . Several of the planes in our Group peeled off and ran the gauntlet back home. . . .

. . . We drew up on our target near Brux. The air was cloudless affording a good view of the target and giving their gunners a good view of us as well! The inevitable black puffs of flak commenced to blossom around us, and it wasn't long before I could hear the "crumph" of the close ones exploding within our formation. Our ship pitched and bucked from the concussion of the big ones and then she commenced to shake and vibrate. We'd caught one in our #4 engine and the wing was covered with dirty black oil. Pohl got the prop feathered and fought to keep us in position as we entered the bomb run. Flak bursts were hitting right under the tail and the fragments

A B-26. COURTESY OF GRAYDON SUBANK

were zinging through the metal skin of the fort as Hervy yelled out, "Bombs away!"

We swung around to the left in evasive action as both Pohl and Etter tried to trim up the ship and get the remaining three engines synchronized. We all snapped on our chutes and prepared to jump as the oil pressure dropped off rapidly. . . .

The ship now flying next to us was unable to close their bomb bay doors and thus presented a promising target for enemy fighter attack. . . .

We didn't have too long to wait for near Chemnitz some twin-engine Messerschmidt 410's drew up on us from the rear. We got set for some more real action and weren't disappointed. About thirty of them formed a long train and came in on us in single file. For the first time, Babicky got a chance to get in the first shots. The MEs were equipped with different weapons than the single-engine German fighters for at a range of about 1200 yards they began to launch rockets at us. The rockets started from under their wings and trailed out a long streamer of grayish-white smoke as they drew rapidly up on us. Every rocket looked as if it was headed directly for our own plane! . . . Three of them just missed our wings and tail.

After firing the rockets, the MEs would close on us with cannon fire, then machine-guns at point-blank range. . . . After finishing their pass, they would tilt one wing up and peel off to left or right, exposing their silver bellies to our gunfire. They were evidently heavily armor plated underneath for I could see bullet strikes underneath them yet none was going down!

. . . The twin-engine jobs were soon joined by some single-engine fighters. . . . Again, the air was full of falling planes and parachutes. At one time, I counted over forty parachutes in the air as five big bombers went down along with several fighters. The white parachutes of the Americans and the colored ones of the Germans were dropping behind us as the wild melee continued to the west. . . .

Finally, their ammunition exhausted, the enemy fighters dropped back behind us. . . .

We flew on, trailing cripples behind us—some of them sinking lower and lower on two engines or one. . . .

When the navigator called out "France below," we all heaved deep sighs of relief. . . . Shortly afterward, a swarm of our "little friends" descended on us...

Little flak was encountered at the coast and we made the trip back to base without incident.

. . . When the final statistics on this strike had been tabulated, a total of 150 fighters were lost by the *Luftwaffe*. Eighty-four had been shot down by our bombers and sixty-six credited to our fighters. But our own toll had been equally as heavy. . . . I have no record of the total number of bombers lost by the Eighth Air Force; I do know that the Third Division alone lost thirty-seven. . . .[4]

May 22—Sixteenth Mission—Kiel (7¾ hours)

. . . A large hole in the clouds was open over Kiel and their defensive smokescreen

4. This was the Eighth Air Force's first mission against oil production targets. German fighters hit the leading elements of the 3rd Bombardment Division heavily. The division sent out 295 B-17s to attack five different targets and lost forty-one bombers, of which fourteen were from the 452nd Bomb Group and twelve from the 96th Bomb Group; the 388th lost one, according to *The Mighty Eighth* by Roger Freeman. On almost every mission, some aircraft never left the ground or had to abort the mission in flight because of mechanical problems or even damage en route to the target. In Cook's squadron, the 561st, eight aircraft either never left or had to turn back, as described by Edward Huntzinger in *The 388th at War*.

Chemical Warfare Troops and the Air War

The following letter to *Yank* magazine from several members of the Chemical Warfare Service (CWS) was published on April 30, 1944.

> Dear YANK:
> We have been waiting for this opportunity to correct an impression that the only job of CWS in this struggle as far as the ETO is concerned is to bother fellow EMs with tear gas and gas mask drill by the numbers.
>
> Let us simply refer you to page 20 of your edition dated April 2, 1944, which reads: "the explosive loads being dumped on the Axis by Allied planes are now averaging 60 percent incendiaries and in one recent raid on Berlin 98 percent of the entire load was fire bombs, Chemical Warfare Service reported in Washington. At the outset of the war incendiaries accounted for only 5 percent of our bomb loads, the Service disclosed."
>
> We're not asking for any credit, but we feel that we are doing our small part, too.
>
> Sgt. Richard F. Wernecke
> Cpl. Thomas A. Sunseri
> 1st Sgt Clifford G. Anderson
> T/5 William F. Fyffe
> T/5 Kerwan L. Mulligan
> T/5 Arthur N. Smith.

Only two of those who signed the letter could be identified from U.S. National Archives and Record Administration (NARA) files. Sunseri was drafted in December 1942 in Altoona, Pennsylvania, and Fyffe was drafted the same month in Boston. There were two Clifford G. Andersons, one from Washington and the other from Wisconsin, and six Arthur N. Smiths.

failed to hide the sub nests. There was no need for PFF bombing with an opportunity like this, so the area was resoundingly plastered by visual means. Flak caught several of our heavies in vital spots and they fell into the city itself. Several others were damaged badly enough to drop out of formation and try for the airbase at Malmo in neutral Sweden. The wily Hun was forever attempting new methods of counter-attack and he had another new one to try out this time. Several of the fighters flew over the bomber formation and released bombs suspended from parachutes, another attempt at air-to-air bombing. Parachutes suspending long trailing wires were also released in an attempt at fouling our propellers. Our escorting fighters broke up their little party.

On May 19, Lt. Douglas McArthur, who flew his first mission in late April, was on his fifth mission, which was a return trip to Berlin. In May, his bomber survived two missions out of sheer luck.

> May 19, 1944 (our fifth mission)—Berlin, Germany—ten 500 lb. incendiary bombs. Lots of flak and enemy fighters south of Denmark. We had good fighter escort cover, but I saw several bombers go down. On both of these missions [his first to Berlin was on April 29] we had to fly old B-17s (at

A cartoon from the April 9, 1944, edition of *Yank* magazine.

high altitude)—hydraulic turbo & prop controls—that made it very difficult to get into formation and just as difficult staying there with all the flak and enemy fighters encountered. We were very lucky to get back to England!

May 19, 1944 (our ninth mission)—Leipzig, Germany—ten 500 lb. bombs, target was an Me-109 factory—lots of flak and enemy fighter attacks. We had good fighter escort, but we lost an engine over the target and had to come back on three engines (approximately four hours over enemy territory). If I didn't stay in formation, enemy fighters would have picked us off. Again, very lucky to get back to England.

The *Luftwaffe* Neutralized?

On January 21, 1944, the *Luftwaffe*, under the direction of Hermann Goering, launched the "Baby Blitz" against London with more than 400 bombers. Although the results were poor, the bombings continued through May. The Germans' bomber contingent of 695 in northern France at the beginning of the year dwindled to only 144 operational bombers in May, according to *Strategy for Defeat* by Williamson Murray. The German bombings also introduced some of the green American troops in England to war. Casualties were few, and the assault amounted to little more than a nuisance, as it did not even interfere with the buildup of Allied troops.

On June 6, Eisenhower told his Allied troops, "If you see fighter aircraft over you, they will be

Airmen Return Home from the War

While the infantrymen and other combat troops fought almost incessantly on the battlefields of Italy and elsewhere around the world, the airmen who flew over enemy territory were given tickets home after a certain number of missions. The foot soldier could expect several days or even weeks of rest, after which, unless he was critically wounded, he was certain to return to the front lines. The airman, on the other hand, in the spring of 1944, knew he would return home from the war after he completed twenty-five missions.

In an article published in *Yank* in April 1944, Sgt. Mack Morris summarized the situation. Once the airmen completed their combat missions, they were sent back to the United States, where they arrived at redistribution stations created by the air forces. Created late in 1943, these stations were located at Santa Monica, California; Miami Beach, Florida; and Atlantic City, New Jersey. Upon his arrival, the veteran airman would be met "at a port of debarkation or at a casual reception center by a liaison officer who informs him of the redistribution station to which he is to report." In addition, he was given a twenty-day furlough before reporting to duty, unless he already had had one and been home. At the redistribution station, the staff determined his next assignment. The physical and mental evaluation took up to three weeks. The returnee could request the type of assignment he wanted next, and if he qualified, he could attend Officer Candidate School (OCS) or become an aviation cadet. In some cases, airmen were sent back overseas, but not within less than three months. In Atlantic City, the redistribution station was the 670-room Ambassador Hotel, the largest on the Boardwalk. In all three stations, which Morris called "Valhallas," the airmen were treated as if they were on vacation, with no other duties than reporting for their orientation lecture, interviews, and examinations.

ours." He could assert this with some confidence because the Allied bombing campaign had begun to pay big dividends. Although the *Luftwaffe* was at its peak strength, Allied attacks against the German aircraft industry had slowed down production. In addition, the raids against oil targets were creating a crisis. As wave after wave of Allied bombers flew over Germany, Goering was forced to pull back the majority of his fighter forces to protect the Reich. As the shortage of fuel became acute, the German commanders drastically reduced training time for new pilots. Thus by June 1944, German pilots had about 150 training hours in the air, whereas Allied pilots averaged closer to 350 hours. A month later, German pilots would be down to 100 training hours. Throughout the spring of 1944, German pilots were shot down quicker than ever before because Allied fighters were able to extend their range for escorting bombers. Their replacements had even less combat time. Before long, German fighters were ordered to go for the bombers. Nonetheless, as reported in the U.S. Strategic Bombing Survey's publication *The Defeat of the German Air Force*, the skies became safer for Allied bombers as long as they stayed within the range of fighter escorts. The *Luftwaffe* still had a considerable force left, but the air now belonged to the Allies.

CHAPTER 5

Deception, Assembly, and Intelligence

Well before dawn on Tuesday, June 6, 1944, two task forces consisting of several convoys carrying American troops assembled with British convoys off the Normandy coast. (British invasion convoys were also assembling just to the east of these.) Task Force 125, designated Assault Force U, under Rear Adm. Don P. Moon, had departed England late the previous morning with the 4th Infantry Division, 70th Tank Battalion, and specialized engineer units. This invasion force was to occupy an approximately 4,000-yard-long beach area designated as Utah Beach, along the east coast of the Cotentin Peninsula of Normandy. Task Force 124, Assault Force O, under Rear Adm. John Hall, sailed on the afternoon of June 5. It carried engineers of the 5th and 6th Engineer Special Brigades, as well as the 741st and 743rd Tank Battalions, with the 1st "Big Red One" Infantry Division, which was to take a 7,000-yard stretch of beach identified as Omaha Beach on the Calvados coast. The 116th Infantry of the 29th "Blue and Gray" Infantry Division was attached to the veteran 1st Division.

Among the assault troops was Sgt. John Robert Slaughter, a Virginia National Guardsman and member of the Blue and Gray Division, which had consisted of Virginians, Marylanders, and Pennsylvanians before the war. The division had become diluted with inductees from other states after 1941 and, unlike the 1st Division, had never seen action before D-Day. Slaughter was a squad leader in Company D of the 116th Infantry. His regiment had reached the embarkation areas with the 115th Infantry of the 29th and the 1st Division in late May. The 3rd Battalion of the 116th boarded the attack transport USS *Charles Carroll*, designed APA-26, along with the regimental commander, Col. Charles Canham, and regimental headquarters. The 2nd Battalion and supporting units were assigned to the attack transport USS *Thomas Jefferson* (APA-30). The 1st Battalion was carried on the British-manned LSI *Empire Javelin*.[1]

Before boarding their transports, the troops had spent a few gray, rainy days in confined camps at the embarkation areas. During that time, John Slaughter and his comrades felt as if they were "incarcerated behind barbed wire, and MPs made sure that no one entered or left camp."

> No soldier inside the compound was allowed to talk to anyone outside; he could suffer the possibility of getting shot. This was serious business.
>
> Brand new equipment was issued, and the new weapons had to be test-fired and zeroed in on the firing range. Unlimited amounts of ammo were given to each of us for practice firing.
>
> Steak and pork chops with all the trimmings, topped off with lemon meringue pie, were items on a typical menu, and it was all-you-can-eat. This caused one of the wags to say, "They're fattening us up for the kill." The officers became friendlier, and it seemed that the men were a bit kinder to each other. First-run movies were shown all day, and *Mrs. Miniver*, with Greer Garson and Walter Pidgeon, was one of the favorites. Touch football, softball, boxing, reading, and letter writing were popular pastimes.
>
> Capt. Walter Schilling briefed us on the big picture and then told us what our particular assignment would be. Lt. William Gardner, company executive officer, rigged up a sand table model of our sector of Omaha Beach, code-named Dog Green. It featured the Vierville Draw, Pointe du Hoc, and most importantly, the Vierville church steeple, which we were to guide on. Electric lights simulated shell bursts to enhance the realism of his handiwork. Our two leading officers, the company commander and the company executive officer, along with three other company officers, were killed in the invasion.
>
> On June 4, loaded down with equipment, we walked up the gangplank and onto the British HMS *Empire Javelin*, an LSI. Weymouth Harbor was alive with activity.

The men of the 1st Battalion, 116th Infantry, climbing the gangplank of LSI-2, HMS *Empire Javelin*, were burdened with over sixty pounds of weapons and supplies, which had to sustain them until a beachhead could be established. These troops were well trained, but none of them had ever been under hostile fire. Being green

1. The 16th Infantry Regiment, 1st Division, was transported on the attack transports *Samuel Chase* (APA-26) and *Henrico* (APA-45) and the British LSI *Empire Anvil*. A battalion of its 18th Infantry was on the transport *Anne Arundel* (AP-76), and the *Dorothea Dix* (AP-67) and *Thurston* (AP-77) carried various other units for Omaha Beach. Five smaller British LSIs carried the 2nd and 5th Rangers, and a sixth carried the Special Engineer Task Force (SETF). The 4th Division and attached units arrived at Utah Beach on the attack transports *Bayfield* (APA-33), *Joseph Dickmann* (APA-13), and *Barnett* (APA-5) and the British LSI *Empire Gauntlet*.

A *Yank* cartoon shows secret weapons for the U.S. invasion of Germany. Note the boxes of Spam stored in the submarine.

> was an advantage; none of us knew what we faced.

T/5 Walter Condon from Worcester, Massachusetts, who spoke with the accent of a New Englander, had National Guard experience. After being drafted, he was sent to the 29th Division to become a member of 3rd Platoon, Company C, 121st Engineer Battalion. His company consisted of three line platoons and a headquarters platoon. The line platoons consisted of three squads each and were assigned typical engineer missions for D-Day. Condon was briefed on his unit's mission about a week before the invasion.

> About six days before the invasion, we were in Dorchester, England, a few miles north of Weymouth, in a camp with barbed wire all around it. We had Canadian guards patrolling the surroundings. They had set up sand tables, and they brought us in five days before the invasion, told us where and when it would be, and showed us our objectives.

Our objective was to blow the wall at the D-1 Exit. Right next to it was a blockhouse with sixteen-foot-thick concrete walls and an 88-millimeter gun shooting down the beach. These two walls blocked the exit from the beach. There were about two feet between them. They were about two feet thick with poured concrete. There was a passageway for pedestrians to go through them, but not vehicles. We were to be on an LCT with a bulldozer and a ton of TNT behind the blade and a jeep. About forty-eight men were to be aboard; we were 20 percent overstrength.

They had cleared out all the prison camps in the U.S. and shipped them over under the gun, and about six weeks before the invasion, all units were increased by about 20 percent overstrength. We also had two lieutenants to each platoon allowing that we would have heavy casualty losses among the officers.

They issued us $4 in French francs, and we used them to shoot craps with. I won all the money and sent it home.

We got up around 3:30 in the morning, got a big breakfast, and moved by truck about seven miles from Dorchester to Weymouth, where the long convoy backed up near the dock, near the hards. There was a priest going from truck to truck to give last rites. If there were any Jews on the truck, he took them off until he had a quorum and had a special service for them before they got back on the trucks. I think he had to have something like nine or ten for a quorum.

We loaded for the invasion at Weymouth at the hards. This was a pebble stone ramp that went into the water. The LCT would pull right up and drop its ramp, and we would march right on in four abreast. It probably took longer to put the jeep and bulldozer on than anything.

We were issued a special first-aid kit called a parachute pack, with about four times the size of our regular first-aid kit. It had a big pressure tourniquet, compression bandages, and the largest dose of morphine you could take. It was in like a tube of toothpaste with a screw-off cap, and there was a needle you would stick in the wounded man and roll up the tube, and then take the tube and stick it in the man's collar so nobody else would give him another dose in twenty-four hours, or it would prove fatal. This was to stop him from going into shock, because there was nothing we could do for the wounded on the beach. I used it when we got into the barbed wire near a road running along the beach and I found a Sergeant Cuberston from Company B. He was lying in the wire, badly wounded, so I administered his morphine to him and stuck it into his collar. Many months later, he returned to his Company B as first sergeant but was still not up to par and suffering from the effects of his wounds.

We were issued two special pills. One we called "My Blue Heaven," because it put us to sleep if we wanted to. The other pill, I guess Benzedrine, would keep us awake if we needed it. We went in as engineers with our flamethrowers, bangalore torpedoes, and all those other items, including two hand grenades on the front of our pack harnesses.

All the people loaded on LCTs were special teams with special missions that day. The infantry went on LCVPs. Because of this, the infantry were loaded on the troop transports and served three meals a day when on ship and did not have to touch their own rations. We were tied up at Weymouth Harbor and loaded on the LCT at about six o'clock in the morning. The LCT moved out into the outer harbor. It had been rainy and overcast for days. There was a long storm that had gone on for days. There were five- to twelve-foot waves in the channel, and this boat was only about two feet out of the water. The bulldozer was not fastened to the deck, and it could slide sideways or forward and back. The boat was battered by big waves and the bulldozer would shift; and the skipper would try to hit on the other quarter to make it move back a little bit. It didn't take much to make this landing craft tilt. It had no facilities, only a two-by-eight in the back over the stern that we sat on if we had to go the toilet. If we had to urinate, we did it over the side.

There were about fifty of us and five Coast Guard crewmen on the boat. We had to stand and couldn't sit, and had to wear our ponchos because it rained continually. We were in the outer harbor tied to a buoy. We had been on this boat about ten hours since early on the morning of June 4, and we were to land on the morning of June 5. About four o'clock in the afternoon, we moved out in a wave of all LCTs. The top speed of these boats wasn't very high, and you can't run at top speed on those kinds of seas. The seas were so rough that the boats on each side of us were probably about 100 yards away, and sometimes we couldn't see them. They did a yeoman job of keeping those LCTs together and going those 120 miles in the dark. Anyway, we are on our way, there is no food or water aboard ship, and we are out in the rain taking a beating. We never got the signal that the invasion had been delayed for twenty-four hours and to turn back until the early morning. We got back to our starting point in the early afternoon. At four o'clock, we turned around and went again. Now we are faced with the problem aboard the boat that we had all used up a good deal of our one-day supply of water, and we all are dying for a hot cup of coffee because we had no hot meal. All we had was a K ration. So they asked the skipper if he could spare some water to refill our canteens. He agreed we could keep all the water we had in our canteens, and he would take all of their water to make us all a cup of hot coffee. I will tell you, that really hit the spot.

Thirty-year old T/4 Clifton Tabor Bitgood, an April 1942 draftee from Connecticut, was also in Company C, 121st Engineer Battalion. He was a serving in the 2nd Platoon as a squad carpenter and had been with the 29th Division since just before the Carolina maneuvers, during which his unit built pontoon bridges over the Pedee River in South Carolina. Next, the division moved into the camps near the ports in May to prepare to board ship for the invasion.

A lieutenant came to me and said one of my brothers was a few miles down the road, and wanted to know if I would like to go and visit him. I said yes. He got a jeep and permission from someone, and away we went. I had not seen him since I had left home in 1942. He trained in Iceland with an antiaircraft outfit having 90-millimeter guns.[2]

A couple days after meeting my brother, we loaded onto landing craft. We had constructed ramps on the deck of the landing craft [LCTs] about eighteen inches high so a tank could shoot its guns over the ramp.

2. Bitgood met his brother in early June 1944. After the war his brother told him that his unit also had its own harrowing experience when, during the Battle of the Bulge, the men leveled their gun barrels to fire directly against enemy tanks in their line of sight.

T/5 Maxwell B. Moffett, a volunteer from Rock Hall, Maryland, served as a company aid man assigned to Company E of the 115th Infantry.

> We were on the LCI for several days. We weren't feeling too good and were glad to get off and get going. Being the "first-aid man," I had my hands full with seasickness. Some of the men had the "shakes of fear" and some didn't know what was about to happen and what they were about to face, even though we had been trained for this. The aid men in all the companies were told not to stop on the beach to fix the wounded; the navy shore patrol would do that. We were just to get off the beach. We were called "pill rollers," but in combat, it was a different story.

Pvt. A. B. Mirmelstein, a draftee from Newport News, Virginia, was a rifleman in Company H, 115th Infantry, of his state's own 29th Division. He kept a diary of the events.

> May 25, 1944: Moved out by truck to Camp Raleigh near Plymouth, where outfit thoroughly briefed for D-Day mission. Placed under guard. Mission was to land at 10:30 A.M., D-Day, as support wave for 116th Infantry. To form in a column, march four miles inland, relieve them.
>
> May 30, 1944: Shuttled by LCVP's to LCI 503, at Plymouth Harbor.
>
> May 31, 1944: Sailed from Plymouth Harbor parallel English coast.
>
> June 4, 1944: Because of rough seas and sea sickness pulled into Weymouth Harbor. [This was the day Eisenhower postponed the invasion because of weather.]
>
> June 5, 1944: 5:00 P.M. sailed for Normandy Beach.

According to Mirmelstein, not all the units of the 115th departed from the vicinity of the 1st Division's staging areas.

PFC Everett H. Kelly of Charleston, West Virginia, was sent to England as a replacement in 1944 and was assigned to the 30th Infantry Division. During the last days of May, he and his comrades were taken out on ships, off-loaded, and returned to shore. Although his division was not assigned to the amphibious assault, he claims to have found his way into the loading area with troops of the 29th Division.

> Everything was so crowded you could hardly walk anywhere because of all the GIs. There was no time to assign me to any outfit. I would have waited perhaps a few days after the invasion and then went over as a replacement. But down on the harbor that night, I began to walk down the boardwalk looking for someone I knew and after walking quite a distance someone was yelling, "Load up!" and I was caught up in the loading of the ship nearest me. I suppose I was the only one who did such a stupid thing as to leave my position and go walking down the docks. Now these men were probably some of the 29th Division, but I did not know this, and about two days later, after we had made the landing, what was left of us were a scattered few. A sergeant rounded us up and we sat down, and he said we would be his group.

Kelly belonged with Company B, 1st Battalion, 117th Infantry of the 30th Division, and returned to his unit after the invasion.

PhM3/C Vincent A. Kordack, with Company B of the 6th Beach Battalion, prepared for the landing like thousands of other men. His battalion had undergone extensive training in Florida before arriving in England. On May 6, his battalion moved by truck convoy down to Weymouth.

Invasion money issued to the troops.

He recorded the events of the landing in his diary.

May 20: The day wasn't out of the ordinary. We were a little excited for we were getting pictures made. We hiked down the road to a large field where we fell into formation. We did not have long to wait before the Old Man's car pulled up. Commander Carusi walked up to the front of the battalion and we had a group picture made. Then during the inspection, we had moving pictures made.

After inspection, we were put at ease and the old man made a speech. It was on our next move, which we were to make. However, his main subject was fear. He said there isn't a man who is normal who isn't frightened on his first battle. But a coward is a person who hides from himself and doesn't overcome his fear after hitting the beach. He said that a coward not only failed himself but by not doing his job, he made it more likely that his buddies would be killed. After the speech, he secured us and we marched back to camp.

May 23: In the afternoon, we were told that we would be lectured by a general. The general's name was Hoge, commander of the 5th Engineer Special Brigade. The title of his speech was fear. . . . He said just because a man is scared he is not a coward. . . .

May 28: We were awakened at 0300 [3:00 A.M.], we had some hot coffee and bread and jelly. This was to be our breakfast till we arrived at D-8.

After turning in our blankets and putting our gear on, we boarded trucks. After a half hour of waiting, we pulled out. We rode for at least a full hour and after we arrived a mile from D-8 we had to wait. We got off the trucks. . . . It was only a few minutes hike and then we arrived at D-8. . . .

The meals here were really delicious; they were served cafeteria style. . . .

June 1: We were told to have our gear packed and we were issued extra rations. Then, at 1731 [5:31 P.M.] we fell in and marched over to the main gate. Trucks were waiting to take us to Weymouth. We arrived at 1800 [6:00 P.M.], and then we had a long hike to the docks.

I can hardly believe it but I am heading for my first invasion, an event that may change my whole life or end it.

As we were marching to the docks, some people would wave at us and some girls even blew kisses. They knew this was what they had been awaiting for five years. If they did not know we planned to make the invasion, they were awful dumb, for guns and vehicles of all types were moving towards the docks. I did not think I would make it to the docks for it was a long hike and I had a heavy pack to carry. The weight of the pack and litter together must have exceeded sixty pounds.

We arrived aboard the USS *Henrico* at 2200 [10:00 P.M.], then we received our quarters and stowed our gear.

June 2: The time and day between the second and fifth are not recorded for we have done nothing but sleep, eat, and stand by for the orders to sail.

June 5: The days have been moving along very fast and most of the men wonder when D-Day will come. None of them seems the least worried about what was going to happen. They played cards and dice, joked about the trip, or talked about what they will do after the war.

I am a little frightened, I know, for I can feel it in my system; but when the time comes, I pray to the Lord that I pull out of it.

The day was running as the rest since we got here—we had our meals and the scuttle was flying fast, but as usual. However, in the latter part of the afternoon, the transports started to leave port. When this started, we knew the time was close. For once we pulled out, the invasion would be the next day. The *Henrico* raised her anchor and set sail at 1745 [5:45 P.M.].

As we moved along the channel, we saw all types of ships and landing craft. They could be seen as far as the naked eye would permit. Some types of craft I have never seen till this day. On the weather, it was overcast and once we left the harbor, the water was very choppy. With all my gear, getting ashore would not be too easy.

Men were gathered around the deck talking about the invasion as if this were a game of some sort; like our side will beat their side. This made the whole thing more fascinating than ever.

After chow around 1900 [7:00 P.M.], the ship's commander read a speech over the speaker. It referred to our treatment of our allies, the French. He also read us a message from General Eisenhower. It said, they are fighters and will use all means to stop us. But the tide was about to turn and when we go in, go in fighting, and don't stop, keep moving.

At the beginning of June 1944, the men of the Provisional Ranger Force, under Lt. Col. James Rudder, loaded up along with the 1st, 4th, and 29th Divisions and all the attached units. Rudder's force included his own 2nd Ranger Battalion and the 5th Ranger Battalion. The 2nd was to launch a direct assault upon the German battery on top of the cliffs of Pointe du Hoc.

The man in charge of battalion communications for the operation was Lt. James Eikner, who had been drafted in Texas while working for the phone company. Before joining the 2nd Ranger Battalion, he had attended OCS. Like many of the men who took part in D-Day, he retained crystal-clear memories of the day he embarked for the invasion.

> We loaded up on June 1. We had several small converted cross-channel steamers, and we trained with them. They rolled out the red carpet for us. In the marshaling area [the previous evening], before we got on the boats, the Germans dropped an egg or two on us, and we lost several people (none of ours) and vehicles in the motor pool. I had picked out a slit trench, and when the bombing started, I ran over to it, but it was full, so I lay down on the ground.
>
> We were locked in, and nobody could get in and nobody out. We arrived at the final staging area in Camp D-5 on May 27. On June 3, we boarded the LCIs at Weymouth, although some people say Portland. I forgot which date it was, but we were bombed again, once we were aboard ship, by a Stuka dive-bomber, and they shot it down.[3]

The 2nd and 5th Rangers embarked from Weymouth on five British LSIs that carried the LCAs from which they would make their assault: HMS *Prince Charles*, *Ben Machree*, *Amsterdam*, *Prince Leopold*, and *Prince Baudouin*.

Deception

Early in the war, the Allies resorted to deception, mostly under the auspices of the British. The FBI and the newly created Office of Strategic Services (OSS) joined with the British in intelligence. The British capture of the German Enigma coding machine and several of the codes for it during the war represented an undeniable asset to Allied intelligence. Many times, however, the information was deciphered too late to be of any use. In other cases, it could not be employed without running the risk of revealing that the British were able to read the German wireless codes.

In 1943, the Chief of Staff to Supreme Allied Commander (COSSAC) planners worked on developing a course of action for the invasion of France, while others prepared a deception scheme, known as Jael, to keep the Germans guessing where and when the next invasion would come.[4] One part of this deception, called Zeppelin, tried to convince the enemy that the main thrust would take place in the Balkans or southern France in 1943, when in reality, Sicily was the main target. According to Anthony Cave Brown's *Bodyguard of Lies*, the object of the second part of the plan, known as Cockade, was to keep as many German divisions as possible pinned in the west in order to relieve the pressure on the Soviets.

As Eisenhower took over the Supreme Headquarters, Allied Expeditionary Force (SHAEF) in January 1944, the Allies gave Jael a new name: Bodyguard. Now the plan was no longer to keep German divisions in the west, but to keep them away from the designated invasion area. The goal of Bodyguard was to redirect the Germans' attention from Normandy. The British XX Committee (double X for double cross) used double agents to feed false information to the Germans. A British double agent, the Spaniard Juan Pujol, known as Garbo, fed the Germans a steady stream of information, indicating that the Pas de Calais was the intended invasion site. Even after

3. This may well have been another type of aircraft, as the Stuka was a slow dive-bomber extremely vulnerable on cross-channel raids after the Battle of Britain.

4. Churchill took the name Jael from a biblical character who used deception to catch an enemy general off guard and kill him.

The FUSAG Deception

The creation of the First United States Army Group (FUSAG) was a brilliant idea that succeeded in misleading enemy intelligence. It was to be led by Gen. George S. Patton and consisted of the following elements:

- Canadian First Army
  - Canadian II Corps with 2nd Division and 4th Armoured Division
  - U.S. VIII Corps with 79th, 28th, and 83rd Divisions
- U.S. Third Army
  - U.S. XX Corps with 4th, 5th, and 6th Armored Divisions
  - U.S. XII Corps with 35th and 80th Infantry and 7th Armored Divisions

During the summer of 1944, FUSAG also consisted of fictitious or phantom divisions. These divisions, which had their own distinctive divisional patches and were used in wireless communication, included the 11th, 14th, 17th, 22nd, 46th, 48th, 50th, 55th, 59th, 108th, 119th, 130th, 141st, and 157th Infantry and 6th, 9th, 18th, 21st, and 135th Airborne Divisions.

Patton had already shuffled around the Mediterranean during the latter part of 1943 to mislead the Germans, who thought he was the most important American field commander. In early May, Eisenhower conferred with Gen. George C. Marshall about relieving Patton, who once again was becoming a political embarrassment in the same way as in Sicily; in April, Patton had given an address at Knutsford, England, in which he said the United States and Britain would rule the postwar world, excluding the Soviet Union. Fortunately, Eisenhower reconsidered his decision, because Patton's presence reinforced the Germans' belief that FUSAG was a real entity. Apparently the German air reconnaissance was too limited to detect the dummy formations, and enemy intelligence did not realize that the wireless traffic had been created for the sole purpose of misleading them. Although most of the units in Patton's fictitious army group were real, a couple of them had not yet arrived in England, and some of them were not actually located in southeastern England. After the invasion, as these divisions gradually moved into France, they were replaced with phony ones, according to *Strategic Military Deception*, edited by Donald Daniel and Katherine Herbig.

the invasion began, he was able to convince the *Abwehr*, German military intelligence, that Normandy was only a diversion.

PFC Fred Bewersdorf, a volunteer from Illinois serving in the 430th AAA (AW) Battalion took part in the FUSAG deception. "We participated with others in a sham thrust towards Calais in April or May 1944," he recalls. "We were loaded aboard an LST and with other ships went towards Calais and returned."

First Sgt. Louis Magnon from San Antonio, Texas, trained for an administrative position when he left the 36th Division.

> [After arriving in England] in the latter part of April, we went to London and from there to Grosvenor Square, where Eisenhower's headquarters was. When I arrived in Wales, a young man came up and asked if I was a typist. I said I could type, and he

The Forgotten Few: OSS Teams

Office of Strategic Services (OSS) teams and British Special Operations Executive (SOE) units took part in the Zeppelin deception. Many Americans participated in these operations, just as they did in France. The OSS teams that went into the Balkans have largely been forgotten, however, along with their mission.

One of the Americans involved in these operations was T/4 Alfred J. Borgman, who had volunteered for service with the OSS because he spoke fluent Dutch and wanted to be sent to the Netherlands. In Cairo, he was assigned to a three-man team going into Greece to harass the Germans and sabotage lines of communication. He received "suicide pills" in case he was captured. He left from Brindisi, Italy, in a C-47 on the evening of June 3, 1944, and dropped into the Pindus Mountains of Greece the next day. His citation for the Legion of Merit reads:

> Technician Fourth Grade Alfred J. Borgman (ASN 37427976), DEML, United States Army. For exceptional meritorious conduct in the performance of outstanding service in occupied Greece from June 1944 to November 1944. As a member of the Allied Military Mission to occupied Greece, Technician Borgman parachuted into Greece on the night of 4 June 1944 to serve as a medical orderly at the Mission hospital. On several occasions, he volunteered to accompany Mission personnel and guerrilla fighters on sabotage operations and attacks upon enemy convoys, in order to provide the necessary medical aid. Always cool, steady and attentive to duty, even while under enemy fire, Technician Borgman did much to maintain the morale of the Allied and guerrilla personnel with whom he served.

Borgman and his comrades were instrumental in preventing a significant number of German troops from reinforcing the Western Front, yet their contribution has been largely overlooked in the annals of history.

> said he was being sent as an aide to some general and I could take his slot. He was a first sergeant at the time and I was a corporal. I went over there and the general interviewed me. He told me the unit was the Electronics Training Group. Its mission was to train American personnel in the installation and use of radar. They were bringing graduates of universities to be trained and sending them back to the United States to train others.
>
> At one time, this unit had 750 officers and 4 enlisted men. My commanding officer was Col. Kenneth Stice, who was a professor at the University of Illinois. There was no physical training for me; we were purely administrative. I knew the code names because I could see the buildup of the paperwork. They attached us to the 1st Division when the invasion came.

This very specialized unit played its role in the deception.

By June 2, 1944, German intelligence grossly overestimated that the British had forty-eight infantry and eight armored divisions, and the

Beach obstacles along a section of the Atlantic Wall. With one or more Teller mines on them and saw-tooth steel blades to cut through the bottom of a landing craft, these log ramps were designed to damage or sink a vessel at high tide. Behind them are hedgehogs and other obstacles.

Americans forty infantry and six armored divisions in the British Isles. Of these, according to Daniel and Herbig, they believed that forty infantry and eight armored were in southern England, ready for the invasion of France, and another thirty-eight American infantry waited in reserve in the United States.

On May 30, 1944, an American intelligence station at Asmara, in the highlands of Eritrea (East Africa), intercepted a radio emission from Baron Hiroshi Oshima—Japanese military attaché to Berlin—to Tokyo, confirming the success of Bodyguard and Fortitude. In this message, the baron revealed that Hitler was convinced that the Allies had assembled eighty to ninety divisions in Great Britain and planned to launch a diversionary assault on Norway or Normandy. According to William Casey in *The Secret War against Hitler*, the Fuehrer believed, however, that the main thrust would take place against the Pas de Calais.[5]

The Ultra intercepts of the British decoding operation at Bletchley Park helped the Allies uncover the German order of battle, but they failed to locate the German 352nd, 711th, and 716th Infantry Divisions in Normandy.

Assembly for Invasion

The troops began leaving their camps in preparation for the invasion by truck, train, or foot at the end of May. The marshaling areas where they moved had been prepared months earlier by the army engineers of the Western and Southern Base Sections, who operated them along with the port facilities reserved for the invasion. Included in these two sections were engineer general service regiments, camouflage companies, water sup-

5. The success of the deceptions can also be seen in Ultra intercepts and in German intelligence documents found at NARA.

ply companies, and small formations to maintain the marshaling areas, according to *Corps of Engineers* by Beck et al. These engineer units also built the concrete ramps known as hards to allow the landing craft to pull up for the embarkation of troops and equipment. The normal port facilities would be in full use at the time of the invasion as well.

When he was planning the construction of the camps, the engineer general estimated that he would need 15,000 troops in addition to the 46,000 men of the Services of Supply (SOS). The 5th Armored Division was cannibalized to provide the additional 15,000 men to work on the marshaling areas. Of these men, 4,500 became cooks, though they were hardly qualified for the position, according to Gen. Omar Bradley in *A Soldier's Story*. The division, which had arrived in England early in the year, was re-formed later to cross the Channel toward the end of July.

There were two types of marshaling camps: large ones, which had a capacity of about 9,000 men, and "sausage" encampments, consisting of fourteen small camps holding about 230 men each. The sausage encampments were strung out for five or more miles along roads. Each of the marshaling areas had railheads for storing all kinds of supplies. In addition, each camp had a complete set of facilities, including quarters, tents for the staff, mess, and briefings, as well as a water-filled concrete tank to test vehicle waterproofing, as described in *Corps of Engineers*.

The Southern Base Section included nine major marshaling areas, one of which was operated by the British and two of which, located in Southampton, were run jointly. Each of these areas was to operate at 75 percent capacity, leaving the remainder to take on reserves. The perimeters of the camps were wired and patrolled by MPs to maintain complete security. The airfields for the paratroopers were similarly guarded, and the pilots and airborne troops were isolated from other personnel on these bases.

The Airborne Assault Force Prepares

A few days before the invasion, Col. Gerald J. Higgins, chief of staff for the 101st Airborne Division at divisional headquarters in Greenham Common, carefully reviewed the plans for the movement of troops from the camps to the airfields for assembly. For months, he had wrestled with the problem of securing aircraft for practice drops, and his current concerns were how to get replacements to bring the division's formations up to strength. During the last week in May, the parachute units moved to the same airfields they had used for Exercise Eagle. By that time, the divisional units that were to move by sea had already reached their marshaling areas, according to Rapport and Northwood in *Rendezvous with Destiny*. Later, Colonel Higgins would have another thorny dilemma to solve, because the high command had no intention of sending replacements to either of the airborne divisions while they were engaged in Normandy.

By this time, the new division commander, Maxwell Taylor, had replaced William Lee, the "Father of the Airborne," who had had a heart attack in February. Taylor was chosen for the post because he offered the division his experience as a veteran of operations with the 82nd Airborne in the Mediterranean. What the 101st's "Screaming Eagles" lacked in combat experience, they made up for in spirit.

The paratroopers who were to go on the attack in the early hours of D-Day had moved from their camps to the airfields from which they were to depart and were isolated from the rest of the world with barbed wire. When the time came to board their aircraft, the heavily laden troopers moved by truck and bus, then made their final preparations.

Pvt. Harold Martino, a draftee from East Liverpool, Ohio, serving with the 401st Glider Infantry Regiment (GIR), was amused by all the predictions for the invasion date made in the media during May 1944. "All activity ceased in Brock Barracks," he recalleds, "save the constant flow of officers in and out of the gates with jeep loads of maps to a special room that was called the 'war room' and was heavily guarded."

He knew the invasion would soon begin, but by this time his glider battalion was already attached to the 327th GIR and confined to its garrison area.

> On the morning of May 24, we were told the invasion was close at hand and the day would be spent in issuing of combat equipment and clothing in preparation for movement to the marshaling area in Plymouth, where we would learn further the details of the invasion. This was it! Everyone was excited and rushing around drawing equipment, checking rifles, taking hand grenades, and making their prediction as to where we'd land on the French coast. No one seemed too nervous, and surprisingly enough, I was unusually calm. I had really expected to be bubbling over with fear and nervousness, but that was to come later, how well I know.
>
> That night, our last in Brock Barracks, it seemed like hours before I fell asleep. Thoughts, horrible ones and pleasant ones, were racing through my brain. Cold beads of perspiration formed all over me when I tried to visualize how it would be. My buddies, whom I had lived so closely with for the past two years, would fall dead or be terribly wounded before my eyes. I wondered if I could stand it. Then me! I wasn't invincible; I could die just as easily as the next man. Then I wondered what Mom and Dad were doing now. If they knew I was sweating out an important step in my life? I drifted off to an uneasy sleep.
>
> The next morning, we were awakened earlier than usual. The parade ground was crowded with buses. As we dressed that morning in combat clothes, everyone seemed cheerful enough, but I suppose they were all like me, singing and cracking jokes, ribbing one another about how they looked in their combat uniforms, to hold back the emotion pent up inside them.

After breakfast, they loaded into buses and departed the camps.

> It seemed as though the entire civilian population of Reading was at the gates cheering, waving, weeping, and wishing us luck. It was almost like leaving home. For some of us, six months had elapsed since we first came to Reading, and in that time, we had made some good friends.
>
> After a five-hour ride, we arrived in the port city of Plymouth. It was then we began to realize that we were to lead the invasion by sea and not by air, as we had all expected, for this was a port camp, not an airport, as it would have been had we been going by air.
>
> Vehicles were waterproofed, equipment checked and rechecked, gas masks waterproofed, additional ammo issued, until every man was a walking arsenal in himself. Orders issued, rescinded, and reissued. Physical exercises were highly stressed, for every man must be in tiptop shape for this great adventure.
>
> The next day, our company was to move to the briefing room to be briefed on our particular mission. This was what we had been waiting for. The next morning, we moved into the briefing room. Maps, hundreds of them, were tacked up all around the room: maps of the Cherbourg Peninsula, with colored crayon marks showing the landing areas of various troops, aerial photographs showing beach installations,

mines, and pillboxes. After a forty-five-minute lecture by the battalion commander on the mission of the battalion, we were taken to a huge sand table re-creation of the entire peninsula made to an exact scale, showing every contour of the ground and each and every shore installation and pillbox. This was it: Company B was to hit Uncle Red Beach on D-Day at 1045 hours, secure Causeway 1, with Poupeville, a small village, as the initial objective.

The morning of June 3, we received our final briefing and final thorough checkup and fell out in company formation, full battle equipment, in preparation for our march down to docks two miles away. It was a hot day, and the heavy equipment seemed to increase in weight with every step. We marched through the streets of Plymouth, lined with civilians waving and wishing us luck. Luck? I wasn't counting on luck alone; each step was a prayer, a prayer for divine guidance. As we marched, over and over in my mind I could see the beaches of Normandy, the mines, the pillboxes.

Finally we reached the docks and as far as you could see, the harbor was lined with LSTs and assault boats, and the sky filled with barrage balloons and fighter planes, circling around, offering protection to the assembled armada. We boarded an assault boat after waiting very little. The LST I was assigned to was a veteran of the Salerno and Anzio landings. That gave me a little confidence in the ship.

As soon as the ship was loaded, we moved well out into the channel and waited for the armada to assemble. Standing on deck, I was amazed at the sight I saw. As far as the eye could see in any direction, there were boats of all descriptions, loaded with men and equipment and a barrage balloon anchored at the stern of each ship. What a sight! What an encouraging sight! The date was June 4; the next morning, June 5, at 1045 hours, we would be assaulting Uncle Red Beach on the Normandy coast. That afternoon, we started to move. This is it, Mr. Hitler!!!

The 81st Airborne AA Battalion, led by Maj. X. B. Cox Jr. from Texas, was scattered in England. On May 15, Battery C departed Basildon to join the 401st Glider Infantry Battalion for a sea voyage to Utah Beach, from where it would travel inland to join the division.

The battery loaded on LSTs and Rhinos on the night of June 4–5 and, after a rough sea ride, returned to port. On the next morning, they took off again.

The battalion headquarters and the medical detachment left Basildon Park on May 17 for a port in Wales where we joined other units of the 101st Airborne Division that were to go in by sea. On May 28, General Taylor spoke to all personnel and disclosed our destination. We also began waterproofing our vehicles, which at that time included twenty-four ¾-ton trucks which we secured for further transportation to our antitank batteries. On May 31, we moved to Cardiff, Wales, and boarded the *Robert E. Perry* on June 2. The ship was crowded, and the food was K rations, plus hot coffee. We sailed on June 5 and joined the convoy going to France.

Batteries A and B left Basildon on May 29, 1944, and went to Aldermaston airport. At one time, we were scheduled to use Horsa gliders, but that changed and we were scheduled to use American CG-4A gliders. Therefore, we had to revise our loading schedules of equipment and personnel. Each battery was to have twenty-two CG-4A gliders and one Horsa glider.

The CG-4A gliders were to go in on the first lift, and the Horsa gliders were to come in the evening of D-Day. On 5 June, all personnel of the 101st were at the airport and addressed by General Pratt, the assistant division commander, who gave them the final briefing.

S.Sgt. Raymond Smith, a twenty-year-old from Thorton, Kentucky, had enlisted in 1940 at age sixteen. He was assigned to and trained with the 4th Division until he attended Parachute School in 1941. He graduated on November 7, he claimed, with then-captain Steve Chappuis. He was considered for Medical Corps OCS but rejected because he had only an eighth-grade education, so he served as a medic in his PIR. Smith boarded his aircraft before dark on June 5, the false start of the previous day still fresh in his mind. He had volunteered for the Pathfinders, because they needed medics, and he had trained with the radar transmitter called Eureka, which the pilots homed in on with their Rebecca receivers after the Pathfinders marked the DZ. He had been thoroughly briefed with terrain maps and aerial photos about the gun emplacements, flooded areas, and obstacles that he might encounter. In addition to his normal combat load, as the medic he carried morphine and plasma along with his tommy gun. On the fateful day, he and his comrades were taken to the airfield, where three planes awaited. They boarded, eighteen men to a craft. Smith's aircraft carried the Number 1 Group, led by Lt. Robert S. Dickson III and Capt. Frank Lillyman, later credited as being the first man to land. Their objective was the area near St. Germain de Varreville. The other two aircraft were to land a few miles on either side of them. "In our Group Number 1, we had three men from the intelligence section of the 101st Airborne," Smith recalls. "Their leader was Capt. [Lt.] Robert S. Dickson, who played football, I believe at UCLA."[6]

A typical beach obstacle included posts like this at Utah Beach with a Teller antitank mine strapped on top.

Before they boarded the waiting aircraft, Signal Corps photographers showed up and assembled their equipment, and then got the members of the group together for one last picture before they flew into history.

First Lt. Robert Dickson, a thirty-year-old commissioned from ROTC years before, was mobilized for the war. He served as a platoon leader in Company E, 502nd PIR, from May 1942 until his arrival in England in September 1943. Then he was transferred to a staff position at the regimental headquarters, where he was also to

6. Smith had enlisted on June 6, 1940, and exactly four years later, "at 7 A.M. on June 6, 1944, I was standing on Utah Beach to welcome the 4th Infantry Division to Normandy." He had served in that division for almost a year until he went to Parachute School.

organize and coach a football team. In early May 1944, his staff assignment resulted in orders for him to join the 502nd's Pathfinder Team in central England. He arrived at the assembly area at North Witham Air Base with the team. He was to jump with that group and his two men from the regimental intelligence platoon. Their mission was to reconnoiter a route for the 2nd Battalion of the 502nd from the drop zone to the main objective, a major coastal gun position overlooking the beach. The Pathfinders had to prepare the panels, lights, and radar equipment they were to use to mark the landing field. The long wait before departure added fuel to their anxiety. Finally, on the evening of June 5, 1944, they boarded their C-47, the engines revved up, and the first load of Pathfinders took to the sky in the fading rays of the evening sun. They were on their way.

PFC René A. Schmidt, a twenty-seven-year-old draftee from Elmsford, New York, was inducted in September 1942. Born in Germany in 1917, he was still not a U.S. citizen, but he was quite patriotic and volunteered for the paratroopers. He was assigned to the 502nd PIR of the 101st A/B Division and vividly remembers the marshaling area.

> It was completely surrounded by barbed wire and patrolled by MP units. We were briefed in a tent that consisted of several large sand tables. We had models on those tables, and they were exact replicas of the terrain and towns where we were going. We were given all the information at that time, except the name of the general area. We didn't know what region it was. We had the replicas of the villages. We knew the number of German troops in them, in some cases the commanders' names. On the wall of the briefing tent was a large situation map, and the information changed almost hourly.
>
> On the night of June 4, we were preparing to enplane. Suddenly General Eisenhower appeared amongst us, stayed there, and just chatted with us for a while. After that, we went across the airfield, got into our planes, and sat there for what must have been an hour or two. Then we were told the mission was scrubbed for that night and we were to go back to bed.
>
> The next night, June 5, was a beautiful evening. We had a full moon, balmy and just as lovely an evening as you could want.

PFC Ray B. Hood, a young paratrooper, had enlisted in 1942 in West Texas before he had reached the legal age for the draft. He was only eighteen years old when he prepared to make his first combat jump. Having joined the paratroopers in search of adventure, he was in the 502nd PIR, which was briefed about ten days before the mission.

> We studied meticulously constructed sand tables, which showed every building, every hedgerow, and every tree surrounding our projected drop zone. We also studied maps of the surrounding area, and we were closely questioned to be sure we were absorbing what we were told and shown. Our mission was to destroy gun emplacements near Ste-Mère-Église and capture the causeways leading to Utah Beach.
>
> The staging area was just outside of Greenham Common, located near Reading. We stayed in pyramidal tents on folding cots. There were no work details. When we were not studying maps or sand tables, our time was our own. We were given and shown details of strongpoints, heavy gun emplacements, unit headquarters, and as much as known about troop dispositions. No nonsense was given about this being a walk in the park. Kill officers and men armed with automatic weapons first. We knew everything about the invasion that we

needed to know—except *when*—and we knew that was very soon.

Earlier, the men had been instructed on how to escape if they were captured, as Hood recalls:

Escape. Escape. Escape. It was emphasized to us that if we allowed time to pass and permitted ourselves to be taken further behind the lines into German-occupied territory, escape would become more and more difficult. We had been lectured to before by British officers who had escaped, and given advice about paying close attention to our guards, watching for any opportunity at all. We were told how to pretend to be injured, addled, confused, and create our own opportunities. We had been instructed on how to hide knives or small handguns near the scrotum because of the average man's reluctance to search adequately in that area.

We had several Jewish men in the company who were most emphatic about not being captured. One, a very young man named Rosenberg, was a very good friend of mine. I remember what he said: "I have more sense than to let the sons of bitches get their hands on *me*. No dice." He meant it, too. They all did. Even then, we were aware of the treatment of the Jewish people in Germany, though I don't think we really knew of the ferocity involved.

The subject of taking prisoners was not mentioned, except casually. At one time or another, several officers passed careless remarks that we might find prisoners too much trouble to contend with.

The camp was surrounded by barbed-wire fences, and guards were posted to prevent any unauthorized trips to town. Roll call was held twice each day. Each man's last name would be called, and he would about-face, then respond with his first name and middle initial. I think I first started realizing just how close to action we were when I saw the care taken with roll call.

We ate in a very large mess tent, and the cooks and the men on the serving line came from a unit that was not going to participate in the invasion. Our own cooks, sensible fellows, did not jump out of airplanes. We were told, in no uncertain terms, *not* to talk with these men. We learned from eavesdropping that they were also under guard.

The gear I carried: I had an M-1 rifle and sixteen clips of ammunition, two—perhaps three—fragmentation grenades, a land mine, a bayonet, a trench knife, canteen of water, first-aid pouch, compass, an entrenching tool, a reel of communication wire, and half of an SCR-300 radio, which makes no sense whatsoever. Why not carry the whole thing and have a working unit, and give somebody else the wire to carry? Ours not to reason why. I also had a musette bag with socks, underwear, a shelter half and tent pegs, a raincoat, and K rations for three days; also a machete and a twenty-foot rope in case of a tree landing (we all carried it).[7] I have no idea how much all this stuff weighed, but I—like most of the others—had to be boosted into the aircraft.

At that time, we did not yet use the parachute with a quick-release harness. A belly-band and three snap fasteners had to be negotiated before the paratrooper became anything like a fighting man. During those frightening minutes while he was getting out of that harness, he was a sitting duck.

7. The musette bag (M-1936 field bag) was a canvas bag usually used for carrying personal items. It could be attached to the suspenders or carried with a shoulder strap.

> Most of us devoted a little time to practice. It seemed to me a prudent thing to do.

Hood also remembers the para-packs, bundles attached to the aircraft that carried mortar tubes, bipods, base plates, ammunition, and other supplies. These para-packs were to be released by the crew chief after the jumpers were out of the aircraft; other equipment packs were to be shoved through the door by the jumpmaster before the parachutists exited. Some men carried their M-1s in Griswold cases, broken down into three pieces: stock, barrel and receiver group, and trigger assembly. It took only a few seconds to assemble the rifle by placing the stock and barrel together and inserting the trigger assembly. Others carried their rifles already assembled.

Ray Hood received a luminous map, but none of the maps or any of the briefings showed or mentioned any of the flooded areas. He and his comrades were told not to load their rifles, because their commanders did not want them to be caught in firefights on landing. It is not clear, however, whether all the participating units were given similar orders.

Although the men in Hood's company were disappointed when the invasion was postponed, their morale remained high. To Hood's later embarrassment, not even the pep talks registered the importance of the invasion in his mind. He did not realize the magnitude of the event in which he would be taking part until a few weeks later.

PFC James D. Purifoy, another draftee from Texarkana, Arkansas, had volunteered to join the paratroopers and was a member of the S-2 section of the 2nd Battalion, 501st PIR, 101st A/B Division. He moved to the staging area with his battalion a little more than a week before the invasion.

> We were ready for the night of June 4–5 and they canceled it before we got out to the planes. The fifth, we knew we would go, but I don't know what time of day we went out to the airstrip.
>
> On the fifth, the S-2 had made a sandbox of the objective we were to take, and everybody studied it. We looked at maps and the sandbox a week before the invasion and kept going over them.
>
> We had one of the best steaks I ever ate in my life, and you could get all you wanted. After that, we milled around and talked. Everybody was anxious or nervous and ready to go. Soon we went to church services and then out to the airstrip, and we sat around the planes waiting to load. I think we loaded at 10:30 and took off after 11. Lieutenant Sefton, Private First Class Goebels, and I were the S-2 on this plane, with some members of the machine-gun platoon and mortar platoon. I knew some of them.

According to Purifoy, in past exercises, it had been standard procedure to assign groups of two or three men from the S-2 section to each of the companies and for these groups to establish radio contact with the battalion. The battalion loaded its aircraft at Merryfield.

For PFC Robert A. Flory from Anderson, Indiana, a rifleman in the 3rd Platoon, Company B, 1st Battalion, 506th PIR of the 101st Airborne Division, the days immediately preceding the invasion were equally memorable.

> During the last week in May, we left our Quonset huts in Aldbourne and departed for the marshaling area. In our case, this was Uppottery Airfield. Here the security was extreme. We were not allowed to leave the company without a special pass. We passed the time by writing letters, which were heavily censored, playing cards, shooting dice, and smoking. The food was excellent,

and we joked about being fattened for the kill.

Briefing began on June 1. Sand tables were set up, and we were drilled incessantly until we knew exactly what our mission was and where it would take place. My platoon's primary objective was to clear the enemy out of the small village of St. Marie du Mont and to prevent any of the enemy from moving toward the beaches. The briefing continued for two or three days.

We were issued $10 of French invasion money. Every man had a three-yard-square silk map, which, when pieced together, represented the entire peninsula of Normandy, and one or two diagrams or overlays of the village or strongpoint his platoon or company was assigned to take. Small brass compasses were issued so that we might orient ourselves on the ground, since this was to be a night jump. In addition, dime-store metal crickets were issued for identification purposes: one squeeze, click-clack, to be answered by two, click-clack, click-clack.

We drew small American flags about three by five inches and sewed them to the right shoulders of our jump jackets. Some shaved their heads; others had Mohawk haircuts with a two-inch strip of hair running from the forehead to the back of their head, the rest of the head shaved. Boxes of machine-gun and mortar ammunition were rolled in equipment bundles and attached to the bottom of the planes. Then we drew Mae West life jackets. We went down to the hangars, drew our parachutes, put our rifles in their cases, and checked our ammunition.

The jumpsuit had one large pocket on each thigh plus two front and two back pockets. The jacket, which reached below our hips, had two side pockets and two breast pockets. The jumpsuit was olive drab, and our jump boots were cordovan brown leather and laced halfway up on our calves. Then our helmet liner and steel helmet with chin strap. Our parachutes were called the T-5 assembly. The main chute was camouflaged nylon, twenty-eight feet in diameter, and the reserve chute was white nylon, twenty-two feet in diameter. The harness consisted of two leg straps that came between the legs and fastened on each hip. The chest strap fastened in the center of the chest. The reserve chute fastened to the chest strap. The T-5 assembly weighed about sixty pounds.

My equipment consisted of the following: an M-1 rifle with a 9-inch bayonet, two bandoliers of M-1 ammo, four hand grenades, first-aid kit, a jump knife in a holster attached to my right calf, a thirty-foot jump rope in case I landed in a tree, a musette bag containing three K rations, four D rations, a carton of Camel cigarettes, gas mask, canteen, and a small Bible sent to me from my sister . . . and, believe it or not, two extra pairs of socks and a change of underwear.

Several fellows jumped with a leg pack that included Gammon grenades and mines. As soon as the chute opened, you pulled this string or rope, and this pack dropped forty feet below you and hit the ground long before you did. So many of them didn't drop; that is why there were so many broken legs. We carried the rifles in a canvas Griswold bag in three pieces.

On the fourth, we were alerted and began to suit up. At about ten o'clock at night, we were waiting at our plane and they canceled. It was rainy and foggy, and we were under the wing. We hoped it would be canceled. It rained most of the night.

On the afternoon of June 5, we were again alerted and were told there would be no cancellation. This time we would go! At

> about 9 P.M., we went to the hangars and began to suit up. By midnight, we were onboard the plane and ready to go. Before suiting up, we had camouflaged our faces by smearing charcoal or chocolate on our cheeks, noses, and foreheads. Lieutenant Minton spotted one of his men who had not darkened his face. He made him go to the exhaust of the plane's engines, collect carbon, and cover his face.

In the meantime, the 437th Troop Carrier Group prepared for the invasion at Ramsbury Air Base. CWO William Hart from Fayetteville, Arkansas, was in charge of some of the ground crew, who had the job of getting all the aircraft ready because their group was carrying units of the 82nd Airborne Division.

> We had open bases, and there were highways running through them. Prior to D-Day, they closed the bases, and nothing went in or out. The airborne troops that moved in had their own guards and kept separate. Our flight crews were kept separated also, and we were not in contact with them. Everything was locked up for a few days before D-Day.
>
> We gave them all the birds we could, some seventy odd. We knew this was D-Day, because you couldn't get into the base. The aircrews were isolated from us. The troops were on another end of the airfield, and we couldn't even see them since it was at least half a mile way.
>
> They got out early and lined up for D-Day on the runway. Two long lines of birds and gliders, a good easy target. Off they went when the word came. Most of the mission came off in the dark. We were ready for several days. I know the planes sat there on the runway. We watched the takeoff, making sure they all got off and everything went.
>
> The aircraft in combat had their lights hooded, and you had to be at a certain angle to see the lights. The lights were on the wings.[8] They had recognition lights they could turn on. The only thing you saw from the ground was the exhaust. It would get white hot and was just like a big lightbulb. They had a big alligatorlike attachment for the exhaust; it helped some in eliminating the light. It was normal for the exhaust to do this after a short time. Those dampeners helped some, but I don't recall if they were put on in time for the invasion.

The 82nd A/B Division moved into its staging areas about the same time as the 101st. The 101st A/B had completed its training with a full-dress rehearsal in the form of Exercise Eagle during the second week of May. The 82nd A/B was denied the same privilege. The division had been scheduled to have its full-scale rehearsal at the end of April, but the exercise was canceled because of bad weather. The 508th PIR did make the drop a week later, but according to William Lord's history of the regiment, the results were poor because the weather was still bad. Fortunately, the 82nd had a number of combat veterans and veteran units, although it also had green units such as the 508th PIR and a fair number of green replacements in the veteran units. Nonetheless, troop morale in the 82nd was as high as in the 101st.

PFC Kenneth Burch was a Texan from Wichita Falls who was drafted in August 1942. In 1943, he completed Parachute School and was serving with the 507th PIR. A friend from his training days at Fort Benning had served with the 504th PIR in Italy and volunteered for the Nor-

8. These were the blue formation lights that remained dimmed when flying over enemy territory in formation.

The 504th Parachute Infantry Regiment Sits Out D-Day

The 504th PIR arrived from Italy too late to participate in the invasion, but many of its men volunteered to fill the ranks of the 82nd A/B Division. PFC Bernard G. Shipton, a New Yorker, was a member of a mortar crew of the 1st Battalion. He had enlisted in February 1942 at age twenty and in May 1943 sailed to Africa with the division. Shipton made his first combat jump in Sicily with the regiment when the 1st and 2nd Battalions lost twenty-three aircraft to friendly fire. He was with the 504th when it jumped at Salerno and when the situation became serious after the invasion. The 504th continued fighting in the Italian campaign, even as the remainder of the division shipped out for England.

Shipton's regiment also took part in the invasion of Anzio on January 22, 1944. Finally, in April, the 504th boarded the *Capetown Castle* and sailed for England. Arriving on April 22, the unit was moved by train to Leicester and bivouacked on Soughton's golf course. It stayed there until the drop into Holland in September 1944, although not all of the men remained there until September.

According to 1st Sgt. Regis J. Pahler of HQ Company, 1st Battalion, 504th PIR, three men from his company—John Dickinson, David Dalton, Bernard Shipton—answered the call for volunteers to jump with other units on D-Day with the Pathfinders. Dalton did not survive the mission, but the other two did.

T/5 James R. Richards from Lubbock, Texas, was a truck driver in Regimental Supply of the 504th PIR in Italy. After their arrival in England, he volunteered to join the airborne invasion force. "We loaded our planes on the night of June 5–6, and everyone had lots of equipment. It was still dark, and there was lots of confusion about which planes to load on. The plane I was in had about twenty-three men."

These and other volunteers helped fill out the ranks of the 82nd A/B Division.

mandy jump. According to Burch, "When we [the 507th] were in England preparing for the invasion, those from the 504th who wished to go could jump with other regiments. Sergeant Grey volunteered for the jump and came into the 507th. I saw him a few times. He knew he was going to die; you could see it on his face. He didn't last the morning. That he willingly gave his life while others in the U.S. griped about food has always annoyed me."

Cpl. Jack W. Schlegel from New York City, a machine gunner in the 3rd Battalion, 508th PIR of the 82nd A/B Division, was born in Germany in 1923 and became a naturalized U.S. citizen. He had enlisted in November 1942 and trained at Camp Toccoa. He had relatives serving in the *Wehrmacht*, but he considered himself an American and had no qualms about the action that awaited him. What puzzled him was that he was in the machine-gun platoon instead of the battalion intelligence section, since he spoke fluent German. One of his memories of the preinvasion days was of his platoon leader, Lieutenant Bodack, prepping the men for the invasion.

> At many of his lecture sessions, he used to say, "One out of every four of you will be dead the first few days of action. If your buddy gets hit, give him a morphine shot and first-aid kit and leave him," and finally, "We don't have time for prisoners." From the last remark, we assumed that no prison-

ers were to be taken since we were behind enemy lines and had no POW compounds or the people available to guard them.

We assumed if we were wounded and unable to escape, we had to give up, but we were told that the Germans don't capture paratroopers. It came down to [the fact that] you had to wait until it actually happened, and it happened to me three times during June 1944 and 1945.

From Nottingham, we went by truck with all our equipment to Folkingham Airport, and we were quartered in large hangars. Everyone was excited, laughing, kidding, but I am sure all felt like I did, afraid, tense, and worried as to the outcome.

When the day came, it was extremely difficult to get the parachutes on over all our equipment. It took two crewmembers at the plane entrance door to get the paratroopers in the C-47. My plane had twenty-four jumpers and equipment bundles. I was the twenty-fourth man in the rear, sitting next to the aircraft's radio operator and navigator.

Also boarding that night was the regimental surgeon of the 508th PIR, Maj. David E. Thomas of Cleveland, Ohio. He had transferred early in the war from the Armored Corps to the paratroopers and had gone to England in 1942 with his new friend, James Gavin, then a captain, to study British methods. He did not go to the Mediterranean with the 82nd A/B Division but joined it in England in June 1944.

We were taken from garrison in Sherwood Forest and trucked to various airfields. At the airfield, we were surrounded with concertina barbed wire. Nobody got out and nobody got in. Outside where we were, there were guys walking around with rifles to make sure nobody got in or out. After we got in there, we had sand tables prepared, and the briefing was given to everybody and shown on sand tables where we were supposed to land. We were told, if it works out this way, great; if it doesn't, it's "cops and robbers, cowboys and Indians," whack 'em where you can, and work towards your objective.

We had two chaplains: a Protestant and a Catholic. While we were locked up in the airfield, they were both doing "sold out" business. I was and still am a big gambler, and I was sitting—never much of a churchgoing guy—in a big-stakes poker game. Interesting story on that: We played IOUs to payday, and come payday, everybody paid off his IOUs. We had an agreement—if a guy got wounded and evacuated or killed, and you had his IOUs, forget about them. I was in a poker game at the airfield, and I wasn't doing very well. I thought, "Hell, I might as well get in and hit a lick for Jesus and get everything on my side I can get." I went into this hangar. We had canvas cots in rows, and Chaplain Elder is up there sounding off, and I am just beginning to occupy the last seat in the last row when Chaplain Elder says, "Now the Lord is not particularly interested in those who only turn to him in times of greatest need." I said to myself, "What the hell am I doing in here?" So I got up and left and went back to the poker game. Our Catholic chaplain never got out of his parachute; he landed in a tree and got shot while he was still in his harness. But Chaplain Elder made it through, and after we were back in garrison at Nottingham after Normandy, I told him the story and he was mortified.

We all had gas masks, which we all left in the aircraft. Everything was uncomfortable, and I think it was gas treated. We had the regular parachutist's uniform with the big baggy pockets and all that stuff. We also had elbow patches on our elbows, and under one of them, we had a little compass and I think $40 in French invasion francs. When I escaped, the first thing I did was open that patch and got my compass, which was all broken to hell, and I didn't have anyplace to spend the money either.

We were equipped with a first-aid kit, pistol belt with a canteen of water and one with ethyl alcohol, but I don't think a drop of that got out of England. The first-aid kit had some morphine Syrettes in it, bandages, and slings—nothing much. The medics did not carry weapons, but nobody argued with them if they wanted to. Their favorite weapon was a pistol. The helmets were marked with a red cross, and we had a Red Cross armband. We wore an American flag on one shoulder and the division insignia on the other.

A lot of guys camouflaged their faces. We had a guy, one of my poker-playing buddies who got commissioned from enlisted status, named Danny Ling, who went in with a Mohawk. He got captured and they pointed at him and said, "Sing Sing," and he said, "Goddamn right, I came here from Sing Sing." He escaped.

Those who were about to die were well fed.

Everything was lined up, they knew where they were going. Every plane had someone who was the troop master for the aircraft. He would have his group, and they would all be assembled and they would have all of their equipment bundles on the aircraft. This was all done ahead of time. We loaded at night, after dark, just shortly before takeoff.

Sgt. Delbert Zane Schlemmer from Canton, Ohio, one of many nineteen-year-olds in the division, enlisted in November 1942. After basic at Camp Blanding, he attended Parachute School in 1943. In the spring of 1944, he served as a forward observer for an 81-millimeter mortar platoon of HQ Company, 2nd Battalion, 508th PIR. While his regiment was camped in Nottingham, it was rumored that the drop would take place somewhere between the Pyrenees and Norway. He recalls the fateful day.

We boarded a group of ancient English buses in all our combat gear and went to the airports. Our battalion assembled at Saltey Airfield, behind a barbed-wire enclosure and behind security. We then all drew combat loads of ammunition. At the time, I was carrying an M-1 Garand .30-caliber rifle mainly because most of my time was to be spent with the frontline companies as a forward observer. We had been informed that the German troops had given priority to eliminating forward observers, officers, and noncommissioned officers, in that order. I carried a rifle and carried my binoculars on the back of my rifle belt to look as inconspicuous as possible.

Other items that we drew were, of course, the ammunition for our mortars and all the other crew-serviced weapons. We also drew fragmentation and thermite grenades. We each drew a Gammon grenade. The Gammon grenades were English and were more or less a cotton sock filled with approximately two pounds of composition C-2, a plastic explosive that was armed with a simple impact detonator. They were super for attacking any armored vehicles, and therefore we called them our hand artillery. The Gammon grenade was also popular with us because a very small piece of the C-2 plastic, when lit with a match, would burn very fast and very hot and smokeless. They were excellent to heat coffee and our K rations tins in the bottom of our foxholes.

So eventually in Normandy, the size of our individual Gammon grenades got progressively smaller each day.

One of the most puzzling phenomena I saw at the time was how each trooper went back for extra ammunition and grenades after everybody had drawn their basic load. Despite the weight of the basic equipment that we had to carry, everyone attempted to increase his potential firepower rather than rely on resupply.

Our waiting time was spent on equipment inspection, cleaning and recleaning our weapons, sharpening and resharpening knives, then rolling our mortars, telephone equipment, and ammunition all into para-pack bundles, which would be dropped from the bottom of our respective planes at jump time.

We went into sand table sessions of our drop area and objectives. We were then informed that German troops had occupied our original planned hill objective and that our mission had been changed. We were also told that we should jump regardless of any kind of circumstance and that we were *not* to return to England with a plane.

The first session with a sand table was without any names, just the terrain. The second session was around the same sand table, but with English-sounding names near the village. That is, Evansville, which in the third session became Étienville; Port Abée, which became Pont L'Agée; and Pickleville, which became Picauville. At this third and final sand table session, we were informed that the invasion site was to be Normandy, France, and that our objectives were to block all German approach routes and their attempts to reach the invasion beach. We were then to hold until relieved.

We were then issued additional items, among which were silk escape maps and small tiny compasses, which we were to sew into our gas-impregnated jumpsuits. We were then issued invasion money in several small French franc denominations in the event we had to purchase anything from the French populace. We were also issued tablets to help keep us awake and alert, as well as a morphine Syrette for self-administering in the event we were wounded. I had no idea at the time of issuing of the tablets or morphine Syrettes that I would use both of them before I left Normandy.

Our M-1 rifles were broken down into several parts and put into a felt container, which we referred to as a violin case. These were then strapped diagonally to our chest under our reserve parachute. I brought along a small .32-caliber nickel-plated Smith & Wesson revolver that I carried just above my reserve chute and just under my yellow life jacket in the event I needed it upon landing.

Weather caused a twenty-four-hour postponement. Finally, about 8:30 P.M. on Monday, June 5, 1944, we assembled by stick. We had eighteen jumpers in my stick, and we traveled across the airfield to our assigned plane, and then we checked our para-packs for the last time. We all had our last relief stop, for once we had our equipment on, it was physically impossible to relieve ourselves.

We then blackened our faces, donned our equipment, put on our chutes, the reserve, and then came the yellow life preserver, our helmets, and our chin straps. We were then each pushed or hauled onboard by the plane's crewmen. Our individual combat load was so bulky and heavy, it was impossible for us to get in the plane by ourselves. The mood of the troopers ranged from nervous chatter to nervous laughter. All minor personality differences between the men were forgotten, and camaraderie pre-

> vailed. I chewed an entire pack of gum from the time of embarking, and I don't have any recollection of what happened to that mouthful of gum. We had some reservations about our plane, which was of C-53 configuration that had relatively smaller exit doors than the standard C-47. I often thought about the engineer that designed the bucket seats in the troop transport plane, because they were definitely not designed for the combat-equipped troops. The pilot and crewmen asked if we would all stand forward for takeoff as much as possible to permit the overloaded plane to become airborne.
>
> In the dusk and incoming darkness of the English evening at the airfield, the motors of the planes started cranking up, each coming to life, idling, coming to life, idling again, and then jockeying into their respective takeoff positions. As the motors of our plane advanced to full takeoff power, it seemed that every loose rivet vibrated in harmony with the engine, and the plane circled down the runway to become airborne. As we lifted off, we could see the airfield personnel all out on the flight line waving the white handkerchiefs, because they knew, as we did, that the long-awaited D-Day invasion was under way.

The 505th PIR was the only veteran parachute regiment of the 82nd Airborne Division jumping into Normandy. PFC (formerly Sgt.) Martin M. Finkelstein of Philadelphia, a member of Company H, 3rd Battalion, 505th PIR, had participated in all the campaigns of the 82nd A/B Division and was only nineteen years old on June 6, 1944. Being Jewish, he had little love for the Germans. In Italy, he had discovered the effects of the Gammon grenade and decided that this was the weapon for him, even though many others were afraid to carry it. When he and his comrades moved to the staging area, they were given briefings. The persistent rain did not seem to be a good omen to the men. Finkelstein, like Hood, was too young to comprehend the importance of the operation in which he was about to take part.

Finkelstein does not remember whether he was told what to do in case they took prisoners. "In the past—Sicily and Italy—prisoners, when taken behind the lines, were interrogated the best we could if we had an interpreter. There was no place to put them, and yes, we just shot them. That was all we could do; maybe not pleasant, but by the same token true." Other veterans have made similar comments about prisoners. Usually, one soldier in a squad executed the prisoners. It was well known that the Germans occasionally executed prisoners and that their mistreatment of prisoners sometimes resulted in death. PFC Kenneth Burch, a Texan serving in the 507th PIR, sums up the situation this way:

> The parachute troops were composed of men who were often streetwise tough, some out of military prisons, some poor folk in it for the extra pay, and a few college kids for honor and country. In general, an unruly lot who couldn't care less until the replacement kids came in after Normandy. Their purpose was to kill or be killed, and not to be gentlemen. In general practice [from what the paratroopers knew], they executed us as prisoners and we them. Both sides knew that.

Although Kenneth Burch's point of view might seem extreme, it was probably closest to the truth in 1944. He knew of men from his unit who had executed Germans in Normandy and considered them murderers. Nevertheless, he thought of himself as being street tough. For him, it was war, and war did strange things.

PFC Finkelstein and other members of his company were told that if they had to surrender, they should rip off their 82nd A/B Division patches and insignias of rank and follow the rules of war.

> What we were doing June 4 and 5 was playing cards and shooting craps in the hangar. The one item that we were briefed on was that we were to capture a machine-gun nest located in a churchyard in Ste-Mère-Église. There were three of us: Stu Northern, Mac McCormick, and myself. Surprisingly, the information given to us was the names of the machine gunner, his assistant, and the guy who carried the ammunition. We were given their wives' names and their hometowns. If I recall correctly, two of them had children. The main reason for this was that if we were fortunate enough to capture them rather than kill them, we were to interrogate them and scare them a little bit by telling them where they were from, their family names, etc. We got this information about two days before the operation.
>
> Unlike the 101st, we had been in combat, and I believe we knew what we were going into. I don't believe I knew anyone that was frightened. We were scared—I think anybody in his right mind would be scared—but we were not frightened about what we were going into. We were more or less looking forward to it. The airborne was taught to be the best, told they were the best, impressed they were the best. We had to live up to what we were being told. Anyway that was the way I felt.

First Lt. Jack R. Isaacs of Coffeyville, Kansas, led the 3rd Platoon, Company G, 3rd Battalion, 505th PIR. Another veteran of Sicily and Italy, he received his mission at his briefing.

> My platoon's objective was to seize those foxholes shown on aerial photos and marked on the sandbox, and use them ourselves to defend against counterattack, which would probably come shortly after. At this point, the objective was not known to us by name. We continued to study our French phrase books, which was a good sign we were going to France, but no one had the foggiest notion where.
>
> Our equipment consisted of light machine guns, 60-millimeter mortars and BARs [Browning automatic rifles], and the new one-piece bazooka, which replaced the two-piece one we used in Italy. We had some carbines, although I did not consider them reliable from my Italian experiences. I chose an M-1 Garand, a more reliable weapon. We had a new type of field uniform, which was olive drab, that replaced the very popular jumpsuit that we used since training at Fort Benning. The jumpsuit of that time was not well suited for field use; it was rather light in weight and sort of tan in color and not good for camouflage. In Sicily and Italy, we had dropped our mortars and machine-gun bundles, and then we had to find them and assemble the weapons. By the time of Normandy, those weapons were actually dropped on the men who were using them. They were placed in a bag that had a thirty-foot riser, which was attached to the man's harness. After his chute had opened, he was to let that bag down, still attached to him. In Italy, we had used a gun case in which the Garand was broken down. In Normandy, we developed a technique where the rifle was carried on the man ready to use when he got out of the chute. We were also to use in Normandy a cricket for identification comparable to a child's toy.
>
> Upon arrival at the airport, we were locked in for security reasons, and here we were told where we were going. It was revealed that our target was Ste-Mère-Église,

France, and our objective was to take and hold the village and deny the Germans the use of the roads through the area, as well as prevent a counterattack towards the beaches.

PFC Raymond Gonzalez, a draftee from Detroit, served in the 2nd Platoon of Company C, 1st Battalion, 505th PIR. He recalls the events leading up to his regiment moving to the staging area.

We knew something was going to happen because they brought in a lot of guards around the compound and the regimental area. One night they told us to pack up everything in the bags, take them to company HQ, and stack them up. We were put on trucks in the morning. We had our combat gear, rifles, clean socks, underwear, etc. They shipped us to an airport; it was secretly done. It was around Nottingham, because I had been to Nottingham before and I could tell. About June 4, I think, they gave us parachutes and reserves. We just sat around cleaning our rifles or going to the movie. We stayed in tents, like four to six to a tent.

Early on June 5, they took us into the hangar, and we laid our chutes down and played cards, joked, read, and loafed around. It was actually boring and we wanted to get going. They took us to tents, showed us the terrain, what was going to happen, where we were supposed to land, and our objective. We were supposed to take Ste-Mère-Église. We were supposed to jump on the fourth, but it was called off. It was just rainy, muggy, and foggy. On the fifth, late at night, we boarded the planes, and there was one accident there when somebody dropped their C-2 explosive and blew their plane up close to me. Anyway, we got into the air; we went around, and around, and around, it seemed endlessly. By that time it was dark, and we moved off.

Also serving with 2nd Platoon, Company C of the 505th PIR, was a mortar man named PFC Allen Langdon from Los Angeles. When he found out their destination was Normandy, for the first time this veteran of the Italian campaign felt that they had a good chance of surviving, because the enemy defenses would be weaker so far from Germany.

Our commanding officer, Capt. Anthony M. Stefanich, gave us a short speech, telling us to put to good use the things that we had learned in Sicily and Italy. No finer man ever lived than Captain Stefanich. He was loved by the entire company and respected by the whole regiment, and as fate would will it, was later killed in Holland. After wishing us good luck and good hunting, we were dismissed, and after a final briefing by our platoon leader, Lt. Gerald N. Johnson, trucks took us to our various planes. Our planeload was made up of S.Sgt. Herman R. Zeitner, our platoon sergeant and jump master; Sgt. Elmo E. Bell; PFC Clarence R. Vinson; PFC John P. Lynn; PFC Steve A. Minarcik, killed later in the Battle of the Bulge; PFC Lyle G. Kohler; and myself. We were joined at our plane by several men from battalion headquarters, mostly medics. We made short work of attaching our equipment bundles to the belly of the plane. These bundles contained our mortar and ammunition for it, one bundle of land mines, one of machine-gun ammunition, and two or three containing extra medical supplies. Each man then selected a main chute and reserve from the pile and began the tedious process of adjusting the harness and trying to figure out where to hang the small mountain of equipment that he carried.

In his history of the 505th, Allen Langdon mentioned that each rifleman drew 160 rounds, two Mark II hand grenades, and a Gammon grenade. The majority of the men preferred to jump with their M-1s assembled, but the Griswold containers were available for those that wanted them. Most of the veteran troopers each carried a pistol, toy cricket for signaling, one unit of K rations (small, packaged combat rations), and two of D rations (high-calorie, almost tasteless chocolate bars).

> When fully loaded, we could barely waddle, and each man had to be helped into the plane. Our pilot and copilot made their appearance, and the pilot, just a young kid about our age and a first lieutenant, apparently caught up in the spirit of the thing, made us an unusual short speech saying something to the effect that if it was humanly possible, he would see to it that we were dropped on our proper drop zone and he wished us good luck. I noticed that he carried a musette bag of personal gear, which looked to me as if he was kind of pessimistic about getting back to England. We were soon airborne.

Pvt. Edward Jeziorski from New Jersey, who had joined the airborne only a year earlier, caught up with the 507th PIR after it arrived in Northern Ireland and moved with it to Tollerton Hall in March 1944. He was assigned as a machine gunner to the 2nd Platoon, Company C, 1st Battalion. The 507th and 508th PIR operated out of nearby Nottingham. His green regiment moved out in the last week of May for its staging area.

> We received our jumpsuits and put those suckers on. I want to tell all they were the lousiest, the coldest, the clammiest, the stiffest, the stinkiest articles of clothing that were ever dreamed up to be worn by individuals. Surely the guy that was responsible for the idea on this screw-up received a Distinguished Service Medal from the devil himself. These things, in no little part, accounted for a lot of short tempers. More than one black eye appeared on troopers who were quite close to each other. It didn't take much difference of opinion to bring out the sporting instinct. We were extremely close to each other as an outfit. These things were forgotten as fast as they occurred.
>
> My recollection of June 1, 2, and 3 are a jumble of maps, overlays, terrain scale models, and mock-ups of our DZs, the surrounding territory, and the areas we were actually to secure and establish positions upon our landing. An admonishment to me was "Remember by damn here's where you go, here's where you set the machine gun up, and by God, you just don't reveal your presence at all till you are ordered to put the thing to use." Of course, that was far from being what actually took place.
>
> On June 3, we rigged our para-packs under our ships and my C-47, its tail number was Z-92422 and chalk number for just company and regimental identification was 22. We were surprised as the dickens to see the white stripes painted on the wings and also on the fuselage. You thought they would be up there like sitting ducks for every ground gunner to try his luck on. We put five para-packs under the ship. They had a total weight of something around 1,300 pounds. Pack number 1, which I was interested in, was my light, air-cooled .30-caliber plus four boxes of armor-piercing ammo. The other packs contained additional ammunition and a small 60-millimeter mortar. On this day, we also got all the rest of the stuff that we would carry personally on the jump. We got K rations, three boxes of them, and then three days of D

rations, as I recall, which were the chocolate bars and quite concentrated stuff that tasted pretty good the first time you ate it. After that, the son of a gun gave you a good case of heartburn or indigestion. We also had our first-aid kits tied to our helmet webbing. Everyone jumped with a Gammon grenade, a phosphorous grenade, two frag grenades, and two bandoliers of ammo for the M-1 rifle. We jumped with the M-1 assembled and slung over our shoulder, with the bellyband around just under the reserve. When we finally loaded up there was an air force guy on each side of us, pushing us up the steps.

After a good breakfast on June 4, we were notified that we would be going in that night. We were told to take it easy and do the things we needed for ourselves. I don't know one of us who didn't attend a religious service by Father Verret. We each made our own peace in our own way. Some of us looked over our main chutes and reserves to see that they had not been disturbed. Some of us piddled around and sharpened our knives and our bayonets. Others wrote letters to the ones that meant the most to us back home. I took my future intended's picture out of my wallet and taped it inside my helmet.

Then, a little bit later that day, we were told that the show was called off and we wouldn't be going until the next day. Some guys, I guess, were relieved a little bit. For the most, I think it was just a true misery to be held over again. I think we were all very anxious to make a move one way or the other.

June 5 breakfast was kind of tough; I don't recall eating too much of it. I also don't remember eating any other meals that day. I thought about home a lot. Kinda hard to shut those thoughts out. I wrote some more letters to Mom and Pop and to my brothers and sisters, and also to the girl that would be waiting for me. I talked to Father Verret very briefly. He asked me if I was scared, and I told him that I didn't think so. I was wondering what might be waiting for us, but I didn't think that I was afraid. Father Verret took me by the hand, and we both knelt down and said a little prayer. At around eight o'clock, someone yelled that the "Berlin Bitch" was coming on the radio. We all gathered around and sat up as she spoke. "Good evening 82nd Airborne Division. Tomorrow morning, the blood from your guts will grease the bogey wheels on our tanks." This I recall very clearly. At around 10 P.M., we began going out to our airplanes, rosters were being called, we carefully checked our equipment, all that stuff, putting it on. Somewhere around eleven o'clock, we began loading up. I figured it would be a tough time to get a case of airsickness, so I took a couple of antimotion pills that we had been issued and popped them in my mouth and swallowed them down. I sure as heck didn't want to be sick up there. We started loading up by jump numbers and settled in our seats, and the engines started warming up, and we began taxiing to takeoff position. Our chalk number, 22, now indicated that in the V-of-Vs flying formation, we would be a lead plane at the extreme left nine of the first twenty-seven planes of our regiment. Lieutenant Parks was our platoon commander, who would jump number one. Gregg Howard, the squad leader, would jump number eight, and I would jump right before Gregg as number seven. Dominic Giacoletti, our platoon sergeant, would jump last. Soon we commenced taxiing down the runways, and then shortly the pilots revved them up and let off the brakes. It just seemed to me that we just rolled and rolled for the longest time before we were able to get the tail lifted and were airborne.

T/5 Abelardo Gonzales, a medic of the 507th PIR's Medical Detachment assigned to Company H of the 3rd Battalion, came from San Antonio. He had been drafted only the previous year and found himself in England preparing for the biggest adventure of his life. After leaving the tent camp at Nottingham and moving to the staging area, he joined Company H for the briefings.

The medical aid men were all with the companies. We were assigned to a company after we went overseas and stayed with the company. I was assigned to Company H. The reason they put us with the company was to know the guys, sleep with them, eat with them, and so on. There were three medics to a company. I was assigned to the 1st Platoon. We were supposed to jump at Amferville, but we never got there. I think the objective was some bridges, but I don't remember, although I know they didn't tell us about the marshes.

On June 4, we were suited up and ready to go, and then they told us to go back. They took us back to the tents on the airfield. On June 5, we just waited. They took us to the planes that were waiting for us at the runway. I had a regular impregnated suit, and it did stink very badly. You got used to the smell. Medical kits—one on each leg—parachutes, my personnel clothing, raincoat, shaving gear, etc. The medical kit had mostly bandages, morphine, tourniquets, and a sort of metal wiring for splints on legs, but mostly bandages. I was not as loaded as the rest of the soldiers. We had three days of K rations. It was little boxes with powdered eggs, lunch meat, toilet paper, chewing gum.

PFC Dick Johnson from Rochester, New Hampshire, with HQ Company, 1st Battalion, 507th PIR, was nineteen years old in 1944.

Around May 15 or so, we got in trucks and they took us up to an airfield at Lechmere, England.[9] We were told that we would stay at least two weeks and would be briefed on the invasion. Prior to this, I only knew about France from my geography and history, and I didn't know where Normandy was until we found out. We were in a big hangar with three or four companies to a hangar—about 600 men in each hangar. We were told it was going to be on June 5.

They gave us maps, a little bit of the French language, and they had the tables laid out with the drop areas on them. They gave us some little things we had to learn in French and German. For those two weeks, it was calisthenics exercising, writing letters to home, having good food, and sitting around. Day after day, they gave us information about where we were going to jump.

Finally June 4 came, and that was the day they told us that at about eleven o'clock [P.M.], we would take off, and about one o'clock [A.M.], we would jump. That night, we had a good meal and sat around getting ready, joking, writing letters. They told us the German soldiers were good fighting soldiers, but where we were supposed to jump, there was not any heavy concentration of enemy. What we feared most was the 88 cannons, Tiger tanks, and the German paratroopers. Around nine o'clock, the

9. Johnson's reference to Lechmere may be a misspelling for a town near Nottingham. The 1st Battalion took off from Fulbock Airfield, while the other two battalions used Barkston Heath. Both were near Nottingham.

weather report came in, and they said the winds were too high to jump in Normandy. The word came down that the invasion was delayed for one day. We all had a sigh of relief, although this is what we were waiting for.

That whole day, we did nothing but write more letters and wait. At about ten o'clock, we were trucked out to the airport with all our gear. We loaded up and about eleven o'clock [P.M.]. I would say there were about eighteen or nineteen men to a stick. They were lined up nine men on one side and nine on the other, and the jumpmaster was with us. We took off a little after eleven o'clock, and it was dark. We could hear the planes and see all the lights through the moonlight; it was a beautiful night, the moon was out, and we could see the planes in the air.

PFC Joseph G. Clowry of Lockport, New York, who served with the 319th Glider Field Artillery Battalion of the 82nd A/B Division, was a veteran of the Italian campaign. He was in one of the few glider units that would go in during the early-morning hours of D-Day.

We arrived in the staging area at the beginning of June 1944, the "we" being the Headquarters Battery of the 319th Glider Field Artillery Battalion of the 82nd Airborne Division, and the "staging area" being an airfield at Membury located roughly midway between London and Bristol, or approximately fifty miles west of London. We had come down from our training area outside Market Harborough, a small town near Leicester in central England.

Arriving at Membury Airfield, our unit was assigned to one of the rather cramped areas, each containing a number of tents, and each surrounded by barbed-wire fences. There we were briefed on the upcoming mission, shown maps of the Normandy area indicating landing zones (in our case LZW, Landing Zone West), issued necessary invasion equipment, and, in general, prepared ourselves and equipment and remained confined.

The 319th was to be part of the Elmira mission to reinforce the division with its landing scheduled near sunset to make the gliders a more difficult target for enemy gunners on D-Day. Clowry's flight, Serial No. 32, consisted of fifty C-47s of the 436th Troop Carrier Group towing forty-eight British-made Horsa gliders and two American Waco CG-4A gliders, scheduled to arrive at the landing zone at 11 P.M. In this flight, in addition to the 319th, were elements of the 320th Glider Field Artillery (FA) Battalion, 82nd A/B Division Artillery, 307th A/B Medical Company and Company A, 307th A/B Engineer Battalion. Clowry's flight was to be followed ten minutes later by the remainder of the 320th Glider FA in twelve CG-4As and thirty-eight Horsas, towed by fifty C-47s from another airfield at Welford.

Part of our waiting period was utilized in loading our assigned Horsa glider with the jeep and trailer, which it towed. The trailer carried such items as switchboards, field telephones, reels of wire, and other communications equipment. The jeep and trailer were secured by rope to lashing rings screwed into threaded holes located throughout the glider floor, and then the springs on both units were blocked with wood wedges to keep them from vibrating and breaking loose in flight. We sewed an American flag on the upper shoulder portion of the right sleeve of our fatigue jacket. We honed our combat knives, which we strapped to our leg. We cleaned our folding-stock carbines and fitted them into the new canvas holsters attached to our belts. We filled clips with ammunition, attached the issued first-aid kit either to the camouflage net on our helmet or on our harness. We packed our K rations, taped grenades to our pack harness, filled canteens, checked our newly issued gas mask and carrying case (many disposed of the mask and used the shoulder-slung case to carry additional rations, cigarettes, ammunition, and other essentials), ate, slept, and sat around waiting.

After the June 5 postponement, we were alerted on June 6 to pack up and leave our staging area for the end of the nearby runway, where the aircraft were all lined up and making ready to depart.

The gliders were lined up in two columns, with each one's nose at an angle of 45 degrees behind the preceding one, so that the wings to the inside of the columns interlaced all the way down. Lined up in front of both lines of gliders were the C-47s. Each tow aircraft faced inward at a 45-degree angle and a 300-yard-long nylon towrope laid out in serpentine manner linked it to a glider. A pair of wires attached by tape to the towrope provided the communication link between the tow plane and the glider. According to *The Glider War* by James Mrazek, the gliders, just like all aircraft flying on D-Day, had three white stripes painted on each wing and fuselage.

Our group entered our designated glider and seated ourselves facing the center of the craft on the benchlike seats that ran most of the length of each side of the body and strapped ourselves in. I was seated across from the previously loaded trailer, slightly to the rear of the center of the craft and on the left side. In addition to our regular equipment, we had been furnished a Mae West life jacket in case we had to ditch in the Channel. Our contingent consisted of a glider pilot and, because of the shortage of pilots, our first lieutenant assisting in the copilot's seat, and a number of enlisted men of various grades.

The 325th GIR of the 82nd A/B Division was not scheduled to go into Normandy until June 7. Unlike the 327th of the 101st A/B Division, most of the 325th went in by glider. T/5 Gerald M. Cummings, a West Virginian already twenty-eight years old, was in the Service Company when the final preparations began.

On May 22, we stood two glider load inspections. On the same day, we had our field jackets dyed, sewed chevrons on, drew ammunition, and left for airports. The next day, Major Taylor, who had planned the glider operation in Burma, was with us.

On May 29, we went to Aldermaston and stayed in a big hangar until we left for Normandy on June 7. On June 2, we were taken to the situation room and briefed on where we would be going. On June 4, we received one British pound's worth of French francs. The next day, we loaded our glider with a quarter-ton trailer and about 450 pounds of antitank ammunition, so we knew that our departure was imminent. As if by magic, planes and gliders were dressed in broad black and white stripes.

On June 6, we put on our battle clothes. We rolled up our old clothes to be sent back to camp. My impregnated pants were an inch too small around the waist, and my shirt was a size too small. The invasion was announced on this day. We knew it was on because the soldiers occupying the other half of the hangar had left during the night.

Capt. Joe Gault, a Texan commissioned from ROTC, led Company F, 2nd Battalion, 325th

Equipment Carried by Paratroopers

A paratrooper carried loads ranging from 60 to 150 pounds, including his individual equipment and additional items carried on bundles and leg packs.

The individual equipment for the Normandy operation included dog tags, pay cards, summer underwear, socks, boots, a helmet, assault gas mask, first-aid kit, raincoat, bag, and pistol belt. The bag was filled with one K and two D rations, toilet articles, basic ammunition loads, two pairs of wool socks, two hand towels, halazone, insecticide, and shoe impregnant. The pistol belt with suspenders included a full canteen, entrenching tool, trench knife, first-aid pouch, and bayonet.

Each paratrooper had to carry one barracks bag to the departure fields with a woolen OD uniform, an impregnated (against poison gas) jumpsuit with a division patch and American flag, one pair each of summer underwear and wool underwear, toilet articles, an extra towel, and a mess kit. In addition, he had to wear a Mae West life preserver with his parachute pack. The men were warned not to inflate it until they removed the parachute harness.

Some of the paratroopers' arsenal consisted of M1 Garand rifles, Springfield 03 rifles, M1 carbines, submachine guns, rocket launchers, and grenades. The light machine gun had to be dismantled into two parts and carried by two paratroopers, the 60-millimeter mortar in three pieces with three men. Each paratrooper with an M-1 rifle carried 176 rounds of ammunition, and each with a BAR or submachine gun took 680 rounds.

One trooper carried the handy-talkie, SCR-536, but the larger radios, such as the SCR-284 and SCR-300, each had to be bundled in separate parts and carried by two paratroopers.

In addition to the items carried by the individual soldiers, supplementary equipment was dropped separately, usually in bundles known as para-packs, equipped with a small battery-powered identification light. Different lens colors indicated the type of equipment they contained. Normally these packs contained a utility handcart with two wheels and a T bar for pulling it. It was used to carry ammunition, weapons, or supplies. The pack also held a light machine gun, 81-millimeter mortar, 75-millimeter pack howitzer broken down into several pieces, and ammunition of various types. The C-47 was equipped with six para-racks located on its underbelly for carrying and dropping para-packs.

GIR. After commanding the company for nine months, he had recently been promoted to the rank of captain. His regiment had moved from Northern Ireland to a tent camp in a cow pasture at the town of Scraptoft. Gault lamented that some of the replacements that had just arrived were of questionable value. Pvt. Richard Weese of Madison, Maine, who was in the 1st Battalion, concurred with his captain. "We had one trooper who drank 'canned heat,' the small can of Sterno which was used to heat individuals' food. He would take and squeeze Sterno into a handkerchief and into a canteen cup and place about an inch of water in it, mix, and drink. By the time he finished the drink, he was in Never-Never Land."

Captain Gault, who had carefully trained his men, was sure they were ready.

> Around June 1, we were moved to a staging area in South England. Each man was involved with his own thoughts, as Company F combat time only served to give them the fears of combat, and we had a very vague idea as to our future.
>
> On the night of June 5, everything was pretty quiet because most of the men hadn't seen combat, but they had spent time in Italy only being shelled. If they were like me, they were wondering what was going to happen. I remember the noise of the aircraft all during the night. They were taking off with paratroopers. It had to be hour after hour. They told us then what was happening, and we assembled the men and told them.

Years later, most of the airborne troopers seem to have forgotten the rainy day preceding the mission, but they vividly remember the excellent fare they were served. From steaks to ice cream, they were allowed to have as much as they desired. The men had mixed feelings about the pending battle and prepared in different ways. Morale remained high, however, and they were ready to have at the enemy. The men of the 506th PIR watched a German documentary showing enemy paratroopers taking the key bridges leading into Fortress Holland in 1940. In his memoirs, *Parachute Infantry*, David K. Webster wrote that Col. Robert Sink, the regimental commander, pointed out how effectively their enemy moved and used cover and concealment. Then the colonel reminded them that Gen. Bernard Montgomery, who had seen both them and the Germans, had maintained that the Americans were bigger and better, which made him feel sorry for the enemy.

Intelligence and the Airdrop

At the end of May, the First Army's G-2 for intelligence received important information about enemy troop movements. Apparently the Germans were shifting their forces in the Cotentin Peninsula, and new units were arriving. At this point, the 82nd A/B Division was to be dropped in the vicinity of La Haye du Puits, and the 101st A/B Division was to land near Ste-Mère-Église. This would allow both divisions to cut the major routes into the peninsula. The 82nd A/B would be more than twenty miles away from Utah Beach. The arrival of these German reinforcements would leave the 82nd in a precarious position where it could easily be isolated and smashed before the breakout from the beachhead could take place.

The question of where to drop the 82nd A/B had already been debated earlier by Gen. Omar Bradley, Montgomery, and Air Marshal Trafford L. Leigh-Mallory. Bradley wanted it placed farther north of La Haye du Puits. The air marshal believed the American airdrop would be a disaster and wanted it canceled. Although Eisenhower pushed ahead with the planned operation, he also had some qualms about it, based on past experiences in the Mediterranean. But he refused General Marshall's even bolder plan for a major airdrop at Évreux, a position well beyond possible support from the invading armies.[10] The army commanders prevailed when Eisenhower made the final decision.

On May 25, Gen. Matthew Ridgway of the 82nd A/B and Gen. Maxwell Taylor of the 101st A/B flew to Bristol to redraw the plans for the airborne operation. The 101st remained with its

10. The site was more than fifty miles southeast of the British invasion beaches and offered a chance to block crossings of the Seine. It would have been very difficult to support, however, especially if the airdrop were as badly scattered as the one on the Cotentin Peninsula on June 5–6.

original mission, while the 82nd would drop north and west of it and take Ste-Mère-Église. While the two generals made their plans, Leigh-Mallory went to see Eisenhower and tried to persuade him to cancel the American airdrop, predicting over 50 percent casualties for the airborne forces. Nevertheless, Eisenhower decided to stay the course.

The troops of the 82nd A/B received their new instructions shortly before the day they took off. On paper, it was the only veteran unit of the two airborne divisions. It should be noted, however, that its two green regiments—the 507th and 508th PIR—were attached, and not originally part of the division. The 505th PIR and 325th GIR were actually the only veteran formations of the eight American airborne regiments earmarked for the invasion.

The planners made the final decision on the locations of the drop zones and landing zones just a few days before the operation, as they had to change plans because of the positioning of new German formations. The 82nd A/B Division took over an area closer to the 101st A/B. The 502nd PIR's objective was to create a larger blocking force in Ste-Mère-Église.

CHAPTER 6

The Assault Divisions Prepare

The Western Naval Task Force (TF 122), under the leadership of Rear Adm. Alan G. Kirk, assembled in southern England.[1] Its main element carried out the amphibious operations for Utah Beach. Force U (TF 125), under Rear Adm. Don P. Moon, transported troops destined for Utah Beach, and Force O (TF 124), under Rear Adm. John L. Hall, carried those headed for Omaha Beach.

According to the U.S. Army's publication *Utah Beach to Cherbourg*, Force U consisted of about 865 ships of all sizes sailing in twelve separate convoys, which took on troops and equipment at nine different points. This group included the warships and bombardment units that would protect and support the invasion. The units they were to transport were from Maj. Gen. J. Lawton Collins's VII Corps and comprised Maj. Gen. Raymond O. Barton's 4th Infantry Division with attachments, including the 1st Engineer Special Brigade, which, at the time, was larger than an army division. It also included the 70th Tank Battalion, with Sherman DD tanks, designed for floating onto a beach from up to 6,000 yards out using their own power.

This massive force assembled between Plymouth, Dartmouth, and Exmouth in southwest England. Of all the invading forces, including the British, it had the greatest distance to travel to its invasion beaches. The units that had to move out first were from the 8th Infantry Regiment, which would make the initial landings alongside the 70th Tank Battalion. The 237th and 299th Combat Engineer Battalions and the men of the combined army-navy demolition teams would also be among the first to land.

The loading began as early as May 30, 1944. The convoys of Force U assembled on Saturday, June 3, but after steaming out of port ahead of the other task forces, as this force had a greater distance to cover to Normandy, the ships had to return or find shelter along the coast when the invasion was postponed because of bad weather. After a meeting with his deputies, Eisenhower decided to call off the operation for twenty-four hours, since the atmospheric conditions were unfavorable to air operations and the naval commander felt that the sea conditions were also too rough. At 5 A.M. on Sunday, June 4, the message went out to Force U to return to port. One convoy of LCTs and LCMs did not get the message until 9 A.M., twenty-five miles south of the Isle of Wight. After three destroyers failed to locate it, a British seaplane spotted it after it had already reversed course, according to Samuel Eliot Morison's *The Invasion of France and Germany*. At 11 P.M., Adm. Bertram Ramsey of the Royal Navy, the naval commander for Operation Neptune, sent the signal for the convoys to sail at the designated times. Early on Monday morning, June 5, the convoys of the TF 125 reassembled and sailed out as the 14th and 16th Minesweeper Flotillas cleared a path for them, marking it with red and green buoys, as recounted in *Utah Beach to Cherbourg*.

The 4th Infantry Division Prepares

T/5 Fred R. Tannery of Raleigh, North Carolina, who served with the 4th Division's 4th Signal Company, moved with his unit to the staging area near Dartmouth several days before sailing.

> I was in Staging Area No. 13 for a few days before we got the news that D-Day was near. We were given details of the landing and issued French paper money. We knew then, this was it. One day, German planes flew over, and one of the planes was shot down. That plane dropped out of the sky and just missed me and my driver, landed in the next field, and blew up. This happened in the daytime, and what a show it was. The pilot had bailed out before his plane crashed, and he was captured by the 4th Infantry Division.
>
> The last few days were spent in waterproofing our equipment. Being a motor messenger, I had a jeep and a driver. We named our jeep *Pop-Tan*. We drove to Dartmouth to load onto *LST-283*.

Pvt. William E. Finnigan, a New Yorker, also in the 4th Signal Company, remembers that they went in groups of eight to ten into a small building, where officers gave them a briefing on the situation.

> We were shown maps of Normandy beach areas. One view was a black silhouette, as though taken from a submarine. "If lost, go to St. Martin de Varreville; there will be directors on the beach"—of course, there weren't! As we left the room, a sign beside the door said, "You now know the Greatest Secret in the World." We were told the

1. The Eastern Task Force carried the British and Commonwealth troops to their three invasion sites.

> causeways across the swamps and the road shoulders would be mined. There were small German signs along the causeway—white with a skull and crossbones with the word "MINEN."
>
> A few days later, naval personnel arrived. We exchanged our British money for French money that was printed by the U.S. and didn't look like French money. I loaded at Dartmouth on *LST 282*. Each LST was so closely anchored you could step over the rail and cross to the others. I did one evening go to confession—I am a Catholic. It seemed all day, and especially in the evening, the sailors wigwagged their flags in conversation with other ships.

The 4th Signal Company embarked for the invasion during the first three days of June.

While the *LST 282*, with the 4th Signal Company onboard, approached the invasion beaches, the soldiers it carried remained largely unaware of the activities taking place.

PFC Guy E. Overbey of Ewing, Kentucky, was a member of the Pioneer & Ammunition Platoon, HQ Company, 3rd Battalion, 8th Infantry. His training was in both demolitions and minelaying and removal. He also qualified as a .50-caliber machine gunner. His platoon's main function was to supply ammunition, water, and food, but patrols were among the men's duties as well. The platoon also included a wire and radio section of about a dozen men. When Overbey and his comrades moved into their staging area, they noticed German aircraft flying over. The day they boarded their vessels, the men were heavily loaded.

> Loading into the LCVPs, my buddy and I had a mine detector, two bags of C-2 compound, a full field pack, and each a carbine. We were to get ashore, get with our command group, and receive instructions on what was necessary. Our battalion loaded on June 4 onto a large ship in the harbor of Plymouth, England. Weather conditions were very bad, with heavy rains and storms. We sat aboard, waiting. There were ships everywhere you could see.

PFC Overbey was lucky to be onboard a transport, because the crossing was much more comfortable for him than for the men on the landing craft. His battalion would be the last in the regiment's assault waves.

PFC Ralph Brazee, a draftee from Connecticut and a gunner in a 57-millimeter antitank company of the 22nd Infantry, anticipated some type of action during the landings, because his crew had used their gun to demolish five walls in the English moors earlier in May. He and his comrades had also tested their gas masks on May 25, as it was feared that the Germans might use gas. During their briefings, they were told about the flooded areas behind the beach.

> We loaded at a small village, someplace near Plymouth, onto an LCT very early in the morning, at daybreak. We rode our half-track through the village in the darkness of early morning, and we all agreed that if we had to be awake, all the people of the village were to also be awake, so we sang as loudly as possible as we rode past the houses. Our half-track and gun were backed up the ramp into the LCT by our track driver. Our sergeant gave him the necessary directions to position the vehicle among the other vehicles.
>
> We were loaded on our LCT on June 1 and stayed in one inlet after another on June 2 and 3. On the fourth, we went out and back into a larger harbor, while on the fifth, we went out into the Channel and back and forth before making our way to our place in the convoy. Before this, I had slept on the hood of our half-track, but on the evening of the fifth, I lost my place and

ended up on a coil of rope in a small compartment next to the loading ramp.

S.Sgt. William L. Conrad, a draftee from Helena, Ohio, as a member of Company F, 2nd Battalion, 8th Infantry, moved with his company to the staging area at Torquay in late May 1944.

We were placed on a transport that was to carry us to within a few miles of the landing site. We were packed on the ship like sardines. Everything was done in shifts, since there were not enough facilities to feed and sleep all of us at one time.

We sailed out of the harbor and dropped anchor, waiting for the other ships to join the convoy. Finally, we set sail; and was it rough! By the second day, we entered into a blackout situation: no light, no radio, no electric gadgets were used. So on the third day, there was a calm.

Sgt. Irving A. Bradbury from Connecticut, a member of Company D, 1st Battalion, 8th Infantry, also headed for the staging area at Torquay.

Here they set up a big tent city marshaling area. We were shown maps with identifiable objects on the beach area in Normandy that we were supposed to go towards when we landed. This went on for days. This tent city was under very strict security: double fence and MPs walking the perimeter as well as the regimental guard unit—twenty-four hours, day-around. We were briefed with current information that was usually only a day or two old and sometimes less than that.

I remember vividly seeing some pictures taken on the beach area where you would actually see Germans horizontal in the air, hitting the beach because they thought they were being strafed, and they didn't know they were being photographed.

I have a ration card, the last one I got in England. It was dated from January 1944 and it terminated June 4, 1944. If we had been intelligent at the time, we could have figured out when D-Day was.[2]

We went on at Torquay, where we marched down across the railroad tracks. Torquay is a big U-shaped inlet. In the town, following the inlet around it, we just marched along the perimeter of it right onto the wooden dock and up on into the ship. I don't remember being paid any money before departure.

I was loaded onto the USS *Barnett*, a Liberty ship. Incidentally, this *Barnett* was the same ship we had done our training on at Slapton Sands. We went aboard. The ship carried LCVPs. We were told at the time of sailing that we would be on the beach at France within eighteen hours after that.

In Torquay, we had one of the things that were typically army: Sometime between midnight and two o'clock, they decided to pull an abandon-ship drill. This was SOP [standard operating procedure] in the army; somebody had a great idea. We had practiced in Torquay to climb over the gunwale of the ship into the landing craft. Then the landing craft would be lowered by winches into the water. When this began at two o'clock in the morning, it didn't work out, because the water was so rough these ships were hitting the bow and some on the stern. Troops were getting legs broken or getting injured, as the water slapped the boat. Now they changed the command.

When Sgt. Vincent A. Angeloni, a draftee from Butler, Pennsylvania, serving with HQ Company,

2. The actual date was not decided upon until the spring.

2nd Battalion of the 8th Infantry, went in for the usual briefing, he was struck by "the blankets strung all over the place, and you couldn't see this big map with the area we were going to hit."

> They swore us to secrecy. One of the officers who swore us in said whatever we were going to see next would not be repeated to anybody, even among ourselves. When we went in the other room, there was this big map, I suppose twenty by ten feet high, and it only showed about a mile and a half of the beach. You could see little ups and downs, and every beach showed every little house with every little thing on the beach as obstacles. Every day we would go up there, they would have more stuff on the map as a result of the planes taking more photographs.
>
> We were told the troops on the beach weren't first-class troops, that they were inducted from Russia and the nations that the Germans had conquered. Of course, they were still there, and as I remember, rumor was we were going to get about 50 percent casualties. That worried us, because you figure one out of two: Am I going to get it or the next guy?
>
> On June 5, we had a downpour. I would say that it was at about four or five o'clock when the sun came out. We then knew it might be the next morning.

For Capt. John E. Galvin, the 8th Infantry's adjutant, the movement to the staging areas and the briefings came as a relief. Now he and the other "Bigots" were not the only men who had to carry the secret that had begun to weigh heavily upon their shoulders. He boarded his LST with other headquarters personnel and steeled himself for the upcoming events.

S.Sgt. Jack W. Carter of Gulfport, Mississippi, was a wire chief in the HQ Battery of the 44th Field Artillery, 4th Infantry Division. His battalion moved down to the staging area near Portsmouth at the end of May.

> My vessel was an LCT loaded with my communication chief Dennis Gray, my wire section consisting of six men, two medics, two 2½-ton supply trucks, four jeeps, two weapon carriers, and one tractor vehicle for getting through sand roads.
>
> We loaded June 1 and sailed up and down the channel to make room for other vessels being loaded. It took until June 4 to load the infantry and other troops. When the flotilla started toward France, it looked to me like everything that could float was in the English Channel. A terrible storm came up, and our boat pitched and tossed all over the channel for approximately one day and a half.

The landing of the 8th Infantry was to be followed by the 4th Division's 22nd Infantry Regiment. PFC Raymond G. Sluder, a draftee from Ashville, North Carolina, was a gunner for a 57-millimeter antitank gun of 2nd Battalion headquarters. "We embarked from Plymouth, England, and were surrounded by a lot of ships. We loaded on a landing craft, which carried three half-tracks, three or four jeeps, three antitank guns, and all our other equipment. We kept waiting for our order for three days. The rough water made everyone on the ship sick."

Pvt. Frank Catalano had arrived in England only in mid-May. This New Yorker had been drafted the year before, at the age of thirty-one, and made the Atlantic crossing in sick bay, suffering from malnutrition. Before he realized it, he was at a staging area near Bournemouth. After a week, he embarked on June 5 on a ship in the group right behind the invasion convoy. He became a replacement for the 22nd Infantry three days later, in an antitank gun platoon similar to Sluder's.

The 12th Infantry Regiment would be the last of the 4th Division's regiments to land. Its new commander, Col. Russell P. "Red" Reeder, had recently been put in charge of the regiment. In his previous assignment, Reeder had been an observer in the Southwest Pacific and had subsequently prepared a special report on troop training. Following that, he had worked in General Marshall's office in Washington and knew the details of Overlord in March 1944. Colonel Henderson, an excellent officer according to Reeder, was removed from command of the 12th Infantry because higher authorities believed he was too old and physically unfit to take part in the invasion. Colonel Reeder flew from Washington to England on April 31, 1944, to take command of the 12th. During the few weeks he commanded the regiment, he earned the respect and admiration of his men. Like several other outstanding regimental commanders, he seemed destined for a higher command, but several days into the invasion, the fortunes of war changed his fate.

Lt. Col. Charles Jackson of Vancouver, Washington, commanded the 1st Battalion of the 12th Infantry.

> On May 16, 1944, the regiment went into its marshaling area in Plymouth, becoming sealed off and guarded by the 5th Armored Division. Here we kept the men busy any way we could within the limits of the constricted area. The officers and noncommissioned officers spent many an hour studying intelligence maps and reports and making tentative tactical plans for the forthcoming assault. On May 20, I received the voluminous top-secret Field Order No. 1 from the 12th Infantry Regiment, and on May 26, I issued the 1st Battalion Field Order No. 1 to my companies (an amendment was issued on May 30). This was the only formal written field order issued by the battalion in any of the five campaigns in which the battalion participated. I also issued aerial photographs for every squad leader and maps scaled 1:25,000 for every platoon leader. After the companies completed their plans, each platoon leader briefed his men as to what would be done, using a huge sponge rubber replica of the landing site made accurate both horizontally and vertically, complete in every detail as to roads, bridges, buildings, fortifications, obstacles, minefields, etc. These were the final training sessions for the men, most of whom had been together for many years, who had trained to a fine fighting edge, who knew each other's capabilities and shortcomings, and who were confident of their ability to successfully accomplish the task they were to undertake.
>
> On June 4, 1944, the 1st Battalion with its equipment and vehicles embarked on four LCI(L)s, three LCT(4)s, and three LSTs. A basic load of ammunition and authorized excess was carried by each person. Riflemen in rifle squads carried one bandolier in addition to ammunition in belts. Each individual carried one each of K and D rations for the landing. Rations were provided while aboard vessels. Mess kits were carried aboard for use in eating the provided rations but were turned in prior to landing. For the landing, each individual carried a full canteen of water and halazone tablets for water purification, carried a gas mask, and wore impregnated fatigue clothes over his uniform as protection against gas attacks. In addition, each person wore a lifebelt.
>
> All units remained overnight aboard the LCIs and did not leave for France until the midafternoon, because D-Day had been postponed by one day. Then each vessel departed with a barrage balloon floating overhead.

The executive officer of Company I, 3rd Battalion, 12th Infantry, was 1st Lt. Thomas Cortright from Aurora, Illinois. His company embarked in Plymouth on a single LCI of the Coast Guard Flotilla.

> On May 15, we were sealed into the marshaling area near Plymouth, England. They were British Army barracks, and no one was allowed in or out of the compound until June 4. We loaded on June 4 because June 5 was supposed to be D-Day. However, it was delayed twenty-four hours, and we sat up on the River Dart for twenty-four hours. We played cards, and I won all the invasion money of all the officers, but I gave it back.

Sgt. William H. Buell, a draftee from Jamaica, New York, was the regimental ammunition sergeant in the Service Company of the 12th Infantry.

> We loaded our boat at 8 or 9 A.M. on, I believe, June 1. It was a small English LST with a crew of five Englishmen. They had a big night before and were still showing the effects. They had forgotten to bring aboard their own rations. This boat held about twenty vehicles, mostly jeeps with no large trucks, mostly vehicles and personnel for regimental headquarters, including Colonel Luckett, the assistant regimental commander. There was no underdeck and one or two one whole heads which filled up the first day. We were all supplied with ten-in-one rations. We all slept on an open deck and in inclement weather under the vehicles. Some of us took fishing gear aboard but were never able to use it.
>
> As for rations, we were also supplied with some English cans of soup that were quite unique. Through the middle of the can was a tube stuffed with some slow-burning substance and a wick at the top. You lit the wick and away it went. Once finished burning, one then opened the can and had some nice hot soup. It was really great.

Sgt. Clarence P. Faria, a draftee from Honolulu, was in the 2nd Platoon, Company L, 3rd Battalion, 12th Infantry. He was probably the first man in the division to become a World War II veteran, as during his first year of service, he happened to be stationed at Schofield Barracks, Hawaii, when the Japanese attacked Pearl Harbor on December 7, 1941. At the time, he was in the 65th Engineer Battalion. In 1944 in England, he was the platoon sergeant for the 2nd Platoon and recalls the preparation in the staging area.

> Twice a day at Plymouth, we were taken to a room with a relief map of our area showing all the terrain information down to the smallest detail. This included the type of enemy units we would encounter, the makeup of the units, ethnic origin. Also, we were told the map was subject to six-hour changes. During one morning session, we were informed of the enemy troops in the area, and then in the afternoon, we were told that a new German division had moved into the area sometime during the night. We were never told at what point of the coast we were going to assault until we boarded our LCT. The complete information as to the beach area and the name Utah, given to the beach sector of the 4th Division, was given by the company commander. He informed us that the area was called Normandy and the largest town was Ste-Mère-Église.
>
> Submarine photo strips taken at periscope depth of the Normandy coast were shown to us to give us an idea of what

> we would see coming into the beach from the landing craft. The relief map was so complete it showed everything.
>
> Several weeks before the planned attack, and moving to the staging area, we were briefed by an intelligence officer as to what to do and say if captured and what to expect as to treatment. Also, the officer indicated that if captured, we should make every attempt to escape.
>
> On June 3 we boarded the LCI and departed the night of June 5. Nothing happened on the crossing during the night.

First Sgt. Donald Sherwood of Whites Plains, New York, was a draftee serving with a collecting company of the 4th Medical Battalion. At the staging area a few days before embarking, he and his men were informed that they would have to face heavy shelling, the beaches would be mined, and they would have to go over a wall. Their mission was to take care of the casualties.

> We had been briefed as to where and when we were going to land. Our American money had been turned in, and we had been issued French invasion money in small amounts. We embarked at Plymouth. We must have loaded and sailed on or about June 3, for our LST developed motor trouble. It was crowded. Many of my company were on the open deck. Our boat came back in, and we were off-loaded and put under heavy guard until the next day, when our boat was again ready to sail. This day and night ashore, a bad storm hit the English Channel and delayed the landing until June 6. We were so afraid we would miss the landing after all the months of waiting and training.

Lt. Peter Triolo, who had come to the 4th Division from the Illinois National Guard, was assigned as a liaison officer with the 82nd Airborne Division.

> What I remember the most about my work as liaison officer was that on June 5, when D-Day was canceled and changed to June 6th I was loaded on a transport and flew down to Plymouth carrying the messages changing D-Day from June 5 to June 6. Upon our return trip to Coventry, England, we were not about ten to fifteen minutes in the air out from Plymouth and were attacked by German fighters. I can recall my pilot yelling, "Mayday, Mayday," and he dropped down to treetop level.

S.Sgt. Glenn Gibson enlisted at Harrisburg, Pennsylvania. He was twenty-nine years old and had a dangerous task for the invasion, since his platoon had special tanks. He prepared his 4th Platoon, Company A of the 70th Tank Battalion, to load their Sherman DD tanks the day before the planned invasion. "We loaded our LCTs with four tanks each, both Companies A and B of the 70th, and moved out from Lupton Camp on June 4. We started across the Channel on June 4, but because of rough seas, we moved into Plymouth Harbor for a few hours. Then we got the word to move back out for the Normandy invasion on June 5."

T/4 Charles J. Myers, a draftee from Baltimore, was also in the 70th Tank Battalion. He was a tank gunner and radio operator in the battalion commander's tank, which was part of battalion headquarters.

> In the middle of May, we moved to Lupton Camp, a sausage camp in the southwest region of Great Britain. We were restricted and remained there until it was our time to load on the ships. There was nothing to see those last few weeks, except field after field of equipment and supplies, and the

An LCT(R) off Omaha Beach on June 7, 1944. These rocket ships created an impressive fire display, but apparently not a great deal of damage.

men slated to use them. Our activities consisted of waterproofing vehicles, checking weapons, and supplies.

On June 4, we traveled to Plymouth and loaded on LSTs. We drove onto the LST, and positioned ourselves according to the unloading scheme. We had self-propelled artillery and half-tracks onboard. If my memory serves me right, on the LST we were on, we had the tank section, three of our assault guns, two mortar half-tracks, several 2½-ton supply trucks, plus vehicles of other units of the 4th Infantry Division, to whom we were attached. The DD tanks were not loaded on LSTs, since they were to be launched at sea, so they were loaded on LCTs. There were four or five tanks on each craft.

Soon after our LST was loaded, we were riding at anchor near Plymouth. Actually, [it was] about sixty-three hours prior to H-Hour, but remember, D-Day was postponed twenty-four hours.

The one thing that stands out in my mind during the Channel crossing is the constant roar of the plane engines as they flew over the convoy. First there were the troop carriers of the airborne troops, then the tow planes for the glider troops. Early in the morning, the bombers and fighters that were to work over the landing areas began flying over.

SF2/C Angelos T. Chatas from Chicago, a twenty-three-year-old navy frogman, served with U.S. Naval Combat Demolition Unit (NCDU) 25. One of eleven NCDU teams that sailed with Force U, this unit was assigned to clear obstacles on Utah Beach.[3]

During the first week of June, in this forest, we broke out the maps. I remember the

3. Twenty-one NCDU teams were assigned to Omaha Beach.

word "BIGOT" on the maps. Honestly, I did not know where Normandy was before the invasion. The date of Monday, June 5, was mentioned. This couldn't have been earlier than June 2 or 3. Some of the last-minute information was that there were wooden stakes put into the ground and mined. It turned out, when we found the stakes, not many were mined. I do not remember any being mined.

We were put on alert on the third, and on the fourth, we were put aboard an LST in Plymouth. Aboard the LST with us were elements of the 101st Airborne Division that came by sea into Utah Beach. I always thought they were elements of the first wave and subsequently manned antiaircraft guns. It was hard to tell who belonged to the 101st and the 4th Division. They were there; I saw them on the LST. We had to spend an extra day, because the invasion was delayed for twenty-four hours. Oh cripes, the storm on Sunday we were in the English Channel [was rough], and very few hardy ones did not upchuck. Boy, the seasickness was pervading the whole ship. We stayed out in the Channel. As far as I was concerned, I was glad, because I had to prepare myself for this invasion emotionally.

The night of June 5, it got a little calmer. This was not a chaplain, but one of the soldiers, I think one of these airborne guys, got back on the stern of the LST and made an announcement that if anybody wanted to have a prayer service to go back there. His message was that [there was] "a lot of talk about secret weapons. We got the best secret weapon there is in our faiths." We broke out into "Onward, Christian Soldiers." We prayed fervently for victory in battle and protection against danger.

The 70th Tank Battalion

The veteran 70th Tank Battalion had converted from the light tanks it used in North Africa to Sherman medium tanks. The battalion included an HQ Company, Service Company, Company D of light tanks, and Companies A, B, and C of medium tanks.

Each tank company consisted of three platoons of five tanks each, two command tanks, and additional supply and maintenance personnel. The HQ Company had three medium tanks, five 105-millimeter self-propelled howitzers, five 81-millimeter mortars, and the battalion and company headquarters personnel with supply and maintenance. The Service Company, a quartermaster unit, handled all supplies, major maintenance, transportation, and minor ordnance problems. The battalion also had a Medical Detachment of about 35 men, giving it a total strength of about 770 men.

Companies A and B included Sherman DD tanks for the first assault wave. The Service Company welded racks that mounted fifteen rockets to the turrets of the tanks of a platoon of Company C. These racks proved unsuccessful, however, and were later removed. The tanks of another platoon of Company C were outfitted with dozer blades designed to clear away obstacles. The tanks of Companies C and D and HQ Company were waterproofed and fitted with engine air intakes and exhaust shrouds, the same type of equipment used on light tanks in North Africa. The shrouds gave the tanks a fording capability of about five feet.

Force U moved toward its destination along with Force O through the hours of darkness during the night of June 5–6.

The Sailors Make Ready

On *LCT 851*, S1/C Myron D. Parsons of Newcastle, Pennsylvania, and his mates began to realize something big was brewing. Since their arrival in April, there had been practice landings. They lost one soldier who drowned during an exercise. Their skipper informed them that they would be taking on infantry on June 4 and nothing else.

> Around June 1, we knew something was going to happen soon, because truck convoys and soldiers were moving all about, heading mostly for southeastern coastal towns and the ports. We were restricted to our ships and the local pubs.
>
> On June 4, we loaded 4th Infantry Division troops. Late that night, we started out for France, but a storm came up and the convoy couldn't see each other in the dark, and our ship finally made it into Plymouth and took shelter. We sat out the storm, and finally, late at night on June 5, we headed for France.

Ens. Walt Treanor, a New Yorker assigned to *LST 58*, was on his ship at Plymouth when it loaded for D-Day.

> I believe it was as early as June 2. We sealed the ship and had no more communications with the shore, except I am sure the captain did. We left Plymouth on June 4, anticipating that we would be engaged in the landing the next day, although it is possible we left on June 3.
>
> One of my worst memories was when we were headed out past the submarine gates, and the gate tenders knew we were headed out toward Europe and wished us good luck. One of our crewmembers said, and I am embarrassed even to recall this, "We will save your Goddamn chicken shit island for you!" This was totally uncalled for. He was very young and did not understand that the British had been fighting for all of us for a very long time.
>
> The weather was very, very bad, and very soon we were called back and moved into an inlet somewhere on the coast of Devon. I believe it was close to the port of Dartmouth. I had to go aboard the Rhino and make sure the cable was secured. That was quite a dreadful trip in an LCVP, as I and three members of the deck divisions went out there to check and make sure the Rhino was well secured to the cable.
>
> The most vivid memory I have of the efficiency of the U.S. military forces of this period is that while we were sitting in this little inlet, waiting for the weather to abate and the decision to be made as to whether we continue on, mail was brought to our ship. This was mail not only for the ship's company, but also for the 4th Infantry Division people that we were carrying across the channel. It was absolutely a miracle, and to this day I cannot believe the great job done, nor will I ever forget the tremendous moral booster that was.

Lt(jg). Eugene E. Eckstam from Madison, Wisconsin, was a survivor of *LST 507*, sunk during Exercise Tiger in April. After that ordeal, the doctor was reassigned to *LST 391*.

> I rejoined it in Falmouth Harbor. We loaded on army troops from the hillside. I was completely overwhelmed by the number of ships in the harbor and the constant flow of

trucks and equipment down the small hillside road loading into the enormous caverns of the LSTs that were present. We had part of the 5th Ranger HQ Battalion on our ship, and all the army officers were full colonels or lieutenant colonels. They were supposed to arrive at the initial beachhead one day after the assault, and therefore we crossed the Channel after the bulk of the ships had gone.

Ens. Donald E. Irwin, a twenty-two-year-old deck officer from Mount Vernon, Iowa, served on *LCT 614* of Flotilla 12. Shortly before the invasion, his ship took on sixty-five men from the 3rd Battalion of the 116th Infantry, with bulldozers, jeeps, and trailers, plus the 149th Engineer Battalion.

The 1st Infantry Division Embarks: The Omaha Assault Force

The veteran 1st Division was reinforced to a strength of 34,142 men and concentrated in the area between Portland and Poole, England. This massive force included the 16th and 18th Regiments of the "Big Red One," as well as the 115th and 116th Regiments of the 29th Division, and Lieutenant Colonel Rudder's Provisional Ranger Force. These units formed the bulk of Force O. Farther to the west, on the other side of the 4th Division's marshaling area, between Plymouth and Falmouth, Follow-Up Force B assembled another 25,117 men and took aboard the 29th Division's 175th Infantry and the 1st Division's 26th Infantry. The 1st began moving into its staging areas as early as May 7 and completed the movement on May 11.

Force O carried some 34,000 men and 3,300 vehicles on 7 transports, 8 LSIs, 24 LSTs, 33 LCIs, 36 LCMs, 147 LCTs, and other smaller vessels. By the afternoon of June 5, the nine convoys of Force O were steaming across the Channel, while a constant stream of aircraft maintained air cover, according to the U.S. Army's *Omaha Beachhead*.

Pvt. Roger L. Brugger, a nineteen-year-old draftee from Ohio, served as a rifleman in the 3rd Platoon, Company K of the 16th Infantry. Appointed assistant bazooka man for the invasion, he carried three rockets.

Sometime before the last two maneuvers, the company changed form. It went from a headquarters section, three rifle platoons, a weapons platoon with 60-millimeter mortars, and light machine guns to five boat groups. In each boat group, there were thirty men. The makeup was as follows: lieutenant, platoon sergeant, machine gunner with ammunition carrier, 60-millimeter mortar team, a flamethrower carried by Sergeant Robey, a bazooka man, and an ammo carrier. The rest of the personnel would be riflemen. [We had] bangalore torpedoes for blowing barbed wire, pole charge—TNT on a pole—satchel charges. These were to be used on pillboxes. The boats were known as LCVPs. They were to carry one jeep or thirty men. During this training, the squad I was in increased from eight men to ten and the platoon from twenty-eight to thirty-four.

We were to wear special jackets called assault jackets, rather than the full field pack, and cartridge belt. The assault jackets had a lot of pockets and pouches in them. They contained rations for three days and a lot of ammunition. We wore a lifebelt under the jacket, which was held together in the front with ties. If you were left off in deep water, you were supposed to untie the jacket, slip out of it, and inflate the lifebelt. We were also issued impregnated clothing, in case the

Germans used gas, and a new type of gas mask that was all one piece with the canister on the left side of the mask.

In early May, we were sent to a marshaling area outside of Weymouth. This area had three strands of concertina wire around the perimeter and was constantly patrolled by British Tommies with Sten guns. At the end of May [June 2?], we were marched to the docks at Weymouth to board the British ship HMS *Empire Anvil* with the rest of the 3rd Battalion.

The ship was unique in that the landing craft were slung in the deck in davits, which meant that the troops didn't have to climb down cargo nets to get into the landing craft. While we were on the ship in the harbor, there was an air raid. It was at night on June 3. The next night, on the fourth, our ship pulled out of the harbor to see if there was any damage. There wasn't any and we returned to port. On the night of June 5, around 10 P.M., our ship pulled out of the harbor to join the other ships for the invasion. We had a late meal on the ship from midnight to about two in the morning. Since this was a British ship, we were again served corned beef.

After we had eaten, a buddy and I went up on deck for some fresh air. Our assault jacket, steel helmet, rifles, and other gear were on our bunks. When we came back to our bunks, I found someone had stolen my steel helmet. I think what happened was someone had lost their helmet while looking over the side of the ship and took mine. I reported my loss to the platoon sergeant, who jovially remarked that I wouldn't be able to make the invasion. He told me not to worry about it.

Pvt. Warren L. Rulien, a twenty-four-year-old veteran of Sicily from a small town in Wisconsin serving in the 16th Infantry's I&R Platoon, considered his briefing too brief.

The day before we loaded on the ships, I was told to get in a long line of soldiers, which passed through one of these tents. When I entered the tent, I could see a long table. On it was sculptured, in miniature size, the whole terrain of where we were going to make our invasion on Omaha Beach and that of Normandy. I tried to imprint in my mind the area in which I was to land so that when we hit the beach, I would recognize the terrain. But they moved us along so fast that it was impossible to really study it.

The next day, they loaded us onto the ships. It seemed the ships were so close together that you could jump from one to another. During the day, as they continued loading the ships, they allowed us to stay on deck. Seeing a cover on one of the openings on the deck, I went over and lay down on top of it, kind of enjoying the warmth of the day. Later on that day, the ships moved out into deeper water and they put us belowdecks, where we stayed for quite some time. Finally we were brought up on deck, where we stood around in groups. I don't recall what time it was, but it must have been very early in the morning, for it was totally dark.

S.Sgt. John B. Ellery from Norwich, New York, of Company B, 1st Battalion, 16th Infantry, was in a staging-area camp guarded by British troops. Like the other units, his company was briefed about the impending battle.

Many hours were spent on a model of our invasion area. We memorized terrain features and landmarks from the model, photographs, and maps. It was impressive and

> exciting. The briefing officers were bright, articulate, and thoroughly confident. I was convinced that we would take the beach, but that we would leave a lot of casualties in our wake, and I was right about that.
>
> The new men, who had never been in combat, were understandably apprehensive and tended to expect the worst. Most of those who had been through it before, the seasoned troops, took everything in stride, or perhaps they were simply resigned. For my part, I was clean, bright, and lightly oiled—loaded and locked, ready for Overlord.
>
> On June 2, we loaded up and moved out. We boarded the USS *Samuel Chase* at Weymouth. She was a lovely ship. Clean, very comfortable for a troop carrier, good food, and plenty of it. We had four days of very easy living. About 0200 on June 6, one of our company cooks brought a crate of apples to our assembly area, and I added several to my load.
>
> Incidentally, in addition to my personal effects, I carried an M-1 rifle with 176 rounds of ammunition—eighty rounds in my belt and two bandoliers of 48 rounds each. A Colt .45 with 21 rounds, three fragmentation grenades, four smoke grenades, a bayonet, an entrenching tool, six K rations, three D rations, a shelter half, a blanket, a pair of field glasses, a 536 radio, and a gas mask. Actually, the load was quite well distributed because we were wearing the new assault jacket, which was something like a hunting vest. There was a large pocket on the back that took the place of a pack. There was another pocket lower down of quite good size that rode on your butt. There were two large pockets in front, one on each side, also low down, below where your rifle or pistol belt would cross. It also had a grenade pocket with a pull-out tab behind each of these.
>
> My assault section, like most of the others, consisted of thirty-one men: a wire-cutter team of four men, a five-man demolition team, a two-man flame thrower team, a four-man 60-millimeter mortar team, two two-man bazooka teams, two BAR teams of two men each, five additional riflemen, a medic, a section sergeant, and a section leader.

PFC Joseph A. Dragotto, a nineteen-year-old native of Utica, New York, was 60-millimeter mortar man with the Weapons Platoon, Company C, 1st Battalion, 16th Infantry. He arrived on the *Queen Mary* as a replacement at the end of 1943 and was assigned as an ammo carrier for one of the three 60-millimeter mortar squads.

> On the third day, Captain Briggs, our company commander, assembled the entire company, ordered trucks, and drove to a large field. In the field were assembled many thousands of American troops, and over a loudspeaker, I heard the word "Attention!" I, with the other troops, snapped to attention, and in the corner of my eye, I could see two men: one wearing an American uniform, the other a British uniform. As they came closer, I recognized them. The American was General Eisenhower, and the other was Field Marshal Montgomery. Both men stepped onto the platform and spoke to the men. General Eisenhower said we were about to embark on a great cause: "the liberation of Europe and God be with you!" Montgomery said almost the same thing, but added that he was grateful for the help, and the troops and supplies from America. After the speech, both men began to walk among the troops, talking to them. Then General Eisenhower stopped in front of me. I thought to myself, "My God, the supreme commander of all the Allied forces in

Europe is going to talk to me!" The general asked where I was from and how long I was in the service. After talking a few minutes, we saluted, and he went down the line.

We then returned to our area, getting ready for what was ahead. One morning, after breakfast, I saw one of the men of my company putting tobacco between two slices of bread, eat it, and then became very ill. He was taken to the hospital. Another one took a rifle and began firing into the pup tents. I asked why, and I then realized they didn't want to go to war. Time was getting close for us to get ready to board the trucks and to be transported through coastal towns to board troopships. Everybody started to do funny things.

On June 5 [4?], 1944, men of Company C, 1st Battalion, 16th Regiment, 1st Infantry Division, assembled in its staging area. We were informed that the division was moving out to a seaport on the coast to board transports. Our transport was the USS *Samuel Chase*, which was manned by Coast Guard personnel. As we boarded trucks for the trip to the seaport, I could not help but think, along with my buddies in the company, of what was going to happen to us in the next twenty-four hours. On boarding the transport, our company was assigned an area where we could get some rest, although we did not get much. As we got settled, officers and noncoms were studying maps of the area where Company C was going to land. The beach area that we were assigned had the code name Easy Red. As we were getting settled, the ship pulled out of the harbor into the English Channel, and a few of the townspeople came out and waved good-bye.

Pvt. Charles H. Thomas, another nineteen-year-old from Chicago, was also in Company C but was a rifleman. He boarded the *Samuel Chase* after about three weeks in the staging area.

It was a great boat, the food was good—the best I had for sometime. There we studied a large map on the floor of the gym. It showed in detail the beaches we would be landing on; ours was Easy Red.

The day before the invasion, I thought about the weight of my pack. I took the ten pounds of TNT and tied it to the pole charge. I had thirty pounds of TNT on the pole. I put a gas cartridge lifebelt around it so that it would float, which helped save my life later.

Capt. Charles M. Hangsterfer of Philadelphia, the commander of HQ Company, 1st Battalion, 16th Infantry, had been with the 16th since 1940, from its practice landings in the United States to its combat landings in the Mediterranean. His company moved into the staging area in May.

When we were in the marshaling area, detailed information was given to us and the field order for the operation. We knew it wasn't a practice, because we were sealed in with orders not to leave the area for any reason. Guards were stationed to insure compliance.

Only general information about the types of fortification that were in place on the Normandy coast was given to our unit before the invasion. Since we were trained in night attack for North Africa and Sicily, at first we were apprehensive about making a daylight invasion. Later we were informed of the big picture with all the support from the air force, navy, special self-propelled amphibious tanks, engineer demolition teams that were to remove obstacles from the beach.

Pictures of the area were shown to us of the fortifications and beach obstacles. A sand

Troops of the 5th Rangers boarding a British LCA at Weymouth on June 4, 1944. On the morning of June 6, they boarded the same landing craft, which was carried on the HMS *Leopold*. COURTESY OF JAY H. MAHAFFEY

table was also provided, with all of the above shown as well as the objectives. There was an approximation of the enemy strength given.

We had about a five-mile drive from the marshaling area to Weymouth, where we boarded the *Samuel Chase*, an attack transport equipped with the latest type of LCVPs and deck-side loading. (This meant we would not have to climb down rope ladders strung along the side of the ship down to the landing craft.)

The loading procedure was no different than loading to go on a cruise, except the troops were combat loaded with the usual combat equipment. Each man was checked off as he proceeded up the gangplank. All of my company boarded the *Samuel Chase* except the Anti-Tank Platoon. The Anti-Tank Platoon was supposed to debark from LSTs and proceed to shore in DUKWs, which transported the men and guns. However, the rough seas sunk the DUKWs, but none of the men was lost.

Our battalion was beefed up with a variety of support groups: naval gunfire observers, air force liaison, Military Intelligence Team, and others. The interpreters of the Military Intelligence Team were to glean firsthand information that might be useful and could be acted upon. They would receive the prisoners before we sent them to the division POW stockade.

When we were aboard the transport ship, we were given the time and date of the invasion. Initially it was June 5, but the weather

HQ Company, 1st Battalion, 16th Infantry

The platoons that made up the HQ Company included the following:

- The Communication Platoon, whose duties included laying wire to the rifle companies, maintaining the battalion radio net, and operating a message center for encoding and decoding messages. This platoon also sent out runners to the rifle companies and regimental headquarters.
- The Pioneer and Ammunition Platoon, which had two sections. The Ammunition Section took care of delivering and storing ammunition. The Pioneer Section laid and removed mines, installed barbed wire, and assisted in defending the battalion command post.
- The Anti-Tank Platoon, which contained the only heavy weapons in the company. These were 57-millimeter antitank guns.
- The Headquarters Section, which operated the battalion command post and included the battalion sergeant major, S-2, S-3, and S-4 sergeants; and the company headquarters, with first sergeant, mess personnel, and clerks. For the Normandy invasion, a non–table of organization and equipment (TO&E) military police group was attached to serve as road guides and perform any other special duties that might be necessary. The MP Section consisted of men who were eligible to return to the States or noncombat assignments but volunteered for this mission. The company commander also served as the battalion adjutant

caused a postponement. My duties on the ship consisted of assigning billets for the officers and men. Also, I was to announce over the ship's speaker system for the boat teams to proceed to their LCVPs for loading, as well as the general functions of a battalion adjutant and company commander.

The harbor was loaded with ships and boats of all descriptions. Many of them had barrage balloons to prevent low-flying aircraft from strafing the fleet.

Sgt. Theodore Aufort, a twenty-one-year-old New Yorker who was an enlisted member of the HQ Company of the 1st Battalion, 16th Infantry, remembers a distinguished visitor to the staging area.

General Eisenhower came walking into our area. Everyone started saluting and he insisted that we be at ease. We formed a circle around him. I happened to be about eight to ten feet directly in front of him. He laid the whole bill of fare on us. We were going to land by sea on the coast of France at a place called Normandy. I know my heart was pounding like crazy. I wanted to know a million details. I guess everyone there did also. He was way ahead of us and explained that all officers and NCOs would be briefed and would relay all information to our men. He then saluted us and said, "Good luck," turned, and left. No doubt he had many areas such as ours to call upon.

Shortly after, all NCOs were called into a large tent for instructions and briefings. There we were told what our objectives were and what to expect in Normandy. We were also told that a lot of men would die. We went over minute details, everything, nothing was left out—what type of landing craft, what to expect in the way of obstacles on the beaches, the water temperature,

> everything was told to us. In the water were I-beams approximately eight feet high, welded together to look like child's pickup jacks, only king size. These were laid out in rows, approximately four rows deep, and were laced with antipersonnel mines. I studied the beaches very closely. After these rows of jacks [hedgehogs], a wide, thick layer of cobblestones [possibly referring to the shingle] was placed along the beach, and after that the natural soft sand.
>
> On June 4, we boarded the *Samuel Chase*. Ships were everywhere. It was unbelievable seeing so many of all descriptions. I briefed the men in my wire team. Each was given certain pieces of equipment to take ashore. I placed three men on the LCVP that was to go in next to me. I did this to make sure one of the two landing craft made it in. My driver was on a larger landing craft with the jeep. They were due to go in later.
>
> Finally the anchors were raised and we, along with all the other ships, were under way. Hardly a word was spoken. We stood there motionless, at least most of us did. The navy personnel were excellent. They treated us like kings. At the evening meal, we were given three types of meat: steak, pork chops, or chicken, which we hadn't had in years. We drank cokes, ate ice cream and candy. This was normally charged for, since it was navy property, but they gave it to us free. They were told to open up the counters—the soda counter and the ice cream bar—and give us anything we wanted. I momentarily thought to myself, a last request just like in prison.
>
> None of us could sleep that night. Those that could were just plain tired. We were exhausted and tired. We didn't know what to expect. Most of us stood on deck just looking out. During the evening, we could hear the aircraft going overhead.

PFC Frank C. Bettle of Lynbrook, New York, was with the 16th Infantry's Cannon Company, which included six 105-millimeter short-barreled howitzers. He had served in the army for almost four years, but this was his first invasion. Bettle did not feel well enough trained for the mission. Like so many others, he boarded his ship at Portland Harbor and departed on June 5.

> We were given, as I remember, two ordinary paper bags. They call them sacks out here, and that was to be used to throw up in. Then we went around and around and around in the Channel. Then it was in the bloody middle of the night and a terribly rough sea. Very rough, terribly rough, and we guys were sick, throwing up terribly—almost everyone; I was one of the few that didn't. I never get seasick. I'm a good sailor in spite of the fact I can't swim. It seems to me that almost everybody but me was sick, and it was because of the pitching.

Pvt. Eldon Wiehe from Missouri had trained with an artillery unit and had been in North Africa as truck driver. Later, in Sicily, he had been assigned to the 1st Division as an infantry replacement. In May 1944, his unit received all new vehicles, which the men proceeded to waterproof in the staging areas.

> About May 26 or 27, I was sent to a hospital in Portsmouth, England, with an attack of malaria. I stayed until the morning of June 4, 1944. That morning, the doctor made his rounds, taking temperature and blood pressure. Everyone that was well and able was told to get his clothes. We were being discharged from the hospital. He did not tell us where we were going. We were taken to a small landing craft. I was the only one to get off on this craft, and when I got aboard, there were thirteen men and seven vehicles.

> The man in charge was a first lieutenant, the rest enlisted men, one sergeant, one corporal, and the rest privates. I missed the briefing, so the lieutenant briefed me on what was happening. We were going to invade Normandy on June 5, the next morning. We sailed out the night of the fourth. Somewhere we turned back and stayed one more day. On the night of June 5, once again we set out to sea. There weren't too many ships around at that time, a lot, but not a great number. We started toward Normandy, and somewhere during the night, we must have met one heck of a fleet of ships somewhere.

PFC Albert Littke, a twenty-year-old draftee from Niagara Falls, New York, was a demolitions man with 3rd Platoon of Company A, 299th Combat Engineers. His battalion was the only engineer battalion to send companies to both Utah and Omaha Beaches. His company and Company C were destined for Omaha Beach. With the help of the naval demolition teams, they were to clear fifty-yard gaps through the beach.

> Around the latter part of May 1944, we had moved into Camp D-6 near Dorchester. Security was tight, and we were confined to the area. We wrote letters and had the best of food—plenty of it—as well as movies. Inspections.
>
> One day we were putting C-2 tetra in old clean army socks. It was a putty substance and we placed about one pound in each sock and carried ten pounds on back and front (twenty pounds overall) over our shoulders like a satchel pack.
>
> We were given the latest information on where we were supposed to land. You could see the steel hedgehogs on the photographs. The pilot must have flown real low, because you could see the German soldiers looking up with startled faces at the plane and working with their teams of horses. You could also see the obstacles with mines attached to these steel tripods. In addition, they had a ramp and steel jagged edges at the top to rip open the bottom of the boats.
>
> From here, on June 4, we were trucked down to the port of embarkation at Weymouth. It was a little chilly and foggy, and it was a slow process going down a slight incline towards the beach. We passed loaded amphibious vehicles and other equipment. There were approximately sixteen waterproofed Sherman tanks, and on the side of the tanks were girls' names. I remember a couple of them: One was Diana and the other Beverly.
>
> Once at the beach, our demolitions and mine detectors were placed aboard the LCM, and we proceeded to load an LCT, which already had four Sherman tanks in the center of the craft in two rows of two. We proceeded to move out into the harbor. We borrowed the ship's glasses and spotted boys making love to the girls on the hillside.
>
> In the early evening of June 4, we started out across the Channel. We went to sleep beside the tanks and woke up the next morning back in the harbor. Since our LCT was one of the first to start the journey, we were one of the last to be told to turn around—pretty close to a point of no return as I was told.
>
> On June 5th, we had hot meals aboard ship and passed the day playing cards (poker), reading books, cleaning weapons, and the usual gossip. We then proceeded across the Channel once again.
>
> At approximately one o'clock in the morning, we were awakened, and we were fed scrambled eggs and coffee, and at about two in the morning, we went over the side of the LCT into the LCM [?], which had our demolition and my detector.

First Sgt. Raus J. Blondo from Detriot was in Company B of the 112th Combat Engineer Battalion, which formed the 1121st Engineer Group together with the 254th and 146th Engineers. "From the D [staging] area, we boarded the LST on June 4 and set sail that evening, only to be put on hold at sea. Then the night of the fifth, we set sail again for Normandy. Arrived there pulling a huge raft with two large outboard motors (Rhinos) and two men aboard having a hell of a rough ride; poor devils."

Intelligence

The British began the process of gathering data on the enemy occupation army and possible invasion areas in 1942. The Inter-Service Topographical Department compiled data from old guidebooks and university professors at the instigation of Lord Louis Mountbatten. According to Warren, Tute et al. in their book *D-Day*, photos were also collected from civilians who had visited the continent before the war. In addition, the RAF flew numerous missions across northwest Europe, photographing virtually everything. Later, reconnaissance aircraft from the USAAF joined the British on these missions. Between the two organizations, a detailed set of maps was produced; however, these maps on their own could not help identify the beaches best suited to an invasion force and the landing of heavy vehicles.

After the Mediterranean campaign, the British decided to create their own special force that could fill the gap in information. These intelligence-gathering units, known as Combined Operations Pilotage Parties (COPPs), consisted of a few men usually traveling in a midget submarine called an X craft.[4] Some of these agents used small surface craft instead. These small commando units patrolled the designated coastal area at periscope depth during the day, making the necessary observations. Typically, at night, a couple of the men swam ashore to take beach samples and examine the type of obstacles the Germans had deployed.

At the end of 1943, the British launched several small diversionary commando missions at sites outside of Normandy to draw the Germans' attention away from the COPPs in the event they should be detected. At the end of January, the 21st Army Group ordered the commandos to cease their operations, as their task was complete. Nevertheless, COPP missions continued. According to Kenneth Macksey in *Commando*, the last three reconnaissance missions, code-named Tarbush, which took place in mid-May, consisted of raids at Les Hemmes, Bray Dunes, Onvial, and Quend Plage whose object was to divert attention to the German Fifteenth Army's front.

The COPPs' work gave the British and American commanders the detailed information they needed about their prospective target beaches. With this information, they could not only make plans to deal with obstacles, but also calculate landing and supply needs. The British used photographs of the coast from sea level taken from low-flying aircraft along with high-level oblique and vertical aerial photographs to prepare models of the invasion areas.[5] In addition, photo strips gave the troops a preview of the landscape they would see from their landing craft.

Although reconnaissance aircraft and their cameras were able to detect large formations, the photographs they took did not allow the photo interpreters to determine the size and composition of such units with any degree of accuracy, unless the enemy was very sloppy. This was a mission for agents on the ground. Members of the

4. These teams were involved in every major landing of 1943 and thereafter. The COPPs and their activities remained secret until their existence in World War II was discovered in 1957.

5. High-level oblique and vertical aerial photographs were mainly used for intelligence and mapmaking.

French Resistance proved invaluable in this field. The Century organization had already provided detailed information on the Atlantic Wall, but as the Germans became more security conscious, it became increasingly difficult to identify enemy formations with precision. Although the Germans restricted access to coastal areas and began removing unit insignias, Allied intelligence was able to maintain a relatively accurate picture of the situation. But after the restricted zone was extended to thirty miles behind the coastline from Normandy to the North Sea, the Allies had to find other methods of gaining intelligence.

As Ralph Bennett details in *Ultra in the West*, this gap was filled by the British operation Ultra, which had captured a German Enigma machine and a few codes, enabling it to read most enemy transmissions. Thanks to this invaluable find, Ultra was able to get accurate, up-to-date information. Each major Allied headquarters had a liaison unit that gave the commander the secret Ultra information. The Allies had to use the information thus obtained very judiciously, however, in order to prevent the Germans from knowing that their coded messages were being intercepted. The Allies managed to keep the secret so well that it did not come to light until long after the war. The major drawbacks were that many Ultra intercepts took days to process, and not all German units used their Enigma machines.

Because of Ultra, more than half of the German divisions defending the coast of France, from southern France to the Channel coast, were identified. Virtually all the panzer divisions were known. In some cases, details on their training status, TO&E, and assignments were also revealed. The major weaknesses of the *Luftwaffe* in the west also came to light. Thanks to Ultra, the Allies realized by late May that their air operations were succeeding in cutting the transportation lines in northern France.

Deception and Intelligence

The greatest success of the Allies' Bodyguard scheme can be attributed to Gen. George Patton. Between January and July, his presence as commander of the decoy formation FUSAG in southeast England convinced the German High Command and Hitler that the Allies planned to launch an invasion on the Pas de Calais. The battalion-size British Fourth Army, aimed at Norway in Fortitude North, and the phantom Fourteenth Army became reinforcements for FUSAG in May. Ultra confirmed before and after the invasion that the Germans continued to believe that this army group led by Patton would soon attack the German Fifteenth Army's coastal positions.

The activities of the French Resistance in France caused some concern for the Allies, who hoped to use them to isolate the battlefield. Some of the resistance units reacted too soon, however. In the spring, the Germans destroyed an armed battalion-size unit of partisans that tried to defend its fortified base on a plateau in southern France. Another unit of the French Resistance, in the Massif Central, decided to fight it out with the Germans and met with some success. In April and May, special two-man Sussex Teams, each consisting of a French officer with a British or American officer, were sent to France to coordinate the activities of the Resistance.

Ultra was unable to ferret out any significant information on the German 711th and 716th "Static" Divisions defending the coast.[6] These static divisions lacked transport and were

6. The Germans had several categories of divisions based on their capabilities for defense and attack. The "static" (or *bodenständige*) divisions, such as the 711th and 716th, had limited transport and were capable only of limited defense. The 352nd Division, on the other hand, was fully ready for both attack and defense. Units were rated for combat effectiveness from 1 to 5: 1 = capable of offensive operations, 2 = limited offensive operations, 3 = capable of defensive operations, 4 = limited defensive missions, and 5 = unsuitable for combat. Static units were mainly rated as 3 or 4.

intended mainly to defend a fixed position. Other sources identified the 352nd Infantry Division in a reserve position south of the Calvados coast but failed to detect its move to the coast at the Omaha Beach invasion sector. When the German 91st Air Landing Division moved into the peninsula during May, however, Allied intelligence was able to alert the planners in time for them to alter the details of the airborne operation.

In May 1944, the Allied G-2 intelligence reports distributed to the major commands taking part in the invasion revealed precisely what was known about the enemy. Little information was held back, in order to avoid later surprises that might have had disastrous consequences. On May 11, 1944, the U.S. First Army headquarters issued its second G-2 estimate. It identified enemy units and their characteristics, including those from the Eastern Front that were battle-worn. The report also identified panzer and infantry divisions that could be brought into the area to reinforce the enemy position. It anticipated that many of the enemy reinforcements might arrive much later than expected, because the Allied air forces and French Resistance had crippled the railroads.

Based on intelligence reports, the assault troops were warned that some of the beaches were defended by two complete lines of hedgehogs, Element C, concrete tetrahedra, and wooden stakes, some just below the high-water mark and others at the low-water mark. Intelligence Analusts believed that the Germans were trying to install a third line between these other two. Some of the obstacles were mined, and in the vicinity of Les Dunes de Varreville, an unidentified line of objects thought to be mines appeared between double rows of hedgehogs and to the seaward side of single rows. One experienced pilot reported a single line of mines half submerged at low water about 400 to 500 yards offshore in the St. Pierre du Mont–Vierville sectors. In the British sectors, stakes had begun to appear in sites suitable for airborne landings. Additionally, the Germans had started digging postholes, presumably to erect posts that might prevent glider landings in the Cotentin Peninsula, and they kept a number of key areas flooded.

The intelligence report also warned that the *Luftwaffe* was husbanding its forces to strike at invasion shipping during the attack and mine embarkation points and ferry routes. More than 70 percent of its fighter force was defending Germany, however. Secret weapons such as the V-1 flying bombs and V-2 rockets posed a concern. The French had reported that the Germans had an amphibious Goliath, a small armored vehicle that was packed with explosives and maneuvered by remote control. These were deployed near the beaches, possibly leading the French to believe they were amphibious. There was also a chance that the enemy might use flammable liquids in inundated areas and on the sea, as the British had planned to do when the Germans threatened to invade England in 1940. Even chemical warfare was considered highly probable. The Allies also thought that the enemy might drop parachutists in Great Britain to disrupt supply and communication lines.

The field order for the 4th Division issued on May 15 included intelligence estimates based mainly on the G-2 reports. In the political section, it speculated that "the survival of the Nazi regime dictates the prevention of invasion of Germany, which, in turn, means determined resistance to our landings in France. Politically, the German hope for victory has dwindled into desire for stalemate."

The same order also reported that "inundations behind the Utah beaches continue to be maintained at an average depth of 3 to 4 feet with possible drop-offs up to 7 feet at ditches or streams." Many veterans claim, however, that they were never made aware of this fact.

CHAPTER 7

Final Preparations

View from the Top

During the spring of 1944, SHAEF headquarters worked out the final plans for Operation Overlord. All the commanders of Eisenhower's air, land, and naval forces were British. His naval commander in chief was Adm. Sir Bertram H. Ramsay, a reasonable choice, as a large part of the naval forces was British. The air commander in chief was Air Chief Marshal Sir Trafford L. Leigh-Mallory, whose assignment might be questioned, since the American Eighth and Ninth Air Forces became the dominant part of Allied air power in 1944. Eisenhower designated Gen. Bernard Montgomery as the ground commander for the initial phase of the invasion, initially placing both American and British forces under his 21st Army Group, which consisted of the U.S. First Army and British Second Army.

During the planning stages of Overlord, the number of landing beaches expanded. The Americans were finally assigned two beaches for a three-division landing force. The British, on the other hand, had three beaches for a similar three-division invasion force. The Americans used three independent tank battalions whose vehicles included special Sherman DD swimming tanks, while the British employed a wider variety of specialized tanks from their 79th Armoured Division. Although the British offered their allies some of their specialized armored vehicles, the Americans turned them down. According to the overall plan, the Americans were to isolate the Cotentin

Peninsula quickly, but the British initially had the greater, and possibly more decisive, task of securing the eastern flank and taking the city of Caen. From the three British beaches to Omaha Beach, however, the Allies failed to achieve many of the post-D-Day objectives.

If events had unfolded as planned, the larger British force, which landed on the Allied left, where there were relatively open beaches with easily accessible terrain behind them, would have been able to advance from the beachhead and lead the breakout, driving across the North European Plain toward Germany. On the other hand, the American forces of the U.S. First Army would have begun their operations from two widely separated beachheads with bluffs backing one and flooded areas behind the other, that could have seriously impeded an advance from the beaches to the few road exits. The famous hedgerows of Normandy proved to be an additional barrier. Logically, however, the Germans would have been forced to concentrate against the greatest threat—the British beachhead—and that they did. The only major seaport within reach that could sustain a continuing buildup was Cherbourg. The mission of the U.S. First Army was to take that port with the troops from the VII Corps that landed at Utah Beach. Montgomery's actions in Normandy demonstrated that he was aware that the primary mission of his Second Army was to tie down the bulk of the German mobile forces in order to allow the Americans to expand their beachhead and take Cherbourg.

By the end of May, all the operational orders had been issued, and the various formations began disseminating the information and making final preparations for the invasion. The most important change or revision concerned the 82nd A/B Division's Field Order No. 6. After intelligence sources identified the German 91st Air Landing Division in the Cotentin Peninsula, it became necessary to change the 82nd's drop zones. SHAEF headquarters no longer considered it prudent to land it around St.-Sauveur-le-Vicomte in order to seal off the Cotentin Peninsula. Chances that the division might be trapped west of the Merderet River and destroyed before the infantry from Utah Beach could relieve it were too great, now that this new German division occupied most of its drop zones. Thus the planners shifted the division's drop zones north of those of the 101st Airborne Division around Ste-Mère-Église.

Eisenhower's Decisions

On May 8, Eisenhower set D-Day for June 5 after his staff determined that only three days in the early part of the month would have the right combination of tides and moon for the landings and airdrop: June 5, 6, and 7. If the invasion did not take place on those dates, it would have to wait until around June 19 before similar conditions would exist again. Meteorologists did not have the means of predicting well in advance that this would be the week of one of the worst storms to hit the area in many years. In the days preceding the invasion, Eisenhower and Montgomery continued to visit as many Allied units as possible.

While the final preparations for the invasion were under way, work on the deception operations intensified. Gen. George Patton had arrived early in 1944 to take part in Operation Fortitude by taking command of the phony FUSAG. His presence with this simulated command in southeast England helped convince the Germans that the Calais area would be the main target. It did not take long before he fell into disfavor with Eisenhower, however, when he claimed in a public speech that America and Great Britain would become the dominant powers of the world, offending the other Allies. On April 30, according to Chandler and Collins's *D-Day Encyclopedia*, Eisenhower cabled General Marshall that he would "relieve him [Patton] from command and send him home unless some new and unforeseen

General Eisenhower inspects paratroopers shortly before the invasion. Notice the censor has obliterated the division markings on their helmets.

information should be developed in the case." He added that he was confident that Gen. Courtney Hodges would make an able replacement for Patton. Nevertheless, he conceded, Patton had "proved his ability to conduct a ruthless drive whereas Hodges has not." Eisenhower soon reconsidered his decision in a dispatch addressed to Marshall on May 3. Thus Patton retained his post, which also included command of the Third Army, whose mission was to land in Normandy after the invasion had progressed. A factor that possibly weighed in Patton's favor was that Eisenhower did not want to lose a commander who had proven his worth as an offensive leader.

Eisenhower had other problems on his mind as well, among them the enemy coastal batteries. In late April, he informed Gen. H. H. "Hap" Arnold that some of these batteries would be targets for the paratroopers. This problem must have weighed heavily on Eisenhower's mind during the next month. He had already made arrangements to keep the British 16-inch gun battleship *Nelson* in the operation, even though it had been scheduled to sail to the United States for maintenance. If the air and naval forces failed to neutralize key German coastal batteries, the Allied paratroopers would have to try to silence them. Up to this point, American airborne operations had not been extremely successful, and Overlord was a night drop, which presented additional problems.

In a cable on May 6, Eisenhower also revealed to Marshall that he was worried about methods for removing underwater obstacles, the production of components for the artificial harbors, the accuracy of weather forecasts, and the coordination of the assault. The extent of the Germans' efforts to defend the coast disturbed him, but he believed that this indicated they had no confidence in their mobile forces. He probably held the same conviction as his enemy, Field Marshal Erwin Rommel, who had told his superiors that the first twenty-four hours would be the most decisive. According to *D-Day Encyclopedia*, aware of the continuing German construction effort, Eisenhower fretted, "I do wish that our assault could get off tomorrow, and on even a broader front."

At the end of May, General Eisenhower sent a cable, reprinted in *D-Day Encyclopedia*, to the Combined Chiefs of Staff, stating:

> As the date of assault approaches it is apparent that two factors operate powerfully to mislead the enemy and hence to further the success of our plans. The Germans overestimate the strength of our seaborne assault and therefore will hold out forces to deal with landings additional to those planned by us. The enemy is also in ignorance of the dependence we place on MULBERRIES and therefore tends to garrison lightly terrain which is critical to us.

His confidence must have been bolstered by the Ultra communications. With only six more days until D-Day, even if the Germans became aware of the purpose of the Mulberries (artificial harbors) or discovered that the FUSAG consisted of phantom divisions, it would be too late for them to redeploy their forces unless they knew the actual invasion site. Only the weather, Eisenhower's other great concern, could ruin the operation.

Capt. Harry Butcher, Eisenhower's aide, wrote in his diary that Air Chief Marshal Leigh-Mallory had warned Eisenhower at the end of May that the American airborne divisions and the Troop Carrier Command would take extremely heavy losses "in full moonlight and over country where ack-ack normally is heavy and in which German troops are now known to be concentrated," referring to the addition of the 91st Air Landing Division. According to Eisenhower's *Crusade in Europe*, the air marshal predicted up to 50 percent casualties among paratroopers before landing and 70 percent among the glider forces, which would result in the "'futile slaughter' of two fine divisions."

For weeks, Eisenhower had watched the weather forecasts. Until June 3, the weather seemed to favor the Allied forces. But as the invasion forces heaved anchors, it began to deteriorate. Group Capt. John Stagg, who led the meteorological team, predicted a ferocious storm for June 5. The previous morning, Eisenhower took this information to a meeting with his air, land, and sea commanders. He finally decided to delay the operation as the paratroopers were already preparing to load for their night mission. Montgomery advocated keeping on track, but Leigh-Mallory's earlier forebodings must have weighed heavily on Eisenhower's mind that morning. The invasion was postponed for twenty-four hours. Later, on the evening of June 4, Group Captain Stagg had some good news: He expected a break in the weather. Eisenhower and his commanders became more positive, and they decided that the landings would take place on June 6. Early the next morning, June 5, at his headquarters near Portsmouth, Eisenhower met again with his commanders as they received another optimistic weather report from Captain Stagg. He gave the order to go ahead. Later that day, he wrote the following message to be sent in the event of failure: "Our landings in the Cherbourg-Havre area have failed to gain a satisfactory foothold and I have withdrawn the troops. My decision to attack at this time and place was based upon the best information available. The troops, the air and the Navy did all that Bravery and devotion to duty could do. If any blame or fault attaches to the attempt it is mine alone."

After the war, Eisenhower wrote in his book *Crusade in Europe* that he had canceled the operation because the weather would have denied air support and limited the accuracy of the naval bombardment. He also mentioned that he had had confidence in Leigh-Mallory and believed in his sincerity and devotion to duty when the air chief marshal had predicted a disaster for the American airborne troops. On the other hand, without the airdrop, as Eisenhower writes in *Crusade in Europe*, he would have had to cancel the Utah Beach landings, and that would have adversely affected the invasion. One can only wonder what he would have decided to do had he known that the German 352nd Division had moved up to Omaha Beach.

The Final Plans: Omaha Beach

The 1st Infantry Division, with its 16th Infantry Regiment and the attached 116th Infantry Regiment of the 29th Division, and 2nd and 5th Ranger Battalions of the Provisional Rangers were ordered to attack 7,000 yards of various sectors of the beach designated as Omaha. The 1st Division's 18th and 26th Infantry Regiments and the 29th Division's 115th Infantry Regiment were to move through the beachhead on D-Day or soon thereafter. Thus the five infantry regiments and other more specialized units constituted an invasion force equivalent to two divisions. Each American division had been reinforced with the addition of some 2,500 troops, and their regiments were turned into regimental combat teams. The regimental combat teams (RCT) comprised armor, engineers, and other noninfantry elements to form a combined-arms unit. The assault forces were to come ashore shortly after dawn, allowing enough time for a naval and air bombardment to clear the way.

The first waves consisted of assault boat teams followed by support boat teams, all traveling in LCVPs or LCAs and consisting of thirty-man units (some claim up to thirty-two men), which were supposed to reassemble into their normal company-platoon formations after the invasion. The assault troops were to land at low tide, just before it began to rise. This would allow them to avoid the German obstacles between the high- and low-tide marks and permit the engineers to clear gaps for the following waves before the tide rose. Minutes after the first assault boat teams of the regimental combat team reached the beaches, the Special Engineer Task Force (SETF), consisting of elements of the 144th and 299th Engineer Battalions and Naval Combat Demolition Units (NCDUs), was to come ashore and begin clearing obstacles. At Omaha Beach, the SETF included sixteen LCMs carrying Gap Assault Teams. These teams each consisted of a thirteen- or fourteen-man NCDU, five of whom were army engineers and the remainder, naval personnel. The SETF had with it two rubber rafts laden with explosives and a twenty-seven-man army engineer unit with two Sherman "tankdozers" crewed by members from the two assaulting tank battalions.

The Sherman DD tanks of the 741st and 743rd Tank Battalions were supposed to come ashore first, a few minutes before H-Hour. They would be followed by LCTs of the two tank battalions that landed on other sectors at H-Hour. At H+01, the LCVPs and some LCAs were to land the first assault boat teams of the infantry regiments. As the infantry stormed ashore, it was to be followed a couple minutes later by the Gap Assault Teams (the NCDU in their LCMs), and behind them the LCTs with the tankdozers. These units were to begin clearing the beaches of obstacles and mines. At H+30, the LCVPs with the support assault boat teams were to land, followed by subsequent waves. The landings at Utah Beach were to follow a similar pattern, but the assault boat teams of the 8th Infantry Regiment were to land first, followed by the 70th Tank Battalion and the Gap Assault Teams.

The beach designated as Omaha consisted of a five-mile stretch backed by bluffs that turned into steep cliffs at both ends of the area. At low tide, about 300 yards of sand beach and German obstacles were exposed. At the high-water mark, the sand was covered by the waves, and a shingle or rock-strewn beach up to 15 yards wide sloped steeply into the sea. Pools and runnels paralleling the shore and varying from 2 to 4 feet in depth posed a serious problem at high tide. A line of dunes skirted the eastern two-thirds of the beach, preventing the movement of vehicles. The shingle of the western portion of the beach was bounded by a stone and wood seawall ranging from 4 to 12 feet in height. In back of this wall, a coastal road ran from Exit D-1 to D-3, and a crude track extended to Exit E-3. Behind the line of dunes and the seawall was a level crescent of sand up to 200 yards wide in the middle. Near Vierville, the area beyond the seawall and sand consisted of marsh and high grass. The steep-sloped bluffs behind the beach ranged from 100 to 170 feet above the invasion area. The four exits from the beach area consisted of draws running through the bluffs. All the roads running along these draws were unpaved except for Exit D-1. A fifth draw, Exit F-1, was located at the east end of the beach, but only a rough trail ran through it. Behind the bluffs, the only major obstacles were the hedgerows that bounded the fields, which had not been considered a serious impedance. Vierville, St. Laurent, and Colleville were within 1,000 yards of the beach, and their stone buildings partially blocked three of the important exits.

The Assault and Support Boat Teams

For the landings in Normandy, the army regiments of the assaulting divisions were reorganized into regimental combat teams so that they would include armor, engineers, medical, and other special troops necessary for a combined-arms operation. The standard infantry company consisted of three rifle platoons and a weapons platoon. Except for the weapons platoon, each platoon numbered forty-one men. The rifle platoon consisted of a four-man headquarters and three twelve-man squads consisting of eight riflemen, a two-man BAR team, the squad leader, and the assistant squad leader. The rifle platoon was not adequate for landing in the initial assault, because the LCVPs could carry only thirty men. In addition, special weapons would be needed in the initial landing. To deal with this situation, the Amphibious Training Center in England developed the assault boat teams.

An assault boat team consisted of a leader and several teams. An officer, as the team leader, was placed at the front of the craft with a rifle team of five men with M-1 rifles and a bangalore torpedo. Behind them sat a four-man wire cutting team, also armed with M-1s, carrying two bangalore torpedoes and wire cutters. Behind them was a four-man BAR team with two BARs. They were followed by a four-man 60-millimeter mortar team with about forty rounds for the mortar. Farther to the rear was a four-man bazooka team with two bazookas and twenty rockets. Adjacent to them was a two-man flamethrower team. In the rear was the assistant team leader, a sergeant, with a five-man demolition team carrying blocks of TNT and pack and pole charges.

Only two boat teams of the 116th Infantry were equipped with flamethrowers and bazookas, but the other two regimental combat teams in the assaults on Omaha and Utah Beaches were fully equipped. On Omaha Beach, much of the heavy equipment was dropped in the water, especially the flamethrowers, only one of which made it ashore.

The support boat teams in the second wave were essentially similar to the first-wave assault boat teams, but they had a six-man heavy machine-gun team instead of the BAR and flamethrower teams and an eight-man 81-millimeter mortar team instead of the four-man 60-millimeter mortar and bazooka teams, according to Jonathan Gawne in *Spearheading D-Day*.

A command boat carried elements of the company's headquarters. The battalions were also reorganized into battalion landing teams.

The only major obstacle beyond the beachhead lay about five miles to the south—the flooded Aure Valley, which stretched from Isigny to Trevières, the largest town in the vicinity of Omaha Beach. Although the inundated valley could be a hindrance for the advancing Allied forces, it would force the Germans to channel most of their arriving reinforcements into the area between Trevières and Port-en-Bessin, which might be blocked if the British advance succeeded. This would afford the assaulting force at Omaha Beach a chance to regroup. The invasion planners identified just two other significant obstacles inland: the Forest of Cerisy, about ten miles south of the beach, and the Vire River.

According to *Corps of Engineers* by Beck et al., the Germans had built thirty-two fortifications between the Vire River and Port-en-Bessin and had strongly defended that town as well as the Vire Estuary and Grandcamp. Twenty-one *Widerstandsnest*, or resistance nests, occupied by a squad- to platoon-size force with one or more machine guns, sat on the bluffs dominating Omaha Beach. In most cases, the resistance nests were not well fortified in this sector, but on the bluffs, they included a system of trenches from which the German defenders could set off explosives and fougasses, TNT charges that threw out rock fragments. The four exits from Omaha Beach were protected by *Stützpunkte*, or strongpoints, a total of twelve of which faced the invasion beach.[1] Most of the positions were sited for enfilading fire. In addition, some of the stone buildings along the beach were commandeered by the Germans for defensive purposes and most of the cottages had been removed. Finally, the Germans had dug antitank ditches ten feet deep and thirty feet wide across the entrances to draws and clustered some of the fortifications around them.

On the beaches were several types of obstacles. About 250 meters below the high water mark, the Germans had placed Belgian Gates or Element C, which had been used as antitank obstacles by the Belgians and, on a more limited scale, by the French at the beginning of the war. Now the Germans used them as antiboat obstacles, as they believed that the landings would take place at high tide. Many were of these Belgian Gates were fitted with mines. A second line of obstacles included log stakes and ramps with mines attached. About 130 yards from the shore was a third line containing hedgehogs, intended to tear out the bottoms of landing craft. Many of these obstacles derived from or were similar to the tetrahedra used in the prewar Czech defenses. The lines of obstacles on the Normandy beaches were not continuous, and they were deployed in an irregular pattern, although in lines. The Germans installed concertina wire behind the shingle beach, where the shingle ended, and along the seawall on the western end. They also laced the beach area with both live and dummy minefields, as well as booby traps.

Pointe du Hoc, about four miles west of Omaha Beach, fell within the area of operations of the Omaha invasion force for the troops landing there. At the very top of the headlands stood a heavy German artillery battery of six 155-millimeter guns, two of which were in concrete casemates, with the remainder on open concrete stands. These guns were capable of firing on the invasion forces at both Omaha and Utah Beaches. Located on the tip of Pointe du Hoc, the battery position was heavily protected by mines and wire, making an airborne assault impractical. The only other approach was from the sea below the cliffs, where a couple of narrow beaches offered the only landing sites. The cliffs rose 85 to 100 feet above them and had to be scaled to reach the guns.

The landing beaches were divided into four sectors: Charlie, Dog (subsectors Green, White, and Red), Easy (subsectors Red and Green), and Fox (subsectors Green and Red). Four battalions, two each from the 16th and 116th Infantries, and elements of two tank battalions were to land in the initial waves across 6,000 yards of beach from Dog Green to Fox Green.

The 16th Infantry Regiment was to land its 3rd Battalion on Fox Green and its 2nd Battalion on Easy Red. The regiment's 1st Battalion was to follow on Easy Red. The two battalions of the first wave were to seize Exit E-3. Next, the 2nd Battalion was to drive to Colleville and the 3rd was to turn east, take Exit F-1, and secure the high ground of the 200-foot-high Mount Cauvin west of Port-en-Bessin. The 1st Battalion was to follow through the beachhead and advance past Formigny to Trévières and the edge of the

1. Along the coast, from the Vire eastward, the strongpoints and resistance nests were designated with a WN-number, in the Cotentin Peninsula with a W-number, and some of the larger strongpoints with an S-number. Some of the *Widerstandsnest* were also designated with a W- or WN-number and were occupied by about seventy men with mortars, howitzers, and antitank guns, according to Joseph Balkoski's *Beyond the Beachhead*.

Paratroopers loading up in England.

flooded Aure Valley. Successive waves on D-Day would bring ashore the 18th and 26th Regiments, which were to push a few miles inland and set up strong defensive positions between Trévières and Mount Cauvin just east of Bayeux in order to secure the beachhead's right flank.

The 116th Infantry Regiment was to land its 1st Battalion on Dog Green and its 2nd Battalion on Dog White, Dog Red, and Easy Green. The 1st Battalion, supported by a company from the 2nd Ranger Battalion, was assigned the ambitious mission of taking the heavily defended Exit D-1, advancing through Vierville before turning west to support the relief of the Rangers at Pointe du Hoc, and continuing to the hamlet of Maisy. The 2nd Battalion, landing on a wider front, was to force Exit D-3 by smashing through the defended hamlet of Les Moulins at its entrance, drive through St. Laurent, and set up a defensive position just beyond Vierville and St. Laurent. The 3rd Battalion, which was to follow it, had to drive upon Longueville and La Combe and set up a defensive position in the flooded Aure Valley. The 115th Regiment was to come next and deploy around Longueville. At that point, the commander of the 29th Division was to take charge of his regiments and remove them from the control of the 1st Division.

Meanwhile, the 2nd Ranger Battalion was supposed to land below the cliffs of Pointe du Hoc and commence the assault by scaling the cliffs. If the 2nd failed in its mission, or if necessary to complete the assault on time, the 5th Ranger Battalion, instead of landing in support, would land on Dog Green and move overland to Pointe du Hoc.

Intelligence reports from mid-May indicated that only one battalion of the German 726th Infantry Regiment occupied the defenses between Grandcamp and Longues, but reserves were nearby. This was partially correct. About one battalion of the 726th Regiment was present, in the vicinity of St. Laurent–Colleville, but unfortunately, the 352nd Division had moved from its reserve position into the coastal sector and placed its 2nd Battalion of the 916th Regiment near Vierville. Rommel had succeeded in increasing the number of obstacles; all he lacked in June was the additional mines he had requested and troops that he wanted moved closer to the coast. Had he received those troops, the 1st Division's landing might have turned into a disaster. With the exception of the Ranger assault on Pointe du Hoc, the plans did not work out the way the Allied planners had hoped, and the beach became known as "Bloody Omaha." The Americans won the day thanks only to sheer grit and courage.

The Final Plans: Utah Beach

The 4th Infantry Division with its three regiments and the 359th Infantry Regiment of the 90th Infantry Division were scheduled to land on Utah Beach. The 8th Infantry Regiment of the 4th Division was to lead the assault. Two of the 8th's battalions and the 70th Tank Battalion were to land on about 2,000 yards of beach. Although the designated assault waves were to establish a beachhead little more than half the length of Omaha, their mission was no less important. It was hoped that six regiments of paratroopers would be awaiting them inland, making this D-Day invasion force the equivalent of three divisions: one assaulting by sea and two that had descended from the air.

The gap teams were organized differently than for Omaha Beach. At Utah Beach, the entire engineer and naval clearing force, referred to as the Beach Obstacle Demolition Party (BODP), included eleven NCDU teams of about sixteen men each using LCVPs, eight gap teams of about twenty-five men each from the 237th Engineer Battalion, and elements of the 299th Engineer Battalion landing in LCMs with tankdozers crewed by the 70th Tank Battalion. Unlike Omaha, the assault boat teams of the 8th Infantry would come in first, followed by the 70th Tank Battalion and BODP.

A firm sand beach occupied much of the east coast of the Cotentin Peninsula running from the Vire Estuary to the vicinity of St.-Vaast-la-Hougue to the north. The beach became soft and muddy at the mouth of the Carentan Canal. The area behind the smooth sandy beach was mostly bounded by dunes ten to twenty feet high and extending inland 100 to 1,000 yards. Beyond the dunes was a wide belt of low-lying land. In the area designated as Utah Beach, and for miles on either side of it, there were no bluffs or cliffs on or behind the beach. The only major obstacle was located between Pouppeville and Quineville, where Rommel had flooded the swampy lowlands one to three miles behind the beach and dunes. There the water was about three feet deep, but the inundated area was also crisscrossed by numerous ditches six to twelve feet wide and six to nine feet deep. Between the Carentan Canal and Quineville, five easily defended causeways crossed the flooded area.

A masonry wall, large parts of which were covered with sand on the seaward side, bordered the invasion beach and adjacent areas forming a natural ramp spanning about 10,000 feet. Only a wire obstacle on top of this wall prevented further progress. German strongpoints along this beach occupied positions that could be quickly isolated if the invaders made it ashore. A second line of defense was necessary at the exit to the causeways across the flooded area to keep an attacking force pinned on the beach. Twenty German strongpoints, two of which overlooked Utah Beach, stood in the area between the Vire Estuary and Quineville. The Germans had completed most of the lines of obstacles, consisting of log ramps, Czech hedgehogs, and a few Belgian gates, between the high- and low-tide marks. The actual beach where the invasion force landed, as a result of an error in navigation, was defended by a single strongpoint, W-5. The water obstacles in this area included Czech hedgehogs and wooden posts. As of early May, however, the work between W-6 and W-5 was far from complete, much to Rommel's annoyance, according to Paul Carell in *Invasion*. Some of the German positions along the Cotentin coast, such as W-5, included small ramps for launching Goliaths, miniature remote-controlled tanks filled with explosives that were designed to blow up landing craft. The position situated on the designated landing site for Utah Beach included most of the features typical of strongpoints, from gun casemates to antitank ditches. Additional strongpoints situated behind the beach guarded the causeway exits. The coastal and field artillery batteries were located a couple of miles inland, on higher ground.

Between Poupeville and St.-Martin-de-Varreville, four main causeways spanned the flooded areas toward the high ground. Not much higher than 200 feet, this was located on the southeastern corner of the peninsula between Carentan, St.-Sauveur-le-Vicomte, and Montebourg. The highest ground was on the northern and western parts of the peninsula. The Douve and Merderet Rivers, whose wide, gentle valleys were also flooded at the time, drained the southwest corner.

Located between La Madeleine and Les Dunes-de-Varreville, Utah Beach was divided into two sectors, Uncle Red and Tare Green. Each of the two sectors was about 1,000 yards wide and included a German defensive position almost at its center. One of these was StP-9 (*Stützpunkt*, or strongpoint, for a company-size unit), and the other was WN-106, also identified as W-8 (for a platoon-size formation). The Germans had completed most of the lines of antiboat obstacles—including hedgehogs, wooden ramps, and stakes—in this area. The forces landing here would have direct access to Exits 3 and 4, to the northwest of the beachhead. To the south, a road located between the coast and the flooded area provided access to Exit 2.

The original plan called for the 101st A/B Division to drop between Ste-Mère-Église and Carentan, with the objectives of disrupting the enemy's line of communications, seizing vital crossing points, and capturing the locks and dams that controlled much of the flooding. The 82nd A/B Division was to land in the vicinity of St.-Sauveur-le-Vicomte, to west of the Merderet. The area was chosen because it contained less flooded ground, allowing the division to make an attempt to block the western part of the peninsula. The airborne regiments were to drop at night, and part of the glider regiments was to arrive on D-Day. Even though some of the glider troops were assigned to arrive on D+1, many, especially those from the 101st A/B Division, wound up traveling by ship instead of glider. Meanwhile, the 4th Division was to drive across the exits and reinforce or relieve the battalions of the airborne divisions.

According to the official plan, after the 8th Infantry Regiment of the 4th Division established itself on the beachhead, it was to be followed by the other two regiments of the division together with the regiment attached from the 90th Division. On May 27, however, intelligence reports revealed the arrival of the German 91st Air Landing Division. The next day, the field orders for the airborne divisions and the 4th Division were amended or revised. The amendment for the 4th Division briefly summarized the role of the airborne divisions:

> 101st Airborne Division will land to the east and south of Turqueville beginning at H-5 hours on D Day and will seize the western margin of the inundated area behind Utah beach between St. Martin de Varreville and Poupeville. It will also seize and hold the crossings of the Canal du Port northwest of Brevands and a small bridgehead east thereof. It will also seize a dam which controls the inundations as well as

> seizing and destroying the bridges southeast of St.-Come-du-Mont on the Douve and Groult Rivers.

The major change concerned the 82nd A/B Division, moving its drop zones back to the eastern part of the peninsula, around Ste-Mère-Église and the Merderet River.

> 82nd Airborne Division will land astride the Merderet River at H-4 hours on D-Day with one regiment east thereof. It will capture Ste. Mère Église and the strong point southwest of Beauzeville au Plain where it will make contact with the 101st Airborne Division It will seize and hold crossings of the Merderet at two points and destroy crossings of the Douve River east of Beauzeville Bastille and south of Pont L'Abbe. Also it will destroy the crossings of the Douve at Nehou and St.-Sauveur-Le-Vicomte, unless already destroyed by bombing and will protect the south and west flanks ofVII Corps along the Douve south and east ofTerre de Beauval.

The 8th Infantry Regiment was to secure the beachhead and neutralize the enemy positions between St.-Martin-de-Varreville and Les Dunes-de-Varreville. The 3rd Battalion of the 22nd Infantry, attached to the 8th Infantry, had the mission of taking Quineville to the north. The 22nd Infantry was to land behind the 8th Infantry, capture Exit 4, and link up with and relieve elements of the 101st A/B Division. The 12th Infantry was to move across the secured causeways, advance on the crossing of the Merderet at Le Port Brehay, a few miles northwest of Ste-Mère-Église, and occupy it. The 359th Infantry (90th Division) was to land and serve as a reserve for the 4th Division.

The Weather and the Enemy

The bad weather may have been a godsend for the Allies. The Germans, who had no weather stations on the North Atlantic, were not able to predict the weather accurately. Although they had tried to run stations in Greenland and even had a weather ship, they could not determine the daily weather for Western Europe that June. For months, Rommel and his officers had diligently directed the establishment of antiship obstacles, certain that the Allied troops' invasion must come at high tide to reduce their exposure to the defenders' fire. No invasion could take place in bad weather. The meteorological conditions on June 4 and June 5 led the Germans to believe that no invasion would take place. This was reinforced by the fact that previous landings had taken place near dawn, and early June would not be optimal for the Allies, with low tide occurring at that time. Rommel rushed home to see his wife and confer with Hitler, while the staff of the German Seventh Army conducted a command-post war game.

The Germans had installed radar stations along the coast and set up a picket line of ships to sound the alarm when the long-awaited Allied armada appeared. As noted by Gordon Harrison in *Cross Channel Attack*, however, the German Navy was convinced that an invasion could not be launched without five consecutive days of good weather. Germany's military intelligence had already sensed, based on BBC messages to the French Forces of the Interior (FFI), that the invasion was at hand, but its military establishment failed to put this information to good use.

When the German 352nd Division arrived in Normandy in May, it completely escaped detection by Allied intelligence. Lt. Col. Fritz Ziegelmann, a staff officer of the 352nd Infantry Division, agreed with Gen. Erich Marcks, commander of the LXXXIV Corps, that the Allies would strike at Normandy with the objective of

2. Since Marcks's corps occupied one of several likely zones for an invasion, it is understandable that he would make such a prediction.

Loose Secrets and D-Day

Early on Sunday morning, June 4, 1944, most of the 7,000-ship armada had heaved anchors from British ports to rendezvous or were already sailing across the Channel when they received word to return. The invasion was canceled for June 5. Detailed operation orders had instructed commanders what to do under these circumstances. The only serious problem was the thousands of seasick soldiers who had been tossed around for hours in the rough seas. Some had been at sea for days and now had to wait another twenty-four hours. One small group failed to receive the message, however, and forged on to its destination before being intercepted and finally turning around.

Late on the night of June 3, as the Allied ships moved into position and long before the final decision had been made, news agencies in North America received an Associated Press message reading, "FLASH . . . EISENHOWER'S HEADQUARTERS ANNOUNCES ALLIED LANDINGS IN FRANCE." The message reached the U.S. news bureaus at 4:39 P.M. Eastern War Time on Saturday, June 3. The news spread, and within minutes, loudspeakers boomed out the message at many of the nation's ballparks. In at least one ballpark, the rival teams and their fans stood up to give a silent prayer. The news was electrifying—at long last, the great invasion was under way. Unfortunately, the same news also reached Moscow and Berlin.

Within two minutes of the initial message, another came over the airwaves demanding, "Bust that flash." The news media received a notice to kill the story. Apparently, a young woman named Joan Ellis, in the London AP office, had been working with a strip of practice tape and did not realize that the teletype machine was connected. On Sunday morning, small headlines in newspapers such as the *New York Times* read, "False Invasion Report," mystifying their readership. In London, although her name was not mentioned, Joan Ellis received extensive coverage in the papers and went home ill that afternoon. Within another forty-eight hours, the whole brouhaha would be forgotten.

Nonetheless, the affair must have been more than embarrassing for Eisenhower and his subordinates. Although the subject is rarely mentioned in books on the invasion, this incident was only the last in a string of episodes that could have given away the secret. Earlier, in March 1944, the FBI notified the military authorities that a parcel found in an army mail office in Chicago had broken open, spilling a number of papers that were stamped "BIGOT" and gave details of the invasion. Sgt. Thomas Kane, who worked in the ordnance section of SHAEF, had accidentally put the wrong address on the parcel and sent it to his home address, according to Jock Haswell's *D-Day Intelligence and Deception*.

A little later, at a dinner party for American Red Cross nurses in April, Maj. Gen. Henry Miller had announced that the invasion would take place before June 15. Eisenhower reduced him in rank to lieutenant colonel and sent him back home. The news media picked up his story shortly after the invasion. In May, Capt. Edward Miles, a naval aide to Adm. Harold Stark, got drunk during a social event and revealed secret information. He was sent home shortly afterward. All these cases involved only

continued

Loose Secrets and D-Day ***continued***

a few people, and thankfully the secret did not get out. In the case of the AP flash, however, thousands of people were informed that the invasion had begun when the ships were actually in the process of being recalled. Fortunately for the Allies, the German radar stations, patrol boats, and reconnaissance aircraft all failed to pick up the mass movement of ships, probably because the bad weather prevented them from noticing something was afoot. Nevertheless, Eisenhower and his associates must have been very concerned. According to Captain Butcher, Eisenhower's aide, when he gave the general a copy of the AP message the next day, "He sort of grunted."

taking Paris.[2] They came to these conclusions during map exercises. Ziegelmann determined that the invasion would take place in May because, according to the German press, the Russians wanted a second front to open soon. In addition, Allied air attacks on transportation lines, radar installation on the coast, and coastal artillery installations increased. Furthermore, a large number of carrier pigeons sent by the Resistance were shot down in the 352nd Division's sector, and a Resistance leader captured in Brittany in early June confessed that the invasion would take place in a few days. Finally, Ziegelmann suspected that the Allies, thanks to their reconnaissance missions, were aware that the coastal fortifications were much weaker west of the Orne than between the Seine and Belgium. In the sector of the 352nd, only one army coastal battery was in concrete emplacements, and a second battery remained unfinished. The infantry had "shrapnel-proof" shelters, which indicated less work had been done here than in the Cotentin. The division's artillery and antitank weapons were in open positions. The required one- to two-mile-deep mine belt and the fortifications were still incomplete because of a lack of materials.

The German Navy had muddled the situation in mid-May. Naval experts had previously claimed that the occupation of the Channel Islands made it impossible for the Allies to invade the west coast of the Cotentin Peninsula, unless they captured the islands first. They had also once maintained that the coast between the Vire and Orne Rivers was not adequate for an invasion. The German 243rd Infantry Division moved from the east side of the peninsula to the west side, making a landing at Utah Beach easier. Rommel wanted all his forces on the coast, so the 91st Air Landing Division and 6th Parachute Regiment (from the 2nd Parachute Division) moved behind the divisions defending the coast of the Cotentin to prevent air landings, eventually interfering with American plans. The sector between the Vire and Orne where Omaha and the British beaches were located was more lightly defended. Except for the 30th Mobile Brigade—bicycle troops stationed between Coutances and St. Lô—there were practically no units to back up the 352nd Division with immediate reinforcements or against airdrops. The 716th Division covered a reduced front and had the 21st Panzer Division at its back at Caen. Both Rommel and Col. Gen. Friedrich Dollmann, the commander of the Seventh Army, theorized that no invasion could succeed without a seaport. Therefore, they concluded, an invasion of Normandy must target either Cherbourg or Le Havre. Thus the 352nd Division took over a sector backed by bluffs and bordered by sea cliffs, where little action was expected.

The Western Naval Task Force

I. **Commander**: Rear Adm. Alan Kirk aboard the cruiser *Augusta*

II. **Mission**: Deliver elements of the U.S. First Army under Gen. Omar Bradley to Normandy.

III. **Components**:

1. Assault Force U
   A. **Commander**: Rear Adm. Don P. Moon aboard the transport *Bayfield*
   B. **Mission**: Land General Barton and his 4th Division with elements of General Collins's VII Corps on Utah Beach
   C. **Elements**:
      1) Minesweeper Group, commanded by Cmdr. M. H. Brown of the Royal Navy with more than 80 vessels, many of them British, including minesweepers, layers, motor launches, and modified landing craft, organized into eight units
      2) Escort Group, commanded by Commander Outerbridge on the destroyer *O'Brien* with 6 other destroyers, 3 British antisubmarine trawlers, 2 French corvettes, and 21 patrol-type craft
      3) Two Assault Groups:
         a) Beach Green Group, under Commander Warburton on *LCH 530*, with attack transport *Dickman*, a British LSI, and more than 100 LSTs, LCTs, LCMs, Rhino ferries, and other specialized landing craft
         b) Beach Red Group, under Commander Wilson on *LCH 10*, with attack transports *Barnett* and *Bayfield* and more than 140 LSTs, LCTs, LCMs, Rhino ferries, and other specialized landing craft
      4) Far Shore Service Group, under Capt. J. Arnold, with 2 steamships, 2 landing barge kitchens, 36 landing barge vehicle, 8 landing barge emergency, 20 landing barge oilers, 1 landing barge water, and other landing craft and DUKWs
      5) Sea Rescue Group, with 10 Coast Guard cutters
      6) Bombardment Group, under Rear Adm. Morton Deyo, with battleship *Nevada*, 3 heavy cruisers (1 British), British monitor *Erebus*, 2 light British cruisers, a Dutch gunboat, 7 destroyers, and 2 destroyer escorts
2. Assault Force O
   A. **Commander**: Rear Adm. John Hall
   B. **Mission**: To land General Huebner's 1st Division with attached units and elements of General Gerow's V Corps on Omaha Beach
   C. **Elements**:
      1) Minesweeper Group, under Cmdr. J. Cochrane of the Royal Navy, with more than 50 vessels, all of them British including everything from minesweepers to motor launches in 4 units
      2) Escort Group, under Capt. H. Sanders, with 6 destroyers (2 British), 3 destroyer escorts, 2 French frigates, 3 British antisubmarine trawlers, and 40 smaller vessels
      3) Four Assault Groups:
         a) Group O-1 for Easy Red and Fox Green, under Capt. E. Fritzsche, with attack transports *Samuel Chase* and *Henrico*, a British LSI, and about 90 landing craft and specialized vessels
         b) Group O-2 for Dog Green and Easy Green, under Capt. W. Bailey, with attack transports *Charles Carroll* and *Thomas Jefferson*, a British LSI, and just over 100 landing craft and specialized vessels.

continued

The Western Naval Task Force *continued*

c) Group O-3 for Fox Green and Easy Red, under Capt. L. Schulten, with transports *Anne Arundel*, *Dorothea L. Dix*, and *Thurston* and about 70 landing craft and specialized vessels

d) Group O-4 for Pointe du Hoc and Dog Green, under Cmdr. S. Dennis, with 6 British LSIs, 1 LCT, and 2 motor launches carrying the Provisional Ranger Force

4) Far Shore Service Group, under Capt. C. Camp, with 1 steamship, a repair ship, 72 landing barges vehicle, 16 landing barge emergency, 2 landing barge kitchen, 5 landing barge water, 20 Rhino ferries, and more than 200 landing craft

5) Sea Rescue Group, with 15 Coast Guard cutters

6) Bombardment Group, under Rear Adm. C. Bryant, with battleships *Texas* and *Arkansas*, 4 light cruisers (2 British and 2 French), and 12 destroyers (3 British)

7) Close Gunfire Support Group, under Capt. L. Sabin, with 69 specialized landing craft including landing craft rocket, gun, and high explosive

3. Follow-Up Force B

A. **Commander**: Cmdre. C. Edgar aboard the destroyer escort *Maloy*

B. **Mission**: To transport the remainder of the 1st and 29th Divisions with General Gerhardt and other V Corps units to Omaha Beach after Force O lands its troops

C. **Elements:**

1) Convoy B-1, under Capt. J. Johannesen on *LST 511*, with 18 LSTs and 46 British LCTs. Escort: 1 destroyer, 3 British destroyer escorts, 3 British antisubmarine trawlers, 2 sub chasers, and 2 Coast Guard cutters

2) Convoy B-2, under Cmdr. T. Cameron on *LCI 414*, with 1 attack freighter, 1 landing craft HQ, and 12 LCIs. Escort: 1 destroyer, 2 British corvettes, 2 patrol craft, and 1 Coast Guard cutter

3) Convoy B-3, under Cmdr. T. Green on *LST 266*, with 34 LSTs towing 26 barges

4) Convoy B-4, under Cmdr. B. Skahill on *LST 515*, with 9 LSTs towing 9 barges. Escort: 3 destroyers (2 British), 2 British corvettes, 3 antisubmarine trawlers, and 2 Coast Guard cutters

5) Mulberry A, under Capt. A. Clark on *Sub Chaser 1329*, with numerous tugboats and associated vessels

6) Salvage and Fire Fighting Group, with 5 British wreck-dispersal ships, 3 American salvage vessels, and 4 tugs with other smaller vessels

7) Area Screen, under Capt. H. Sanders on destroyer *Frankford*, with other destroyers and escorts of Escort and Bombardment Groups, Lieutenant Commander Bulkeley's 12 PT boats, and several British vessels, as well as other patrol craft

Source: Samuel Eliot Morison, *The Invasion of France and Germany*.

This gave the division the possibility of shifting east to reinforce the 716th Division or west to the Cotentin, depending on the point of invasion. This is how it came to pass that the 352nd was occupying the coast as a reserve position and wound up defending the Americans' target, Omaha Beach.

The Invasion Fleet Sails

Most ships took on their cargo of materiel or men at the end of May or the first days of June. Approximately 150,000 troops prepared for the invasion, many of them sailing in an armada of 7,000 ships with an air umbrella of about 11,500 aircraft.

The mass movement of troops to the sausage-shaped assembly areas was finished. Replacements and other divisions waited for the invasion force to leave so they too could move forward and prepare for their own departure. The great invasion fleet began to assemble in the English Channel.

After Group Captain Stagg predicted favorable weather, Eisenhower met once more with his staff at 4:15 A.M. on June 5 and declared, "O.K. We'll go." The sailing orders had already been issued the previous night, an hour before midnight. The invasion would take place on the morning of June 6 or have to wait another fortnight.

Rear Adm. Alan Kirk's Western Task Force consisted of three landing groups with supporting elements. The assault troops loaded up at ports between Falmouth and Poole in southwest England. Rear Adm. Don Moon commanded Force U, which would carry the 4th Division to Utah Beach and sailed in twelve convoys from eight ports. Rear Adm. John Hall's Force O carried the 1st and 29th Divisions departing from several ports in nine convoys destined for Omaha Beach. Cmdre. C. Edgar's Follow-Up Force B, with the remaining elements of the 1st and 29th Divisions and army engineers, departed from Fowey and Falmouth in the southwest. The British Eastern Task Force began moving its three task forces out of ports in southern and southeast England between the Isle of Wight and Harwich. Force G sailed for Gold Beach in sixteen convoys with the British 50th Division, Force J carried the Canadian 3rd Division in ten convoys to Juno Beach, and Force S departed for Sword Beach in twelve convoys with the British 3rd Division. A follow-up force carried the reinforcements for the beachhead. Not including landing craft carried on ships, the Western Task Force consisted of more than 930 ships, and the British Eastern Task Force almost 1,800, according to Samuel Eliot Morison. Some of these vessels had made a false start on June 3, but they set out again on the morning of June 5 to assemble off the English coast. By that night, they began their crossing. No armada this vast and awesome had ever been seen in the Channel before and probably never will be again.

The huge flotilla was preceded by minesweeping units, mostly British vessels that were assigned to each assault force, even American Forces O and U. They cleared the required number of lanes for the convoys following them, working fast, since the main minefield in mid-Channel was not well maintained by the Germans. There was only one casualty during this operation: The American minesweeper *Osprey* was lost when it hit a mine north of the minefield.[3] The seas were not as rough as the day before, but they were still choppy, making the troops in the smaller craft uncomfortable. A couple of X craft, British miniature submarines, awaited the invasion fleet off the Norman coast in order to guide it toward the shore. Overhead, the air was filled with the constant drone of the aircraft flying cover. This time, there were no mistakes like those in the Mediterranean. The ships' antiaircraft guns remained silent, as all Allied aircraft were clearly marked with white stripes for the invasion to prevent them from being mistaken for enemy planes. Shortly after midnight, waves of transport aircraft carrying the three airborne divisions flew over the invasion flotilla.

The Germans in Normandy, still on alert, noticed that the bad weather of June 5 was slowly letting up but felt that there was nothing to worry about. The seas were too choppy and the morning tides too low. Had Rommel not predicted that the Allies would arrive at high tide? Suddenly, after midnight, they heard the drone of the first wave of aircraft. Was the RAF on another bombing mission? they wondered.

3. According to historian Joseph Balkoski in *Utah Beach*, the Germans began laying the minefield in March 1944 and employed conventional mines only because Hitler refused to let them use the secret pressure mines lest they be captured by the Allies. Thus the existing minefield was largely ineffective.

CHAPTER 8

The 101st Airborne Division on June 5–6

A Night of Deception

The Allies launched air attacks on German radar stations along the coast of northern France before the beginning of the invasion. Although they achieved some degree of success, it could not be expected that all the radar sites would be out of operation when the invasion fleet arrived. This being the case, they worked out a masterful stratagem in the form of Operations Glimmer and Taxable.

As the invasion fleet sailed toward Normandy, a much smaller fleet of eighteen launches towed balloons with radar reflectors across the Channel coast, covered overhead by Mosquito night fighters. The group was divided, with nine vessels designated Glimmer moving toward Boulogne, while the other nine known as Taxable proceeded toward Cap d'Antifer. According to *Bodyguard of Lies* by Anthony Cave Brown, a squadron of RAF bombers and night fighters accompanied each unit, flying around the simulated fleet to intercept intruders.

Pvt. Paul E. Pachowka's stick from the 82nd Airborne Division poses in front of its aircraft on June 5, 1944. COURTESY OF PAUL E. PACHOWKA

The radar reflectors projected the image of a 10,000-ton transport ship, and the ships carried electronic equipment that created the illusion of many ships on enemy radar. In addition, the bombers flying overhead began dropping "Window" aluminum strips to confuse enemy radar. At daybreak, aircraft spread a smoke screen, while the small boats used sound amplifiers to broadcast the noises associated with ships preparing to unload troops from an invasion fleet. German shore batteries opened fire on the small ships near Cap d'Antifer. The Germans sent out aircraft and the small ships at their disposal to intercept the invasion fleet, which turned around and raced back toward England.

As Brown described it in *Bodyguard of Lies*, the little fleet drew German coastal fire, units of the *Luftwaffe*, and the small units of the German fleet stationed on the Channel. In the meantime, the actual invasion fleet off the Norman coast went largely undetected until just before H-Hour. The diversion may not have altered the situation off Normandy, however. Had they detected the invasion force sooner, the Germans would have been unable to take decisive action against it. They had few aircraft in the immediate area, and their air units were closer to the Pas de Calais and probably would have been unable to reach Normandy in the early morning even if they had not been diverted by Glimmer and Taxable. The German naval units that challenged the small Allied fleet had a considerable distance to cover before reaching Normandy, so the delay was a minor one. But the units at Le Havre and Cherbourg were not affected by the Allies' ruse. The vessels at Dieppe went out in search of the nonexistent fleet and were unable to return in time to support the naval forces at Le Havre. The ruse succeeded in convincing the Germans that the Allies' target was the zone held by the Fifteenth

Army. In their postwar accounts, some of the more prominent German leaders do not mention whether these operations might also have affected the decision to hold back the panzer reserves. According to the standard accounts, Hitler was asleep, and Gen. Alfred Jodl refused to awaken him to ask for permission. The Fifteenth Army also alerted its formations after intercepting the last part of a BBC message to Resistance forces to begin their operations.

Before the invasion, Allied air strikes took out all but eighteen of the ninety-two radar stations along the coast belonging to the German Navy and *Luftwaffe*, including most of those on the Normandy coast. Glimmer and Taxable were intended to deceive the surviving stations, the majority of which were north of Le Havre, about the target of the invasion. Even though one radar station on the northwestern end of the Cotentin Peninsula detected a large concentration of ships across the Channel, the German leadership at headquarters took no steps to verify or act upon the report. Finally, in the early hours of June 6, Adm. Theodor Krancke, on an inspection tour in southern France, issued the order for his small units to take action.[1] The S-boats operating from Cherbourg turned back after they failed to catch up with the diversionary Allied fleet. In the meantime, Force U slipped by unscathed, opposed only by naval mines. The *Möwe*, *Jaguar*, and *T 28*, of Henrich Hoffmann's Torpedo Boat Flotilla 5, sped out of Le Havre, while smaller patrol vessels lumbered toward the British Eastern Task Force. Hoffmann's S-boats succeeded in launching their torpedoes and escaped under a hail of naval shells raising geysers of seawater all around them, according to *Defeat at Sea* by C. D. Bekker. In the fray, the S-boats managed to hit and sink the Norwegian destroyer *Sevenner* about thirty-five miles northwest of Le Havre at around 4:40 A.M. The remaining vessels of the German coastal defenses searched out the decoy fleets off the Channel coast.

Meanwhile, the invasion fleet had crossed the Channel. During the night of June 5–6, most of the invasion convoys moved to a point about thirteen miles southeast of the Isle of Wight known as Area Z, which covered a ten-mile-diameter region and was also called Piccadilly Circus. The invasion forces sailed toward France through five lanes marked by lighted buoys. At about the halfway point each line split into two lanes, one for the faster convoys and the other for the slower ones. On the eastern side of the Cotentin, for some unknown reason the lighthouse at Pointe Barfleur, the tallest in France, cast a welcoming light, according to Samuel Eliot Morison's *The Invasion of France and Germany*.

The minesweepers did their job well: Few vessels succumbed to an underwater explosion. On the evening of June 5, the American minesweeper *Osprey* was lost when it hit a mine while clearing a lane. The invasion fleet began to move into position off the Normandy coast early in the morning with no other interference than the S-boat attack from the east. There was no significant German response until a few minutes after 5 A.M. when an enemy coastal battery at St. Vaast opened fire on two American destroyers off the Cotentin Peninsula. About 6 A.M., one of these destroyers, the *Corry*, still under fire from the coastal guns, struck a mine; it sank within an hour. Rear Adm. Morton Deyo, commander of the Bombardment Group, gave the order to begin the naval bombardment at 5:36 A.M., which was before the scheduled time, to counter the enemy artillery fire that he had been receiving since 5:05 A.M. As the naval forces engaged the enemy, everyone, sailor and soldier alike, realized that the battle had begun.

1. Krancke went on this inspection tour as he did not expect an Allied invasion in early June because of the weather.

The Airborne in Operation Overlord

The aircraft of the IX Troop Carrier Command departed England late in the evening of June 5, 1944, carrying the paratroopers on the "The Night of Nights."[2] The amphibious landing of the troops was set at 6:30 A.M. (H-Hour), about five hours after the main body of paratroopers hit the ground.

On the night of June 5–6, the route of the aircraft carrying the paratroopers and gliders was marked by a number of checkpoints with beacons. The 52nd Wing, which carried the 82nd Airborne Division from airfields in the vicinity of Nottingham and Leicester, more than fifty miles north of London, assembled at checkpoint Atlanta, flew on to checkpoint Cleveland, north by northeast of Bristol, and turned southward. Meanwhile, the 50th Wing and 53rd Wing, which carried the paratroopers of the 101st A/B Division, began taking off after 10:15 P.M. All the paratrooper elements were airborne by 11:30 P.M as they assembled in the darkening skies over southwest England. They passed over checkpoint Flatbush, the last checkpoint for all of the wings as they departed the coast of England located at the Bill of Portland. After passing Flatbush, all aircraft turned off their navigation lights, and the crew chiefs made sure that there were no other lights in the cabins. All the planes flew south along a ten-mile-wide corridor at 500 feet above the water. The downward-facing amber recognition lights were turned off and the formation lights dimmed to the lowest setting at checkpoint Hoboken, marked by a submarine with a signal light. After having maintained a southeasterly course across the Channel, the aircraft turned toward the Cotentin Peninsula at Hoboken. They also began to climb to 1,500 feet to keep out of range of most antiaircraft batteries on the coast. After crossing over the coast, they were to drop down to 500 feet so that the parachutists would not have a long descent after they jumped, according to Gerard Devlin in *Paratrooper*. To find the drop zone for the Pathfinders, the lead aircraft had to rely on the GEE radio navigation device and visual recognition.

From Flatbush, it took the Pathfinder aircraft, flying at a speed of 150 miles per hour, forty-nine to fifty-four minutes to reach their drop zones. The planes of the 101st A/B Division, flying a distance of 136 miles at 140 miles per hour, took an estimated fifty-eight minutes to reach their drop zone from Flatbush. The craft of the 82nd A/B Division were to cover 122 miles in about fifty-two minutes from Flatbush to their DZ. The interval between the first and last aircraft of the 101st A/B Division was about fifty-five minutes. Finally, the aircraft transporting the 82nd A/B Division closed the cortege about fourteen minutes later. On approaching the DZ, the pilots throttled back to 110 miles per hour or less, dropped the paratroopers and the para-packs, and accelerated to 150 miles per hour for the return trip. The ideal drop speed was considered to be about 90 miles per hour, but since the C-47s were overloaded, their speed was raised to prevent them from stalling out.

The Pathfinders began dropping into Normandy at about fifteen minutes after midnight. A little more than an hour later, at about 1:30 A.M., the first of more than 6,600 paratroopers of the 101st A/B Division in Albany Mission began jumping into Normandy from their 423 C-47s. Albany Mission was followed at about 2:30 A.M. by Boston Mission, consisting of more than 6,400 paratroopers of the 82nd A/B Division in 378 C-47s.

Once the paratroopers were on the ground, Chicago Mission began. Elements of the glider regiment of the 101st A/B Division began landing at about 4:30 A.M. The troop carriers that towed the gliders followed the same route across the

2. This phrase was first coined by Col. Robert Sink in a speech to his 506th PIR as they prepared for the mission.

A Waco glider.

Channel until they reached a midway checkpoint called Gallup, the first boat marker on the route between Flatbush and Hoboken. Here they executed a 90-degree turn and flew to the Spokane checkpoint, where they turned southward toward Utah Beach and their landing zones. The aircraft flew at 115 miles per hour and required sixty-four to seventy-one minutes to reach their designated landing zones. Fifty-one CG-4A gliders loaded with 165 troops, including General Pratt, as well as artillery and vehicles, landed in the dark just before dawn. They were followed a few minutes later by Detroit Mission, consisting of 52 more craft from the 82nd A/B Division's glider regiment, with 220 troops and similar equipment.

The paratroopers who survived the confusing early-morning hours heard the German artillery batteries booming at the invasion fleet just after 5 A.M. and the answering fire of the Allied warships at 5:50 A.M., reassuring them that the invasion had not been postponed again. Just after 6 A.M., when the Army Air Force began its bombing missions over the beaches, the airborne troops realized that relief was not far off.

In the evening of June 6, Elmira, the next glider mission for D-Day, brought 176 gliders with almost 2,000 troops and a great deal of equipment for the 82nd A/B Division. Keokuk Mission, which took place at 9 P.M., at the same time as Elmira, numbered 32 Horsa gliders carrying 165 troops. It was followed at 7 A.M. on June 7 by Galveston Mission, with 104 gliders, more than 960 men, and additional equipment. At 9 A.M. came Hackensack Mission, with 100 gliders, more than 1,300 troops, and the final load of artillery, vehicles, and equipment.

Eagles in the Night Sky: The 101st Airborne Division

As the first aircraft carrying the Pathfinders crossed the Channel late on the evening of June 5 and flew toward the western coast of the Cotentin Peninsula, advance elements of the British 6th A/B Division approached the Norman coast from the north. The British paratroopers had the vital mission of securing the eastern flank of the British Second Army. Among these first aircraft, however, were several on a special mission named Titanic. These broke away from the rest to fly toward several inland sites and drop several hundred quarter-size dummy paratroopers known as Rupert. With them were several soldiers from the SAS, who were to land behind enemy lines and set up noise making devices, detonate small explosives, and send up Very lights in order to divert the Germans' attention from the actual British and American parachute forces.[3] Unlike the American Pathfinders, these SAS men did not expect reinforcements. According to Brown's *Bodyguard of Lies*, some of the men involved in the Titanic missions were dropped in the vicinity of Yvetot, Harfleur, Lisieux, and Lessay. The objective was to attract the Germans and make them believe that each group was an element of a parachute brigade. Beyond that, the SAS men were to survive as best they could. Thanks to their efforts, the Germans concluded that landings had taken place in the area between Rouen and Coutances.

Titanic's success may have saved the lives of many men of the American airborne divisions, because a number of the Pathfinder units were scattered and most of the paratroopers that followed were off target and also scattered. As the greater part of Normandy appeared to be subjected to paratrooper landings, and the French Resistance went into action by cutting communication lines, the Germans throughout the region were totally confused.

In the early-morning hours of June 6, Gen. Friedrich Dollmann, commander of the German Seventh Army, who was expecting his subordinates to arrive for a map exercise, realized that something was wrong and ordered them back to their units. The Fifteenth Army headquarters had intercepted the BBC's signal alerting the French Resistance that the landings would take place within forty-eight hours, but OB West had failed to relay the warning. The naval radar station near Cherbourg also reported unusual activity on the other side of the Channel to Krancke's headquarters, Naval Command West. The information failed to reach the Seventh Army, however, because German Naval Command did not believe that anything suspicious was happening at the time and saw no need to inform Field Marshal Gerd von Rundstedt, who had already received the Fifteenth Army's warning of the impending invasion on its front. Thus, while the divisions of the Fifteenth Army went on full alert, the Seventh Army had no inkling of the impending invasion until the parachutes of the Allied forces began to bloom in the night sky. Dollmann canceled the maneuvers a little too late. When the first paratroopers began to land, the Seventh Army units in Normandy had problems not only with communications, but also with command and control. Furthermore, the enemy seemed to be everywhere.

On the Allied side, each regiment of the 101st and 82nd A/B Divisions sent out an advance group of Pathfinders to mark its assigned drop zones. These groups consisted of a handful of highly trained men who carried equipment to mark the DZs with panels, lights, and radar homing equipment designed to direct aircraft to them. If any of these groups failed in its mission, its regiment would have to depend totally on the skill of the aircrews.[4]

At 12:15 A.M. on June 6, 1944, Capt. Frank L. Lillyman of the 101st A/B Division became the first Pathfinder to set foot in France as part of the D-Day invasion.[5] As he made his jump, the British launched their Titanic missions, and

3. The Special Air Service (SAS) was created by Capt. David Sterling during the North African campaign. It became what is referred to as the British Special Forces.

4. According to Steven Zaloga in *D-Day 1944*, the Pathfinders in turn were helped by half a dozen two-man OSS teams accompanied by three British commandos for protection who had arrived on June 3 to mark their landing sites. It appears this was a planned operation that was never executed.

5. According to Mark Bando in *101st Airborne*, this claim is disputed by Pvt. John McFarlen, who maintains that as a result of some confusion, he actually went first. Lillyman, who was considered too much of a showman by his superiors, was not promoted.

Boarding aircraft on June 5, 1944.

bombers dropped aluminum strips of "Window" to confuse the German radar. Ahead of the British Pathfinders came a group of gliders whose mission was to land in a very confined space and capture by surprise two guarded bridges over the Caen Canal and Orne River. This became the most successful mission of D-Day. Although the British Pathfinders faced some problems, the brigades of their division made relatively good landings and secured most of their objectives. The British flank was secure even though their airborne division landed relatively close to the 21st Panzer Division. Some of the American Pathfinder teams were less fortunate, being dropped too far from their objectives.

The Pathfinders of the 101st A/B Division had to mark three drop zones and one landing zone. DZ A, located east of Ste-Mère-Église, was meant for the 502nd PIR with the attached 377th Parachute Field Artillery Battalion. This regiment was to secure causeway Exits 3 and 4 and destroy a German coast artillery battery at St.-Martin-de-Varreville. DZ C, located near Hiesville, was assigned to the 506th PIR, which was to secure the other two causeway exits, 1 and 2. The 501st PIR, with the 326th Airborne Engineer Battalion, had the most difficult task of landing in DZ D, the farthest south, just north of the Douve River. They were to secure the locks of La Barquette on the river to keep the Germans from destroying them and causing further flooding. They also had to set up a defensive line on the river to prevent German reinforcements from arriving on the southern flank of the beachhead. Supporting units accompanied by Brig. Gen. Donald Pratt, the assistant division commander, landed later, at dawn, on LZ E, near Hiesville. The general died when his glider crashed.

According to Gen. Maxwell Taylor's report of July 15, 1944, the conditions were not ideal.

> The parachute plane formations crossed the channel in a formation of the V of V's [groups of three aircraft] keeping on course and making a landfall on the western coast of the Cotentin Peninsula as planned. The weather up to this point had been clear, but upon crossing the Norman coast, heavy cloud formations were encountered which continued to the Merderet River. The clouds caused the tight formations to scatter as flank lanes tended to diverge to the north and south. As the formations emerged from the cloudbank at the Merderet, flak was encountered. That this ground fire was gen-

erally ineffective is shown by the fact that of the 1656 sorties flown by the Troop Carrier Command . . . on D-Day and D+1, only 46 planes or 2.8% were lost. Nevertheless, this fire had considerable volume and produced an unfortunate effect on the pilots who had never before seen action. As a result, many formations became widely scattered, and many ships took evasive action. This latter greatly increased the difficult and hazard of jumping.

The 82nd A/B Division Pathfinders, commanded by Capt. Neal McRoberts, also had to mark three drop zones and one landing zone. The mission of the 507th PIR was to land at DZ T and take up a position on the west side of the Merderet River north of Amfreville, while the 508th PIR was to land south of the same town at DZ N. The veteran 505th PIR was to use DZ O, east of the Merderet, and capture the bridges at Chef-du-Pont and La Fière in order to link up with the other two regiments. The 505th also was to land near Ste-Mère-Église and capture the town, which was at a key road junction. LZ W, in the vicinity of Les Forges, south of Ste-Mère-Église, was to serve as a landing field for the gliders carrying General Ridgway, division commander, and supporting units, including artillery. Additional gliderborne units from both airborne divisions were scheduled to alight in the evening of June 6. These were to be followed on the LZ by the bulk of the 325th GIR of the 82nd A/B Division the next day. Most of the 327th GIR of the 101st A/B Division, on the other hand, was to disembark at Utah Beach.

The Pathfinder operations had mixed results:

101st Airborne Division
- 501st PIR—DZ D—not on target
- 502nd PIR—DZ A—not on target
- 506th PIR—DZ C—marked an area almost on target
- Gliders—LZ E—marked LZ correctly

82nd Airborne Division
- 505th PIR—DZ O—marked DZ correctly
- 507th PIR—DZ T—not on target
- 508th PIR—DZ N—not on target

Some of the teams were unable to set up or turn on their equipment because they were not properly sited or enemy forces were in the area. Although they did the best they could, the Pathfinders faced problems beyond their control that affected not only them, but also their regiments, which soon followed them.

About half an hour behind the Pathfinders came a force of almost 13,000 men traveling in more than 900 C-47s flying in formation toward the west coast of the peninsula. The lead aircraft of each formation of nine C-47s carried a Rebecca set, which was to home in on the signals from the Pathfinders' Eureka sets. If that aircraft were lost, the remaining pilots would use a T panel of lights to guide their aircraft visually. These lights were also intended to help the lead aircraft find the correct drop position within a couple miles' radius. Each DZ was assigned a different color of Holophane lights. For instance, the 505th PIR's was marked with green lights, the 507th PIR's with red, and the 508th PIR's with amber. Later, 500 gliders carrying an additional 4,000 troops flew almost directly over the invasion armada to approach the peninsula from the east.

The American Paratroopers Arrive

Although many of the paratroopers made fairly good landings, some were dropped so low that they hit the ground almost as soon as their chutes opened, others got snagged in obstacles such as trees and were forced to cut their way free, and yet others landed in flooded areas and had to struggle to get out of their equipment to avoid drowning. To add to their woes, many of the paratroopers either immediately faced enemy fire or were still looking for their weapons while the enemy approached. Fortunately for some, more than once the approaching "enemy" turned out to be a cow. After releasing their harnesses and gathering up their gear, the troopers had to find the other members of their stick. The men of the airborne divisions used little toy clickers to make contact and the password challenge "Flash" and response "Thunder." When members of the two divisions ran into each other as a result of the scattered drops, there was some confusion in making recognition, and it is unknown how many may have been accidentally shot because of it. Ironically, most of the Pathfinders faced fewer problems on landing than the men who followed them.

First Lt. Robert S. Dickson III of the 502nd PIR departed with the Pathfinder group of the 101st Airborne Division at about 9:30 P.M. on June 5. He was accompanied by two men from the S-2 section. This was his first combat jump, and he had received little preparation for this mission. After having spent many months working with the regimental football team, he had been assigned to this mission only three weeks before the invasion. His task was to reconnoiter the route for the 2nd Battalion from the DZ to its objective, the coastal gun position of St.-Martin-de-Varreville, which overlooked Utah Beach with four 105-millimeter guns.

> We departed England in daylight—a three-plane echelon, which I believe consisted of Pathfinder teams representing the three 101st Division regiments. The flight was completely uneventful: no flak, no fuss. Everyone seemed relieved, but with very little of the usual banter going on. I suppose we had our personal thoughts, but one couldn't help but be somewhat apprehensive. When passing the Channel Islands, a huge searchlight was turned on but quickly extinguished. Next came the French coast, which was overcast—the plane gave a slight bump and then broke through to clear skies. The plane then turned on its final leg, and Captain Lillyman stood up to start jump procedures. I am a little vague on this but I believe there were eighteen of us (I have a photo taken by Captain Lillyman showing seventeen bodies). The Pathfinder team included a security detachment to do the main fighting while the others set up their vectoring aids. I was not present, but I understand there was a firefight and Captain Lillyman was slightly wounded.
>
> I "pushed the stick" with the two recon men directly in front of me. I observed when we loaded the aircraft that, as so often occurs, the smallest man was carrying the biggest load. In fact, he could hardly waddle and needed help getting on the plane. His position was directly in front of my group, and when he reached the jump door, he fell down and we had to assist him in leaving the plane. This caused some delay, and by the time I reached the door, the plane was starting to pick up speed and turn for home. As a result, I was dropped well beyond the designated drop zone and spent very little time in the air. I clearly remember that bright moon; it was almost like a daylight jump. I had an easy landing in a small field surrounded by hedgerows.
>
> On landing, I set my M-3 [.45 submachine gun, the "grease gun"] down in the tall grass, got out of my parachute, repacked a few things, and started off. By the time I reached the end of the field, I realized I was missing something: no gun. Now any fool knows you can't fight a war without a gun. So, back to the drop spot on my hands and knees, and after much patting the ground and cursing my stupidity, it was finally found. What a relief. Walking back along the line of flight, I met my two men.

For the first twenty to thirty minutes after landing, everything was quiet in Dickson's area; all he heard was the normal sounds of the countryside. When he found his two men, he suddenly had an unsettling moment thinking that the invasion might have been postponed once again and there had been no time to recall the Pathfinders. This feeling quickly fled, however, when "about then, all hell broke loose as the main body of aircraft flew in." It looked like a "regular Fourth of July in the distance, with tracers shooting through the sky and the whole countryside lighting up as a C-47 went down." Suddenly he realized that he did not have enough time to accomplish his recon mission, since there was an interval of roughly one hour between the drop of the Pathfinders and the drop of the main body of their units. The unit he was supposed to recon for was the 2nd Battalion, which was so dispersed that only a dozen of its men were able to regroup and were unable to complete the task of attacking the battery of four 105-millimeter guns at St.-Martin-de-Varreville. Dickson subsequently learned that the coastal battery had been wrecked by the aerial bombardment. Later that day, he discovered that the range of his grease gun was insufficient to be effective in a firefight and had to replace it, first with an M-1 rifle, and then with a carbine.

S.Sgt. Raymond Smith (then listed as a private), a medical technician assigned to a Pathfinder team of the 101st A/B Division, was also on Captain Lillyman's aircraft with Lieutenant Dickson. In addition to the medical supplies, he carried the M1928 M-1 Thompson submachine gun (the tommy gun), one battery, and three days' supply of K rations.

> Almost every man in my plane was anxious to be taking part in such an enormous mission and was well prepared. In our group, Group No. 1, we had three men from the Intelligence Department of the 101st Airborne. Their leader was Captain [Lieutenant] Dickson. Captain Lillyman told us after we boarded the plane and flew around England for what seemed like hours that we were doing this to confuse the enemy.
>
> Since we were burdened down with so much equipment, and we were flying in at 500 feet altitude, we asked Captain Lillyman if we could discard our emergency chutes. He agreed, and off they came.
>
> We couldn't see anything but the horizon. I landed in an apple tree in a churchyard and broke a bone in my left foot, but I had no desire to sit down or shirk my duties, so I rejoined our group as quickly as I could. Every man from our group gathered within fifteen minutes and did the mission as planned. The number 2 and number 3 plane crews had real problems. One planeload landed in the shallow water a few miles from their objective; they all survived but did not get together in time to set up their radar and lights.

Pvt. Paul E. Pachowka boarded one of the last Pathfinder aircraft. It carried the team for the 507th PIR. He was the number eight man on the aircraft.

> I carried an M-1. It was not broken down, and I carried it under my reserve parachute. I also carried a knife, canteen, K rations, change of underwear, socks, a battery and a light attached together in a sealed unit, 300 rounds of ammo for the rifle, four fragmentation grenades, one white phosphorous and one Gammon grenade, one land mine, bayonet, two first-aid kits, cigarettes, and a couple of black chocolate candy bars. When I got on the scale, I weighed a little over 300 pounds. My normal weight was 168 to 170 pounds. This amount of equipment was more of a hindrance than a help. It weighed all of us down, and we could not get rid of

> it fast enough once we landed. One trooper was designated to jump with the radar, and six of us each jumped with a battery and a light.

There were nineteen men in Pachowka's team, and when their aircraft crossed the Channel, it flew so low that he thought that the waves would hit the aircraft. "I had a pint of gin, which I passed around, and when emptied, I threw it into the Channel." Finally, as it approached France, the plane climbed to jump height, and it was not long before they received the signal to stand up and prepare. It was a bad drop. Ten of nineteen men were killed as soon as they hit the ground. Private Pachowka landed in an apple orchard, his parachute snagged on a tree limb. "I saw two Germans coming out of the woods, and they opened fire with machine pistols. How they missed me, God only knows; the apples were hitting my face and the bullets whizzing by me like bees." He dangled limply in his harness, hoping the Germans would think him dead. When they turned away, "I reached into my boot for my knife and cut the risers. I was so nervous I cut my hand very badly and didn't even notice the blood. The Germans started firing again and hit the tree trunk. I dropped down and went behind another tree. They came into my sights and I killed them." Pachowka later learned that he and his comrades had missed their objective by about three miles, landing in a German bivouac. Since half the team had been killed, they were unable to mark the DZ. Pachowka ran into Fred Burns, one of his teammates, who had a broken leg. Burns told Pachowka to leave him behind to wait for the medics to pick him up. Pachowka left him with an extra grenade, and it was quite a while before the two met again.

> I saw the main drop. The sky was covered with planes and dropping paratroopers. I will never forget it. I joined up with other troopers from various units, and we followed a railroad track. We met Gen. James Gavin and Col. [Lt. Col.] Edwin Ostberg of the 1st Battalion of the 507th PIR. My clothes were soaked from wading through a flooded area. Gavin's clothes were soaked also, and he asked me if I had a dry cigarette. I remembered I had a pack of Old Golds in my helmet liner, and we both had a smoke. Colonel Ostberg joined us, and it was then that General Gavin said we must take the village ahead. A short time later, Ostberg was shot through the throat, and I saw a medic giving him aid.

Ostberg reached the railroad station at Chef-du-Pont at about 10 A.M. and led a charge to the bridge southwest of the town, where he was shot, fell into the river, and was rescued, according to Phil Nordyke's *All American All the Way*, Pachowka later saw the colonel in Nottingham, England, when they returned from Normandy. Edwin Ostberg was placed on the division staff, but he returned to lead a battalion in 1945 when another battalion commander fell.

About half an hour after the Pathfinders left North Witham, the craft carrying the regiments of both airborne divisions began to take off and form up for their flight across the Channel. So that the Allied troops could readily identify the aircraft as their own, they each sported freshly painted white invasion stripes. All the aircraft carrying American paratroopers across the Channel followed the same route, turning toward the west coast of the Cotentin Peninsula as they flew over the enemy-occupied Channel Islands. The craft towing the gliders, on the other hand, flew along the east coast of the peninsula.

On the night of June 5, 1st Lt. William M. Thompson, a draftee from Missouri who had earned his wings, was flying for the 85th Squadron of the 437th Troop Carrier Group attached to the 436th Troop Carrier Group at

Newbury. He and his fellow pilots had been briefed at about 4:00 P.M. on June 5. According to the briefing, it was to be "a piece of cake," but reality turned out to be quite different, remembers Bill Thompson. His aircraft took off sometime near midnight, in the pitch of night. Painted on its nose was *Terror of the Ozark*, a name that was branded in the memory of one young paratrooper of the 101st A/B Division. Almost a year later, when Thompson was flying American prisoners out of Germany, one of the newly liberated POWs turned to his buddy and said, "Oh no, that is the goddamn airplane that brought me into this mess." Thompson, on the other hand, did not recognize the young man; on the night of June 5–6, when he "looked back into the aircraft, it was just a bunch of faces."

Lieutenant Thompson carried members of the 502nd PIR destined for DZ A, which was supposed to have been marked by Captain Lillyman's team. Of the three regiments of the 101st A/B Division, the 502nd was the most widely scattered, its sticks of paratroopers landing miles north of Montebourg, along the east coast and as far south as DZ C. A few sticks landed around DZ A, but none on it. Although Lillyman's team was not to blame for all the aircraft that ended up going off course that night, it was responsible for misdirecting the planes that used its beacons, which were set up a mile from their intended position.

For virtually all the men of the 502nd PIR, this was to be the first combat jump. Lieutenant Thompson, who had boarded the aircraft before they arrived, glanced back at them after they had all embarked and saw that "they were expressionless, and they knew it was serious, as we all did."

> There wasn't much talking, everybody was to their own thoughts. The takeoff was routine. I don't remember anything unusual. It was a moonlit night, and when we hit the shoreline, there were low-lying clouds at the altitude at which we had been briefed to fly the mission. You could look down and see the Channel, but I don't remember seeing any ships, just water. We went into the cloud with an airplane on each wing, flying in close formation, and I was leading the left-hand side of a big formation of forty-five ships. They all went out of sight. We had a procedure where we were to make a 45-degree angle for thirty seconds. In my case, I was on the left hand side, so I turned 45 degrees left and flew it for thirty seconds, and then picked up my original heading and started flying straight ahead. It put me out of the corridor through which we were briefed to fly. The next thing I saw was searchlights coming up. I let down a little bit, trying to make contact with the ground, to see if I could see the ground, then the searchlights picked us up. Then you could see the tracers coming up, and they had our altitude. I could see the tracers in front of us; they were leading us too much, since they probably were not used to firing at slow-flying aircraft.
>
> We did not get hit, so finally I let down some more and broke out of the clouds. I could see the water on the other side and I knew I had to turn right to get back to the drop zone, which I did. The troops in all three airplanes were organized as one unit, and all their equipment had to go down together for them to be an effective unit. Intelligence had briefed us not to drop our troops in the water. My right wingman, flying off of me, saw the water and I guess he got excited and started dropping them before I signaled him to. He didn't realize that I was going to turn south to get them on the drop zone, which I believe was about two miles away. When he started dropping his troops, my reaction was to get them all down together, so I put the signal

> on and dropped all three planeloads of troops. On the other side of the formation, other planes were doing the same thing, so we scattered troops all over the countryside.

Lieutenant Thompson and the two other aircraft in his group, like many other C-47s carrying the 502nd PIR, were dispersed across the peninsula because of the cloud cover. As a result, the 502nd PIR had the worst drops of any of the six regiments in Normandy that night. Fortunately, the three sticks of Thompson's group came down close together, even though they dropped in the wrong place. After the drop, the aircraft flew on across the Cotentin Peninsula.

> It was dark when we flew over the fleet. I thought I was hit, because we had these para-packs under the airplane. When you drop them, they leave these strings, which pull the parachute. I felt a vibration on my airplane after we made the para-drop, and I thought momentarily we had bullet holes in the bottom of the airplane, but it was these cords popping against the airplane. It was about two in the morning when we got back to England.

To his amazement, Thompson learned that all forty-five aircraft made it back to base.

First Lt. Sidney M. Ulan from Chester, Pennsylvania, was a twenty-four-year-old C-47 pilot in the 99th Squadron of the 441st Troop Carrier Group, 50th Wing. Two years earlier, he had been an aviation cadet at Maxwell Field, Alabama. He arrived in England in March 1944, and after some additional training, he prepared for his first combat mission.

> Shortly before midnight on June 5, we took off loaded with paratroopers of the 101st Airborne Division. Our drop zone was just north of the town of Carentan [DZ D]. As we crossed the invasion coast, we were flying in close formation in order to drop the paratroopers together into the drop zone. Suddenly all hell seemed to break loose. The sky was filled with red and green tracers, and searchlights beamed up at the planes just ahead of me. I could also feel the vibration of flak coming up and shaking the plane. I was chewing gum, and the saliva in my mouth completely dried up from fright. It seemed almost impossible to fly through that wall of fire without getting shot down, but I had no choice; there was no turning back. After dropping our paratroopers, I hit the deck to avoid the flak and ground fire, and flying at treetop level, finally ended up just above the Channel, skimming the water, then pulling up to re-form our formation. The baptism of fire was over, and I breathed a sigh of relief. After landing at Merryfield, we looked over the plane, and it just had a few small holes from ground fire.

Like so many other pilots, Lieutenant Ulan wondered how accurate his drop had been. Most pilots never found out. Ulan carried elements of the 501st PIR destined for DZ D. "We were trained to give the 'green light' to the troopers as soon as we saw parachutes coming from the planes in front of us," he says, because the navigators, who had the Rebecca sets, which homed in on the Eurekas of the Pathfinders, were in the lead aircraft. If a formation became split, the pilots had to try to locate the Pathfinders' signal lights laid out in a T.

A red warning light was supposed to light up about four minutes before the jump, but in some cases, according to the veterans, it went on much earlier than that. As soon as the light came on, the paratroopers stood up, hooked up their static lines, checked each other's equipment, and on command, sounded off to indicate that everything was OK and ready. Meanwhile, the pilot

throttled back to decrease his speed to no more than 110 miles per hour. When the green light went on, the jumpmaster pushed out the bags and guided the parachutists out the door before jumping himself. The crew chief released any para-packs under the plane.

Much of the mix-up over the peninsula resulted after the aircraft entered a cloudbank when crossing over the French coastline. Many formations broke up while the pilots strove first to avoid collisions and next to regain or locate their formations. In the resulting confusion, some forgot to turn on the red warning lights for the parachutists. According to George Koskimaki, who interviewed many veterans for *D-Day with the Screaming Eagles*, the 101st A/B Division was particularly beset by this problem. On one plane, the pilot went to the back cabin to inform the paratroopers that he had lost the lead plane and didn't know where they were, but reassured them that they were over land. The stick decided to jump. On Koskimaki's plane, the pilot waited too long to put on the green light. The pilot of another plane overflew the entire peninsula before he about-faced and flew back to the designated DZ. Yet another pilot still refused to turn around altogether and took the paratroopers back to England despite their protests. This was only one of two planeloads of paratroopers that returned to England. The pilot of the plane carried Robert Huerge, a member of the 82nd A/B Division headquarters, dived to treetop level and flew across the coast without giving the green light. Then he turned back and flew for the amount of time prescribed by one of the paratrooper officers onboard before putting on the green light.

The pilots were not the only ones who had problems. The paratroopers had their own share of troubles, although comparatively minor. According to the mission report of the 314th Troop Carrier Group for June 6, one paratrooper refused to jump. Two of the men on another aircraft fouled their static lines and were unable to jump. On a third plane, a paratrooper fell and was hit in the groin; by the time he recovered, the aircraft was already speeding off, so he lost his opportunity to jump. There were problems even before the group left its airbases, such as when one paratrooper refused to board the aircraft. But in spite of everything, almost every paratrooper who was able to do so jumped that night.

Later, many paratroopers complained that their pilots lacked experience and had panicked. Even though many of the pilots had no combat experience, however, they were all qualified and had taken part in many training missions. As the after-action reports indicate, the cloud cover made it difficult to fly in formation, and near collisions forced many of the pilots to break away by diving or gaining altitude to avoid running into aircraft adjacent to them. None of the C-47s had self-sealing fuel tanks, because Gen. Hap Arnold had previously refused to authorize them. The para-packs carried on the belly of the aircraft held ammunition that could explode if hit by flak, turning the plane into a fireball. The planes' fuselage offered no protection against ground fire. If they were hit, the pilots, radio operator, and crew chief had little chance of escaping until the paratroopers were out. As one paratrooper pointed out, if the pilots who missed the drop zones had truly been in a panic and were trying to save their skins, they could have turned on the green jump light at any time, even over the water, since they were not supposed to bring any paratroopers back.

The 506th PIR did not land as accurately as the 501st, but many of its sticks came down close to DZ C or near Ste-Marie-du-Mont. Its 3rd Battalion was assigned to DZ D, and even though it was on target, it was hit heavily by the enemy. Among these paratroopers was PFC Robert A. Flory, a rifleman with the 3rd Platoon, Company B, 1st Battalion of the 506th PIR. During the precombat briefing, he and his comrades were informed that many of the enemy troops were from Russia and the Balkans and had been recruited from prison camps. Rumor had it, however, that the Germans soldiers would not surrender. They were also warned about the "Rommel asparagus" posts planted in the ground.

> Before suiting up we had camouflaged our faces by smearing charcoal or chocolate on our cheeks, noses, and forehead. I remember Lt. Herbert Minton spotting one of his men who had not darkened his face. He made him go to the exhaust of the planes engines, collect carbon, and cover his face. When we entered the plane, we were issued Dramamine pills, which were to ward off airsickness. I threw mine away and was glad later that I did. Many of the men became drowsy and uncoordinated because of them.
>
> Shortly after 11 P.M., planes started taking off. I'll never forget the roar of hundreds of planes taking off and circling to get in formation. At last we were airborne. The men

Summary of Operations of 101st Airborne Division

The following is a summary of the 101st A/B Division's operations on June 6–7 from a report submitted by Gen. Maxwell Taylor on July 19, 1944:

DEPARTURE

The airborne lift consisted of the following echelons:

- 11 C-47s for Pathfinder mission
- 432 C-47s, Mission Albany, carrying about 6,600 paratroopers arriving at H-5
- 51 CG-4A gliders, Mission Chicago, carrying 148 troops arriving at H-2
- 32 Horsa gliders, Mission Keokuk, carrying 165 troops arriving at H+15

The Pathfinder serial departed first and was followed half an hour later by the main body of paratroopers. The aircraft and paratroopers departed from seven airdromes in the Newbury-Exeter area, beginning at 2215 hours on D-1.

PATHFINDERS

None of the teams were dropped at predesignated point, but all came close.

MISSION ALBANY

The aircraft flew in V-of-V formation. On their way to the Norman coast, the clear skies turned to heavy cloud cover over the Channel. The tight aircraft formations became scattered in the cloudbank. As they emerged near the Merderet, they ran into flak, which fortunately was mostly ineffective. Only forty-six planes, or 2.8 percent of the total air fleet, were lost. The barrage of fire caused many of the aircraft to scatter again, however, and as a result, two sticks of paratroopers failed to jump and 1,500 men dropped outside the perimeter of Ravonville, Ste-Mère-Église, the Cherbourg-Carentan railroad, and the Douve River and were either killed or captured.

The 502nd PIR's mission was to capture Exits 3 and 4 and the battery at Varreville. The 2nd Battalion landed on DZ C instead of A, and the 1st Battalion assumed its mission of taking out the battery, previously destroyed by air assault. The 3rd Battalion and 377th Parachute Field Artillery (FA) Battalion scattered, with the 377th recovering only one gun.

The 506th PIR's mission was to capture Exits 1 and 2 from DZ C with the 1st and 2nd Battalions from DZ C, but the 2nd Battalion was scattered. The 3rd Battalion was to land at DZ D and seize two bridges near Le Port on Douve, but it landed in the face of opposition and took heavy losses.

The 501st PIR's mission was to destroy bridges north of Carentan and seize locks at La Barquette. Although the 2nd Battalion landed on DZ D, the 1st Battalion was scattered. The 3rd Battalion was sent to DZ C to act as the division reserve, but it too was scattered. About 250 men under the regimental CO, Colonel Johnson, managed to take the locks, but they were too weak to reach and destroy the bridges.

Of the 6,600 paratroopers that jumped as part of Mission Albany, only about 1,100 dropped on or near their objectives. As the scattered groups began to coalesce, the division reached a strength of about 2,500 men by the end of D-Day.

continued

Summary of Operations of 101st Airborne Division *continued*

MISSION CHICAGO

This night landing of fifty-two Waco gliders suffered only five fatalities, which included General Pratt.

MISSION KEOKUK

In this daylight landing of thirty-two Horsa gliders at 2100 hours, fourteen men were lost, and many of the gliders were damaged, but their contents survived in good condition.

MISSION MEMPHIS

On D+1, this on-call resupply mission landed at 0635 through a misunderstanding, and 118 aircraft dropped supplies that were widely scattered and mostly lost, since the division was not expecting this delivery.

AFTER-ACTION REPORT

The after-action report concluded that since 60 percent of the equipment bundles were lost, less equipment should be carried by the paratroopers and in rack loads in the future. In addition, it recommended that the parachutists have quick-release harnesses and carry pistols for self-protection upon landing. Furthermore, the airborne division could not be expected to function as fully operational force in less than twenty-four hours after landing.

The report concluded, however, that an airborne landing at night, in the presence of the enemy, was not as hazardous as previously thought. Although it resulted in sharp fighting and the loss of some men before they were able to use their weapons, such an attack had a devastating effect on the enemy, upsetting command organization and preventing movement of the reserves and artillery. Even though they may not carry out all their prearranged tactical plans as scheduled, the airborne troops had a disruptive effect on the enemy, which compensated for the disorder in their own plans.

were very quiet. Some were chain smoking, lost in their own thoughts. Strapped in my harness, I was thinking of home.

Lieutenant Minton, our platoon leader, spent most of the trip standing in the door. Every once in a while, he would walk back to the center of the plane and yell at the top of his voice, "Is everybody happy?" And we would reply at the top of our voices, "Yes!" Lieutenant Minton was much admired and respected by the men under him.

It was a cool, damp night with clouds frequently obscuring the moon. I got up once; I had to have help and went forward to look out the door. I got the immediate impression that every C-47 in the Air Corps was on the way to Normandy. As far as I could see in every direction, there were troop transports.

As we crossed the coast of France, we came under intense fire. I saw the flak coming up from the door, and that is when Lieutenant Minton called for everybody to stand up and hook up, because when you come under fire like that, you better get ready to get out of the plane. I moved back to my position, which was between Bill Martin and Don Patton. The plane was weaving from side to side, and it was very difficult to keep our balance. It didn't seem very long, but it must have been ten or twelve minutes before the green light came on and we bailed out. When I went out the door, there was flak, and you couldn't believe how noisy it was. It seemed like explosions all over the sky, and the machine-gun tracers lit up the whole sky. In the distance, you could see the 88 muzzle blasts. I remember the sensation of falling, but I don't remember the opening shock. I looked up and saw my camouflaged chute, and I saw planes coming in—some were on fire. The sky was just full of parachutes. I looked down and went immediately into a state of shock. I was over water! My first thought was that the SOB pilot had dropped us over the English Channel. Then I looked to my right and saw a herd of dairy cattle grazing. About that time, I landed in water up to my chest. I was in a salt marsh. It seemed like an eternity before I could get out of my harness and wade to dry land. All this time, the gunfire was deafening and planes kept roaring over. A plane came over, directly overhead, about 600 or 800 feet high, took a direct hit, and exploded in midair, so he must have been carrying a lot of explosives.

Since I was twelfth in my plane, I started crawling in the reverse direction of the flight. By then I had gotten rid of my gas mask, jump rope, and gun case. My M-1 was loaded and the safety off. I looked at my watch and saw that it was 0130. I was dying for a smoke but didn't dare light up. I crawled up to an embankment and lay there. All of a sudden, I heard a cricket: click-clack. I had completely forgotten about mine, and I was unable to find it. "Don, is that you?" Don Patton started cursing, so I knew I was all right. Later, Bill Martin came crawling up. We had no idea where we were or which way to go.

We decided to crawl toward a hedgerow about 100 yards west. As we crawled up to the hedgerow, we could see a sunken road on the other side. Then we heard voices—German voices! A patrol of about fifteen or twenty German soldiers was approaching from the south. After a whispered conversation, we decided that each of us would throw a grenade at the same time and take off toward the north at top speed. The German patrol was marching in formation. As they drew abreast of us, we each pulled the pin, threw our grenades, and took off at top speed. After running for about 150 yards, we came under machine-gun fire and had to go to the ground. We could hear the screams and cries back down the road but didn't dare go back and finish off the survivors. For the next hour, we crawled up and down the hedgerow looking for some of our buddies. Machine-gun and rifle fire was all around us. We finally located two more troopers and were shocked to find out they were from the 82nd Airborne.

As it began to get lighter in the east, we found three more from our platoon, one with a broken leg, and we moved out of the hedgerows and onto a dirt road. At a crossroad, we left the man with the broken leg and assumed he would be found by the medics. We started moving west and shot three more Germans, who had been sleeping in a barn. They refused to give up and started running from us. We found out later that they were told paratroopers didn't take prisoners.[6] We had no choice but to shoot

6. American paratroopers were supposedly briefed on how to take and treat prisoners according to G-3 Operational Memorandum #23 "Final Briefing of Division Personnel," dated May 22, 1944, from 101st Airborne Division headquarters. Many veterans claim they were told not to take prisoners.

> them. As it began to get lighter, all hell broke loose behind us. The navy had started bombarding the beaches. Up ahead of us, we could finally see a familiar sight: a church steeple. We knew from our briefings that we were approaching the village of Ste-Marie-du-Mont.

At this point, remembers Flory, the three of them buried all their gear near the town and proceeded into Ste-Marie-du-Mont, where they found it difficult to distinguish friend from foe. "Then we ran into a group of about fifteen or twenty from our company, under the command of Lieutenant Minton. It was like old home week. I attached myself to PFC Lee Rogers, who was the oldest man in our platoon, age twenty-eight, and who won the Distinguished Service Cross later that day. He killed eight Germans and captured fourteen single-handedly in breaking up an apparent ambush."

Soon Flory's group grew to more than seventy-five men from different units, and they received the order to take the town of Ste-Marie-du-Mont. The men, who were organized into squads, began a coordinated attack on the town. Flory does not remember whether the group had any mortars, but he is sure it had machine guns on each flank. They found two equipment bundles outside of town in a pasture and brought them in. The naval bombardment had already ended. The Germans counterattacked but withdrew after about an hour. Flory counted thirty-two dead. A few hours later, Colonel Sink, the commander of the 506th, arrived in a jeep and met with Lieutenant Colonel Turner of the 1st Battalion, directing him to secure Exits 1 and 2 from the beach.

> We had plenty of grenades, and if we received any fire from the houses, grenades were tossed through the windows and doors. I will never forget this guy, Clarence Hibbard from Kentucky, running down the street firing his M-1 from the hip, knocking bricks off the buildings as he ran. I remember two fellows with a bazooka, dashing down the street, stopping, aiming, and blowing the front door off the church. Shortly after that, a white flag appeared and about a dozen Germans surrendered. We cleared the town in less than an hour. The surviving Germans retreated towards Carentan, leaving behind many dead and wounded. We did not pursue them but set up a roadblock.

More stragglers joined the American force at Ste-Marie-du-Mont. As they set up the roadblock, recalled Flory, they found one of their buddies "hanging in a tree, still in harness, hanging about six feet off the ground." The Germans had bayoneted him in the groin. A shot rang out from the direction of the church, and another of Flory's pals collapsed, killed by a sniper.

An American lieutenant and two GIs found a battery of 88s about 1,000 yards east of town. Two of the guns had been wrecked, but the third was still serviceable. They turned the gun around and bore-sighted on the church tower. One round and the church tower disappeared along with the sniper.[7]

When the American paratroopers fired the German gun on the church steeple, Sgt. David Rogers of the 1st Battalion's HQ Company (506th PIR) was in the sanctuary with four other paratroopers who had landed near the town. One of them was battalion sergeant major, Isaac Cole.

7. Accounts vary, but according to Gordon Harrison in *Cross Channel Attack*, the town was the headquarters for the 2nd Battalion of the 191st Artillery Regiment that had three batteries of four 105-millimeter howitzers each in the area, one of which was captured. According to Harrison, one of the 105-millimeter guns was used against the church, not an 88-millimeter. There was also a battery of 88s at a nearby farm.

They had entered the church in the darkness and left several troopers on the ground floor as they stationed themselves in the steeple. At dawn, Rogers was able to watch the invasion of Utah Beach unfold. From their vantage point, the paratroopers eliminated several German soldiers who entered the center of town. Early in the afternoon, they spotted an American tank drive up from the beach and stop within a couple hundred yards of the church. Rogers hung out a flag to let them know Americans were inside. At that moment, the artillery piece captured by Flory's group opened fire, mistaking the Americans for Germans. According to one source, the second round hit the steeple, but Flory and Rogers both say it was the first. The clock on the tower was frozen at 1:10 P.M. when the round hit. Rogers, Cole, and their comrades quickly scampered out of their position before another friendly round could topple it. By evening, they reached the village of Holdy, where Captain Patch, Rogers's company commander, was stationed with the gun that had fired on the church, according to Georges Bernage and Dominique François in *Utah Beach, Sainte-Mère-Église, Sainte-Marie-du-Mont*. The first American tank Rogers and his group had spotted was followed by more tanks with troops of the 8th Infantry, which had crossed the causeway leaving Utah Beach through Exit 2. Flory's group spent the remainder of the day cleaning up German pockets in the area. The next day, June 7, D+1, Lieutenant Colonel Turner took over one of the tanks and was standing in the turret when a sniper's bullet felled him. (Flory confused the date of Turner's death with D-Day.)

Meanwhile, the 1st and 2nd Battalions of Col. Howard Johnson's 501st PIR landed in DZ D on D-Day, while the 3rd Battalion was supposed to land at DZ C but missed. The regiment's mission was to secure a position along the Douve River to secure the southern flank and seize the locks of La Barquette to prevent the Germans from increasing the flooding level in the area.

Even though the drops on DZ D were the most accurate of the day, it turned out to be the most difficult drop zone for the Allied paratroopers, because it was located in an area occupied by the German 3rd Battalion, 1058th Regiment of the 91st Air Landing Division. The 3rd Battalion of the 506th PIR landed at DZ D as planned but met heavy resistance. Nonetheless, one small group successfully carried out its mission by taking the northern bridge at Le Port, though it held on with difficulty. The 1st and 2nd Battalions of the 501st PIR encountered similar troubles. The main problem was that the units that dropped in DZ D were largely disorganized and ineffective during their first hours on the ground. Lieutenant Colonel Johnson managed to take the important locks of La Barquette but had to call in artillery support from the cruiser *Quincy* to maintain his position. The remaining units failed to destroy the bridges north of Carentan and take St.-Côme-du-Mont.

The 501st PIR had a hard time because it was the farthest away from any possible support from the beachhead. Many of the paratroopers were killed or wounded before they could rejoin their units. Sgt. William G. Davis of the HQ Company Communications Platoon, 1st Battalion was soon captured by the Germans. PFC James D. Purifoy from the S-2 Section of 2nd Battalion, 501st PIR, had boarded the aircraft with his leader, Lieutenant Sefton; another enlisted man from the section, named Goebels; and elements of the Machine Gun Platoon, Mortar Platoon, and battalion headquarters.

> It seemed like we circled around for an hour or two over England before crossing the Channel. It was light enough to see the water and the ships below. In about ten minutes or so, we got hit by antiaircraft fire. As we were flying along, we were packed in the little seats, and I tried to look back through the window. I saw the plane on our left

explode in the air (I was in the center plane) just as we crossed into France. The plane blew all apart into a ball of fire. I don't think any of them got out. Two or three minutes later, our plane went up on its side, veered to the right about 90 degrees, and it was apparently hit. The pilot leveled off, and I looked out and could see the tip of one wing was gone and the engine was on fire on the right wing (I was on the left side). Then about that time, they started ringing the emergency bell to get out. Lieutenant Sefton was the jumpmaster, and I could hear him. They had some equipment bundles, which they had to kick out. They got one hung in the door, and all the time the plane was coming down fairly fast. I heard Sefton say, "Oh my God, if we don't get this thing out of here, we are all going to die." We all got a little bit scared; the bell was still ringing. The next thing I knew, we started going down to that door as Lieutenant Sefton sent us out. He was the last one out, and he later said that by the time he got out and his parachute opened, he just about hit the ground. He said he saw the plane go on in, crash, and explode. I don't think the crew survived.

As I went out of the plane, just before my chute opened, it seemed the air was afire with tracer bullets. I counted about seven or eight and hit the ground, then the firing stopped. We were in the second wave, so I guess they were firing on the third wave. I got on the ground and landed amongst some cows in the field with hedgerows and ditches filled with water. I jumped with the strap of my weapon across my neck, and when I hit the ground, I had a tank mine hanging on my hip and a roll of maps tied onto each side of my legs. I landed close to Goebels. Some shells started coming in, and I jumped into a ditch full of water. I thought it was knee-deep, but it came up to my neck. A bunch of us had antitank mines. After we got out of the ditch, we were all wet and we just sat around there; we didn't know which way to go. We heard a lot of shooting. We saw a barn and house, and some GIs around there. The farmer was giving apple cider, so we filled our canteens. Then we heard a lot of fire in another direction. There were probably eighteen to twenty men, and a sergeant who told us we should go over there. It took a couple of hours. On the way over, we captured a German Air Force officer dressed in a uniform and a little cap.

When we got to where all the shooting was, we found our regimental CO, Colonel Johnson, was there with forty or fifty men. They called it "Hell's Corner," the Locks. It was not one of our objectives. [It was an objective of the 501st PIR.] They were fighting when we got there, and soon things calmed down. In the early afternoon or evening, a large group of Germans, maybe 500 to 600 came across the field at us. By then I think another forty or fifty paratroopers assembled; we must have had 150 men there under Colonel Johnson. There were other officers there also. We got our machine gun set up, and they started firing back at the enemy. We had some mortars. It could have been late afternoon or early evening, I would say four or five o'clock. It took two hours or so to get there, and I don't know what direction we went in, I was completely lost, and so was Lieutenant Sefton, whom I saw several days later. It could have been earlier, but it was still daylight. They attempted to surrender and put up a white flag. Colonel Johnson hollered for everyone to cease fire, so we did. He walked out towards the German officer with an NCO and white flag, then all of a sudden the guys started shooting again and Colonel Johnson hit the ground. He then ran back toward the barn. He thought the captain ordered the shooting, but he didn't—everybody was trigger-happy. Finally he got the firing to stop, went out again, and brought the German in. Then the German sent the NCO back out, and he returned with others who surrendered, probably 150 to 200. We had killed the others in that open field; the rest of the 600 were dead or wounded. We put the prisoners in the house for several days, until we got some vehicles from the seaborne forces. The fighting stopped.

During the fighting that afternoon, one guy named Tantello was laying on a manure pile shooting Germans as we both chewed away on tobacco. I took a bite and offered Tantello some, and he said he didn't want any and asked, "What do you want me to tell your folks when I go down to Arkansas and see them?" I said, "I plan to be there myself to tell them." It couldn't have been a half minute after that he was hit right between the eyes and killed instantly. I had lost a best friend.

I was assigned as a guard for the prisoners, and when we lined them up on the road, the Germans started throwing mortars and killed a few of their own men. I jumped in a ditch, and these Germans piled in on top of me; they were as scared as we were. One of the sergeants I knew got his kneecap blown off, while another guy asked me to look at his back. I pulled his shirt off, and his back looked like hamburger meat, little old tiny pieces of shrapnel all over.

Purifoy's ordeal took place on D-Day and D+1. The Germans he mentioned surrendered on D+1 at about 3 P.M. and the official history records that Colonel Johnson was met by two German privates, who claimed that they wanted to surrender but their officers were shooting those who spoke of doing so. One of the two privates was sent back with a message that they would be annihilated by superior forces in thirty minutes if they didn't give up. When the time expired, a group of Germans moved toward American lines, followed by another 350 into the evening. Finally the German battalion commander, with 150 of his men dead or wounded, came to discuss surrender terms. Of the 250 Americans at the locks, 10 were killed and 30 wounded. Thus the German 6th Parachute Regiment suffered a serious defeat at the hands of American paratroopers who were desperately holding out, awaiting relief.

The 502nd PIR had the only properly marked DZ of the division, but not one of its sticks landed on target. This regiment had the honor of a visit by Eisenhower at its air base before departure. According to PFC Rene Schmidt, a member of the 502nd PIR, the trip to France was uneventful until they ran into a barrage of anti-aircraft fire, which "drove many of the planes off course. We had only been over land for about three minutes, so when the flak hit us, many aircraft caught fire. My aircraft was hit, and I later found out that it returned safely." When he jumped, Schmidt says, "I had a great opening shock and lost all of my equipment, with the exception of a trench knife and a hand grenade." Apparently the aircraft was traveling too fast. "On top of that, I made a tree landing. That was my introduction to Normandy."

PFC Ray B. Hood of HQ Company, 2nd Battalion, 502nd PIR, had just turned eighteen and was finally of legal age to serve in the army he had joined two years earlier with a forgery of his father's signature. When he boarded his aircraft, he carried his M-1 rifle, sixteen clips of ammo, two or three fragmentation grenades, and a land mine. In addition, like most of the others, he carried a bayonet, trench knife, canteen, first-aid pouch, compass, entrenching tool, machete, and twenty feet of rope in case of a tree landing. He also had a reel of commo wire and half of an SCR-300 radio, which could be used only if he found the person with the other half. In his musette bag, he carried socks, underwear, a shelter half, tent pegs, a raincoat, and three days of K rations. Like most of his comrades, he was unable to climb aboard the aircraft without help. Later, General Taylor commented that it was useless to overload the paratroopers because much of the equipment got lost, and the sheer load of the equipment prevented the men from operating efficiently when they landed. The trooper's parachute was equipped with a bellyband with three snap fasteners that had to be removed before he could get out of it. "During those frightening minutes while he was getting out of that harness, he was a sitting duck," says Hood, "and most of us devoted a little time to practice since it seemed prudent to do so." In his July 1944 report on Operation Neptune, General Taylor in fact recommended that these harnesses be replaced with the new quick-releases. According to Hood, the flight of the 502nd PIR into Normandy was quite eventful.

> The 2nd Battalion, 502nd PIR, led the invasion. The C-47s flew in a V of Vs. I was in the lead aircraft of a group of three on the left of the leading group of three aircraft. The planes flew across the Cherbourg Peninsula from west to east, and as soon as we reached the coast, we were subjected to heavy (but not particularly accurate) antiaircraft fire. The pilots, I am sorry to say, definitely did *not* hold formation, and did *not* reach the correct drop zones. We were scattered all over an area twenty miles in diameter, and at least one pilot jumped his men in the sea.
>
> The last minute in that airplane will stay with me forever—the noise, the erratic motion, the difficulty of remaining erect. The normal procedure was that five minutes away from the drop zone, a red light would come on near the exit (turned on by the pilot). At that time, the number one would give the command "Stand up and hook up." The jumpers would hook up the snap fastener on their static lines to the anchor cable that ran down the center of the aircraft's roof. The next command was "Check equipment." Each jumper checked his own gear in front, and then checked the backpack of the jumper in front of him. Then came the command "Sound off for equipment check." The last man scheduled to go out the door would answer first: "17 OK," then "16 OK," and so on. The stick was then ready to go. The number one man stood in the door ready to go. The other jumpers stood very close to each other, crowded, left foot forward. When the green light came on, there was no command—we just went, fast.
>
> All this stuff did not happen in my plane over Normandy. The anti-aircraft fire evidently caused our pilot to panic.[8] The airplane was all over the damn sky, and I had a very difficult time staying on my feet. There was a combination of engine noise, yelling, and the sound of exploding shells. The roller-coaster ride—I cannot convey my feelings. *I wanted out of that airplane.* And all of a sudden, we went. We were very low. The time elapsed between the opening of my chute and my hitting the ground was shockingly brief. I don't think I swung more than once or twice before I hit the ground. My left fibula was broken, and movement was greatly curtailed.
>
> I landed approximately five miles from my scheduled drop zone [DZ A]. We had

8. Ray Hood, like many paratroopers, blamed the pilots for flying erratically and breaking formation, but from their position in the aircraft, there was no way they could see what the pilot saw or know whether the pilot had avoided a collision with another C-47.

been instructed not to load our weapons until daybreak, since mistakes in identification could easily cause small wars between units of Americans. I had been in the army long enough so that I did not automatically believe everything I was told, and I damn well loaded my M-1. If mistakes could be made with a rifle, they most certainly could be made with hand grenades—even bigger, noisier mistakes. Each man carried a "cricket," the small metallic toy that children use, and this was used in the dark as identification.

I hobbled and lurched, and it is most difficult to describe my feeling of frustration. The communications equipment I carried would be needed, perhaps badly. I knew how important it was, but I was absolutely lost. I did not know where the hell I was, and that realization was most unpleasant. I stumbled into another man from the regiment. We knew that we were supposed to have jumped somewhat southwest of Utah Beach, so we started generally north, moving slowly and carefully, staying off the roads, and walking near the hedgerows near the open fields. We had two brushes with the enemy before daylight and on one occasion solved the problem with grenades.

We heard men approaching on the road just the other side of the hedgerow from where we were. They seemed to be making no effort to be quiet, and the number of voices indicated several men. They were either recruits or the dumbest soldiers in the German Army. The hedgerow was about six feet tall, and we waited until they were even with us, and then lobbed grenades gently over the hedgerow into the middle of the formation. While all the screaming, yelling, and shooting were taking place, we quietly walked away.

Lt. Col. Benjamin Weisberg's 377th Parachute Field Artillery Battalion was assigned to the 502nd PIR. Each of the three batteries carried four 75-millimeter pack howitzers, and each piece was broken down into six large packs and carried under a C-47. The battalion's antitank battery was to arrive with six 37-millimeter antitank guns. Although DZ A was the destination for the fifty-four aircraft carrying the battalion, the drop was widely scattered. Eventually only one of the 75-millimeter howitzers was recovered. When the artillerymen were finally able to gather enough weapons to support the regiment, they used a couple of captured Russian guns and a 105-millimeter howitzer. They used these guns until about June 12, when they ran out of ammunition and the 105-millimeter needed repairs. Either Taylor or McAuliffe sent orders to relieve Weisberg and tried to put the blame for the battalion's losses on him, according to Bando's *101st Airborne*.

Sgt. William D. Gammon from Arkansas was with Battery B of the 377th Parachute Field Artillery Battalion when he took off from Newbury. His stick included the battery's commo section: Cpl. Herbert Ostien; Harvey Poehls, the switchboard operator; Denley Fisher; Wilmer Bean; and a few others. Their job was to establish communications among the battery, fire control center, and forward observer.

> They split us up on different aircraft. There were about six from my section in my plane, and we had the switchboard and reels of wire. The 502nd PIR had the mission to knock out the coastal guns, and we were supposed to support them with artillery fire. There were twelve planes in our group—Battery B.
>
> I was the jumpmaster. Crossing the Channel was pleasant. They had the amber and red lights on the wing, and when we crossed the Channel, they blacked them

out. There was a moon that night, and you could see well, including the boats flashing code to us. We cut into the Cotentin Peninsula. When we approached the peninsula, the pilots panicked and scattered. The red light came on and I gave the commands: "Stand up! Hook up! Check your equipment!" When we got the green light to jump, we had only about fifty seconds to the Channel, so we had to unload right away. I had six rack loads and a door load. I had a solenoid to release the racks underneath and a manual if it didn't work or one hung up. We cleared the plane quickly; it was rocking with the flak. I was the last one out. We yelled, "Bill Lee!"[9] There were tracers coming up and it seemed like I was going toward them. I made my only tree landing in Normandy and was strung out there like a turkey and couldn't get to anything.

I discovered a lieutenant from the 82nd Pathfinders with a Eureka on his leg; he was shot up. That night, I heard the burp guns shooting at him. I thought they were shooting at me, so I took my knife off my leg, cut my suspension lines, dropped on a limb just under me, broke the limb, and fell about another twelve feet. It seemed I was in the tree an eternity, but probably not too long. That lieutenant was still hung up in the tree the next morning. [He was dead.] I could see the tree-lined road and an apple orchard.

I was carrying six grenades, some blocks of amatol and a detonator, my carbine, a pack, and a gas mask. When I got out of there, I wandered around till almost daylight. I walked up the road and heard a patrol coming down the road, so I jumped facedown in the ditch and ran my face in this stinging nettle. My heart reminded me of the old diesel pump, pumping at the station back home. They marched on by, and I got up and found a thicket of brier bushes where I had a good view of the open field. I stayed there until I got nervous and couldn't stand that. Then I heard some guys talking; they were from the 82nd. It was still night, and I could hear them talking a good distance. I had the cricket.

We moved toward Ste-Mère-Église, and I served with the 82nd for three days. Lt. Edward Mitchell from our unit, and later killed in Normandy, who had jumped with the 502nd as a forward observer, joined with us. The group was led by a lieutenant from the 82nd, and he made me scout one while Lieutenant Mitchell said he would be scout two. We went into Ste-Mère-Église. The Germans had pulled out, but we still had a little skirmish with a few of them. It was about 6 A.M. The French people came out, and we thought we had won the war right there. They gave us wine and sausage. I walked to the corner of the street, and here came two German tanks. The guy hanging from the church was already down. The tanks came down and we scattered.

The tanks were knocked out by men from the 101st with bazookas, but they in turn were killed by enemy machine-gun fire. Sergeant Gammon and the remaining Americans "dug in and then went to a big star-shaped jagged trench that went about a block, which the Germans had dug." They remained there about a day and a half. Gammon did not rejoin his unit until five days after he jumped. His battalion had been dispersed more widely than any other unit and lost all of its artillery.

Thus began the 101st A/B Division's "Rendezvous with Destiny," predicted by Gen. William

9. William Lee was the original commander of the division.

Lee before he had been incapacitated in 1944 and sent home. General Lee, considered the "Father of the Airborne," was the first commander of the division, but during the invasion, he was in the United States recovering from two successive heart attacks. Later in June, he heard the news that many of the men of his division had shouted his name as they jumped from their aircraft.

The 82nd A/B Division experienced the same problems as the 101st during its night drop. In fact, most of the units were incomplete, and many men wound up serving with other battalions or even with the other division. Since this was the largest airdrop the Americans had ever organized up to that time, it was to be expected that some confusion would ensue. Because the paratroopers had more objectives than in past drops, it was not possible that all of them would know what to do if they landed in the wrong zone. During the predawn darkness of June 6, many of the men began to coalesce into improvised units to move against objectives that were not part of their original mission, but were critical to the success of both divisions. The ultimate completion of the mission can be attributed to the ingenuity of field-grade officers who improvised ad hoc formations and went on to fulfill their missions. Regimental and battalion commanders such as Colonels Robert Sink, Howard Johnson, William Turner, Robert Cole, Patrick Cassidy, Steve Chappuis, and Julian Ewell were able to rally the men of the 101st and win the day, although they managed to reassemble only about 2,500 men out of the 6,600 who had dropped before daylight.

CHAPTER 9

The 82nd Airborne Division on June 5–6

The 82nd A/B Division, including only one of its veteran regiments, followed the 101st A/B Division into Normandy. Its airdrop was code-named Boston. By the time it landed, the vast air armada carrying the 101st A/B had fully alerted the Germans. Its Pathfinders had been almost as unsuccessful as those of the 101st. The veteran 505th PIR, which had the critical mission of establishing the link on the east bank of the Merderet, landed first. The other two parachute regiments were supposed to land west of the same river. The 505th PIR had the most accurate drop of the division, which was lucky, since it had one of the most important missions, including capturing the crossings of the Merderet near La Fière and Chef-du-Pont with the help of the 1st Battalion. In the meantime, the 3rd Battalion was to occupy Ste-Mère-Église, and the 2nd Battalion was to secure the northern flank.

The 47th Squadron of the 313th Troop Carrier Command, a veteran unit of Mediterranean operations, was one of the many squadrons carrying elements of the 82nd A/B Division into Normandy. It consisted of twenty-six crews and eighteen aircraft. Among its veterans was twenty-year-old 1st Lt. Allen Braem of Marshfield, Wisconsin.

After we took off, we had to get in position with other groups. We then had to get organized, one troop carrier group after the other, and that was a bit of a hassle for us. Once you are up there, you are busy on the wing of somebody else. I was not a flight leader at the time, only a pilot. There were three aircraft in a V, and even the flight leader is flying on somebody else. Flights of three were flying on the lead flight of three, manned by the squadron commander. We had very tiny blue lights on the top of the wings of the plane, which would guide you in your formation.[1] All you are doing is concentrating on that wing on which you are flying. You could hardly see the plane itself unless the moon was out. When we got over France, we were supposed to drop down to 800 feet to make the drop. When we reached the French coast, we flew through some clouds that were not supposed to be there. It caused us to lose sight of the lights on the plane we were on, and we got scattered so we wouldn't run into each other, so we never dropped as a full squadron.

According to other members of Lieutenant Braem's squadron, the British had sent aircraft to draw the enemy antiaircraft fire away from them. Braem corroborates this fact.

Over the city of Cherbourg, I saw a great big Lancaster bomber sitting in the searchlights, drawing all the fire, and we were not subjected to too much although we did have some.

We did find the drop zone, which was marked by Pathfinder groups. There were lights there and a radio beacon, so we dropped individually on that, and then everybody headed for the deck and flew toward the coast about 100 feet above the ground. After we left the drop zone and made for the shore, we got some ground fire.

Second Lt. Lyle Foutz, a twenty-four-year-old from Colorado, was another veteran of Mediterranean operations who flew with Braem's squadron that night.

We took off from Folkington, and the whole flight must have taken about six hours. When we went into Normandy, we turned off the wingtip lights. The only lights we had were three little blue lights, and you could only see them if you were in the proper position. It took complete concentration; you didn't know where you were going. You paid attention to the airplane you were flying on. Your copilot was the one who was supposed to look around, because the pilot did not have time for anything extra. It was quiet over the drop zone except for small-arms fire. [On the return trip,] when we passed the coast, we could see miles of ships. After returning to England, we were debriefed and we went to sleep.

Second Lt. Paul Cody from Illinois, who joined the 47th Squadron in April 1944, was on his first combat mission. It was the first time he and his fellow crewmen received flak vests to go with their usual helmets and side arms. When he flew past the Channel Islands and approached the coast, he ran into trouble.

1. Sets of three formation lights were on the wings and fuselage. They were dimmed and partially shielded so they could not be seen from all directions. The field order stated: "Navigation lights, formation lights and downward amber recognition lights will be ON to a point four (4) minutes beyond 'FLATBUSH,' at which point navigation lights will be turned OFF and a check will be made to see that all cabin and cockpit lights are extinguished. Downward recognition lights will be turned OFF at 'HOBOKEN' and formation lights will be turned to lowest practicable intensity."

> We got scattered in a cloud base, and I lost my flight leader in there. We had three little balls of light [the blue wing lights], and the thin clouds were just enough to lose sight. I was in the first echelon, Dilks and Stephens were leading the squadron, and we lost them completely. I lost Dilks just before we got into the drop zone, so we went in alone and came out alone. We saw the Pathfinders' markings. They had flares on the drop zone.

T.Sgt. John Birchman from Wisconsin, twenty-eight-year-old crew chief on Lt. Fred Fischer's aircraft, was another Mediterranean veteran. He claims that on the night before the drop, when his aircraft flew over Normandy, he kicked some type of radar out the door before the aircraft returned home.[2] On the evening of June 5, as they prepared for the airdrop, the paratroopers "were just lying under the wings and on the ground before boarding, and we visited. Some of them slept, or tried to; you could hardly talk to them, the way they were worked up. They were all really scared, more so than we were. We were all frightened." After crossing the Channel, the pilot told Birchman to go back and open the door before putting on the red warning light. Some aircraft made the crossing with their doors closed, while others kept them open.

> On the flight in, everybody was nervous and tense, and they hardly spoke; they were just in deep concentration. When it came time for hookup, when the red light went on, everybody hooked up, and then I went up front and stood between the pilot and copilot as I always did.
>
> It was the 82nd we dropped. Each aircraft had a jumpmaster. They were supposed to unload in eleven seconds once the green light went on. I was little, about 107 pounds, and I hung on and pulled in the static lines, two at a time, after the paratroopers were gone. The ack-ack started coming up at us. Once they got out, we would make our turn and let out a sigh of relief. I would go up, stand between the pilot and copilot, and watch the fireworks.
>
> There was one thing about Fred Fischer that always sticks in my mind. He always had in his flight knapsack Milky Way candy bars, and he would give each of us one to eat if we made our turn. My radioman, Merv Chambers, could tell you they came from his ration he saved up, and it would take your mind a little bit off of everything. We flew together all the way through the war on the same plane, *Lady Katy*.

Even the most experienced pilots had some difficulties that night. Although many paratroopers accused the young, inexperienced pilots of cowardice and blamed them for scattering the troopers all over the peninsula, the facts do not support these charges. Although it is true that a large number of the paratroopers were not dropped on their DZs, and some even landed many miles from their objectives, the majority ended up within a five-mile radius of Ste-Mère-Église.[3] Considering the facts that the cloudbanks limited visibility, that in some cases the pilots encountered heavy German flak and had to take evasive action to save their passengers, and that many of the Pathfinders were not in the correct positions or not operating their equipment, the results were acceptable. If the pilots had not done

2. It has not been possible to verify whether John Birchman actually did this or confused this mission with another drop at another time and place.
3. The majority of the paratroopers of the 82nd A/B Division landed within three miles of Ste-Mère-Église, concentrated just to the west of the town, while a large percentage of paratroopers from the 101st A/B Division landed within two miles of Ste-Marie-du-Mont. Many others landed near St.-Martin-de-Varreville.

a relatively good job, the troops would have been scattered even farther, and many more would have been dropped in the Channel or returned to England without jumping.

The 505th PIR had one of the most successful drops, with about 1,000 of its 2,200 men landing in DZ O and many others nearby. The 505th's three battalion teams of Pathfinders, led by Lieutenants James J. Smith, Robert B. Bales, and Michael C. Chester, set up their equipment within ten minutes and had the lights ready shortly after that. The 2nd Battalion, leading the regiment, picked up the Eureka signal fifteen miles out. However, after running into the cloudbank, many of the scattered aircraft were flying at 2,000 feet or higher and were going too fast. As a result, they dropped their troops from too high when they spotted the Pathfinders' T lights. In addition, a slight wind scattered many of the men around the DZ. In the confusion, Lt. Col. Edward Krause spotted a new danger in the form of a flight of C-47s below him as his stick floated down to earth. Maj. Frederick Kellam of the 1st Battalion, the last of the 505th to drop, assembled most of his troops quickly and moved against the bridge over the Merderet at La Fière, but he did not have enough men to move on the crossroads and bridge at Chef-du-Pont at the time. Lieutenant Colonel Krause managed to regroup only 25 percent of the men of his 3rd Battalion before he moved against Ste-Mère-Église.[4] By 4:30 A.M., they occupied the town, but they were far too late to save the American paratroopers who had floated down in the town earlier and for the most part were shot by the German garrison before they reached the ground.

Lt. Col. Benjamin Vandervoort of the 2nd Battalion, the first of the regiment to drop, set up a defensive position on the north flank as planned. At 6:14 A.M., the commander of the 505th, Col. William Ekman, who had had no news from Krause, ordered Vandervoort to capture Ste-Mère-Église. At 9:30 A.M., Ekman countermanded his order when he received news from Krause. Vandervoort turned the 2nd Battalion around again to move on Ste-Mère-Église when the Germans launched a counterattack with armor against the paratroopers holding the town. One of Vandervoort's platoons carried out part of the battalion's original mission by occupying Neuville-au-Plain, less than two miles north of Ste-Mère-Église. Even though they were outnumbered five to one, Vandervoort's men held off an assault from the direction of Montebourg by a German force advancing on Ste-Mère-Église to help other enemy troops trying to recapture the town. The 505th accomplished its mission at Ste-Mère-Église and made it possible for the 4th Infantry Division to link up with the 82nd A/B Division that day.

The accidental drop of paratroopers on the town of Ste-Mère-Église was a D-Day tragedy caused by a series of unfortunate events. A fire broke out in a barn at Ste-Mère-Église, and the townspeople went out to fight it. When they continued to fight the fire well after the curfew hour, part of the German garrison came out to investigate. At approximately the same time, about a dozen aircraft, missing their DZs, dropped elements of the 506th PIR, 101st A/B Division, just east of the town—about two miles too far north and at least a mile short of any of the 101st A/B's drop zones. Half an hour later, the aircraft carrying the mortar squad of Company F's 2nd Platoon, 505th PIR, overflew DZ O, dropping its stick on the town. The men came down within 200 yards of each other, many being shot before they landed or as they touched the ground. One even landed right on the town square, where he was killed. Private First Class Blankenship met his end by landing in the burning barn. Two men got snagged on the church steeple and one of them,

4. Major Kellam was killed and Colonel Krause was wounded on June 6 near the bridge of Manoir, also known as La Fière Manoir, as it was about half a mile from the town of La Fière.

C-47s Hit by Flak

Although most of the C-47s came through unscathed, some of them were hit by flak and plummeted to the ground, where they burned like small, ominous bonfires, according to Allen Langdon. Rumors and rancor spread among the paratroopers, who accused the pilots of cowardice and of wanting to get rid of the troopers as fast as possible so they could make good their escape. Most veterans also became convinced that everyone had been forced to jump regardless of conditions because the pilots had been ordered not to come back with any paratroopers aboard. In fact, at least two aircraft returned to England carrying troopers of the 101st Airborne Division. These pilots did not drop their troopers in the Channel simply to avoid having to explain why they missed the DZ.

More than one aircraft was hit because the pilot stayed on course so the jumpers could get out. S.Sgt. Herman Zeitner and his mortar squad of the 2nd Platoon, Company C, 505th PIR, was on a C-47 that took several hits that knocked all the men off their feet as they stood in the aisle, waiting for the green light to signal their jump. One engine of the plane was knocked out and the para-packs caught fire as the aircraft began to dive. The pilot released the burning cargo and tried to regain altitude. Zeitner led his men out the door as soon as he felt they had reached a safe altitude even though his men had wanted to go earlier. After he jumped, he recalls years later, "My chute popped and my ass hit the ground."

Another aircraft carrying the 1st Squad of Company B, 505th PIR, took three hits, the first of which wounded a few of the men. Eventually half of the stick was injured. The uninjured troopers were not able to clear their way to the door in time to jump before the plane reached the Channel, so the pilot brought the entire stick back to England. All the transports that had carried the 505th PIR returned safely to England, but many other squadrons were not so lucky.

Pvt. John Steele, was taken down by the Germans and imprisoned. Pvt. Kenneth Russell dangled from the steeple for a while, playing dead. Later, he cut himself down and escaped, virtually deaf from the ringing church bells.

PFC Martin Finkelstein, a veteran of the Italian campaign, departed England with Company H, 3rd Battalion of the 505th PIR. In Normandy, the battalion had the key mission of taking Ste-Mère-Église. Because Finkelstein was the radioman and officer guard, he was placed in the number-two position in the aircraft. Unlike the rest of the regiment, his stick did not have a felicitous drop.

> Directly across from the door, lying on the floor, were a bunch of Mae West life preservers; then the bucket seats began, with a row on each side of the plane. I was in the first set, opposite the door. I purposely did this because I felt that if the plane were hit, I could get out the door. I didn't want to die up there. I didn't want to die at all, but I surely didn't want to die in an airplane. That is why I volunteered for radioman and lieutenant guard.
>
> On the trip across the Channel, I sat on the Mae Wests instead of the bucket seats. It was more comfortable. When you went into combat, you had your main chute; your reserve chute, which I had ditched; and your gas mask, which I had taken out of the pouch and filled with socks. We were in

plane number one of a nine-plane formation that carried our three platoons in three V formations. Flying over the Channel, I was looking out the door, and the weather at that point was so-so. All of a sudden, it got quite bright, and the moon came out of the clouds as I was looking down (through the door) into the water, where I saw thousands of white lines. We weren't that high and I could see there were ships—the invasion fleet. What a phenomenal sight!

As we got closer to the mainland, I saw another white line, but this one was vertical. I soon realized it was the breakers on the beach, it was the white foam. Just at this time, everything disappeared. We entered a cloudbank. It was frightening. I didn't think we could have been more than 400 or 500 feet flying in. When everything disappeared, I got up on my knees a little bit, and I was ready to go out this damn door. I could not swear how long it lasted, but I would say we were in that cloudbank five minutes or maybe longer. In those situations, time has little meaning. We finally cleared the cloudbank. I was still looking out the door. The plane to our left and to our rear, opposite the door, just about had his wingtip in our door. I knew we were going to have a midair collision; there was just no way of getting away. At this point, I was just about ready to dive out the door by standing up and hooking up. It seemed to last forever, but it was only seconds, for as soon as our pilot saw what was happening, probably just as the other pilot did, they took what I am assuming was a predetermined maneuver to avert a crash. Our plane started to dive, and the other one began to climb. I saw the wingtip go straight up. We were really diving, and at this point, everything became black, and again I thought sure as hell we were going to crash, when we got the red light. The other men in the plane knew something was wrong. Lieutenant Stone was trying to look out the door from his position without standing up, and when the red light came on, I was yelling to him it was on. The lieutenant was close to the door, and he knew we were too low. You could almost see the treetops. I was right behind him, and everybody behind me was ready to go, and then the green light came on.

At this point, things got really hairy. Lieutenant Stone stood in the door and just braced himself. Everybody was pushing against me, and I was pushing against him. I had my hands on the inside of the door, trying to stop them from pushing us out. We held our position, and I think they finally realized we were too low and the pressure was relieved behind me as our plane started to climb. We had the green light, he was looking out the door, and I was yelling, "Don't jump, we are too low," but he knew that without me saying it. He went and I followed, and I am sure the rest of the stick went.

We were taught to count "one thousand, two thousand, three thousand," and if the chute didn't open, then pull your emergency chute. I didn't have an emergency chute, so counting was out of the question. I just yelled when I went out the door. It wasn't "Geronimo!" When my chute opened, I also hit the ground simultaneously. The first thing that hit me was that Lieutenant Stone did not make it, because I don't think his chute had time to deploy fully. I never knew what happened to him.

We were taught when you hit the ground, to look at the direction of the plane and walk backwards to where the officer would be. I automatically, without giving it a thought, pulled my chute up to me at the same time I looked at the plane. I was out of my harness, pulling my chute together, looking for someone else, but saw nothing at all, just the plane. I thought there were other planes, but I only saw ours. The next thing I saw were two lights, similar to the landing lights of an airplane and coming straight down. First thoughts were that a plane was coming down and would crash right where I was. As I glanced around, I realized I was in an antiglider field; there were poles sticking up all around. I could see what I later learned were hedgerows, which we were not told about before we jumped. I started to run to get away from this crash site, looking up at this plane, but regardless of which way I ran, it kept coming towards me. I turned around and ran the other way. I kept running back and forth, frightened to death, when I finally realized that these goddamn things were not coming down that fast. I stopped and paid attention, and then I realized that they were two flares coming down side by side, and I could just see the little chute above.

I walked back, looking for the others, but I was alone in the field. Eventually there were eleven of us from the aircraft that got together before we were captured. Three of the men had been shot, captured, or wounded. It was a very trying time, for the simple reason that we realized we were nowhere near our drop zone. We didn't believe it at first. I think we felt we were just a little off the beaten path. Finally, we got to the point we were convinced. We later learned we were twenty miles from the drop zone and had landed in the midst of a German battalion or regiment. We only had the ammunition we jumped with. That was quite a bit. Besides my M-1 ammunition—I had four bandoliers of that—I also had ten clips of .45-caliber pistol ammo, my grenades, and the Gammon grenade. After the first ten hours of almost continuous combat, we were kind of running out, and we eventually ran out. That is when we were taken prisoner. We did hold out and fought almost continuously for eighteen hours. At about 6 P.M., we had no ammunition left, and it was either give up or get killed.

Before we were captured, we had killed quite a few of the enemy, knocked out one tank, and disabled another. At one point, about 4 A.M., a command car came down the road. We were lying in a ditch on each side of it. At that time, there were still about ten of us, maybe eleven. The command car stopped up the road in front of us. There were two German officers sitting in the back of the car and a driver in the front. The top was not up. Stu Mulligan was right in front of me and said, "Come on Blackie (they called me Blackie because in Africa I got very dark), let's get these Jerry so-and-sos." I replied, "Come on, Stu, cut it out," and he went. I wasn't going to let him go alone, because he had saved my life at one time, so I went with him. When we got near the command car, Stu took out his trench knife, which we carried in our boot, and I took mine out. Where the driver had gone for so long, I don't know. I was waiting for him to come back and get in the command car, but he didn't. We finally got up behind these two Jerries, Stu grabbed the one on the right, and I got the one on the left. Stu slit his throat. I grabbed him around the mouth and got him in the back; I just couldn't get his throat. Just as they were lying on the ground behind the command car, the driver came out of the woods. We were trying not to fire. At that point, we were trying not to let the enemy know where we were, because there were so many of them around. He saw us and went in the woods yelling in German, and then all hell broke loose in the hedgerows on either side of us. We tried to take the command car but couldn't get the goddamn thing started.

There were still eight of us when we surrendered. (Stu Mulligan was dazed by the explosion of a grenade during a firefight and wandered away from the group during the action.) We stood up with our hands up. There was an awful lot of Jerries around. They were searching us, with one Jerry standing in front of each of us. One guy started searching, and the next thing you know a shot rang out and one of them hit the dust. He was hit. The rest, of course, hit the dirt. They were lying down and looking around, and we were standing there. They must have stayed on the ground a full minute until one guy got up and then another. We are still standing there with our hands behind our heads. They were searching us again when another shot rang out and another Jerry was hit. Just at this time, one of the Germans yelled out, "Look for the knives." [Martin Finkelstein was Jewish and happened to speak Yiddish, which was similar to German.] It dawned on me that it probably had something to do with those two officers Stu and I killed. So when the second shot rang out and everybody hit the dust, we did too, and I yelled out to the guys to get rid of their trench knives. We threw them in the ditch. The Germans never noticed. During the search, they took cigarettes, candy, invasion money, and everything we had. After a few minutes, we were almost ready to be marched away when another shot rang out and I got hit. I was hit in the shin—not badly; it was a grazing shot. When you're hit, it burns. I had been hit before with a piece of phosphorous grenade and I was yelling for all kinds of help. They finally got us together and marched us off.

First Lt. Jack R. Isaacs of the 505th PIR jumped with the 3rd Platoon, Company G, 3rd Battalion. His battalion's mission was to take Ste-Mère-Église, and his regiment had one of the best drops of June 6. Lieutenant Isaacs had been with Company G in Sicily and Italy, so he knew what to expect.

My platoon objective was to seize those foxholes (indicated on aerial photos) on our objective and use them ourselves to defend against the counterattack, which would probably come after we were on the ground. At this point [in England before their final briefings], the actual objective was not known to us by name.

Our equipment consisted of light machine guns, 60-millimeter mortars, BAR, and the new one-piece bazooka. We had some carbines, but having used them in Sicily and Italy, and failing me twice, I was of the opinion that they were not reliable weapons. This was my third combat jump and my twenty-eighth jump.

Company G of the 505th was the lead company in the 3rd Battalion. As the 3rd Platoon leader of the company, I had the left V of three planes—it took nine planes to fly a company. As we approached the coast, we hit a rather dense fog bank, forcing some evasive action on the part of the pilot to avoid running into other planes. I knew my flight of three planes was veering to the left, and I would probably be off the target.

Breaking free of the fog, some three or four miles inland, I saw no other planes. There were a few floating clouds, a goodly amount of German antiaircraft fire, both light machine guns and 20-millimeter and some 88-millimeter I am sure. Whether you looked north or south, east or west, you could see plenty of antiaircraft fire.

The red light came on at approximately the correct time for the drop, and then the green light came on. Knowing I was over land, it was my duty to take the stick of eighteen jumpers out. This I did on receiving the green light. I could see as I approached the ground in the dark that I was coming into a fairly good-size field for Normandy, about 150 by 250 yards. I subsequently learned it was bounded on the east by a blacktop road, on the south by a gravel road, on the west by a country lane, and on the north by a common hedgerow. All of the sides had hedgerows. I could see that there were cows in the field as I came down. That was reassuring, because if there were cows in the field, there would be no mines.

I got out of my equipment and set out to roll up the stick and find my men or any men I could, and take command of them, then move on my objective. I found one man immediately. I didn't know him, but this indicated that there were probably other planes in the area; I just didn't see them. Shortly after finding this man, we heard the sound of an approaching motor vehicle, and I didn't know at that time that the field was bounded on the east by a blacktop road. We immediately set out for the sound of the vehicle, knowing it would be German and that we should ambush it. The vehicle was speedier than we were, and it had passed us before we could get there. We did take up a position in case another vehicle came along, since we determined it was a road, which carried quite a bit of traffic. We didn't spend more than five or ten minutes in this position, and nothing else came along.

I then set about gathering up what men I could. It was then that I began to hear the sound of a cricket. Following the sound, I came upon a man who was badly injured. The Germans had staked out the large fields in Normandy to prevent glider landings, and they set the poles in the ground about ten to twelve feet high, and I am sure they sharpened them. This man landed on one of those poles and broke his leg midway between the knee and hip. He had a severe fracture of the thigh and was in great pain. He was effectively out of the fight, and there was no way I could take him with me. Each man carried a first-aid kit that contained morphine. I took his morphine and gave him a shot of it. I took his rifle with the bayonet on it and put it in the ground with his helmet on the butt of the rifle. This was sort of a universal symbol that a man was out of action and did not intend to fight. Then I went on trying to find additional men.

Moving to the north side of the field about an hour after I had landed, I came across another American parachutist whom I did not know. Continuing on along the hedgerow on the north end of the field, I eventually came upon Lt. Patrick B. Ward, who at one time at Forts Benning and Bragg had been in G Company. He was now the S-2 of the 3rd Battalion. He had gathered up a few men, and we combined forces.

We did find two or three equipment bundles and gathered those up. About daylight, we discovered a small house. We gravitated to that house and used it as an assembly point. We were sending out one- and two-man details to see if we could find additional jumpers in the area. Ultimately we gathered up about thirty-five men, the bulk of whom I did not know. From my own platoon, I had Cpl. Quentin Echols of Tulsa, Oklahoma. He had a broken ankle but great determination. He was unable to do anything but hobble along. There was Private Whistler from my company and my own runner, Pvt. Robert Treet. One man I found, who remained with me a long time, was an artilleryman from the 101st.

About dawn, while we were around this small French house, a Frenchman came out

Summary of Operations of 82nd Airborne Division

The following is a summary of the division's operations on June 6 from a report submitted in July 1944 by Gen. Matthew Ridgway, who wrote, "33 days of action without relief, without replacements. Every mission accomplished. No ground gained ever relinquished."

Force A, led by Gen. James Gavin (assistant division commander), with 6,396 parachutists included:

- Pathfinders in 9 C-47s
- Various HQ detachments in 9 C-47s
- 505th PIR, 507th PIR, and 508th PIR each in 117 C-47s (total of 351 aircraft)
- Company B, 307th Airborne Engineer Battalion in 9 C-47s

Force B, led by General Ridgway, included:

- Divisional HQ Company, Division Artillery HQ and
- Signal Battalion in 46 gliders
- 325th Glider Infantry Regiment in 172 gliders
- 319th Glider Field Artillery Battalion in 40 gliders
- 320th Glider Field Artillery Battalion in 54 gliders
- Three batteries of 80th Airborne Anti-Aircraft Battalion in 57 gliders
- Company A, 307 Airborne Engineer Battalion, in 10 gliders
- 307th Medical Company, 82nd Recon Platoon, and other support in 49 gliders

Force C, led by Gen. George Howell (commander of the 2nd Airborne Infantry Brigade), included the remaining elements of the division and attached units arriving by sea beginning on D+2.

Parachute units dropped between 1:00 A.M. and 3:15 A.M. All parachutists landed by 3:12 A.M.

The 505th PIR and attachments were to land east of the Merderet River about 1,000 yards northwest of Ste-Mère-Église. The 505th PIR landed generally in the vicinity of its drop zone. The 3rd Battalion entered Ste-Mère-Église at 4:00 A.M. and secured the town in an hour. The 2nd Battalion joined in the defense of the town, and the 1st Battalion moved against the bridge at La Fière at 6:30 A.M. and secured the east side by 8:30, but enemy fire covered the western approaches.

The 507th PIR was to land west of the Merderet River about 1,000 yards north of Amfreville. However, the unit was scattered between Montebourg and Carentan and east of the Merderet. By 3:12 A.M., the entire regiment was on ground, mostly east of the Merderet River and was fairly dispersed. Small groups assembled to form small task forces until the regiment could assemble. One of these forces on the west bank attacked Amfreville, but it was forced back to Flaux by an overwhelmingly superior enemy. A patrol sent to the western end of the La Fière Bridge made contact with elements of the 505th PIR on the eastern end at 2:30 P.M. However, the enemy recaptured Flaux, driving this patrol from the western end of the La Fière Bridge. Another element of the regiment joined with Force A HQ at 11:30 A.M. and attacked to secure the Chef-du-Pont Bridge, meeting severe resistance. The eastern end of the bridge was secured by nightfall.

The 508th PIR and the HQ units were supposed to land west of Merderet about 1,000 yards north of Picauville. Unfortunately,

continued

Summary of Operations of 82nd Airborne Division ***continued***

it was scattered and most of its parachutists dropped east of the DZ while some landed not so far to the north. It managed to reassemble in four separate groups. One was in the vicinity of La Fière, where it fought along the railway and attacked the La Fière Bridge. Two other joined forces west of the Merderet River in the vicinity of Picauville after taking part in heavy fighting around Gueteveille and north of Picauville. An officer of one of these groups shot and killed the commanding general of the German 91st Division. The combined group next seized the high ground west of the Merderet River during the night of June 6–7. The fourth group, which dropped in the vicinity of Ste-Mère-Église, fought with the 507th PIR to take Chef-du-Pont Bridge and later organized a defensive position covering the bridge.

MISSION DETROIT

Its 52 gliders, carrying the batteries of the 80th Airborne Anti-Aircraft Battalion and other detachments, began landing at 4:04 A.M. Because of fog and flak, the gliders were scattered and many were damaged when they crashed into small fields and high hedgerows.

MISSION ELMIRA

Its 100 gliders, carrying artillery, engineers, and special troops, as well as a company of the 325th Glider Infantry Regiment, began landing at 9:10 P.M. A company of the 746th Tank Battalion began landing at 2:00 P.M. at Utah Beach and moved inland at 4:00 P.M.

MISSIONS GALVESTON AND HACKENSACK

At 7:00 (Galveston) and 9:00 A.M. (Hackensack) on June 7, these missions brought in the remaining elements of Force B, including the 325th Glider Infantry Regiment.

MISSION FREEPORT

This resupply airdrop took place between 6:11 and 6:29 A.M.

Source: Robert Anzuoni, *"I'm the 82nd Airborne Division!"*

of his house and was surprised to find his barnyard occupied by Americans, who certainly had not been there the night before. There was a great deal of consternation on his face and I am sure alarm at what our intentions were. We subsequently learned his wife was in the house with his daughter of ten or twelve years of age. At this point, our French phrases, which we had studied, would have come in handy, but neither Ward nor I could remember a single one of them. So with sign language and a great deal of pointing and looking at the map, with the help of the Frenchman we found out we were about six miles north of Ste-Mère-Église. So then our objective became one of getting organized and moving towards the town.

Lieutenant Isaacs's exact location was somewhere near DZ O, northwest of Ste-Mère-Église. Allen Langdon's history of the 505th places them within sight of Montebourg, but Isaacs could not have been far from LZ O (adjacent to DZ O) because one of the gliders from Mission Detroit landed at his location shortly after 4 A.M.

The gliders started coming in. One of them chose this field I had landed in to make his landing. With unerring accuracy, he hit one

This glider has fallen victim to obstacles placed in an open field by the Germans.

of those antiglider poles, demolishing the glider of course, and his load, which was a jeep and some other equipment, and injuring every member of the glider. So these people, rather than being reinforcements to my little group of thirty-five, became a liability to us. Shortly after this, we managed to get the wounded glider men to the little French farmhouse. Shortly thereafter, we noticed a German soldier step out onto the field over on the east side and approach the injured man we had left there. He came over to him, looked him over, and then shot him. Of course, this infuriated all our jumpers, and he did not survive the trip back to the hedgerow.

About 7 A.M., the Frenchman through sign language indicated he was going to a large farmhouse. It was only a few yards from where I had landed, but I had not seen it in the dark. It was about fifty yards south of us. The Frenchman indicated that he was going and did. I was not particularly alarmed, because he left his wife and child in his farmhouse. When he did not return, I picked Private Voges from my company and another man and went down there on a recon. We moved along a small lane on the west side of the field, and on the way, I discovered our supply sergeant in a ditch. (He served with the service company to keep our company supplied.) I directed him back to where I left Lieutenant Ward and the others.

We made a T intersection and turned east along the gravel road. Private Voges was about five yards behind me, and the other man about ten. We were nearing the French house when Private Voges threw a pebble to get my attention. When I turned towards him, he frantically motioned me over to the other side of the road. He pointed to the farmhouse. The Frenchman was standing there talking to some German officers, and there were about thirty-five or forty ranks standing about in the farmyard. From my experience in Italy, I concluded this was a battalion headquarters.

Lieutenant Isaacs intended to return to his group and attack the headquarters. He had two light machine guns, one BAR, and one 60-millimeter mortar. Before he could move back, however, he was discovered by a German, and his small group fled back to the others. Within a few minutes, he and Lieutenant Ward prepared to attack the German position, which was only about 100 yards away. But before they could do so, a group of about twenty-five Germans approached and opened fire. The only escape route was to the west. Isaacs's group tried to fight off the enemy. Private Treet was killed following him across the road. After taking several casualties, the two lieutenants decided to make a retreat to the west. Isaacs stayed with the rear guard. When he caught up with the group, he was told Lieutenant Ward had been captured. Private Voges became separated from the group and somehow made it back to the battalion.

> This firefight had lasted perhaps three or four hours. Not being pressed by the Germans at this time from any direction, I decided to set up a perimeter defense. We had moved about eight or nine fields west, or about 1,000 yards, and we had a little elevation. Looking back towards the east, we discovered a rather sizable column of German foot soldiers moving towards us. As I put my glasses on them, it appeared that they might be up to 250. It was too big a force for us to attack. We prepared to defend ourselves. As the Germans got within 500 yards of us, they took another lane, went in a different direction, and bypassed us. We had no further contact with them.
>
> I made a personal recon and found another field I thought better suited for defense. I moved the group there. We set up a perimeter with the remaining force of about twenty men. The casualties during the retreat were lost and became POWs. Sometime well after dark, I was awakened by the sound of enemy armor. I knew that we were within yards of enemy tanks, and immediately looking to the road on which we were positioned, I saw an enemy column moving up. They were not in combat formation, but in a close-march formation with supply vehicles, half-tracks, and thin-skinned vehicles. My immediate intention was to use our weapons and grenades to block each end of that road by knocking out a vehicle, and then to attack the jammed-up vehicles in the defile. It was a perfect ambush spot. We had Gammon grenades to knock out the armor. I set out to organize this with what men I had and discovered that I had no men other than the artilleryman from the 101st and Corporal Echols. I was quite surprised. I had posted guards on the perimeter before I took a rest. I learned from the two men still with me that the others had decided—with some encouragement from two other men—that I did not have the foggiest idea as to what I was doing, and that I would get them killed or captured. They had deserted. I subsequently learned that all these men were captured.
>
> With only three men, there was nothing I could do about the enemy column but watch silently as it passed by. The next morning, we observed a German *Nebelwerfer* battery move into position and go into action, firing several volleys before loading up and moving away because of counter-battery fire.

Several days later, Lieutenant Isaacs was put in command of Company G when the regiment took St.-Sauveur–Le-Viscomte on June 16.

PFC Joseph Bean from Pine Bluff, Arkansas, a twenty-seven-year-old veteran of the Mediterranean campaign, was in Company G, 3rd Battalion of the 505th PIR. His drop, like many others, was off target: "Our plane missed the target by a few miles, so after jumping, we had to hike the distance back to the town, cutting lines of communications as we went. By the time we got to Ste-Mère-Église, many had been killed or wounded. The battle was still raging when we arrived, so we dug in and continued to fight."

PFC Raymond Gonzalez of Detroit joined the 505th PIR in England. He was with the 2nd Platoon, Company C, 1st Battalion, at the time his aircraft approached the coast of Normandy.

> We picked up speed going up, and then the plane dipped down and we were standing. The green light came on to jump. My lieutenant, 2nd Lt. Richard Harold Brownlee, wouldn't go, and I was the second man, so I said, "Lieutenant, the light's on," and finally he took off and we jumped. It seemed like the chute opened and I hit the ground. I didn't have time to set myself to hit the ground. I hit something, but I think when I landed I hit on my knee and chest. I lay on the ground for maybe fifteen or twenty minutes; I could hardly get my breath. Finally I checked around and found nothing was broken, so I unhooked my chute. I saw some hedgerow maybe 100 feet from me. I crawled over there and lay down and tried to get my breath. I looked to see if any other troopers were around. Then I noticed two chutes coming down and they landed right close to me, maybe 100 feet from me. They were supply chutes, so I decided to go over there. The lights were still on the supply chutes, and I figured if I left them on, the Germans were going to come over. I crawled up to the chutes and tried to turn them off.
>
> After about fifteen minutes, I heard a couple of guys coming down the hedgerow. I joined them and we went to a farmhouse and found a couple more troops. As we went on down the road, we picked up a few more, until there were about sixteen troopers altogether. One of the officers decided we should go to a roadblock close to Chef-du-Pont. By the time we got there, it was early in the morning. While we were sitting there I was talking to a trooper from another company. As I was talking to him, he got hit in the head with a bullet, and I didn't know he was hit. He was talking to me before, and since he wouldn't answer my questions, I turned around and this gray matter was coming down his head, and I knew there was a sniper around. I got on my stomach, crawled away, and joined some other fellows.
>
> About two hours later, I saw my captain coming down the road with some men from the company, and he gathered us all up. We didn't have a full company, and we were all disoriented. My captain told me we had to knock out a roadblock at a farmhouse. We took positions and tried to charge the farmhouse. My captain, Stanley Stefanich [Anthony Stefanich, killed in Holland], got hit a couple of times, and a couple of other boys got hit. We stayed there until we finally knocked the Germans out and took that position. When we took that position, we established a roadblock there.

Lieutenant Brownlee was injured on the jump and was left with about twenty others in a farmhouse north of Bandienville—a few miles north of Ste-Mère-Église—where Major McIlvoy's Regimental Medical Team set up an aid station and marked it with Red Cross flags. Two days later, the troops of the 4th Division came to their rescue.

PFC Allen Langdon, a draftee from California who was in Company C, 1st Battalion, 505th PIR, was in an aircraft with Platoon Sgt. Herman Zeitner and mortar squad leader Sgt. Elmo E. Bell. On board with them were a few men from battalion headquarters, mostly medics.

> Most of us slept or smoked quietly on the long three- to four-hour ride. I thought of my home and family, recited the Lord's Prayer and the 23rd Psalm to myself, and felt resigned to whatever would come, knowing that it was out of my hands anyhow, and dozed off. Something aroused my attention,

perhaps a slight throttling back of the engines, and I looked out of the window just as we came over the coastline, and there in the bright moonlight, through scattered clouds, was my first glimpse of France. It was so quiet and serene it was hard to believe that it was German-occupied territory. Shortly thereafter we got the red light, the signal to stand up, hook up our static lines, and check our parachutes. About this time we heard the first antiaircraft fire, but it seemed so far away and innocuous that I'm sure no one thought too much about it. We had been standing for several minutes, ready to jump, when all hell seemed to break loose. Antiaircraft fire had hit our plane, causing the starboard engine to quit and setting our equipment bundles, beneath the plane, on fire. Our heavily loaded plane immediately began to fall, and we, of course, all fell in a tangle in the aisle. I managed to crawl up onto the seat, and as I lay there, I thought to myself, we're going to hit the ground in a moment, and I'm going to die.

During this time, our skillful and busy pilot had managed to salvo our bundles and had gotten the stopped motor running again—although it was running so rough it felt like it would shake the plane apart. As he righted the plane, everyone got to their feet and began screaming to Zeitner to jump. He later said that at this time, we were barely clearing the hedgerows, and had we jumped, we would have all been killed. He remained braced in the doorway until he felt that we had gained sufficient altitude, and out he went with the rest of us right behind. I'm sure we set a new record for emptying a plane that night. What at the time seemed to take many minutes probably took less time than it takes to tell. I guess we were hit by the fire in the vicinity of Amfreville. The antiaircraft fire must have disrupted our whole serial, and strangely enough, our planeload landed quite near the area where most of our company had jumped just moments before. As near as I can figure we landed somewhere just south of Beuzeville au Plain and overshot our drop zone by two or three miles.

As I went out the door, I knew from the prop blast that I was really in for a jolt, and I wasn't disappointed. The opening shock actually made things go a little gray for me and I knew that my parachute must have blown some panels, so I first looked up at it, saw some section ripped but not enough to cause me any problems, looked down at the ground, and hit at that moment. I judged that we jumped at not much over 200 feet, our normal jumping height being 600 feet. I landed in a pasture all by myself, not far from the hedgerow, and immediately, without unbuckling my parachute, ran over and crouched in the shadow of the hedgerow. Expecting the worst, I carried a small pistol that I had liberated in Italy strapped to one of my boots, and as I crouched there, I got it out, expecting to be attacked at any moment. When everything remained quiet, the greatest feeling of exultation came over me, and I thought to myself, "I'm alive and I'm in France." I then got out of my parachute harness, assembled and loaded my rifle, hooked my pack on properly, and was ready for business. About this time, I began feeling a little lonely, so I looked up at the planes still going over (this is how we determined direction) in order to rendezvous with my buddies. All of this, time antiaircraft guns had been firing from the direction of Beuzeville, and just as I looked up, I could see shells going into one of the planes, and suddenly, in a tremendous flash, it just disappeared. I could see about six parachutes in the air, and most certainly the ones still in the plane were killed instantly. Apparently their bundle of land mines was hit.

I started down the hedgerow in the shadow, and I had just gone through an opening into the next field, when I was challenged. I immediately recognized PFC Lyle Kohler, who had jumped just ahead of me. He had landed in the hedgerow, broken his knee, and was still hung up there in his harness. I helped him out of it, and as he could still hobble, on we went. We soon contacted other members of our squad and Sergeant Zeitner. One of them had run into someone else who knew where the company was assembling—in a farmhouse about a half mile away—so we made our way there, and sure there was about half of our company, although the only officers that I can recall were Captain Stefanich and Lieutenants Gerald Johnson, Richard Brownlee, and Stephen Waseka. Brownlee and Waseka had both broken their legs on the jump.

Our battalion's objective was the bridge across the Merderet River at La Fière, and since we had missed our drop zone by so much and had a long ways to go, we soon started out without waiting for the rest of the company. In the maze of roads in that area, we were soon lost, and the captain sent another fellow and me, since we could each speak a little French, over to a large farmhouse to get directions. It was completely dark, and not knowing whether it was occupied by Germans or not, we knocked on what seemed to be the main door and jumped back in the shadow with our guns ready. The door was opened a crack, and a very French voice asked, "Who is it?" We explained who we were. Inside, as I recall, were five people all dressed and awake. When we asked directions to La Fière, one young fellow about our age offered to show us the way. He took us to the crossroad on the main highway just south of Neuville au Plain and I believe left us there after telling us to continue straight along that road to La Fière. While we were stopped there at the crossroad for a moment (it was just starting to get a little light), we saw a German army truck speeding towards us. Everyone scattered for cover, and as the truck came up to us someone cut loose at it with a BAR, and it piled up in the ditch at the southwest corner. Someone else threw a Gammon grenade at it, blowing the whole side in, and it seemed to be filled with radio equipment of some kind. The two German soldiers that had been driving it were wounded, and one of our medics patched them up a bit, and the last I saw of them, they were lying in the ditch.

We were soon on our way again and came to the railroad crossing and on to La Fière. By this time, we were running into quite a few other troopers from various units and had collected quite a force; however, we were still short of equipment, as most of our bundles had been lost. As we got a little past the small farmhouse that was just north of the bridge and on the river side of the road, we came under machine-gun fire, apparently from the Manoir buildings.[5] Captain Stefanich told me and another fellow named Joseph Fitt (killed a couple days later) to follow him, and we would see if we couldn't outflank the machine gun from the upper road. We followed a hedgerow up to the upper road, and I was following the captain down the ditch toward the Manoir buildings when Fitt, who had been following me, walked across the road as if he owned it, without drawing a shot, and through a little lane into the field beyond. He had no sooner disappeared from sight when he started fir-

5. Referring to the buildings at La Fière Manoir, where the bridge on the Merderet was located.

ing his BAR at full automatic. The captain stopped and I told him that I had better give Fitt a hand, and without thinking, I started back across the road at a run.

Just about the time I got to the center of the road, a machine gun opened up on me from the direction of the Manoir, and I felt a light blow on my shoulder. I turned and dove back into the ditch and was just congratulating myself on a near miss—I thought it had just grazed my shoulder—when I started coughing up blood and felt blood running down my chest. The captain came back to me, gave me a shot of morphine, and tried to put a compress on my shoulder to stop the bleeding. As it was a difficult place to bandage, he told me to stay put and he would send up a medic. I was having difficulty breathing, and the coughing was making me bleed quite badly, and as I lay there, for the second time that morning I wondered if I was going to die. After a while, a medic came crawling up to me, patched me up, and we both crawled back to the cover of the hedgerow and made our way back down to the lower road. We really did crawl, because by that time, the Germans were really blistering the road and hedgerow. I never did find out what Fitt saw in that field or what happened to him there.

They had set up an aid station in the small farmhouse I mentioned before, and after some further bandaging and another shot of morphine, they laid me in the barn part of the house in some straw. I was quite drowsy, due to the morphine, but I clearly remember some of my buddies coming in to see me before they went on. Sometime in the afternoon, the Germans started shelling the house from across the river, and two of the medics came running in, threw me into a GI blanket, and with each one holding one end of the blanket, down the road they went with me bumping along at every stop. I am indebted to several individuals for incidents that undoubtedly saved my life on several occasions, and these two medics are two of them. I distinctly remember telling them to put me down—that I could walk. They carried me about 300 or 400 yards down the road to a place that had been scooped out above the road to catch water, and there we stayed for two days and nights. On the third night, a stretcher jeep evacuated me, and when I awoke in the morning, I was in a large kitchen of a farmhouse. I was lying next to a friend of mine, Robert H. Fridley, who had been hit in the throat with a piece of shrapnel, narrowly missing his jugular vein. Apparently this place was used as a collecting station, because that day a GI truck, which was fixed to take stretchers, took us down to the beach, where we were put on an English hospital ship.

The 507th and 508th PIRs had the worst of all the drops of that night as many of their men landed east of their DZs in the flooded areas of the Merderet and ended up serving with the 505th PIR or the regiments of the 101st A/B Division for several days.

A number of men from the 504th PIR volunteered to jump with their division, the 82nd A/B, since their regiment had only arrived late in April 1944, after being engaged on the front at Anzio, and was not ready to make a combat jump. Among those who volunteered to jump were Bernard Shipton, John Dickinson, and David Dalton. Shipton and Dickinson went in with the Pathfinder teams of the 82nd A/B; Dalton was killed during the operation.

The 508th PIR had the mission of securing a defensive position on the west side of the Merderet. German troops in the area prevented the Pathfinders from successfully carrying out their mission, however, resulting in the regiment's paratroopers being scattered. Several sticks landed close to Utah Beach, but most of the others scat-

The 81st Airborne Anti-Aircraft Battalion in Normandy

Maj. X. B. Cox's 81st Airborne AA Battalion, 101st Airborne Division, included six companies that were split up for the Normandy landings.[6] Anti-Tank Batteries A and B, originally scheduled to use British Horsa gliders, were placed on CG-4As. The loading schedule was quickly revised. Each battery, with eight 57-millimeter guns, had twenty-two CG-4A gliders and one Horsa. The CG-4As were to land with the first lift, and the two Horsas would arrive on the evening of D-Day. The batteries departed from Aldermaston Airfield at about 1:18 A.M., and the first glider was in Normandy by 3:58 A.M. Because the landings were scattered, it took until the afternoon before both batteries were fully functioning. Battery A was assigned to a parachute regiment, and Battery B to the 327th Glider Regiment. Battery A, with its 57-millimeter guns (British 6-pounders), was the first to claim the destruction of enemy armor, including three German tanks southeast of Carentan during the first days of action.

Anti-Aircraft Batteries D, E, and F, each with twelve .50-caliber antiaircraft machine guns, were assigned to land with the amphibious troops on Utah Beach. They arrived at H+15 minutes with the 8th Infantry Regiment in twenty-nine landing craft. Within one hour, sixteen guns were in action, and by 1 P.M., thirty guns of the batteries defended the beachhead. These batteries, which were commanded by Capt. Robert Jackson, remained attached to the VII Corps until June 11, 1944. During the week of defending the beaches, they shot down one FW-190 and one ME-109. They also shot down one American P-51 on D+3. That aircraft narrowly missed a hospital tent when it crashed, and its pilot survived.

There were not enough gliders available for AT Battery C, so it also went by sea. It landed at 4 P.M. and went into division reserve until June 9, when the battalion headquarters under Major Cox went into operation. The headquarters with the medical detachment sailed on the *Robert E. Perry* and were scheduled to land on D+1 on Uncle Red but were mistakenly taken to Omaha Beach. They stayed there until D+2, and then moved to Utah Beach on D+3. After setting up their headquarters, it took a few days to contact all the dispersed units.

6. Major Cox took command of the battalion in March 1944 but did not receive his promotion to lieutenant colonel until July.

tered between St.-Sauveur-le-Vicomte and Ste-Marie-du-Mont.

Sgt. Delbert Z. Schlemmer was the forward observer for the 81-millimeter Mortar Platoon of HQ Company, 2nd Battalion, 508th PIR.

> On June 6, 1944, 0001 hours in British time, we were approaching the English Channel with no door on the plane and the prop wash created a nice cool feeling. There were eighteen troopers in my stick. Lieutenant Halbertson, one of our officers, led them in, and I being the sergeant and second in command jumped last in the stick. As we reached the Channel, it was getting dark, with wave patterns distinguishable, and it seemed that as we hit the Channel, the mood changed from the shattering bravado, and the scene became very quiet, and all of us were very pensive. The only lights that I saw were several glows of cigarettes. From where I was, next to the cockpit bulkhead,

by standing I could see through the cockpit windshield, and I could see the blue and white tips of the formations ahead of us in our serial. After flying over the dark waters of the Channel for some time, and then a left bank, I saw two small blackened islands appearing off our left wing (the Channel Islands). Soon thereafter, our plane crossed the French seacoast, and it seemed we could see the roads, fields, the small houses which stood out in a reddish brown color. We then hooked up our parachutes to our static lines and prepared our equipment to be prepared to jump should any problems arise. The red light came on.

Then suddenly, without any warning at all, our plane was engulfed in the middle of a cloud or a dense white fog, and we were concerned because all we could see outside the plane was white. You could not even see the blue wing lights at the end of our plane's wing.[7] This caused the pilots of the planes of our wing to disperse to avoid a midair collision with other planes of the formation. Suddenly the cloud cleared as rapidly as it had engulfed us. At that time, we experienced the German flak and small-arms fire, which, when it hit the plane, sounded like gravel hitting a metal roof. It was quite an unmistakable sound. Our equipment check proceeded; we then closed the stick up for exit and waited for the green light. During this time, I had time for personal thoughts. The first was to get the hell out of the plane as rapidly as possible, since I was the last one to jump.

A trooper can anticipate the green light. The pilot will throttle back the plane to jumping speed and raise the tail of the plane slightly. Not this night; the green jump light flashed on, and out the door went the stick in a very well-rehearsed sequence. The opening shock of my parachute was quite violent, but very much a welcome feeling. My helmet jarred forward over my face to the extent that I had to push it back in order to see. The sky seemed alive with pink, orange, and red tracer bullets, which would arc up gracefully and then snap by with little tugs as they went through the parachute canopy. I kept wondering what ratio the tracer bullets were to the ordinary bullets. In the distance to the east, the direction the planes were flying, I could see a sizable fire burning the ground. This must have been Ste-Mère-Église, although I did not know it at the time.

We had jumped extremely low to minimize the time we had in the air, and I hit in a Norman apple orchard and came up with very sore bruised ribs from the impact with all the equipment I had strapped to my body. I cleared my chute harness quickly and assembled my rifle and tucked my little revolver away. The moon at that time was behind broken clouds, and the tracer bullets on the glowing clouds created a reddish sky against which I could see. The flak and small arms at the time had been switched to the next flight serial which was coming across. I could not discern any sign of life either in the field or the little house. Down the lane and in a westerly direction were a group of buildings, obviously a German stronghold.

There was no possibility of recovering the para-pack bundles. I later learned that Lt. Albert Smith, who was our jumpmaster, had been immediately captured and taken prisoner and subsequently killed during an American fighter plane strafing attack. At that moment, as I went from the field out through the lane, a very large orange ball of

7. Schlemmer was one of the few paratroopers who were in a position of the aircraft where they could verify the problems the pilots faced when the cloudbank concealed the dim wing lights, forcing them to disperse the aircraft to avoid collisions.

> fire appeared overhead, coming in a steeply descending easterly line of flight. It looked very much like a meteor, but it was accompanied by the roaring whine of two runaway full-power plane engines, obviously a troop carrier going down. My immediate thoughts were of the troopers and of the crew still aboard. Later on D-Day in daylight, I saw the burned-out hulk of a C-47 in the Merderet River marshes. Whether this was the burning C-47 I have never been able to ascertain.

Sergeant Schlemmer did not know he had landed in an area occupied by the German 91st Air Landing Division, and he was surprised at the size of the hedgerows, which he had been told were supposed to be similar to those in England. Most shocking, however, was the fact that there had been no indication of the flooded valleys during the briefings and on the models. When Schlemmer landed, he was alone and lost.

> I was unable to assemble with my stick due to the German-occupied farm building directly in my path. So I quickly laid my antitank mine in one of the tracks on the lane and covered it over with brush and pulled off the ring clip device arming the land mine, and I headed across the large pasture in a southerly direction in order to flank the occupied farm stronghold. Near the far hedge of the next field, I came across a sergeant from the 101st Airborne Division who was just as bewildered as I was as to where we were. Both of us were far from where we should have been. We then heard small-arms firing from the southeast and decided that meant there were others of us nearby. We headed that way.
>
> We suddenly came across an east-west lane or road. In the ditch alongside this road, we found parallel wires along the route. It was obviously military communications, so we clipped the wire and rolled up about 100 feet of it and clipped it again, and threw the cut piece of wire over a hedgerow to keep it from being used again. Just ahead, the road came to a little turn, which led into a causeway over the flooded marsh with a large house back in a group of trees where the firing was originating from. It was obviously another German stronghold. So we continued easterly on the causeway until we came to a small masonry bridge, some darkened houses along the road, and finally an intersection railroad track. I knew that the only railroad village in the area was a town called Chef-du-Pont. The bridge, the railroad, and the town were all on our model sand table. That meant that I had landed some one and a half miles southeast of our designated drop zone, which wasn't bad compared to others. It also meant that I was on the wrong side of the Merderet River.
>
> With this orientation, the sergeant from the 101st decided to continue southeast towards his division's operation area. I then knew I was on the wrong side of the river, so I doubled back over the small bridge. By that time, there was considerably more German fire coming in my direction from the big house, which was a chateau. So I was forced to detour along another partially flooded roadway, which went in a northerly direction from the main road that I had originally traversed. There was sporadic small-arms fire in all directions, but I was not able to tell whether it was friend or foe, or all intended for me. Just as I reached the edge of the flooded marsh, I heard a glider crash against the tall trees bordering the field somewhat distant from me. We had been told several gliders carrying baby bulldozers would come in before dawn. The sound of hearing this glider hitting the tree was similar to smashing 1,000 matchboxes all at once. I could just visualize the poor glider

pilot with the baby bulldozer behind him. I suddenly found myself cold and shivering; whether it was from the dampness of the marsh, the coldness of the night, or whether I was just plain scared, I don't know.

Shortly after, by using the frog clicker, I came across three other troopers, one of whom had already been wounded, another with a broken leg, and both requiring medical attention. We put them under an overhanging hedgerow on a roadside ditch, and the other trooper came along with me.

At dawn, we left the road and the lane and went to the fields, for we had been instructed that after D-Day morning, we should stay off the roads and out of any houses or buildings, because our artillery would zero in on these. We came across additional troopers who were in the various fields waiting to ambush any Germans using the roads and lanes. Each field tended to become a separate battle ground. Before entering it, we would examine it to clear the hedgerows. If there were any cows, we were certain these fields were not mined. Also, by watching the cows, which by nature are curious, we could tell whether there was anyone else in those fields.

We could tell the sound of the German hobnail boot on the Norman roads from that of the rubber-soled paratroopers' jump boots. So we were able to ambush many patrols merely by the sound they made on the other side of the hedgerow. Also, we were soon able to distinguish between the different rates of fire of the automatic weapons.

By midmorning, more and more troopers—and always the walking wounded-assembled, and we found that we had no mortars, few machine guns, few bazookas, and fewer radios, with little medical supplies other than what the troopers carried.

Finally, a message from our colonel informed us to break it off and assemble on Hill 30, which overlooked the flooded marsh which I had crossed in the dark that morning. We converged on the hill, from which we could theoretically control the two causeways across the Merderet River. However, they were covered with hedgerows and apple orchards. I was assigned an outpost, and I spent most of the following four days and nights at this fighting outpost on the Hill 30 perimeter. This was Colonel Shanley's group.

Directly west of Chef-du-Pont and west of the Merderet River, Hill 30 overlooked the flooded terrain and the river crossing. The defense of Hill 30 by Shanley's 2nd Battalion of the 508th PIR and elements of other units, with a combined strength of about two companies, may have saved the weak and scattered airborne units from being rolled up by German counterattacks. According to Gerard Devlin's *Paratrooper*, Shanley's men beat off several strong assaults, apparently by elements of the 91st Air Landing Division, in the direction of Chef-du-Pont.

The flooded valley of the Douve River was the widest between Beuzeville la Bastille, just to the southwest of Chef-du-Pont on the other side of the valley, and Carentan. This obstacle hampered German efforts to strike back between Carentan and Beuzeville la Bastille and advance on Utah Beach. North and northeast of Carentan, the German 6th Parachute Regiment failed to push back the 506th PIR. In the meantime, elements of the 508th PIR held on to Hill 30, and the 505th PIR hung on near Neuville-au-Plain, blocking German troops advancing from Montebourg in the north. Thus the paratroopers denied the Germans the opportunity to bring large forces to bear against the scattered airborne forces on D-Day and sealed off the advance of amphibious-landed troops from Utah Beach.

Cpl. Jack Schlegel was a nineteen-year-old machine gunner in HQ Company, 3rd Battalion, 508th PIR.

> The trip across was at first full of talk and laughs, but then settled into silence with the occasional passing of the slop bucket. Most of the time, the guys threw up on themselves. It was very tense in the C-47. I talked mostly with Ward, the radio operator of the C-47, since I was practically in his seat.
>
> The first action I saw before jumping was when the plane was hit by flak. I don't remember hearing "Stand up," but I saw everyone getting up, and I remember screaming "24 OK" (there were twenty-four in our stick). The next few moments found me standing alone at the rear of the C-47 and racing to the door as fast as the equipment on me would allow. I exited the plane at about 600 feet. The opening shock was hard due to the heavy load we carried. I remember quite vividly looking up at my chute and seeing the departing C-47 explode in a fiery flash (it must have sustained a direct hit). The next moment, I hit the ground and rolled over. I landed in a large field, and the next object to approach me was a large cow. Had it been a German, I would have been dead, since I was still tangled up in my chute and equipment.
>
> I landed in a large cow pasture at approximately 1:25 A.M. The first trooper I contacted was my assistant gunner, Leonard Sacharoff, and within ten minutes, we had more than ten troopers with us. A firefight shortly after that dispersed us all.

During the first minutes after landing and skirmishing with the enemy, Lieutenant Bodack's words at the briefing rang in Schlegel's mind: Only one out of four of them would survive the first few days, and they wouldn't "have time for prisoners." The men of his company were dropped in the wrong place, but they fought with such fierceness that the Germans nicknamed them "Red Devils."

> The first house we hit was a farmhouse where I saw a light. I pounded on the door and when it opened slightly, I said in my best army booklet French, "Je suis American paratrooper, où est la Ste-Mère-Église?" We stayed five minutes, had a bottle of wine, and between hand signs and French-English-German, got the directions to Ste-Mère-Église. At this time, I gave my parachute wings to the Frenchwoman. We (about six of us) proceeded along a road with tall hedgerows on either side towards Ste-Mère-Église—we were actually near Picauville.

Corporal Schlegel marched behind his company commander, Lt. Malcolm D. Brannen, whose stick had jumped from another aircraft just as—by some miracle, he thought—the cloud cover had lifted. Brannen's landing was not without mishap, however.

> I landed in a tree. It was difficult to get out of my harness. I took out my knife, which was sharp as a razor, and it still took me a half hour to get out. Every few minutes, I had to stop because I heard people talking, so I finally stopped when I realized they were Germans. I thought, if they see me here, they will kill me before I get out of my parachute, so I took my time and finally got out. Then I went to a road and met some of our engineers and others mixed with them. Before I met them, I looked up into the sky and heard a terrific roar and a boom; one of our planes had been hit, and it was crashing.

Lieutenant Brannen and this small group cut up some wires running along the road in the direction of Picauville. Along the way, Brannen's group grew to about twelve men, as he remembers. According to the official history, however, he had only three men with him. Shortly afterward, they skirmished with the Germans and lost one man. As they continued on their way, they came across an empty command post and proceeded to destroy its radio and telephone equipment, as well as cut the tires of a motorcycle parked nearby.

Eventually Brannen's small party reached a three-story house. Only Lieutenant Brannen, Lieutenant Richards, and one enlisted man approached the dwelling. They knocked on the door and, when someone finally opened, asked for directions. All of a sudden, they heard a car coming down the road. Brannen sent the group for cover behind the house before he went out and raised his hand to stop the car. Suddenly some shots rang out. His men opened up on the vehicle, which crashed into a stone wall. A German major in the front seat was instantly killed. The passenger in the rear was ejected and dropped the pistol in his hand. As he tried to crawl toward his weapon, Brennan shouted, "Halt! Halt! Halt!" The German officer yelled back, "Don't kill! Don't kill!" but continued to reach for his pistol. As he grabbed it, Brennan shot him. Brennan also shot and wounded the driver, a corporal, who was trying to escape, and took him prisoner. He also took the officer's hatband for identification and later discovered that he was a general.

It turned out that Brannen had ambushed and killed the commander of the German 91st Air Landing Division, Gen. Wilhelm Falley. The general had been on his way back to his headquarters near Picauville after the cancellation of the map exercise at the German Seventh Army headquarters. Thus it was that the 91st Air Landing Division lost its commanding officer early in the battle. This single action of the 508th PIR's "Red Devils," even though it came about through a stroke of luck, may have had a major impact on the early moves of one of the most important German divisions responsible for dealing with enemy air landings in the Cotentin.[9] Brennan's group continued its meanderings, but then split up after another skirmish. The German prisoner escaped and Brannen was left with two men. He was separated from these two in a subsequent skirmish and hid until Saturday, June 10, when he encountered troops of the American 90th Division.

Corporal Schlegel's group of four, which was near the same road, ambushed two German motorcyclists who were following General Falley's car. As the four men moved up the road, they came across the general's vehicle and the bodies of the occupants on the ground. They were reaching for a briefcase and package in the backseat, when they heard a group of soldiers approaching and dived for cover. The newcomers turned out to be men from the 505th. Schlegel opened the package and found a huge German flag that had belonged to Falley's headquarters. Shortly after this, the corporal and his comrades ambushed another group of Germans, killed several, and captured a soldier of the German Air Command. "He was my age," Schlegel recalls, "and pleaded not to be shot. He seemed relieved when I spoke to him in German. I always kept the German prisoner next to me and Privates George Donohue and Stephan Fallet."

During his march across the fields, Schlegel, like Brannen, noticed that there were too many Germans in the area. He and his group picked up three German prisoners at a farmhouse. When Schlegel realized that they were in the midst of a

9. After the campaign, Brannen was criticized for not taking the general prisoner. According to other witnesses, however, Brannen and his companions had been instructed not to take prisoners. Brannen claims to have written to General Gavin, and that the general replied that he had done the right thing, because the German general might have shot him, and there wasn't much chance of getting the officer back through the lines.

strong German position, he hid the captured flag in one of the buildings before departing with his comrades.

> At one point, while crossing a field towards a hedgerow, we came under intense small-arms fire from two German positions. Several of our group were hit as we ran to the bank of the hedgerow. We crawled to the top of the hedgerow, which had a growth of small brush on it. At this point, a German weapons carrier with machine guns blazing approached us. The German gun was practically level with the top of the hedge. Bullets cut into our group, hitting several more men. I still remember Donohue, my buddy, yelling, "What are we going to do, Schlegel?" To use the army term, I was scared shitless, and so was everyone else, including our German prisoner. With three dead and others wounded, I told the German kid to stand up and tell his Germans that we surrendered. The kid got up yelling in German and was at once shot in the arm. The armored vehicle drew up to us and took us prisoners.
>
> I heard the Germans yell, "Shoot them! They're paratroopers!" Our German prisoner, bleeding, kept yelling, "Stop, I'm shot, but it was you not them. The American speaks German, and he treated me well."
>
> We were taken and escorted to a farm where about another 150 Allied prisoners were being held. It is hard to believe, but we were never searched. I had my jump knife, other articles, and a Gammon grenade for three days. I got rid of the Gammon grenade at a bridge crossing while on a forced march.

Maj. David Thomas, the regimental surgeon of the 508th PIR, like most of the others in the regiment, took off from England on his first combat jump.

> We took off and headed out over the English Channel. As far as you looked to the rear, all you could see were C-47s. We got no flak until we passed the Channel Islands. We got a little flak at that point, but it didn't amount to much. Shortly thereafter, we did a left flank and went into Normandy. When we turned in to the peninsula, we got into clouds and couldn't see anything. When we got out of the clouds, we could not see another airplane in the sky. We were one little C-47 taking on the whole German Army all by ourselves. On our aircraft, we had the 1st Battalion commander, whom I jumped behind, and troops from HQ Company.
>
> So we came out of the clouds and nobody else was around, and we are looking and looking. Only the first aircraft in the echelon had the equipment to home on the Pathfinders' radar; we didn't. The pilot didn't know where he was either. We had been briefed about the Douve River coming down to meet the Merderet and when we saw this river going that way, I said, "This has got to be the Merderet, and we got to get the hell out of this aircraft." Colonel Harrison said OK, so we jumped. It was just like any other parachute jump; you clear the aircraft and check your canopy, and then look around and see where you are. After I landed, I saw something and I wondered what the hell it was. I went creeping and crawling up to it, and it was a cow. You could hear aircraft all over, but I didn't see any around us.
>
> The first guy I met was Bill Ekman [Lt. Col. William Ekman], and I haven't the faintest idea how he got there. Bill Ekman was the XO in the 508th, and when Jimmy Gavin was promoted to assistant division commander, they moved Bill from the 508th to command the 505th. I had known

him ever since I went into the airborne. We looked and could see his troops jumping on Ste-Mère-Église. Bill said, "Dave, why don't you come with me?" I said I would like to, but I was due down at the bridge at Chef-du-Pont, so I better head that way. He went his way and I went mine.[10]

Out of that stick, I only picked up a couple of people; I don't know where the rest went. I saw the CO later. We headed down towards Chef-du-Pont, since we had landed near a place called La Fière. We were supposed to be closer to Chef-du-Pont, but if we had waited longer, we would have been in the ocean. We fumbled our way in the darkness, and by dawn, I had gotten with a group that was surrounded.

We had maybe sixty people. We were out in the country in the hedgerow. We had this area we were occupying, sort of rounding up the wagons, and we were getting a lot of fire. We had a lot of German prisoners, a couple dozen. We were manning the ditches of the hedgerows. We put the Germans in the middle of us, gave them some entrenching tools, and told them to dig in if they wanted to, and they did. We were surrounded all day long. There was a little farmhouse with a thatched roof, so I used it as my aid station until the Germans shot some incendiaries on the roof and burned the thatch off.

I had very little; only what I had carried on me: a scalpel, a few hemostats, a few bandages, and that kind of thing. We had a soldier that got hit in the knee and the only thing holding the leg on was his patellar tendon. In the ditch, I said, "Son, just bite the bullet." It was the only way I could do it, and I cut off the tendon and we got him out of there. I had a fair number of casualties and no place to go with them. That night, we moved. We had radio contact and moved to a larger group.

The 507th PIR was scattered as widely as the 508th, but a large number of its sticks came down along the flooded valley of the Merderet, between DZ T and DZ O. It suffered a series of setbacks, however, as the diary of Pvt. William D. Bowell—excerpted with the permission of C. Hugart, *507th PIR News*—indicates.[11]

As the C-47s left the ground, we were on our way to make history. The long awaited invasion was taking place. Our "stick" in the plane was silent; it was a moonlit sky with a few spotted clouds here and there. I was a battalion radio operator assigned to a crack demolition team. All around us we would see the dark shapes of other C-47s as they hovered over the field, maneuvering into tight formations. Finally, with all the paratrooper-laden ships in the air, we made our history-making flight across the channel and into France. The silence in the ship was suddenly broken by the German manned ack-ack guns. The flak was heavy, it was bursting all around us, small burning pieces were piercing the fuselage of the plane. Underneath the ship, hanging from the bomb-racks, were six bundles of explosives. A hit there would send us to Eternity and blow the plane into a million small pieces—we were going through clouds. Abruptly the plane seemed to do a back flip, and then it was steady. We seemed to be losing altitude. "Stand up and hook up," every man

10. It appears that Major Thomas actually landed either north or northeast of the Merderet, past the flooded area well beyond his drop zone, DZ N, to the west of the Merderet.

11. The paratroopers were not supposed to take diaries or cameras with them on the Normandy airdrop, as a matter of security in the event they were captured. Several men, including Bowell, ignored this directive.

> rose mechanically, this was the moment for which we had all waited and trained for two years. A funny sick feeling in the pit of my stomach, murmured prayers, "May God be with us!" At that same moment the ship hit another flak area, we received a bad hit and the plane gave another lurch and began to vibrate. Our plane was going down. We were very low to the ground; "Go" the jumpmaster gave the signal. I was the 11th man in the "stick." Number 7 slipped and fell, then 8, the rest of us right down to the last, fell down on our knees. Somehow, we managed to get out the door. We all were weighted down with ammunition and heavy equipment. Some of us crawled out.

T/5 Abelardo Gonzales of the 507th PIR was assigned to Company H, 3rd Battalion, as one of its medics.

> We were supposed to jump at Amferville, but we never got there. I think the objective was some bridges. They didn't tell us about the marshes; we found out about that after we got to Normandy. They didn't drop us anywhere close to our DZ.
>
> I slept most of the time during the flight. It was dark and I could see nothing out the window. When they told us to "stand up and hook up," I woke up after sleeping most of the journey. We hooked up and waited for the green light. The jumpmaster couldn't see anything, and as soon as the pilot gave us the green light, we went out. We never knew if we were in the right area or not. It was like every jump—scary. No problem when I jumped, no enemy fire that I remember. Everything went smoothly.
>
> I landed on a highway; it was more like an alley. I broke my kneecap. Both my knees were swollen, and I thought both were broken. When I joined the rest of the people that jumped with me in the plane, the lieutenant asked if I could walk. I said yes, but I couldn't run or walk very fast. I told him what was wrong with my knees. There were only about ten or fifteen guys, mostly from the same aircraft. I was the only one injured when we landed. The lieutenant, just as soon as it was daylight and we could see, found a house. He went to the house, and since there were no Germans in there, they took me in and told me to stay there by myself. Then some French people brought in Robert McCarroll, who they found injured. He was from my company.
>
> That day about noon, we could see the trucks, tanks, half-tracks, and trucks full with troops. I was watching through a keyhole in the door. All these were heading toward the beachhead, past the front of the house. We were inside the house but were not prisoners. That afternoon the Germans were coming back, they were retreating. They came into the house and took us prisoners. McCarroll had a broken leg, and we had no weapons. We stayed there for two to two and a half days. They never spoke to us and just kept a guard in the front of the house. They did not even search us and caused us no problems. I know that some of the guys that were captured at Larange [?] in a church were killed, and the surgeon was killed there where he set up an aid station. They didn't give us food; they only kept a guard out there. Then the American tanks came, and the Germans just left us that night. When I went to look, there was no guard. They took us on tanks back to Ste-Mère-Église and then to the beachhead for evacuation.

Young PFC Dick Johnson of Rochester, New Hampshire, was in HQ Company of the 1st Battalion, 507th PIR. On his flight to Normandy, he was struck mostly by the beauty of the moonlit night.

> As we flew over, we started getting hit by some ack-ack. When we stood up, we could see there was water down there. Then there was more ack-ack coming up. The pilot must have decided there was too much Ack Ack and started to turn the plane. When they did, our lieutenant said we better get in the door and jump out. I was the only guy that landed on dry land. About fifteen to twenty of us got together.
>
> When I took my chute off, I heard someone holler, "Help!" I ran down the little field, jumped over a hedgerow, and landed in the water. The gas mask gave me buoyancy and helped me get over to the other side. When I got over there, I still heard him hollering for help. I looked up there in the tree and saw one of my fellow paratroopers. I think his name was Jack Cavanaugh. He was just hanging there, about eight feet off the ground. I climbed up the tree and cut his static line, and he dropped to the ground. In the process of trying to get down, he had almost cut his thumb off. It was bleeding quite badly, so we took the sulfur in his first-aid kit, put it on, and bandaged his finger the best we could. We couldn't do anything else, since there was no aid station.

During the day, Johnson's group skirmished with the Germans and eliminated a few machine-gun positions. They decided, however, that it was the better part of valor to shun a confrontation with a large number of German reinforcements charging down one of the roads.

Pvt. Edward Jeziorski, a machine gunner in the 2nd Platoon, Company C, 1st Battalion, 507th PIR, had feared getting airsick and had taken the airsickness pills he had been issued before boarding. The next day, he discovered that some of his pills had dropped inadvertently into his canteen, fouling his water. His aircraft was on the far left of the formation of the first twenty-seven aircraft of the regiment, and the lead of a group of three. He was the number eight man, and his platoon sergeant, Dominic Giacoletti, would jump last. When he looked at his watch on takeoff, it read 11:50 P.M.

> On the way over the Channel, I don't know why, but it slipped my mind about a strict and total blackout, and I lit up a cigarette. Boy, I will tell you, orders came down to "put that damn thing out real fast!"[12]
>
> Flying between the Isles of Jersey and Guernsey, flak started coming up. It just seemed that as soon as we hit landfall, the sky simply lit up with a lot of multicolored antiaircraft fire. This fire was intense and accurate and sounded like heavy hail. Then shortly after, we were in some clouds, and the flak eased off a good bit. But the airplane was bounding up and down and sliding from side to side. It seemed like when the red light came on, it was hard as anything to balance or to even stand up. As a matter of fact, I went down to my knees, and several of the other guys did also. After we had checked equipment, we began coming on down at a fairly good rate of speed, much too fast. As the ship leveled off, the green light came on, and Lieutenant Parks yelled, "Are you ready?" and the answer was "Yes!" And then came "Let's go!" and out the door we went.
>
> Just as I peeled out, very vivid in my mind, it seemed that the whole world lit up

12. According to some men, smoking was allowed on their aircraft, but others said it was forbidden. It is likely that it was forbidden, but apparently many violations took place.

right underneath me, a tremendous ball of fire, and a bunch of black smoke mixed in with the red fire, just a great fireball. I exclaimed to myself, "The bastards are waiting for us!" I tried to slip away from the thing, and tracers were coming up and through the silk. They were coming up in colors and in streams. I can remember them being so close that I actually pulled my legs up as far as I could, my knees into my stomach, to get away from a string of tracers. I slammed into the ground, and I was immediately pinned down by machine gun fire. There was no way to rise up. Every time I tried to turn, the machine gun would open up. I'm sure that's what it was; it couldn't have been *Schmuezzer*, not with that kind of fire coming out of it. At any rate, every time I tried to move, there would be a burst. Apparently I was between the great fireball, which I later found out was a C-47 that had been shot down, and was silhouetted so I couldn't move. I only was able to bring my right leg up close enough to where I could get my jump knife out of my boot. I cut the harness loose and the bellyband off, as well as the reserve. I couldn't get any of the darn hardware loose and couldn't get it to release. We had tied ourselves in so snugly and pulled the straps up so tight that now I couldn't get the bugger unhooked. Finally I did. I cut all the restraints.

In the meantime, this guy is shooting. Every time I make a move, he's letting a burst or two go. When I had cut loose, I rolled over into a little depression. Fortunately, it was deep enough. I had my hand on my rifle, and I was able to squeeze off a couple of rounds from where the fire was coming, and he stopped. I'm sure I didn't hit him, but at any rate, it got his attention. A little bit after that, there was a good deal of thrashing going on over on the other side of the hedgerow from where I was. The sound was as though something or somebody was coming on through the underbrush. I still held my rifle real tight, and I just pointed it at the sound and lay prone. When the sound got very close, I said, "Flash!" and the countersign "Thunder!" came back. It was my assistant gunner, Grover Boyce. There were the two of us together now, and it seemed like a better world all of a sudden. By the next half hour or forty-five minutes, we were joined by Tony Guzzo and the aid man, Andy Manger.

By around 4 A.M., we located a parapack, and believe me, we were fortunate. One of the packs we opened had a machine gun. We got it out and a couple boxes of ammo. We really felt pretty good having that thing in our hands. That was all of us who got together from our stick of eighteen troopers on D-Day. From that point on, there just weren't any more of the 2nd Squad and 2nd Platoon out of Company C that we came across.

According to Jeziorski, his platoon's assigned mission was to occupy a road fork near Le Manoir, while the regimental objective was the high ground west of the Merderet. He was nowhere near that area, however. Instead, he was almost on top of Utah Beach. The supporting fire of the battleships took him by surprise, because he had not been warned about it during his briefings.

At that time, we didn't know the shells coming in were from the battleships. They were mighty big suckers coming over, sounding like freight trains, and then going off in a distant flash and a "whoomph." I had set my gun, and we formed a little defensive position. We didn't know where we were, but we knew we weren't anywhere near where we were supposed to be.

As it turned out, we were in a little community by the name of Hébert, which was very close to the beach on the east side of the peninsula [located between the exits of causeways 1 and 2; they had landed far from their DZ]. I guess, given another five seconds, we'd have been in the water. As I set the machine gun up, and before dawn broke, a Jerry half-track started coming down the road. I had anchored the legs of the machine gun pretty solid down in the ground so the thing wouldn't be bouncing all over and give me a pretty decent field of fire with a degree of accuracy. The darn half-track was coming down the pike, and I was trying to get the gun turned around, but I couldn't do it. In desperation, I pulled out the Gammon grenade that I had, took the cap off, and heaved it. I missed him by a mile, there is no doubt about that, but I know he was scared as hell, because you could hear the thing rev up, and then he was moving down the road in a hurry.

After this little episode, things seemed to be going our way. We heard some firing off in the distance, so I said, "Let's go on over there and see what is taking place." Grover got the tripod, and I put the gun up on my shoulder, and we were heading out for whatever it was. There was a little cluster of houses ahead of us. Some fire came from these houses, so we set the machine gun up and I kicked back, and a German bailed out of the house that was nearest us and raised his hands, and that was it. Dante was trying to interrogate him, and it just looked like the face of the Jerry simply disappeared. From one of the houses, apparently one of his friends just took a pop at him so that we wouldn't get any information. He didn't die instantly, but Andy gave him a good dose of morphine and told us he wasn't going to last much longer; so much for our first prisoner.

We were puzzled as to what could have done so much injury to the Jerry with such a small entry hole on the right side of his face. As we cleared out the village, we found many clips of wooden bullets in the homes which were more rounded at the nose than regular ammo and were colored purple. Apparently our prisoner was shot with one of these.

We went through that little community, and the houses were cleared in a hurry. No one else was left, Germans or civilians. I don't know where they had gone. We found two more troopers from the 101st Airborne, who joined with us. We cut out all wires we found and were getting ready to go ahead and set up some sort of a decent roadblock when somebody yelled, "Here come the Krauts!" A little stone fence or hedge, if you will, was leading on into the end of the town. There was about a squad of Germans that were following the hedge towards us. Guys popped their rifles at them, and they fired back at us. By then I was ready with my light machine gun and turned loose a couple of bursts, and they gave it back with an MG-42. We just traded for a couple of bursts back and forth. I took the Jerry out. There wasn't any noise from him. We moved on after that. As we backed off about 200 yards, here came another group of Germans. All of D-Day, we just moved, moved, and moved; never seemed to get away from activity; it was one firefight after another. We were on the road between two of the causeways for Utah Beach, and the Germans were actively patrolling the thing.

After a day of many skirmishes, none of us in the group were wounded, but I found my best buddy and cut him down where he had been shot in an apple tree where he had gotten entangled. My squad leader, Howarth, who jumped in back of me, was taken prisoner. We lost Giacoletti and the lieutenant.

Pvt. Kenneth Burch of the 1st Battalion, 507th PIR, was accompanied by a friend of his, Sergeant Grey of the 504th PIR, one of many volunteers from that regiment who jumped on D-Day.

I was the company runner, and my immediate job upon landing in Normandy was to find the captain, who jumped from another plane. I did find him within about ten minutes. He had bounced badly and broken an ankle and since there was so much machine-gun and rifle fire nearby, I was sent to find out "What that gunfire is about." As I went, it was becoming early dawn, and I could hear the distant booming of naval fire and see the sky light up.

About that time, I saw General Gavin, alone, carrying an M-1 rifle and wearing no insignia. He stayed with us for a short time and then vanished along there somewhere.

Two other paratroopers and I became pinned down in a mud hole by sniper fire. Looking in an effort to locate which tree the fire was from, the soldier next to me said, "Oh, I'm hit!" and clasped his hand to his chest. As he removed his hand, the slug fell into the palm of his hand; it had hit the mud just in front of him and then him. That was a guide to the particular tree, which all of us fired into, and the sniper fired no more.

Upon returning for the captain, I found he was gone, and I joined the group under my battalion commander moving on Chef-du-Pont. It was a village in the shape of a T, with a fairly large river and a German pillbox at the intersection. As we went into the village, no shots were fired until we were inside the houses on both sides of the road, then the opposition opened up. The only escape was to go into the houses, which we did. Finally the enemy withdrew across the river.

Our captain had managed to get there somehow and had half his face blown off, while the battalion commander was dead.[13] Sniper fire continued as we carefully searched each house. We found one paratrooper who had landed on a slate roof and crashed through and apparently had a German bayonet rammed through him, which pinned him into the floor. He was dead. I removed the bayonet, dragged the body to a window, and lowered him to the ground with his parachute, which was still attached.

We cleared the town, and an officer, a major, wanted a prisoner. A young blond German soldier was brought to him and came to attention before the major. The major, without a word, raised his carbine and shot the German in the belly and walked away. I saw my first of many murders, and so had the German troops just across the river. It became then a no-holds-barred affair. After that, the days became blurred, and I can't remember which action took place first.

The American paratroopers received glider reinforcements at dawn, just as the seaborne invasion began.[14] Lt. Peter P. Triolo, from the 1st Bat-

13. Lt. Col. Edwin Ostberg had advanced with a mixed force to take Chef-du-Pont at about 10 A.M. and led an attempt to rush the bridge. He was one of two officers shot and fell off the bridge into the river, where he was rescued. Lt. Col. Arthur Maloney, commander of the 2nd Battalion, may be the red-headed officer Burch believes replaced Ostberg since he was also at Chef-du-Pont.

14. Mission Chicago, in fifty-two Waco gliders, landed at about 3:45 A.M. at LZ E, with Brigadier General Pratt and 155 men of the 101st A/B Division, sixteen antitank guns, twenty-five vehicles, and a bulldozer. Mission Detroit, in another fifty-two Waco gliders, landed at about 4:10 A.M. with 220 men of the 82nd A/B Division, sixteen antitank guns, and twenty-two jeeps. Each mission carried several tons of ammunition and supplies, according to Alan Wood's *History of the World's Glider Forces*.

talion of the 12th Infantry, 4th Infantry Division, had been assigned as the liaison officer to the 82nd A/B Division and arrived in a CG-4A glider of Mission Detroit early on the morning of D-Day.

Our destination was near Ste-Mère-Église. The plane was to fly toward Ste- Mère-Église. As we hit the mainland, we were flying over at a low altitude, and you could see all these tracers coming up to us and hear this pluck, pluck, pluck. The colonel, who was chief of staff, sitting next to me, informed me that bullets were coming through the canvas of the glider and said, "Why don't you sit on your shovel?" I realized all the people were. He said, "You got to protect your family jewels." So naturally I did the same thing. It was funny to realize somebody was actually shooting at you. When we did land, it was a sad experience. We had no casualties, but because we landed in an area of small trees, the British gliders cracked up and splintered, and the men became casualties with plywood splinters.

I assume we released at about four o'clock, and I believe that made me the first member of the 12th Infantry Regiment to land in Europe. We landed east of Ste-Mère-Église and had to march back. Upon arriving in Ste-Mère-Église at about 4:35 A.M., we set up in an apple orchard just outside the famous church with the paratrooper hanging from the steeple. I was there at daybreak when they took him down.

Around nine or ten in the morning, we received a heavy bombardment in the town. At the time of the bombardment, I found myself in a ditch along the highway with half a dozen other members of the 82nd A/B. After crawling back in forth in the ditch during the barrages, one of the soldiers said, "Hey, Lieutenant! Your legging is bleeding!" I looked at my leg, and apparently a piece of shrapnel had cut my canvas legging. It was not more than a scratch. He said I better go to the aid station. I asked where the aid station was, and he said he didn't know. I replied, "I don't know either, and I am not leaving this trench until after the bombardment." By the time all the excitement ended, my leg dried, and I never did go to the aid station. I can't say I was wounded, because it was an ordinary scratch, as I remember.

Early in the afternoon, two columns of German troops were heading toward Ste-Mère-Église. The commander of the 82nd A/B asked the air force liaison officer if he could get air protection and an air strike. He was informed that the weather was overcast and could not. The naval liaison said if he could contact the USS *Texas*, he could get us naval fire. The air and naval liaison officers and I went up in the steeple of the church to direct the fire. The Germans looked to be about two miles away from Ste-Mère-Église. The USS *Texas* fired a first round, which fell short. They gave them another coordinate reading, and the second round fell long. Then they gave him a fire for effect. I will tell you, it sounded like the whole world was coming apart, like freight train after freight train was coming overhead from the USS *Texas*. It was just marvelous to see how gunners who could not see their target could hit it so effectively. They hit both heads of both columns and stopped them in their tracks, due to the fact they were in road with hedgerows on both sides, which caused them to stop when the head of the column was knocked out. Shortly after that, a half hour or forty-five minutes later, we got clearance from the air force that they could send planes in, which they did. The air force had a field day.

The scattered airdrops of the two American airborne divisions served to confuse the Germans. The majority of the paratroopers roamed the countryside, raising havoc, while they tried to find their units. This prevented the Germans from obtaining a clear view of the situation, allowing them only to conclude that Normandy was the target area. Slowly the airborne units began to re-form and move against their objectives or take on new missions. After the actual amphibious landings took place at Utah Beach, the 4th Infantry Division rushed up from the beaches to make contact with the paratroopers. At the same time, the naval and air units provided fire support to the airborne units that were preventing the Germans from breaking through to the beachhead.

Meanwhile, the C-47 transports returned to their bases in England. For a few squadrons, some aircraft were missing. CWO William Hart, the aircraft maintenance officer for the 84th Squadron, 437th Group of the Troop Carrier Wing, could not sleep that night.

> I was up around operations, because that is where the news would come from. First thing we knew about what was going on is when they came back early in the morning. We were counting birds. We were surprised that they came back in good numbers. One bird came back with a wingtip that looked like somebody put a hole punch through it about one to two feet in diameter. We got them back into operating condition and ready to turn around for another mission.

At the Ramsbury Air Base, many of the C-47s had to be refueled and made ready by 8:30 P.M. for their third and last mission of D-Day, according to Frank Guild in *Action of the Tiger*. After that fateful day, their missions involved a variety of duties from delivering supplies to evacuating the wounded. Hart's group also flew several missions to recover gliders from Normandy. A couple C-47s of the squadron were each equipped with a removable wooden boom rigged out of the cargo door for a cable with a hook attached to a winch. As the plane flew low over the glider, the crew used the hook to snag a looped rope attached to the glider held up by raised poles. According to Hart, they "picked up less than a dozen gliders on the far shore and found that it didn't really pay."

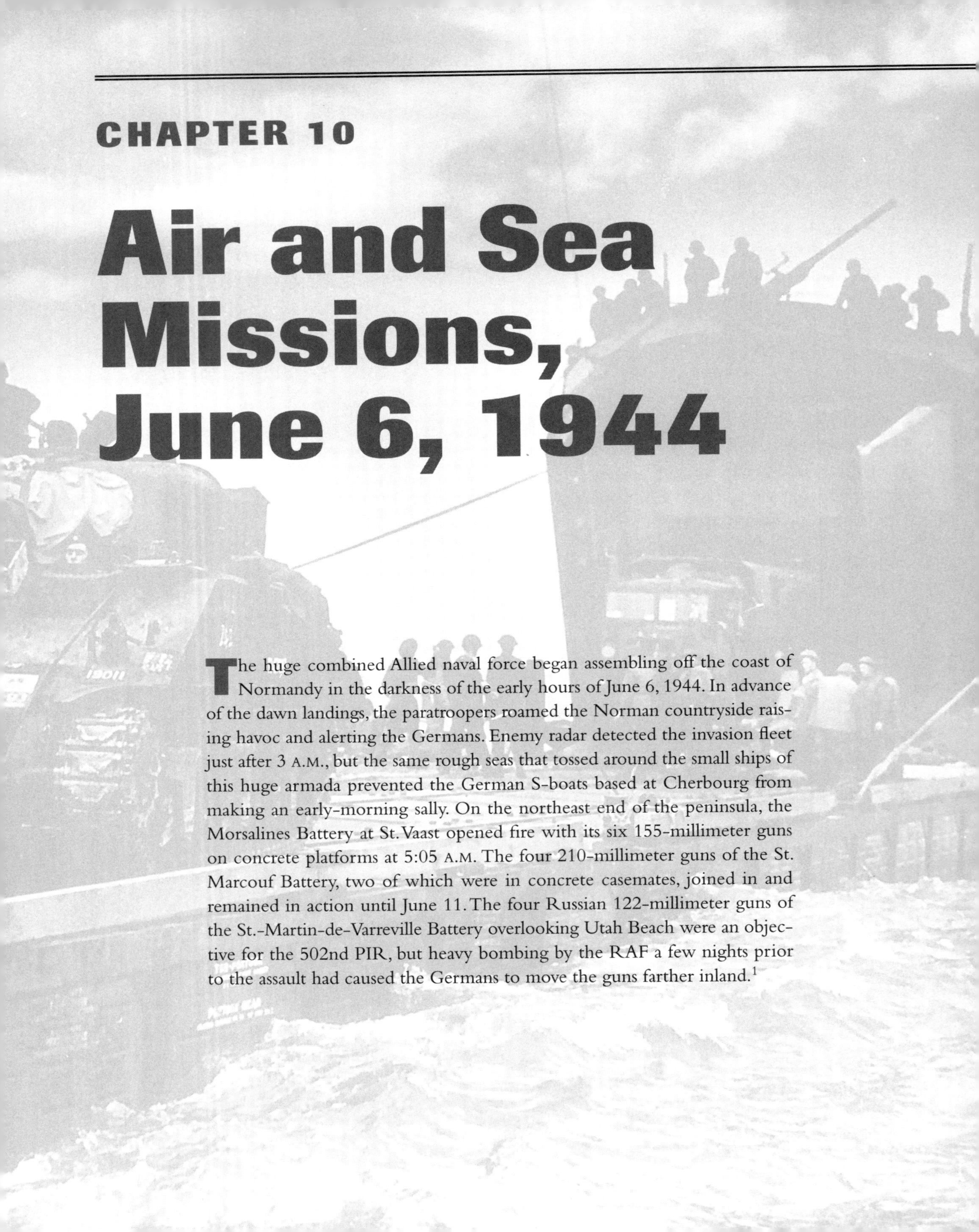

CHAPTER 10

Air and Sea Missions, June 6, 1944

The huge combined Allied naval force began assembling off the coast of Normandy in the darkness of the early hours of June 6, 1944. In advance of the dawn landings, the paratroopers roamed the Norman countryside raising havoc and alerting the Germans. Enemy radar detected the invasion fleet just after 3 A.M., but the same rough seas that tossed around the small ships of this huge armada prevented the German S-boats based at Cherbourg from making an early-morning sally. On the northeast end of the peninsula, the Morsalines Battery at St. Vaast opened fire with its six 155-millimeter guns on concrete platforms at 5:05 A.M. The four 210-millimeter guns of the St. Marcouf Battery, two of which were in concrete casemates, joined in and remained in action until June 11. The four Russian 122-millimeter guns of the St.-Martin-de-Varreville Battery overlooking Utah Beach were an objective for the 502nd PIR, but heavy bombing by the RAF a few nights prior to the assault had caused the Germans to move the guns farther inland.[1]

In early June, the RAF conducted night-bombing missions against batteries in the Pas de Calais area to divert attention from Normandy. On the night of June 4–5, the RAF carried out another diversionary mission, but targeted the Maisy Battery between Utah and Omaha Beaches, near the Pointe du Hoc Battery. The next night, the RAF Bomber Command flew more than 1,200 sorties to support the invasion, striking at nine of the most important batteries in Normandy—including St.-Martin-de-Varreville, Maisy, Pointe du Hoc, Longues, and Merville—right before the first airborne troops landed. The American Ninth and Eighth Air Force reached the beaches at dawn.

Once German coastal observers sighted the invasion fleet after a night of confusion, the defenders scurried to their fighting positions. The units held in reserve on the peninsula had to contend with the American paratroopers, however, who seemed to be everywhere. In addition, the key panzer divisions, which were located deeper inland and were under the direct control of Adolf Hitler, could not be released without the Fuehrer's permission. At the time of the invasion, Hitler was still asleep and General Jodl refused to disturb him, keeping the German armor units frozen until it was too late to change the course of events.

Forces U and Force O reached their assembly areas at about 23,000 yards off Utah and Omaha Beaches at 2:30 and 3 A.M. respectively, just as the C-47s were flying away from the Cotentin Peninsula. The white invasion stripes painted on the wings of the planes clearly identified them to the antiaircraft gunners, who held their fire so there would be no repeat of the 1943 disaster in Sicily. After these C-47s were gone, other Skytrains towing the gliders arrived, and another hour or so later came the bombers intended to soften up the beaches.

The invasion troops on the transports ate an early-morning breakfast, picked up their gear, and loaded into their landing craft shortly after 4 A.M. But the soldiers who had crossed on the fleet of flat-bottomed landing craft such as LCIs and LCTs were not as fortunate. After being tossed around for hours on the rough seas, they were drenched by the waves crashing over the decks, many were dreadfully seasick, and most felt wretched even before they hit the beaches in the first assault waves.

When the concealing sea mist lifted in the early light of dawn, it unveiled a vast armada to the German observers peering through the observation slits of their bunkers. The uneasy silence that had fallen after the night parachute drops and the departure of the Allied transport aircraft ended, shattered by the booming of the big naval guns. The landing craft stopped circling near their transports and headed toward the shore. The German Morsalines Battery opened fire at 5:05 A.M., the main counterbattery riposted after 5:45, targeting the German coastal battery sites. The German 210-millimeter gunners of the St. Marcouf Battery scored many near misses against the three heavy cruisers of the bombardment group. At 5:30, German batteries near Port-en-Bessin aimed at the battleship *Arkansas* off Omaha Beach. The battleship responded about twenty minutes later. To the soldiers heading for the beach, the roar of the huge battleship guns sounded like a freight train passing overhead, but it filled them with confidence. To the paratroopers already on the battlefield, the thunder of the guns heralded the arrival of their relief.

The enemy soldiers manning the coastal defenses, on the other hand, especially the foreign troops from the east inducted into German service, lost some of their confidence as they beheld the vast spectacle unfolding in front of them. At

1. The bombing on the night of May 28–29 resulted in heavy damage, so the RAF's bombing mission on the night of June 5–6 should have been canceled. The guns were mounted on open concrete platforms.

LSIs crossing the English Channel during the invasion with barrage balloons trailing.

about 6:10, about five minutes before the first waves landed, the naval bombardment shifted to the beach defenses. Shortly after 6 A.M., before the invasion force reached the beaches, vast Allied air armadas swooped overhead, damaging enemy morale more than they did the coastal defenses. Smoke and clouds obscured the view of the bombardiers of more than 400 B-24 Liberators of the Eighth Air Force flying over Omaha Beach, forcing them to delay releasing their bombs for about thirty seconds in order to avoid hitting the friendly forces coming ashore. According to Joseph Balkoski in *Omaha Beach*, they carried only small 100-pound bombs, as larger ones would have cratered the beach area making it impassable to vehicles being landed. Most of the bombs were dropped far inland because the bombardiers waited an extra thirty seconds. The 300 B-26 Marauders of the Ninth Air Force faced a similar problem, but the pilots dived through the cloud cover, coming in at 6,000 feet or lower to seek out targets on Utah Beach.

Although several of the German gun batteries stood up to the Allied invasion force, two of the most important positions failed to do so. The gun battery at Merville, on the eastern flank of the British invasion beaches, had been taken by British paratroopers during the hours of darkness. It turned out to be less formidable than reported by the intelligence service, however, because it consisted only of 75-millimeter guns occupying a large casemated artillery position. The other important objective was the battery at Pointe du Hoc, whose 155-millimeter guns in open and casemate positions presented a threat to Omaha and Utah Beaches. While other American troops landed on the main beaches, the 2nd Ranger Battalion launched its assault on Pointe du Hoc by scaling the cliffs to eliminate this battery. After a heroic climb to the top, the Rangers managed to drive back the defenders, only to discover that the guns were gone. Apparently, days before the invasion, the Germans had moved the six 155-millimeter guns a short distance back to protect them from the intense Allied aerial bombardment, which had left the site pockmarked with craters.

No special troops were sent against the casemated German battery of four 150-millimeter guns at Longues between the British beaches and Omaha Beach, possibly because they could not fire directly on the beaches. A British cruiser and some destroyers opened up on the battery during the landings, knocking out two of its guns by 8:30 A.M. The remaining two guns, also behind steel shields mounted in concrete casemates, went back into action against ships off Omaha Beach in the afternoon. Finally a French cruiser put the battery out of action. A fourth heavy battery of four 122-millimeter guns at Varreville, near Utah Beach, was targeted for elimination by paratroopers, but it had been withdrawn a few days earlier after the raid by the RAF Bomber Command.

The *Luftwaffe* had pulled back earlier to defend Germany, leaving few aircraft in the Normandy area. On D-Day, only two German fighters flew over the beaches and made a single strafing run. Except for a brief S-boat raid on the British from Le Havre early in the morning, the German Navy made no effort to stop the invasion fleet on June 6. The Allied troops were able to land with full naval and air support, encountering serious opposition only from the German coastal strongholds on Omaha Beach. At about 6:30 A.M., the battle for the beaches began in earnest as the first wave landed at Utah Beach, a few hundred yards to the south of its designated landing area. The defenses here were lighter, so only a few landing craft were damaged or sunk by mines or enemy fire. At Omaha Beach, however, where the defenses were much stronger, the first waves of soldiers were badly mauled.

The Western Task Force off Normandy

The bulk of the troops of the first wave on Utah and Omaha Beaches disembarked from LCVPs and LCAs.[2] The American attack transports carried most of the troops bound for Utah Beach and the British LSIs, the men bound for Omaha Beach. In both areas, the first-wave LCTs transported the Sherman DD tanks. At Omaha Beach, the tanks tried to come ashore just before H-Hour, whereas at Utah Beach, the LCTs carrying them came just behind the LCVPs. The arrangement of the two landing forces was also different. At Omaha, the engineers arrived on the LCMs, right behind the first wave. At Utah, however, several waves of LCVPs or LCAs disgorged thirty-man infantry assault teams before the LCIs in the fourth wave brought the engineers.[3] About an hour after the initial landings, additional engineers disembarked. They were followed about an hour later by DUKWs and additional LCTs and LCMs. During the next three hours, the LCVPs and LCAs continued to drop their cargo and return to the assembly area. Many of the transport ships were unloaded and returned to England by nightfall, picking up a new load of troops, although some of their LCVPs stayed behind to continue supporting operations in Normandy. On the late afternoon of June 6, the follow-up convoys delivered more troops and equipment.

2. About seventy British LCAs took part at Omaha Beach, including eighteen LCAs of the British 551st Flotilla from the LSI *Empire Javelin*, which brought in the 1st Battalion, 116th Infantry, and the *Empire Anvil*, which carried the 3rd Battalion, 16th Infantry.

3. In the first four hours, more than twenty waves were scheduled, but often these waves were grouped so that the first wave referred to the waves scheduled to land between approximately 6:30 and 7 A.M., and the second wave those between 7 and 8 A.M. and so on. The U.S. Army history, *Omaha Beachhead*, states, "Beginning at 0700, the second group of assault waves touched down in a series of landings that lasted 40 minutes."

Rhino barge loaded with trucks.

Few of the Coast Guard Flotilla of LCIs that sailed from England fully loaded with troops were assigned to the same beach sector. Twenty-year-old MMM2/C Warren Hotard from New Orleans was a coast guardsman on *LCI 320*. His ship had loaded an infantry unit at the docks of Southampton. The sailors, like the soldiers, had to wear gas-proof clothing over their dungarees. The seamen wore light coveralls. Shortly before the invasion, Hotard was promoted to motor machinist mate second class and no longer had the lowest rating on the ship. Prior to this, in Sicily, the lowliest and most disgusting chores had fallen to him.

> The troops we carried always got seasick. I was a fireman, and the lowest rate. During Sicily, my job was to clean the toilet compartment, or at least fix them, because I was in the engine room and knew a little bit about mechanical work. I had to clean these pressure toilets. The soldiers got so seasick they would use magazines, handkerchiefs, rags, anything they could find when they went to the toilets. They got stopped up, and you had to pump it out because you had to pump the waste up. All the screws and fittings were brass and broke very easily. It was my job to fix it, and there was quite a deal to see 200 troops with half of them seasick and vomiting.

In England, as new firemen took his place, it was no longer Hotard's job to clean up. The Channel crossing was beset with the same problems as the episode in Sicily, however. As his LCI crossed the Channel, Hotard manned his duty station.

We were at sea for quite some time. Once they posted the notice, I had the twelve-to-four watch. At midnight, I went down into the engine room and handled the controls. We had four GM motors on each shaft. We controlled them with two round handles that went up and down, and the captain would tell us 400, 200 rpm or whatever. We had a dial which showed us how fast we were going. It was pretty rough, as I remember. Our ship only drew six feet of water forward and eight feet aft. After the twelve-to-four watch, it was calm and nothing unusual about it. I was the only man in the engine room, which was normal for night operations. After my watch was over, I went topside, where it was blacked out. I opened the waterproof hatch, got up topside, and saw ships for as far as you could see. Dawn was breaking and revealing thousands of ships. After leaving the 120-degree temperatures of the engine room, I felt a little chilly and got a cup of coffee from the radioman. I then went down to the compartment, but I couldn't sleep.

When daylight came, I saw the USS *Texas* not too far from us. When they opened fire, I could feel the vibration come up my pants leg. When they started the bombardment, a big ring of smoke went out, and then you heard this sound, a tremendous sound. I didn't think anything could stand up after they let go with the big guns.

When they called for our landing stations, I went up to the forward 20-millimeter gun. The 20-millimeter had a round magazine with something like sixty or seventy shells, and every third one was a tracer. I normally strapped myself into it, while another man operated the trunion to make the gun move up and down, and another man worked it side to side. During the landing, I was up there by myself, because everyone else had something to do. We received notice that some Me 109s were coming in to strafe the beach but soon discovered that they were our own planes. I don't remember whether we opened fire or not.

We couldn't go all the way in. The shells were popping all around. They brought some LCMs alongside, and we off-loaded the troops on these. We couldn't get closer because of enemy fire.

Chief QM John Gatton Jr. of Louisville, Kentucky, served on *LCI 96*, which sailed not far from Hotard's *LCI 320*. For him, too, the sight of the old American battleships shelling the beach was unforgettable. He steered his LCI toward a flat area with no hills and only a few structures on the beach. The landing maneuvers of his craft proceeded smoothly, with no hitches. SC1/C Leon Rodriguez in *LCI 323* also went into Utah Beach, but compared with other operations he had taken part in, such as Gatton, he found nothing extraordinary occurring, so he barely remembers one of the most important events of the twentieth century.

Twenty-eight-year-old SM1/C Edward Matousek of Chicago was one of the older crewmen on Coast Guard *LCI 84* as it approached Omaha Beach with troops of the 6th Engineer Special Brigade. Before the landing, he was in the conning tower snapping his camera, but he was later disappointed.

Most of my photos were ruined. I counted 736 bombers in the air coming from England, coming in waves of 36. As soon as they got into French territory, you saw the flak go up. It seemed like thousands of puffs of smoke, you would see a big flash, and you knew one plane got hit . . . those poor guys!

We carried all infantry. On our first approach, we hit a sandbar and they put the

> ramps down. Four troops went down on each side, and the water was too deep. The water was over their heads, and the eight men drowned. The captain pulled us off, and we went to another part of the beach. They got off here OK. On the beach, it was chaos. Guys were running everywhere.

CMOMM Ralph W. Gault, another twenty-eight-year old from Chicago, served on the Coast Guard *LCI 88*. On the morning of June 6, the vessel churned its way toward Omaha Beach carrying a load of troops—Platoon C-8 of the 6th Beach Battalion and engineers of the 5th Engineer Special Brigade—but the chief motor machinist's mate saw little of the action on deck until after the ship came under enemy fire.[4]

> The engine room was my world, and that was where I stayed. We went into Easy Red at H-Hour+65, or at about 6:30 in the morning [part of the ninth wave scheduled to land at 7:35]. We had several casualties, and I had to turn my board [controls] in the engine room over to Les Wooley, because the officers called me up on deck. We had rations in the wells on either side—canned milk. When I came up on deck, we had flesh and milk, and whatever you have, splattered over the front of the conning tower. Our boatswain's mate, who was supposed to be in charge of the deck at the time, was hanging on to the rail and sick as all get-out. All I could do was grab hold of a handy billy, which was a gasoline-powered fire pump, grab a short hose, and wash all the remains of all these people over the side. Other than that, I can only tell you that my engines were running good and hot.

S1/C Robert McCrory from Louisiana was aboard Coast Guard *LCI 93*, which carried a company of the 18th Infantry, 1st Division to Easy Red of Omaha Beach. He faced no special problems during the crossing other than a lot of seasick soldiers.

> We went in at about 7 A.M. [probably after 9 A.M., when the landing was scheduled, although it was delayed until about 11:30 A.M.] with what was supposed to be the second wave [twenty-first wave]. It was very disorganized. We went through an opening that had already been made through the obstacles and was just about wide enough for a ship. We had a few feet to spare on each side. The skipper showed some excellent seamanship. We lowered the ramps and started discharging the troops. There was heavy machine-gun fire. We didn't get hit by any large shells, although quite a few were landing all around. Quite a few of our troops were killed going down the ramps. We got off without taking any heavy hits and went back out to one of the transports. They loaded us up with an engineer outfit. Although we normally carried about 200 troops, they gave us 400, a double load.[5] We had them stacked in the troop compartments, on the deck, and anywhere we could put them. They said they needed them on the beach badly. So we started back in to the beach and were stopped because some destroyers were running up and down the beach firing rapidly into the beach, trying to knock out the pillboxes. We finally started in, and just before we got to the beach, they got the range on us and began lobbing the shells in. I don't know

4. Albert B. Vernon, commanding Coast Guard Cutter 28, one of sixty operating in the Coast Guard Rescue Flotilla in Normandy that plucked survivors of vessels sunk or damaged during the landings, wrote that *LCI 88* was hit by armor-piercing shells from an 88. One went through the wheelhouse without detonating. Vernon was assigned to *LCI 88* in July.

5. Footnote to come?

One of five gooseberries formed off the Normandy coast. Number 1 and number 2 were formed off Utah and Omaha, respectively. The gooseberry was an artificially breakwater formed of blockships.

how many times they hit us, but I have heard anywhere from seven to thirteen times. According to the skipper's report, which I found in the navy yard in Washington, D.C., they were using 88s and 105s. We hit one or two land mines [?]. We wound up with the starboard engine lying on top of the port engine where one of the mines hit. We got most of the troops off. A lot of them were lost in the water.

The quartermaster and the motor machinist were in the pilothouse when an 88-millimeter armor-piercing shell came right between them. They got a lot of wounds, not from the shell, but from where it pierced the bulkhead. Another shell passed through the officers' quarters and took off the mess attendant's leg. I was on the bow, and when I realized everybody on the bow had gone to the stern, I did too. The only place to hide back there was behind an ammunition ready box. So that is where I hid, but they soon stopped shelling us.

When they finally quit shelling us, we were sinking. Actually, we were on the bottom in about ten feet of water. The skipper gave the order to abandon ship, and we did.

The ones that were not wounded swam with the ones that were. When I went over the side, I went underwater a good ways. They dropped the boatswain's mate to us; he had five pieces of shrapnel in his neck. We did not lose a man of the crew. The worst casualty we had, our mess attendant, lost his leg where an 88 hit him. They tried to get the destroyer *Emmons*, which was about a half mile away. The skipper had the signalmen signal over to the *Emmons* and asked that some boats be sent to pick us up, but they wouldn't do it. Of course, I didn't blame them, but they did get six volunteers to come in with motorized lifeboats. They couldn't come in and stayed at least 1,000 yards or more away from where we were. We had to swim out to them. I towed the boatswain's mate out to the small boat. We spent the next five days on the *Emmons*.

According to McCrory, many of the army engineers they carried were lost, even though the LCI went down only a few hundred yards from the beach. Shortly before they were hit, one of the engineers had asked him what it was like on the beach, and he had answered that it was

Coast Guard *LCI 85* sinking off Omaha Beach on June 6. COURTESY OF ELMER CARMICHAEL

"real hot." The engineer told him that they were not supposed to do any fighting, just come in and clean up, according to plan, and McCrory quipped that things just were not going according to plan. McCrory was up front during the shelling and later found a lot of shrapnel in his life jacket. Thankfully, none had reached his body.

BM2/C Elmer Carmichael of Crescent, Oklahoma served on Coast Guard *LCI 85*, which moved toward Omaha Beach with troops of the 16th Infantry, 1st Division, onboard and was scheduled to land at 8:30 A.M. in the sixteenth wave. The four troop compartments were furnished with one bunk per soldier. The main problem on this long journey was feeding the passengers.

> Most of them ate C rations from a can, and they also had K rations. The troops and crew ate the same food. After loading, it was uncomfortable after day one. The troops had a patch with a red "1," but they were not infantrymen; we had mostly medics.
>
> After leaving Weymouth, I saw ships from horizon to horizon. There wasn't any direction you could look and not see ships. There was one other thing new to us: Each ship was flying a barrage balloon to protect us from aircraft.
>
> We had half our crew on duty all the time. Each vessel had a small light on the stern that the ship behind used as a guide to stay in single columns. It was still dark when we rendezvoused at the debarkation area, which was about ten miles offshore, and we just went in circles until daylight. When it came time for us to go ashore, the closer we got toward the shore, I could see we were probably in trouble because there was a lot of smoke hanging on the shore on

Summary of After-Action Report for *LCI 85*

Lt. Coit Hendley, USCG, submitted an after-action report on the loss of his LCI during Operation Neptune.

The USS *LCI(L) 85* on June 6, 1944, arrived at the transport area with the other ships attached to Assault Force O and circled in the LCI collecting area until times to make the run into the beach. The ship was scheduled to hit Omaha Beach, sector Easy Red, at K plus 120 or at 8:30 A.M. At 8:20 A.M. we arrived at the line of departure. The primary control vessel for Easy Red beach called to us by loud hailer and told us to go into the beach at this point. As a result of the strong tide running along the beach, the control vessel had drifted until it was almost past Easy Red beach.

We actually landed in the left flank of Easy Red or the right flank of Fox Green rather than the right flank of Easy Red as scheduled. We grounded at 8:30 A.M. and put out both ramps, but the water was too deep for the troops to wade ashore so we retracted both ramps and began to back off. As the anchor was secured, something hit the aft winch causing her to stop running. There were no LCVPs in sight to help unload so we went about a hundred yards to the right and made another beaching.

This beaching was made without the anchor as the winch would not start. As the ship grounded a Teller mine exploded under the bow splitting the void tank. The port ramp went down and the troops began going ashore. Shells and machine gun fire began to hit us. About fifty troops got down the port ramp before a shell hit it and blew it off the sponsons and over the side. As the starboard ramp had not gone down and the wounded men were jamming the deck, we backed off the beach again.

We had approximately 15 dead and 30 wounded men all in the forward part of the ship. We had been hit approximately 25 times by shells. Fire was starting in troop compartments 1, 2, and 3. Water was coming in slowly from shell holes below the water line and the hole made by the mine. No hits had been suffered from the engine room aft.

We backed off the beach and stood off about 200 yards. The damage control party began fighting the fire and within 30 minutes had them out. In compartments 1 and 2 the fire had been bunks, blankets, etc. burning. In compartment 3 oil from a punctured fuel tank was also burning.

We were carrying several Army and Navy doctors and our pharmacists' mates, so the wounded received immediate care. All but about 30 of the troops that were able to go ashore were sent in by LCVP. We proceeded to the USS SAMUEL CHASE to unload the casualties. We went along the CHASE about 12:00. We had a bad list from the water in the compartments forward.

The damage control party was making an attempt to pump out the water with three Pacific Pumpers but it was not too successful. The strainers on the

continued

Summary of After-Action Report for LCI 85 ***continued***

pumpers would clog up after five minutes running and would have to be cleaned. By 1:30, all the wounded and dead were transferred to the CHASE. We backed away from her and were taken in tow by the *AT 98*. We had such a bad list that the tugboat captain and I decided to try to pump the water rather than make the beach. The *LCI(L) 85* capsized about 1430. The crew scrambled on board the tug before she went over. A demolition charge was put in her stern and she then went down completely.

Casualties to the crew were four men wounded. These men were placed on the CHASE for treatment. Confidential publications and confidential material on board was on the bridge in a weighted sack and went down with the ship in 14 fathoms of water.

our section, Easy Red of Omaha Beach. It was sometime after 7 A.M. We went in and discovered the water was too deep, and there was too much debris around for us to get either ramp down. Our seaman did go ashore with the anchor to assist our troops in landing, and when we started backing off, he came back aboard and we moved down the beach a little further. Our skipper, Lt. Coit Hendley, saw another opening, and he went in there, making a pretty fair beaching. We got our port ramp down, but our starboard ramp came down upon debris and a hedgehog, and cantered up in the air so our troops could not get on it. Our troops started down the port ramp and were machine-gunned as they got in the water. We couldn't see how many of them got ashore, but some of them did. Then we started getting hit by 88-millimeter and 75-millimeter guns and we caught on fire. We had a fire in our Number 3 troop compartment. I could see a lot of dead laying around the decks. The skipper saw we weren't doing any good there—everybody was getting killed going ashore—and so we backed off and went out a little ways. We were fighting the fire in the number 3 hold and with the handy billies—portable pumps. We pumped water into the hold to put out the fire. Another handy billy was used to pump the water out to keep from sinking. I was in charge of trying to get a collision mat over a big hole we had on our starboard side. It was probably three feet across. We got the collision mat over it, and it really worked. The mat was about ten feet square and had pieces of rope we called "froming" sewed on one side. The idea was to work it over the hole, and the pressure of the water would push it in enough. It was secured with lines to hold it in place. It worked pretty good while the LCVPs came alongside.

The LCVPs came alongside and took off the troops still in commission and left the wounded and dead onboard as they proceeded to take the others ashore. We started back to the rendezvous area. When we got under way, we couldn't hold the collision mat in place, and it washed away. We continued to take water and listed heavily on the starboard side. We pulled alongside the USS *Samuel Chase*. We had to go along the lee side, because the swells were pretty bad. We put all our wounded in litters, and they took them aboard on slings. The skipper of the *Samuel Chase* told me he wanted to unload the dead and told us to take them back ashore. Our skipper said we weren't going to make it back ashore, so they took the dead off. I think we had fifteen dead and forty wounded, from what I have read. We had some of our crew slightly wounded and they stayed aboard. After unloading, we started back in an attempt to beach it. A big navy tug, *AT 89*, pulled alongside us and tied up to us. Her pumps went to work to try to save us. They couldn't gain on the incoming water. They passed the word to abandon ship, and finally it rolled over and sank. When I got aboard the tug, I sat on the ready box and the bow of our ship was still showing. They sent a crew over and put a demolition charge on it and blew a hole in it.

I had left my cigarettes on the ship so I asked somebody for a cigarette. One of the navy guys on the tug gave me a cigarette and some matches, but I got to shaking so bad I could not light it. I had been pretty cool and calm prior to that. It kind of hit me what had happened and I started shaking, so they had to light the cigarette for me. We stayed on that tug the rest of D-Day and all night.

Twenty-eight-year-old Lt. Ed Fabian from Los Angeles commanded *LCI 86* after being transferred from his *LCI 89*. The *LCI 86* was turned into a communications ship for duty off Omaha Beach. Virtually every compartment was filled with radiomen from the navy and their equipment to communicate with the troops on shore and direct fire support missions. A similar LCI was prepared for operations off Utah Beach. These were probably the only LCIs that did not tow a barrage balloon to deter enemy aircraft. During the day, Lieutenant Fabian's LCI moved up and down parallel to the beach, and the radiomen were fully engaged. Captain Sabine of the navy, who was in charge of the communications operations, directed the lieutenant on what course to take. As the battle raged ashore, Fabian received the news that virtually everyone was pinned down on the beach, and the commo exchanges seemed to indicate a great deal of concern that the troops would not get off the beach. Despite this dismal picture, he never heard any word of evacuation. "We had German aircraft strafing the beach in Sicily and Italy, but I didn't see any here," Fabian recalls. Mostly, "there was so much noise."

All day long, the tugboats towed over the blockships, placed them in position, and sunk them, all the while under fierce fire from the shore. That night, Lieutenant Fabian tied up alongside the elderly British warship *Centurion*, destined to become a blockship, to use it for cover. When he boarded the old battleship, he discovered that it was largely intact and even had all its lightbulbs. The skeleton crew that had sunk the ship had long departed on the tug. Other smaller ships also used the *Centurion* for shelter. At low tide, a good deal of its keel was exposed, since it sat on the bottom.

Y2/C George Gray of McFall, Missouri, was also aboard Coast Guard *LCI 86*, which served as the deputy task force commander's headquarters. His duties were to carry the orders or requests of the commodore to others onboard. In his idle moments, he had time to observe the operation. Thus he witnessed the opening salvos in the early morning, since his vessel operated close to shore. His memories differ from Lieutenant Fabian's, however.

The naval bombardments lit up the sea from the left horizon to the right horizon. From out to sea, it was mostly battleships and cruisers, with destroyers further in and rocket ships close to shore. Gunfire from

Adm. Alan Kirk.

the ships was joined by bombs from planes. The entire shoreline was lit up.

During daylight, the shells of the battleships' gun turrets could be seen in the air when one was behind the line of flight. If in front of the fire, an LCI felt as if it would be lifted from the water. The noise was terrific but didn't seem oppressive unless a person was close to it. The destroyer fire was more of a "crack" than a "boom," and during daylight, much of the fire was, or appeared to be, line of sight.

Rocket ships fired banks of rockets set beam-to-beam in what appeared to me to be LCTs. The fire was continuous and drew parallel lines of red against the shore as our view was behind them. Smoke from the explosions, and sand plus rock dust, created a boiling cloud onshore. All in all, it was quite a show as most rocket attacks stopped at dawn, at least in our area.

As H-Hour began, it became difficult to determine where fire originated until explosions occurred on the beach. Those were mortars, 88s, and other guns fired by the Germans until they were too far away or had targets much more threatening close to them.

As D-Day wore on, the battleships fired at targets further and further inland. This could be discerned just by following the line of flight from the shells. Destroyers moved close inshore and attacked targets giving trouble to our troops from the base of the bluffs on Omaha Beach to the crest.

One LCM drew alongside Gray's LCI and unloaded two dead soldiers who remained under a tarp on the fantail for a couple of days. The things that struck Gray the most on that day off Omaha Beach were the constant explosions of mortar and artillery shells on the beach, as well as the large amount of materiel and great number of small ships, DUKWs, and landing craft lost to the mines and enemy fire. The dazed look of the coxswains on LCMs as they returned to pick up more men from the transports, after having left their first passengers on the beach, and the frantic radio calls from those on the beach for a variety of items, mostly artillery ammunition, left an indelible impression on him.

Eighteen-year-old naval S1/C Myron Parsons from Newcastle, Pennsylvania, was aboard *LCT 851*, one of many vessels that transported vehicles and infantry across the Channel. This crossing was far more uncomfortable than for those in the navy or Coast Guard LCIs. Parson's vessel carried a load of infantry to Utah Beach in the second wave, about two hours after the first had landed.

At about 150 feet from the beach, we put out our anchor, and when we ran out of anchor cable, we dropped our ramp and the

> men of the 4th Division headed in. The water was about four feet deep. Some of the soldiers went under, and most of them regained their balance and headed for a two-foot concrete wall that ran the full length of Utah Beach. German 88s were hitting all around, and machine-gun fire was going off around us. Some soldiers were getting hung up on the underwater obstacles, and a lot of them were stepping on land mines. Because the tide was going out fast, my ship got hung up on the beach, and we had to go ashore and dig foxholes and stay until the next tide. Most of us went up to the concrete wall, about 300 feet away, and we hid behind it while we waited.

Ens. Don Irwin, skipper of *LCT 614*, departed from Portland with one other officer and a crew of twelve, transporting sixty-five soldiers of the 112th Engineer Battalion with bulldozers, jeeps, and trailers to Dog Red, Omaha Beach. They were scheduled to land one hour after H-Hour. Irwin's was one of four LCTs with an LCVP carrying elements of this battalion that landed in the eighth wave, coming in behind the 3rd Battalion of the 116th Infantry.

> The rough sea did not make a pleasant journey for the soldiers, but little else happened until dawn as they watched the bombardment and specially fitted landing craft firing salvos of rockets at the beaches.
>
> When dawn broke, the Normandy beach lay ahead, and not much was to be seen but haze and smoke. Ships were everywhere. I had my executive officer on the conning tower. The crew was at battle stations. We were so heavily attired that even with life jackets, I fear we would have gone straight to the bottom had the ship sunk. As I recall, in addition to my life jacket and helmet, I had on navy foul-weather gear, and on top of that impregnated clothing for protection against poison gas. In addition, I had my gas mask slung, a .45 pistol on my belt, and a pair of binoculars around my neck.
>
> We headed toward the beach, abreast with four other LCTs. Things began to happen. The most ear-splitting, deafening, horrendous sound I had ever heard—or probably will ever hear—took place. It was the guns of the battleship USS *Texas* firing over our heads and into the beach. As I looked back over my shoulder, it looked as if the *Texas*'s giant 14-inch guns were pointed right at us, but of course they weren't. Their trajectory to reach their targets on the beach was so flat, it just looked that way.
>
> Then I thought, as we stood on the conning tower, how tranquil it seemed heading in. Perhaps the briefing officer, a U.S. Navy captain that briefed us shortly before we left port, was right when he said, "There won't be anything left to bother you guys when you hit the beach. We've thrown everything at the Germans but the kitchen sink—and we'll throw that in too." Then he went on to state how much aerial bombing would be carried out and how much shelling the USS *Texas* and USS *Arkansas* would be doing.
>
> But things did change, and how! As we approached the beach—we were still quite a distance out—the sea seemed to get much rougher, and the current was getting much stronger as the tide was coming in. What I then attempted to do was to get close enough to the beach so that I could drop my ramp and get the sixty-five troops and equipment ashore in relatively shallow water. I had already dropped my anchor so that I would have help in pulling away from the beach. As I tried to get in closer, I saw the water starting to splash ahead. I thought the battleship firing behind us was firing short,

The battleship *Nevada*, built just before the U.S. entered World War I and a veteran of Pearl Harbor, firing on German positions on D-Day.

but no such thing; the Germans had started to open up with 88-millimeter guns. We finally dropped our ramp. Then all hell tore loose. We came under intense fire, as did the LCTs to the right and left of us.[6] Most of the fire seemed to be rifle and machine-gun fire. I found I still couldn't get the soldiers and equipment off, because the water was still too deep. We spent about an hour trying to get our landing craft closer to the beach. As I recall, a couple of bulldozers were driven off the ramp in pretty deep water but did reach the shore, only to be blasted by German gunners with phosphorous shells which started them burning.

Then some of the soldiers, with a couple of officers leading, took off from the ramp in water up to their armpits, with rifles held high over their heads, and headed for shore. As soon as a few of the soldiers left the ramp, two of them got shot just as they stepped off the ramp. They were quickly pulled back aboard ship. One was shot in the back, but it appeared to be more of a grazing type wound and not serious. The other was shot in the stomach, a more serious type wound, and the bullet just missed a rifle grenade on his belt.

The German fire grew so intense I was standing behind the chart house for protection with a member of my crew. Suddenly I saw him reel and start to fall. Blood was coming from beneath his eye. I caught him before he hit the deck, thinking of course that he was fatally wounded. He regained consciousness shortly, and after the flow of blood was stemmed, he seemed to be in good shape. Apparently a piece of shrapnel from a mortar round had slashed him as neatly as a knife, and the impact caused him to lose consciousness. (He refused to leave the ship and go aboard a hospital ship.)

Now, with the soldiers getting shot going off the ramp, I had a problem. The rest of the troops refused to leave. I had orders that I should disembark these troops and equipment here and now. It had been stressed that to fail to do so could jeopard-

6. There should have been three LCTs to his right, carrying elements of the 121st Engineer Battalion. They were scheduled to land at Dog Green but moving eastward like most of the waves in front of Irwin's to land mainly at Easy Green.

ize invasion plans. It was even suggested that if necessary, orders were to be carried out at gunpoint. I could in no way force human beings to step off the ramp to almost certain wounding or death, because by now the situation had grown worse.

The shellfire became even more intense. The sea continued to get rougher. Pandemonium seemed to be everywhere, with lots of smoke and explosions. There were bodies in the water. It was evident the invasion force at Omaha Beach was taking a bad beating.

Every once in a while, ahead of us on the beach, we could see U.S. soldiers huddled at the base of a cliff. They weren't moving inland. The Germans were firing at them from the front, and the heavy tide was bringing the sea ever closer to them from behind. At this point, we ourselves had come under intense rifle and machine-gun fire.

The men in my crew, who were still at their battle stations, and who had been standing erect on our way to the beach, were now flattened out against the ship as if they were a part of it. A couple of my crew yelled, "Skipper, let's get out of here!" After an hour of trying to get my load of troops and vehicles off, I was ready.

Finally, a reprieve came. Orders came over our radio from our command ship to retract from the beach.[7] The beach was described as being too "hot" from German gunfire, and our orders were to withdraw, go out into the English Channel, anchor, and await further orders. What welcome orders! But little did I know that my troubles were just beginning.

When I gave the command to raise and secure the ramp, I noticed what appeared to be a German mine bobbing in the water close to the end of the ramp, but it never made contact with the ramp. If it had, we never would have made it out of there. With the ramp up and secured, we attempted to retract from the beach by winding in the anchor cable with our gasoline engine-driven winch and backing down (reversing) with the three screws on the stern of the landing craft.

At about this time, we rescued four or five sailors from drowning near our landing craft by pulling them out of the sea. They were completely fatigued and as blue from the cold water as any living human being I've ever seen. They had their LCVP blown out from under them by the Germans while they were trying to put some troops or equipment ashore. We found out later they were from the USS *Caroll*, a navy attack transport anchored out in the Channel.

As we continued to try to back away from the beach, we were suddenly stopped and found that we were hung up on a German underwater obstacle. After some tense moments, we got free of the obstacle, but in the process, it rendered useless one of the outside screws of our LCT, so I had only two screws to operate with. We were indeed fortunate to get free from the underwater beach obstacles.

[Sometime during the landing,] I saw two soldiers nearby that were trying their best to survive. One of them had his arms around one of the large wooden post obstacles that the Germans had driven into the beach. Hanging on to his waist was another American soldier. They were using the post as protection against the German rifle and machine-gun fire. So accurate was this fire

7. After those in the initial landings faced problems on the beach such as vehicles and equipment piling up for lack of exits, the landings at Omaha were temporarily stopped.

The *Nevada*'s 14-inch guns firing a salvo on D-Day.

that the bullets were splintering the log on the sides. And to add to the perilous position of these two men was the incoming tide, which was raising the water ever higher on the log. I often wondered if they survived.

Just as we had the anchor cable nearly all in, the moment came when our large anchor should be coming into sight, but the anchor wouldn't lift. It was hooked onto something, and our thoughts were that we were sitting ducks for German fire and we could get entangled into more obstacles. Try as we might, we couldn't free the anchor. I gave the command for "All engines ahead, full!" This caused the anchor to move, and soon coming to the surface was a small landing craft that had been sunk by the Germans, with our anchor hooked into it. As we made a turn away from the beach, with our two operable engines still ahead at full speed, the wrecked craft finally pulled free from our anchor. What a relief! We pulled the anchor in, secured, and then headed out into the English Channel, where we anchored awaiting further orders. We still had most of our troops and equipment aboard.

We got the order around two o'clock that afternoon that we should proceed to the beach and attempt once more to get off our troops and vehicles. This time around, the German shelling and gunfire had been much reduced. We still had trouble getting in close enough to the beach so that our troops could wade ashore and the waterproofed vehicles could make it. In fact, many of the vehicles didn't; they simply "drowned out" in the water and stalled. One sergeant I had aboard said he was sure he would lose his jeep and trailer in the water, so he chose to stay with his jeep and trailer until we beached again. But we didn't beach again on the American beaches, and not until we were at the British invasion area did he and his equipment get ashore.

Hundreds of small craft sailed across the Channel along with the larger transport ships, warships, and other support units. The LSTs, too large and vulnerable for the first assault waves, stood offshore waiting, with none initially scheduled to land before 11:30 A.M.

Among the multitude of ships were the naval tugboats, which were armed with little more than a 3-inch gun and a couple of 20-millimeter antiaircraft guns. S2/C Theodore Gaydos served on the *ATA 125*, an auxiliary tug.[8] During the hours of darkness, his little ship towed an unmanned ammunition barge across the Channel. Unlike the crews of most of the other ships, the men of the

8. Gaydos transferred to the army during the invasion of southern France and retired as a lieutenant colonel.

The LCT and Other Landing Craft

According to Ens. Don Irwin, maneuvering the LCT was like operating most large landing craft. "On the way to a beach, a large anchor was dropped off the stern. The anchor was fastened to a large wire cable that was fastened to a winch onboard the vessel. When it came time to retract from the beach, the cable was wound on the drum of the winch, which helped to pull the craft off the beach." Irwin describes the LCT:

> The whole ship was built like a pontoon. It was one flat layer of pontoons. The water that got so many infantrymen wet on the deck came through the ramp, and not through the pontoons. None of those ramps was completely watertight. We had to unbolt two-foot round hatches for each of the pontoons to check for water inside. I would have to go down into each pontoon and check, but there was never any water in them. The air in them was stale from being sealed and is hard to forget. We had a billy pump in case there was any water in the pontoons.

The aft section of the LCT included the wheelhouse. Belowdecks was the engine room, and behind it at the stern were the quarters for crew. The LCT(5) was about 112 feet long and 32 feet wide and consisted of three watertight sections. It could carry three to five tanks, depending on their size, or nine trucks. Since it had no accommodations for passengers, the infantrymen who crossed the Channel on it had a rough ride on the open deck. The vessel also carried two 20-millimeter guns and its crew numbered one officer and twelve men. The LCT(6) was slightly larger and could be loaded from the stern. Except for the locations of the wheelhouse and crew quarters, there was not much difference between the two vessels.

The LCM was designed to carry a tank or a vehicle. Types 2 and 3 were similar. They

LCTs on the beach.

continued

The LCT and Other Landing Craft *continued*

ranged from 45 feet to 50 feet in length and were 14 feet across. Both needed a crew of four and mounted two .50-caliber machine guns.

The transports carried LCVPs, small craft that were about 36 feet long and 11 feet wide. Manned by three men, they were armed with two .30-caliber machine guns and could carry up to thirty-six soldiers or one vehicle.

The larger landing craft included the LCI and LST. The LCI(L) was an oceangoing vessel designed to carry troops or cargo. It had a length of 160 feet and width of 23 feet. With a normal crew of three or four officers and twenty-one to twenty-five men, it could transport approximately 200 troops and mounted four or five 20-millimeter antiaircraft guns for protection. There were slight differences between the first and second series of these craft in size and crew.

The LST was about 328 feet long and 50 feet across, but later models were slightly larger. The crew consisted of eight to ten officers and just over 100 men. The type and number of weapons onboard and the number of davits for landing craft were variable. According to naval documents, the LSTs were designed to carry up to 165 soldiers, but on D-Day, they carried more than 500 men on short trips. Their armament consisted of a dual purpose .50-caliber or a 40-millimeter gun, plus six 20-millimeter guns. The ship was designed to carry and land tanks and vehicles.

Specialized versions of the above-mentioned vessels also existed. Not all of the British models were similar to the American.

ATA 125 took few special measures for the invasion, and the sailors on deck wore no distinctive clothing or flak jackets, other than having dyed their white caps blue. For Gaydos, it was a memorable day he never forgot.

> We could see high cliffs up ahead. It was Omaha Beach. We saw Rangers assault the cliffs and watched the tin cans and battlewagons fire on the shore. We cut our barge loose and it drifted to shore, where it was unloaded. We never saw it again.
>
> We received an emergency call for salvage and went to Utah Beach, where an LST had hit a mine and was beached. We sent our towline over to the LST with our small boat, and it was attached to the LST. The only people I saw on the LST were three men on the bow who attached our cable to their ship and then left. I'm sure everyone was evacuated before we began towing the LST. We started to pull it off the beach and got it going at pretty good speed when she started to sink. Our boatswain took an axe and cut the cable with one blow. The LST then slid beneath the water.

The warships dominated the scene, thanks to their guns. The *Augusta*, a heavy cruiser, served as the headquarters for the Western Task Force. The mission of its 8- and 5-inch guns was to back up other supporting ships if necessary. Its two scout aircraft were not carried onboard for this mission, and the pilot, Lieutenant Cahill, flew a British aircraft out of England. The *Susan B. Anthony*, a troop ship that was following the *Augusta* during the crossing, sank after it struck a mine. Fortunately, all but half a dozen of the men it carried survived, and most were rescued by the *Augusta*.

LCI 85 being abandoned just before sinking off Omaha Beach. COURTESY OF ELMER CARMICHAEL

Lt. John L. Evans of Tupelo, Mississippi, the *Augusta*'s disbursing officer, stood at his battle station in the coding room, which was below Admiral Kirk's quarters in the forward section of the ship. "When I decoded a message to deliver to Admiral Kirk, I had to climb metal ladders and open a metal door to get to the deck where his quarters were located, and invariably our 8-inch guns would fire just as I opened the door. The vibration would shake the door, causing bumps and bruises on me, which were not pleasant."

Carl J. Hummel, a radioman on the USS *Augusta*, also remembered that day quite vividly.

> Jack Hudgins and I were in the plotting room. He worked a key with fire control parties, and I worked voice with the British and American planes. The plotting room usually had two officers and half a dozen enlisted men. As I recall, the officer in charge was a Lieutenant Rowan. All firing of 8-inch guns was controlled in this room. In most cases, the planes worked in pairs, with one above the other to protect the plane that was doing the spotting. The pilots worked with their mikes open, and you could hear the rat-tat-tat of their guns as they were diving down. It was like listening to a war picture at the movie house. Guts, they had.
>
> As we carried on our conversations, we were in the plot room, which was air-conditioned. We were sweating like we just got out of a swimming pool, especially when the shells would land in the water close to the ship and rock her. Scared? You can bet your life we were.

Communications with Spotting Aircraft

Carl Hummel provides the following example of typical communications that might have taken place on an aircraft:

> Pilot: This is Red 3. I have a target!
> Hummel to Pilot: Roger, Red 3.
> Hummel to Lieutenant Rowan: We have a target!
> Rowan to rest of men: Prepare to fire!
> Pilot to Hummel: This is Red 3, 26W 44N.
> Hummel to Rowan: 26W 44N.
> Rowan to crew: 26W 44N.
> Pilot to Hummel: Fire when ready!
> Hummel to Rowan: Fire when ready!

At this point, the men would have been making adjustments on the dials of their equipment, looking much like a bunch of guys playing pinball machines.

> Rowan: Fire. Time of flight, 26 seconds.
> Hummel to pilot: Fire. Time of flight, 26 seconds.

Hummel would then watch the clock, and at the twenty-six second mark, he would say, "Splash!" so the pilot would know when to look to see the shell land. If the aircraft went down, Hummel would have to locate another spotter, American or British. According to Hummel, "The conversation between pilots was not fit for the average churchgoer to listen to."

Most of the men belowdecks probably shared Hummel's feelings while the battle raged above them.

Lt. William H. McDaniel from Los Angeles had served as a fleet marine before the war. At twenty-seven years old, he served aboard the USS *Augusta* and commanded an antiaircraft battery manned by his marine detachment. From his duty station, he had an excellent view of the course of events.

> We were off Omaha Beach and at H-Hour, after the preliminary bombardment, we withdrew to a position back a few miles from the beach. Later that day, we did go in close to the beachhead, I think for the benefit of the admirals and generals, who wanted a closer look at what was going on.
>
> We engaged in fire missions some period of time after June 6. The reason for that was that our ship was newer than most of the gunfire support vessels in the area, and our guns could be elevated to a higher degree. Many of the old ships, particularly the old British ships, that were brought there to support the invasion could not elevate to a high degree. We were called upon to fire our main battery, the 8-inch guns, in support of the landing. There was one very irritating aspect to those of us in the AA battery and that was the fact that whenever the ship fired the main battery, the ship would go to general quarters, which meant that all of us had to be at our battle stations whether we had anything to do with the main battery or not. One of the primary problems, particularly after being there so long, was that we were drowsy from lack of sleep. We would take any advantage that was offered to us to get a few minutes' rest.
>
> One thing particularly bothersome to me was that my battle station was in the after main mast, which was pretty much

> over turret 3. Turret 3 was immediately below us and aft of us, and when those 8-inch guns would train up to a high elevation and out to port or starboard, as the case would be, those of us up in the crow's position, up in the top of the main mast B, weren't very many feet from the end of those barrels. As a result, when they fired, we got a tremendous blast—you almost had to hang on. On one occasion, a first-aid box from the concussion was ripped off its position on one of the supports, and we had gauze and bandages flying all over the place. It was very disturbing to us that we had to be in those battle station positions during the firing missions.
>
> As an officer of an AA battery, I had to be at my battle station even though enemy aircraft rarely came in. They would come in at night.

As the cruisers, battleships, and one monitor pounded the coastal positions with big guns ranging in caliber from 8- to 15-inch, the faster destroyers moved closer to provide more direct fire support from their smaller batteries. Their support must have been welcome to the soldiers already onshore, because in the early hours of the invasion, it had been possible to bring only the lightest of guns, and those were not enough to turn the tide.

As the British and American Naval Task Forces moved across the English Channel, the RAF and USAAF concentrated their entire effort on operations related to the invasion. The paratroopers dropped in Normandy were already roaming through the countryside while the men of some of the bomber units ate an early breakfast, drew their equipment, and headed for their briefings. Before the first assault troops landed on the beaches, waves of bombers flew past the fleet toward the coast of Normandy. The skies were so crowded that the bomber units were ordered to abort their missions if they could not identify their targets on the first run, because there was no room to turn around and try again.

During the darkest hours of June 5–6, as the transport aircraft carried the paratroopers across the Channel, British Bomber Command sent 551 Lancasters, 412 Halifaxes, and 49 Mosquitoes to hit ten of the main coastal batteries in Normandy, including La Pernelle, Maisy, Pointe du Hoc, Longues, and Merville. Amazingly, they lost only three aircraft in this operation. Some aircraft screened against enemy night fighters or took part in the simulated invasion operations along the coast between Boulogne and Le Havre and dropped dummy paratroopers. At the end of day on June 6, another 1,065 aircraft of Bomber Command launched a night operation against lines of communication and transportation centers in Normandy, according to *The Bomber Command War Diaries* by Martin Middlebrook and Chris Everitt.

The previous day, 464 B-17s and 206 B-24s of the Eighth Air Force had bombed the coastal defenses of the Pas de Calais region and Cherbourg. Every bomb group participated on June 6, as 882 B-17s and 543 B-24s flew toward coastal targets lying between Le Havre and Cherbourg. The B-24s of the 446th Bomb Group were recorded as the first over the coast followed by hundreds of other Eighth Air Force bombers. They dropped their bombs on coastal positions at 5:55 A.M., before the first troops landed. The cloud cover forced them to drop their bombs too far inland, however, in order to avoid accidentally hitting the assault troops. An additional 84 B-17s and 296 B-24s followed the first waves of aircraft, flying toward Argentan and other towns behind the front. Six aircraft had gone down on June 5, but only three were lost during these morning missions. According to Roger Freeman in *The Mighty Eighth*, one of these downed planes was a B-24, the only aircraft of the Eighth Air Force to be shot down by the Germans that day over France.

Destroyer Action

The following description of the actions of the USS *Frankford* under the command of Capt. James L. Semmes appears in the book *Semmes America*:

> On Tuesday, June 6, 1944, D-Day, his ship was among the destroyers that formed a screen 5,000 to 6,000 yards offshore, with the assignment of bombarding enemy land positions using directions from Army artillery spotters on the beaches. Semmes's *Frankford* was assigned the Omaha Beach sector.
>
> It didn't take long for the artillery observers to realize that they could not locate the German targets in the midst of the confusion and the intense enemy fire. Semmes himself surveyed the beach with his binoculars. "We could see wounded and dead men all over the sand and smashed landing craft everywhere," he recalled. "There were thousands of troops huddled at the base of a hill, pinned down. It was heart rending to see all those bodies littering the beach. We thought the invasion was falling on its face."
>
> Hundreds of other landing craft that had not yet beached were milling in circles, unable to go in because of the heavy German fire and because the beach was already jammed with soldiers who could not move further inland. Some of the vessels were hit by Nazi artillery, and the *Frankford*'s sailors took several badly wounded men aboard their ship for medical care.
>
> When the "Hot Dog," as the men called her, could not get coordinates of targets from her assigned fire control party ashore, she set to work on so-called "targets of opportunity." At about 9 A.M., Semmes, realizing the magnitude of the situation on the beach, took the initiative to move his destroyer as close to the beach as possible, about 1200 yards from the shore.
>
> "I just wanted to see if we could do something to help," Semmes said later. "Through binoculars and our gunnery telescopes we could see the flashes of machine-gun fire on the slope, and we opened fire on them."
>
> He gave orders to turn the ship broadside to the beach and bring her four five-inch guns to bear on the Germans on the ridge above the beach, especially on the Germans' heavily-defended gullies, which the Allied invaders needed in order to get off the beach and move inland.
>
> At one point during the invasion, when it was observed that the whole beachhead was stopped completely by several well-concealed enemy batteries, the admiral directing the fire support group pleaded frantically for someone to locate the deadly enemy positions. After many suspected locations had been shelled, a sharp-eyed "Hot Dog" lookout finally discovered the real enemy emplacement, and the "Hot Dog" commenced firing.
>
> She hurled salvo after salvo of shells into the camouflaged enemy emplacement. When the firing ceased, the "Hot Dog" crew watched breathlessly as one

continued

Destroyer Action *continued*

brave infantryman crept up the hill toward the dangerous spot. Other soldiers followed him. There was no enemy fire. The first man reached the top of the hill unharmed and waved his comrades on. The "Hot Dog" crew heaved one long sigh of relief.

Visually observing the enemy surrendering to American troops, the whole crew cheered as the announcement came over the ship's loudspeaker that 22 prisoners were being herded down the hill toward the beach from their demolished position as a result of the *Frankford*'s gun fire.

The *Frankford* continued to cruise up and down the beach until 2:30 P.M., but by midday, some progress had already been seen in the troops' movements. They were finally able to climb the hill and begin to move inland. Throughout the action German mortar and cannon fire splashed near the *Frankford* but failed to hit the lucky ship. Semmes explained that the Germans were more interested in trying to knock out the landing craft than the destroyers. . . .

Rear Admiral Alan G. Kirk . . . commented that the destroyers *Frankford*, *Doyle*, *Harding*, *Thompson*, *Baldwin*, *McCook*, and *Emmons* ventured in so close to Omaha Beach, that "they had their bows against the bottom."

That afternoon, several bomb groups with 73 B-24s returned to bomb targets at Caen; another 409 B-17s and 300 B-24s hit the coastal area one more time, losing only one aircraft. This time, the cloud cover forced 528 aircraft to return to their bases with their bombs. Of the more than 1,700 Eighth Air Force fighters that continually flew escort and patrol missions, only 25 were lost, and an additional 400 were used as fighter-bombers.

The U.S. Ninth Air Force also sent 800 A-20s and B-26s against the coastal defenses and communication centers, and more than 2,000 of its fighters participated in various missions that ranged from escort to bombing. It lost 30 aircraft.

Beside air operations against Normandy, the U.S. Fifteenth Air Force in Italy diverted the *Luftwaffe*'s attention by continuing shuttle-bombing raids. On their return from the USSR, 105 B-17s hit Galati. Another 570 bombers struck at the oil refineries at Ploesti and other targets in the Balkans.

First Lt. Douglas G. McArthur, a twenty-five-year-old draftee from Newport, Washington, was in the 561st Squadron, 388th Bomb Group. On his twelfth mission, he piloted his B-17 across the Channel during those early hours of the invasion.

> We carried twelve 500-pound bombs and were in the first wing of the heavy bombers that went in that day.[9] We encountered lots of enemy tracking flak and ground rockets, but we were able to make it home with none hurt.
>
> Our mission (number thirteen) that afternoon was to Pont-L'Evêque, France. The target was a main road-railroad junction. We again carried twelve 500-pound

9. These should have been 100-pound bombs if their mission had been to hit the beach area.

The Destroyer USS *Meredith*, DD 726, and the Last D-Day Convoys

The first USS *Meredith* went down in the Pacific war during the Guadalcanal campaign of 1942. The following are excerpts from the official secret report from the summer of 1944 written by Cmdr. George Knuepfer of the second USS *Meredith*, which was launched in December 1943.

> The *Meredith* arrived in the United Kingdom on the 28th of May [1944], after having escorted a convoy from the United States. . . . Around 29 May I received all the information for Operation Neptune. We received a special briefing in the old theater at Plymouth, where the whole operation was explained to us, and I, in that operation, was assigned as Escort Commander of Convoy U-3 which consisted of 16 LSTs, and six Rhinos, the whole convoy containing about 7,500 troops.
>
> Among my escorts were two French corvettes, the *R'Achit* and the *Renoncule*, three British trawlers and four U.S. Coast Guard Escort ships, quite an assortment of Allied Escort vessels. We started out the day before D-Day from Torquay, England and made our way across through swept channels across to the invasion coast.
>
> The weather was quite rough, heavy overcast and a moderate sea. As is well known, the tides in the English Channel, particularly as you approach the French coast, average sometimes as much as 6 knots at full flood. And I had a 6-knot convoy, so that at many times in order to make the course good, I had to steer 86 degrees off the base course to make my path good.
>
> . . . This crossing with the slow convoy was probably one of the most hazardous of the trip. . . . We were able to keep our fixes by radar and arrived in the transport area, with the convoy intact and on time. While crossing during the night, we saw innumerable ships illuminated by star shells and snowflakes which indicated the presence of E-boats but none of them approached close enough to my convoy to entail any real danger. . . .
>
> The sight of these thousands of ships crossing the channel was something that I never hoped to see. Being a slow convoy, we started before many of the others had to start so they passed us in the channel. . . . My ship . . . being one of the newest . . . received particular comment from the British forces that passed me, telling me what a fine ship I had, good luck and happy hunting.
>
> We arrived in the transport areas . . . on time. . . . I turned over my convoy to the Task Force Commander . . . and was assigned to screen the northeast of the transport area. This area was about five miles from the French coast. During the night we patrolled the entire area along with about five other destroyers, hoping for an E-boat attack so we could eliminate of few of those that had caused quite considerable trouble to ships crossing.

The *Meredith* took most of the day to arrive off the Norman coast and spent the remainder of the night of June 6–7 on the defensive screen. On June 8, while on patrol, the ship struck a mine and was towed away. German aircraft sank the *Meredith* the next day.

bombs. Colonel David, the base commander, led our group on this mission. There was lots of enemy tracking flak, ground flak. Ground flares identified the target. Because of weather, this mission took seven and a half hours, much longer than originally planned. We were running low on fuel by the time we got back to the English coast and had to land at the P-47 base at Boxtead, England, and refuel. Before flying back to the 388th base, we had to let down through 2,000 to 3,000 feet of solid cloud cover and still stay in formation. There was a standard procedure for this, but it's still a bit scary with so many planes in the air!

This was the only time our crew had to fly two missions in one day. On this day, two things impressed me: We had to drop our bombs within two minutes of a preset time or go on to a secondary target to avoid hitting our ground troops. Secondly, we had to fly back to England fifty miles south of the invasion point.

First Lt. Chester Pietrzak, a twenty-two-year-old from Erie, Pennsylvania, served with the 563rd Squadron of the 388th Bomb Group. On his twenty-third mission, he flew aboard a B-17 as a bombardier. He wrote in his diary that on the previous two days, his squadron had bombed coastal batteries on the Pas de Calais in weather that was better than predicted at the briefing. They dropped their bombs visually, with fair results, encountering no enemy aircraft and only moderate flak, which damaged two aircraft. These easy missions, or "milk runs," left the crews relatively fresh for June 6.

We went to bed early the night of June 5th since we were alerted to be ready for our 23rd mission the next day. Each of the crew members was slightly elated that our last two flights had been "milk runs" (of short duration) and we were hoping for more. Much longer missions seemed to be our order for day previously; these were to Poznan, Berlin, Brux (Czechoslovakia), Fredrichshaven, and others.

We were awakened very early (soon after midnight) the morning of June 6th, 1944. There was considerable discussion about the need for this earliness. Consensus declared another "long" one in order. That did not set in too well.

Getting organized was a real chore. Barracks were cold and clammy. The latrine was at least 300 feet away—a long walk on a cold morning. What to wear was a problem. It gets -50 degrees at 23,000 feet altitude, that's cold-cold. You better be prepared for anything and everything.

In the back of our minds, we were always aware of possible abrupt alterations in our lives. We were hardened to the ways of aerial warfare with the *Luftwaffe* and German flak, plus the weather taking their toll. We would lose a portion of our formation or our squadron would be torn apart, yet we had to go, and to go back the next day tougher, wiser and full of prayer. "Courage was fear that had lots of prayer."

With a couple exceptions, we hardly knew the men in the planes that flew with us. We saw them exploding on take-offs, on landings, in mid-air by enemy aircraft or bursts of flak. Some were gone after their 1st mission, some on their 25th (originally we flew 25 missions in the Eighth Air Force and were done, but later this was raised to 30 and then 35).

Now, after being awakened, dressed and having eaten breakfast, all paths led to the briefing rooms for a look at the mission for the day. There was a map on the wall, and it was still covered with the line up of air-

LST 21 unloading a British Sherman and trucks onto a Rhino barge off the coast of Normandy.

planes (crews) and their positions in formation.

"Ten-hut!" We rose to our feet as the Operations Officer took over the briefing. "At Ease! Take your Seats!" the intelligence officer at the command of the Operations Officer pulled aside a curtain that covered the map of Britain and Western Europe. There a red line stretched across the Channel to the coast of Normandy and back—but not the same way—out to the Atlantic near the Isles of Jersey and Guernsey, then back to England and our base.

There were cries of joy, elation and surprise—three "milk runs" in a row. Smiles and cheers prevailed. But, suddenly the voice of the Operations Officer with a very, very serious voice proclaimed, "Yes, this will be an easy one for you guys, but down below you there will be thousands and thousands of men who won't have it easy at all. Gentlemen, today is the day—the invasion of Europe."

Suddenly there was a tremendous hush and for one quick moment a sudden paralysis in all the faces, but with no command, no gesture, all these men, as one, fell to their knees, bowed their heads, and surely prayed.

Our primary targets were on the coastline in direct support of the Allied invasion forces, which were to land immediately after the bombing. After a "That's all!" everyone scrambled to their feet and headed for their areas, additional specialized briefing, then on to the airplanes. We were more than ready. Soon we heard the sounds of the warm-up generators and explosive roar of propellers, and we were on our way heading for the English Channel and Normandy.

Sgt. Melvin F. Larson was a toggalier in the 388th's 560th Squadron.[10] Toggaliers were enlisted men serving as bombardiers, but without bombsights. The D-Day mission wound up being less eventful than the "milk run" before D-Day. Lt. Mike Soldato was seriously wounded on a mission over Paris on June 4, but he did not tell his copilot to take over until he was about to lapse into unconsciousness because of the to loss of blood. He died four days later.

> June 6, 1944, was my twenty-second scheduled mission, and we had a very early briefing at 11:30 P.M. on June 5, 1944. Col. William B. David, the base commander, personally conducted this special briefing. "In a few hours, the Combined Allied Forces will be making history, and we shall be part of it. Bombing on the primary target will be carried out within the strict prescribed time limits. No second bombing run will be made on the primary targets. Takeoffs will be accomplished according to the strict schedule—regardless, and I do mean regardless."
>
> The 388th Bomb Group was to furnish the A and B Groups and would be the first and second waves, respectively, to be over the target area. I was flying as toggalier with Lt. George Montgomery and crew, and we would be in the A [Group] that would lead the Eighth Air Force on today's historical D-Day invasion. Our aircraft would be the fourth one to cross over the landing zone.
>
> We were airborne at 2:30 A.M., and the target was to be bombed by PFF Pathfinder because of the 10/10 cloud coverage. Lt. Col. Chester A. Cox, the deputy commander of the 388th Bomb Group, was flying in the lead PFF aircraft, and he was also the lead commander. His aircraft would be the first aircraft to drop bombs in support of today's D-Day invasion. Piloting the lead PFF aircraft was Capt. Ray Campbell.
>
> We dropped our bombs at 6:56 A.M. from an altitude of 15,000 feet. We were disappointed, as we could not see the ground or the English Channel to observe the massive invasion forces because of the solid cloud coverage. We saw no enemy fighters and no flak on today's mission. We landed back at Knettishall by 10:45 A.M. We were later informed by the second group, which bombed later, that the cloud coverage had broken and it looked like you could almost walk across the English Channel because of the saturation of LSTs and ships involved in the invasion.
>
> The 388th Bomb Group performed three support missions for the Allied invasion today. The last mission was under the command of Colonel David, and his group dropped their bombs at 2100 hours [9 P.M.], and they did not return back to the base until 0010 hours [12:10 A.M.], 7 June 1944.

Their second mission was against a tactical target on the peninsula, and the third mission was against Pont-L'Evêque

Twenty-three-year-old S.Sgt. Byron Cook, a left waist gunner from Ohio on one of the 560th Squadron's B-17s called *Little Boy Blue* undertook his twenty-fourth mission on June 6. He had been wounded in April over Germany on his tenth mission and he had missed the next few, returning to duty on May 7 for a mission to Berlin. On June 6, 1944, his wife received a message informing her that he had recovered and had been back on duty since April. The D-Day mission was a short hop, but it took about eight hours because of the prescribed routes.

10. After the war, Larson was ordained as an Episcopalian minister. In the 1990s, the reverend became the archbishop of the northwestern United States. He passed away in fall 2008.

An LCVP on D-Day.

At 2300 hours [11 P.M.], on June 5, we were called into the briefing room and, in an atmosphere electric with suppressed excitement, were given the news so long awaited—D-Day was at hand! All Allied planes had been painted with identifying stripes; any plane without them was to be fired upon. The targets were to be bombed visually by individual squadrons. Everything that could fly was to be thrown against the enemy the following morning. We took off about 0200 hours and flew up to northern England to make rendezvous with our squadron. Such a tremendous volume of bombers was scheduled to bomb just ahead of the first wave of assault boats that the many rendezvous points were scattered all over the country and the ships were to fly at many different altitudes, a precaution against collision. All through the darkness could be seen the running lights of the bombers, green and red dots on each side of the bluish exhausts.

After several hours of circling the splasher beacons, the great armadas of planes set out through the awakening dawn towards Fortress Europa. The waters near southern England were covered with landing craft headed towards the French coast, but before we were halfway across the Channel, we passed over 10/10 cloud undercast, which remained unbroken all the way to the enemy coast. The division, wing, and group formations all split up into squadrons to attack their respective targets. The dense clouds made PFF bombing imperative, as well as denying me a view of the drama being enacted at the coast below. Our 388th Group was the group scheduled to be the first over the Normandy coast. *Little Boy*

> *Blue* was flying number 2 position in the Composite Group [C Group]. There was little glory to it, however, for the PFF set on our lead ship went out just before reaching the headquarters of a German infantry division at Caen, which was our objective. There was no chance of taking another run on the target. . . . Our squadron banked around and rejoined the group formation, backtracked over the Channel. All the way back, I was straining to see something of the great assault, but there were no breaks in the undercast until nearing the English coast. The group landed and refueled, many of the planes soon taking off on small squadron sorties, which went on all day, but our crew wasn't fortunate enough to be assigned to any. Many RAF Lancasters and Halifaxes, normally night bombers, were seen passing overhead during the day, as our combined Allied air offensive was thrown full strength against the enemy.

Byron Cook was awarded the Oak Leaf Cluster to his Air Medal the next day. That same day, he flew a mission against a railroad bridge at Nantes, flying once more over the invasion fleet.[11]

T.Sgt. Javis Roberts, a twenty-one-year-old draftee from Louisiana in the 561st Squadron of the 388th Bomb Group, was the flight engineer aboard the B-17G named *I'll Get By*, piloted by Lt. John McNicol with Lieutenant Mergenthaler as copilot. Lt. Gus Arnoff was the navigator, Lt. Harry Tingey the bombardier, and Leonard Gill the radioman. Woodrow Whitecotton and Harry Pennington were the waist gunners, Ted Cook was in the tail, and Joe Marandino manned the ball turret. Since its first mission in March, this had been a rather lucky crew.

> On D-Day we took off early in heavy fog at 2:27 A.M. The English Channel had solid overcast, except a break in the clouds before we got to the Sword Beach area. All we saw was a bunch of ships for about two minutes before the clouds closed in again. Bombs were away at 6:56 A.M. at 15,050 feet. All we saw was several rockets way off to our left, very ineffective as they usually were then. All our aircraft were back at base by 10:43 A.M.

June 6 and the days before and after were easy ones for the 388th. Before the end of the month, the group would be flying long, dangerous shuttle missions to Russia. Some aircraft, like the one in which Javis Roberts flew, never returned from Poltava, because the *Luftwaffe* caught them on the ground.

Among the hundreds of B-17s that flew on D-Day was the one piloted by 2nd Lt. Jack R. Sargeant from Cincinnati, serving with the 326th Squadron of the 92nd Bomb Group. Like the others, Sargeant was briefed about his mission just before midnight on June 5. His squadron was to bomb a road intersection at St. Lô and had a second mission against a German command post. He prepared for this mission just like the others, putting on his long john underwear, green pants and shirt, flying suit, and A-2 jacket. Over all this, he strapped on his Mae West and parachute harness. He preferred to use a chest pack, which he placed alongside his seat. Before reaching the enemy coast, he donned his flak suit, of which the pilot and copilot wore only the front portion. He was fortunate enough to get a glimpse of the

11. In July, the crew was flying another B-17. On July 17, on Cook's thirty-first mission, his plane sustained several hits over the coast of France, and the crew bailed out when the crippled aircraft reached England. Because of a few minor injuries, his crew did not fly the next day and another crew took up their *Little Boy Blue*. While the planes assembled in the air, there was a midair collision, and the tail of their craft broke off. Only the tail gunner and another crewman managed to bail out before the aircraft crashed and exploded. Cook flew two more missions, completing his tour with his thirty-third

fleet below, as well as the vast air armada of which his aircraft was a part.

> We were assigned a certain altitude and a certain track, and we were allowed to vary, I think, a half a mile either way from the track, and that was the course because the sky was full of airplanes at all altitudes. I could see the B-26s and B-25s going in just below us. There were aircraft everywhere you looked, with fighter cover over the top of us. There was no way the enemy could get through to us, I thought.
>
> One of our bombs hung up in the bomb bay, and Bill Hocutt, our engineer, got back there with the bomb bay open and no parachute on, and he kicked the bomb out. It landed in the water.

T.Sgt. Alvin Anderson, a twenty-one-year-old flight engineer of a B-17 from the farm lands of Monticello, Indiana flew with the 525th Bomb Squadron, 379th Bomb Group, and had an interesting experience the evening before the invasion.

> On the evening of June 5, after we came back from a short run to France, we got a pass and went into Bedford. I was standing on a street corner talking to some English girls, and one of them said tomorrow will be D-Day.
>
> We got back towards midnight and went into the barracks. We got into bed and the CQ [charge of quarters] came through, got everybody up, and told us to go down and eat breakfast.
>
> We left the mess hall and went down to the briefing rooms. All the crews had gathered there, and as the briefing officer got up in front of us, he said, "Well boys, today is the day; this is D-Day." I looked at my pilot and said, "My gosh, I heard that in town last night." The briefing officer went ahead and cautioned all of us not to mention a word to anyone, including the ground crew, although they knew something was up because this was shortly after midnight and we were all gathered at our planes.
>
> We put our machine guns into the turrets. The pilot, copilot, and I helped preflight the plane, checking all outside appearances, the controls, and everything else. Then we got inside the plane. As we received the orders to taxi out to take off, we started the engines up. Just before we started down the runway for takeoff, we had to run the engines up and check all the controls again. Again, we checked our mags to be sure everything was proper. We took off down the runway, and shortly after clearing the runway, the gear came up and we climbed to our designated altitude and circled all the way up. When we reached our altitude and coordination points to assemble, we finally headed out over the Channel for our target. It was foggy that morning, extremely foggy. We had a Pathfinder ship, a B-17 equipped with radar to pinpoint the place to drop our bombs. Our orders were, if we could not drop our bombs at a certain time, to bring them back, which normally we didn't do—we always dropped them in the Channel.
>
> After getting our altitude and forming our formation, we headed for France and couldn't see anything below us. There was absolutely solid overcast. We did drop our bombs where the Pathfinder ship did.[12]
>
> Consequently, I didn't see anything on the ground that day. There were no enemy

12. A Pathfinder ship was an aircraft, usually carrying special electronic equipment to locate the target for the main body of bombers that followed it.

> fighters. According to my information, we might have had a few rockets fired at us at Guernsey Island, but for flak over the target, there was none. It was a "milk run." That afternoon, they ran another flight over France, but I wasn't on that one. There were two men in our crew that did fly that one.

The Eighth Air Force sent twenty-one heavy bombardment groups of B-17s and nineteen of B-24s: twelve groups of B-17 Flying Fortresses from the 1st Bombardment Division, fourteen groups of B-24 Liberators from the 2nd, and nine groups of B-17s and five of B-24s from the 3rd. There were sixteen squadrons of P-38 Lightnings, P-47 Thunderbolts, and P-51 Mustangs of the VIII Fighter Command and eighteen squadrons of P-38s, P-47, and P-51s. The Ninth Air Force's IX Fighter Command also participated in the action. In addition, joining this massive air force was almost every available aircraft of the thirteen troop carrier groups (C-47s and C-53s) of the IX Troop Carrier Command and its IX Bomber Command with its bombardment groups of A-20 Havoc light bombers and eight bombardment groups of B-26 Marauder medium bombers.

Twenty-eight-year-old 1st Lt. Frank Gallagher from Des Moines flew as a bombardier on a B-26 Marauder of the 450th Squadron, 322nd Bombardment Group. Flying below the heavy bombers, Gallagher was treated to a good view of the fleet. "I took pictures of the ships in the Channel—it was impressive. On June 6, we were bombing a coastal gun site, which I believe was on Omaha Beach [more likely Utah Beach]. Sometimes we did four missions a day: briefing at 4 A.M., takeoff at 5 A.M., back by 11 A.M., and so on. When we hit the target, it was daylight, maybe 9 A.M. We watched the bombs fall—no fighters and no flak."

This first mission was a flight of one hour and fifty-five minutes; the second took just over three hours, as it was farther inland. Two weeks later, Gallagher undertook his seventy-fifth mission, which completed his tour.

One fighter pilot of the Eighth Air Force who took part in the action on D-Day was Maj. Robert S. Johnson of Lawton, Oklahoma. One of America's leading aces, he served in the 62nd Fighter Squadron, 56th Fighter Group. In April and May, he flew cover on No Ball missions. He flew his last mission, number ninety-one, on May 8, shooting down two aircraft, which brought his total to twenty-seven. Instead of returning home, he went to rest in Scotland. On June 3, he called Col. Bob Burns at his unit's headquarters and requested to be sent home or back into combat. Colonel Burns told him to report back to headquarters for his papers to return home.

> At 6:30 A.M. on June 6, 1944, I was shaving—the phone rang. I said, "Hello." Colonel Burns then said, "Bob, turn your radio on. Good-bye and good luck!" and hung up.
>
> D-Day! I called him back and begged, pleaded, threatened, and cried. "Put me back in combat for just two weeks; I want to see this thing!" He again said, "Go home and get fat!" and hung up. I was never allowed to go back into combat, even in Korea.

Except for the spectacle of the vast air and sea armada, Johnson did not miss out on any action that day as he flew home on a C-54 Skymaster, since the *Luftwaffe* did not appear. Only a couple of German fighters showed up during the day, as most fighter squadrons had largely been withdrawn to defend Germany before the invasion.

The Allied air plan called for five groups of the IX Fighter Command to fly high cover over the assault area, one group of P-38s in conjunction with four from the VIII Fighter Command to protect the convoy area, and two groups of P-38s and four of P-47s to give direct air support to the army. Six P-47 and three P-51 groups from the

An LCVP from the *Samuel Chase*, carrying troops of the 16th Infantry in the tenth wave, takes a hit.

VIII Fighter Command escorted the IX Bomber Command. In addition, four groups of P-47s and two of P-51s in reserve for the Ninth Air Force were assigned missions as fighter-bombers. During the campaign, the *Luftwaffe* flew an estimated seventy sorties against the Allies.

The 1,077 heavy bombers dropped 3,096 tons of bombs on Normandy between 6 and 8:30 A.M. The 1,347 fighters of the Eighth Air Force flew inland and covered the area between the Seine and Loire and along the flanks of the air armada. By the time the Eighth arrived on the scene, the 770 C-47s Skytrains of the Ninth Air Force were already home or on their way. Most of the light and medium bombers of the Ninth Air Force flew below the squadrons of the Eighth Air Force and provided cover for the air armada, although some of them flew fighter-bomber missions.

Capt. Jack Ilfrey, a twenty-four-year-old Texan, had unofficially become the first P-38 ace in March 1943 during the North African campaign, when he shot down his fifth enemy aircraft. After that, he was sent back to the United States for one year to train pilots. Upon arriving in England in April 1944, he was given command of the 79th Fighter Squadron of the 20th Fighter Group of the Eighth Air Force. He had already flown seventy-two missions in the Mediterranean when he began the first of seventeen missions in a P-38 Lightning in late April. During his third mission over Berlin on May 24, he shot down two Me 109s. The second one he hit collided with him and took a five-foot chunk out of his right wing. Most of his missions were over Germany, but one was as far as Poznan, Poland. On June 2, he was sent over Paris, and the next day, he was assigned his shortest mission, over the Pas de Calais area. Between June 5 and 11, he operated over the English Channel. He flew three missions on June 6, ranging from three hours and ten minutes to three hours and twenty-five minutes in operational flight time. His squadron, with the 77th, sent three flights of four P-38s to patrol ahead of the convoys on the first escort mission of the invasion. The 55th, 77th, and 79th Fighter Squadrons rotated throughout the day. The 20th Fighter Group saw little action on D-Day, but the pilots had a great view of the invasion. Ilfrey describes the life of the pilots as having followed a strict routine.

> In the early-morning hours, the group intelligence officer and his personnel would receive the order for the day's mission. Usually the squadron commander would have already turned in a list of the pilots who would fly that day. Those on the list plus a few spares would be awakened and get over to the officers' mess for breakfast. Lots of times, we would have been awakened earlier due to the noise of several hundred bombers forming up in our area at Kingscliff. It was important that we heed the call of Mother Nature, and some of us would get a fix quick for this at this time.
>
> Then we would be taken over to the briefing room, where the intelligence people had been working on a map on a board with the details of our mission for that day. We made our notes on pads on our knees, after intelligence was through; the group leader for that mission would give us his thoughts and answer questions. Sometimes the squadron commander (me) would give his views.
>
> At the end of the briefing, we would all synchronize our watches, go out in front of the headquarters building, and meet with the chaplain, who would offer a prayer for our safe return. I personally did not think much of this. When you think about it, we had a license to kill, and I did not want to be prayed over for that. Some of the others thought the same way.
>
> We would go to our respective squadrons' operations building and put on our flight gear for the mission and then would be taken out to our aircraft, where we usually had a chat with our crew chief.
>
> We had three types of missions: penetration, escorting bombers in to the target; target area support; and withdrawal, escorting bombers out from target. After we were through with these missions, we were free to hit the deck and ground-strafe targets of opportunity, which meant anything if we were in Germany. We used discretion while in other countries.
>
> Upon return to base in England, all of us would be somewhat to very tired after five and a half to six hours or more being strapped down tight. We were given medicinal whiskey, went to briefing, and we were briefed by the intelligence people about the mission. After the briefing, we would gather in the officers' club and have drinks and dinner while we shot the bull. More drinks for some of us, and back to the barracks and bed to wait for the morning call.

He was back over Normandy the next day.

Some of the Eighth Air Force fighters who patrolled beyond the target area were luckier. Near Évreux, the Allied fighters shot down one German fighter and encountered a few others. A flight of P-51s took out eight to ten Stukas, and seven more were destroyed in the air. In the afternoon, an ammunition and a troop train were strafed, and the ammunition train was destroyed. Also in the vicinity of Évereux, four of ten FW-190s were shot down as they landed. By the end of the day, the VIII Fighter Command accounted for twenty-six German fighters but had lost the same number of its own, according to Hess and Ivie in *Fighters of the Mighty Eighth.* The American fighters suffered more losses than the bombers. Nevertheless, on June 6, the Allies dominated not only the sea, but also the air.

CHAPTER 11

The Landings on Utah Beach

After the first blow to German morale in the predawn darkness when the paratroopers landed, the Allies dealt the enemy a second one several hours later, when the guns of their vast armada and the fleet of bomber squadrons were unleashed against the coastal positions. Although the explosions shook the concrete structures and rattled the nerves of many of their occupants, they alone could not bring victory. The Allied assault troops had to breach the German defenses by wading ashore from hundreds of landing craft, storming across the beaches past enemy obstacles and mines, and neutralizing strongpoints they could not bypass. The survival of thousands of parachutists depended on their establishing a beachhead and breaking through to the troopers.

Details of the Landings

The 4th Infantry Division, reinforced with a regiment of the 90th Infantry Division, was assigned the relatively flat terrain of the eastern side of the Cotentin Peninsula identified with the code name Utah Beach. A Bigot-Neptune analysis on April 21, 1944, described the beach as 9,655 yards in length, low-lying, with no distinctive terrain features.1 The report also noted that the beach was backed by a masonry seawall, except for a couple-hundred-yard stretch, and behind the central part of this wall were sand dunes ranging from 10 to 25 feet in height and extending southward about 150 yards inland. Inundated lowlands lay beyond the beach. Few roads passed through this barrier.

Shortly after midnight, the transports that followed the minesweepers toward the assembly points reduced their speed. By 2 A.M., the troopships had dropped anchor about twelve miles from the beach, just beyond enemy artillery range. The 1st and 2nd Battalions of the 8th Infantry Regimen would be the first waves of infantry to land, with the 1st aboard the attack transport *Joseph T. Dickman* and the 2nd on the *Barnett*. Each transport carried more than a dozen LCVPs.[2] About an hour and a half before dawn, the first troops began climbing down the landing nets to board LCVPs, which had been lowered from the ships. The rough seas made the loading dangerous, and the soldiers had to take care not to fall between the ship and LCVP as the vessles bounced against each other. Some army commanders asked the naval officers to disregard orders and load the LCVPs before lowering them, in order to reduce the risk to the troops, but according to Gawne's *Spearheading D-Day*, the naval officers refused to comply.[3]

As the loaded LCVPs of the first waves of the 8th Infantry began circling, a special force from the 4th and 24th Cavalry Squadrons was assigned the mission of assaulting the Îles St. Marcouf, two small islands flanking the landing site, to eliminate a possible enemy observation position or a site that might be used for detonating controlled sea mines. The assault took place at 4:30 A.M., but no Germans were there, and land mines caused the only casualties. The troopers secured the islands by 5:30 A.M. In the meantime, the soldiers of the 4th Division in their landing craft were tossed around by the seas as the circling ended, and they formed into assault waves before heading toward shore.

The landing control vessels, one primary and one secondary for each beach, departed for their stations just before 5 A.M. The primary control vessel for Red Beach, *PC 1261*, was sunk by a mine, and the secondary control vessel was delayed when a buoy fouled its propeller. At 6 A.M., a mine exploded, sinking *LCT 597*, which was carrying DD tanks that followed the primary control vessel for Green Beach, *PC 1176*. *PC 1176* was also sunk by a mine as the secondary control vessel, *LCC 60*, moved over to take

---

1. The expanse of beach covered in the report was greater than the sector selected for the landings.
2. One source, *D-Day Encyclopedia*, edited by David Chandler and James Collins, states that the *Dickman* carried thirty-three LCVPS and 1,750 troops and the *Barnett* and other APAs carried twenty-six LCVPs and two LCMs with 1,400 troops. These numbers are reasonable, as a Coast Guard history states that the *Dickman* carried thirty landing craft in Operation Husky, but at Normandy carried more than 1,960 troops (mentioning only the loss of seven LCVPs and not the total number carried). According to Malcolm Willoughby's *The U.S. Coast Guard in World War II*, the *Bayfield* was listed as carrying nineteen LCVPs and two LCMs, and twelve of these LCVPs were sent to unload the *Barnett*. The U.S. Navy listed the *Bayfield* as having a capacity for about 1,200 troops, twelve LCVPs, and four LCMs, and the *Barnett* with at least twelve LCVPs. In *U.S. Amphibious Ships and Craft*, Norman Friedman states that the *Bayfield* and *Barnett* could each carry about twenty-five LCVPs and two LCMs.
3. The British LSIs, essentially similar to the American army transports, had stronger davits, so the landing craft could be loaded on deck before lowering them.

charge of the craft heading for Red Beach, which no longer had a control vessel.[4] The loss and delay of the control vessels, the effects of currents, the smoke and haze left by the naval bombardment, and the barrage of 5,000 5-inch rockets delivered against the beaches by LCTs just before the landing created a state of relative chaos. In the confusion, the assault waves hit the wrong beaches, a few hundred yards south of their designated targets.

Companies E and F of the 2nd Battalion were the first to come ashore on the new Uncle Red Beach at 6:30 A.M. Companies B and C of the 1st Battalion landed about fifteen minutes late at the new Tare Green Beach. Initially there was some confusion onshore, because the assault troops were not able to identify the strongpoints they were supposed to attack. The only recognizable landmark was an old windmill that should have been on their left but was to their right. Several officers quickly realized that they had landed in the wrong place. The error was fortunate since the Germans manned more heavily fortified positions at the intended landing sites. The son of the former president, Brig. Gen. Theodore Roosevelt Jr., landed with the first waves. General Roosevelt held an honorary position and served as an extra brigadier general. He had insisted on going in with the leading waves, which put him in a real command position early in the landing as an assistant division commander. Once onshore, he made one of the most important decisions of the day. After conferring with the battalion commanders, he ordered the subsequent waves to continue landing on the wrong beach, designated the new Red and Green Beaches. In the first waves, there were little more than a dozen Comanche "code talkers," who radioed back that it was the wrong beach. According to the after-action report of the 8th Infantry, the regiment eliminated strongpoint W-5 at the end of road U-5 at H+25 minutes, encountering little opposition. Within three hours, the remainder of the beach defenses had crumbled.

The landings went relatively smoothly, because the B-26 Marauders had effectively bombed all the strongpoints from W-3 to W-10, which encompassed both the intended landing site and the actual one. W-3 had only three men left. W-5, located on the actual landing site, had suffered particularly heavily from the bombing. This position included 50-millimeter guns, 47-millimeter antitank guns, machine guns, and a Tobruk with a French tank turret mounting a 37-millimeter gun. To the rear of W-5 were W-4, an unfinished position, and W-7, the site of the German commander of the 3rd Battalion, 919th Regiment, which defended this section of coast. Farther up the beach stood the well-armed W-8, which was stronger than W-5 and blocked access to Exit 3 on the intended invasion beach. Just beyond W-8, on the other side of the intended beach, was StP-9, enclosed on the landward side by an antitank ditch and mines. The most heavily defended position in the area, it included two casemates mounting 88-millimeter guns in flanking positions, one of which may have been the 88 that had been observed pounding the invasion site early in the day. This strongpoint included five turret positions, like W-5, and a 50-millimeter automatic fortress mortar in the cloche of a bunker.

W-5 was easily taken, and its elimination meant that no serious opposition was found on the beaches. Most American casualties were caused by the coastal batteries farther north firing into the area. The Germans' own water obstales effectively cut off the defenders from relief and reinforcement, since the Allied paratroopers on the other side prevented the enemy from reaching the causeways.

4. The PC (patrol craft) was a 173-foot boat used as the primary control vessel. It was supported by an LCC (control craft), a 36-foot boat equipped with radar and radio equipment.

Sherman tanks with fording gear and troops coming ashore in follow-up waves.

The twenty-eight Sherman DD tanks of Companies A and B of the 70th Tank Battalion, attached to the 4th Infantry Division, disembarked from their seven LCTs 3,000 yards offshore instead of the planned 5,000 yards. A mine on the way in had destroyed the eighth LCT. The 8th Infantry spearheaded the landing, with thirty-man assault teams of the 1st Battalion in ten LCVPs landing at Tare Green Beach and ten more of the 2nd Battalion at Uncle Red Beach, while the Sherman DD tanks were still swimming behind them. Companies A and B of the 70th Tank Battalion supported the 1st and 2nd Battalions of the 8th Infantry, respectively, stretched over a front of about 2,200 yards. The 8th Infantry's Companies E and F hit Red Beach at 6:30 A.M., and Companies B and C landed on Green Beach at 6:45 A.M.

The second wave, five minutes behind the first, consisted of thirty LCVPs carrying most of the remainder of the 1st and 2nd Battalions and army engineer–navy underwater demolition teams (UDTs) in twelve of the LCVPs.[5] The demolition gap assault teams had the mission of clearing obstacles and creating four fifty-yard gaps among those on each beach. The third wave, which was to land at H-Hour plus fifteen minutes, included ten LCTs ferrying the tanks of Company C of the 70th Tank Battalion (less a detachment of tankdozers) on both beaches. This tank company was ordered to start firing from a range of about 3,000 yards in support of the landings, but it was told to hold its fire after H-5 minutes so as not to endanger the leading waves. The tanks of Company C actually landed ahead of its battalion's leading companies, however, whose Sherman DD tanks were still swimming toward the beach. Company C was assigned to the Beach Obstacle Demolition Party and was to return to the control of the 8th Infantry later.

The fourth wave, consisting of additional engineer units of the 237th and 299th Engineer Bat-

5. Some sources prefer to group the waves together and call all the formations in the first hour the first wave. In the plans, however, each line of landing craft was considered a separate wave.

talions, came two minutes behind Company C of the 70th Tank Battalion. Successive waves brought ashore the 3rd Battalion of the 8th Infantry, the 22nd Infantry at about 10:30 A.M., the 12th Infantry, the 1st Battalion of the 401st Glider Infantry, and two battalions of the 359th Infantry Regiment of the 90th Division.

The first vehicles landed at about 9 A.M. while elements of the 1st Engineer Special Brigade were beginning to organize the beachhead. The original landing plans were discarded, because they were on the wrong beach, and the commanders had to improvise. Gen. Henry Barber, the 4th Division's assistant division commander, came ashore with elements of the CP at about 9:30 A.M. Gen. Raymond Barton came ashore about half an hour later and took over.

During the first hour, the demolition teams of the Beach Obstacle Demolition Partyunder the command of Maj. Herschel Linn of the 237th Engineer Combat Battalion from the 1106th Engineer Group began clearing the gaps among the obstacles. Major Linn was onboard an M-29 Weasel, a small tracked cargo vehicle, which sank on its way to the beach. The major's XO had to take over until Linn arrived the next day.

After a couple hours, the 8th Infantry of the 4th Division reorganized and began moving inland along the causeways in the marshes. Although the planners had meant to use two roads on the originally targeted beach, only one road, U-5, was available in the new invasion area. The route through the inundated area was a narrow road that included a culvert blown up by the Germans. A German antitank gun crew near the culvert took out the first Sherman advancing up the road before 10:00 A.M. The tank platoon pushed the destroyed tank into the flooded area and forded the small creek. Other vehicles from the 70th Tank Battalion destroyed the German position, and personnel from the 1106th Engineer Group repaired the culvert. Company D of the 70th Tank Battalion, scheduled to arrive several hours after the initial landings, came ashore with its light tanks and prepared to drive toward the airhead of the 101st A/B Division at about midday. Meanwhile, vehicles crowded at the assembly areas and created a huge traffic jam. The narrow road became heavily congested as some units blocked it and the engineers stopped their vehicles to unload pontoons. Two tanks tried to get around the blockage and became stuck in the swamp. When two more tanks tried to advance, they created another obstruction on the road. The soldiers were able to move on, but supplies and armor support fell behind. In the meantime, the Germans fired only at the beach area instead of these bottlenecks.

The 2nd Battalion of the 8th Infantry reached Poupeville at midday against light opposition and soon took up position on a hilltop. The 1st Battalion advanced to Reuville by late afternoon without opposition. It cleared the town and moved south until it was stopped by German troops at Turqueville. The 3rd Battalion was held up at Germain, where it encountered a defensive position with several 88-millimeter guns and small arms. The battalion attacked the position, killing about 50 Germans and taking 100 prisoners. Next, the 3rd moved to a point south of Ste-Mère-Église. The battalion's Company K was sent toward Chef-du-Pont. Thus the 8th Infantry successfully achieved most of its objectives for D-Day.

By the time the 22nd Infantry landed, after 10 A.M., the Germans were having more success hitting the new waves of troops. A mine destroyed a battery of the 29th Field Artillery, blowing up its LCT. The 3rd Battalion of the 22nd Infantry headed up the beach to destroy the German strongpoint blocking road T-7. The 1st and 2nd Battalions of the 22nd moved northwest through waist-deep swamps crisscrossed by unseen deep ditches and holes. It took seven hours to go two miles because fortified positions on the coast firing across the low terrain delayed the advance of the 22nd Infantry. The regiment finally reached St.-Martin-de-Varreville late in the afternoon.

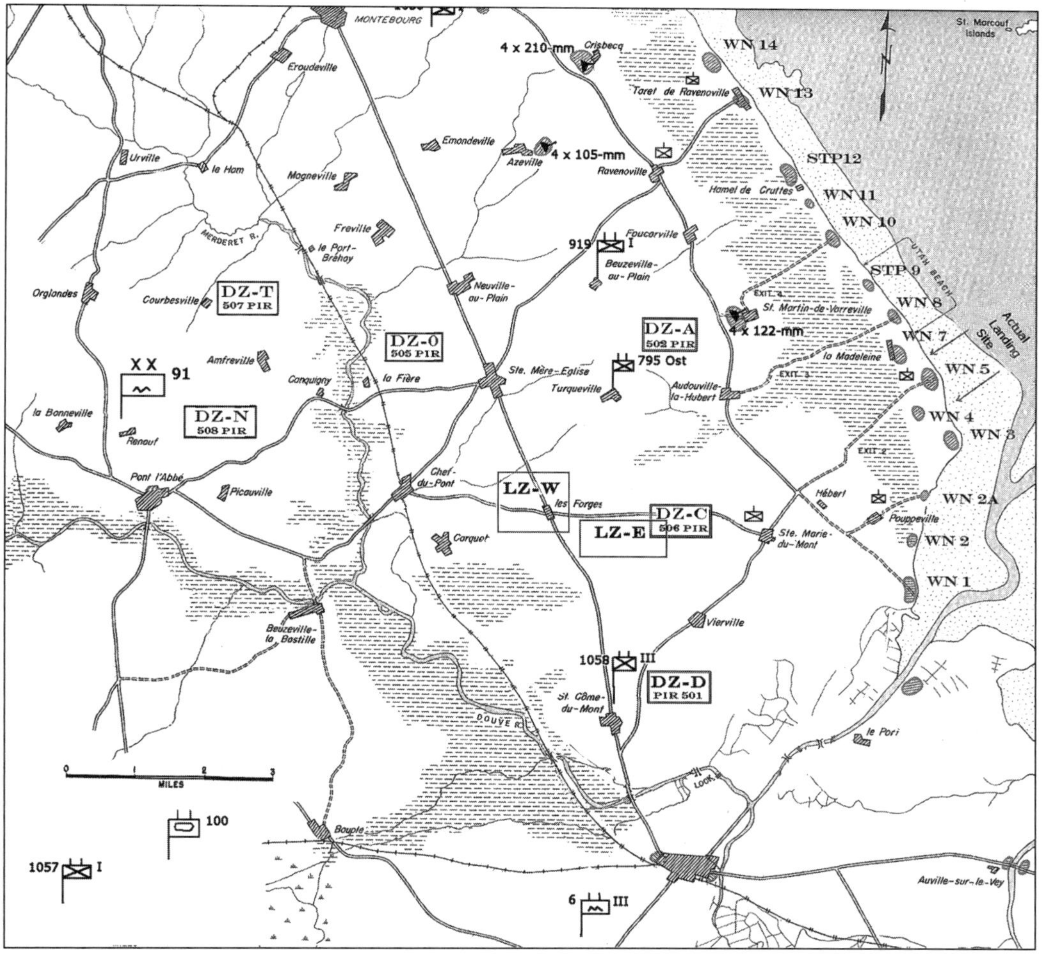

UTAH BEACH and Airborne

Drop Zones & Landing Zones

German Defenses

709 Division:
729, 739 &
919 Regt.
(919 Regt.
defending area
shown)

91 Air Landing
Division:
1057 &
1058 Regt

6 Parachute Regt

The 12th Infantry Regiment landed early in the afternoon, moved through the inundated area, and came to a stop near Beuzeville-au-Plain after reaching elements of the 502nd PIR. As with the 22nd Infantry, its advance was slow. Neither of these two regiments secured its objectives for June 6. The 3rd Battalion of the 22nd Infantry and a battalion of the 359th Infantry became the division reserve that night.

Accounts of the Utah Beach Landings

At about 1 A.M. on June 6, 1944, troops fortunate enough to be on the larger transports were awakened and served an early-morning breakfast. Although some considered it an unusual time to eat, for most of the men it would be a long time before they would have another prepared meal. After eating, the troops assembled their gear and prepared to depart from their transports. S.Sgt. William L. Conrad, a draftee from Ohio of Company F, 2nd Battalion, 8th Infantry, was onboard the *Dickman*. "We went over the side with full packs," he recalls, "down the net to await our bobbing ship below." After each man leaped onto the LCVP, the craft moved out to begin circling. The guns of the battleships boomed and plane engines droned overhead as the LCVPs headed toward shore. After hitting the beach at Uncle Red, Sergeant Conrad led his platoon against a German position. "Soon there were Germans coming out with white pieces of a sheet or some type of fabric waving, and we sent about ten of them to the rear to be guarded." Conrad's battalion moved south along the beach toward Pouppeville to link up with the paratroopers. His company came under mortar fire after the first couple hours. They later were pinned down until supporting guns eliminated the enemy artillery that held them up. Finally they broke through to meet the paratroopers near Pouppeville.

Pvt. Raymond Griffis, a twenty-five-year-old draftee from Trenton, New Jersey, was a rifleman in the 1st Platoon, Company E, 2nd Battalion, 8th Infantry, who also landed in the first wave. His landing craft approached the Normandy coast amid high swells and a crowd of ships. Hitting the beach was "a hell of an experience," he says. From there, he and his platoon hurried inland.

PFC John A. Plonski, a twenty-six-year-old from New York City who was drafted in February 1941, was a BAR[6] man in the 2nd Platoon of Company E. As he hit the beach, he looked at his watch; it was 6:42 A.M. His memories of that day are jumbled images of a landing craft blowing up, soldiers felled by enemy fire, men hollering, and weapons being fired. He and his comrades of the 8th Infantry were among the first Allies on shore on D-Day, and this was their first combat experience. Before long, however, after one day of fierce combat followed another, the memories of that first day blurred and merged with those of the succeeding days.

For T/5 Vincent A. Angeloni, the twenty-eight-year-old chief of the message center of the HQ Company, 2nd Battalion, 8th Infantry, the dawn of June 6 presented quite a contrast with the drenching downpour of the morning of June 5 when the invasion was postponed.

> I came out on the deck and could see these bombs and shells hit, and although about eleven miles out, I could even hear them.
>
> I went over the ship on the rope ladder, and the water was bouncing up and down, with the boat and ship separated by between six to eight feet. You had to make sure when the boat came up that you jumped on. We lost two or three guys with broken legs. With ninety pounds on you, you had to make sure you hit at the right time. My back got sore as the devil because I hit at the wrong time, as the boat was going down.

The second wave of LCVPs carried the remaining companies of the two assaulting battalions and the gap assault teams. On the way to shore, it passed the Sherman DD tanks that had started behind the first wave but had not yet reached their destination. Over the side of his LCVP, PFC Harper H. Coleman of Company H, 2nd Battalion, watched the other landing craft circling under the cover of the big-gun battleship *Texas*. He saw the LCVPs of the first wave move off and pass a small overturned vessel with men clinging to its side. Coleman was a gunner in a six-man squad with a .30-caliber machine gun on a support boat team. When his group reached the shore, he says, he saw "General Theodore Roosevelt with his cane almost pushing men across the beach." Coleman moved across the beach, his main concern avoiding the land mines he knew the Germans had planted. His memories of the town of Pouppeville are small-arms fire and artillery. Before long, his unit engaged the enemy in fierce combat.

The 1st Battalion, 8th Infantry, where Sgt. Irving A. Bradbury was a radioman in Company D, departed early onboard the USS *Barnett*. The battalion had practiced loading onto the LCVPs before the invasion, but things did not always work out as planned.

6. The .30-caliber BAR, or Browning automatic rifle, served as a squad light automatic weapon. Developed during World War I, it weighed just over nineteen pounds and had a twenty-round magazine.

Troops of the 4th Infantry Division scamper over an antitank seawall at Utah Beach.

When we began, it was 2 A.M. We had practiced loading over the gunwale of the ship into the landing craft, and then the landing craft would be lowered by winches into the water. It didn't work out, because the water was so rough. Troops were getting legs broken or injured as the water slapped the boat. Now they changed the command. As my turn came up, we got the honor of being the first troops over the side to climb down the rope the way we were trained in England on these rope nets. You had to be very careful, because you had to hit the boat at the right moment, as it came up on the swell and just started to go back again, so you didn't break your legs when you jumped, with ninety pounds on your back, off the rope net into the boat. Many guys got hurt that way, while many others got sick for the first time as they experienced motion sickness.

Once you got in the boat, you moved away from the ship, and you just hung around a while going in circles. We were to go to the marshaling area and join up with a group of boats we were to go in to the beach with. Sometime during this period, the bombing on the beach started. There were colors coming from land that I have never seen since or before in my life. A rainbow didn't have as many colors. While we were in the landing craft, the planes were coming over to do the bombing. It looked like an umbrella of planes, and you could actually hear the roar of the planes on these noisy landing boats, which were going round and round, slapping the water.

Waves broke over the landing ramp, splashing everybody up front, where I happened to be the first one in the corner behind the ramp. The gas mask came in handy when the spray came in over the

Gap Assault Teams

The gap assault teams were special units that combined army and naval demolition experts and whose mission was to clear a path or gap through the beach obstacles. These special units were assigned to both invasion beaches. The beach obstacles, located between the low-tide mark and the seawall, included small concrete pyramids, concrete steel sections called tetrahedra (not found on Omaha Beach), Czech hedgehogs, Element C or Belgian Gates, stakes mounting Teller mines (antitank mines activated by pressure plates), and mined timber ramps. In addition, barbed-wire obstacles and mines lay beyond the high-tide mark. Concertina barbed wire was strung along the seawall at Omaha Beach. At Utah, only a wire fence ran on top of the eight-foot-high masonry seawall. At Omaha Beach, the Germans had positions on the heights overlooking the beaches from which they could detonate hidden explosives such as old French naval shells and TNT charges that blew out rock fragments, known as stone *fougasses*.

Even if the infantry with its limited armored support successfully established a beachhead, it could not make any sustained advance inland until additional units with supplies and support echelons could come ashore. According to the official U.S. Army history, *Corps of Engineers*, the gap assault teams, referred to as the Special Engineer Task Force (SETF) at Omaha Beach and the Beach Obstacle Demolition Party (BODP) at Utah Beach, had to land right behind the initial infantry assault waves to clear the way.

> Combined Army-Navy boat teams of thirty-five to forty men carried in LCMs were to undertake the task. The sailors were to destroy the seaward obstacles, the soldiers to handle those landward and to clear mines from the tidal flat. First on the scene would be the assault gapping team (one to each gap), composed of twenty-seven men from an Army engineer combat battalion (including one officer and one medic) and an NCDU [Naval Combat Demolition Unit] augmented to thirteen men by the attachment of five Army engineers to help with demolitions and two seamen to handle the explosives and tend the rubber boats [at Omaha Beach].
>
> The assault teams were to be followed by eight support teams, one to every two assault teams, of about the same composition. . . . Each assault team was to be supported by a tankdozer [from one of the assaulting tank battalions] to clear obstacles. All boats were to carry some 1,000 pounds of explosives, demolition accessories, mine detectors, and mine gap markers.

The NCDUs sent to Utah Beach consisted of about fourteen men—eight navy men, their officer, and five army engineers. Similar teams were sent to Omaha Beach. The army demolition teams consisted of twenty-three to twenty-five men, an officer, and a medic.

> ramp. I remember vividly the overhead planes and the explosions on the beach as we came in.

S.Sgt. Glenn E. Gibson, the platoon sergeant of the 4th Platoon of Company A, 70th Tank Battalion, was in the first wave and assigned to Beach Tare Green. Company B, on the left, was destined for Uncle Red Beach. Each LCT carried a platoon of four Sherman DD tanks, which were to be launched several thousand yards out. Each of the company's platoons was loaded into four LCTs. Of the eight LCTs, all but one successfully launched their swimming tanks, which moved slowly to shore while the leading infantry units outdistanced them. Sergeant Gibson happened to be on the one LCT that failed to launch its tanks; its ramp struck a mine when dropped, and the vessel sank.

> I had the misfortune of my LCT [*LCT 597*] hitting a large naval mine. It blew up and sank our LCT with all four tanks and my crews. Out of about thirty-seven men, I am the *only army* survivor. I believe a couple of navy men survived, although I am not sure. I was picked up out of the Channel by assault engineers going in to blow the seawall. I was wounded in the head and legs and was taken back out to a destroyer. I was transported back to England, where I remained in a hospital for a few weeks.

Sergeant Gibson had been standing on the rear deck of his tank, preparing to direct the launching of his platoon's tanks. He was thrown into the water by the force of the explosion, while the sixteen tank crewmen were trapped and drowned. He swam back to the section of the LCT still afloat and tried to rescue a seaman trapped near the pilothouse, but the vessel capsized and he was plunged into the water again. About twenty minutes later, the sergeant was picked up by an LCM. He recovered from his wounds and returned to his unit in Normandy later in the month. His platoon suffered more heavily than any of the others, as Gibson was the only member to survive of the landing, and none of his men ever had a chance to fire a shot that day.

At Utah Beach, army-navy engineer and UDT assault teams followed the first waves of infantry. SF2/C Angeleos T. Chatas, a navy frogman, came ashore with other members of NCDU 25 with the mission of clearing a gap in the obstacles on the seaward side of the seawall.

> Aboard the LST with us were elements of the 101st Airborne Division that came by sea to Utah Beach. As we approached Normandy—we didn't get very close—I saw off in the distance flashes of light. We got off our LST while it was still dark. I was supposed to make sure all of us got out of the LCVP. As we proceeded in the LCVP to the beach, we could see the planes. The sky was full of planes.
>
> There were five men and an officer in the Naval Combat Demolition Unit (NCDU). For the purposes of the Normandy invasion, there were three men from the fleet assigned to us, whom we quickly gave a smattering of training back in England, plus five combat engineers. This made fourteen in the unit. We called this JANFU—Joint Army Navy Foul Up.
>
> We went in to the beach. Utah Beach had a grade that was very slight, so the zone between low and high tide was more than a mile. We came in right after ebb tide. We frogmen didn't go in wearing our swim suits, but in full battle gear with explosives on our backs. Right before we left the ship, after we were given last-minute instructions, the commander of the navy frogmen going into Utah Beach said, "Remember men, that cap has got to blow even if you got to hit it with a rock."

> Our objective was to blow a fifty-yard gap up to the seawall. We successfully did this and everything went off all right. For a while, we had a problem with German 88s.

The obstacles Chatas and his comrades first encountered as they approached the actual landing beach were scattered three-legged wooden ramps, whose longest leg measured 14 feet. Between these ramps were six unconnected Belgian Gates. The task of the naval personnel of the team was to destroy the Belgian Gates with the Hagensen Packs, each of which consisted of a 2¼-pound block of C2 plastic explosive inside a footlong canvas tube.[7] Since these tubes were not available in sufficient numbers, the demolition men used socks instead. According to test results, it was estimated that sixteen Hagensen Packs wrapped around the beams of a Belgian Gate and connected by prima cord linked to a blasting cap would flatten the gate. In reality, it took eighteen to twenty-two charges. The next line of obstacles consisted of six-foot-high reinforced concrete posts in some locations and six-foot-high concrete tetrahedra with 4-foot sides in others. There were three rows of concrete posts spaced at about 35 feet between posts and 40 feet between rows. The last line of obstacles consisted of three or four rows of wooden stakes spaced about 30 feet apart with 40 feet between rows running the length of the beach. This last obstacle was usually located at the high-water mark and up to 200 feet from the sea wall. To destroy one of these concrete posts, one or two charges were placed at the base. The tetrahedra also required several charges, with two to three placed at the base of the wooden posts and two fixed at the apex of the ramps. The destruction of hedgehogs, shaped like toy jacks, and similar obstacles required a 15-pound satchel filled with 2¼-pound blocks of the explosive tetrytol. Once the obstacles were wired, the demolition team detonated a group at a time to clear a gap. No mines were found with these obstacles at Utah Beach.

The other gap assault units proceeded to clear their required gaps among the obstacles for the waves of troops and vehicles that followed. The men assigned to this dangerous mission at Utah Beach were lucky that resistance was light; however, sporadic German artillery fire inflicted some losses. The successive waves brought in the tankdozers of Company C of the 70th Tank Battalion, which easily pushed the beach obstacles along Utah Beach. Since things were going so smoothly, the demolition teams proceeded to clear as much of the landing area as possible instead of cutting fifty-yard gaps. About 700 yards of the beach were cleared and ready for the afternoon high-tide landings. Later in the day, at the next low tide, another 900 yards were cleared. According to *Engineers in the Normandy Invasion*, a manuscript written by the Society of American Military Engineers, six soldiers and four sailors of the gap assault teams fell on Utah Beach.

Col. Eugene Caffey of the 1st Engineer Special Brigade made an unauthorized landing with the initial assault waves. He was with General Roosevelt when the decision was made to continue the landing on the wrong beach. The commander of the 1st ESB, Brig. Gen. James E. Wharton, landed on the beach at 7:30 A.M. to find his XO already there. The units of the 1st ESB included the 531st Engineer Shore Regiment, 24th Amphibian Tractor Battalion, the 286th Joint Assault Signal Company, and other service companies, according to *Down Ramp* by William Heavey. The 1st and 2nd Battalions of the 531st Engineers soon began disembarking. The 531st sent a reconnaissance platoon for each of its company areas, which corresponded to the areas of the battalions of the 8th Infantry. These recon platoons brought beach markers, explosives, mine

7. Named for Lt. Carl P. Hagensen, U.S. Navy, who invented it in February 1944.

The Code Talkers

On May 9, 2002, a bill was introduced into the Senate to authorize the president to award a gold medal to Choctaw and Comanche code talkers of both world wars. Although the Navajo who had served in the Pacific War had been recognized for their service, the Native Americans from other tribes who had served in Europe had been forgotten. At the time this congressional act was passed, only one Comanche code talker, Charles Chibitty, was still alive. He passed away in the summer of 2005.

After the attack on Pearl Harbor in December 1941, Native Americans volunteered for service. Fourteen Comanche Indians served in the 4th Signal Company of the 4th Infantry Division as code talkers. Since the Comanche language did not exist in written form and the enemy did not know it, radio or telephone messages in that language were safe from interception. Two Comanche code talkers went ashore on D-Day with each regiment to help with fast communications; the remainder arrived with the headquarters. Chibitty arrived with the later waves on D-Day and spent the first night in a foxhole making peace with his Creator while waiting for his unit to advance in the morning.

One of the first messages sent in Comanche was that the landing had taken place south of the intended invasion site. The Comanche code talkers had to develop words for military terminology that did not exist in their language. One term was *posah-tai-vo*, which referred to Adolf Hitler. It meant "Crazy White Man." Comanche had no words for many military terms such as tanks and bombers, so the code talkers used the Comanche words for "turtles" for the former and "pregnant airplanes" for the latter.

Sources: Michael Dodson, "Last Comanche 'Code Talker' Recounts War," *News Star*, June 13, 2002; Vicki Lockard, "Code Talkers," *Canku Ota: A Newsletter Celebrating Native America*, June 3, 2000; Dennis Ryan, "Last Comanche Code Talker Visits Arlington," *Pentagram*, November 8, 2002.

detectors, weapons, and other equipment. After reaching shore, they quickly set about their work, even though the landing did not go smoothly for all the men.

First Lt. Sidney Berger, a twenty-three-year-old Baltimore native, led the 3rd Platoon of Company A, which served as the recon platoon of the 531st Shore Battalion and was over strength for the operation. His battalion was brought by the APA *Bayfield*. "In the transport area, we transferred to an LCVP rendezvous for one and a half hours and then transitted to shore," after which the battalion spent another hour and a half moving toward the beach in "very miserable" conditions "that left everybody terribly sick." The individual load for most of his men was an M-1 rifle (Berger carried a carbine), hand grenades, extra bandoliers, and a field pack holding two canteens, a two-day supply of C rations, two first-aid kits with morphine, an entrenching tool, mine detectors, and beach markers. Each man also carried about forty pounds of composition C explosives.

Berger's LCVP grounded before it reached the designated beach, and he and his men had to trek for more than a mile to reach it. As they landed sometime after 8 A.M., the 237th Engineer Combat Battalion and a company from the 299th Engineer Combat Battalion breached the sea wall and moved into the dunes. Lieutenant Berger and his men followed them to make a recon and determine where to breach the seawall. They detonated explosives against the seawall, set up beach markers, and began mine-clearing operations on the exit. During the mine clearing, his platoon came under enemy fire. A shell landed in the midst of one of his squads, which had an unsettling effect on the others. He ordered the other squads to keep clearing mines and sent for medics to attend to the injured. Soon another enemy round exploded in the area, inflicting additional casualties. The lieutenant exposed himself to enemy fire to keep his men working on the clearing operations. He later received a Silver Star for his distinguished service.

During these operations, his platoon cleared mines from a site for an AA gun. As the AA guncrew occupied its new position, one of the naval 5-inch rockets that had been fired before the landing exploded. He helped the gun crew handle the casualties and get their gun into operation. According to Berger, although many of the naval 5-inch rockets turned out to be duds, they presented an additional hazard for his men. His platoon successfully removed many mines, but the type of mine in a wooden box proved difficult to locate. He also assisted his company commander in getting a reserve dozer and tools to replace the ones that were lost when the LCT carrying them was sunk. As the day wore on, he ordered his platoon to direct traffic on the beach, because each time a bottleneck created a concentration of vehicles, the enemy fire targeted them.

The two other platoons of Company A and the HQ section landed at the extreme left of the beach. Their LCTs approached the beach on a rising tide, and one carrying the company's dozers and other equipment was sunk. Meanwhile, Company C cleared the roadway up to Exit 2, the only causeway leading directly away from the new invasion site, according to Joseph Balkoski in *Utah Beach*. Pvt. Otway Burns from Sarasota, Florida, at twenty years of age was already a veteran of the Mediterranean war. A truck driver in Company A of the 531st Engineers, he landed in Normandy with the LCTs carrying the first load of vehicles for the battalion.

> We had two D-4 bulldozers, two trucks loaded with ammo for beach defense, maintenance trucks—two with cranes. I was driving one of the trucks with ammo for Company A. The cranes were mobile units for unloading; they were like a 5-ton truck with a crane. We landed in the morning. We were on a British LCT, and the captain dropped the anchor too far off, probably because they were shelling us. One guy got killed looking up over the side from an exploding shell. They opened the doors and put the ramp down. The bulldozer went into a shell hole. They removed the towed gun from the truck and pulled it back aboard the boat and got it restarted. Meantime, all the other boats that had been unloading had left. The German guns were shooting at us as we were left there by ourselves. So we got the bulldozers off, and I was the next vehicle out. We had everything: explosives, TNT, .50-caliber and .30-caliber, bazooka shells, etc. We were the first truck off.

As Private Burns drove his truck ashore, he came under artillery fire. The second truck in line, which was heading in the designated direction, blew up. As fate would have it, Burns had turned in the wrong direction. If not for this mistake, his truck might have been hit instead. After that, an officer directed him to an assembly area in the dunes.

PFC John P. Gallagher, a twenty-year-old from Cleveland drafted two years earlier, landed in the morning with Company D of the 531st Engineers. As enemy artillery shells hit around them, fear spurred him to dig as deep a foxhole as possible, from which he was to guard the beach perimeter. He spent most of the day watching the massive buildup. Half of his company worked on the beach, while the other half occupied the perimeter.

The 286th Joint Assault Signal Company (JASCO) disembarked with the 1st ESB, which was divided into teams—one for each battalion and brigade headquarters. T/4 Hyatt Moser from Greensboro, North Carolina, had joined the army in 1940 at age twenty and was a radio operator in this signal company.

> On landing, my job was to go in with a walkie-talkie, then radio back to the ship when we got on the beach. There were two other men doing the same job, so if any got killed, one would get the message back. This was the first-wave job. The second wave would come in with a larger radio. As the day progressed, our big radios would come in on the trucks, and we would fold up our little ones and start our radio nets with the larger ones. This was the same routine for the other invasions [the brigade had taken part in Mediterranean invasions].
>
> I left England on a Coast Guard LCI, but they had to bring in smaller landing craft, and we loaded off the LCI for the beach landing. The most vivid memory I have was that I almost missed the boat. The head was in the front, and I had all my equipment on and was all ready to go. The people were loading onto the boats, and I had to go, bad. I said I was not going to go in to the beach and mess my pants up, so I ran into the head to have a good old crap before going in. I had to hurry and get my pants back on and get all this stuff back on to get back into the boat.
>
> We got off the LCI on these ramps. We then went around and around, and the waves got a lot of people sick. I was on the boat with Major Hayes, whom we all hated. This son of a bitch, who never made an invasion before, was a total fanatic, and he sat in the back of the boat with his pistol cocked and said, "Anybody that don't get off of this boat, I will shoot him." I think he did this because he knew if he were in the front we might shoot him!
>
> I was attached to Company B of the 531st Engineer Shore Regiment. When I hit the beach, I had a radio, an extra battery, a pack with three days' rations in it, a change of underwear, gas mask, 200 rounds of ammo, and an M-1 rifle. I hit the beach slightly to the right of where the 1st Engineer Brigade monument is today. I moved across the dunes, as instructed, and set up my radio station. I stayed there until the next wave came in with a larger radio. The larger radio put us in communication with all the other battalions. The only message I sent with the walkie-talkie was back to the ship to say we had landed. Before the day was over, a DUKW came over with an SCR-399 [or 299?], which had two generators mounted on it. With it, we could communicate anywhere.
>
> That afternoon we were strafed, and our AA shot down one of our aircraft behind the German plane. He was one mad pilot, cursing like hell.

Tech/5 Henry E. Sunier, a twenty-five-year-old from Washington, D.C., who had enlisted little more than a year before, was also in the 286th JASCO and crossed the Channel on an LCI.

> The crossing had been very rough, and I got very seasick. The only relief I could get was to lie down in my bunk. Sleep was very fitful, and whatever I could get was appreciated. When I got up at daybreak, the Channel was still rough. We didn't have any breakfast, so it was acceptable. We made the

Behind the beach.

invasion at about H+4 hours and were glad to get ashore. A friend in front of me had some difficulty with his wire pack, and he struggled in the water. I was able to assist him to land and we moved inshore. The defense of the coast at that time was not too dramatic. The naval boys manning the DUKWs were very clever individuals. They stood offshore and watched the 88s firing on the shoreline. They came in, unloaded their troops, and backed off; they were safe and we were ashore.

When I got ashore, I immediately went to the seawall, which was very well sheltered. At about 10:30 A.M., we were ashore in France and made the landing without unnecessary casualties. We went about our duties of providing communications between the front line and rear echelons. My duty was to set up a radio and telephone communications in the area. We were also to find any available cable in the area which we might use. We had the heavy wire, about 50 pounds of W-4, and we carried it in and set up telephone communications with the outposts. Our first duty was to establish communications with the front-line troops back to the beaches.

Like Moser, Henry Sunier witnessed the Allied antiaircraft battery shooting down one if its own planes instead of the German aircraft it was pursuing. It was a Spitfire, he thought.[8]

The ground units had to maintain communications not only with each other, but also with the naval element. The 1st ESB with the 2nd

8. According to Kenneth Werrell's *Archie, Flak, AAA, and SAM*, despite invasion markings, on D-Day after 8 P.M., Allied antiaircraft weapons accounted for downing at least four friendly aircraft, plus hitting one Spitfire that left the scene with smoke pouring out as it lost altitude.

Telephone Communications at Utah Beach

According to Moser, the first wireman ashore landed with a metal stake, reel of small telephone wire, and field telephone. The first thing he did was attach one end of the wire to the stake and the other end to the telephone. At the same time, down the beach, wiremen for the two other battalions did the same thing. The wireman then followed the first infantry platoon leader to hit the beach, letting out his wire with the telephone as he went. This happened all down the beach with every platoon leader at the same time: Every infantry platoon leader had a wireman following him with a reel of wire and a telephone, and the other end of the wire was attached to the stake.

When the second wave came in, the wiremen in this wave each had a six-position switchboard. This switchboard operation took the end of the wire secured to the pole and attached it to his switchboard. This happened simultaneously at all the other positions down the beach. Thus, within a few minutes, the wireman following the infantry platoon leaders had communication with all the other infantry platoon leaders up and down the beach. The company commanders were usually followed by the infantry communication people, who set up similar switchboards at the command posts. Within a matter of an hour, all the infantry platoon leaders and company commanders were linked by telephone.

Later on, when division headquarters came in with larger switchboards, and still later corps headquarters, they just kept getting bigger radio sets. The telephone system worked beautifully until the first tank came ashore. The tankers seemed to take great delight in getting right in the middle of these telephone wires, spinning the tanks, and tearing up the wires. Immediately the wire crews had to go out and restring the wire while supervised by a communications chief. The communications chiefs kept getting killed because they had to run up and down the beach, supervising.

Naval Beach Battalion was in charge of maintaining this contact. A naval communications group was formed to support the naval officer in charge (NOIC) and the beachmaster from the 2nd Naval Beach Battalion. The forty-seven men of the group landed at 10:30 A.M. with three trucks full of radio equipment. The next day, the army demolition teams cleared a bunker so they could set up their communications equipment there.

The 3rd Battalion of the 8th Infantry landed with a battalion of the 22nd Infantry, after the leading waves carried in the 8th Infantry's 1st and 2nd Battalions, the BODPs, and engineers. Twenty-four-year-old 1st Sgt. Samuel D. Norris from Piedmont, South Carolina, who had received a battlefield commission in December, boarded an LCVP with some of his comrades. He moved off the beach with the 3rd Battalion onto the traffic-packed mile-long causeway of Exit 2, which led to Houdienville. "We were on the beach only a short time. After leaving the beach, our first main contact was a horse-drawn artillery unit coming up for support. We had very little trouble with this unit but did have trouble cleaning out a farmhouse where the Germans were hiding as well as the small buildings around it. The gliders started coming in very late in the afternoon with supplies, and we stopped for the day at about 10:30 P.M." These were the last glider landings of the day. For Sergeant Norris, the greatest problem on D-Day was getting mortar and artillery support for his company.

PFC Guy E. Overbey, a twenty-two-year-old draftee from Ewing, Kentucky, was a light-truck driver in the P&A (Pioneer and Ammunition) Platoon of HQ Company, 3rd Battalion, 8th Infantry. This platoon was assigned various tasks ranging from demolitions and clearing minefields to bringing up supplies for the battalion. Overbey and his comrades had prepared to disembark from their transport onto the waiting LCVPs early in the morning.

> Loading into the LCVPs, my buddy and I had a mine detector, two bags of C-2 compound, a full field pack, and each a carbine. We were to get ashore, get with our command group, and get instructions on what to do.
>
> Our planes were bombing the coastline; the battleships, cruisers, and destroyers were shelling. You could see great flashes and hear the missiles being hurled overhead. We stayed in the rendezvous until it was light; getting the signal, we headed for shore. I was in the boat with our battalion commander, Col. E. H. Strickland.
>
> When the boat ramp went down, it was everyone for himself. I jumped off into the water, went into a bomb crater going to the bottom. Having a lifebelt on, I broke a gas cartridge that inflated the belt, bringing me to the surface. About thirty [?] feet from the water was a seawall, which everyone tried to get against to protect them from shelling.

The battalions of the 22nd Infantry landed behind the 3rd Battalion of the 8th Infantry about one hour after the first waves. As they came ashore, the engineers were finishing clearing most of the beach obstacles and destroying the Belgian Gates that blocked access to the beach exits. The 3rd Battalions of both the 8th and 22nd Infantry Regiments began landing at 7:45 A.M. The 2nd Battalion of the 8th Infantry had already eliminated strongpoint W-5 at La Madeleine and moved toward the causeway over a small inundated area at Exit 1, which led to the town of Pouppeville. The 1st Battalion also easily eliminated enemy opposition on the beach and moved against the long causeway of Exit 3. The beachhead was largely cleared of enemy resistance by 9:30 A.M. The newly arrived 3rd Battalion of the 8th Infantry and tanks of the 70th Tank Battalion advanced down the center of the beachhead and took the causeway at Exit 2, which quickly became jam-packed with vehicles. The battalions of the newly arriving 22nd Infantry moved north, attempting to clear the coast road and enemy strongpoints to secure Exit 4. Many of its companies moved through the flooded sectors.

Second Lt. Nathaniel K. Helman, a twenty-eight-year-old draftee from Colton, California, had risen through the ranks. He had left the 40th Division in Hawaii in 1942 for Officer Candidate School (OCS). In 1944, he was with the 22nd Infantry, leading the 81-millimeter mortar platoon of Company D, 1st Battalion into Normandy, having arrived in the twelfth wave aboard an LCVP. He moved with his men into the inundated area shortly after landing, trying to reach Exit 4. "I encountered a few dead soldiers on the beach. We crossed the swamps using ropes to aid us. We moved by foot carrying the mortars and ammunition (two mortar shells on each man). We met some paratroopers while moving inland and dug in for the first night."

Gen. Raymond Barton, commander of the 4th Division, was concerned about the scarcity of antitank weapons delivered to the beachhead and ordered the available weapons moved out to support the advance. He wanted to give priority to AT units. Pvt. Frank Catalano, a thirty-two-year-old gunner, was one of the soldiers who manned the 57-millimeter antitank guns. Even though the situation was relatively well in hand by this point, as the landing craft in which he was sitting raced toward the beach, the roar of its engine was drowned out by the whining pitch of an enemy shell that exploded nearby.

> A piece of shrapnel about four by six inches with sharp edges hit the side of the helmet of the man in front of me, cut through his backpack, and landed at my feet. The pilot of the vessel asked to see how big it was. I picked it up, like a fool, only to drop it because it was so hot. On landing, the pilot dropped the gate in five feet of water, which reached my shoulders. I waded in soaked and wet. We were regrouped and marched up an embankment to a road nearby. Both sides of the road were flooded. We were taken to the antitank company amid the shelling and assigned to a squad, which had lost a few men.

PFC Ralph Brazee, another gunner in an antitank unit of the 22nd Infantry, crossed the Channel in an LCT that carried his half-track. He had slept on the vehicle until the night of the crossing, when lost his place and had to sleep on a coil of rope near the ramp. Finally, after the morning bombardments and initial landings, it was his turn to disembark.

> We went in, the ramp went down, and a Weasel took off. It was a last-minute addition to our vessel and was not part of our platoon. It went straight down and out of sight. Our LCT backed up and went in again, closer this time. Our track was next, and it went off into about five feet of water with all of us right behind it. The waves were just high enough that I lost my footing several times. The shore was sandy with a wall fifty feet ahead. The only enemy activity was an 88 firing down the length of the beach.
>
> The problem the first day was to get clearance or authority to get on the one causeway to our objective. After we crossed the causeway, we encountered a sniper in the steeple of the village we were passing through.

PFC Brazee's platoon, one of three in the antitank company, was assigned to guard against tank attacks and saw little ation after the first day. Brazee employed his gun against a church tower the Germans were using as an observation position. After shooting a few rounds of high explosive (HE) at that target, he seldom fired his gun again in Normandy.

The 12th Infantry Regiment came ashore after noon. The 22nd Infantry landed at about 10 A.M. and moved to the right, behind the 8th Infantry. One battalion from each regiment secured Exits 1, 2, and 3. The 22nd sent two battalions across the inundated area, where the water was mostly waist-deep, toward Exit 4 and St.-Martin-de-Varreville. In the meantime, its 3rd Battalion moved up the coast clearing out the German strongpoints just past Exit 4: W-8, StP-9, and W-10. Many troops continued to move through the inundated area. The 12th Infantry passed through the center of the front and pushed inland toward Montebourg.

At thirty years of age, Lt. Col. Charles L. Jackson commanded the 1st Battalion, 12th Infantry. His battalion sailed to Normandy aboard four LCIs, three LCTs, and three LSTs.

> As dawn broke on June 6, 1944, we were able to see an awesome sight of battleships, cruisers, destroyers, other combat and combat support vessels, APAs, all types of landing craft, and many other types of vessels. With barrage balloons swaying overhead, planes flying to and returning from beach and inland targets, and the planes in orbit to provide protection for the armada against enemy air attacks, one was confronted with

> an unforgettable spectacular picture beyond description.

Jackson watched his men transfer from the LCIs to LCMs and LCVPs. This had not been part of the landing plan, but the conditions of the new landing site early that morning made it necessary. As a result, some of his platoons and squads were distributed among different landing craft. When the craft were within 200 yards of the beach, there was a sudden lull in the enemy shelling. Jackson moved his battalion across the flooded area on a broad front to save time, instead of taking Exit 3, the only causeway in his path. When the last elements of his battalion were about 200 yards inland, the German bombardment of the beach resumed. If he had ordered his unit to move along the small road, it would have been caught in the shelling. Once they crossed the inundated area, the men of his battalion dropped their lifebelts and reorganized, moving all the while on St.-Martin-de-Varreville. After shifting into battle formation along the road to Montebourg, they attacked on the orders of Col. Russell "Red" Reeder, the regimental commander. The 1st Battalion advanced on the right side of the road and the 2nd Battalion on the left.

Lieutenant Colonel Jackson earned the admiration and loyalty of his men because of his sincere concern for their welfare as well as his sangfroid under fire. But he had not been as sure of himself as he appeared to his men. "A fear that had gnawed on my mind for many months was how I would react when I saw wounded and dead men. From childhood, I had a feeling of nausea whenever I saw the sight of blood. I found out that I was so busy and my mind was so occupied with what was happening or what had to be done that I had no time to dwell on such sights other than to have a sense of sorrow."

Capt. Robert B. Kaye, who had joined the 4th Division in August 1942, was with Company I of the 12th Infantry on D-Day. During the Channel crossing, he had taken a cold saltwater shower and then taken care of his spiritual needs.

> I was down in the compartment with my troops, at which time I decided to make use of a New Testament I carried in my pocket. I proceeded to read some of the scriptures. The men were generally quiet and subdued with their own thoughts. One voice piped up and said, "Hey Lieutenant, if what you're reading is any good, how about sharing it with us?" which I did. I read John XIV: "Let not your heart be troubled, you believe in God also believe in me." That watchword followed me all my life. We all needed to believe in something, mostly ourselves, for what we faced we were not sure of.
>
> As daylight broke and we saw what was happening, we moved into line and disembarked to an LCM landing craft. I was in the bow of the boat as we approached the beach, slowly but surely bouncing as we did; no one seemed to have got seasick. As we went ashore and crossed one sandbar and through a second sandbar, the coxswain running the boat said, "Lieutenant, this is it!" With that, they dropped the ramp. As we had all been trained before, once the ramp is dropped, you get off the boat. A voice behind me said in a high, squeaky voice, "After you, Lieutenant!" That was a big laugh. We went into chest-deep water and waded ashore. Successfully we made the beach, to the concrete wall and sand dune line. We began to bunch up, which was poor military technique. We spread out and I moved over the dune line to find a combat engineer sweeping with a mine detector in the dunes. I asked where it was clear. He said, "It is clear as far as you can see; from here on, it is your own baby." So I took no alternative but to strike out with the troops to move out behind me, which they did.

Men flood the beachhead.

For T.Sgt. Clarence P. Faria, who came ashore with his 2nd Platoon, Company L, 3rd Battalion, 12th Infantry, Utah Beach was a far cry from the beaches of his home in Hawaii. At least this time, he could shoot back at his enemy instead of feeling as helpless as on December 7, 1941, when the Japanese attacked his unit at Schofield Barracks. He came to Normandy onboard an LCI.

> The tide had started to change, and therefore the LCIs were not able to get close enough to the shore, and we were advised by the skipper of the craft that we had to transfer to LCMs, which we did. In going in, I had a chance to look over the ramp, and the area in front of us looked just like the photo strips taken at periscope depth by submarines which were shown to us before the invasion.
>
> There was hardly any action on the beach. I saw one truck burning just above the waterline. I don't recall any firing. I moved forward immediately to the sand dunes directly in front of us, where I observed the first casualty: a dead American soldier. I saw some prisoners with their hands on top of their heads. I didn't waste any time on the beach, just moved forward, and then we came upon the flooded area. We were provided with short pieces of rope with loops on the ends, and when joined together they would form a long rope. I swam every ditch there was with all my equipment on and my lifebelt inflated. When reaching the other side, they would toss me an end of the rope, and I would hold it until several other men came across the rope and then moved to the next ditch. Upon reaching the far shore at the end of

> the flooded plain, we located the balance of the company and moved forward until darkness. We spent the night in a pasture bordered on all sides by banks of dirt with hedges growing on top.

Company I of the 3rd Battalion, 12th Infantry, also arrived by LCI. Its twenty-six-year-old company XO, Lt. Thomas Cortright, had a rough ride.

> The Channel was choppy, and our LCI could not go in because of this, or possibly it drew too much water, so we had to transfer to three LCMs. As we headed toward the beach, a soldier came up and said, "Lieutenant, I have to crap; what can I do?"[9] I said, "Do it in your helmet and throw it overboard."
>
> Near the beach, I peeked over the side of our craft just in time to see an LCVP alongside of us get blown completely out of the water.

After landing on the beach, his company moved inland, across the inundated area. "This water was mostly about two feet deep, but if you stepped into a ditch, it was over your head. Fortunately, I did not, but several of the men did. The water was only about a mile, but it took us several hours to negotiate it. As we were coming out, we were fired on from a house to the left, but that was silenced after a few rounds from our riflemen and BARs."

Pvt. Dalton Coffin, a twenty-three-year-old draftee from Ashland, Maine, and two other men from the Intelligence and Reconnaissance (I&R) Platoon were attached to Company C, 1st Battalion, 12th Infantry. Coffin was a radio operator and carried an SCR-300.

> At 4 A.M. on June 6, I was on deck and in my assigned radio net. I was seasick and the Channel was still rough. We came in after our 22nd Regiment. Due to obstacles, we had to off-load on the LCMs.[10] We were dumped in water up to our necks. We crossed the beach, the sand dunes, and grassy hillocks, and then a large inundated area that we also waded through. Some dropped out of sight in deep holes in the flooded area. We finally got a bit of sleep in a horse stable in an orchard or field. I left the radio open and outside the barn door. A day or so later, I rejoined the I&R Platoon.

Sgt. Leonard Herb, a twenty-four-year-old draftee from Philadelphia and a member of the I&R Platoon, HQ Company of the 12th Infantry, crossed the Channel on a British landing craft (probably an LCT) carrying jeeps, with the motto "To Hell with the Enemy" painted on its side. According to Sergeant Herb, the British captain delayed their landing, forcing the men onboard to wait until the tide changed several hours later. There was "much debris constantly floating by, including human, while shells were constantly falling at targets closer to the beach." It seemed that "the Germans ignored us," says Herb, "and when we finally landed, it was uneventful. . . . We were held up briefly on the beach and several small pieces of shrapnel pinged off the jeeps." Everyone took cover. Soon they moved inland toward Ste-Mère-Église, but later their mission was changed.

For twenty-seven-year-old Sgt. William Buell, a regimental ammunition sergeant who came

9. The M-1 helmet replaced the old World War I–era bed pan style helmet by mid-1942. It consisted of the steel helmet and a removable fiber liner that was adjusted with inside straps to fit the head and could be worn without the steel pot. The steel helmet acquired functions never dreamed of by its designers, serving as a cooking pot, a shaving bowl, even a chamber pot.

10. According to Lt. Col. Charles Jackson, because of the conditions of the new beach, the troops had to be off-loaded onto smaller craft when the 1st Battalion arrived.

ashore with elements of the Service Company of the 12th Infantry, the Channel crossing was relatively uneventful.

> I have no bad memories of the crossing. Maybe there was something wrong with me, but I enjoyed it. Early on June 6, the sight of many planes and gliders was an unbelievable sight.
>
> Once we landed, all was well for the first fifteen or twenty minutes. Then some enemy artillery landed on the beach. For the first time, I felt fear. On marching off the beach, I saw my first sight of a war casualty, a Norman woman split wide open by a shell. That day, I dug three or four foxholes. I believe for the rest of the war, I dug only one more. One felt safer in a foxhole than anywhere else, but they were a lot of work.
>
> Finally, toward evening, I got in the back of a jeep with Capt. Victor Vrable and Maj. Kenneth Lay. We reached the 12th Infantry regimental command post, which was near the preplanned objective. On the way, we came to a crossroad where a bunch of Frenchmen were wildly waving at us not to take one of the roads. We had no confidence in Major Lay's map reading and proceeded the way they warned us against. I was sure it was the end. This time, the major was right. Incidentally, I always thought of Major Lay as one of our best officers.
>
> That night, I slept on the cobblestones in the creamery barn room of the command post.

CWO-2 Larry Knecht, a twenty-nine-year-old from New Orleans who had joined the army during the Great Depression and served many years in the 8th Infantry Regiment, was the assistant adjutant of the regiment. He too was on an LST that morning.

> I was standing on the deck, and there was my partner, Capt. Walter Hollis, and another good friend. We were close enough to see the beach, and we were about to transfer over to an LCVP. Before that happened, I noticed an LST [LCT] on our right on which someone was waving. I thought he was waving at me. Captain Hollis had field glasses on, so I said, "Walt, give me those field glasses. I want to see something." He gave me the glasses, and I am looking at the deck of this LST [LCT] when all of a sudden, there is a big explosion. I heard the explosion first. Looking through the field glasses, I saw this LST [LCT] split in two, right in the center, and both the stern and bow went straight up in the air like in slow motion and came down. Everybody ran over to the right side where I was standing. The water was just boiling up and coming up with bodies, and the water just turned red. There were people on the other side with hooks, anything they could get their hands on, throwing it into the water. I don't know what was picked up.

During the day, the artillery battalions of the 4th Division began to land. Only one, the 20th Field Artillery with 155-millimeter guns, did not arrive. In the morning, the 29th Field Artillery came ashore. One of the LCTs blew up, causing numerous casualties. This may have been the vessel that Larry Knecht observed. The other two 105-millimeter artillery battalions, the 42nd and 44th, arrived later in the day.

Col. Russell "Red" Reeder Jr., the commander of the 12th Infantry, came ashore with his regiment and directed operations to get them moving inland in as fast as possible. Like Lieutenant Colonel Jackson, he was well respected, but as was the case with many men and junior officers of the 4th Division, he was wounded within a few days.

S.Sgt. Jack W. Carter, a wire chief in the HQ Battery of the 44th Field Artillery, was responsible for laying wire to each battery in the battalion and to other units they would support. Forward observers from his headquarters were attached to the three battalions of the 22nd Infantry. They too had access to his telephone lines. He went to Normandy in an LCT with his wire section of six men, two medics, two 2½-ton supply trucks, four jeeps, two weapon carriers, and a tractor vehicle.

> The morning of June 6, we could see orange-colored flames coming from the battleship guns, bombs bursting, and all sorts of sickening noises. However, most of us were so seasick we didn't care too much what happened.
>
> One of my new men had a piece of chalk with him and in an effort to cheer us up, he scribbled on the loading ramp, "It's too late to worry now!" As we were nearing Utah Beach, I was glad to be getting off that damned LCT. I could hardly wait for them to drop the ramp. As soon as the ramp dropped, I jumped off before we hit land. I was loaded with my field pack, rifle, etc. I jumped into water over my head. Thinking fast, I used my lifebelt and treaded water until I felt the good earth under my feet. I directed my vehicles toward a more protected area. One of the first men I saw on the beach was our assistant division commander waving his arms toward land and yelling to me, "Get those goddamn jeeps off the beach!" We did, in a hurry.
>
> After landing, I saw several bodies lying on the beach. I couldn't believe this was happening. I saw a man walking along the beach and unbelievingly asked him, "Are these men dead?" He looked at me in disgust and said, "What do you think, Sarge?"
>
> While on the beach, I discovered that most of the underwater obstacles had been removed by the time we landed. We finally found safe cover right off the beach near St.-Martin-de-Varreville, where a couple of pillboxes had been knocked out. We dug in to wait for orders to move inland. While we waited to move, the 42nd Field Artillery was landing. I looked up and saw a German mortar drop in the middle of one of their open-turret self-propelled 105 [105-millimeter howitzer] pieces.
>
> We moved to our headquarters, and it was time for my men and me to lay our telephone lines. By the time we had laid to the firing batteries, it was dark and time for us to lay lines to the 22nd Infantry. We started laying our line, and I was helping throw it out of the roadway when I stumbled over a German motorcycle and a dead German lying in the middle of the road. Getting over that scare, we proceeded on toward our destination.

The 42nd Field Artillery Battalion and its self-propelled guns landed to support the 12th Infantry. S.Sgt. Murphy Chustz from Livonia, Louisiana, was the chief of the instrument survey section of Battery B.

> When daylight came, I could see landing craft of all kinds around us. We were supposed to land in two feet of water, but the ship's captain made a mistake and let his anchor out too far away. When the ship got to the end of its cable, we were still in five feet of water. The four M-7s made it to shore, but our wheeled vehicles drowned out.[11]
>
> When we got on the beach, we had to wait for the engineers to blast a hole in the

11. The M-7 Priest was a 105-millimeter howitzer mounted on the chassis of the M-3 Lee medium tank. It also mounted a .50-caliber machine gun on a ring mount for use against aircraft. The crew consisted of seven men: four cannoneers, a gunner, a driver, and the section chief.

An infantryman from the 4th Division inspects a bunker on Utah Beach. COURTESY OF LAWRENCE KNECHT

> seawall so our M-7s could get through. We went over the flooded area on one narrow road under heavy artillery fire.

Charles Bergeron, a friend of Sergeant Chustz's from his hometown who served in Battery A, believes they arrived in the eighteenth wave.

> At one time when we were going in, I looked to my left and saw one of the LCTs blow up. I said, "Oh no, there goes Murphy!" It was a mistake; it wasn't Battery B, it was Battery C of the 29th.
>
> Just before we got to the beach, the landing craft stopped. They said, "This is it, boys; we can't go any further." We started to unload and got into about five feet of water. As soon as I hit the beach, they started shelling it. It looked like it was raining shrapnel. We jumped off our M-7s and got under them. Some of the boys got wounded. Out of about nine men when we got on dry land, there were three of us left: myself, the tank driver, and one more man. We managed to get the waterproofing off of our equipment and went into position. Our impregnated clothes made us very hot.
>
> At about 2 P.M. [?], we got a fire mission. The two other boys and I managed the 105. Our first target was a church steeple. We shot three rounds and demolished it. We sat there for about an hour. At that time, late in the afternoon, the paratroopers started coming in with gliders. Prisoners were coming in to the beach also. At about nightfall, they said we were moving in.
>
> Behind the beach was a flooded area. We managed to get through it, traveled through the night, and passed a little town before we got into position. The next morning, just

> before dawn, we had a fire mission. We were sitting there firing, and all at once an 88 hit our M-7. We jumped off of it, ran for cover, and our M-7 went up. In just a few hours, we had another one to replace the one that had blown up. That same night, on June 6, they hollered, "Gas!" and we had to put our gas masks on and worked for about forty-five minutes with it on. We did not sleep; we were too damned scared to sleep.

Some members of the 8th Infantry's regimental staff landed in the afternoon. Capt. John E. Galvin, adjutant of the 8th Infantry, crossed on an LST.

> We were fortunate, but the Channel was very rough. Believe me, when we hit the beach, I stepped on land and I couldn't believe it. There were about thirty men with me. We got on the beach and everything was quiet, nothing was happening. This was about 5:30 in the afternoon. There were a couple of people you could see on the beach who were cleaning up the craters [?] on the beach, and one man with a bulldozer opening up more roads and exits to move inland. In an instant we heard a terrific crash, and I looked over at the bulldozer. He didn't have any tracks any longer, and there wasn't an operator on it. I never have known what happened to the operator. That woke me up, and I thought this is it. We moved inland for a while and waited overnight for someone to come down from regiment to guide us into our command post.

Donald V. Sherwood, the first sergeant of a collecting company of the 4th Medical Battalion, 4th Infantry Division, arrived in an LST with most of his company. They were supposed to land about two or three hours after H-Hour. Their vehicles and supplies were not scheduled to land with them. On that first day, his company was scattered, and it was impossible to account for all the men.

> Our landing was uneventful, and all aboard got off safely. However, the landing craft next to ours took a direct hit from an 88 and received heavy casualties. The water was very cold, but the heavy underwear was some protection. We moved rapidly up the beach and regrouped behind a concrete retaining wall, about chest-high. In a few minutes, we climbed over the wall and started inland. Several land mines were detonated. A jeep and driver were blown into the air. We rendered aid and continued inland.
>
> Our company at this point had no transportation. We continued to walk and render aid as needed. We came upon glider troops who had crashed upon landing the previous night [actually early that morning]. They were in bad shape. All casualties were given aid, tagged, and readied for evacuation back to the beach. Our point of progress was near Ste-Mère-Église. We came upon a few dead Germans along the way.
>
> The minefields on the beach had been marked by tape, but the landing vehicles and equipment had made these markings useless. The fear of land mines was very great and real.
>
> The first night ashore, a gas alert was sounded. After several hours [?] of gas mask wearing, the alarm proved to be false.

Pvt. William C. Montgomery, who served as a litter bearer in Company A of the 4th Medical Battalion, crossed the Channel with his company on the British LSI *Empire Gauntlet*.

> We were offshore of Normandy when we unloaded from the LSI into an LCI at about dawn on June 6. We joined a large group of

The Medical Battalion

A medical battalion numbered over 400 men and consisted of four companies. One was a clearing company, which gathered the casualties from each of the other companies and moved them to the rear. The other three were collecting companies, which were attached to each regiment of a division. Each collecting company was commanded by a Medical Corps officer with a staff of two captains and a lieutenant. The company included several platoons and sections, such as a litter platoon, ambulance platoon, motor pool, supply section, and clerical section. This gave the company a strength of about 100 to 120 men. The Litter Platoon consisted of several squads that operated from battalion aid stations, which sometimes carried the wounded on jeeps. From there, ambulances from the collecting company picked up the casualties.

In the 4th Medical Battalion of the 4th Infantry Division, Pvt. William Montgomery recalls, the rest of the company avoided the litter platoon.

> Ours was not an attractive situation. We had no spokesman at the commissioned officer level. We controlled nothing useful like vehicles, supplies, or medical alcohol. We had the fewest and lowest-ranking noncoms. We had all the newcomers and the youngest, greenest guys. We had all the misfits and dummies. We had all those who had been busted or were being punished. And we had hard, dangerous work.
>
> But because our work was between the aid station and the front line and contrasted dramatically with what the rest of the company did, we thought of ourselves as combat elite.

A medical unit wades ashore.

The company aid man was not part of the medical battalion. "He is the hero of everything I know about combat medicine," says Montgomery. "He lives and dies with the infantry. But he is actually a member of the medical detachment and under the command of the battalion surgeon."

LCIs, circled briefly, pitching and rolling, then headed for the beach.

I was in front, close to the ramp. In the landing craft were dozens of troops. We were cautioned not to climb up the ramp to look at the beach, for fear of being wounded, but I heard a loud explosion and I couldn't resist. I looked over the top and saw a four-by-four truck on the beach somewhat off to my left burning and exploding. It must have been full of ammunition.

I heard a voice from the right and above me: "Get your fucking head down, you stupid son of a bitch!" I looked up and it was a coast guardsman hunched on the rail, preparing to operate the mechanism that lowered the ramp.

We hit the beach at what I recall as 8 A.M. on June 6, although why I say 8 A.M., I don't know. It was in the morning. The ramp went down and we piled off. I had the front end of the folded litter on my shoulder, and Bill Rohloff had the back. I think the Coast Guard guys running the LCI may have been in to the beach once before and were anxious to get in and out fast. We went down the LCI ramp into chest-deep water, waded ashore, and ran across the beach and up the metal ramp the engineers had laid in the sand through the gap in the seawall. Almost at the top of the dune, something caused us to hit the ground.

I used to recall it as a strafing German airplane. Now I doubt it because of what I've read since. More likely it was that truck I saw burning on the beach as we approached. I hit the deck because of the explosions and immediately began to breathe something unpleasant and choking. I thought, "Gas!" because of all the warnings we had had, and began to fumble for my gas mask. In doing so, I discovered I was lying on the ramp with my face inches from the tailpipe of a jeep, which the driver had abandoned temporarily to take cover. I was breathing exhaust fumes.

When we got across the top of the dune and looked down behind, we saw a very busy sand lane parallel to the dunes, jammed with vehicles heading west [*sic*] a couple of hundred yards or so, then inland up over another line of dunes. I looked back and was dumbfounded at the fleet behind me. It looked dense enough to walk across clear to the horizon, and the sky was full of barrage balloons.

We saw none of the landmarks we were supposed to follow. We regrouped in a ditch along the lane, near the intersection (where the traffic jam began), and tried to figure out what to do. While we were puzzling over it, there in the sun, there was a big explosion, and a jeep which was partway up the road inland was blown into the air. I've never been able to figure out how all that traffic passed over that mine before it finally went off.

We decided to head inland ourselves. Somewhere during this trek, the glider troops flew over [near dusk]. This time, the sky was filled to the horizon, black with tow planes and gliders. Some planes were towing two gliders. Later, when we began to catch up with them, I realized I was not seeing a single undamaged glider. We saw a number of glider pilots heading towards the beach.

We must not have done any "medical work" that day, because the next thing I can recall is nighttime. We were mixed in with paratroopers, still looking for our company. We wandered around late into the night, at one point running across a comrade from another medical company who was tending a small circle of wounded on stretchers beside a road. He was waiting for others from his company to evacuate them. He whispered a warning to us not to go further down the road, that these men had been wounded in an ambush just around the bend. We finally drifted into a cobblestone courtyard in front of a French farmhouse at the intersection of two roads and fell asleep near the well pump, sitting propped up against the house.

By the end of the day, Private Montgomery reached Ste-Marie-du-Mont where contact was made with the paratroopers. He had crossed Exit 2, where traffic had piled up because a culvert in the middle of the causeway had been damaged.

Elements of the 4th Signal Company of the 4th Division began landing during the day. Among them was Pvt. William E. Finnigan, who served in the field-telephone wire section. He went to Normandy in *LST 282*, which towed a Rhino barge across the Channel.

> I was in the kitchen in the evening when a captain asked for some sandwiches for his underwater demolition team. I had seen them loading explosive charges in small boats [LCVPs] hanging in the davits in the afternoon of June 5. The cooks weren't too anxious to make sandwiches until the captain said, "Most of these men won't be coming back." The sandwiches were immediately prepared. In the morning, the davits hung empty. They had gone in the night [early morning, probably about 3 A.M.]. Dawn was just light enough to see the enormous number of ships of all kinds and sizes. A new-looking destroyer went by very slowly close to us. No lights, no sign of life, although you knew every man was awake and at battle stations, as ours were. Our LST pulled the Rhino barge around to the front of the ship, and after a long struggle with it banging into the LST doors, it was secured to the ship. The LST doors had to be repaired in England.
>
> I was on the tank deck—the lower deck—so I was in the first group off. During this time, a battleship constantly fired its big guns with big clouds of dirty yellow smoke. The Rhino had two big engines, like two giant outboards, but the water was too rough, so a small boat pulled us away, and later an LCI arrived. Approaching the beach, there were trucks on fire, beached boats, and shells landing from a German gun further to the right.
>
> There was a long concrete wall, and we came to a place that had been blasted through. I saw a new mine detector and its open case lying in the sand and thought, "What a waste!" We threw away our lifebelts—everybody had one of them around their waist.
>
> One American tank had slid off the causeway and went on across to dry land beyond the swamps. A young German, a boy, came up to the group of us. He was wet from the waist down from the swamp. He handed his rifle to someone, and while standing there, a group of prisoners came by. He gave a little wave to them but got no response.
>
> The first dead man I saw was an American and then a German. I was to see many dead in Normandy. Later in Europe, I saw a handmade sign outside a graves registration area: "Bring your bodies here, Allied or otherwise.

T/5 Fred R. Tannery, a messenger in the 4th Signal Company, was on the top deck of the same LST, "watching the action along the landing area."

> I was watching our battleships shell the coastline. One shell hit an enemy ammunition dump. It was a very large ammunition dump, from the size of the explosion. Quite a sight! Some enemy shelling was landing close to the LST I was on. During all this action, I saw the wounded being loaded on boats and returning to England for treatment. Seeing the wounded really shook me up, and I realized this landing was the real thing and I would wind up being wounded.
>
> After landing, I noticed two men carrying wire cages, which contained two homing pigeons. Later that day, messages were delivered to the men in charge of the pigeons. At once they attached the messages to the legs of the pigeons, and one pigeon

was tossed into the air. He got his bearing and flew toward England. The other pigeon was released but did not respond as fast as the other. He flew to a tree, a truck, and his cage and hopped around on the ground before he was able to fly high so he could get the correct bearing for his flight. He finally did his duty and was on his way.

Late in the afternoon, I ran into one GI not from my company, but from an infantry company. He started talking to me and said he wanted to show me something. I went with him, and he showed me three Germans who had been shot during the invasion. This was my first encounter with the enemy who were dead. While trying to get over this experience, I noticed the GI take a piece of rope, attach it to one of the Germans' legs, and start to pull to see if the bodies were booby-trapped. Then he jumped into the ditch and started to remove jewelry from their fingers. I was too dumbfounded to think and said nothing to stop him. I felt guilt because I knew this was wrong and did nothing. I understand this GI was involved in many unusual matters. Once he stole a German command car, drove it around, and nearly got shot by his own men.

The 8th Regiment's communications officer, Capt. Herbert M. Krauss, a twenty-nine-year-old draftee from Chicago, landed with his radio section, wire section, and message center section during the day. All he remembers about the crossing was that the food was not very good and that he had a sergeant thrown in the brig for tossing a cigarette butt over the side. When he landed, his jeep was missing. He and his driver went back and found it. Soon after this, he stumbled across his first two dead Germans.

The 70th Tank Battalion came ashore with the first waves of the 4th Division to give it support. Its remaining elements arrived later in the day. According to the postinvasion account of the 70th Tank Battalion, "After overcoming coastal defenses, the companies advanced inland over the causeways crossing inundated areas toward STE.-MARIE-DU-MONT. Companies "A", "B" and "C" together with elements of the battalion forward echelon, spent the night in assembly area vicinity ST. HUBERT—northeast of STE.-MARIE-DU- MONT."

Company D, 70th Tank Battalion, equipped with light Stuart tanks, was transported on an LST. Its tanks, like all other vehicles, were waterproofed. Each light tank had an engine air intake and exhaust shroud that allowed it to operate in five feet of water. T/4 Charles J. Myers, a twenty-six-year-old draftee from Baltimore, served in the HQ tank section (three tanks) and was the ranking NCO, radio operator, and gunner for Lt. Col. John C. Welborn, the battalion commander. The second tank was for the XO, and the third tank of the HQ section was for artillery observation and usually operated with the assault gun platoon. The HQ and Company D were loaded on an LST, and Myers vaguely recalls that the vessel had three of their assault guns, two half-tracks with mortars, several 2½-ton trucks with supplies, and vehicles from other units of the 4th Division. Charles Myers spent most of the day aboard the LST, watching the operations on Utah Beach.

What stands out in my mind during the Channel crossing is the constant roar of the plane engines as they flew over the convoy. First there were the returning troop carriers, then the tow planes for the glider troops. Early in the morning, the bombers and fighters that were to work over the landing areas begin flying over. I saw the most ships that I had ever seen before my eyes when dawn arrived. Next was the naval shelling, and I prayed they were hitting their targets to make the landings a bit easier.

Loading *LST 282*.

> The HQ tank section did not land until about 1630 [4:30 P.M.] on D-Day. The battalion CO was not with us, as he was anxious to know what was going on with his command, so he hitched a ride on an LCI earlier in the day and was with a part of the unit when we landed.

When the headquarters section landed the beach area had already been cleared, and there was only sporadic shelling from a German battery near St. Marcouf.

> Upon landing, we were directed to a remote spot on the beach where the waterproofing equipment was removed. One of our recon men then led us to an assembly area where we spent the night. Each of the assaulting companies had a supply truck that was landed after the beach was cleared. These trucks loaded at the supply dumps and delivered the loads at the assembly area, where the tanks were refueling and the ammo expended was replenished.

Tank losses include five Shermans of Company A and four of Company C at sea and three more of Company A, two of Company B, and two of Company C during the land operations. The 70th Tank Battalion lost a total of sixteen medium tanks on D-Day. Nineteen men of the battalion died during the first day, including sixteen on S.Sgt. Glenn Gibson's LCT.

Twenty-five-year-old 1st Lt. Ralph E. Lingert had been drafted in South Dakota in 1941 and left the 6th Infantry Division to attend OCS in 1943. He was subsequently assigned to the 4th Division, and in 1944 he was in the Service

Company of the 12th Infantry, serving as assistant regimental motor officer.

> I was given charge of our rear-echelon troops—kitchen personnel, etc.—so the regimental motor officer, who was the company commander, left most of the motor officer duties to me, WO Lester L. Crist, and the regimental motor sergeant. We were loaded on boats ten days before June 5 and spent those days in the English Channel.
>
> The English boat captain took us to Omaha Beach. I refused to get off and forced him to take us back to Utah Beach. Our vehicles were transferred to Rhinos—a flatboat affair powered by outboard engines—so that we could unload as close as possible to the beach. It took about two Rhinos shuttling back and forth. We landed about three-quarters of a mile out in the afternoon, several hours (about four hours) late. The water was rough. I embarked into the water 229 vehicles all capable of running in several feet of water. One jeep (my vehicle) got ashore. The rest were drowned out.
>
> We were led off the Rhinos in theoretically six feet of water and my jeep hit the water when the ramp went down and we found we were in ten to eleven feet of water. By using my hands over the snorkel, we were able to get the vehicle to shore by dodging the potholes the propellers had made and bomb craters. Looking back, 229 vehicles of the 12th Infantry had gone underwater and were drowned. I went to the beach commander and asked for the use of a DUKW and a diver to salvage my vehicles. He said nothing doing. There was no DUKW or diver, and as far as he was concerned, the vehicles could rot.
>
> As I cruised the beach area for some distance, I was fortunate enough to meet Teddy Roosevelt Jr., whom I knew personally. I explained my problem and told him I needed a DUKW or two and divers to get the vehicles ashore so we could get them and supplies to the 12th Infantry. He said the supplies were most important and he didn't think I could salvage the vehicles. I said, "Oh yes, we can salvage the vehicles." He went to the beach commander with me, he introduced himself, and the beach commander stood at attention. He told him, "Give this lieutenant two DUKWs and four divers, two for each DUKW." He added that he would give them back. He asked him if that was understood and the colonel said, "Yes sir, understood." I got my DUKWs and went to work. They started pulling my vehicles ashore. We pulled them to the back part of the beach, and my mechanics dewaterproofed them and cleaned them up to see if we could get them back in running condition. Our mechanics worked the whole night and well into the next day to get the vehicles running again. At two o'clock in the afternoon (D+1), we had the first convoy ready to go up into the Monteburg area for the command post that the Service Company was going to establish. I sent WO Les Chris up there with the first convoy. I brought in the last convoy at about four that afternoon. Every one of these vehicles that had been underwater was serviced by us completely through the whole war with no problems. By the time the war was over, they had lost their seals, had bad front ends from water contamination, and they were burning oil quite profusely. However, I know they saved the 12th Infantry from quite a few headaches.

Lt. Tom Cortright of the 12th Infantry moved inland at the head of his Company L with the regiment until about dusk.

As I was standing talking to the company commander, we saw tracer fire coming from every direction. The tracers were firing at gliders—our gliders were coming in. They really made a scary sound, kind of a whirring noise coupled with the small-arms fire from the firefight in front of us. The captain of the glider troops deployed his men in a field where they landed, which was to our left, facing the enemy, and I never heard any more out of them. At that time, the leading platoon experienced a frontal attack. The captain deployed the 3rd Platoon and one mortar squad off to the right in the direction of the attack. After they deployed, the men from the leading platoon became confused and pulled down the main road, and what I saw could have become a rout. I ran about forty yards to the rear to the next crossroad and hedgerow and stopped everyone there and deployed the men on either side of the road. The 3rd Platoon was still deployed and isolated about sixty yards forward of my main body of men. I had five mortars and put them in battery and fired them by command of the Weapons Platoon lieutenant, who was up and cut off with the 3rd Platoon. I also had two .30-caliber air-cooled machine guns that I fired over the heads of the men in the field from the hedgerow in front of us. This way we were able to extract the 3rd Platoon.

The glider troops were the last airborne units to arrive on June 6. The first evening mission, code-named Keokuk, departed from Aldermaston at about 6:30 P.M. The gliders airlifted more than 150 troops of the 101st A/B Signal Company of the 101st A/B Division and the 326th A/B Medical Company, as well as vehicles, guns, and supplies, destined for LZ E. According to Wood's *History of the World's Glider Forces*, most of the thirty-two Horsas missed the landing zone; about one-third of the troops they transported were injured, and fourteen were dead. Flight Off. Eddie Anderson from Ozark, Arkansas, flew with the 73rd Squadron, 434th Group, and piloted a glider on this operation. His squadron attended a briefing before June 6, during which the intelligence officer displayed aerial photographs of the individual landing areas. In addition, the pilots were shown sand tables that included the hedgerows, but they were not told that these hedgerows had bases of up to thirty feet and had been in use for hundreds of years, serving as walls to separate individual fields. Thus most of the pilots clipped into them, believing they would come apart like those they had encountered in England.

The photo display at the briefing had included the town of Heisville where division headquarters would be installed, so Flight Officer Anderson had no difficulty recognizing the features when he came down.

Col. Mike Murphy was in our unit, and we would get the best information available, because Mike was going to get it for us. We also learned that Mike would carry in Brigadier General Pratt of the 101st Airborne Division early in the morning of June 6. We left the briefing room with a feeling of exhilaration and excitement. As we walked out past the MPs we were placed under guard and marched back to our BOQ [bachelor officer's quarters]. Later on that day, we were called and told it was off: "You're not going in." What a letdown. Later we were told it was on again.[10] Then we really began to get to work.

We went to the supply room, and each glider pilot was issued three hand grenades, ninety-six rounds of .30-caliber ammo for

10. Anderson is not clear whether this message was given on June 6 or the day they were briefed by Colonel Murphy.

his M-1 or carbine, and those with a .45-caliber Tommy gun got six clips.

For my flight, I was assigned to one of the big Horsas on a mission called Keokuk. My copilot was Jack Tucker, the squadron engineering officer. He was one of the finest fellows you could meet and a graduate of a Texas university. Old Jack had a little eye problem. If he had ever had to take a strict physical, he would have been grounded. The rest of us all took up for him. When it came his time to fly, one of us would fly with Jack, and he would get his flying time in.

Our load consisted of a jeep and an anti-tank gun, which I believed was called a British 6-pounder, with a five-man crew. We also had a demolition crew with about forty-five pounds of high explosive, headed by a sergeant whose name I believe was Schafer.

Just before takeoff, Colonel Whittaker drove up beside my glider and handed me two notes. One was addressed to me, and it was wrapped around a rose. It was from an American Red Cross girl who was a very kind person and a good friend, not from a romantic relationship. The little note said, "Take care of yourself you big lug and hurry back. . . . God Bless You." That touched me. The other note, which I did not open, I was to deliver to Colonel Murphy after landing.

Takeoff time was about 1830 hours [6:30 P.M.]. We got our troops onboard. Finally our glider pulled into position, and then came the moment of takeoff. We formed into a circle around Aldermaston and put our formation all together, then headed south. The major who briefed us didn't miss it when he told us we would have the best seats to see the "Big Show."

Our flying time was two hours and thirty minutes to Heisville. Jack Tucker and I took turns at the controls. From time to time, we allowed the airborne troops to come up on the flight deck to see the sights. It took a lot of power and muscle to fly that big thing because we did not have a hydraulic assist on those big ailerons and controls. It was pretty much all done by leverage and muscle, and after about thirty minutes of that, you got a little tired.

As we approached the Normandy coastline, we were at about 700 feet. We could see the activity all along the beach. The battleships *Arkansas* and *Texas*, were firing their big 14-inch guns. Shortly before we reached the coastline, we received small-arms fire. As we crossed the coastline, I took control and began to look for our designated field. We crossed the swamp, and then I recognized our landing zone and picked my field. I remembered that Colonel Whittaker had told me just before the takeoff, "Andy, try to make a 360-degree approach if possible; it will give you a chance to look the field over to make sure there are no obstacles." As we crossed over the boundary of that field at about 560 feet, I told Jack to "cut" [the towline]. I flew the length of the field; at the end of it, I made a 90-degree left turn and almost immediately another 90-degree turn downwind. Being in the left seat, I had the opportunity to look the field over as we went down the field. We were doing great, losing the proper amount of altitude, then another 90 degrees onto the base leg. At this time, I got down to about 250 feet of altitude and I thought, "This is perfect!" as I made my final turn onto the final approach. I was watching the ground activity, and Jack was calling out my airspeed and altitude, and after I made this 90-degree turn, which put me perpendicular to my landing path, Jack hollered, "Look out!" Just as he did, I looked up, and I was in a banked attitude of the air-

> craft, and here comes another big British Horsa at about 100 miles per hour, flying just perpendicular to my flight path. He flew under me; I jerked the controls up and just barely missed him. By jerking the controls back, I almost stalled the aircraft, which dissipated my speed. To regain speed, I had to shove the controls forward and make a different angle of attack with my wing, which almost caused us to hit the ground. I didn't have enough altitude to make the final left turn, so I did the next best thing—I just landed straight ahead. I grazed over a hedgerow and set the glider down on the ground without putting a scratch on it. I had landed exactly 90 degrees from the path I intended.

As soon as Anderson's glider was down, it was greeted by a hail of small-arms fire. After taking cover on the ground, the passengers returned to the glider to unload it by taking off the entire tail section.

> It has a ring that goes around it. You pull this ring and pull the tail section off. There are two big tracks that run out the back so you can run the jeep and gun out. We did that and got our gun unloaded and the men cut out. We were scared and out of our element now that we were on the ground. We got our weapons and started moving out. As we neared this hedgerow of about ten feet height, I believe there were three German soldiers walking along the hedge. Unexpectedly, we all met at the gate in the hedgerow. There we were, and there they were. For a moment, everybody stopped. We fell down on the ground. One of the Germans had a potato masher, and he threw it in a haphazard way. It exploded, and I received a little scratch on my right wrist. At that time, a couple of paratroopers on the other side saw what was going on, and they started shooting. Immediately the Germans gave up. One of the paratroopers said he would take the prisoners in. We got our jeep on the road and started toward the divisional headquarters. I had the map and knew exactly we were going.

At headquarters, the glider pilots were given various missions. That night Anderson and a few other pilots set up a perimeter defense on the east side of the 101st A/B headquarters and captured a few German paratroopers from the 6th Parachute Regiment, which was in the area.

In England, twenty-two-year-old veteran PFC Joseph G. Clowry, a telephone lineman in the wire section of the HQ Battery, 319th Glider Field Artillery Battalion, was given the alert to pack up and prepare for departure on the afternoon of June 6. His group moved onto the runway, where the gliders stood in two columns at a 45-degree angle from each other. Facing these columns was a line of C-47s similarly angled. A 300-yard-long towrope linked the tail of the C-47 transports to the gliders they were to tow. As Clowry approached his glider with his comrades, he braced himself for the great adventure.

> Our group entered our designated glider. We seated ourselves facing the center of the craft on the benchlike seats that ran most of the length of each side of the body and strapped ourselves in. I was seated across from the previously loaded trailer, slightly to the rear of the center of the craft and on the left side. In addition to our regular equipment, we had been furnished Mae West life jackets in case we had to ditch. Our contingent consisted of a glider pilot and, because of the shortage of pilots, our first lieutenant assisting in the copilot's seat, and an unremembered number of enlisted men of various grades.

> Outside, the engines of the tow planes were warming up, and the noise was such that any verbal communications had to be shouted. Soon the roar of the lead C-47 was heard, and it was off at 2037 hours [8:37 P.M.]. Soon it was our turn. The towrope unraveled, tightened, and with a slight jerk, our Horsa began to roll forward. We gathered speed, and shortly the rumble of the wheels on the runway was silenced and we were airborne. We were veering off and climbing to the preset altitude for assembly.
>
> At last, this was it; this was what we had been training for, and we were finally ready to go. Sitting there, I had a feeling of anticipation. How would the flight go, the landing, and after? There wasn't any internal or external sign of fear—this was a great adventure, and after all, what could happen to a twenty-two year old? It could happen to the person across the way, or the one next to you, but never you!

Clowry was in the first serial of the second wave of Mission Elmira, which took off from Membury with forty-eight Horsa and two Waco gliders. The first wave had departed more than an hour earlier in two serials from Ramsbury and Greenham Common, with fifty-four Horsa and twenty-two Waco CG-4A gliders. It had headed for LZ W carrying some 400 troops, sixty-four vehicles, thirteen antitank guns, and other supplies. The second wave also had two serials and took off from Welford just a few minutes after Clowry's serial, which included the 319th Field Artillery Battalion with 418 troops, thirty-one jeeps, and fifty-one tons of supplies, according to *History of the World's Glider Forces*. It was followed by thirty-eight Horsa and twelve Waco gliders carrying the 320th Field Artillery Battalion, with 319 troops, a dozen 105-millimeter howitzers, twenty-eight jeeps, and fifty-five tons of supplies. For the troops at Utah Beach and on the ships off the Normandy coast, these waves of C-47s, gliders in tow and fighter escorts at their sides, were truly a sight to behold. The Germans greeted them with small-arms and machine-gun fire. As LZ W was not secure, only a few gliders landed there; the remainder looked for other landing sites. Clowry's serial had to be diverted.

> Our troop carriers were unaware that the 82nd Division was diverting our flight to LZ O instead of LZ W because of supposedly better landing conditions and because LZ W was covered by German weapons. The two serials joined up in a column of fours as we headed across southern England and the Channel for France. We were accompanied by groups of Allied fighter planes. Apparently because of the approaching darkness, the fighters turned back before the glider train reached the French coast. The flight over the Channel was relatively uneventful. By turning my head to the left, I could peer out of one of the portholes lining the length of the Horsa. Over the Channel could be seen the lines of tow planes and gliders droning over the increasingly darkening water below. Soon we were approaching, and then over, an armada of fighting ships below, the larger ones, parallel to the shore, belching great balls of yellow and orange flames toward the shore. Rapidly we passed over the fleet, the beach, and headed inland. As we approached Utah Beach, the rushing noise of the wind passing over the wings and the side of the glider increased. The gliders were usually towed at about 100 miles an hour, but as we approached shore, the C-47 pilots increased their speed to what felt to be about 125 miles an hour so that they could get in and out as fast as possible.
>
> The sun had set a few minutes before we reached the beach, and as we headed inland,

the ground began to become darker, and it was more difficult to make out objects below, even at 500 feet. I continued to look out the window, and about three miles inland, I could see what appeared to be a group of fireflies milling about on the ground in the creeping darkness and then ascending in single file, increasing in velocity as they approached in streams until, with a swish, they whizzed by the window. Realizing they were tracer bullets, I felt that I had nothing to worry about because they could be seen; it was the other four or more bullets between each tracer that you had to look out for. The intensity of the ground fire increased as we proceeded, and more and more fireflies were streaming by. The glider pilot finally cut loose, the noise of the rushing wind silenced, and starting a 180-degree right bank, began to descend into the darkness. I continued to peer out of the porthole, searching for any recognizable land feature. That was the last thing I remember.

The first glider release in our serial occurred at 2255 hours [10:55 P.M.], ahead of schedule by five minutes. A large portion of the gliders released over a mile short of LZ O, while six gliders released at least five miles east of the landing zone. LZ O was marked with green panels forming a T, green smoke, and a Eureka beacon. The change in landing zones took the tow planes and gliders over German concentrations north and northeast of Ste-Mère-Église and into heavy ground fire.

Clowry's serial and the one that followed missed LZ O for the most part. Of eighty-four Horsas, fifty-six were destroyed and thirteen landed without damage. The fourteen CG-4As were either damaged or destroyed, but forty-two jeeps were still serviceable. As put forth by *History of the World's Glider Forces*, ten pilots were dead and another twenty-nine wounded. Of the 1,190 troops carried in the Elmira Mission, only 157 were wounded or dead, according to Zaloga's *D-Day 1944*. Unfortunately, Clowry was among the casualties.

The next thing I recall is total darkness and the continual sounds of what seemed to me to be the crunching and splintering caused by someone jumping off the roof of a house into a large pile of wooden matchboxes. Then I heard the splintering noise of someone tearing away plywood from on top of me and anyone nearby; then some dim shadows with arms extended to assist in extricating me from the rubble. There were two others in the pile, one on each side of me, so that I was sandwiched between them, and they must have absorbed some of the impact. I saw a 4th Division insignia on one of the rescuers. While laying on my side in the wreckage, my glance spotted, about ten to fifteen feet away, the jeep tipped over on its side, with a complete oval-shaped section of the glider floor still attached to it by the tie-down ropes. I felt relief that it had not landed on me. Blood was running down my face, and my entire body was sore and aching. I had a swelling and a gash about an inch above the outside corner of my left eye and a number of slashes across the top of my head in an ear-to-ear direction. Someone bandaged me up with two compression bandages: one across the top of my head and tied under my chin, the other over my left forehead and tied in back.

Amid the usual din of war, in the darkness, I made my way to a nearby stone wall about three feet high separating the next field. I pulled up about me an abandoned parachute I found nearby, leaned in a seated position with my back against the wall, and waited, hardly moving to prevent aggravat-

> ing the soreness I felt all over me. There I sat back to see what the six hours of summertime darkness might hold in store.

On the night of June 4, Flight Off. Charles V. Gauntt of Fort Worth, Texas, heard erroneous reports on the radio that the invasion had begun. He had done most of his flying in Horsas and was to pilot a glider for the 435th Troop Carrier Group assigned to carry troops of the 82nd A/B Division on June 6. During the briefing preceding the flight, the intelligence officer tried to convince the skeptical pilots that they would have plenty of room to land. Gauntt was assigned to the second serial of the second wave, which departed from Welford at 8:40 P.M. His serial carried more than 300 troops of the 320th A/B Field Artillery, twelve 105-millimeter howitzers, twenty-eight jeeps, and other supplies. The guns were carried in CG-4As. Gauntt took off before the CG-4As in his serial. The other serial, which left from Membury, carried the 319th Airborne Field Artillery.

At about 11:00 P.M., when they passed over the French coast, it was already dark.

> Everything was pretty quiet, then all hell broke lose. All the AA was sitting there, waiting for us. They had stirred up a hornet's nest that morning and the Germans moved back in there and took over these open fields. We had to change landing zones because the Germans had recaptured ours. We were in two lanes, and my flight leader was leading the left lane and I was leading the right. The flight leader turned in toward Ste-Mère-Église and ran into a brick building. He was too close in and I guess he didn't see it in time. The guy immediately behind me turned on his landing lights and saw what he was going into, veered off to the left, and landed in an apple orchard. He lost his wings and all that. I saw the lieutenant in front of me. He made his turn and we turned in behind him. I saw him going down in this little field and pile into the trees. By that time, we were busy. Lieutenant Azworth all of a sudden veered off to the left where he saw a little field over there and was going to go through the opening. The opening wasn't big enough for the Horsa, and unfortunately his aim wasn't too good and he hit a tree head-on, right where I was sitting. If I had been two feet this way, I would have been all right. We hit that tree at least going 90 miles per hour with the 88s popping at us. When we got on the ground, the machine guns started firing at us. We were catching machine-gun fire when we touched ground. An antitank gun blew our landing gear and tail to hell and back. Of course, when we hit the tree, about five feet from the pilot, the wings came off and there was nothing left but the fuselage where the troops were. The only other ones to get hurt were a captain and a lieutenant who had the poor judgment to sit immediately behind the pilot. The sergeant had to take over. One had a broken back and the other a broken leg. The rest of the troops were all right. I was the copilot, and I had a broken leg while the pilot had two broken legs.
>
> I sailed through that nose when we hit the tree, seat and all. I guess that is what saved me. I had a helmet on and a flak suit. When I went through the nose of the plane for seventy feet or so, I scooted along the ground with part of the wood and chicken wire of the nose section wrapped around me, and I couldn't move. A board or something got under my neck, and I couldn't breathe. I finally kicked my way out and turned on my side so I could breath. The troopers had cut me out. There was a German trench about twenty feet from where

we stopped; it was about five feet deep and two feet wide. They put all the injured there. We stayed there for two nights, and on the third night they evacuated us.

As the last gliders lifted off from Welford early in the evening of June 6, some men felt greatly disappointed to be left out. Second Lt. William D. Knickerbocker was detached from the 314th Group with others from his unit for service with the 435th at Welford Park. "We sat in the officers' club, watching them take off. They had assigned all the glider pilots without us. I was on the verge of tears. I watched several years go by, and here is combat, and I have twenty missions in the Mediterranean pulled out from under my feet. The sky was full as they were up there getting their formations together. I don't know about the other guys, but it broke my heart."

As the sun set behind Utah Beach and the Cotentin Peninsula on D-Day, the German coastal defenses were shattered, and the beachhead was well established. Many of the men of the two airborne divisions were scattered, and the bulk of their equipment and supplies were lost. Most of their glider units were not scheduled to land until June 7. The contingent of the airborne divisions was less than half strength. Of the 6,600 men dropped that morning, the 101st A/B Division had accounted for only 2,500 by day's end.[11]

On the other hand, most of the elements of the 4th Infantry Division had come ashore with reinforcements, which included the 359th Infantry Regiment of the 90th Infantry Division, 65th Armored Field Artillery Battalion, 87th Chemical Mortar Battalion, 899th Tank Destroyer Battalion, 70th and 745th Tank Battalions, and elements of the 1st Engineer Special Brigade. More than 20,000 men and 1,700 vehicles had successfully landed at Utah Beach. The entire division had suffered only 197 casualties, of which 118 were in the 8th and 22nd Infantry Regiments and 60 were men of Battery B of the 29th Field Artillery who were lost when their landing craft blew up.

One of the few problems on Utah Beach was establishing communications between the combat elements and higher headquarters, but this was not serious compared with the events unfolding on Omaha Beach.

11. A report from the 101st A/B Division headquarters summarizing the events of the month of June 1944 stated that by 6 P.M. on June 6, the 502nd PIR had a strength of about 500 men around Varreville, the 506th PIR about 350 near Culoville and the 377th Parachute Field Artillery Battalion 85 men and one howitzer near Foucarville. At that time, there was no information from the 501st PIR or the 3rd Battalion of the 506th PIR. By midnight, the division had accounted for 50 percent of its combat troops, although the 501st PIR's situation was still unknown except for 120 men from its 3rd Battalion at the division command post. On June 7, about 600 men from the 2nd and 3rd Battalions of the 501st PIR were accounted for but the remainder of the 501st PIR and the 3rd Battalion of the 506th were still missing. The next day, the first contact was made with the rest of the 501st and elements of the 506th's 3rd Battalion located north of the Douve River and east of Carentan.

CHAPTER 12

The Landings on Omaha Beach (Part 1)

The troops assigned to the assault teams for Omaha Beach began loading their landing craft at about the same time as those of Assault Force U. The veteran "Big Red One" 1st Infantry Division was selected for the attack on the section of the Calvados coast designated Omaha Beach. The 116th Infantry Regiment of the 29th Division was attached for the initial landing.

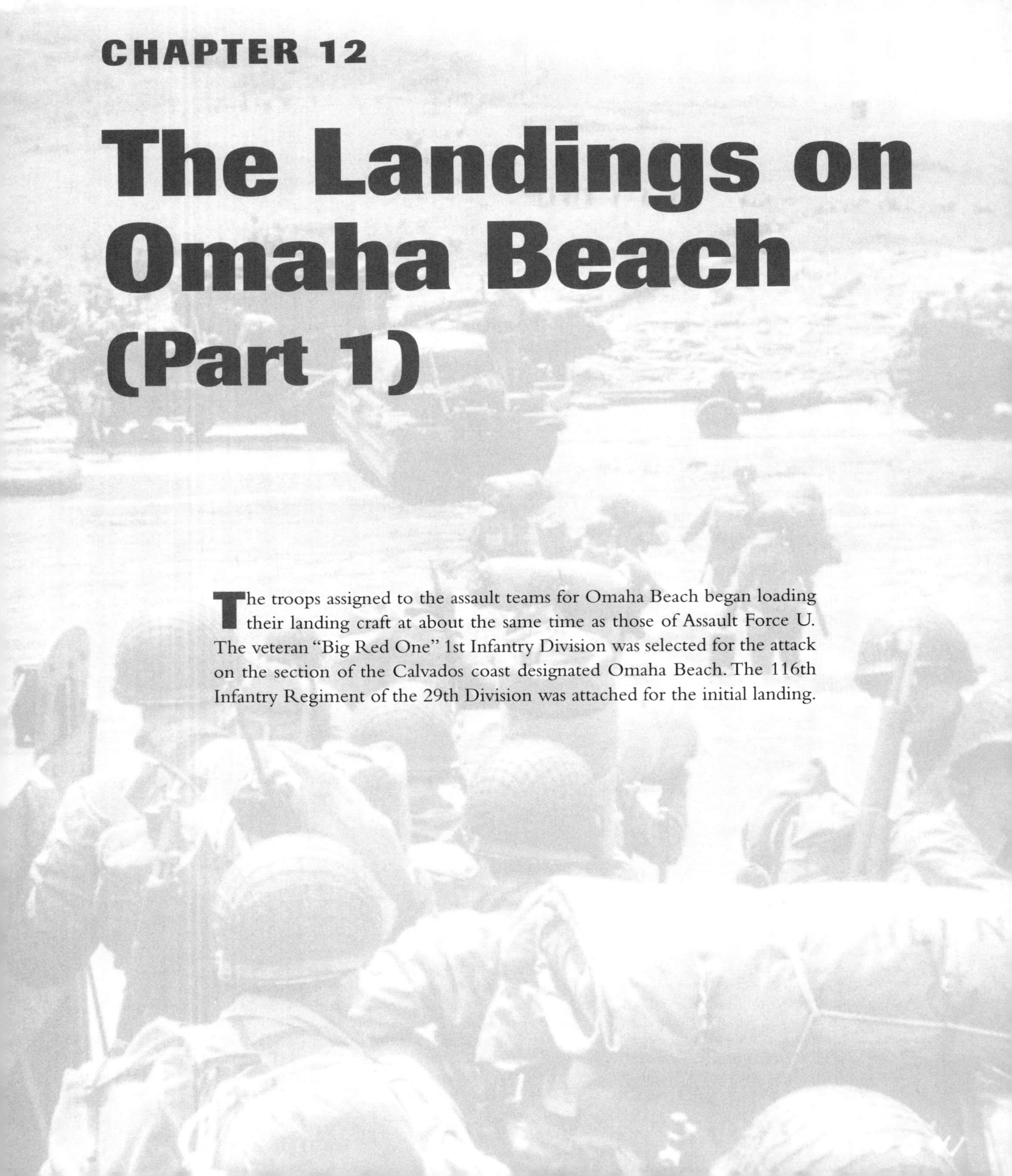

For the assault, the two companies from the 2nd Battalion and two from the 3rd Battalion of the 16th Infantry, carried on two transports—the USS *Henrico* (APA 45) and the large British LSI *Empire Anvil*—would lead the first wave onto Easy Red and Fox Green Beaches. On the right, the 116th Infantry was to land Company A of the 1st Battalion on Dog Green. At the same time, the 2nd Battalion would send one company each to Dog White, Dog Red, and Easy Green. These battalions crossed the Channel on the British LSI *Empire Javelin* and the attack transport *Thomas Jefferson* (APA 30). Farther to the west, the 2nd Ranger Battalion, which was to storm Pointe du Hoc, arrived with its troops on the small British LSIs *Prince Charles*, *Ben Machree*, and *Amsterdam*. The Special Engineer Task Force (SETF), whose mission was to destroy the beach obstacles, was to come on the heels of the first waves and arrived on the British LSI *Princess Maud*. Next came the 3rd Battalion of the 116th Infantry on the attack transport *Charles Carroll* (APA 28) and the 1st Battalion of the 16th Infantry on the *Samuel Chase* (APA 26). The 5th Ranger Battalion was onboard the small British LSIs *Prince Leopold* and *Prince Baudouin*. Additional troops were waiting aboard the transports *Anne Arundel* (AP 76), *Dorothea Dix* (AP 67), and *Thurston* (AP 77). This lineup numbered more than eighty LCVPs and eighteen LCAs carrying boat assault and support teams; fifty-plus LCTs, some of which transported Sherman DD tanks for the first wave; twenty-four LSTs, six of which carried units for the initial assault; and thirty-three LCIs, five of which were to move into the landing area after the first waves had landed. Assault Force O totaled 34,000 men and 3,300 vehicles. The success of the operation, however, depended almost entirely on the several thousand men of the first waves.

When the time came, the LCVPs were lowered into the water from the transports and the LCAs from the LSIs. After circling for some time, they began to move into landing formations and head toward the beaches. By the time the sun was peeking over the horizon, the naval bombardment was already under way. The Sherman DDs were to leave their LCTs and swim to shore before the first wave hit at H-Hour, approximately 6:30 A.M. as at Utah Beach. Some Shermans in the first wave were equipped with wading trunks on the engine compartments to prevent flooding their engines, since they were expected to leave their landing craft in shallow water.

LCVP Boat Teams

Each of the infantry companies in the first wave was assigned seven LCVPs to deliver its men and equipment to the beaches. The company headquarters landed on the heels of the boats leading the assault. The standard company consisted of three rifle platoons of 41 men each, one weapons platoon of 35 men, and the company headquarteres for a total of 193 men. The LCVPs had a capacity of 30 to 31 men each, so seven could carry about 210 men.

The troops of the first wave for Omaha Beach had been reorganized and given special training with additional weapons and equipment for the assault. The infantry companies had reorganized into six thirty-man boat landing teams (BLTs) each led by a lieutenant with five riflemen, a four-man wire-cutting team, two two-man BAR teams, two two-man bazooka teams, a four-man 60-millimeter mortar team, a two-man flamethrower team, five demolition men, a medic, and an NCO.

The strength of the infantry companies was raised from 193 men to about 210 men, not counting the attached medics. Each of the six BLTs was in effect a small platoon assembled from men drawn from each of the company's three rifle platoons and its weapons platoon.

Troops wade ashore from their landing craft.

Farther to the east, the British troops made their own preparations while awaiting news of the American landings, since their H-Hour was not until 7:30 A.M. Unlike the Americans, the British spearheaded their landings with a variety of specialized armored vehicles from their 79th Armoured Division. They had offered some of these vehicles to the Americans who turned them down, according to some sources. It has also been suggested, however, that the British industry was not able to produce enough of these modified tanks. Be this as it may, the Americans accepted only enough swimming Sherman DD tanks to provide immediate fire support for the assault troops on the beaches.

The American 4th Infantry Division, the Canadian 3rd Division, and the British 3rd and 50th Divisions faced relatively level terrain in their assault area. Like the 4th Division, the British 3rd Division, which landed at Sword Beach on the east flank, had to advance rapidly inland to relieve or rescue the British airborne forces. Led by Gen. Leonard Gerow, the American V Corps, which landed at Omaha Beach, had no such noble rescue mission. This was fortunate, as its mission became one of survival as soon as the assault waves hit the beaches.

A successful landing on Omaha Beach would make it possible to link the other beachheads and prevent the Germans from sealing off the 4th Division in the Cotentin Peninsula. This American beachhead was also necessary to protect the construction of a British artificial harbor near Arromanches and allow the American Mulberry to be established at Omaha Beach, which were intended to be the locations of the main supply lines.

An unpleasant surprise awaited the first waves of American troops at Omaha Beach. The Germans had reinforced their overextended 716th Division with the 352nd Infantry Division in the planned landing sectors, but Allied intelligence sources had reported that the 352nd was still in reserve near St. Lô at the time of the invasion.

The area selected for the assault made the situation even more difficult, as it consisted of a crescent-shaped 7,000-yard stretch of beach bounded by bluffs. On the bluffs overlooking the beach, the Germans had set up strongpoints with casemated gun positions that could sweep much of the landing area at both points of the crescent. Wn-73, armed with mortars and machine guns, was on the western side, dug into the cliffs, which gave it a measure of security. Its single French 75-millimeter field gun was able to enfilade most of the beach. A little farther to the west, at Pointe de la Percée, stood Wn-74, with two 76.2-millimeter guns. The bluffs were easily defended, with half a dozen draws offering exit points from the beach. Only half of these exits were suitable for vehicles and strongpoints, and all were blocked with antitank ditches, barriers, or both. A network of slit trenches linked many of the concrete positions. Neither the preparatory bombardment nor the aerial by the Allies succeeded in neutralizing the German strongpoints before the arrival of the first waves.

The site designated as Omaha Beach was divided into eight beach sectors. The distance between the high- and low-tide mark for most of this expanse of beach was 300 yards. At high tide, part of this tidal flat was 18 feet underwater. An assault at low tide would allow the landing craft to avoid the obstacles, which included Belgian gates, logs with mines on top planted at an angle, and log ramps placed in broken lines. The Belgian Gates were located at about 250 yards from the high-water mark, the mined logs 20 to 25 yards. About 100 yards from that line and 130 yards from the high-water mark were 5½-foot-high hedgehogs. The assault troops would have to negotiate the 300 yards of tidal flat in the face of enemy fire coming from the bluffs, which stood 200 yards or more from the high-water mark. In addition, the flat had runnels paralleling the coast, and the troops could accidentally fall into these when they were covered with water.

The tide was expected to come in soon after the first waves landed, so the SETF needed to work quickly to clear paths through the lines of obstacles on the tidal flat. Once the first troops reached the high-water mark, they had to cross a 15-yard-wide expanse of shingle that spanned the eastern two-thirds of the invasion area. Consisting of pebbles about three inches in diameter, this presented a serious obstacle to vehicles. On the other side of this expanse lay some sand dunes, and the Germans had placed concertina and other wire obstacles just behind the shingle. A seawall topped with wire obstacles crossed the remaining third of the beach on the west side and ended by Exit D-3 at Les Moulins. Ranging in height from four to twelve feet, it would offer some degree of protection to the assailants who managed to reach its shelter.

Behind the wall and dunes was a shelf, or beach flats, that included a mixture of marsh and high grass. This area was defended by some real minefields and many dummy ones. Between Les Moulins and Exit D-1 to Vierville, the Germans had destroyed several villas to prevent them from being used as protection. Several structures in Exits D-1 and D-3 were defended by the Germans. The coastal shelf was bordered by bluffs that were very steep and rose to 170 feet in some sections. Many of the German strongpoints were located on the edge of these bluffs and included mines, wire, extensive trenches (mostly slit trenches), concrete bunkers, Tobruks with machine guns, mortars, and antitank guns.[1]

Only four draws large enough for vehicles cut through this wall of bluffs from the beach. On

1. A Tobruk was a small concrete position with an open circular firing position in the roof designed for a machine gun or mortar. One constructed to hold a machine gun usually had an opening large enough for one man to stand with a light machine gun. Tobruks were often attached to bunkers, but many stood alone.

The German Strongpoints on Omaha Beach

Twelve strongpoints located along the beaches and just behind them faced the American invasion force. Farther back were two more strongpoints at St. Laurent and Colleville. Some of these positions were built on the bluffs and the slopes leading toward the beach in order to create enfilading fires. All were classified as resistance nests, or *Widerstandsneste* (WN). There were no major strongpoints (StP) like the one on the planned Utah Beach. Compared with the other sections of the Calvados coast and the eastern Cotentin Peninsula, this section of beach was relatively easy to defend.

Wn-60, on the bluff on the east end of the beach, was occupied by forty enemy troops on June 6 and had trenches, bunkers, Tobruks, and old French tank turrets. Its weapons included four mortars, a 20-millimeter flak gun, an automatic flamethrower, and a 75-millimeter gun whose field of fire covered the beaches a little short of Pointe-de-la-Percée. This site guarded the F-1 exit.

Wn-61 and Wn-62, which blocked Exit E-3, were the last positions to fall on June 6. Wn-61, located on the shelf below the bluffs, included an 88-millimeter casemated gun that enfiladed the beach to the west and an antitank ditch that ran in front of it and across the entrance to E-3, with minefields on both sides. Only a dozen troops defended this position. In addition, there were a few smaller positions, including one for a tank turret and two for 50-millimeter antitank guns. On the west side of the exit, facing Wn-61, was Wn-62, a very strong position surrounded with barbed wire and minefields. It extended down the slope toward the sea, where two of its casemates armed with two Czech 75-millimeter field guns facing west provided flanking fire across the beach. On the east site of Wn-62 were two 50-millimeter antitank guns that covered the exit, machine guns, mortars, a flamethrower, Tobruk positions, and concrete bunkers. Surprisingly, only thirty-one men occupied this position.

Wn-64, located on the bluffs on the east side of exit E-1, and Wn-65, sprawled between the bluffs and the shelf on the west side, covered the road. The armament of Wn-64 consisted of a Russian 76.2 field gun, a 20-millimeter flak gun, two mortars with Tobruk stands, trenches, and an unfinished gun casemate. It was manned by about twenty soldiers. Wn-65 included two 50-millimeter antitank guns, one of which was in casemate and covered the exit; two 50-millimeter mortars; and a 75-millimeter gun.

Exit D-3 at Les Moulins was covered by Wn-66 on the east side and Wn-68 on the other. Wn-66 included an old French tank turret and a couple of mortars. A 50-millimeter antitank gun on the lower slope at the end of the antitank ditch blocked the entrance. An antitank wall stood in the entrance, between the two strongpoints. Behind it was Wn-67, which was armed with Nebelwerfer multiple rocket launchers, which fired on the Allies on D-Day. Wn-68, which sprawled from the bluff toward the seawall, had a 50-millimeter antitank gun on the west end of the anti-tank ditch and two French tank turrets to the rear.

Wn-70, which stood mainly on the bluffs between Exits D-3 and D-1, had a casemated 75-millimeter gun, a 75-millimeter gun in a field position, a 20-millimeter flak gun, and two mortars. The machine guns at this position presented a serious setback for the Amer-

continued

The German Strongpoints on Omaha Beach *continued*

ican soldiers who managed to reach the beach on D-Day.

Finally, the Vierville exit, D-1, was defended by Wn-71 on the bluffs overlooking the east side. It included a number of concrete bunkers and some Tobruks. Its armament consisted of two mortars and one small cannon. Wn-72 sat across from it, on the shelf blocking the exit. This position included a flanking casemate with an 88-millimeter gun that faced east and covered most of the beach and a 75-millimeter antitank gun. Another bunker containing a 50-millimeter gun stood to the west of this casemate. Wn-72 was the most heavily defended position on Omaha Beach. Finally, Wn-73, just west of Exit D-1, included a 75-millimeter field gun in casemate that could enfilade the beach and three mortars. Its seaward side was protected by cliffs.

These resistance nests, with a total contingent of about 250 to 400 troops, faced the Americans on June 6. The fact that all these positions survived the bombings relatively unscathed made it possible for their few pieces of artillery and numerous machine guns to nearly bring to a halt more than 2,000 American soldiers arriving in the first wave and 1,500 or more arriving in the second wave.

All the resistance nests were manned by German troops from the 726th Regiment of the 716th Infantry Division. Two companies of the 916th Regiment of the newly arrived 352nd Infantry Division were stationed between St. Laurent and Colleville. Additional companies stood farther back, by Formigny. Three batteries of four 105-millimeter guns of the 352nd Division stood behind the coastal villages.

These German defenses were formidable compared with those at Utah Beach, where there were just three resistance nests, only one of which—W-5 with a 75-millimeter gun, a 50-millimeter gun, and a mortar—was well armed.

the west side, a paved road passed through Exit D-1 to the town of Vierville, located behind the bluffs. Farther down, a dirt road went through D-3 to the town of St. Laurent. In the center, another unpaved road passed through E-1. Near the east end, yet another unpaved road passed through E-3 and led to Colleville. Finally, the small Exit F-1 also allowed a way off the beach.

If the troops reached the bluffs, they could secure the landing beaches. On top of the bluffs, the terrain was open for a short distance and favored the assault force. The towns of Vierville, St. Laurent, and Colleville, however, could serve as German strongpoints to keep the invaders in check. The D-Day planners had hoped that the V Corps would be off the beaches and two miles or more inland by evening. They wanted the troops to link up with the British near Port-en-Bessin on the east flank and reach the Vire on the west flank and the flooded valley of the Aure River to the south. Unfortunately, none of these objectives was attained on D-Day.

At Omaha Beach, the Germans had completed most of the main lines of obstacles, whereas at Utah Beach, they had not. As a result, the American assault force at Omaha faced fifteen strongpoints, some of which were located on the bluffs and slopes to provide enfilading fire. The enemy had also covered all the exits, blocking them with antitank obstacles and ditches. Because Omaha Beach bowed inward, the Germans could easily cover the tidal flat and much of the beach area with fire and observation from the flanking bluffs. To the east of the invasion area and Port-en-Bessin, the German Longues Battery became problematic for both the Americans and British during the morning. On the west side of Omaha Beach and within range of the landing areas stood the German battery at Pointe du Hoc with its six 155-millimeter guns. Two nearby batteries at Maisy threatened Utah Beach and perhaps Omaha Beach as well. To take out the battery at Pointe du Hoc, the 2nd Ranger Battalion was to land below the cliffs and then scale them as the first waves came ashore on Omaha Beach.

Details of the Landings

The tank-carrying LCTs crossed the Channel in the convoy of Capt. Lorenzo S. Sabin, which, according to Samuel Eliot Morison, included 11 LSTs towing barges and 161 LCTs. As at Utah Beach, the thirty-two special Sherman DD tanks were to lead the way. They came from two tank battalions attached to the 1st Division and were to be launched 5,000 to 6,000 yards from the shore in the first wave. Eight more LCTs, also from the two tank battalions, followed the DDs carrying sixteen additional Shermans and eight tank dozers, with two tanks and one tankdozer per LCT. Wading trunks protected the air vents on the tanks' decks. All these vehicles preceded the assault troops of the first wave.

Lt. D. C. Rockwell, the naval commander in charge of the vessels carrying the 743rd Tank Battalion, concerned that rough seas and unfavorable winds would curtail his missions, ordered the LCTs to carry the Sherman DDs right up to the beach. The LCT carrying the commander of Company B was sunk, and only eight of the company's sixteen tanks made it ashore at Dog Green. Although the antitank guns of Wn-72 and Wn-73 took a heavy toll on them, forty of the American tanks made it to the tidal flats. The troops of the 116th Infantry who followed the tanks were decimated by the fire coming from the German strongpoints defending the beach.

The 741st Battalion with a similar armored force designated for the sectors of the 16th Infantry, was even more unfortunate. Despite the adverse conditions, the two company commanders ordered the yellow flags up, the signal to launch the tanks. The vehicles rolled off the LCTs 5,000 yards from the beach at about 5:40 A.M. and sank one after the other when their canvas curtains failed. Most of the crews drowned. Only two tanks from one company made their way to shore. Ens. H. P. Sullivan, commander of *LCT 57*, pulled up the ramp after watching the first tank roll off and sink. After trying to rescue the first tank crew, he carried the remaining three tanks to the beach, according to *The Story of Vitamin Baker* by Lanier et al. The other eight LCTs with the remaining sixteen Shermans mounting wading trunks also took losses bringing them ashore. Only eighteen tanks from the battalion finally reached the beach, where they were subjected to heavy fire. In minutes, the situation went from bad to worse.

Fortunately, the quick thinking of several officers, including Lieutenant Rockwell and Ensign Sullivan, eventually saved the day for the Americans at Omaha Beach. So many things went wrong that it took individual initiative and grit during the next six hours to turn the tide. Many troops arrived ashore as a leaderless rabble, usually in sectors to which they were not assigned, and they had to be taken quickly in hand if they were not to panic.

The first wave consisted of about 1,450 troops, including the SETF. The defenders, having weathered the earlier bombardments, manned their strongpoints and directed devastating machine-gun, mortar, and artillery fire against the landing craft and the troops pouring out of them. After the ramps dropped on the LCVPs, the soldiers who were not cut down by enemy fire had to negotiate more than 300 yards across the tidal flat,

U.S. Rangers at Pointe du Hoc after the position had been stormed.

where only the German anti-invasion obstacles offered cover. The next available shelter was offered by the few tanks on the beach, the seawall, and then the dunes, where they were still subjected to enemy small-arms, mortar, and artillery fire. Beyond that, they had to breach the barbed-wire obstacles and the minefields in order to approach the bluffs. To add to their woes, most of the assault companies of both regiments landed in the wrong sectors as a result of currents that pulled them eastward and other navigational problems.

During the first minutes of the landing, withering enemy fire left scores of American dead or wounded, decimating many of the assault companies, especially the engineer units, and earning the beach the nickname of "Bloody Omaha." Many of the officers, who were the first to jump off the LCVPs and LCAs when the ramps dropped, were cut down by enemy fire. Company A of the 116th was one of the few to land on the correct sector, in front of the Vierville Draw. It would have been better off if it had drifted eastwards like most of the others. Instead, like the tanks that preceded it, it was shot up and soon reduced to a rabble of leaderless troops scrambling for cover. Other companies of the 2nd Battalion of the 116th Regiment missed their sector and clustered in front of the strongpoints at Exit D-3, also taking heavy losses. One company was scattered along two of the 16th Infantry's sectors.

The 16th Infantry fared no better. The two assaulting companies of its 2nd Battalion were spread out between the sectors designated for both battalions of the regiment. One of the two companies of the 3rd Battalion landed on Fox Red, a sector in the shadow of the cliffs where no landings had been planned. The other company went too far east and took an hour and a half to return to Fox Green. The gap assault teams suffered heavy losses. Some units were almost wiped out as they worked on the tidal flat, unprotected from enemy fire. In some cases they found it difficult to blow up the obstacles, because many soldiers, especially those who were wounded, had sought refuge behind the hedgehogs and ramps. But despite this problem, they managed to clear four gaps in the obstacles on Easy Red, the sector of the 16th Infantry of the 2nd Battalion. In the 116th Infantry's sectors, they managed to open a gap on Easy Green where many troops had clustered. They also opened a gap on Dog White where no assault troops had landed, as the designated units had drifted too far east. This last gap would be important for succeeding waves. A shortage of equipment made the engineers' task all the harder since only six out of sixteen dozers made it ashore. The SETF sustained more than 40 percent casualties in the first few hours of the landing.

The first wave of troops was to be followed by a second, due at about 7 A.M. By that time, many of the soldiers onshore had sought cover behind the tanks and any other object that offered protection, including the shingle and the seawall. Some of those who cowered behind the tanks became prime targets for the defenders. The bombardment had set the vegetation on the shelf on fire, and the resulting smoke masked the view of the German gunners in some locations, allowing the Americans the opportunity to find shelter, penetrate the minefields, and work their way up to the bluffs. With most of their officers and NCOs dead, the troops were paralyzed. Added to this, the Germans started picking off incoming landing craft, and the tide began to come in as many troops still struggled across the tidal flats. Soon dead bodies began floating toward the beaches.

The situation did not improve as the second set of waves made their way ashore. Company B of the 116th came in directly behind Company A and suffered badly as it joined the remnants of the other company. The coxswains strove to maneuver their landing craft through sections that had not been cleared by the SETF. The situation continued to deteriorate.

At about 7:40 A.M., while the beach was still under intense enemy fire, several LCIs headed for shore. The Coast Guard–manned *LCI 91*, followed by *LCI 92*, was hit at Dog Red and Dog White at about 8 A.M. *LCI 91*, which carried the alternate headquarters for the 116th Infantry, took a direct hit as the troops began to disembark. *LCI 92* hit a mine, which caused its fuel tanks to explode. Both wrecks burned for hours and had a high number of casualties. Enemy artillery beyond the bluffs to the west rained down shells on the beaches of the 116th, adding to the destruction and disorder among the survivors of the landing. Meanwhile, on Fox Green, *LCI 85* received a fatal blow, but its gallant crew withdrew from the beach and evacuated the casualties before it went down.

Company C of the 2nd Ranger Battalion was intended to land on the right flank of the 116th Infantry and take out a radar position to the west. Elements of the company landed on Charlie sector on the extreme west side of the beachfront. At the same time, Company A of the 116th ran into serious trouble. Lt. Col. Max Schneider's 5th Ranger Battalion landed at Dog White, with the attached Companies A and B of the 2nd Rangers on the eastern side of Dog Green, when their mission to Pointe du Hoc was canceled. They were welcome reinforcements that would help turn the tide and break the stalemate.

The 116th Infantry's regimental commander, Col. Charles Canham, and Gen. Norman Cota, the assistant division commander, had come ashore after 7 A.M. with the second waves. They began to rally the troops they encountered and urged them to get off the beach. Cota sternly warned them that if they stayed there, they would surely die, and exhorted them to face death on the bluffs instead. When the 5th Rangers landed,

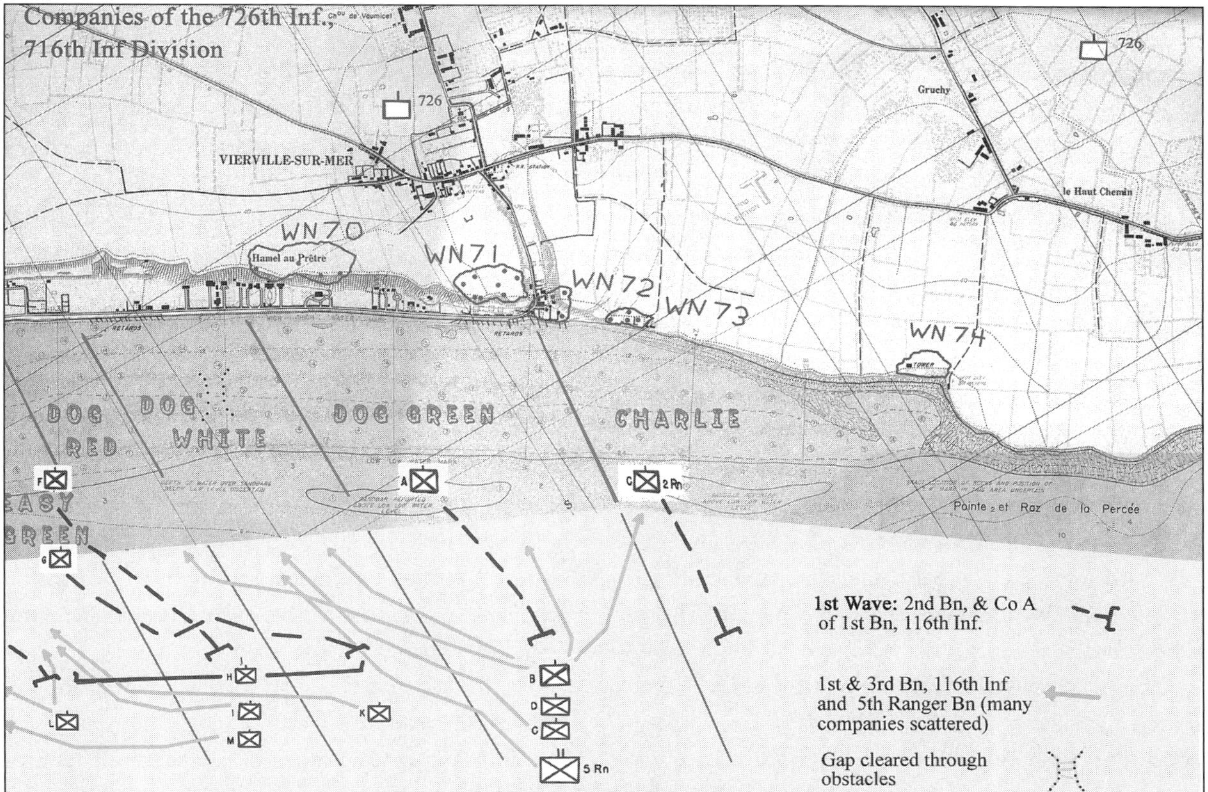

Landings on Omaha Beach by 116th Inf, 29th Inf Division

General Cota told one of their captains that he expected "Rangers to lead the way."

When the wire was finally breached, Cota with the 5th Rangers and troops from the 116th swarmed up the bluffs between Wn-70 and Wn-68. Canham had moved farther east and rallied more troops to follow them up the bluffs after 8 A.M. Company C, 2nd Ranger Battalion, had moved around Wn-73 but did not have enough men to go on. Maj. Sidney Bingham of the 2nd Battalion took over the leaderless Company F and led the assault on Wn-66, which dominated Exit D-3. His men were held in check by enemy fire, however, until they eventually worked their way around the position, according to Joseph Balkoski's *Beyond the Beachhead*.

On the far eastern end of the beach, 1st Lt. Robert R. Cutler Jr. took over Company L of the 16th Infantry, which had landed on Fox Red and a sector not designated for a landing. They moved west along the cliffs toward the main beaches. Cutter maneuvered elements of his company around the German strongpoint Wn-60, at Exit F-1. This position, which was manned by forty men, included a 75-millimeter gun and three mortars. In spite of its overall strength, it was unable to cover the immediate area in front of it, which allowed the Americans to maneuver around it. Company L, with support from two Sherman tanks and the destroyer *Doyle*, reduced the strongpoint and took thirty-one prisoners before 9 A.M. Having cracked the first enemy strongpoint facing the veteran 16th Infantry, Company L moved forward. Its success was due to the fact that it had landed on the wrong beach. In the meantime, the troops that struggled ashore on Easy Red and Fox Green still had to penetrate and remove the centers of German resistance facing them.

Lt. John Spalding led a couple dozen men from his Company E through a gap the engineers had opened to the west of Exit E-3. Capt. Joseph Dawson pushed his Company G through the same gap. Spalding's ad hoc group was the first to penetrate the wire and minefields and get to the top of the bluffs, despite withering small-arms fire from Wn-62. From there, Spalding moved to attack Wn-64 from the rear and took the position shortly after 10 A.M., capturing twenty-one Germans. Meanwhile, Company G advanced on Colleville, and other units followed Spalding's path up the bluffs.

On the beach, Col. George Taylor, commander of the 16th Infantry, came ashore and began to rally his troops at around 8:30 A.M. He admonished his men, saying that there were two kinds of people who would remain on the beach: "those who were dead, and those who would be."

The beachmaster and the men of the 7th Naval Beach Battalion had their hands full as men, equipment, and vehicles began to pile up, since no exit had been opened to allow them to clear the beach. He ordered a halt to the unloading of vehicles at 8:30 A.M. Slowly, both regiments began to move from the beaches, and by noon, the remaining German strongpoints were cut off. Generals Eisenhower, Bradley, and Gerow, aboard ship, were finally relieved to know that the evacuation they had contemplated during the first hours would not be necessary. Earlier, when the situation along the Calvados coast had seemed ominous, General Gerow, commander of the V Corps, seriously considered a withdrawal from the shores of Omaha Beach. Only the leadership and gallantry of a handful of officers and NCOs finally tipped the scales in favor of the Americans.

As the situation improved on Omaha Beach, the 18th and 115th Infantry Regiments began to approach the beaches in LCIs at 10 A.M. The vessels carrying the 115th Infantry drifted eastward and finally set their troops ashore in the sector of the 18th Infantry of the 1st Division. Exit E-1 leading to St. Laurent, partially cleared by Lieutenant Spalding, was the first one opened by the end of the morning. Warships bombarded the German positions at Exit D-1, forcing their defenders to surrender at 2 P.M. The American soldiers took Exit E-3 at 4:30 P.M. The garrison of Wn-62 retreated but was soon encircled and forced to surrender. The first tanks clanked through E-1 at 5 P.M., and the key Exit D-1 at Vierville at last opened to traffic at 6 P.M.

The 26th Infantry of the 1st Division came ashore in the evening. By then, with the beachhead secured, the V Corps had suffered an estimated 2,400 casualties, including 1,190 from the 1st Division, 743 from the 29th Division, and the remainder from V Corps troops.[2]

As the Omaha Beach landings proceeded, farther to the west, the leading assault companies of the 2nd Ranger Battalion began scaling the cliffs of Pointe du Hoc under a hail of fire from the top. When the Rangers made it to the top and cleared out the defenders, they found that the enemy artillery was gone. When it appeared this daring assault might have failed, the Ranger reinforcements diverted to land with the 116th Infantry, so the troops at Pointe du Hoc were on their own.

By midday on D-Day, the battle had shifted from the beaches to the bluffs and farther inland. The infantry began moving beyond the direct support of the tanks, and M-7 self-propelled guns assembled on the beach.

The naval shore fire-control parties, which had come ashore early in the landing, had become ineffective after suffering heavy personnel and equipment losses. The lack of anticipated support from the field artillery, antitank, and antiaircraft units was disappointing, as their landings had been delayed for the most part. Col. Donald V.

2. Sources vary on the actual number of casualties, because it was difficult to get a proper count for several days. Some troops listed as missing had attached themselves to other units, and the dead still had to be collected and identified after June 6.

The stream of men and equipment continues.

Bennett, who came ashore on Fox Green ahead of the M-7s of his 62nd Field Artillery, found a disorganized mess, which he describes in his book, *Honor Untarnished*. Like Colonel Taylor and other officers, he began organizing the troops, together with Capt. Kimball Richmond of Company I, 16th Infantry. Finding an abandoned light vehicle from an antiaircraft unit that mounted .50-caliber machine guns, he directed his XO to put them into action against the Germans on the bluffs while he went with Richmond. Later, Bennett left Richmond on the bluffs and went back to meet the first of his M-7 self-propelled guns, which were due to arrive at about 8 A.M.[3] The LCTs carrying his battalion had been forced to turn around and wait for the situation to improve. The first M-7s did not land until 3 P.M.

The situation on the beach delayed their arrival until after 3 P.M. The Cannon Company of the 16th Infantry was sent in at 8:30 A.M., but it could get no closer than fifty yards from the beach. The 7th Field Artillery (FA) Battalion of the 1st Division lost six of its 105-millimeter howitzers in DUKWs and awaited the remainder, which could not land. The 5th FA Battalion attempted to land at 10:30 A.M., but three of the LCTs on which it

3. Colonel Bennett received the Distinguished Service Cross for his efforts as did General Cota, Colonel Canham, Colonel Taylor, Captain Dawson, Captain Richmond, Lieutenant Spalding, Lieutenant Cutler, and more than fifty other officers and just as many enlisted men. Lieutenant Monteith posthumously received the Medal of Honor for his action at Omaha Beach.

had crossed the Channel struck mines. Earlier, at 8:30 A.M., elements of the 197th and 467th Self-Propelled AA Battalions managed to land but took heavy losses. It was one of these battalions' quad .50s that Bennett found on the beach.

The 116th Infantry attempted to land its AT Company, but one of its platoons, which came ashore with three 57-millimeter guns, was pinned down for hours on the beach. The 111th FA Battalion, 29th Division, lost virtually all of its 105-millimeter howitzers, which were carried in thirteen DUKWs. Five of the DUKWs went down right after leaving their LCT, and another four sank while circling before heading for the beach. This partially explains why the troops onshore lacked supporting firepower. The remaining vessels dashed for the beach under a barrage of fire. One DUKW sank, but not before a Rhino ferry with a crane managed to lift off its gun.

Few of the tanks that made it to the shore with the first wave survived long, but they continued to support the troops on the beach. Farther down the beach, naval gunfire had intervened on E-1, helping Lieutenant Spalding capture Wn-64. At about 10 A.M., the engineers bulldozed the first gaps in the dunes. About an hour later, Colonel Taylor, commander of the 16th Infantry, ordered the last three tanks to attack E-3, but the German gunners soon knocked them out.

After the first GIs penetrated the bluffs and elements of the 16th Infantry began moving forward, the 2nd Battalion, 18th Infantry, came ashore just west of E-1. Enemy obstacles had accounted for most of the losses to its landing craft. LCIs carrying troops of the 115th Infantry missed their beaches and came in at Easy Red with the 18th Infantry. By 11:30 A.M., the 16th Infantry had neutralized the German defenders of E-1. This section of Easy Red became the main landing site. The 1st and 3rd Battalions of the 18th had to delay their landings until 1 P.M. while the 2nd Battalion moved off the beach before noon, using both sides of the draw at E-1. The 115th could not exit the beach until 2 P.M. At 1:09, the V Corps reported the first good news to the First Army commander, Gen. Omar Bradley: "Troops formerly pinned down on beaches Easy Red, Easy Green, Fox Red advancing up heights behind beaches."

The 18th Infantry moved inland, toward Colleville, while the 115th turned toward St. Laurent. Both regiments gave welcome support to the strung-out battalions of the 16th and 116th Infantries, which had led the way off the beaches after taking heavy losses.

Naval support became more effective after 10 A.M. as two destroyers moved within 1,000 yards of shore to strike at the strongpoints holding up the 116th at D-3. Most of the tanks of Company A of the 743rd Tank Battalion and some of the remaining Sherman DD tanks fired in support from hull-down positions in the surf, with only their turrets visible above the water. Some of these tanks were eventually lost to the rising tide. Naval support became critical as tank support diminished. The Joint Assault Signal Companies (JASCO), which included an army communications section, an air liaison party, and a naval shore fire-control party, might have been of great value, but it was quite a while before those ashore could establish effective communications. The 116th Infantry moved behind the draw at D-3 and toward St. Laurent before noon as elements of its 2nd Battalion and the 5th Rangers moved into Vierville. As at E-1, the critical exit at D-3 remained in German hands. The exit at D-1 leading to Vierville fell at 1 P.M. Colonel Canham of the 116th Infantry, held the 5th Rangers near Vierville, because they were the strongest and best-organized force available. Enemy fire from the first line of hedgerows had already slowed down the Rangers' advance. Canham's orders put an end to the units' mission to relieve the troops of the 2nd Rangers holding Pointe du Hoc. A platoon under Lieutenant Parker separated from the battalion, however, and moved on to carry out the relief, not

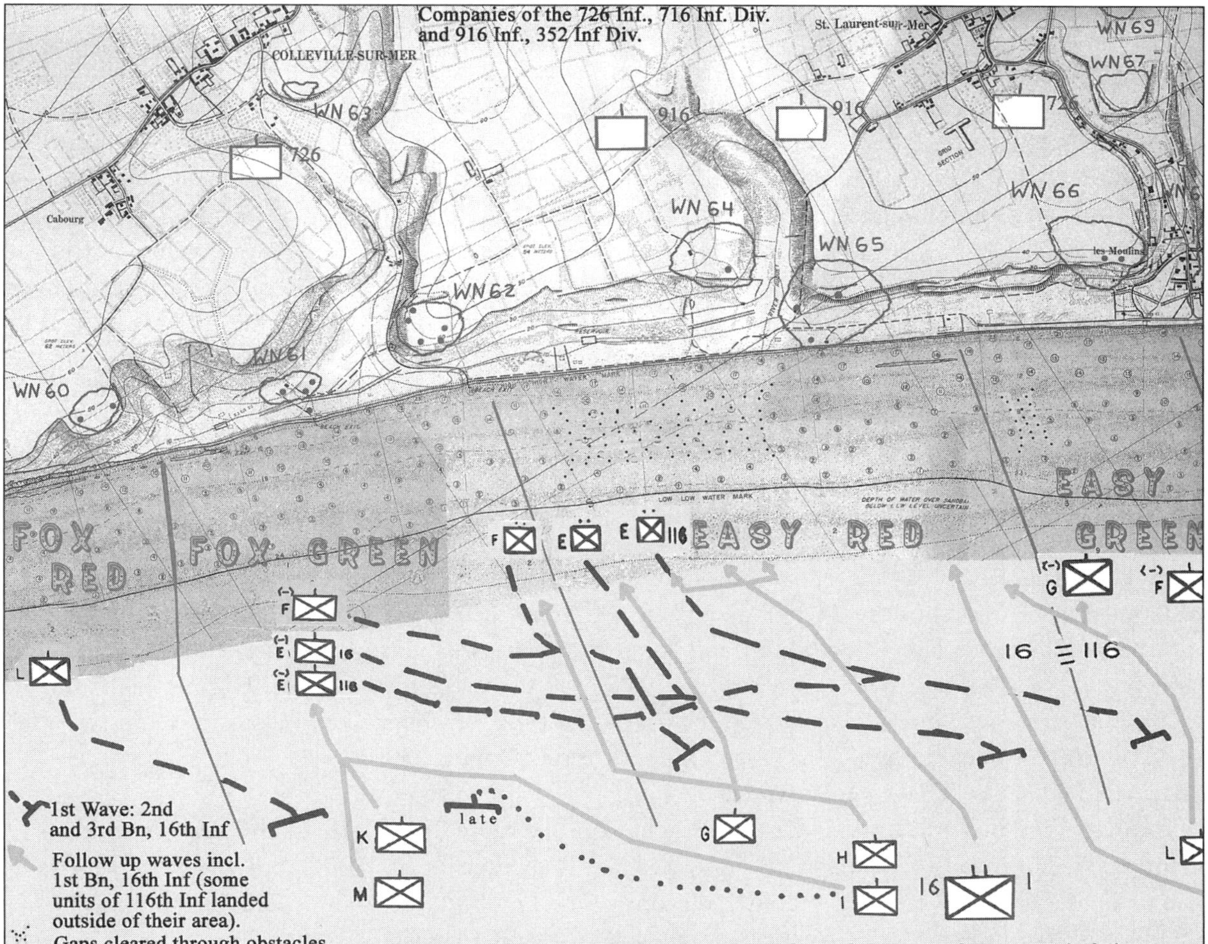

Landing on Omaha Beach by 16th Inf., 1st Infantry Division

knowing the mission was temporarily canceled. By nightfall, after an encounter with the Germans, Parker's platoon broke through to its objective.

The final infantry reinforcements consisted of the 26th Infantry Regiment of the 1st Division. The transport vessels turned up at 1 A.M., but did not receive orders to land near E-3 until 6 P.M. The regiment began to disembark at 9 P.M. Its 2nd and 3rd Battalions moved inland to a point between the 18th and 115th Infantry, south of E-1, while the 1st Battalion moved to a point north of Cabourg and Colleville to secure that part of the front. The battalion of the 16th Infantry, on the division's east flank, headed for Le Grand Hameau. The 745th Tank Battalion had landed at Fox Green at 4:30 P.M. and moved inland by 10 P.M., only three hours after the 741st Tank Battalion had left the beaches.

The artillery finally made it to the shore later in the afternoon and slowly moved into supporting positions. Five artillery battalions—7th and 32nd FA, 58th and 62nd Armored, and 111th FA—took up position on the beachhead before the end of D-Day, but they had lost twenty-six of their seventy-two guns.[4] Only the 7th Field Artillery actually took part in the fighting that day.

4. The 7th and 32nd FA Battalions were from the 1st Division, the 111th FA was from the 29th Division, and the 58th and 62nd Armored FA Battalion were nondivisional units.

General Wyman, the assistant commander of the 1st Division, had disembarked earlier in the day. General Huebner, the division commander, did not come ashore at Easy Red until 7 P.M. General Gerow and V Corps headquarters landed at 10:30 P.M. Enemy artillery fire continued to harass the troops landing on the beaches and moving out along the exits most of the day. By evening, the engineers had cleared thirteen gaps and removed about 35 percent of the beach obstacles.

Accounts of the Landings of the First Waves on Omaha Beach

Early on the morning of June 6, the tank crews of Companies B and C of the 741st Tank Battalion were still queasy after their rough and wet ride across the Channel in LCTs. Many of the men, feeling seasick and unwell, rested before they prepared to leave their LCTs with their Sherman DD tanks. They were to precede the first wave of the invasion force at Omaha Beach. Capt. James Thornton of Company B contacted Capt. Charles Young of Company C by radio on their LCTs, and despite the rough seas, they agreed it was worth the risk to launch their tanks. So at about 5:35 A.M., Companies B and C launched their tanks at 5,000 to 6,000 yards from the beach. The tanks of Company B moved toward Easy Red, and those of Company C aimed for Fox Green. Five of the tanks of Company B reached the beach, but only two actually swam in; the other three were delivered by their LCT.[5] All the tanks of Company C, on the other hand, sank beneath the waves.

Cpl. Wardell Hopper of the 1st Platoon, Company B, rode off in the lead tank on his LCT. The men of his platoon had started up their engines at 4:45 A.M. The previous day, Lt. Patrick O'Shaugnessy, the platoon leader, had told the men on the LCT that they were to launch at 5 A.M. (?) and should swim to the beach by 6:20 A.M. But seeing how rough the waters were, the lieutenant radioed his company commander, Captain Thornton, to determine whether to launch the tanks. The company commanders had already decided, and the ramp had already been lowered to begin launching at 5:35 A.M. The driver of Hopper's tank, Gordon Crouse, allowed it to slide off the vessel, because the accelerator was stuck and he did not want to risk a rapid entry by starting the engine. As the Sherman moved off the LCT, it suddenly lurched back when a wave hit the vessel. In the resulting chain reaction, three other tanks collided with each other, damaging their canvas supports, so the boat commander, Ens. H. P. Sullivan, decided to deliver all the tanks to the beach. Hopper's tank, in the meantime, chugged its way toward shore through the choppy waters.

> Crouse was down in the driver's seat; the lieutenant and PFC Bill Merkert tried to hold up the then collapsing canvas skirt while I steered, so that three of us were on top of the tank. The water was really rough. So when we saw we couldn't make the beach, I yelled to Snike in the turret to come out, and Merkert yelled to Crouse. We tried to pull the canvas back, and one side caved in. The life rafts were little fold-up things stored alongside the skirt, and they stayed there when the skirt went up. We got one life raft partially inflated as the tank sank to the bottom. We had to use our Mae Wests. The lieutenant and Merkert were on the one raft, as Snike, Crouse, and I went to the bottom with the tank. I will never forget my cigarettes coming out of my pocket and going up past my face; that is when I

5. Captain Thornton's tank sank. Like many others in his company, he was rescued, and he joined the remnants of his company on the beach the next day.

> started breathing water, and I thought I was gone. The three of us managed to make it to the surface. One rocket boat passed me, and the commander saluted me, but that didn't help me any! The LCT I had been on tried to pick me up as I floated around. Every time a wave raised me up, I could see everything going on around the beach. Then the LCT threw me a line. I had to wrap it around my arms, because my hands were too cold. They pulled me aboard and I passed out. They picked up the four of us, while Crouse was taken aboard another ship. We thought he had drowned, since he didn't know how to swim.

Sgt. Walter Jutkins, who was on the same LCT as Hopper, was from Illinois, like his comrade. Neither man had seen any body of water larger than Lake Michigan before entering the army. Jutkins, a draftee, must have wondered how he ended up in such a strange tank unit. The platoon sergeant, Paul Ragan, asked the boat commander to pick up the crew of his lieutenant's tank. They threw a life preserver to Hopper, who tried to hold on to it. "We had to yell to him after he came up to put his arms under it," Jutkins recalls. "We pulled him and the lieutenant onto the LCT." Jutkins does not remember if there was enemy fire when the LCT made the run to the beach, lowered the ramp, and let the three tanks roll off to maneuver through the beach obstacles. When the enemy opened up fire on them, the infantry had just begun to arrive. An enemy round blew the .50-caliber out of Tech 5 Williams's hands, leaving him with a shrapnel wound. Jutkins administered first aid to him while the tanks struggled forward through the tidal flat.

> We got hit again when we started to move up the hill. A hit by the track cut the track. The assistant driver jumped out, went down towards the beach, and was wounded in the chest. We couldn't do much of anything. The infantry was by us. After we got hit, we just went off with the infantry at the bottom of the hill. They were going up the hill, but I would say it was a few hours before we were hit and abandoned the tank. We were firing at enemy positions before that and fired ahead of the infantry. After the tank commander was hit, I was on my own. I only had radio contact with the other tanks, and I don't think we got any directions. After abandoning the tank, we just dug in near the hill not far from the tank. We were right below the hill [the bluffs].

Williams was evacuated the next day, and Jutkins and the other two men repaired the track of their tank.

As Sgt. Paul Ragan drove his tank off the LCT and hit the beach, he could see one of German pillboxes. His tank unloaded about forty rounds into it as he maneuvered through the obstacles. Like Jutkins, he saw a lot of enemy fire coming in among the assault troops that had landed. Although a minefield and an antitank ditch blocked his path, he continued to fire, and he claimed to have knocked out an enemy mortar. Ragan, whose lieutenant evacuated after his tank sank, was in command, but his radio was not working, which was why Jutkins received no instructions. Ragan's tank was trapped on the beach where the shingle broke their tracks. The third tank was knocked out while attempting to neutralize an enemy gun.

Of the two Company B tanks that actually swam ashore, one belonged to S.Sgt. Turner G. Sheppard, who watched Captain Thornton's tank and others sink. When he reached shore, he was joined by Sgt. George Geddes in the only other tank to swim ashore. Geddes took credit for destroying two 75-millimeter guns at Wn-62 overlooking Exit E-3 by 8:30 A.M. At about 7 A.M., he saw the remaining three tanks of Ser-

Troops wait to disembark.

geant Ragan's platoon disembark from their LCT. Meanwhile, Company A came ashore in LCTs at 6:40. Sheppard's tank expended its ammunition against various targets and destroyed a 75-millimeter and an 88-millimeter gun. The only 88-millimeter gun nearby was a casemate facing west in Wn-61.

To judge from numerous individual accounts and unit histories, the situation appears to have been confusing for most of the troops involved. Easy Red, where elements of the 16th and 116th Infantry were present, was under fire from positions at Wn-61 and Wn-62. The soldiers in this sector found some relief only when Sergeant Geddes in his Sherman knocked out two 75-millimeter guns at Wn-62. Wn-61, located below the bluffs, with an 88-millimeter gun in a casemate that flanked the beach to the west, was in the Fox Green sector. S.Sgt. Frank Strojny of Company F, 16th Infantry, called for a bazooka team to take it out, but none was available. He found a damaged one, and after collecting several rounds of ammunition, he scored eight hits on the casemate, finally knocking it out. According to the after-action report, he then rallied his men and led them forward until he was stopped by the wire obstacles. He ordered one of his men to cut the wire. He went on to clear the minefield barring the way and led more than a dozen men forward. The initiative and valor of Strojny and several others like him carried the day for the American troops. He received the Distinguished Service Cross for this action, according to Balkoski's *Omaha Beach*.

Meanwhile, Sheppard, whose tank's ammunition was expended, reloaded from one of Company A's tank trailers and moved on to clear the road toward the east. He ran afoul of a German antitank gun—probably a 50-millimeter gun at Wn-61—which took out his tank, killing his assistant gunner and injuring him. Besides the Purple Heart, Sheppard also received a Silver Star for his actions on D-Day.

Company A moved ashore by 6:40 A.M., losing only two tanks and one tankdozer, which went down when their LCT exploded at 2 A.M. for unknown reasons. The Sherman tanks of Company A, their engine compartments covered with wading trunks, had to be delivered close to the beach.[6] When Company A came ashore on the edge of Easy Red and Fox Green, it was able to engage the enemy strongpoints right away. As the fighting raged, three of the four tankdozers of the Dozer Platoon, led by Lt. Frank Klotz, came ashore and began clearing the beach obstacles under heavy enemy fire. The fourth tankdozer did not make it ashore that day because its LCT had mechanical problems. One tankdozer was destroyed by an 88-millimeter gun, probably the weapon that Sheppard later knocked out, and its wounded crewmembers were evacuated. At 11 A.M., as the fight for Exit E-3 continued, Colonel Taylor ordered all operational tanks to move into position against the German strongpoints defending it. The German gunners destroyed two of the three tanks that had moved into position, but the amount of their fire was somewhat reduced when Lieutenant Spalding, Captain Dawson, and their men reached the top of the bluffs and penetrated behind the German positions.

The following accounts and details given by members of Company A in *Unit Journal of the 741st Tank Battalion* reveal the hardships they endured once they reached the shore. The experiences described in this section are also based on this source.

> At 0625 hours . . . firing in movement 2nd Lieutenant Barcelona and Sergeant Nicol with tanks and crews landed directly in front of Easy Three [E-3] exit. Upon debarking from Naval LCT Lt. Barcelona turned right while Nicol's tank turned left to clear ramp for debarking the bulldozer . . . 200 yds. beyond beach obstacles, Sgt. Nicol's tank was hit in the left front drive sprocket, damaging the sprocket and breaking the track. Cannon fire from Sgt. Nicol's tank was then directed to a stone house to his right front [this appears to have been Wn-62]. Direct hits were scored until Sgt. Nicol was completely satisfied that any gun emplacement in that building was silenced. Fire was then shifted to gun emplacement in Easy Three exit. Extent of damage was unknown. . . . After firing 150 rounds of 75-mm and numerous .50 Cal., driver and assistant driver were forced to move into turret basket because of water 2 ft. deep in their compartment. Water seeping in through damaged sprocket where rivets were torn out. At this time, large waves of incoming tide broke over the turret hatch, drenching all crew members. The command to "abandon tank" was then given. Under enemy machine gun fire, crew members, one by one plunged into 7 ft. of water to make their way to shore. The tank commander and gunner abandoned tank at 0745 hours [7:45 A.M.].

Sergeants Ball and Coaker landed at the same time and headed for bunkers and a 75-millimeter gun at Exit E-1, which they silenced. Next, they moved toward E-3. Coaker's tank, which was hit by what he believed to be an 88-millimeter gun, was unable to move fast. When the tide came in, Coaker's and Nicol's crews moved up to the side of the hill, where they dug in. Meanwhile, Ball's tank rolled on to Exit E-3 under mortar fire, fol-

6. The wading trunks covered the engine compartment and projected upward, allowing the tank to cross through water up to about seven feet deep.

lowed by Sergeant Sheppard's tank, which was soon knocked out by a German 88-millimeter gun. Ball's tank located a 50-millimeter gun and eliminated it but had to withdraw from E-3. Soon its engine drowned out, and Ball and his crew had to abandon the tank under enemy fire.

Lieutenant Klotz's tankdozer arrived on the LCT at the same time as Ball's and Coaker's tanks. The tankdozers of his platoon came in on four different LCTs. Klotz fired on the enemy positions while he cleared obstacles from the beach. He was hit during the operations when his crew dismounted to remove obstacles that they dragged away with cables. When Sgt. George A. Habib and his tank dozer arrived at about 8:00 A.M., he found the beach very crowded. An officer soon ordered him to a point where they could knock out the obstacles. After several hours, Habib's vehicle threw a track, but after the necessary repairs were made, his tank crew resumed the task of clearing obstacles and burned-out vehicles until 9 P.M.

S.Sgt. Thomas Fair's and Sergeant Larsen's tanks were on an LCT with a tankdozer. They missed their landing point and came in near E-1. "The ramp was dropped in pretty deep water, and we left the craft. I was in number 1 tank and Sergeant Larsen number 2 tank and the dozer number 3," recalls Fair. Only days before, the engine compartments of their tanks had been equipped with wading trunks and made watertight. The water was so deep it "was up over our turret ring," says Fair. Fair and Larsen did make it to the beach, but "we stayed in the water enough for protection. Our bow gunner and [turret] gunner started spraying the trees and hillside with .30-caliber while, with no aid of the snipers and shrapnel, we looked for antitank guns and pill boxes." When Fair found a machine-gun emplacement, he directed his gunner to open fire on it. Although the first shots came in low, they finally blasted the German position away. But the tide rose quickly and the tanks moved forward. "All of a sudden, hell broke loose in front of us; they had made a hit on the boat obstacles where there were Teller mines. We moved into a new position to the left and began firing in the direction we thought it came from."

As the tide closed in, Fair realized that he and his men would be trapped, since the bluff was in front of them and casualties were pilling up all around. He moved his tank down the beach in search of Lieutenant Barcelona, their platoon leader. "The going was slow, for we had to weave in and out among bodies, sometimes stop till the medics cleared them from our path. On the way down, we accounted for two machine-gun nests, which the infantry located for us." Fair finally found a platoon and moved into firing position near E-3. Just then, Larsen's tank took a hit from a 57-millimeter round between the gun shield and the armor plate.[7] His gunner was wounded, and the breach and recoil mechanisms were smashed. Larsen sustained powder burns on his face. He ordered his crew to abandon the tank. Fair came across PFC Robinson, who was wounded, and carried him up to Larsen's group. A little later, Fair's tank moved onto the shingle, where it became stuck. He unhooked the trailer his tank was towing so he could back his tank off the shingle. His efforts came to naught, however, when his tank threw a track. Having fired its last HE rounds, the crew dismounted and took cover behind the vehicle.

First Lieutenant Edward S. Sledge II describes his platoon's experiences.

> Landed at 0635 hours vicinity of Easy01. . . . One tank under S/Sgt Kark destroyed just after debarking. Lt. McDonough and Lt. Sledge's tank fired on two emplaced French 75-mm guns on hill at left flank of Fox-

7. Much of the information from the 741st's history, from which the accounts in this section have come, seems to have conflicting details.

> Green [Wn-60 with one 75-millimeter]. Claim credit for destruction of guns at 0715 hours. Infantry pinned down by enemy machine gun and sniper fire from the same position. Tanks could not locate these targets from beach, but could not advance due to mine fields. Upon assault of C Co 16th on his hill by flanking moving up Easy-1 Exit, four tanks (Lt. Sledge, Lt. McDonough, Sgt. Carlson, Sgt. Rieman) moved west on beach to cover this advance. Tank of Lt. Sledge hit teller mine at this time and knocked out of action. Tank of Lt. McDonough hit in gas tank by 88-mm and burned. Sgt. Rieman's tank brought fire to bear on machine gun positions on Easy-1 exit. One DD tank under S/Sgt. Sheppard proceeded up Easy-3 exit followed by tank of Sgt. Carlson. DD tank destroyed and burned by 88-mm located in pill box on west slope of Easy-1 exit. Tank under Sgt. Carlson claims credit for silencing gun—does not believe gun completely destroyed but did not fire further. Tank of Sgt. Carlson threw track and temporarily put out of action.

Sergeant Call's and Sergeant Skiba's tanks moved quickly to support the infantry, firing at a German gun emplacements and spraying the ridge with machine-gun fire when a captain from the 16th Infantry requested it. Captain King of Company A finally came up to them and directed them to a rally point. Call was wounded, and Corporal Short took over as they advanced toward the E-3 exit, where the tank struck a mine that demolished the suspension system. Captain King ordered his crew to dismount. Skiba's crew tried to repair the track on their tank. Skiba was killed at about 10:45 A.M. when his tank was hit, and Cpl. Steve Hoffer took command. They had thrown a track while moving out with Call's tank on Captain King's orders. The crew tried to make repairs, but they were ordered to make for the bivouac area.

Cpl. William Schiller, in Lieutenant Barcelona's tank, nicknamed *Always in my Heart*, continuously fired on targets as they approached the beach. The crew of this tank engaged a house to the right of E-1 as their main target. After they left the landing craft, they turned their guns on a casemate with a 75-millimeter gun, neutralizing it with a few HE rounds. While they moved down the beach toward E-3, they were hit five times by a another gun, which they later destroyed. Shortly, their tank threw a track. While they were repairing it, they reloaded it with ammunition from the trailer they were towing and continued firing. It took several hours to finish the repairs, move out to Exit 1, and get over the crest of the hill to support the infantry.

The 741st Tank Battalion supported the 16th Infantry in its difficult position, and at the same time sustained heavy losses among its companies. The 743rd Tank Battalion suffered the lightest losses during the approach to the beaches, because it did not launch its Sherman DD tanks at sea.

The LCVPs and LCAs of the first wave came ashore on the heels of the tanks. T/5 Albert Mominee, a twenty-nine-year-old draftee from Southbridge, Massachusetts, boarded an LCA from the British LSI *Empire Anvil* with his landing team from Company I. Their objective was Fox Green, but the LCAs drifted too far eastward missing their objective. As Mominee's LCA was lowered from the *Empire Anvil*, the sea became very rough.

> It would get even rougher as we went along. Each soldier had been given a large paper bag to take along with him to be used if he became seasick. We hadn't been out too long when I, and I am sure just about everybody else, became very sick. This is when the bags became very useful. I kept vomiting until all I had coming up

were dry heaves. If at a time like this, known the insurmountable danger I was facing in landing on a hostile shore, I was supposed to experience fear, I did not, because it never materialized. I was too sick and hurt to care.

The craft that I was in carried the command post [CP] section, which comprised the CP group, communications group, executive officer, and the company commander. Before leaving the transport, the men put on a special designed combat jacket [the assault jacket especially designed for the assault teams]. We could put all our things we had in the old pack [into the assault jacket] and more. It fit like a vest. One good feature that I liked was that in an emergency, it could be removed quickly by pulling on the straps which held it together. Besides carrying my carbine and other equipment, I was given two boxes of .30-caliber machine-gun ammunition to carry onto the beach. The other men in the CP group had the same load.

The assault craft carried thirty-five men plus the coxswain. Each man had to sit between the legs of the man behind him with all our equipment on. It felt like we were squeezed tighter than sardines in a can. There was nowhere we could move until the craft came to a stop at the beach area and the ramp was let down.

The rough sea with spray from the waves coming over the bow made it difficult for the coxswain to maneuver the craft in a position with the other assault craft awaiting the signal to go into the beach. The coxswains directing the other craft were experiencing the same difficulty. So right from the beginning we were in trouble.[8]

It seemed to me that we were going in circles. It looked like the coxswain couldn't make up his mind where he wanted to go. Finally, he started towards the shore. He got close enough for us to land and he lowered the ramp. A machine gun, which had been well concealed, opened up. The coxswain immediately pulled the ramp up, but not before he was hit. Luckily for us, he was not wounded seriously enough that he could not maneuver the craft.

So back out we went to get out of range of the machine-gun fire. Because of all the setbacks, valuable time was lost, putting us behind the scheduled time we were supposed to hit the beach. The landing had been planned for 6:30 A.M. The company commander, Capt. Kimball Richmond, realizing the ever-mounting risk and danger of prolonging the landing, decided to select a site and directed the coxswain to it.

As we were already two hours late, the tide had already started to coming in, and the water was not deep enough to cover the obstacles in our path. About 400 yards from shore, the craft gave a sudden lurch as it hit an obstacle, and in an instant an explosion erupted, followed by a blinding fire. The LCA was enveloped in flames. Flames raced around and over us. The craft slowly sank and then stopped, coming to rest on an obstacle buried on the sandy bottom, which prevented it from sinking any further. It happened so quickly. The first reaction of thought when one gets in a situation like this is survival. The immediate instinct is the will to live. Being experienced in the ways of combat also helped, for my first impulse was to get out of the craft, as did all the other men who could manage it. Not all

8. At this point, the boats carrying Company I had drifted east away from their objective and were preparing to return, which was not until more than an hour later at about 8 A.M.

Wounded troops are aided to shore.

could, or did, especially the men who had the flamethrowers strapped to their backs. They never had a chance.

Before I knew it, I was in the water. The first thing I did was to pull the straps on my combat jacket and let it slip into the water. Next, I inflated the life preserver around my waist and moved away from the craft towards the shore. By this time, the Germans who were inside of a bunker on top of the cliff overlooking the beach directed machine-gun fire toward the men in the water and those who had left the craft. At least those of us who were in the water kept moving, making it more difficult for the Germans to pick us off.

About fifty yards from shore, I found the water was shallow enough for me to wade. I was exhausted and in shock. A few times, I stumbled, picked myself up, and struggled trying to force myself to continue. Thirty yards to go, and then twenty. I started to catch my breath, when I heard a voice shouting, "Come on, little one! Come on! You can make it!" It was Lieutenant Anderson, the executive officer shouting encouraging words to me, urging me on. It seemed like someone had awakened me from a dream. I looked ahead and saw him at the water's edge. I lunged towards him, and as I reached him, he grabbed my hand and pulled me out of the water, then practically dragged me to the cover of the overhanging cliff.

Most of the men gathered. They were wounded or still suffering from shock. Most of the casualties there were from Company I, in the craft in which I was. Only six of thirty-five escaped unharmed. Luckily for me, all I received were burnt eyelashes and my hair was singed up to the rim of my helmet.

As I sat underneath the safety of the cliff, the realization that I had been spared brought me back to reality. Looking around, all I could see was a scene of havoc and

> destruction: abandoned vehicles and tanks, equipment strung all over the beach, medics attending the wounded, chaplains seeking the dead.

Albert Mominee made it ashore from his destroyed landing craft, procured a "rifle from a casualty and despite heavy mortar, artillery, and machine gun fire courageously joined a successful attack upon a numerically superior foe," earning him a Bronze Star. After the elimination of the enemy fortification, his group went to the base of the cliff, not realizing that on either side of them troops of their regiment had already gone over the bluffs and outflanked the Germans. He did not find out until the next morning.

The SETF, which was to clear the beaches, followed the leading waves of the 16th Infantry. Companies A and C of the 299th Combat Engineer Battalion were assigned to Omaha Beach, while Company B went to Utah. PFC Albert W. Littke, who was in the 3rd Squad of the 3rd Platoon of Company A, 299th Engineers, was delegated to carry one of the unit's mine detectors ashore. His unit had crossed the Channel in an LST (although he stated it was an LCT) carrying four tanks, one of which was named *Diana* and another *Beverly*. His mine detector and Hagensen Pack, socks filled with C2 explosive designed for blowing up obstacles, had been placed aboard the LCM before it left Weymouth. On the morning of June 6, he descended the rope ladder into the LCM.

> Once loaded, we started off in a large circle with the other LCMs following. They had letters A, B, C, D, E, and F. I believe E and F were in reserve. Once completing the circle, we then headed towards the beach. I was assigned to assault boat A. I was the first man off once the ramp was dropped, because I had to clear the beach of mines. I was on the starboard side.
>
> Going in, the battleships and smaller boats were laying down a huge barrage. Looking out to my right, I noticed another LCT with large tubes—rocket launchers—on it. I watched them firing towards the beach. They fired clusters of rockets, which you could see for a split second, coming out of the tubes about every two seconds. A cluster of about thirty-four came out at the same time. I saw a fountain of water going up into the air between the rocket launchers and us. I assumed it was German artillery. At this point, I stepped on my tiptoes, peeked around the ramp, and saw the coast of France and the rockets exploding on the beaches. One member of my squad named Raleigh was seasick and blaming the damn Germans for being here. The LCM slowed down a little, then vibrated and stopped. The ramp was lowered. The navy personnel fired .50-caliber machine guns over our heads.
>
> I inflated my lifebelt (by cartridges), put my M-1 rifle over my left shoulder, grabbed the suitcase in my right hand, and started down the ramp. At the base of the ramp, the water was knee-deep. I looked down and saw sand ripples underneath the water, but after a couple of steps, I looked up towards the beach and stepped into a tank trap [more likely a runnel]. I was going down; I released my suitcase, started to kick, and came to the surface, then dog-paddled a few yards until my right knee hit solid ground. I got up and started back towards the beach minus my suitcase—the life belt saved my life.
>
> I hit the beach, where I rested for a few seconds on my stomach. I saw nothing in front of me but the obstacles. I turned to my left and saw GIs coming onto the beach, so I got up and proceeded. I dropped my demolition charges at the base of an obstacle and

continued on to the break wall, where I lay down on my left side and turned to my right and noticed a GI drop his rifle with both hands clutching for his throat. Lying there, the beach was being crowded with other soldiers. At this point, one of my squad members, George Reiss from Rochester, was beside me and we agreed to cover each other. Jumping up to the top of the break wall, there was a single roll of barbed wire. I jumped sideways in order to straddle the wire, but my crotch and the inside of my right leg got caught up with some of the barbs, and it seemed like an eternity being there before I broke through free and ran down towards a brick wall. The brick wall was red in color and about eight feet high and ten feet long. It was part of a wall from a house. On reaching the wall, I looked back towards the break wall and noticed a steel helmet standing on its edge, then fall over flat on the ground. A white marking was on the back of the helmet. Following directly behind me and now lying facedown and not moving was an officer.

Littke apparently landed on Easy Red between Wn-65 and Wn-62. He fired his rifle toward the top of the bluffs and moved to another position, where he came under enemy machine-gun fire. He took cover in the sand dunes and began to dig in. Finally, he spotted *Achtung Minen* signs, took out his bayonet, and began probing for mines while he used the white tape he carried to mark a path. He had barely started this task when the Germans started dropping mortar rounds, forcing him to scurry back to his foxhole. After chewing on his chocolate ration, he looked back toward the beach. An LCI, which may have been scheduled to land about sixty-five minutes after H-Hour, was disgorging infantrymen "on the port side, but not on the starboard side, because of the angle of the boat."

I noticed they were coming directly for me. Two lines of men were spaced with no bunching up. All of a sudden, I saw a blue flash with different colors—a direct hit on the steps [ramp] of their LCI, on the port side where the GIs were unloading. Then there was a cry for help and medics. Coming towards me, the two lines of infantry passed beside my foxhole, and a sergeant said, "Kid are you all right?" and I answered, "Yah!"

They were making for the top of the escarpment. At this time, I decided to join them. A voice called out and said, "Limey!" I was born in the States but had my education in Canada. I recognized the guy; he was in my platoon, but in the 2nd Squad. He asked me to help him and a wounded soldier. We made a shallow foxhole for him, grabbed him by the shoulder and side, and placed him in the foxhole. I didn't recognize him until the corporal said, "Are you all right, Fatty?" and he answered. He was one of my best friends in my squad. He told me to look for my squad up the beach. Leaving him, I ran into a one-star general or some guy in a trench coat, who stopped me and said, "Son, how do I get to the top?" I told him to follow the white tape. I continued down the beach and ran behind a couple of Sherman tanks firing towards the top of the escarpment. They were spaced about fifty feet apart. Then another barrage came in, and I threw myself down. I then noticed a GI coming up from the beach, placing himself behind the tread of the second tank nearest me. All of a sudden, the tank commander standing halfway out of the tank yelled, "Let's get the hell out of here! They are zeroing in on us!" Before he was in the tank, it backed up, pushing the helpless GI down into the sand. Getting up, racing back from where I came from, some-

> thing was slapping my thigh. Looking down I saw the hose from my gas mask was hitting my leg—half my gas mask was missing, so I just unbuckled it and let it drop. I also noticed another GI sitting and laying back against a sand dune with both of his legs gone at his thighs as well as his left arm. I looked at him for a second and continued on my way. There were quite a few of those scenes down there that day.
>
> Late in the afternoon, I proceeded with the infantry until I got to the top of the escarpment, when a sergeant in my platoon yelled for me. He was trying to round up some of our company. Later on, I found out that of the eleven men in my squad, five were killed and two wounded. I was fortunate that I transferred to the mine detector, because setting the charges on the obstacles and using the prima cord was hazardous when incoming German rounds prematurely detonated them. That night, I went to sleep in a foxhole.

Like Littke, the first waves of engineers in the gap assault teams had a great deal of difficulty that day. Nevertheless, they managed to clear five of the eight intended gaps on Easy Red, Fox Green, and Fox Red. Only two of the assault teams could not be located after the initial landings, but they were found by 9 A.M. According to the unit history, some of the engineer teams actually landed before the infantry. They worked throughout the day clearing the beaches.

Nineteen-year-old Pvt. Roger L. Brugger of the 3rd Platoon of Company K, 3rd Battalion, was in the wave that followed the engineer group. His company crossed the Channel on the British LSI *Empire Anvil* with most of the 3rd Battalion. They boarded their LCA onboard ship and were lowered into the water from davits. Someone had stolen Brugger's helmet during the night; some of the soldiers apparently had lost theirs over the side. He told his sergeant, who took care of the situation when they moved to their boarding stations.

> The sergeant grabbed a British helmet that was hanging on the bulkhead and gave it to me, saying, "Now you have a helmet!"
>
> We were issued a puke bag for seasickness, and as it turned out, one wasn't enough. We kept going around in circles, rendezvousing, and by this time, everyone in the boat had used their bag and was throwing up on the deck.
>
> The British LCAs differed from the American-made boats in that the British had about a thirty-inch covering on each side, while the American boats were all open. Also, the British had an armored-plated covering in front that the coxswain stood in to steer the boat. As we approached the beach at about 6:30 A.M., the shells were dropping in the water and machine-gun bullets whizzing over our heads. Sergeant Robey told the coxswain to run our boat right up on the beach. He did and we got off on dry land. We ran straight for a shale wall. I remember thinking as I ran from the boat and saw the bullets tearing up the sand on either side of me, "This is like a war movie." After we got to the shale wall, I looked back at the boat we had just left, when an 88 artillery shell hit it in the engine compartment and it blew up.
>
> I watched another boat come in, and as the guys came running to the wall, one guy got a direct hit with a mortar shell, and all I could see of him were three hunks of his body flying through the air.
>
> We were all sick and scared. The tide was coming in, and our beach was getting smaller. We could see the bodies of the dead rolling in the surf. Our company commander took a shrapnel wound to his left

leg that was so severe the medic couldn't stop the bleeding, and he bled to death. The company executive officer took over, and he had the company for less than an hour when a sniper got him. We only lost one man in our boat group; he got hit in the shoulder. The Germans were using wooden bullets, and they made a very nasty wound.[9] After what seemed like an eternity, we started up the draw to the top of the cliff overlooking the beach. This was about 10 A.M. On the way up from the beach, a wounded man from Company L gave me his helmet and took the British one I had been wearing. We had just got a good start up the draw when we were pinned down by a machine-gun emplacement built in the side of the cliff.

A medical unit wades ashore.

Next, Brugger saw a warship, probably a destroyer, move close to shore and direct its forward gun turret against the enemy position, knocking it out with a couple of shots. Finally his group reached the top of the hill.

There was a path through the minefields, but it was laid with barbed wire. We had to crawl through this or else step on a mine. After we got through the minefield, close to a road, there was a blanket or piece of tarp that looked like someone might be under it, so our squad leader, Sergeant Robey, told us to fire into it with our rifles. Out of the eight of us in the squad, only four of our rifles would fire, the others being clogged with sand. As it turned out, there wasn't anything under it anyway.

A little further up the road, I saw my first dead German. His helmet was off, and I could see the name Schlitz printed in it. We had to crawl through the hedgerows to get from one field to another. We gave each other covering fire to make the machine-gun crew, which fired through the opening, keep their heads down, then three or four of our men could dash through. As we crawled through the hedgerows, we would have to crawl over the dead and wounded.

At about 1:30 P.M., we came to a large stone barn and farmhouse. We had a chance to eat some of our rations and clean our weapons. Most of the 3rd Battalion and some troops from the 116th Infantry were in and around the barn. We set up a defense perimeter and dug in with two men to a foxhole. Patrols were sent out throughout the rest of the afternoon and after nightfall. I went on one of the night patrols. They were very scary.

9. A number of veterans refer to wooden bullets being used by the Germans. These were supposed to be for training, but apparently the Germans employed them in some combat situations.

> After the patrol, I returned to my foxhole, where the rest of the night was spent two hours on and two hours off. At midnight, I realized that I had made it through the day.

The next day, Brugger's battalion advanced toward Port-en-Bessin to link up with the British 50th Division. Some of the troops of Company K hitched a ride on the tanks of the 745th Tank Battalion. They were surprised to find that the British had fresh eggs, something they had not seen during 1944, and they traded their cigarettes for this small luxury.

The 1st Battalion was to follow the other two battalions at about 7:30 A.M. S.Sgt. John Blaise Ellery of Company B, 16th Infantry, a veteran of North Africa and Sicily, crossed the Channel the APA *Samuel Chase*. He boarded an LCVP at about 4 A.M. and after waiting quite a while at the rendezvous, he and his wave "headed for the beach at about five knots."

> The sea was a bit rough, with three- to four-foot waves. It wasn't long before every man was soaked through. Many of them, perhaps most, were seasick, but I wasn't. We must have been in the boat for about three hours, when we finally lined up for our run for the shore at full throttle, and dropped the ramp at about 0700. We walked right into heavy machine-gun fire. Three or four men went down immediately. The water was waist-deep, and it was a struggle to reach the tidal flat. Here the sand was fairly firm for about 200 meters before we ran into soft sand and swampy marsh, then there was another 100 meters or so to the shingle bank. All of this under the greatest concentration of mortar, machine-gun, and artillery fire that I have ever seen—direct fire, plunging and grazing, and flanking fire, and at the end of the beach, a minefield. I was aware of men falling around me, but it was not until I reached the base of the bluff that things began to come into focus. I had to peer through a haze of sweat, smoke, dust, and mist. There was a man beside me who was dead. Another was on the ground about fifteen meters behind me. I ran back to him and started dragging him to some cover. A medic ran up and helped me, and he took over. From the looks of that wounded man, I doubt that he lived.
>
> I didn't spend any time looking for people or rounding up troops on the beach. Several men collected around me however, and I told them that we had to get off the beach, and that I'd lead the way. After the war, I read about a number of generals and colonels who are said to have wandered about, exhorting the troops to advance. That must have been very inspirational! I suspect, however, that the men were more interested and more impressed by officers and NCOs who were willing to lead them rather than having some general pointing out the direction in which they should go. I didn't see any generals or field-grade officers in my area of the beach, but I did see a captain and two lieutenants who demonstrated courage beyond belief as they struggled to bring order to the chaos around them; they managed to get some of the men organized and moving forward up the hill. One of the lieutenants was hit and seemed to have a broken arm. It hung limply at his side, but he led a small group of six or seven to the top. It looked as though he got hit again on the way. Another lieutenant carried one of his wounded men about thirty meters before getting hit himself. These young officers provided leadership in a measure that was truly filled up, pressed down, and running over.
>
> I decided it was time to head to the high ground. I started up the bluff with four or

five men behind me, and about half to two-thirds of the way up, a machine gun opened up on us from the right front. Everyone hugged the ground. I scurried and scratched along until I got within ten meters of the gun position. Then I unloaded all four of my fragmentation grenades, and when the last one went off, I made a dash for the top. Those other kids were right behind me, and we all made it. I don't know if I knocked out that gun crew, or if they bugged out. In any event, those grenades were all the return fire that I provided coming off the beach. I didn't fire a round from either my rifle or my pistol.

Our D-Day objective was approximately three miles inland, near Trévières. We didn't get there. I should think we probably covered 1,000 meters or thereabouts from ramp to the hedgerow where I found myself at dusk on D-Day.

During the day, I was about to climb through a break in the hedgerow, and as I did so, an ID bracelet on my right wrist got hung up on a rather sturdy piece of brush. I slid back down and broke off the branch to get loose. Meanwhile, a fellow from company who had joined my group decided to pass by me and go on over. As his head cleared the top of the hedgerow, he took a round right in the face and fell back on top of me, dead. That was about as close as I came to stopping a bullet during the invasion. In any event, two men and I went looking for the sniper. At last, we found him. We found a soldier that I thought was a sniper, and I evened the score. It was a clean shot, and the only one that I fired on D-Day.

The first night in France I spent in a ditch beside a hedgerow wrapped in a damp shelter half and thoroughly tired, but I felt elated.

Company C of the 1st Battalion, slated to land on Easy Red, came in after Companies G and H of 2nd Battalion, which had taken heavy losses in men and equipment. The 1st Battalion disembarked between 7:40 and 8 A.M. and did not suffer as badly. It landed near the point where the 2nd Battalion troops had begun their climb of the bluffs between Wn-62 and Wn-64. S.Sgt. Albert Nendza and Privates Buddy Mazzara and Frederick Erben moved through the obstacles barring the way up the bluffs. Mazzara carried an 82-pound flamethrower, and Freddie Erben the explosive charge. Despite his heavy load, Mazzara managed to pull another soldier from the water on the way to shore. The bodies floating in the water, the stench of death and gunpowder, and the mutilated bodies of his comrades cut down by enemy fire and mines were forever sealed in Sergeant Nendza's memory. Weighed down with bangalore torpedoes, he had to be helped to the beach by Larry Brown, one of his men. When he saw the men bunching up, he knew he had to get them moving. Mazzara saw no living officers around; only Nendza was organizing the men and moving them along the beach. Nendza, Mazzara, and Erben approached the enemy wire. Nendza set his explosives, blew a thirty-foot gap in the wire, and cut the remaining wire with his cutters.

Mazzara and Erben were the first of the team to go through the gap and approached a German bunker. Erben used his pole charge, which sent the two men inside to come out yelling that they were Polish. Their names were Wisniewski and Boleslaw. It turned out that Wisniewski had been a schoolmate of Nendza's stepbrother, and he knew him. This encounter may have taken place on the western side of Wn-62.

Some of the troops on Easy Red reached the bluffs and scaled them; a few actually penetrated Wn-62, only to be captured. When the Germans retreated late in the afternoon with their prisoners, they found themselves isolated and surrendered to their prisoners, according to *Omaha Beach* by Georges Bernage.

As Sergeant Nendza continued to climb the bluffs with his men, his rifle jammed, so he started throwing rocks at the German positions, yelling, "Grenade!" This novel approach to fighting earned him his second Silver Star.

After the troops got over the bluffs and penetrated the coastal defenses, patrols were sent out. Freddie Erben and a few comrades crossed a hedgerow, to be met with a hail of enemy small-arms fire. Erben, wounded by a German grenade, fell unconscious to the ground. Mazzara dragged him back under the hedge a few inches at a time. When he finally made it back, Carl Wooden came over to congratulate him. As Mazzara turned around to respond, a sniper's bullet felled Wooden. After Erben was taken down to the beach, where he waited for a transport to carry him out, Gene Greco bandaged him up. Back on the bluffs, Mazzara looked back at the beach and the thought struck him that Erben had received the "million-dollar wound." He was more concerned, however, that his friend might be killed before a landing craft could get him out to cash in on it.

Pvt. Charles H. Thomas, a young draftee serving as a rifleman in Company C, carried a pole charge to which he had attached about thirty pounds of TNT and a lifebelt in case the water was deeper than expected. When his LCVP reached the beach, the problems began.

> The coxswain was killed trying to open the ramp from the outside. A lieutenant named Scott was hit in the shoulder while reaching over and trying to open the ramp. They finally got it open. I was the last one off the boat, because I had the pole charge and it was in the corner of the boat. As I was getting off the boat, I stopped to pick up a smoke grenade, as if I didn't have enough to carry. The guy running the boat yelled for me to get off. I guess he was in a hurry, so I jumped in the water. It was up to my hips, and then it went over our heads a little further in, but I managed to get in with all the equipment except my pole charge. A guy came up next to me who couldn't swim and almost drowned me, so I gave him the pole charge to hang on to. I saw him a little later on the beach. The bullets were hitting all around us, and when I finally got to shore, there were dead and wounded floating by. We were told not to stop to help anyone, because the medics would handle it. I made it to the layer of shale with many other guys, but we were getting hit pretty hard before we got a bangalore torpedo under the barbed wire. That didn't happen until about 10 A.M.
>
> I went up to a second layer [of shingles], which was crowded with GIs all being wounded or killed. A bullet went through the helmet of one of my buddies next to me. He pulled it off and looked at it. He had a pair of socks, and the bullet ricocheted around his head and didn't hit him. Another one had a chunk blown out of his buttocks. There was no medic available, so we poured sulfa powder on him and he was laughing.
>
> We could see smoke, and very few could see the top of the hill, but the enemy could see us easy, because they were dropping mortars and artillery on us. I crawled back down on the first layer of shale towards the water, and I had lay on my side. I opened my fly; I had to urinate. I don't know why I did that, because I was soaking wet anyway and I was under fire.

Private Thomas also saw a couple of knocked-out Shermans on the beach and a third continuing to fire on the Germans. He helped pull in some 4.2-inch mortars with their ammunition and load them on carts. These weapons belonged to one of the chemical mortar battalions, possibly the 81st Battalion, as the infantry division had only 60-millimeter and 81-millimeter mortars. Thomas then found a large group of men from his company taking cover near the remains of a house. A Sergeant Ninza from his company had crossed the wire and attempted to follow a path up the hill, but he came running back, yelling that the area was mined. They moved forward and emplaced their bangalores to blow the wire. After that, they began to move out one at a time, between machine-gun fire.

> I ran for it, tripped, and fell in the wire, but crawled through all right. I had all of my equipment, and it was heavy. When we were going up the cliff, a GI stepped on a mine, and two guys ahead of me fell wounded. I think the guy that stepped on it might have been killed.
>
> Before we reached the top, they told us to stop, and they brought in a mine detector. They taped off the mines as we walked up the hill. We finally got to the top, and we could see the whole beach. It was a real mess. The landing craft were trying to come in, but they were being shelled. On top of the hill, we weren't being hit. I think it was about 11 A.M.
>
> My best buddy, David Jacobson, put on his glasses and said he could now see the enemy. Ten minutes later, he was killed by a sniper going in a barnyard. It made me sick. The first night, we captured a couple of machine-gun nests, and it quieted down. We were in the ditch off the road. I ate my apple from breakfast and tried to get some sleep as it got dark. That night, two or three German planes came over and bombed the beach, so we didn't get much sleep.

PFC Joseph A. Dragotto, a member of a 60-millimeter mortar crew in a Company C weapons platoon, also had vivid memories of the landings at Omaha Beach. The smell and sight of death surrounded him as soon as he hit the beach. "As the landing craft got closer to the beach, shells began to explode around us. The craft next to us hit a mine and exploded, sending bodies into the water." His vessel grounded on a sandbar and he had to wade ashore like so many others. He saw the regimental commander, Col. George Taylor, exhorting the troops off the beach. His group stopped and waited for the engineers to clear a minefield before they moved through it. The company commander, Captain Lykes, assembled the remnants of the Company C as they moved forward. Dragotto's mortar crew had lost its mortar and had to pick up enemy weapons. Their objective was Colleville. About 1 P.M., the battalion began to advance over the bluffs, and Dragotto was relieved to leave the bloody beach behind him.

HQ Company of the 1st Battalion followed the wave, carrying its two leading companies. Capt. Charles M. Hangsterfer, another veteran of the African and Sicilian campaigns, was in command. Beside a 57-millimeter antitank gun and small arms, this company had no weapons. It was necessary, however, to get its Communications Platoon, its Ammunition and Pioneer Platoons, and headquarters ashore to set up operations for the battalion. Naval observers, Air Corps liaison personnel, a military intelligence team, and others were attached to the company. Since there was a possibility that the 57-millimeter guns of the AT Platoon would be needed for defense, the platoon was ferried on an LST so that DUKWs could carry the guns ashore. The rest of the company was aboard the transport *Samuel Chase*. The rough seas swamped the DUKWs, but fortunately, none of the men were lost. When these elements arrived, the situation on the beach seemed ominous.

> As we approached the beach, some of the LCVPs from the 2nd and 3rd Battalions

were heading back to the transport ships. All was quiet until we were about 500 yards from shore. At this time, I could hear the sound of battle over the roar of the LCVP's engine. The edge of the beach was crowded with troops, and the tide was coming in. To our surprise, the beach obstacles were not removed. There were still mines attached to the wood poles, and some of our LCVPs blew up when they hit these mines. Machine-gun fire raked the beach, which delayed our letting down the ramp of the LCVP. It was forty years later that I found out that the battalion XO, Maj. Albert Smith, didn't give the order to lower the ramp because we were being targeted by enemy machine-gun fire, while all the time I was shouting for them to let the ramp down so we wouldn't get blown up by one of the mines. After the ramp was dropped, half the men got off before more machine-gun fire hit our boat. We were in waist-deep water. Several men were wounded. I helped one man off who had been hit in the leg. None on my LCVP was killed. It was about 0730 on June 6 when we landed on Easy Red. The terrain was as described to us on the sand table; however, the pillboxes were still operational, since they were not touched by the air strikes. The DD tanks sank on the way in, so there was no fire support from heavy weapons that we were supposed to have. Small-arms and heavy-weapons fire was constantly being brought to bear on the troops and follow-up landing craft. On the beach were still elements of the assault battalion (the 2nd).

However, our Company A [on Hangsterfer's right near E-1] had breached the barbed wire and blazed a trail through a swampy area and up the escarpment to the top of the hill. Our boat team was together, and in a few minutes, we found a gap in the barbed wire and went through the opening into the swampy area. This exit led us to what is now the cemetery [between E-1 and E-3]. I could see a trail, which was littered with bodies of men from Company A, who had been shot or stepped on a land mine. Major Smith had a small bottle of scotch and gave me a swig. I also ate an apple, which I saved from breakfast. Somewhere along the route, I lost an orange I had saved. At this time, Major Smith told me to go back to the beach to round up anyone I could find from our battalion.

I went alone and moved up and down the beach looking for people. To add to the confusion, elements of the 116th Infantry had been forced to land on our beach [from the first waves] or were mislanded there. I saw the beachmaster's command post and received permission to use a handheld bullhorn they had there. I announced, "All Dagwood Red personnel report over here!" (Dagwood was the 16th Infantry telephone call word.) In this manner, I was able to gather up people from our battalion and lead them through the path I had come from. While I was going along the beach, I noticed Bob Capa, the photographer from *Life* magazine, taking pictures from behind one of the disabled self-propelled tanks.[10] There was another exit that the remainder of my company had taken, so when I arrived back with Major Smith, most of my company was settled down behind a hedgerow, which served as our command post for the balance of the day and first night. At the command post, telephone lines were laid to our rifle companies, and the

10. Robert Capa was on Easy Red near Wn-62 and Exit E-3.

regiment laid a wire to our switchboard. The radio net was established.

When I was walking up and down the beach, a mortar shell hit close by me, and I was hit by flying stones rather than shrapnel. Six days later, this caused me to be evacuated from beach. The pillboxes were not destroyed by air force bombing; however, one of our destroyers came close to shore to fire point-blank at the pillbox, thereby knocking out one of the main holdups to a more rapid advance. In order to use the naval gunfire, we gave their observer a mission to fire on a suspected enemy command post. We had captured a prisoner, and he pointed out on a map where it was located. So a fire mission was ordered, and we could hear the outgoing shells, which is by far more pleasant to hear than incoming shells. The observer wanted to know what the effect of the salvo was. I was on top of a hedgerow and told him to fire again, but he had to see for himself, and when he could only see 100 yards or so to the next hedgerow, he wouldn't fire unless he could see the effect. I told him the sound was all the effect needed to bolster the morale, but he didn't go along with this idea.

Sometime in the afternoon of the sixth, my motor sergeant came back to the command post with over fifty prisoners. He told me they had surrendered to him when he was looking for a possible site for the motor pool for when our vehicles arrived. Since the prisoners outnumbered my group in the command post, I quickly got rid of them by heading them down to the division command post. I don't know whatever happened after that. During the night of June 6, all through the area was heard the sound of German machine pistols, very easy to distinguish by their rate of fire from that of our weapons.

As always, I was looking for something to eat besides the D rations. With all of the hedgerows having to be cleared one by one, it was slow going, so our battalion command post didn't move very much from the place we stopped after clearing the beach, which was across the road which ran parallel to the beach [just to the west of Colleville which the Germans held into the evening].

Another 1st Division veteran of Africa and Sicily, T.Sgt. Theodore G. Aufort, landed with HQ Company of the 1st Battalion. He was a wire chief in the telephone section. He heard his company commander, Captain Hangsterfer, calling out instructions over the loudspeaker on the bridge of the *Samuel Chase*: "Now hear this: Boat teams number 25, 26 . . . Proceed to your assembly areas!" Earlier, the captain had turned the microphone over to John McVain, a radio correspondent who was preparing an eyewitness account of the events, to read the messages from Eisenhower, the prime minister, and the president. Aufort moved to the port side to prepare for loading.

I had split my crew into two sections: I had seven men, three men in one and four men in the other with me. Each man was assigned specific pieces of communication equipment to carry onto the beach. We stood off, and when the whistle blew or somebody yelled, it was time for us to go down the cargo nets, which hung over the side of the ship. The LCVPs were down below, and we were told to release from the net when the landing craft came to its highest point, and you would meet the craft coming up as you were coming down. I don't know how many legs were broken, but I understand there were a few. I got three-quarters of the way down the net to wait for the landing craft. I jumped as it was going down and made it OK. We were given barf bags and were told to keep our heads down.

The boat leaped forward, and every once in a while I would peek over the side. We gathered up with other landing craft into a big circle, and then we spread out and all the craft headed for the beach at the same time. I was no hero; I was scared just like everyone else. The engines were pounding wide open, and a coast guardsman was in a steel compartment with just slits to look out of as he operated the landing craft.

They dumped us off just as we got to the obstacles [hedgehogs]. When the ramp went down, I yelled to the guys to grab their equipment. I was the last one off the craft, and I happened to look back and saw a six-drop switchboard, which weighed about 60 pounds. The party who was assigned to take it ashore left it there. I ran to the other end of the vessel and grabbed it, because we had to have that switchboard. Meanwhile, the Coast Guard crew started backing out. I jumped off the ramp with it, and the water went over my head.

As Sergeant Aufort struggled to reach the shore, soldiers were being hit by enemy fire, including a man to the right of him named Lemcheck.

I grabbed him by the back of the neck, and then I rolled him over with his face out of the water, still walking him ashore. Somebody was yelling at me, "What are you carrying that thing for?" What I didn't know was that a bullet had hit the other side of the switchboard. As soon as I saw it was destroyed, I dropped it right there on the beach. Then I grabbed Lemcheck and dragged him up a few feet out of the water and just dropped him there and ran for the beach. I went over the cobblestones, which were a foot and a half or so thick. I found a tank with its track standing out on the rock and the belly of the tank lying on the rocks, making the tank helpless. I worked my way up onto the beach behind the barbed wire until I reached some protection, where we all crowded behind. This was when I heard this colonel yelling at the tank operators—they had abandoned their tank. He yelled at them to get back in their tank and start shooting. They crawled back into their tank and started shooting at targets.

The heavy strands of barbed wire prevented us from going in further, so somebody yelled, "Bangalore torpedoes!" I saw Sergeant Ford from one of our line companies. He stepped on a Teller mine as he went through the barbed wire. It was a horrible sight to see him laying there with all the meat blown off his legs and just the bone hanging there. He didn't last long—he died.

After we got to the top of the bluffs, I started looking for my men. I found two guys; they had telephones, and one of them had a roll of wire—W-130 wire—one roll for a half mile. I didn't think it would be enough, so I told them to stay there and look for any other guys they could find while I went back to the beach. I found two telephones and another roll of wire lying down near the water. I checked them over and they looked in good shape. I went up the hill again the same way I came down. While I was on the beach, I heard somebody call me. It was one of the fellows from the I & R [Intelligence and Reconnaissance] Platoon. He was a Jewish fellow, but I can't remember his name. His left arm was blown off at the elbow, and somebody had put a tourniquet on it. I lit him a cigarette, stuck it in his mouth, and gave him the rest of the pack. That was the last I saw of him before he was taken off the beach.

By the time I got back, I found the rest of the men and my jeep had arrived from an LST [LCI?]. My jeep and driver showed up with all the necessary equipment.

Pvt. Warren L. Rulien, another veteran of Africa and Sicily, served with the Intelligence and Reconnaissance Platoon of the 16th Infantry. He was so seasick that he could hardly wait to disembark.

As we got nearer to the shore, bullets began hitting the sides of the landing craft but could not penetrate as we ducked down low. It wasn't long after we stopped when the ramp of the landing craft was lowered. For a few seconds, everything seemed quiet and nobody moved. Someone shouted, "Let's go!" Instantly we began pouring out of the craft. As I stepped off of the ramp, I dropped into water up to my chest. This threw me off balance, and I lost my rifle. I floated for a few seconds trying to find my rifle, then gave up and began wading in to shore. On both sides of me were many soldiers coming from other landing craft, all wading in to shore. In front of me were steel rails driven into the bottom of the seabed, which extended about six feet out of the water. On top of them were mines. They were wide enough apart so troops could easily walk between them. By the time I got to the steel rails, the water was about up to my waist. There was a sandbar, which was perpendicular with the shore. About fifteen or twenty feet of it extended above the water. Bullets began hitting the water only a few feet in front of me, so I stepped behind one of the steel rails and squatted down. The rail was only about six or eight inches wide. A young replacement about nineteen years old, who was from my platoon, shouted at me, "Hey, Rulien, here I go!" and began running toward shore. He stepped onto the sandbar, and machine-gun fire opened up and he dropped into the water on the other side.

I took one of the bodies that was floating in the water and pushed it in front of me toward the shore. I had only gone a short distance when three or four soldiers began lining up behind me. Seeing this, I stood up and shouted, "Don't bunch up!" and walked off, leaving them with the body. I got down as low as I could in the water until I reached the sandbar, and then I crossed the sandbar on my belly. When I got across it, I noticed that the water was deep again, about up to my chest. I kept moving forward until I reached the beach. About two yards in from the beach was a sandbank, which was about four feet high and ran the whole length of the shore. Behind this, soldiers from each direction began bunching up. About 100 feet further onshore were two rolls of barbed wire. There the terrain began getting steeper and continued to rise. Halfway up the hill was a pillbox, but there was no gunfire coming from it.

In the back of the pillbox was a path leading up to the top of the hill. A German soldier who came out of the back of it began running up the path in back of the pillbox. Small-arms fire from American soldiers began pouring in on him. He turned back around immediately and ran back into the pillbox. Between the barbed wire and the pillbox were many land mines. Lying beside me, on his back, was an American soldier who had been shot in the stomach. He held his hand over his stomach, moaning—but only for a short time. Then he died. Seeing his rifle lying beside him, I picked it up, threw back the bolt, and looked down the barrel to make sure that sand hadn't been jammed into the barrel. I put a clip of ammunition into the gun, looked up the hill, and saw German soldiers running along the crest of the hill. At the distance that I was from them, they looked about two inches high. I began firing at them. On the shore, there were officers sitting there stunned. Nobody was taking command.

Landing craft were continuing to bring waves of soldiers in, and they were bunching up on the beach. Finally, out on the water, coming towards the shore, walking straight up with a staff of officers with him, I recognized Colonel Taylor, the regimental commander. He stepped across the sandbar, and bullets began hitting the water around him. He lay down on his stomach and started crawling towards shore, his staff officers doing the same. I kind of chuckled to myself, thinking, "Crawl on your stomach, like I did." When he got to shore, he sized up the situation immediately. I heard him say to the officers, "If we are going to die, let's die up there." It seemed to take effect, because the officers began moving their men along those two yards of beach to reach their objective.

A soldier from my platoon came up to me and said, "Follow me! We're going down this way." I let him take about a twenty-yard lead and began following him. I ducked down low as I walked down those two yards of beach. I had gone quite some distance when the soldier in front of me stopped. I stopped too, thinking he was getting his bearings. The lieutenant from my platoon came up to me and asked why I had stopped. I said I was following the soldier in front of me. The lieutenant continued on, and I saw him stop and talk to that soldier and continue on down. When we got there, I saw ten to fifteen men from my platoon there. There was a white band of tape down in that gully going up over that hill. We began in single file, following the tape up and over the hill. When we got to the top of the hill, I saw that there were trees, and along these trees were foxholes dug by the Germans. The sergeant in charge told us to stay in these holes for the time being. I got into one and began eating one of the boxes of K rations. I stayed in the foxhole until it was dark.

One of the sergeants came and told me to follow him. We met two other NCOs; one of them was carrying a stretcher. All of us began walking along the road towards the enemy. I saw a lot of red tracers in the sky and mortar shells exploding. None of them was falling near us. After we had gone some distance, we came upon our lieutenant, who was lying along the side of the road. He had been wounded. It looked like he had been hit by mortar shells, for some of the fragments had hit his face and he was blind. We picked him up, put him on the stretcher, and carried him back towards the side of the hill from which we had come up from the beach. We left the lieutenant next to the rest of the wounded and went back to our foxholes.

Sgt. John Souch, a veteran of Sicily from Warstall, Pennsylvania, served in Company D. After studying maps and a sand table the previous day to get familiar with Easy Red, Souch was unable to get much sleep. That night, he and most of his companions got seasick. His company was the last one of the 1st Battalion, 16th Infantry, scheduled to land on Easy Red an hour an a half after H-Hour. During the trip, Souch believed he saw Robert Capa on deck several times and thought the photographer looked Hungarian. If he had known Capa was a fellow Hungarian, he would have tried to speak with him.

Although many others remember having a rather full and satisfying early-morning breakfast on the *Samuel Chase*, Souch seems to recall being served only the soft-boiled eggs that were not cooked properly and were served just before the men loaded up and disembarked.

> We had our field packs, which I thought were heavier than I was. I was the first to go over the side down the rope ladder from my platoon. As I let go of the rope ladder, a landing craft went down. With the waves, it was so rough that I fell onto the landing craft, landing on my back. The full field pack helped me from getting a serious injury. My buddies told me to complain that I hurt my back and I would miss the invasion. I responded by saying I wanted to go with them.
>
> We went to a rendezvous area. All you could see was a lot of craft going in circles, waiting for the signal to go and hit the beach. We were supposed to stay down in the craft, but we tried to stand up and take a peep to see what was going on. You could hear the machine-gun bullets hissing by and the water splashing all over us as we made our run in.
>
> Finally the ramp went down in the water. The landing craft didn't even come close to the beach. We went off the ramp and into the cold water, holding our rifles above our heads. Shells were exploding in the surf and machine-gun bullets were whipping up spurts of water, and mortar shells exploded all around us. You could hear the naval gunfire over our heads. As we moved inward, there were jagged barrels of steel rails [hedgehogs] and rows and rows of barbed wire, which were pretty high, concrete blocks and what-not, planted by the Germans.
>
> It seemed like a long time before we finally hit the beach. There were bodies lying all over the beach. Some were wounded and others were dead. They told us to dig in. You couldn't dig in on the beach, as it was nothing but rocks the size of potatoes [probably the shingle]. We were brought in at the wrong part of the beach. Then I had diarrhea and no place to go. So I crawled under between the barbed wire until I found a small open place. It was difficult, because you had to take all the equipment off your back; the toilet paper was wet, along with everything else; and we had gas-impregnated uniforms on.
>
> There was an amphibious tank on the beach, but it wasn't operable and many of us were huddled in back of it so as not to be hit by machine-gun fire or mortar fire. Then we moved out, behind this wall where we huddled and then the officer in charge had us push a bangalore torpedo on the barbed wire. We were shaking from being afraid of getting killed or wounded and could hardly screw the pipe torpedo together. Finally we started getting organized to move up the hill. The bulldozer made a hole through the tank trap and mines were cleared. There was a man-made canal [antitank ditch] to trap the tanks. We had to wade through the water, which was up to our chests. The gas mask in front of my chest helped to hold me up as we were going across it. It was about fifty to seventy-five feet wide. We started up the hill, going zigzag very slowly. If we saw a mine, we were supposed to put a marker on it with anything we had.
>
> A GI in front of me whose name was Marolla said, "Souch, I think my foot is on a mine." It was his right foot. It was an antipersonnel mine. We were sweating it out. I told him to take his weight off slowly

> and shift his body to the left. If the mine goes off, he would only lose his foot or the heel of his foot. I told him to slide his foot off real fast, which he did, and the mine didn't go off. We placed a white cloth on it.
>
> It was a slow process walking up the hill. To the right of us, there was a GI who must have been in shock, since he was wounded and cutting off his leg with his bayonet. We finally reached the top of the hill and reorganized and went to our objective. Everyone was cold and damp. A lot of the guys were missing. Our uniforms were still soaked and weren't drying. It was getting dark. You couldn't sleep.

Thus ended Souch's first day on Omaha Beach.

PFC Frank C. Beetle served in the Cannon Company of the 16th Infantry. Like so many of his comrades, he had suffered from seasickness during the crossing and had put his brown paper bag to good use. His group reached the shore in small landing craft sometime after 9 A.M. The short-barreled 105-millimeter howitzers were to be brought in on larger vessels later, but they failed to arrive. When the ramp was dropped, everyone had to jump into the water to reach the beach. The tide was rising, and Beetle was up to his neck in water.

When he reached the beach, he first noticed that most of the troops dispensed with their gas masks. Then he saw dead men everywhere among the survivors. Enemy small-arms fire was peppering his area. He got rid of his carbine and picked up an M-1 rifle, which he considered to be more reliable than his own gun. Everyone moved quickly to the base of the cliff and huddled for cover. Many of the riflemen were already there. The officer from Beetle's group was trying to radio back for instructions. Artillery rounds were dropping behind them on the beach. Eventually the company was attached as infantry to what Beetle thought was the 2nd Battalion, since the battalion appeared to have suffered very heavy casualties.

On the beach, prisoners were coming back, and Beetle was surprised to observe one with Oriental features, probably a member of an *Ost* battalion, a unit formed from prisoners and volunteers the Germans shipped from Eastern Europe and the Soviet Union. He could see the paths through the minefields marked by the engineers with little white pieces of cloth and was shocked by the number of badly wounded men missing legs, whose bodies, he thought, must have done more to clear the German minefields than the mine detectors.

Eventually his group moved inland and dug in for the night. Sometime late in the day or during the night, at least one of the howitzers arrived, but without ammunition. During the first two days, his company had no ammunition to fire, as far as Beetle can remember.

Pvt. Stanley Stypulkowski, a twenty-two-year-old from New York, drove a half-track with a 57-millimeter antitank gun of the Anti-Tank Company of the 16th Infantry in tow.[11] His detachment crossed the Channel on an LCT and was to land an hour after the initial landings. Only Stypulkowski and the squad leader remained from the original group that had crossed the Atlantic to invade North Africa.

> Going in to the beach was very difficult. There were many underwater obstacles that sank other landing craft, as well as disabled craft that had been knocked out by artillery fire. The firepower coming down from those cliffs was tremendous. We could see

11. The 57-millimeter antitank gun was much heavier and more difficult to maneuver than the less-effective 37-millimeter antitank gun, and a three-quarter-ton truck or half-track was needed to tow it, unlike the 37-millimeter, which required only a jeep.

bodies floating by, as our naval coxswain looked for an opening through the obstacles.

The coxswain finally maneuvered around obstacles, sunken barges, as well as a few Sherman tanks that never made it. He got us in close enough and dropped the ramp. I revved up the engine, hoping the water wouldn't be too deep. We got to the beach OK. I drove the track about 300 yards down the beach, and I was stopped by our engineers, who were still trying to remove land mines. We were directed to take cover.

My squad at this point became separated. I took cover near a burned-out Sherman tank. As I took cover behind the tank, I soon found myself sitting on the ground beside a wounded soldier with a severe leg wound asking for help. I called to a couple of medics nearby, and then I attempted to aid him. I found I was unable to move my arms. At this point, my mind didn't quite function as it should have. "Why can't I help this poor fellow?" I just sat there, kind of numb. The medics came over, and one worked on the severely wounded soldier while the second asked me how bad I was hit. I told him I didn't know I was hit. He removed my gas mask, which was worn chest-high for buoyancy, and showed me a hole through it and then a hole in my shirt. He cut away my shirt and undershirt, and this is when I saw a hole in my chest the size of a silver dollar—no bleeding. The medic advised me that it didn't bleed because I was apparently hit by a large piece of shrapnel that was still red hot and sealed the blood vessels as it entered my body.

The medic dressed Stypulkowski's wound and helped him back toward an LCT, which was discharging troops.

Halfway out in the surf, small-arms fire got very heavy. The medic told me to try to make it to the boat on my own, and he then left me to go back to the beach. After taking a few shaky steps in the surf, the salt water got into the wound, and I apparently passed out. When I came to, I was laying on my back on an inflated raft, looking up at two sailors who apparently had pulled me out of the surf. The LCT took me back to a ship, where I was placed in a body basket and hoisted aboard. It was the *Dorothea Dix*.

That was the end of Stanley Stypulkowski's war experience. Like many other wounded soldiers that day, he was eventually sent home after just one fateful day on Omaha Beach.

CHAPTER 13

The Landings on Omaha Beach (Part 2)

The 116th Infantry, 29th Division, landed on the western sectors of Omaha Beach at the same time as the 16th Infantry came ashore on the eastern sectors. Company A, which arrived in British LCAs, took heavy losses on its assigned sector of Dog Green. The other companies of the first wave drifted farther east than planned before landing. The remaining companies of the 1st Battalion landed behind Company A.

As described by Joseph Balkoski in *Omaha Beach*, Captain Schilling of Company D died when his LCA was hit by an 88-millimeter gun that penetrated the ramp and steel doors behind it. Before the landings, he had informed his men that he was proud to lead them into battle and warned them that the enemy would be ready, but said that intelligence estimated that only a couple of the twenty-two bunkers in their sector would be occupied with low-quality troops. Sgt. J. Robert Slaughter remembers well that last briefing. "On D-Day, I was the squad leader of the 2nd Squad, 1st Platoon. I was confident in our ability to do the job. They awakened us at 2 A.M. for breakfast by sounding the general alarm. Breakfast consisted of steak, gravy, white bread, and coffee. I wasn't hungry but ate anyway."

Slaughter's Company D and the remainder of the 1st Battalion stood on the deck of the British LSI *Empire Javelin*, where they received a printed version of General Eisenhower's message, which was also read over the ship's loudspeaker. Each soldier carried more than pounds of equipment, including a quarter pound of TNT for making foxholes and eliminating enemy strong points. The men of Company D, including Slaughter's squad, climbed into their LCA, and they were lowered onto the heaving seas by means of davits. Lt. George A. Athanasakos commanded Slaughter's LCA.[1]

> The cold spray blew in, and soon we were soaking wet. I used a gas cape—a plastic bag used for protection from poison gas—as shelter from the spray. Lack of oxygen under the sack caused seasickness.
>
> A few thousand yards from shore, we rescued three or four survivors from a craft that had swamped with water and sunk. We left the rest in the water, as we did not have space. I could see the battleship *Texas* firing its 14-inch guns. In minutes, the giant swell from the recoil of those guns nearly swamped us and added to the sickness and misery. The bilge pumps couldn't keep pace with the incoming seawater, necessitating manual help: helmets and pumps.

Meanwhile, Company B in LCAs had already landed on the heels of the engineers and ahead of Company D in LCVPs. PFC Harold Baumgarten, a rifleman in his boat team, had recently transferred from Company A to Company B, but his company was not to escape the bloody fate that befell Company A.

> Clarius Riggs was hit in front of me as he exited the boat. As I ran through the water, carrying an M-1 rifle at port arms, a bullet hit the receiver plate. I was able to fire the gun one time, and then the stock broke in half. I threw the thing away. Pvt. Nicholas S. Kafkalas picked it up, handing it back to me, thinking I had given up. Bullets ripped through my field jacket, and one glanced off my helmet. I left my assault jacket on the landing craft. As we worked our way to the sand, I noticed three amphibious tanks; two of them were knocked out. Many Company A soldiers were hanging on to the tanks, one of which was firing its 75-millimeter gun into the pillbox to the right flank of Dog Green. The bunker just kept firing back.
>
> When I reached the seawall, blood was gushing from my left cheek. My gums were lying on my tongue. I met PFC Dominic Surro, who was then unhurt [later KIA]. He tried to help, but we were under intense fire from that pillbox to the right.
>
> Pvt. Robert L. Dittmar was hit in the chest and soon died. Pvt. Nicholas Kafkalas was wounded and dazed. Bullets were ricocheting off the ground, and 88 shells were exploding. S.Sgt. Clarence E. "Pilgrim" Roberson was to my left and behind me. He was shot in the forehead and helmetless. He was on his knees as if praying. Twenty yards to the left front, I saw Sgt. Bedford Hoback, who received shell fragments in the face. The same explosion got me in the cheek.
>
> As I crawled toward the seawall, I picked up another M-1 rifle and followed Surro, who was moving left toward the Vierville draw. We were seeking safety from the deadly pillbox to the right. I then found my best buddy, PFC Robert L. Garbett, lying facedown and dead. Men from Company A—PFC Harold Weber and some fellow

1. The accounts in this chapter through that of Randolph Ginman are from Slaughter's original manuscript.

> named Gilbert Pittenger, Herbert Kaufman, and Frank Symzac, all of Company A—were at the slanted seawall with me. We noticed two more amphibious tanks knocked out.
>
> My adrenaline was pumping, and I got up to cross the road above the wall and the beach, when Pittenger tackled me and probably saved my life, because, just as I started, a hail of bullets came my way, barely missing. I helped Sergeant Frazier (Company A), who was wounded and paralyzed, to get behind the slanted seawall. That was the last I saw of him.
>
> A mortar shell exploded; three pieces of shrapnel got me in the left side of the head. My helmet had three holes but probably saved me from much worse.
>
> More mortar shells began falling nearby, so we dived back behind the wall. One of the medics, T/5 Cecil G. Breeden, leaned over me, shells and bullets flying, and applied a pressure bandage and sprinkled sulfa powder onto my face wound. I tried to pull him down to safety, but he refused, saying, "You're hurt now; when I get it, you can take care of me.

Baumgarten watched Breeden patching up the wounded and about half a dozen "of our boys trying to take that damn pillbox," none of whom survived, according to his estimation. Later, he worked his way toward the draw where a command post had been set up. There Breeden gave first aid to Colonel Canham, who earlier had been shot through the hand.

PFC Robert L. Sales of Company B, who served as Capt. Ettore Zappacosta's radio operator, had trained with the 29th Rangers.[2] Zappacosta chose him for his bodyguard as well. As they approached the coast, the English coxswain of the LCA told the captain they were as close as they could get and dropped the ramp. The captain led the way toward the beach, right into enemy machine-gun fire that was targeting the boat. The disembarking troops were hit one after the other as they left the boat. Sales, who was the fourth in line, caught his heel in the ramp and fell to the side. He heard Zappacosta cry that he was hit and tried to reach him, but without success. Sales dropped his radio and assault jacket and clung to a timber post with a Teller mine that was floating by. Eventually the log drifted to the beach and he came ashore, the only survivor of his boat team. The second wave was hit as hard as the first.

From his place on the beach, Sales watched other landing craft approach the beach under a hail of bullets. The battalion surgeon, Capt. Robert B. Ware, was cut down by machine-gun fire before his very eyes. Sales made his way to the sea wall, passing many dead, dying, and badly wounded men. Dog Green proved deadly for every wave of the 1st Battalion that tried to land there.

As Company B struggled across the beach, Sergeant Slaughter's Company D approached in LCAs.

> Two or three hundred yards from shore we encountered artillery fire. Near misses sent water skyward, and then it rained back on us. The British coxswain said he had to lower the ramp and for us to quickly disembark. I was stationed near the front of the boat and heard Tech Sergeant Norfleet counter, "These men have heavy equipment, and you *will* take them all the way in." The coxswain begged, "But we'll *all* be killed!" Norfleet unholstered his .45 Colt pistol, put it to the sailor's head, and ordered, "*ALL THE WAY IN!*" The craft proceeded, plow-

2. The Provisional 29th Ranger Battalion was formed from the 29th Division in December 1942, but it was disbanded in the fall of 1943, and the troops returned to the division.

ing through the choppy waters, as far as it could go.[3] My thinking: If this boat didn't hurry up and get us in, I would die from seasickness. This was my first encounter with this malady. Wooziness became stomach sickness and then vomiting. Thinking I was immune to seasickness, earlier I had given my puke bag to a buddy who already had filled his. At this point, death is not so dreadful. Minus the paper bag, I used the first thing at hand—my helmet. I didn't care what the Germans had to offer, I needed to get to dry land. Nothing is worse than motion sickness, except maybe 88s and MG-42 machine guns.

About 150 yards from shore, I raised my head despite the warning. I could see the craft to our right taking a terrific licking from small arms. Tracer bullets were bouncing and skipping off the ramp and sides as they zeroed in on the boat, which touched down a few minutes before we did. Had we not delayed a few minutes to pick up the survivors from the sunken craft, we might have taken the concentration of fire on that boat too. Great plumes of water from enemy artillery kept sprouting close by.

As we approached the beach, the ramp was lowered. Mortar shells exploded on land and in the water. Unseen snipers concealed in the cliffs were shooting down at individuals, causing screams from those being hit. The water was turning red from the blood. The smell of cordite was something that would forever become fixed in our minds, always associated with death and destruction.

The ramp was in the surf, and the front of the steel craft was bucking violently up and down. As my turn came to exit, I sat on the edge of the bucking ramp trying to time my leap. I stayed there too long, causing a bottleneck and endangering myself as well as the men that followed. The one-inch steel ramp was going up and down in the surf, rising as much as six feet. I was afraid it would slam me in the head. One of the men was hit and died instantly. There were dead men in the water with the living. The Germans couldn't tell which was which. All were coming in with the tide. It was extremely hard to shed the heavy equipment. I had to inflate my Mae West. I helped Pvt. Ernest McCanless, who was not a very strong swimmer, get closer in so he wouldn't drown. He still had one box of precious .30-caliber machine-gun ammo.

I crouched down to chin-deep in the water when I saw mortar shells zeroing in at the water's edge. Sand began to kick up from small-arms fire from the bluffs. I don't know how long we were in the water before the move was made, but I would guess close to an hour. Initially I tried to take cover behind one of the heavy timbers and then noticed an innocent-looking mine tied to the top. Getting across the beach became an obsession.

While lying on sand behind one of the log poles, I watched a GI from another landing craft trying to cross the beach about fifty yards to our right. He screamed for a medic. One of the aid men moved quickly to help him, and he was shot. I'll never forget seeing that medic lying next to the wounded GI and both of them screaming. They both died in minutes.

The tide was rushing in, and later waves of men were due. I believe I was the first in my group, telling PFC Walfred Williams, my

3. There are several stories of officers or NCOs threatening coxswains, but it is not possible to determine whether they are exaggerated or embellished.

Troops of the 29th Division take shelter at the base of the bluffs.

number one gunner [who still had his 51-pound machine-gun tripod] to follow. I had my rifle ready to fire, with safety off, and had also fixed the bayonet before disembarking.

I gathered my courage and started running as fast as my long legs would carry me. I ran as low as I could to lessen the target, since I am six-foot-five. I had a long way to run, about 100 yards or more. As I ran through a tidal pool with about six or eight inches of water, I began to stumble. I finally caught my balance and accidentally fired my rifle right by my foot, continuing on to the seawall.

Reaching the slanted seawall, I looked back for the first time and got a glimpse of the armada. It was a sight to behold. I also saw that Williams, Pvt. Sal Augeri, and Pvt. Ernest McCanless were right behind. I didn't see Norfleet until later. Augeri had lost the machine-gun receiver in the water, and I had gotten sand in my rifle. We still had one box of machine-gun ammo. I took off my assault jacket and spread my raincoat so I could clean my rifle. It was then I saw bullet holes in my raincoat. I didn't realize I'd been shot at. I lit my first cigarette—they were wrapped in plastic, as were the matches.

All of the squad crossed the beach unscathed, except Pvt. Robert Stover and medic Pvt. Roland Coates, both of whom were killed. I don't know what happened to these men.[4]

I organized our squad. We finally made it to the base of the hill and out of range of flat-trajectory small-arms fire. Here stragglers from other companies congregated.

4. Records show that Coates died of wounds on June 7.

> About midmorning, we met some misguided machine gunners from Company H who had a receiver but no tripod. Combining our assets, we finally had a machine gun. We observed 88s firing from a pillbox to the right and up on the bluff. We set up the gun and opened fire at the concrete bunker. I acted as observer, Williams was the gunner, and Augeri the number two man. They placed tracer bullets directly into the embrasure of the gun emplacement. I could see tracers ricocheting around the opening, and simultaneously, the 88-millimeter fired at incoming landing craft. Our gun soon jammed, so we moved before return fire was implemented.

M.Sgt. William Presley of Company B led a small group off the beach and encountered a dead naval forward observer. He took his radio and called in naval fire from one of the American destroyers in the Channel. Sergeant Slaughter notes that they had observed a *Nebelwerfer* unit firing on the beaches, and that Sergeant Presley directed the destroyer's guns against them. The German rocket launchers were on the bluffs at Wn-65, blocking the end of Exit D-3, leading to Saint Laurent.

> Soon came the screaming of the large shells, whistling over on their way to the German tormentors. Ker-whoom-ker-woomker-whoom! The ground trembled under us. The exploding shells saturated the area to our right front, some of them landing too close for comfort to our position.
>
> Later that afternoon, we still hadn't gotten farther than the top of the hill. German bicycle troops appeared, riding down the road paralleling the beach, as if they were on a Sunday outing. We surprised them with some well-placed rifle fire that separated some of them from their vehicles.

S.Sgt. George A. Kobe, who was in Captain Schilling's landing craft, was a mortar man with the Mortar Platoon of Company D. When the vessel began to slow down about 600 yards from shore, Schilling, who stood behind the ramp, turned around and said, "You're not going to drop the ramp here!" Suddenly a large-caliber round, or possibly a mine-on-a-pole obstacle, struck the ramp, killing the captain and blinding the mortar platoon sergeant, John Stinnet, in one eye. PFC Bernard "Rocky" Latakas, Schilling's radioman, saw the captain and a British sailor, who yelled at them to get off the boat, fall. Latakas, who could not swim, lost much of his equipment but made it to shore. After he moved behind an obstacle, he discovered his rifle was jammed. He met up with Lieutenant Dixon, who he thought had been killed on the landing craft, the only Company D officer in the area. The two moved with others toward the bluffs and began taking prisoners.

Corporal Crimone, on the same landing craft, saw not only the captain killed in the explosion, but also First Sergeant Obenshain and other comrades. As he left the sinking ship and inflated his life preserver, Sergeant Kobe came along and tried to help Crimone make the shore, since he couldn't swim, but the corporal let go because he was pulling Kobe under. Eventually Crimone drifted about 500 yards to the east and sought cover behind an obstacle. Soon he was rescued by Lt. Verne Morse and S.Sgt. Edward Fatula. Together they moved up the bluffs and captured a Polish soldier in a foxhole. While Crimone drifted eastward, Sergeants Stinnet and Kobe and three soldiers made it to the seawall.

PFC Randolph Ginman, a gunner in a mortar squad, remembers the heroic English crew of the LCA that brought his group within 100 yards of the shore. The Germans fired at the occupants, killing the two British sailors, who lay dead in their vessel while Ginman and the others quickly disembarked and struggled to shore.

The 121st Engineer Battalion in LCTs came in with the waves following Company D. The battalion was split into several waves, the first elements arriving with Company C. As Capt. Robert W. Stewart and his men headed for the shore in an LCT, an LCVP took a direct hit. As their vessel came closer to shore, it had to plow through the dead bodies that had been carried back out to sea. The ramp came down and German small arms fire rained down on the men as they left the LCT. Only twenty-one of them reached the beach, which was littered with bodies. Other elements of the 121st Engineers also took heavy losses.

T/5 Walter Condon went into Dog Green with the 3rd Platoon of Company C, 121st Engineer Battalion. Their objective was to blow up the concrete wall that sealed Exit D-1. Condon's LCT carried a bulldozer with a ton of TNT on it, a jeep, and about fifty men. The platoon was overstrength for the landings; Condon believes that many of these new men had been cleared out of the prison camps in the United States. As his LCT moved in, he wasn't able to see much.

> It was certainly overcast, and the smoke was pouring up off the beach over the hill. On the way in, two Canadian LCTs collided and turned upside down right in front of us. The men on those two boats were the 2nd Ranger Battalion; they had a jeep on each of those boats, but no heavy equipment.[5] We fished two boatloads of Rangers between ourselves and our other platoons. Some with their life preservers did not want to get pulled out and waved to us. The boat could only turn around two or three times to pick these men up, and then we had to resume our run in. We picked up maybe fifty men or so. Now we were real crowded.
>
> By the time we landed on the beach, we had been on this LCT roughly two and a half days, and no place to sit down. You couldn't sit down on the deck, because there was an inch of water. As we were going in, we finally landed at Exit D-3. We were supposed to land just to the left of Exit D-1, which was our objective. We tried going down the beach toward D-1 with our bulldozer, but we got bogged down several times. Our company commander was Capt. Svend A. Holmstrup, and he was killed right on the ramp of the boat with the 1st Platoon. All of our officers were lost the first day. We took a tremendous beating as we tried to work our way down the beach. We finally got to D-1 with our bulldozer. By then, the 88, which had controlled the beach had been knocked out. Sometime during the afternoon, we placed the charge between the two walls and blew the two big walls out of there so our vehicles could start moving off the beach. We moved up to the D-1 transit area and checked it for mines and dug in. Company B dug in on the other side of the hedgerow.

By 3:30 P.M. in the afternoon, they had blown the concrete wall that sealed the Vierville draw at D-1 and opened the exit. The AT ditch was filled in and the mines were removed.

Before the invasion, T/4 Clifton T. Bitgood of the 2nd Platoon, Company C, 121st Engineers, was on an LCT. There were two tanks in the front, which did not belong to his battalion, and four 2½-ton trucks with canvas-covered cabs that did. He had fashioned a bed between a camouflage net and the canvas cover on a cab and slept through what was a rough ride across the Channel. At about 5 A.M., the sound of gunfire awoke him. Soon those on the LCT were preparing to land, and Bitgood assembled his equipment, which included a mine detector in a case that he

5. The 2nd Rangers arrived on British-manned LCAs.

estimated was about eighteen by thirty by ten inches. He asked a member of the Coast Guard crew if they would get wet and was assured they would be landing high and dry. The landing was forever seared in his memory.[6]

> Our captain was hit in the head and killed. Then the first man off went in the water up to his neck, so I put the mine detector case in the water and got on and paddled to shore on it. Our landing craft was hit and burned most of the day.
>
> I saw five beach engineers go down on the beach to blow an obstacle, and an 88-millimeter shell hit near them and only three came back. I saw one whose head was completely severed and rolled off of his shoulder.
>
> We started digging in as soon as we were up on the beach beyond where the water would be at high tide. About 2:30 P.M., I got in the rear of a tank with about twelve others and started up, away from the beach, and made it to the top of a bluff. That night, I slept in a trench that the Germans had used. A buddy was beside me, and I heard a shot close by. He said he had fired because there was a German soldier near one of our trucks and that he thought he got him because he was not moving. I slept good that night.

Lt. Col. Max Schneider waited a quarter of an hour past the deadline for the signal that Rudder's troops at Pointe du Hoc had succeeded in taking the position and were waiting for him to reinforce them. When no message came, Schneider took his 5th Rangers and Companies A and B of the 2nd Rangers to reinforce the 116th Infantry at Omaha Beach. They followed the first wave of the 121st Engineer Battalion.

The 5th Rangers had loaded its landing craft on the HMS *Prince Leopold* and HMS *Prince Baudouin*. The unit landed on Dog White to the east of Dog Green because of the difficulties the units on the beach were encountering. Lt. Jay H. Mehaffey recalls the landings.

> [The day before,] Col. Max Schneider, commanding the 5th Rangers, called the officers to the wardroom and pinned first lieutenant bars on myself and several others. The promotions had come through that morning, and he jokingly told us, "I hope you live long enough to draw a paycheck." We went over the battle plan: The 2nd Rangers would land at the base of Pointe du Hoc at H-Hour, 0630, and assault the cliffs. If they achieved a foothold they would signal the other three companies [Companies A and B only; Company C was already assigned to land behind the 116th] of the 2nd and our six line companies of the 5th Rangers to land at Pointe du Hoc, and from there we would proceed inland to expand the position. If no signal appeared from the Rangers at the Pointe, the 5th Battalion would land at Omaha Beach and then proceed up the coast paralleling the coast and attack Pointe du Hoc.
>
> On board HMS *Prince Leopold* during the early hours June 6, 1944, the Rangers made a final check of equipment and weapons and had their "final meal," as it was jokingly referred to. Breakfast was served at 3 A.M., with fresh eggs and all the trimmings. We took our boat positions on deck about 4 A.M. When the first streaks of dawn appeared, we went over the side into the assault craft. The sea was quite rough, with waves running over five feet high. H-Hour

6. The 121st Engineers were in five LCTs and two LCMs. They were scheduled to land at H+50 and H+60 at Dog Green, but after Company A of the 116th Infantry was decimated, the follow-up waves tended to drift east toward Dog White.

Command post for beachmaster from 2nd Naval Beach Battalion on Omaha Beach.

was 0630, and we were to make our approach from twelve miles off the French coast. Because of the heavy seas, the horizon was limited, and the only boats in sight were the other Ranger assault craft. I glanced at my watch and it was nearly 0630, H-Hour. Arriving late, as we finally approached the coast I could see on the horizon the reddish brown cliffs with a mask of haze and smoke. At 0655, I could see Pointe du Hoc jutting into the Channel far off to the right, and it became obvious that we were now going into the Dog Green sector of Omaha Beach, as we had prepared for in our alternate plan.[7]

Omaha Beach was protected by three rows of beach obstacles. To the everlasting credit of the British coxswain who took us ashore, we survived this horror that smashed the earlier assault waves. He maneuvered around and through the obstacles, until he finally had to drop the ramp and we jumped into the surf. We were in waist-deep water that was cold and chilled us on this gray and chilly dawn. Held down by the weight of extra equipment, we slowly waded ashore, where we were immediately taken under fire by German machine guns enfilading our landing area from the right flank in the direction of Vierville. At the water's edge sat a tank. My platoon sergeant and myself, along with several others, took cover beside it and surveyed the situation to our front. Ahead of us was a small seawall

7. They actually landed farther east, because of the unfavorable situation on Dog Green.

> that offered some protection from the mortars and artillery which began to drop as we landed. The German machine gunners were firing long bursts and would then pause. I told the men we would have to outguess the space between bursts, so after the next burst, I made a dash for it and made the seawall.

The battalion landed on Dog White, and all but one of Lieutenant Mehaffey's men made it to the seawall.

> One took an embarrassing wound through his buttocks. He was shot at such an angle that he had four separate holes in his rear end. If we had any illusions about the grand design of D-Day, they died at the seawall. Around me was Company C of the 5th and part of Company D, along with the battalion commander and his staff. We were beyond visual sight of the rest of our battalion.
>
> We were pinned to the seawall unable to move until after 0800. Out in the Channel, the only ships we could see were the ones burning at the water's edge with no indication other waves were coming in. You could not see much and most of the noise seemed to be German fire, and I had the impression that the invasion had failed and that all other Americans had been killed or captured. Off to our right flank, a few inspired leaders had rallied the stragglers and survivors of the initial assault force and began to engage the German pillboxes on the bluffs. The machine guns that had us pinned to the seawall stop firing, and Brig. Gen. Norman Cota of the 29th Division came up the beach to where we had taken cover. I was the first officer he spotted, so he took cover beside me. He asked me, "How many Rangers got in?" to which I replied, "We got about two companies here; I don't know about the rest." He told me, "Get 'em up the cliffs; it's suicide to stay here!" I referred him to the battalion commander, who was a few feet away, and he gave him the same order.
>
> Beyond the seawall was a double apron of concertina barbed wire. The first sergeant of Company D jumped the wall and placed a bangalore torpedo under it and blew a gap several feet wide. Then, one by one, we moved up the bluff. It was 0830; D-Day was two hours old. I had a gas mask strapped to my leg, and it snagged on the wire as I moved through it. I took a slug in my pack, so I unhooked the mask and left it hanging on the wire. As we moved up the high bluff, we drew more machine-gun fire, but the grass was on fire and the smoke gave us some concealment. At the crest of the bluff was a dead German, the first Kraut I had seen dead or alive. We moved across a heavily mined field and into our first hedgerow. As I climbed through the hedgerow, I saw a lieutenant and three men from the 116th Infantry taking cover in it, so I told them we had gotten ashore with most of our weapons and they should join up with us. Those troopers, shocked from what they had seen on the beach, looked at us and shook their heads, refusing to move on.
>
> Moving up the bluffs we moved opposite the Chateau de Vaumicel, a fortified stone villa [a few hundred yards south of Vierville], where one of our platoons with several men from the 116th Infantry had begun to engage the defenders in a firefight. We deployed along the coast road leading into Vierville and parallel with the beach, and after taking positions along the ditches, I made a cup of instant coffee.
>
> As we waited to move into Vierville, a Ranger came down the road with eight

Watching the invasion unfold.

German prisoners, their hands clasped over their helmets. We stopped them in the middle of the road and lined them up opposite an opening in the hedgerow from which a German sniper had just shot one of our people. They stayed there motionless until we moved off down the road. We didn't have time to fool with prisoners, but these had moved through their own minefields back to the beach.

As we moved through Vierville, our D-Day objective, Pointe du Hoc, was still three miles up the road. Unable to advance any further that day to assist the 2nd Ranger Battalion and complete our mission, we had to dig in on the western outskirts of Vierville and wait while Company B of the 5th cleared the German strongpoints on the road ahead of us. We held this position the rest of the day. As the sky darkened that evening, Company C, 5th U.S. Rangers, bedded down in a hedgerow west of Vierville. We hadn't seen a German plane all day, but they bombed the beach about midnight. After that, there was absolute stillness.

Sgt. Victor H. Fast, who served as Colonel Schneider's German interpreter, also had vivid memories of D-Day.

The first glimpse I had of the French shore was when Colonel Schneider tapped me on the shoulder and said, "Hey, Vic! Take a look at the beach and the cliffs!" Smoke was rising from the hillside on Omaha Beach, exactly where we were supposed to land. Colonel Schneider then ordered the British flotilla commander to land east of Dog Green, because he saw the intense fire the German defenders were putting on the troops who had landed on our designated beach. The colonel's decision saved a multitude of lives, and I am thankful to the good Lord. I saw some of the LCAs overturned hitting some of the underwater obstacles. Some hit the Element Cs, tetrahedra, and hedgehogs with Teller mines attached.

Colonel Schneider jumped into the water and went under, followed by all the men in our LCA. We had to all swim to shore. When I crawled up to the beach and then to the seawall, I had an M-1 rifle, two bandoliers of ammo, and several grenades, no helmet, no gas mask, no pack. I had peeled all those off so I could swim. I retrieved a helmet from a dead buddy, only to find it half full with the remains of his head. I quickly found another and wore it along with a .45 automatic through the remainder of the war.

We were lying behind the rock seawall, regrouping, when General Cota walked up

> and then promptly hit the beach when a machine gun opened up. He said to Colonel Schneider, "I am expecting the Rangers to lead the way." We started inland through smoke haze and a minefield.

Before long, Sergeant Fast had an opportunity to interrogate some prisoners as the 5th Rangers moved up and over the bluffs. Separating the lowest-ranking and youngest German from his lieutenant and the other prisoners, Fast told the young man to give him the information he wanted, or he would turn the prisoner over to his Jewish friend, Herb Epstein. The sergeant looked over toward Epstein, who then nodded. "Herb had not shaved for a day and was big and burly. He had a .45 strapped to his hip, a Ranger knife on his boot, and a Thompson machine gun, so he looked mean enough to scare the living daylights out of anybody. He was the colonel's intelligence sergeant and knew Yiddish, not German, but knew more about the invasion than our intelligence captain."

Other than telling Fast about the German S-mine, the "Bouncing Betty" antipersonnel mine, the prisoner divulged little information, claiming that there were no troops in Vierville and there were many panzer divisions inland.[8] He may have tried to intimidate his interrogators. Nonetheless, Fast rewarded him with a D bar. A little later, Fast and his comrades proceeded to the Vierville draw, where they came under sniper fire from a church steeple. Colonel Schneider called for naval support, and a warship promptly demolished the steeple. They found a girl sniper in the rubble.

> That night, Colonel Schneider set up the battalion headquarters in a chateau [Château de Vaumical] with a courtyard front and back. I dug a foxhole (slit trench) just outside the front door and stood guard while medics tended the wounded inside. GI blankets hung from the windows, and candlelight was used inside.
>
> Jerry came over and bombed us that night, and Father Lacy bailed out of the headquarters building right on top of me in a prone position in my foxhole. Soon after, Colonel Schneider received reports from the company commanders that they were short of 60-millimeter and 81-millimeter mortar shells. I was called in, and the colonel ordered me to get down to the beach and get all the ammo I could and bring it back to the command post. I was not allowed to finish asking how I was to do this. I found a Frenchman with a horse and the two-wheel cart that was in the courtyard. We went down the draw and loaded the cart with 60-millimeter mortar shells that were still on the backs of fallen Rangers and the members of the 116th Infantry. I brought the horse and cart back to the command post while watching the moon moving in and out of the clouds that night. I went into the colonel's sleeping quarters, awoke him, and told him that his ammo was out back. He thanked me and went back to sleep.
>
> The bad memories from D-Day included a GI I came across with a gaping stomach wound. I lit a cigarette for him, shot him full of morphine, and left. I am sure he bled to death. Two very close buddies of mine died on D-Day, Sgt. Walter J. Zack and 1st Lt. Dee C. Anderson. Dee was a young clean-cut Mormon from Salt Lake City. He caught a bullet in the side of the head leading his platoon across an opening in a hedgerow. Walter was killed on the beach directing traffic, when he was splattered by a direct hit from an 88 on the beach. One moment I saw him, and the next I didn't.

8. Once a "Bouncing Betty" mine was tripped, it propelled its time-delayed explosive charge about waist-high, which then detonated.

The 5th Rangers on June 6th 1944

The after-action report of the 5th Ranger Battalion was compiled about a month after the landings. What follows is a brief summary of the battalion's operations.

> At 0530 hours the Fifth Ranger Battalion loaded into LCAs from the mother ships, HMS *Prince Leopold* and *Prince Badouin*, and started the ten mile run to the coast of France. The morale of the men was excellent, the weather cloudy, and the sea very choppy.
>
> About five miles from shore, one LCA containing the First Platoon and part of company headquarters of Company F had shipped so much water that it was forced to drop out. . . . This platoon did not make the assault . . . but did land near the St.-Laurent-sur-Mer Beach exit at 0900 after transferring to a passing LCT.
>
> The beach was protected by a large number of underwater obstacles. . . . Mortar and artillery shells were bursting in the area of these obstacles and a heavy concentration of small arms fire swept the beach. A four foot sea wall ran laterally along the beach about 75 yards from the water's edge. Friendly troops were observed utilizing the protective cover afforded by this wall. A pall of smoke obscured the sharply rising ground immediately in the rear of and overlooking the beach. . . .
>
> The LCAs slowly threaded their way through gaps in the lines of obstacles at H+75, 0745, the first wave consisting of one half Battalion Headquarters, Companies A, B, and E, landed on Omaha Dog White Beach at . . . approximately 800 yards East of Exit D-1. . . . Lieutenant Colonel Max F. Schneider, had ordered the flotilla commander to touch down his craft east of the intended landing point, Dog Green, because of the tremendous volume of fire which covered that portion of the beach was inflicting a large number of casualties on the preceding wave.
>
> The first wave crossed the beach in good order with few casualties, halted temporarily in the rear of the sea wall, and immediately reorganized.
>
> The second wave, consisting of one half Battalion Headquarters, Companies C, D, and one platoon of Company F, duplicated the feat of the first wave.
>
> At the signal from the Battalion Commander, the leading echelon scrambled over the wall, blew gaps in the protective wire, and protected from enemy observation by the curtain of rising smoke, advanced unhesitatingly to a point near the top of the hill. Here the smoke had cleared and the topographical crest was being swept by effective automatic weapons fire. First Lieutenant Francis W. Dawson, Company D, led his platoon over the top and wiped out a strongpoint thereby enabling the battalion to advance.
>
> Because of numerous minefields the battalion now changed into a column formation and, after winding through their intricate pattern, the leading unit, Company B, reached the St.-Laurent-sur-Mer–Vierville-sur-Mer road at a point approximately one kilometer east of Vierville-sur-Mer. During the advance numerous Germans, well concealed in weapons pits constructed in hedgerows, were killed.
>
> Company B advanced toward Vierville-sur-Mer receiving heavy sniper and machine gun fire. Several direct hits from enemy artillery on the rear of the battalion column caused numerous casualties. Company E attempted a penetration to the South but was halted by intense machine gun fire. An

Type H667 casemate for a 50-millimeter antitank gun that fired on the eastern portion of Omaha Beach and the E-1 exit to St. Laurent. Troops of a naval beach battalion occupy the position after June 6, 1944.

81-mm mortar concentration fired by Company C knocked out several of these positions but they were rapidly replaced and the advance remained halted.

The weight of the attack was shifted toward Vierville-sur-Mer and, after overcoming considerable sniper resistance, the battalion advanced through the village to its western outskirts where it was again held up by a large volume of . . . fire. At this point contact was established with the Commanding Officer First Battalion 116th Infantry and approximately 150 men of his unit. Dusk was falling and the battalion was ordered to dig-in a perimeter defense for the night. Companies A, B, and C of the Second Ranger Battalion, numbering approximately 80 men, also assumed a portion of the defense area. Tanks of the 743rd Tank Battalion moved within the defense. . . . Except for occasional exchanges with enemy snipers and machine guns the night was one of little activity.

One platoon from Company A which became separated and after crossing the sea wall proceeded through Vierville to the rallying point southwest of the town, arriving there at 4:00 P.M. In accomplishing this feat they captured 12 Germans and killed at least an equal number. Leaving the rallying point shortly thereafter this unit fought its way through to Pointe du Hoe [Hoc] (the Battalion objective) and contacted the Second Ranger Battalion, arriving there at about 2200 hours [10 P.M.].

The platoon for F Company, which landed near St. Laurent . . . [sent a patrol] to locate the Fifth Battalion but were unable to gain contact. Attempting to move along the beach toward Vierville this platoon was subjected to artillery fire receiving 8 casualties. After advancing 600 yards to the West the unit was . . . pinned down. When darkness fell the platoon retained this position.

The results for the first day were about 100 prisoners taken, 150 enemy dead and approximately 60 Rangers killed and wounded.

On the heels of the 5th Rangers and the 121st Engineer Battalion came waves consisting of DUKWs launched from LSTs, carrying the first guns toward the beachhead established by the 116th Infantry. The 111th FA Battalion launched twelve DUKWs from three different LSTs. Each of these LSTs carried four of the DUKWs, which were loaded with one battery of 105-millimeter howitzers and carried fourteen men with fifty rounds of ammunition and one 105-millimeter gun. They were launched from their LSTs between 4 and 6 A.M. After several hours at sea, the rough waters had swamped many of the amphibious trucks. The surviving DUKWs with the remnants of the 111th FA formed up for the assault on Easy Green, joined by additional DUKWs from the same LSTs carrying the AT Platoons of the 2nd, 3rd and 1st Battalions and the Cannon Company of the 116th Infantry. The German gunners destroyed the remainder of the 111th FA's DUKWs. Only one 105-millimeter gun was rescued by a Rhino ferry.[9] Behind this wave came LCTs carrying the regiment's AT Company and the 467th Anti-Aircraft Automatic Weapons Battalion. They were followed by additional DD tanks in LCTs and the 461st Amphibious Truck Company in DUKWs. As the invasion plans went awry, the follow-up waves were delayed until the congestion on the beaches could be relieved. As a result, the men in these areas were forced to endure the rough seas as well as enemy artillery fire longer than had been expected.

The Anti-Tank Platoon of the 1st Battalion headed toward Dog Green. Among these men were S.Sgt. William Lewis, his squad, and its 57-millimeter antitank gun onboard a DUKW. Lewis's platoon had crossed the Channel in *LST 408* with the Anti-Tank Platoon of the 2nd Battalion and one battery of the 111th FA. Lewis remembers nothing unusual about the crossing and says no one suffered from seasickness. Sergeant Lewis and his eleven-man squad were on one of three DUKWs carrying their platoon, along with the platoon leader, Lt. Leo van de Voort; his radio operator, Richard Jeffries; and a 57-millimeter antitank gun.

> We left the LST before daylight so we could rendezvous. We had to go out in a big circle, round and round and round, and of course we lost half of them there. They would just turn over and sink. The DUKW would ride up a swell, and instead of coming back down, it would go in—the gun and the whole bit. If it had been clear weather, we wouldn't have had any problems.
>
> We headed in, and I saw the battleship *Texas*. They fired a broadside when we were still not too far from them. It was a god-awful terrible explosion that went out when they turned loose. The smoke ring, it passed us, it looked like a tornado, it kept getting bigger and bigger, and finally it disintegrated, and by then they fired another round. We were about a block or so from it. I don't believe we should have been that close even. Anyway, there were the *Nevada* and the *Arkansas* also firing. One French cruiser, a camouflaged thing, did a good job and got in awful close; he was inviting them to do battle with him. He shelled the hell out of them. We saw the destroyers come in close to the beach.
>
> The DUKW was like a truck. We were down heavy with a big load on there. The

9. This gun finally arrived ashore and was used by another battalion since the 111th had lost all of its guns.

guy [driver] was busy trying to keep it heading in. He would let the waves come behind it and push it along. If you should cut across, there you were going to turn over sure as hell in a big storm. When we got to the metal obstacles out there, I saw a man hanging on to one of them. He was hollering for help. We were going by, but you can't control that boat very well, and we got pretty close to it and Lieutenant van de Voort yelled at him, "We are out here to kill people and not to save lives. Jump if you want on this damned thing!" He jumped and came onboard with us. We were going along and sheared a pin just like a motor-boat. We were in the area with Teller mines and were adrift. The mines were sticking out two or three feet above the water or partially in it. We drifted sideways and hit a mine more than once. We kept bumping it, but I guess the salt water deteriorated it, since it did not explode. The mine was strapped right onto the log. The Germans began to machine-gun the things, so we jumped out of it. There went the DUKW, the antitank gun, and everything. When it went in, I jumped in and could stand on my toes, except when a wave crashed over me.

The natural assumption was that the closer you went, the more solid it was going to get. That wasn't true, because sand had built up on these obstacles, and I just stepped off into a hole. You cannot swim with this weight we carried, including a gun and two bandoliers of ammo, a full field pack, helmet, and boots. Every time a wave crashed over you, you would feel for the bottom and keep paddling. You didn't go very far before you could touch the bottom again. I wasn't about to go back the other way; PFC Lewis Lorditch and I just kept coming in. We just kept coming in with the water, just dancing to that damn machine-gun fire around you. Lorditch ran towards a landing craft (appeared to be an LCT) for cover. It had turned on its side (landed in earlier waves). They shelled it immediately when Lorditch was in it. A big boom went off, and he came back out. The landing craft was set afire. He had run in there just as a shell hit it, and he came back out and then joined me.

A unit history of the 116th Infantry Regiment's operations in Normandy was prepared by division personnel in September 1944. Like many other histories put together after an operation, it includes many individual accounts that contradict each other. The account for the Anti-Tank Platoon of the 1st Battalion, based on an interview with Sergeant Balanski, who was in another DUKW, does not agree with that of Sergeant Lewis. According to Balanski, only two of the platoon's three DUKWs moved toward the beach. The third was swamped, and another vessel rescued the survivors and returned them to an LST for a trip back to England. As the two DUKWs moved forward, one of them lost power, and supposedly its squad transferred onto the other DUKW. Sergeant Lewis has no recollection of such a difficult transfer at sea, but there is no reason he should, even if it did occur, since he was concerned about the problems his DUKW was having at the time. Balanski's DUKW finally started up again and returned only to reach the DUKW that had broken down more than a mile from the beach. According to this confused story, Lieutenant van de Voort eventually changed DUKWs, but Sergeant Lewis recalls the lieutenant being onboard as they drifted among the obstacles. Supposedly, Balanski's DUKW landed later in the afternoon on Easy Red, whereas Lieutenant van de Voort and Bill Lewis's squad landed in the morning on Easy Red. Judging by Sergeant Lewis's description, he was on or near Dog

Green. The fact that his squad was rounded up later in the day by Maj. Tom Dallas and moved up through the Vierville draw to the chateau on the outskirts of Vierville corroborates Lewis's story.

Once on the beach, Sergeant Lewis and his squad finally made it to the seawall, cold and scared.

> Larry Vogt piled in there on top of us. He said, "Is that you shaking, Sarge?" "Yeah, damn right!" I replied. He said, "My God, I thought that was me!" and I looked at him and he was shaking like me. We were huddled there just trying to save our lives. You couldn't do anything. The fire became heavier. As they [the other landing troops] came along, they could all see the seawall, so they got on top of you trying to get below the damn thing. So that is when old van de Voort, a real tough cookie, said, "Let's go, goddamn it! There ain't no use staying here, or we are all going to get killed!" He took Larry Vogt and a few others, and he told me to stay behind because I looked like I needed some rest. The first thing he did was to run up there to a gun emplacement, and he threw a grenade in there and brought back about five or six Germans with him. Larry stayed with me and the squad, and the lieutenant disappeared, going back against the Germans. We spent the remainder of the morning pinned on the beach.

Sergeant Lewis's squad suffered no losses on June 6. Lewis knows of no other losses in the platoon, although he and his squad did not rejoin it for several days. This would explain why Lieutenant van de Voort disappeared that morning after bringing back the first prisoners.[10] With just one badly shaken squad onshore, without a gun, and armed only with rifles, the lieutenant probably felt he would not be able to carry out his original support mission. So van de Voort moved on to see what he could do to get the troops off the beach.

Sergeant Lewis's men spent most of the morning behind the seawall.

> On the beach, all the guys were walking back and forth with shirts stained with blood. That afternoon, a bulldozer came on in and hit a land mine, and there was nothing but two pieces of track where that baby hit.
>
> A 1st Division sergeant, a veteran, arrived in the afternoon and told us to get some fire on that bunker [a large one near the exit]. He told everybody to get up and start firing on the embrasures. He took some men and went up there, but I didn't go. They went up there and took some bangalore torpedoes and put them under the bunker. It stopped the fire that had been murdering us.

Bill Lewis is not really sure when the 1st Division sergeant arrived, but he is certain it was before Lieutenant van de Voort went out and brought back the first prisoners they saw that day. Later in the day, a messenger from Maj. Tom Dallas, the battalion XO, told Lewis to move his men up the beach and through the draw to Vierville.

Major Dallas had landed with the 1st Battalion headquarters. His group was lowered on an LCA from the British LSI *Empire Javelin*, only to get hung up under the outlet for the heads. After they were trapped there for a while, with effluent spilling all over their vessel, they finally got the ship's davits to function properly. His vessel came in slightly east of the Vierville draw where some Rangers had already landed. Here his small group was trapped a good while at the base of the cliffs. Later in the day, he made it off the beach and

10. He also received the Distinguished Service Cross for his actions that day.

rounded up those left behind to form up near Vierville, where Sergeant Lewis saw him.

During the morning, 1st Lt. John A. McAllister of Battery C, 227th FA, transferred from the LST in which he had crossed the Channel to a landing craft (he is not sure what type) to land ahead of his battalion as a forward observer. His battery remained onboard the remainder of the day. On the LST, he had been able to see the events unfolding on the beach, but once he boarded the landing craft, the beach was out of sight. His team, armed only with carbines, was the first off when the ramp came down. It was followed by the infantrymen, who he believes had deliberately put his forward observervation team in front to avoid being first out. They had to wade toward shore under enemy fire. Once they reached the beach, they spent a good part of the day pinned down. Eventually McAllister's team exited through the Vierville draw and joined with elements of the 2nd Battalion. In his opinion, none of the forward observers from the 29th Division had much success that day.

The Navy Comes to the Rescue

Several destroyers were stationed at 5,000 to 7,000 yards from the beach for naval fire support after the landings began. The American *Satterlee* and the British *Talybont* supported the Rangers at Pointe du Hoc. After 8 A.M., as the situation ashore deteriorated, Capt. Harry Sanders ordered his destroyers to move closer for better support. The *McCook* approached at about 1,300 yards from shore to help the troops of the 116th Infantry pinned down near the Vierville strongpoints. The *Carmick* moved within 900 yards, seeking targets of opportunity in the 116th Infantry sectors. The *Doyle* supported the troops on Easy Red.

On D-Day, Lt. Cmdr. James L. Semmes, whose brother commanded another destroyer in the Pacific, brought his destroyer, the *Frankford*, within 800 yards of the shore, risking being grounded, to pound the enemy positions near the Colleville exit and farther down the beach.

> We could see wounded and dead men all over the sand and smashed landing craft everywhere. There were thousands of troops huddled at the base of a hill, pinned down. It was heartrending to see all those bodies littering the beach. We thought the invasion was falling on its face. Through binoculars and our gunnery telescopes, we could see the flashes of machine-gun fire on the slope, and we opened fire on them.

The 5-inch guns of Semmes's ship concentrated on a ridge above the beach where German positions protected the exit. After blasting away an enemy position, the ship's crew watched a soldier move cautiously up the hill and wave to his comrades to come on. A little later, as the sailors watched, the ship's loudspeaker announced that twenty-two prisoners were being led down the hill. The crew let out a triumphant shout. The *Frankford* continued to support the troops onshore for hours. The German gunners put a number of rounds near the intrepid destroyer but never scored a hit.

According to Rear Adm. Alan G. Kirk, aboard the flagship *Augusta*, the destroyers ventured so close to Omaha Beach that "they had their bows against the bottom." The *Thompson* took out the radar position at Pointe de la Percée, the objective of Company C of the 2nd Rangers, which was tied up near Vierville at the time. The *Thompson* was also credited with the destruction of the *Nebelwerfer* battery at about noon. The *Baldwin* was the only destroyer actually hit by the enemy, but it sustained little damage. All these ships had to fire at targets of opportunity, because the shore fire-control parties had taken many casualties and were unable to operate for most of the day.

Many years later, James E. Knight, a member of the 299th Engineers, wrote in a letter to a member of the *Frankford* crew, reprinted in *Semmes America*:

> I landed on Omaha at H-Hour plus three minutes as a member of a Special Demolition Team of the 299th Combat Engineer Battalion, with the mission of blowing eight, 50-yard gaps in all three rows of obstacles in front of the 1st Infantry Division's eastern half of Omaha Beach.
>
> This was to take place after . . . 26 or 28 amphibious tanks touched down on the beach to pick up the fire and keep the Germans, now reeling from the devastating bombardments . . . hopefully pinned down while we attempted to accomplish our mission.
>
> Unfortunately, things didn't go anywhere near the way they were planned. The air bombardment landed way inland . . . as did most of the naval shells. The shell and bomb craters that were to provide us cover when we set off our charges were practically nonexistent and only one of the amphibious tanks made it in. . . . Nearly all units landed from a few yards to a few hundred yards from their designated objectives. . . .
>
> The first few hours half of several thousand men that managed to survive and reach the dune line were pinned down. . . .
>
> I landed on the eastern end of Omaha and was fortunate to be where the sandy dune line was replaced by a rock formation that gradually rose from a few inches to over a hundred feet high, being about seven–eight feet high and providing excellent cover except for mortars. As a result I was facing the channel during the first few hours. All of a sudden, at about 10:00 or 10:30 (my guesstimate), out of a sea swarming with dozens of various size and type landing crafts and DUKWs, a destroyer loomed, headed straight toward me. My first thought was that it had either struck a mine or had taken a torpedo, and though it wasn't listing or smoking, it must be damaged bad enough that they are beaching it. While I was coming up with the reasons for it heading in, it started to turn right and before it completed its turn to be parallel to the beach, all its guns opened fire simultaneously.
>
> The shells landed just a few yards above my rock cover. As it proceeded toward the western end of the beach, I continued to watch it and wondered how it could be so close and not be taking any artillery or mortar hits. As I watched it go farther and farther from me, I expected to see it pull out to sea, when suddenly I realized it was backing up, and its guns had yet to pause since commencing fire. It backed up almost to where it had started, went dead in the water for a second time, still to my knowledge, without taking a hit, and again headed toward the other end of the beach, with all guns still blazing. When it reached the western section of the beach it pulled out to sea.

In 1989, another member of the 299th Engineers, Barton A. Davis, corroborated much of Knight's account of the *Frankford*'s action.

> Apparently Jim was in the same section of beach as I. . . . How well I remember your ship coming in so close. . . . As I recall, the gun position just above where I was pinned down . . . would fire at you, and your ship would answer with at least two turrets forward, and possibly stern guns as well. I recall seeing a spout of water just in front of the bow and thought, "Boy, that was close!"
>
> The gun in the pillbox . . . couldn't bear on us on the beach directly, since we stayed close to the slight cliff. . . . Your ship not only knocked out the pillbox but also the

mortar positions above us. The infantry could then attack up the hill.

Both James Knight and Barton Davis, whose account appears in *Semmes America*, reported that the *Frankford* sailed in closer than any other destroyer, and that its devastating fire made it possible for the 16th Infantry to get off the beach. It appears from their account that they were in a position near E-3.

The Provisional Ranger Group and Pointe du Hoc

As other units prepared to make their early-morning assault on June 6, 1944, the Provisional Ranger Group, under the leadership of Colonel Rudder, readied for a nearly impossible mission. The Provisional Ranger Group was formed from the 2nd and 5th Ranger Battalions and consisted of three forces labeled A, B, and C. Companies D, E, and F of the 2nd Rangers formed Force A, which numbered approximately 225 men. Company C, led by Capt. Ralph Goranson, formed Force B. The remaining companies of the 2nd Rangers, as well as those of the 5th Rangers under Lt. Col. Max Schneider, formed Force C.

Force A's main objective was the German battery on top of Pointe du Hoc. The success of its mission depended on the air and naval bombardment, which was to pin the Germans in their shelters long enough for the Rangers to land on the narrow beach and scale the cliffs. Force B was to land to the right of the 116th Infantry, scale the cliffs, eliminate a German radar position and a strongpoint near Pointe de la Percée, and advance on Pointe du Hoc. Force C would reinforce Force A on Pointe du Hoc only if the leading companies of the 2nd Rangers signaled that they had been successful.

At 6:10 A.M., after the naval bombardment ended, eighteen medium bombers from the Ninth Air Force bombed Pointe du Hoc. Colonel Rudder decided to personally lead Force A ashore below Pointe du Hoc. After launching the LCAs from the British LSIs *Ben Machree* and *Amsterdam*, things did not go well. *LCA 860*, carrying Capt. Harold K. Slater and twenty men of Company D, was swamped. The survivors, who were rescued, returned to England. Next, one of the LCAs carrying supplies went down. A second one was in danger of being swamped, so the men dumped all of the packs it carried for Companies D and E. The Rangers on the other LCAs had to bail out water to keep their vessels afloat. Most of the Rangers and their scaling equipment were soaked before they even left their landing craft, and the entire group drifted too far east. When Colonel Rudder discovered the error, he ordered the coxswains to move back toward their objective. Meanwhile, the air bombing had stopped and the Germans emerged from their shelters and began firing on the assault force. By then, the element of surprise was lost. Rudder's Rangers landed thirty minutes behind schedule, and the Ranger companies of Force C waiting to reinforce the assault failed to receive the signal they awaited. Lieutenant Colonel Schneider stayed in position an additional ten to fifteen minutes, waiting for the signal, before he diverted his battalion to land in the sector of the 116th Infantry, leaving the three companies of Rangers at Pointe du Hoc without reinforcements.

As it moved west toward the cliffs, Rudder's force lost one of its DUKWs to German fire coming from the positions on the cliffs it was paralleling. In the meantime, the British destroyer *Talybont* closed in to support the Rangers by bombarding the German positions on the cliffs for fifteen minutes, while the American destroyer *Satterlee* fired on German troops concentrating above Pointe du Hoc.

The bombardment had pockmarked the beach with craters that the supporting DUKWs were unable not negotiate. The Germans continued to fire down upon the Rangers as they scrambled

Omaha Beach with the dead still washing ashore after the invasion.

for the base of the cliff. The *Satterlee* kept spraying the cliff tops, keeping some of the pressure off the Rangers. The naval bombardment tore chunks out of the cliff. Company D was supposed to land on the west side of Pointe du Hoc, Company E and F on the east side. But since the battalion's LCAs were off course and had to move back toward the point, Company D landed on the east side, between the other two companies. The wet, slippery clay of the cliffs added to their woes. Undaunted, the Rangers took on the cliffs with their special ladders, toggle ropes, and other scaling equipment. The rocket-launched rope ladders were a great asset for many groups in their ascent. The debris from the naval bombardment of the cliff face gave the Rangers a platform to begin their climb, shortening the distance to the top. Two DUKWs with extension ladders for scaling the cliffs were not able to get past the cratered surface, and the ladder on one DUKW could not be raised high enough to reach the cliff. S.Sgt. William Stivison clung to the ladder of another DUKW, firing a twin Vickers machine gun eighty feet in the air, swaying with the waves, and looking like a circus performer as he drew enemy fire.

Despite all the problems, within ten minutes of the initial landing, the first six Rangers, including Lt. T. E. Lapres Jr. of Company E, climbed over the top. They quickly moved against their objective, a large observation bunker at the end of the point. The German strongpoint looked like a lunar surface, with all its recognizable features gone and its open emplacements and most of its casemates badly damaged or already destroyed. To the Rangers' disappointment, the German battery of 155-millimeter guns was not there.

According to the War Department Historical Report: "The climbing parties had gone ahead with speed, determination and resourcefulness, ready to improvise when necessary. This was the main reason for their success, and for the fact that within 30 minutes from touchdown all the attacking force was on top except for casualties, headquarters personnel, and some mortar men (30 to 40 Rangers out of about 190)."

Elements of three Ranger companies, each numbering only about sixty-five men at full strength, moved against the German force defending the fortified position, drove it back, and prepared to withstand enemy counterattacks without any reinforcements from the sea. Lieutenant Lapres's group attacked the observation bunker, only to find that another group of Rangers had preceded him from the other side. Later, another group spotted the Germans still firing from the bunker. The next day, the Rangers brought up explosives, believing that they had forced the remaining Germans into underground tunnels linking the bunker to other positions, from which they got reinforcements. By 9 A.M. on June 6, the Rangers had cleared most of the German positions, with the notable exception of the antiaircraft bunker on the west flank, which became a serious problem. Groups of Rangers moved across the fields bordered by hedgerows all the way to the hard-surfaced coast road. Small groups of Germans infiltrated behind them, however, and captured one small party of Rangers, who were never seen again. PFC William Cruz found German weapons stacked up near one of the abandoned gun positions, and warned his superiors that the enemy was using underground tunnels, which may only have been partially covered communication trenches.

The Rangers astride the main highway eagerly awaited the relief force consisting of the 5th Rangers from Omaha Beach. Little did they know that most of the troops on Omaha Beach were still pinned down, and that only one small Ranger platoon, by error, had actually left the beachhead perimeter and would arrive later in the evening.

After 9 A.M., 1st Sgt. Leonard Lomell and S.Sgt. Jack Kuhn went out on a two-man patrol. They discovered the five missing 155-millimeter guns reportedly about 250 yards inland, in position to fire on Utah Beach and with no Germans on guard while the gun crews were in bivouac nearby. Sergeant Lomell disabled two of the guns with thermite grenades and smashed the sights on another. The two Rangers went back for more thermite grenades and returned to finish sabotaging the remaining guns.[11] Meanwhile, another patrol, under S.Sgt. Frank Rupinksi, discovered an ammunition dump south of the German battery and used explosives to detonate it. The explosion startled Lomell and Kuhn, who hastened back to their group. On their way back, they glimpsed a large force of Germans, most likely the crew from the battery, that appeared to be reorganizing about 100 yards from the guns. Lomell and his dozen Rangers held an advance position and silently watched as about 130 Germans filed past them through a hedgerow opening, heading toward the point, according to Ronald Lane's *Rudder's Rangers*.

As night drew near, the 2nd Rangers, led by Colonel Rudder, had a tenuous hold on Pointe du Hoc. They occupied positions along the coast road, but their supplies and ammunition were low, and in a number of cases they had to rely on captured German weapons and grenades. That evening, Lieutenant Parker's platoon from the 5th Rangers reach Pointe du Hoc. The platoon had left Omaha Beach from the rendezvous point mistakenly believing that the battalion had

11. The thermite grenades were relatively silent and did not alert the nearby Germans already distracted by other sounds of battle. The high heat created by one of these grenades would have left a molten mass, which might have been on the mechanism controls or in the breech, depending on where the grenade was placed, making the weapon unserviceable. Recent research by Texas A&M University has concluded the guns were about half a mile or more away from the point, not 250 yards, and sited to fire on Utah Beach.

already moved out to relieve Rudder's men. Parker's men helped defend against the German night assaults, which finally drove the 2nd Rangers back from the road to the battery position on the point. Some Rangers were captured during the night battle, but the remnants of the three companies held out.

First Lt. James W. Eikner, who served as the communications officer for the 2nd Rangers, was with the companies assaulting Pointe du Hoc. He was a member of the Headquarters Detachment with Lieutenant Colonel Rudder and was greatly disappointed with the behavior of Capt. Cleveland Lytle, the battalion XO, who was supposed to lead the assault force against Pointe du Hoc. Apparently, while he was still on the ship, Captain Lytle received intelligence indicating that the guns had been removed from Pointe du Hoc and that his unit was on a pointless suicide mission. After getting drunk, he argued with the medical officer over the importance of the mission. Colonel Rudder temporarily relieved him of duty, because he felt that Lytle might cause the mission of Force A to fail if he did not believe in it. Rudder, against the wishes of Gen. Clarence Huebner of the 1st Division, decided to take command of the force, attacking the point himself.

According to after-action accounts, Lieutenant Eikner and his group came ashore in *LCA 888* with Lieutenant Colonel Rudder, although James Eikner does not agree with those accounts and recalls the events as follows:

> On D-Day morning, we got up about 2 A.M. We had a light breakfast and coffee. The colonel and I, we decided rather than load up the headquarters people as scheduled that we ought to split our people up in case one boat was hit. History said I was in the colonel's boat, but I wasn't, although I was supposed to be. I was in one of the Company E boats, I think *722*.[12]
>
> It seemed like we were on the water forever. We were watching the naval gunfire. Here came the rockets—a beautiful thing to see—and then the first thing you know, some of the damn things are falling around us.
>
> Just as daylight broke, we could make out the headlands. We were heading for a point jutting out into the sea, but it didn't look right. Colonel Rudder was the first to notice that we were headed for Pointe de la Percée. The British had three small craft giving us protection for this run in and taking care of navigation—two little gunboats with a half-pounder cannon and another British boat with something heavier. Anyhow, we were taken to the wrong damn point, so we had to turn right and parallel the shore, while already in small-arms range, for a couple of miles to get to Pointe du Hoc. The Germans were shooting at us like in a shooting gallery. When the first bullet hit our craft, it went through one of the boxes. We had six in each craft: two up front, two amidships, and two aft. Somebody said, "What's that?" I looked up and saw a little round hole in there. We had all been standing, looking, stretching our necks. "Get down, boys!" came the command.
>
> Of course, when we turned right, we turned into the waves. These boats were heavily loaded, and the water was coming in the front. We had to take our helmets and bail. So there we were, being shot at and using our helmets to bail. Some of the boys were sick and puking. We had already lost one boat, that of Captain Slater. He was our most "gung-ho" Ranger company com-

12. Ronald Lane noted in *Rudder's Rangers* that Eikner came ashore with a cloverleaf of mortar rounds, so it may be that he was on *LCA 722*, since it carried a 60-millimeter mortar, although Lane placed him on *LCA 888*.

mander. Most of his men were saved. I had a radioman with him, and he broke radio silence and said, "Sinking, sinking, sunk!" He couldn't even swim, but his Mae West saved him. Then we lost a supply boat to this bad weather. Our other supply boat had to throw off about half of everything they carried to just stay afloat. We wound up with no packs or supplies, hardly anything.

A British destroyer noticed our difficulty and took the enemy under fire. They could see the Germans rushing to the edge of the cliff and shooting. We didn't see them standing at the guns, but I remember distinctly the 20-millimeter incendiaries coming close by.

I was in an LCA. We had to change the landing pattern, because originally Company D was going to land on the west side of the point and Companies E and F on the east side. Since we lost one Company D boat and we had to approach Pointe du Hoc laterally, it screwed up the plan, so we had to land everything on the east side. We landed thirty-eight minutes late. The Germans had time to get up out of their foxholes and find out what was going on. They were up on the cliff shooting at us.

I was the last man off of my boat. Many of us had something to take off, like extra ammo. I agreed to take off a cloverleaf of 60-millimeter mortar shells. When it came my time, I was running along, and I saw the other guys splashing along in the water. The shell holes from the bombing were filling up as the tide was coming in. I stepped in one of those and went down. I fished the mortar shells out and set them up under the cliff. I saw ropes right in front of me with a couple of guys going up, so I went up right behind them. I could see the Krauts bending over the top shooting at us. About that time, a terrible explosion occurred and I don't know how it affected those two guys, but I remember the dirt and rock coming down. It knocked me down, and I caught on a ledge before hitting the bottom and was covered up to my knees. I was looking for my tommy gun, and I took a bead on the German up there and tried to fire. It was clogged up and full of clay. It seemed humorous to me then.

I looked around and looked in that cliff. I saw an antenna by a small cave, sticking out. We had already sent the signal to authorize the main force to turn back and land at Omaha Beach—the code word for that was "TILT."[13] I had assigned the phrases. This was sent out, I think, by Colonel Rudder's radioman. I saw this radioman down there, but I didn't know who he was. Later, I sent the code word that the first man was up the cliff. When all essential people were up, the code was "PRAISE THE LORD."

I came across several wounded guys, to one of whom I gave a shot of morphine. I got some stones to give him protection. I took the radioman and went down and ran into Colonel Trevor, the British commando colonel, and said that we'd better be careful, since we were under fire. He told some of the guys, "They can't hit you if you change your stride" and "You take a long step, then a short one!" It wasn't long before he had a patch on his head after one creased him right under his helmet.

I found my other two communications boys, and we found a shell hole. We had our big hand-cranked generator set ready on the beach within five minutes after we had landed. We were available for communications at that time, but nothing was coming in, because everything was in a mess on the

13. Schneider's group indicated that no signal was sent. Later, in his account, Eikner mentions that the "TILT" code was sent late.

POWs evacuated from Omaha Beach.

main beach. We had no one with whom to communicate.

Higher headquarteres gave us thirty minutes to knock these guns out, and if the escalade were not successful, the main force would land down on the main beach and hike up. In addition to the "TILT" code, we were going to fire a white flare from a mortar. They received no notification, but the "TILT" was sent late.

I monitored with my SRC-300 radio all up and down the line, trying to find somebody. When I would find somebody, I would break in on him, but I couldn't find anybody who would do business with me. We had a challenge and reply system in code words. You had to consult your little book and see what your response would be. I was challenged two or three times and gave the wrong response. The trouble was, they had changed the signal operating instruction and had not notified the Rangers.

[After ascending the cliff,] we set up over an underground bunker and used it for an aid station. I was up there about 7:30 or 7:40 A.M. We were in this shell hole facing the sea. The toggle ropes and steel ladder were already there when I went up. We were busy as hell with messages coming in from the companies and getting messages out. About midmorning, I set up the World War I–era signal lamp. About an hour later, the guns

> were knocked out [Lomell had found them farther inland and destroyed them], and we sent a message back: "Mission accomplished, need ammunition, food and reinforcements." We had to send that two or three times by every means: radio, pigeons, signal lamp. Finally, the message came that all Ranger forces had been committed—in other words, "Sorry boys, no reinforcements!"

Lieutenant Eikner remembers two German counterattacks that afternoon, each involving small arms and machine guns. The Rangers, on the other hand, had a lone 60-millimeter mortar that was missing its sights. Eikner sent two of his radiomen, Louis Lisko and Stephen Liscinsky, down the cliff to retrieve ammunition from the sunken vessels. They recovered about seventy-five rounds which the mortar crew put to good use.

During the morning, three paratroopers from the 101st A/B Division who had dropped far from their objective joined forces with them. Except for Lieutenant Parker's platoon from the 5th Rangers, there were no other reinforcements that day.[14]

The Follow-Up Units on D-Day

The 16th Infantry of the 1st Division was followed by the 18th Infantry, and the 116th Infantry by the 115th Infantry of the 29th Division. Numerous supporting units also disembarked during the day. The main landing area was on Easy Red for both follow-up regiments. Later in the day, the 26th Infantry of the 1st Division landed at Fox Green. If not for German fire, the follow-up waves would have been an anticlimax. The 115th Infantry moved up Exit E-1, which opened in the afternoon, and by evening it had deployed south and east of St. Laurent on both sides of the main road. The 18th Infantry landed its 1st Battalion at 12:30 P.M. on Easy Red and Fox Green. Its 3rd Battalion arrived after 1 P.M. under German artillery fire. These battalions moved over the bluffs, near the site of the present-day American Cemetery, and took up positions on the south side of the main road between St. Laurent and Colleville. In the meantime, the 2nd Battalion moved to a position south of Colleville between elements of the 2nd Battalion, 16th Infantry, on the west edge of Colleville, still in German hands, and the 3rd Battalion, 16th Infantry, at Le Grand Hameau. The 26th Infantry's 2nd and 3rd Battalions moved to a position between the 115th and the 18th Infantries, while its 1st Battalion took up positions just north of Cabourg, also still in enemy hands, to protect the approaches to exits F-1 and E-3.

Exit D-1 at Vierville and Exit D-3, which were the only hard-surfaced roads off the beach, were the last to be cleared. D-3 was the last to fall, late in the day. Exit E-1 required some work to make it passable to vehicles, since it was closed by two concrete walls more than eight feet high and six feet thick, with a tank trap in front. Sgt. Noel Dube, at the head of a squad from Company C, 121st Engineers, was assigned the task of moving from Easy Red to Dog Green to blow up the wall, with several men and two dozers from his company. The squad placed ten cases of TNT against the objective and blew away both walls in the afternoon. None of the men can say with certainty, however, at what precise moment they accomplished their mission.

A few supporting units, such as tank battalions, struggled forward to support the infantry

14. Twenty-five of the 153 Distinguished Service Crosses awarded for actions in Normandy from June 6 to 8 were given to officers and men of the 2nd and 5th Rangers: Lieutenant Colonels Rudder and Schneider; Major Sullivan; Captains Goranson, Arnold, Masny, and Whittington; Lieutenants Dawson, Kerchner, Lacy, Moody, and Parker; Sergeants Belcher, Belmont, Courtney, James, Johnson, Lomell, Moody, and White; Tech 5s Clark and McKissic; and PFCs Alexander, Dreher, and Stephens.

regiments that night. Fortunately, the Germans were not able to launch any significant counterattack in the morning or afternoon. Although the American invasion force failed to reach its assigned objectives, which included an advance south of the main road running from Bayeux to Isigny, the Germans were unable to move enough troops to a point from which they could launch a counterattack against the Omaha Beachhead. The successful British landings at Juno, Gold, and Sword posed too serious a threat for the Germans to divert sorely needed units toward Omaha Beach. At the same time, the forces at Carentan and in the Cotentin Peninsula had to deal with the successful landings at Utah, with the invaders advancing to reinforce the scattered airborne units.

The 115th and 18th Infantries landed at about noon on Easy Red. Pvt. A. B. Mirmelstein of the 115th Infantry's Company H recorded the day's events in his diary.

> June 6, 1944, went up on deck 9:30 A.M., in combat formation preparing to land. First sight of European continent three to four miles offshore, high cliffs and great columns of smoke. Overhead thousands of planes and many other ships in convoy, all types; LCVP's to battleships. Our ship began to circle because of inability to land. Confusion on beach. At 10:40 A.M. ship land. Went down the ramp 20 yards offshore into five feet of water. Threw ammunition overboard in order to get to shore. Took shelter behind rocks. Cut off life preserver. Company gained top of Easy Red, Omaha Beach, with only one casualty. Took first town and fought way inland against moderate resistance. Snipers in trees serious threat.

T/5 Maxwell B. Moffett of the Medical Detachment was assigned as aid man for Company E, 2nd Battalion, 115th Infantry.

> I had my hands full with seasickness. Some of the men had the shakes of fear, some didn't know what was about to happen and what they were about to face, even though we had been trained for this. Aid men in all the companies were told not to stop on the beach to fix the wounded, since the navy aid men would do that.
>
> What I remember is the smoke that was laid down from the marsh grass that was afire. Small-arms fire once in a while and mortar shells would land. But we were told on the boat to hit the beach and keep moving to the high ground. Follow the white engineer tape through the minefields were the instructions. That night, D-Day was about the biggest fireworks I had ever seen. No sleep, even though we were dead tired.

Second Lt. Charlie A. Miller from Baton Rouge, Louisiana, the 1st Platoon leader of Company I, 3rd Battalion, 115th Infantry, remembers the skipper of the vessel yelling at him and his men to get off, while the control party onshore shouted for them not to because the water was too deep.

> We landed. The beach was filled with men. The dead and wounded were all around. My company landed at noon and by evening had moved single file off the beach and into the hills. Some of the wounded soldiers, some seriously, seemed to be not too worried, and pleased. They were not in much pain, because they had been administered morphine. As we moved up to higher ground, the tanks were moving through minefields. Numerous enemy rounds were fired at them.

Sam Zittrer of New York, who had enlisted in 1940 and taken part in the North African campaign, was in the HQ Company of the 1st Battalion of the 18th Infantry. He was assigned as a bazooka man and had an assistant to carry a couple of rounds. He left the LCI on which he had crossed the Channel for an LCVP. His group was scheduled to land at H+195. His first sight of Omaha Beach was unforgettable.

> I saw a lot of broken-up landing barges on the beach. I saw the shells coming in. They were using a great deal of mortars on us. The LCVP opened up the front gate, and we proceeded to go off and up to our necks in water. I'm glad that I put all my valuables in my parachute gas mask—we called it a parachute gas mask because we held it under our chin. It was a black miniature gas mask. It was waterproof, and I put all of my valuables in it. We got to the beach, and we proceeded up the beach to where there was a long row of pebbles [the shingle]. For some reason, we stopped and hit the pebble beach. The stuff was coming in pretty fast. I hadn't even loaded my rifle. As we got up to proceed inland, I got hit. I believe it was a mortar. I got hit pretty bad in both legs. My bazooka man got a big cut, and I told him he'd be all right. They moved on and I just stayed where I was. I took off my pack, my bazooka, my M-1 rifle, and bandoliers of ammunition. In about twenty minutes or so, a medic came over. He wanted to bandage me, but I told him he had better get in a prone position. The shells were landing, and there was shrapnel flying all over the place. He bandaged me and inserted a morphine Syrette, which we all carried. He left to bandage other men around us, and I happened to notice about fifteen to twenty yards away, where I had left my pack and gas mask, that all of my valuables were in it. But I didn't want to take the chance to get up and get it.
>
> I laid up on that beach all day. I saw the entire show. Every time a tank would come by, which wasn't too frequent, we would motion them to keep on going, because we figured the artillery would sight the tanks and miss them and hit us. At about 5:30–6:00, a couple of soldiers took pity on me, put me on a rubber raft, and brought me onto a small boat. I stayed there for a while then we went out into the channel and transferred to an LST—it might have been an LSM.

Duwaine Raatz, a twenty-five-year-old draftee from Twin Rivers, Wisconsin, was assigned as a messenger in the 1st Battalion of the 18th Infantry. He was a veteran of two other invasions with the 1st Division. He landed shortly after noon near Exit E-1 on Easy Red, where confusion reigned. Although he thought he knew what to expect, he was unprepared for the situation he found on the morning of June 6.

> When I saw the beaches of Normandy, France, my spirits dropped. There were stakes, ramps, obstacles, and curved rails sticking out of the water. That is when I started to pray and think about what I was going to do. I was the jeep driver for the message center.
>
> After the guns and engineers got an opening to go through, I finally got my jeep off of that LST [more likely an LCT] and made it to shore, but not very far because of the sand. Many of my buddies were killed and wounded. I sure prayed, sweated, and cried the rest of the day. I was wounded twice before, and I figured, like the old saying, three times and out. The beach was full of tanks, jeeps, bulldozers, and equipment, so I could not go anyplace. I laid under my jeep until a shell would hit close, then I would run from one vehicle to another, back and forth, because I could not dig a foxhole in the beach sand. It seemed

> like the longest day of the year. I thought about home and everything else, but most of all about getting my jeep and myself off the beach.
>
> Then the navy [?] blew an opening in the hill, and the engineers got some wire mesh laid down upon the sand and over the hill, so some of my buddies and I lifted my jeep upon the wire mesh, so I could drive my jeep over the hill and off of the beach. Thank God for that!
>
> When I got to the top of the hill, I drove into a minefield, but lucky for me, the Germans had them all marked with a little yellow flag with skull and crossbones on it. Then I looked back at that beach. It sure was a mess. How I got off of there was with the help of the Almighty. There was more shelling, mortars, machine-gun fire, fires, dead bodies, knocked-out equipment, more than you can imagine. I hope I will never see anything like that again.

Eldon Wiehe, a truck driver in the 1st Division, had returned to his unit after a bout with malaria that had him hospitalized. He was assigned to a landing craft carrying seven vehicles, a lieutenant, and about a dozen other troops. His group was to land about an hour after the invasion, but after one of the landing craft near his was hit, the skipper of his vessel turned away and did not attempt a landing for a couple of hours. When they returned, they came under heavy fire, and the craft turned back out to sea once again. At about noon, a small vessel came out and ordered the skipper to take his craft in and unload. As the ramp went down, it came under enemy fire. After the first vehicle drove off and sank, the lieutenant yelled at skipper to take them in closer. The skipper refused, however, and ordered them to unload. The remaining trucks drove off the ramp and sank one by one. Next, the men waded in and heard incoming artillery fire as they reached the beach.

> I jumped into a shell hole without looking; I didn't have time. When the shell burst, I got up and I guess I panicked. I started crying. There was a ship to our right, and my buddies got me behind that ship, where I cried for what seemed like hours. I cried until tears would no longer come. Suddenly I felt a warm feeling go through my body, and I came to my senses.
>
> There were four pillboxes, but we were sheltered by this ship. Soon we saw two bulldozers headed for the pillboxes with their blades up. They were successful in closing the holes the guns were shooting out of. On the return trip back to the road, one of them took a direct hit. The man on it seemed like he flew all to pieces.

They were stranded on the beach until about 4 P.M., when their lieutenant decided to go find a way off the beach. He returned soon and led them off the beach under enemy fire.

Clyde D. Strosnider, from West Virginia, was a twenty-two-year-old veteran of two invasions and served as a BAR man in Company I, 3rd Battalion, 26th Infantry, the last regiment to land on D-Day. He arrived on an LCI and disembarked in waist-deep water. His landing, although hectic, was much easier than the preceding ones. Strosnider and his company struggled through the surf, crossed the beach, and passed single file through a minefield. His squad reached its assembly point beyond the beach well ahead of the rest of the company. Their radio did not work, however, and they became lost. Suddenly both Americans and Germans began firing on them.

> Finally a troop truck came along, and in the cab was a man and woman soldier. From the camouflage job on it, I thought it was one of those British lorries. But after it got by, I realized it was German and I opened fire on

Taking care of the wounded at Fox Green sector on Omaha Beach.

> it, but my gun jammed on me because of all the sand and water in the gun.
>
> We tried to contact our troops by hollering to them that we were American, but they wouldn't believe us. They kept asking us questions. "The Germans know how to speak English too," they said. They asked us questions like who played on the New York Yankee teams and who played for Baltimore.

Strosnider's squad occupied a position near a hedgerow. Some enemy soldiers were located just a few hundred yards away in a clump of trees but did not give them much trouble. Strosnider and his squad settled down for the night. They had survived another invasion.

The engineer units from the gap assault teams that arrived during the day with the first wave took heavy losses trying to clear the enemy obstacles under fire, but their work was critical in clearing a path on the beach for the successive waves. They had to clear the mined area at the exits and remove and destroy the obstacles before high tide that morning.

Units such as the 336th Combat Engineer Battalion were temporarily attached to the 348th Engineer Beach Group and had specific duties for their landing on the afternoon of D-Day. This battalion's Company A serves as an excellent example. According to the plans, it was to land on Easy Red and move laterally in an easterly direction along the beach, if possible; otherwise, it was to move inland. After that, the company was to divide into Security, Mine Removal, and General Engineer Platoons. The Security Platoon was to set up two .50-caliber machine guns on the high ground to the left of Exit F-1. Two other .50-caliber machine-gun teams would be held in reserve. The mine removal section was to move out with a patrol along the cliff line and clear it of mines. It was also to send a section with a shoreline patrol and a third section inland with a third patrol. The road through F-1 was to be cleared in time for a platoon of engineers to complete a road before H+12. After this mission was completed, a DUKW park and battalion maintenance area was to be cleared.[15] The General Engineer Platoon was to land with a couple of dozers and other engineering supplies.

As is often the case in war, however, not everything went according to plan. Company A, as part of the 5th Engineer Special Brigade, landed at about 3 P.M. Among its men was T/4 Byron C. Ruyle, who came ashore on Easy Red in his D-7 bulldozer towing a six-ton Athey trailer filled with the company's explosives. He touched land about 2,500 yards west of his original destination, because that was the only section of the beach where the obstacles had been cleared. While he moved along the beach behind the engineer column, a second bulldozer was hit and exploded. As soon as he reached Fox Red Beach at about 5 P.M., he began operations to open a road through Exit F-1. According to the history of the engineer group, Ruyle and Pvt. Delbert H. Hattrup received a Bronze Star because they "courageously performed their tasks without regard for the fact that bulldozers, as well as tanks, were 'drawing fire' from the enemy." They had traveled a distance of a mile and a half over open beach "while completely exposed to heavy enemy shell fire." The success of Company A in opening Exit F-1 was due entirely to the bravery of these two men.

That afternoon, the 336th's Company C arrived in two LCTs and also landed on Easy Red about 3,000 yards west of its objective. It was pinned down by enemy fire, but 1st Sgt. Harry C. Kaiser took charge and moved it across the beach to its designated objective. Still under heavy fire, with the help of several of his men, he began to salvage mine detectors left behind by the first-wave infantry troops and used them for mine-clearing operations at the exit. Before embarking at the marshalling area in England, he and a group of men had asked John Ready, a forward observer from the 1st Division and veteran of North Africa, what combat was like. Ready had told them, "Each guy sees it differently, but don't ever let yourself think that your number is up—that's when you will get it." Sergeant Kaiser took his advice to heart and received a battlefield commission for his leadership. Later, Kaiser was distressed to find John Ready buried at the nearby cemetery.

The 112th Combat Engineer Battalion was assigned to the sector of the 116th Infantry on Omaha Beach to support the operations of the 121st Combat Engineer Battalion of the 29th Division. The first elements of the battalion, with the mission of opening Exit D-3 and the road leading to St. Laurent, were to arrive by LCM by H+40. Company A landed at H+30 with the mission of clearing the roads of mines and setting up a motor vehicle transit area. Company C came in at the same time with the mission of acting as an assault company with the 2nd Battalion of the 116th Infantry, which attempted to clear the lateral road along the beach. Company B did not arrive until H+170 and had the mission of clearing roads inland from the beach.

The dozer drivers of the 112th Engineers wore flak suits obtained from the Air Corps, which protected them effectively while they were exposed during their road-clearing opera-

15. On both Omaha and Utah Beaches, general (noncombat) engineer units were to help in establishing maintenance and depot areas for the buildup. These included Class I, II, III and IV depots.

German prisoners being marched away above shattered position on Omaha Beach.

tions. The dozers arrived in LCMs that also carried many of the battalion's men. Many of the battalion vehicles were unloaded from their landing craft in deep water, and their engines flooded out. The battalion took heavy casualties on June 6. The battalion history describes the situation:

> The rising tides and uncleared obstructions made it difficult for the crafts to get close to shore but they boldly maneuvered through the obstructions as far as they could go, braving murderous fire.
>
> It was our first encounter with combat and our surroundings indicated that we had fierce resistance. Our troops were weighted down with a goodly store of engineer supplies and equipment, vital cargo to break through the outer crust of the enemy defenses.
>
> Some crafts had to unload in deep water. The waves charged in and men struggled and staggered as they pushed towards the beach. The landing was made under heavy enemy fire. The beach was under sporadic shelling and machine guns and snipers cut loose from the hills. The troops were pinned to the beach at the high water mark and as the tide came in, they inched their way forward.
>
> An Intelligence estimate . . . indicated one German Infantry Battalion . . . however, it was learned later that one offensive German Division was training in the area. This was the reason for the determined resistance and our delay in advancing inland. Defenses on Beach Exit D-3, Les Moulins, were especially reinforced with elements of this enemy division. This was the exit this

Landing craft and ships off Omaha Beach.

Battalion was to clear of obstacles for vehicular and tank movement.

Assault units of the battalion landed on OMAHA BEACH commencing H+30 to H+70. . . .

Our assault forces organized briefly on the beaches and courageously went over the top in the face of a seemingly hopeless position, through the mine fields and obstacles. More troops poured in from the boats. Shells continued to fall with devastating effect on the crafts, vehicles, beach exit and personnel.

Our Battalion reorganized on the beach during the afternoon. Our Battalion Commander, Major Richards, was killed early on D-Day. Major Bateman, Executive Officer, then assumed command and we prepared to move inland.

Several attempts were made by our units to perform their assigned missions early in the afternoon, but enemy resistance caused us to withdraw from the work until direct fire on the working parties had been neutralized.

At about 2000 hours [8 P.M.] on D-Day, our exit was opened by our units for traffic, roads were made passable. Work on one transit area had begun and the remainder of our battalion moved to the vicinity of St.-Laurent-sur-Mer to a suitable bivouac. . . .

The troops dug in, expending much effort digging deep into the hard ground in the black of night until early D+1. Our security was posted and the remainder of our command crawled into their foxholes to relax and rest after their first grueling day of war. The night air was cold and the wet clothing didn't add to the comforts of a foxhole. Sporadic fire by snipers in the vicinity of our bivouac area kept the guards and troops on the alert. Intermittent firing and

> shelling continued through the night. A few enemy planes encircled above, through our umbrella of anti-aircraft fire, working their way in to bomb the beach, which was lit up by smoldering fires of burning vehicles. . . .

First Sgt. Raus Blondo, of Detroit, the top NCO of Company B, 112th Engineers, who had been nicknamed "Fangs" by the company commander, Capt. Grandison Bienvenu, crossed the channel on *LST 410* loaded with DUKWs of the 461st Amphibious Truck Company. He wrote to his captain later:

> Arrived pulling a huge raft called Rhino with two large outboard motors and two men aboard having a hell of a rough ride. Poor devils. We were about twelve miles out when we unloaded into landing craft. The raft was to take on the motor vehicles we had aboard. We were supposed to land H+30, however we messed around at sea and did arrive ashore around nine thirty. I watched the warships and rocket launchers send their gifts to Hitler and trained the glasses ashore and saw them strike. Water was rough. Everyone was in a good mood and immediately shut up as two bodies floated by us.
>
> I was the ranking member aboard our craft. We had some of H&S personnel also. I never saw you [Captain Bienvenu] from the time we left the LST [on an LCVP] till I met you in the Orchard in St.-Laurent-sur-Mer.[16]
>
> The ramp went down and we were waist deep in water. We walked ashore. No shelling at that time. Just the zip, zip of small arms fire going by. Lots of smoke. Pappy Glen Kloth (at the edge of the water) asked me to cut his life preserver loose and I started to do so when an "88" shell came over and exploded a hundred yards away into the sea. I found myself standing there with my knife in my hand and Kloth was gone as were all the others. Just running like hell for the protection of the bluff which had many men crouched and glued to the sand, or digging in like mad. Many wounded around on litters waiting to be picked up and sent back to the ship.
>
> It did not take much encouragement for me to start my run for the safety of the vertical dirt at the base of the bluff. I was the last man off the beach and all men were ashore and no one was injured. The shells and small arms fire was now increased. I would run like hell and flop down awhile and up and run again.
>
> At one point I dove with hands outstretched and found myself beneath a body. Departed that area in a hurry and dove under a machine, a bulldozer that was stalled. Some of our men were calling to me and pointing up. I rolled over and looked up and was astonished to see that the rack on the top of the dozer was loaded with land mines. I did not fool around staying there. I left in a hurry with lead flying and nipping sand all around me. I made the protection to find our troops (Company B) strung out all to my left as I faced the Bluff.
>
> I can still see this very young GI with the Red One on his shirt sitting there with his teeth chattering and shivering in a state of shock. I do not think he was wounded. He would not talk to me. I tried to encourage him to dig in. He would not. I assigned one of our men to dig him a hole and pushed him into it.

16. Captain Bienvenu and many other men loaded onto the Rhino barge which carried many vehicles including two cranes. These probably did not land until late in the day.

I told the men to pass the word all along to the Captain wherever he might be, that we were all ashore and no casualties. I saw none of our officers. I made George "Punchy" Lazar my runner. Having no instructions yet I dug a hole. In doing so I was looking at the Dozer and all of a sudden there was a big explosion and the dozer was gone—a direct hit. M.P.s were walking German Prisoners down the beach. As soon as a craft would touch down the "88s" would go at it. I saw several small craft pulling the stalled Ducks [DUKWs] ashore. Many of them were drowned out. Landing craft were stuck ashore with bodies draped over the machine guns. Death was all around us.

I do not think I ever got to use my hole when word came to me that we were all to move to the north and exit the beach. I was informed to bring up the rear and to be assured that all B Company got off the beach. That turned into a chore. Most of the men started to move to the North and we did fine till we reached the exit. Shells started to come over and several of our men jumped off to the left into a German mine field. I had to yank them out of there and kick butts and threaten some to get them moving. Never forget who they were either. I warned them that they would not have to worry about a shell; they better worry about me because I was ready to leave that hot beach and they were not going to take up too much of my time. Some of those poor bastards got to me I guess. Hell, we were all afraid, so what was new.

We got them up to the top of the Exit (Draw) and came to a halt with everyone in the left side ditch. Word came back that snipers were working us over. I can see the English officer with his Aide walking briskly past up on the dirt road. I called to him regarding the snipers, but he ignored me. I can still see that poor devil on his way back down the road with the seat of his pants all bloody.

In a short time word came back from you (Captain Bienvenu) to move out. I had to kick some more A—— but we all were running like hell, cutting to the right across a field and into this Orchard. I remember hiding behind trees and jumping from tree to tree as I saw you all hunkered down in a nice deep ditch at the base of a large hedge row. I was jumping over mutilated German bodies. I made the ditch and this is where we met again. Did a head count and we were missing some personnel. I remember Gaddy was one of them. Sgt. Fields's squad was not there either, but they came in later in the day. Gaddy came to us the next day. Said he was fighting with the infantry. Never took that seriously. We were facing a church across a field about 150 yards. Thought that we were taking fire from the tower so set up a .50 cal. and Sgt. Pitchler did some shooting. We were still taking sniper fire. Derby and I inspected the house and the large Sand Table set up with all the ranges and gun positions built on it. I made out my Morning Report and sent it to HQ. You then dispatched Sgt. Al Rasche and his squad to make a recon towards Formigy to see if the roads were clear. He reported that it was all clear. Sgt. Fields was using the latrine and almost hit by sniper fire. We were told to dig in for the night and prepare the next day for a counterattack.

Gravel type ground, but very hard to dig in. Sgt. Derby and I dug together and did not get very deep. We faced each other with legs over the other's shoulders. Lots of automatic weapons fire all night. No shells came our way. They sent them to the beach. We slept from exhaustion.

Herbert Campbell, who served in one of the companies that formed the 5th Engineer Special Brigade, transferred from his transport ship to a landing craft.

For that day, we were dressed in gas-proofed clothing. Of course, we had our rifles, steel helmet, combat pack, and grenades. With all this gear on, it made moving about difficult, but with all the German shells going overhead and exploding, and our shells going in towards the Germans, you didn't worry too much about it.

If anyone tells you that he was not scared that day, I just don't believe it. I know I was scared. When the German shell hit our landing craft, it killed a sailor that was approximately three or four feet from me, and the man that started down the ramp ahead of me had his arm almost completely severed from his body. I didn't see him after that; I don't know whether he survived or not. I got hit in the legs and the left and right side of my body. I can still remember the supply sergeant going past us saying, "Men, let's get off of here or we'll all be killed!"

In those moments, I recall as we were pulling in to the beach that there was a house on the sands there. Incidentally, the beach we landed on was called Easy Red. I remember the rockets from our side going towards the Germans, the warships blasting away at them, all the wreckage on the beach, dead bodies there, and I feel very lucky to have come out of it the way I did.

It seems to me that the navy medics were there just within moments after I was hit. They gave me first aid and then they put us on a barge, and I can still remember the navy corpsman saying, "Let's get this out of here before the Germans strafe us again!" We went out into the channel. They put me on a stretcher; it was a wire arrangement of some kind, it looked like a basket. Anyway, here I was. They ran a rope out to the hospital ship, and I was pulled onto the ship in this stretcher. And I tell you, that was a wild ride.

The 5th Engineer Special Brigade was responsible for beaches Easy Red, Fox Green, and Fox Red. According to the after-action report, by 7 A.M., "craft could still unload men seaward of the obstacle belt, but the rapidly rising water was making such landings increasingly difficult. . . . The accuracy of enemy artillery fire was deadly, particularly on the eastern half of the beach where many of the approaching craft were immediately hit." The 37th Engineer Battalion, with the mission of clearing E-1, landed the remainder of its assault group around 8:30 A.M. The units of the 348th Engineer Battalion, assigned to clear F-1, landed near E-1. The 6th Naval Beach Battalion and the 293rd and 294th Joint Assault Signal Companies came ashore near E-1, but not without taking losses.

On the sector of the 6th Engineer Special Brigade (116th Infantry's beaches), the situation was not much better before 9 A.M. Many vehicles were clustered in front of Exits D-3 and E-1, mainly because these were the only sectors where enough obstacles had been cleared for landing. The concentration of vehicles invited enemy artillery fire, however. Although enemy fire continued to hinder the brigade's operations throughout the afternoon, the engineers continued clearing operations on Exits E-1, E-3 and D-1. The German strongpoints at E-3 were only partially neutralized, and the enemy troops continued to slip back into the defenses. Although it was open, Exit F-1 was of limited use while the dozers of the 336th strove to clear it late in the day.

At noon, the 459th Amphibian Truck Company and the 131st Quartermaster Mobile Battal-

A beached LCVP.

ion, both part of the 5th ESB, began to land their preloaded DUKWs, which had been slated to land sixty-five minutes after the beginning of the invasion. It took more than two hours for all the DUKWs to land, but enemy fire began to slacken.

By 3 P.M., German artillery fire still covered all exits from the beach and D-1. Enemy units still defended some strongpoints at D-3 in the 116th Infantry sector. E-3 still remained closed, but vehicles moved through Exit E-1. It was not until the morning of D+1 that most of the exits were opened to traffic.

After suffering heavy losses of the morning, the remnants of the gap assault teams from the 146th and 299th Engineer Combat Battalions regrouped during the afternoon. They salvaged their equipment, gathered some from other units, and continued their beach-clearing operations. Attempts to blow gaps in the obstacles had slowed, because too many soldiers remained in the area. Only single demolitions could be done. Nonetheless, the engineers managed to remove Teller mines from the obstacles and send in the dozers to remove the obstacles. By late in the afternoon, they had cleared five large and six small gaps in the obstacles, five of which were located between Exits E-1 and E-3.

The engineers were the hardest hit at Omaha Beach. Statistics reveal that about one out of four of the approximate 2,000 casualties was an engineer.

In addition to the combat engineer battalions, the beach groups included naval beach battalions, whose mission it was to organize and operate the beaches and coordinate the incoming quartermaster and ordnance units of the group. The 6th Naval Beach Battalion, assigned to the 5th Engineer Special Brigade, arrived during D-Day, and its companies were assigned to each of the beach groups.

Each platoon of Company C, 6th Naval Beach Battalion, was assigned to a company of the 37th Engineer Combat Battalion. The battalion commander, Cmdr. E. C. Carusi, who landed with the first waves, provided exemplary leadership. On the way in, one of the LCIs hit a mine and casualties were taken. Other vessels were also hit by the enemy or encountered obstacles. Company B arrived later in the morning, followed by Company A. By noon, they had cleared lanes in the field of obstacles, marked them for the incoming landing craft, and set up ship-to-shore communications. All the while, the medical teams handled the evacuation of casualties.

Company B landed with the 348th Battalion Beach Group, with the original objective of assisting the operations of the 18th Infantry. PhM3/C Vincent Anthony Kordack of Platoon B-6, Company B, 6th Naval Beach Battalion crossed the Channel on the USS *Henrico*. Since he was not too hungry at breakfast, which consisted of sandwiches, coffee, and apples, he stowed much of it away, not knowing when he would see food again. After that, at about 3 A.M., he watched the infantry of the 1st Division depart the ship. They seemed calm, he thought. At H-Hour, he went below and slept until 8:30 A.M., when his buddy Jerry awoke him to inform him it was time.

> So I put on my aid kits and a few other odds and ends and went topside. We then climbed down the ladder into an LCT. An army officer told us to get comfortable, for we had a long ride, for it was ten miles to shore.
>
> The men were all excited, for they could see our big guns still firing upon the beach. Then all of a sudden, a craft pulled up alongside of us and said to stand by offshore. He said that the Jerries were on the hill and were keeping the infantry on the beach. So all morning long, we drifted about a mile from shore.
>
> We found rations onboard, and I fell asleep around noon and did not wake up till 3 P.M. When I woke up, they said that the infantry had made a charge and went over the top.
>
> The second wave went in around 4 P.M., then they asked us what kind of troops we had onboard. The skipper of the LCT said engineers were aboard, so orders came from the command post on the beach to come in.
>
> Our craft hit the beach at 4:45 P.M., and as the ramps went down and the troops left, the Jerries opened up. A machine gun opened up to our left, then the 88-millimeter laid four or five projectiles around us. When the first 88 hit, I was more stunned than anything else, for I did not know what was going on. But when the second hit, I took cover under a jeep. All the time they fired, it was so close I could hear shrapnel hit my helmet, and sand blew on us.
>
> That was the first time I realized our danger. I could tell I was scared, for my mouth just dried up like a prune. When I left the craft, I had had to wade in water up to my waist for about twenty-five yards. It was the last time I saw any of the corpsmen from B-6 that night. I noticed several DD tanks half underwater.
>
> After I got on the beach and the shelling stopped, I left the jeep and started to dig in. I gave up, for there were only ten yards of sand for us to dig in, and there was a lot of gravel in the sand. I took army packs off two dead soldiers and made a barricade around me. Every time I started to take a few steps, I would trip over a body, for they were scattered all around us. After I had my barricade made, I started to take care of casualties around me. Several of them had arms or legs missing—one body was missing a head. When I returned, the tide was almost at my barricade, so I started to move it. As I was working the Germans started firing again. No wonder they call the 88 the "whistling death," for you can hear the projectiles whistling through the air. They put a few around us, but no one was seriously wounded.
>
> I heard an explosion in the waters, so I stopped and looked around and saw a small

> boat which was hit. Men were running all around the beach. Aboard were casualties, and none of them had life preservers. They were calling at the top of their lungs. One of them was hanging by a rope from another craft. He was hit, and I knew aid had better be gotten to him before long. The water was cold, and he would not last long. The men tried to send rubber boats out to them, but the tide was too strong. One of the fellows and I swam to him and pulled him out. A small boat came and rescued the rest of the men.

As the day continued, Kordack continued to work on the wounded while still under enemy fire. The Germans opened up several times on the area he was in. He saw "an LCT that was knocked out and had been set on fire. On it were six half-tracks; only one ever got off but was hit leaving the ramp. As it burned, the ammunition was set off, and bullets went flying everywhere. The flames shot up at least twenty feet in the air and lit up the whole beach all around us as it grew dark."

Kordack spent part of the night sleeping on the beach, until he was awakened at about 1 A.M. and told they were moving up the hill. He and his comrades followed a path up, nervously dodging mines. At the top of the hill, they began to dig in, only to find that the ground was too rocky. For him and his comrades, the "Longest Day" had extended into the early morning of June 7.

PhM3/C Frank D. Snyder Jr., a nineteen-year-old from Cocoa, Florida, was a member of Platoon B-5 of Company B, 6th Naval Beach Battalion. He was part of the platoon's medical section and had crossed the channel on the APA *Windsor*. He and his fellow sailors were to land on the beach in green fatigues and helmets with the rainbow symbol designating the beach battalion units painted on the front. They boarded their landing craft at about 7 A.M. and circled in the rendezvous area until about 10 A.M., when they received the signal from a patrol craft to form up at the line of departure.

> Upon closely approaching our designated landing site, Beach Fox Green, the patrol craft signaled the boats to stand off and circle up again. This was at a distance of about one mile from Omaha Beach. Smoke of exploding shells on and immediately adjacent to the beach was very heavy, but occasionally the wreckage of boats and other equipment could be seen.
>
> We watched an old four-stack destroyer [there were no old four-stackers at Omaha] move so close in to shore that we wondered how it didn't become grounded. That old tin can opened fire on the high bluff with every gun it had and fired continuously for about five minutes. The air was filled with a steady stream of tracers and the bluff was blanketed with explosions and soon disappeared in a cloud of smoke dust. During that period of heavy fire I imagined that the German defenders could do nothing more than take cover. That old destroyer did take a few hits but soon moved off to deeper water. I feel certain that any man that made it safely ashore that day was directly as a result of the heroic action of the old four-stacker.
>
> Our LCT, with about seventy-five men of the 6th Beach Battalion aboard, grounded ashore several thousand yards to the left of our designated landing point at Fox Green Beach. As the ramp dropped, even before the first corpsmen could disembark into the water, two explosions, either mortar or 88-millimeter shells, bracketed the boat, and shrapnel zinged off in all directions around us. Before jumping off the boat myself, I assisted two army medics carrying aboard an army major whose left arm was gone. Then, making a mad dash for cover, I sought refuge between a knocked-out light tank

[probably a Sherman, as no light tanks had come in yet], but was quickly advised to get away from there, because the enemy had it zeroed in and were occasionally firing at it. In the ensuing confusion, I was unable to find any other men of my platoon, but did locate an aid station that consisted of nothing more than four small Red Cross flags on three-foot-high pegs stuck in the sand outlining a rectangular area about twenty feet by thirty feet. The aid station was manned by four or five medics, one of which was an army doctor.

We worked together. The doctor in charge received orders around noon to move his aid station inland. He said to me, "Get your equipment together, soldier, and let's go!" I replied, "I am not army, sir!" He then said, "Who the hell are you?" I gave him my name and navy rating, and he told me to find my own outfit. I left my field pack with him, since he would probably need it more than I would.

During the course of the afternoon and evening of D-Day, I joined up with other enlisted men of my platoon, and under the direction of two doctors of the 5th Engineer Special Brigade, assisted in loading the wounded who came through their evacuation station onto the landing craft for transport to various ships offshore. As night fell, those of us who had not found our own units were allowed to take refuge in some foxholes already dug in on the side of the bluff overlooking the beach.

Kordack's and Synder's experiences were repeated hundreds of times as the troops reached the beach and milled aimlessly around amid the utter chaos. At least the medics knew that their job was to take care of casualties, and they performed their duties to the best of their abilities. Most of the other soldiers who landed were disoriented or trapped and strove only to survive. As they dashed for cover, they dodged missiles that blew their comrades to pieces and ran past badly mutilated dead and dying soldiers. To add to the horror of the day, the incoming tide started washing ashore the corpses of the troops that had been killed at sea. The few who survived the attack on Omaha Beach felt as if they had to gone to hell and back.

Nightfall brought some degree of relief as the fighting began to slacken. That first night left a lasting impression on some of the survivors, however. "T/4 Al Brown has slept indoors only one night since D-Day . . . and that night he couldn't sleep!" announced the *Dozer Blade* news sheet of the 1121st Engineer Combat Group on March 31, 1945.

That evening, Follow-Up Convoy B, carrying the remaining regiments of the 1st and 29th Divisions, rode the waves offshore. Originally it had been slated to land most of these troops after noon. Because of the reverses suffered by the initial assault waves and the need to clear the beaches and land equipment, however, the landing of these units was delayed first until late afternoon and then until the next morning on D+1. Among these waiting troops was 1st Sgt. Ernest Lee, whose friend Sgt. Bill Lewis was already on the beach. They had been together from the time they had transferred from the 36th Texas National Guard Division in 1942 to a special intelligence unit in Maryland until they volunteered for the 29th Division. Lee was a member of the I&R Platoon of the HQ Company of the 175th Infantry Regiment. His platoon had been slated to board an LST, land its jeeps at noon on D-Day, and drive inland as far as St. Lô to conduct a reconnaissance. After the debacle on the beach, its orders were changed. Meanwhile, according to 1st Lt. Carl Hobbs, the S-2 of the 1st Battalion, 175th Infantry:

We weren't all that close to the beach. We were probably out three or four miles, and

Landing craft move in during the buildup off Omaha Beach.

we could not see the individual soldiers on the beach. If the first troops had gone in with little resistance, we would have gone in earlier. We expected to go in later the first day or in the night, but it was not to be. While aboard ship, I looked through the operations book for Overlord. It was a huge book of about 200 to 400 pages, with lots of maps and details including on supplies, equipment and the landings.

Review of Events on Omaha Beach

At the end of D-Day, Omaha Beach was littered with dead and wounded soldiers and abandoned or wrecked equipment and vehicles, as the survivors of this near-debacle sought shelter as best they could. Nonetheless, the infantry regiments managed to create a sort of beachhead perimeter only about a mile or so inland with the support of elements of tank battalions that had survived the landings. The supporting units such as the quartermaster units and beach battalions, under the direction of the engineer special brigades, began to organize and operate the beachhead. Without these units, the whole invasion would have been doomed.

Some of the vital exits from the beach were opened. The strongpoint guarding D-1 at Vierville was silenced at about 1 P.M. The guns of a destroyer blew to pieces the German position at Pointe de la Percée, which had resisted for most of the day. The 121st Engineers blew up the anti-tank wall, and traffic finally began to roll through Exit D-1 by 5 P.M., although enemy artillery fire continued until dark. The important exit at D-3 remained closed to the Americans on D-Day, because the German strongpoints continued to hold out.

German resistance at St. Laurent tied up traffic exiting from E-1, but by 4 P.M., the engineers cut a detour to the coastal highway, although the naval fire support team and destroyers tried without success to locate and neutralize an enemy battery firing on E-1. At 5 P.M., the 336th Engineers finally reached Exit F-1 and began to clear it and cut a road through the draw. The 745th Tank Battalion moved through this new exit by 8 P.M. to support the left flank. The surviving tanks of the 741st and 743rd Tank Battalions moved forward in the center of the beachhead and at Vierville.

The artillery made it to shore by the end of the day, lending its support to the beleaguered troops already there. The surviving 105-millimeter howitzer of the 111th FA Battalion joined with the 7th FA Battalion in the early afternoon and fired the only mission from the beachhead at 4:15 P.M. The 62nd FA Battalion fired supporting missions from LCTs in the morning and finally landed six M-7 self-propelled guns at 6:30 P.M. Two other howitzers were lost, eight landed at Fox Green in the evening, but no shore missions were fired. The 32nd FA Battalion landed in the evening, losing two guns and twenty-five vehicles. This brought the total to five artillery battalions on shore by the evening with a loss of twenty-six guns. Two AAA (AW) Battalions had been slated to land during the day to support the beachhead against air attack, but they had to wait until D+1 to land.

The supply situation did not develop as planned either. Only 100 out of 2,400 tons actually reached Omaha Beach that day. The DUKWs played a critical role since 90 of 110 carrying badly needed supplies landed successfully. The quartermaster units and beach battalions expedited the movement and distribution of the vitally needed supplies, and had the situation well in hand by the next day. Fortunately, each infantry unit carried additional ammunition and the tanks towed ammo trailers. The loss of fifty landing craft and ten larger vessels and the damage to many others made resupply more difficult, however.

General Huebner, the commander of the 1st Division, was ashore at Easy Red by 7 P.M., and General Gerow, with his advance headquarters for the V Corps, landed after 10:30. The last regiment ashore that day was the 26th Infantry, which arrived at 11 P.M. It was badly needed, since the V Corps had suffered between 2,000 and 3,000 casualties. The 16th and 116th Infantry Regiments alone had lost about 1,000 each. The inability of the Germans to launch a serious counterattack saved the day for the Allies. As darkness fell on the bloody battlefield, twenty-two aircraft of the *Luftwaffe* launched a night raid against the fleet, but with little success.

CHAPTER 14

U.S. and British Perspectives on D-Day

The only surprise about what has been known as the greatest amphibious invasion in history was its timing. The Germans grossly overestimated the threat of the massive land, air, and naval force, which served to validate Field Marshal Erwin Rommel's prediction that the invasion must be defeated in the first twenty-four hours or the Reich would be doomed. The actual number of Allied divisions was smaller than those the Germans had faced in the west in 1914 or 1940. This time, however, there were only a few dozen German divisions, of variable quality, many of which were static formations lacking mobility, to defend the hundreds of miles of coastline. In the West, the news media kept the public informed of the situation. But the media commentators' speculations did not alarm the security services as much as did fortuitously coincidental items such as a crossword puzzle containing the words "Utah," "Omaha," and "Neptune" that appeared in a newspaper.

In January 1944, the leading news magazines in the United States began speculating about the "Big Invasion of 1944." *Time* magazine reported at the end of the month that Gen. Omar Bradley and George Patton might each lead an army in the coming invasion. The Germans were concerned about Patton's appearance in England as commander of the First U.S. Army Group (FUSAG), not realizing he and his command were decoys. The media unwittingly helped the Patton ploy succeed.

Media Reports from the Winter of 1943–44

U.S. News and World Report published an issue on secret weapons early in January 1944. Since an invasion by a massive Allied force would take place that year, almost everyone in the West was confident that their armies would be unstoppable unless the Germans had some surprises in store. Since 1942, the Germans had been defeated on every front facing the Western Allies. Even secret weapons, such as the glider bomb, had failed to stop the Allied invasion at Salerno. Older and not-so-secret weapons, such as the dive-bomber, the Tiger tank, magnetic mines, and even the American bazooka, no longer had the advantage of surprise. Berlin announced that "tremendous rocket guns" installed along the English Channel were aimed at important targets in Great Britain. The Germans were possibly alluding to their secret V-3 project. The construction of the first of fifty huge rocket launchers had begun at Mimoyecques, near Calais, in late 1943. The Allied Bomber Command began bombing this location in November 1943, however. It seems, therefore, that the announcement, which came a month after D-Day, was most likely a bluff on the part of the Germans, as the new weapon site could not have been completed at that point.

Another secret weapon mentioned in German sources was a "projectile that exhausted the oxygen for miles around and would suffocate all human life within the area." This weapon, they claimed, could obliterate entire divisions. They were probably hinting at an atomic weapon, but Allied commandos had already brought to a standstill Germany's development of this kind of weapon when they struck at the enemy's heavy water supply in Norway.

For a while, the Allies had feared the possibility of gas warfare, but because the Germans no longer dominated the sky, this was ruled out as a serious threat. Nonetheless, both Allied and German troops continued to carry gas masks. The Western media also considered briefly, but ruled out, Germany's ability to conduct bacteriological warfare, particularly after a Swedish university professor, Louis Backman, postulated in a February 1944 article in *Time* that the flu epidemics occurring in Europe might have been caused by organisms arriving from Venus, Jupiter, or Mars.

The newspapers and magazines were full of reports on events from around the world, especially the Allies' bombing missions against German targets prior to D-Day and the campaign in the Italian peninsula. Occasionally, a few seemingly unimportant items found their way into the news, but what might be reported in one country was not always considered of significance in another. Thus on April 8, 1944, the *London Times* reported that the Turkish supply of chrome in England was falling as it increased in Germany. The Germans were even loaning the Turks additional rolling stock to move the vital mineral along the old Baghdad-to-Berlin railroad. On April 21, the British news reported that the chrome shipments to Germany had stopped. A week earlier, the *Times* had also reported that the Allies were pressuring the Swedes to stop selling ball bearings to Germany. None of this seemed to cripple the German war machine.

Not surprisingly, however, the anticipated invasion of France dominated the news. At the beginning of April, *U.S. News and World Report* stated that England was bulging with thousands of tanks, guns, and other vehicles. The buildup, it claimed, was not a secret; only the landing site of the invasion was.

The date of the invasion was of the utmost concern for most people. At the end of March, the media announced that a ten-mile-deep strip of coast covering the length of Southern England had been closed to civilian visitors, and that the civilian airmail service to Europe and Africa had been stopped.

Even foreign diplomats soon found themselves trapped in England. Tension was building in antic-

The wounded wait to be evacuated.

ipation of the invasion. On April 10, *Time* magazine speculated that if the invasion did not take place in April, it would be a serious blow to Hitler's prestige, because he had withdrawn troops from the east, in the face of advancing Soviets, to bolster the defenses in the west. The magazine also claimed that French civilians were being evacuated from the Calais coastal area and flooding was taking place in the Low Countries. The media correctly reported that Hitler had shifted the 10th SS Panzer Division from France to the east, having withdrawn many troops (an overestimate) a few days earlier from Norway, where morale was low. The media also reported that a surprise attack had disabled the battleship *Tirpitz* in its Norwegian anchorage, disquieting the German troops stationed in Scandinavia. In a press conference, Rommel informed the German media that tides and weather conditions would favor an April invasion. No invasion materialized, however.

The correspondents in England set up their own betting pool to select the invasion date. The Soviet correspondent from *Tass* predicted the earliest date, April 20. The British reporter from Reuters went to the other extreme, with September 1. The Swiss estimated that the invasion would take place between May 6 and June 7. An editor in Madrid calculated that the landings would take place the first week of May, at either 4:41 A.M. on Saturday or 4:39 A.M. on Sunday. The Finns, on the other hand, reported that the invasion had already begun.

The May 1 issue of *Time* announced that "Berlin had a profound case of jitters," and the

Germans were desperately fishing for information. In Berlin, the media reported that the German forces were on the highest state of alert and knew that the Allies were moving to the invasion ports. A girl assigned to a barrage balloon joked that the Allied buildup was so heavy that "England would sink if you cut the balloons lose." A *Time* reporter claimed that the island was "groaning from the vast weight of men, machines and materiels pile up for D-Day, there was tension." The May 5 issue of *U.S. News and World Report* noted a shift in the air war. Soon the papers were full of stories about bombings of numerous targets in Western Europe, especially in the vicinity of the Pas de Calais, which they claimed indicated that the invasion was imminent.

It is clear that German intelligence also relied on American and British news sources, as some of the captured enemy files contained clippings referring to units in training or transit. The Germans certainly must have been dismayed in mid-May, when articles calculated quite accurately the strength of their infantry and armored divisions in the west. *Time*, for instance, estimated that the German forces included about forty divisions in Denmark, the Low Countries, and France, without counting fifteen infantry divisions and five to seven panzer divisions held in reserve by Rommel and twelve divisions in Norway. The same magazine also speculated that landings could not take place in areas with cliffs, bluffs, or marshes. In addition, the invasion had to be be near a port, the closer to England, the better. The Germans apparently embraced a similar theory, deciding that the area between the Somme and Ostend would be the most likely target. Despite all the speculation, however, the Allied High Command succeeded in keeping secret from everyone—including the Germans—the actual date and location of the invasion.

On May 16, the *New York Times* informed its readers that the Germans were increasing their aerial surveillance over Britain, and that twenty Nazi aircraft had been shot down. "Twin sweeps by the *Luftwaffe* over the South and Southeast coasts of Britain last night [May 15] during which 15 German planes were shot down, now appear to have been for the purpose of recon rather than attack . . . as D-Day draws nearer."

Also on May 16, reporter Drew Middleton wrote from London that the Germans, helped by the cloud cover and bad weather, were concentrating aircraft and ships in Northwest Europe to launch an attack on the Allied invasion forces as soon as they rendezvoused for their journey across the Channel. He also reported that the *Luftwaffe*, "despite serious losses, is continuing its new offensive against Britain which is aimed at south coast towns."

In mid-May, German radio stations surmised that the great air offensive was the harbinger of a major invasion. The Allies' intelligence and counterintelligence intercepted two foreign radio reports that confirmed that their efforts to mislead the enemy were succeeding. In the first, a Nazi-controlled radio station claimed that the Allies were massing fifty divisions and 80,000 paratroopers for the invasion. The second was a Swedish transmission, supposedly using German sources that reported that the Allies had assembled fifty British and forty to fifty American divisions with combined air forces of 10,000 aircraft.

On May 27, the *London Times* said that according to the German news service, "Eisenhower has again missed the invasion bus," because it would be another month before the weather, moon, and tide conditions would favor an invasion from England. Thus, the Germans concluded, General Eisenhower had not yet completed his invasion preparations.

The Last Days of Anxiety: Reports from June 1944

As the month of June began, it seemed as if the "world was holding its breath," except for the

Off the Normandy beaches, the fleet antiaircraft guns open fire during a night attack.

soldiers, sailors, and airmen fighting in the Mediterranean and on the fronts against Japan. The soldiers in England, who had moved at the end of May into the "sausage" or "cigar" camps near their ports of embarkation or to the isolated sections of airfields, knew that the fateful day was on hand. Even the civilians in England could sense that something was afoot. Fortunately, this secret remained confined to the island. The Germans, however, were fairly confident that the weather and tidal conditions would not be right during the first week of June, even though their intelligence sources had intercepted signals for an uprising of the French Resistance. Amazingly, they disregarded information stolen from the British embassy in Turkey by a spy code-named Cicero, which pinpointed the invasion points with some degree of accuracy.

During the first days of June, the press continued to focus on preinvasion bombings along the French coast, especially between Boulogne and Dunkirk. Drew Middleton wrote another article warning that the Germans were increasing their strength in the west, including the number of panzer divisions and that two German army groups were already stationed there: one under Rommel and the other under Blaskowitz. Middleton also expected the Germans to launch a counter-offensive within ten days of the invasion. An Allied officer, he wrote, had warned that it was a mistake to equate a successful landing with victory and ignore the danger of a serious counterattack.

According to the German press, their armored formations were prepared to spend the first days of the invasion disposing of the "airborne bridgehead." It seems that the German press fully expected a heavy concentration of airborne troops well inland, behind the seaborne forces, especially near Paris. General Marshall had indeed

Photographing the War

First Lt. Arnold N. Delmonico from Moosup, Connecticut, reached England in the spring to take command of a photography unit with thirty-three enlisted men of the 490th Bomb Group's HQ Squadron. He had enlisted in the army in 1939 and took part in offshore patrols looking for U-boats before the United States entered the war. Later, he became an officer. In the late spring of 1944, he led a photographic team equipped with aerial and ground cameras. The team's sole mission was to photograph anything that might be of interest at the base or in the air. Although most of his men were not anxious to fly on combat missions, they did so out of necessity.

Before each mission, Delmonico mounted a camera on the floor behind the bomb bay. The camera was programmed to continue clicking at eleven-second intervals after the bombs were released, long enough to follow them down. Each of the group's squadrons carried three mounted cameras. "Since none of the boys wanted to go, and I wasn't going to force them, I took on the job on my own for selected missions," confesses Delmonico years later. When he went, he took along his personal Speed Graphic K-20 camera, a 35-millimeter Leica camera, and a 16-millimeter Bolex movie camera. He would fly in the waist of a B-24 aircraft or up front in the nose of a B-17, which had more room than the B-24. He filmed from both positions in either type of heavy bomber.

He flew his first mission over enemy territory in late May, shortly after his unit went into operation. He did not realize that these were the prebombing missions for the invasion, an event he could not miss. During this first mission, he pushed his luck while flying in the waist of a B-24.

> I was unaware as to what to expect. As we approached the French coast, we were informed to put on our flak suits, which consisted of vests and an apron that hung down to your knee. I was sitting on the lower part of the vest, and the next thing I knew an announcement came over the intercom, "Flak at ten o'clock," and that was my first view of flak with its black puffs and explosions. Immediately after that, one went off underneath, and I hit the ceiling because a piece of shrapnel hit below, and I was scared as anything. I quickly reached for the lower part of the flak suit to put it on, and there was a nice big hole in the bottom of the aircraft. I put that flak suit back over it because it saved me once and might do it again.

The biggest photo opportunity of all presented itself to Delmonico only about a week after his first mission, on June 6. He knew he could not pass it up.

> We were scheduled to fly two missions on June 6. I went on the first mission, and there was heavy cloud cover as we went over the Channel. There was one small break in the clouds, and as I looked down, I could see the water. I have never seen so many ships in my life and could see nothing but wakes as they approached the landing points. It was a

continued

Photographing the War ***continued***

sight to behold. We went on to our target, dropped our bombs, and came back. It was light when we left France.

The weather and darkness prevented him from photographing the fleet. During the remainder of the day, he recorded various activities on the base. Later that day, he flew on the second mission over St. Lô, where he photographed the dropping of the bombs, but not much else. The photographic material proved to be no more spectacular than that from later missions. Few aerial photographs exist from the morning of the invasion.

contemplated an airborne invasion in the vicinity of Évreux. Was it just a coincidence that 12th SS Panzer Division was stationed in that area? In fact, some panzer units were intended to deal with landings behind the beach area.

Later in early June, the media shifted its attention to operations in Italy, where the Allied armies were on the move and Rome lay in their path. Other news items began to supplant the possible invasion. American bombers were using bases in Russia, and Marshal Tito successfully eluded a major German strike against his headquarters in the mountains of Yugoslavia. Hidden in the back pages, however, were snippets of information of concern to Allied airmen. One article, titled "German Admits Fliers' Lynchings," mentioned that German officials reported that irate mobs of citizens, supposedly "primitive country folk," had on occasion lynched fliers who came down in their area. The German minister of propaganda, Joseph Goebbels, tried to blame these actions on Allied pilots who practiced "man hunting" from their aircraft. The Allies strongly condemned these acts. Swedish news sources, on the other hand, dismissed them as mere fabrications of the German propaganda machine.

On June 1, the American public was informed of a new wave of terror sweeping through the west as the Gestapo arrested and executed hundreds of "patriots." In London, news spread that the Germans were "ravaging" the Dordogne Department of southwest France. The report was not exaggerated; the 2nd SS Panzer Division with the help of local French Fascist units were the culprits.[1]

The next day, the news of a poison gas attack in Brooklyn that had killed a thousand people splashed across newspapers around the United States. Despite the mass hysteria, however, it turned out that it was not a German secret weapon; instead, a steel cylinder full of chlorine gas had leaked while in transit.

When it was announced on June 2 that mail was delayed in reaching the United States because of "transportation and pre-invasion censorship of mail," the American public realized that events were taking a serious turn. Some people had not received mail for up to two weeks. Allied intelligence officials did not seem concerned, however, that this official statement might let the cat out of the bag.

On June 3, the newspapers around the world were brimming with invasion warnings. *The London Daily Mail* reported that according to the paper of a Spanish town on the French border, successive pinpoint bombings of secret military

1. On June 10, several days after the invasion the 2nd SS Panzer Division slaughtered the inhabitants of the village of Oradour in retaliation for the activities of the French Forces of the Interior (FFI).

headquarters in The Hague and France had made officers of German invasion headquarters in Western Europe extremely uneasy.

On June 4, the media reported a great deal of activity in Western Europe and the arrival of American forces in the outskirts of Rome. The Calais area was being blasted by the Allied air forces, and "the most battered section of Hitler's Atlantic wall and daily target of Allied air attack for almost fifty days, received morning and afternoon batterings yesterday." As Americans read these reports over their morning coffee, the invasion fleet was leaving British ports, but then turned back because bad weather.

On June 6, the British public first learned about the invasion from radio announcements, whereas Americans read about it in late editions of their daily newspapers. Most details were not forthcoming until the June 7 editions, however. The headline of the *New York Times* trumpeted, "Allied Armies Land in France in the Havre-Cherbourg Area; Great Invasion is Under Way." The paper also carried Communiqué No. 1 from Allied headquarters (SHAEF): "Under the command of General Eisenhower, Allied naval forces, supported by strong air forces, began landing Allied armies this morning on the northern coast of France." The news had been released at 6:30 A.M. London Time, 12:30 A.M. Eastern War Time in the United States.

The German agency DNB reported that Allied invasion operations began with the landing of airborne troops near the mouth of the Seine and maintained that the "center of gravity" was at Caen. At 10 A.M., the DNB said that the Anglo-American troops had been reinforced at dawn at the mouth of the Seine River in the Havre area, Germans shock troops had moved to meet the Allied airborne units and the first clashes ranged between Cherbourg and Le Havre. Furthermore, the DNB claimed, large-scale amphibious landings had taken place between the Seine estuary and the mouth of the Vire (there were no landings near the Seine), most parachutists who were dropped in large formations near airfields were already eliminated (no major drops took place near any airfields in Normandy), and the British 1st Airborne Division was "badly mauled" (actually, the 6th Airborne Division was dropped with relatively good results, and the 1st was not used).

Capt. Ludwig Sertorius, the German DNB commentator, announced that the "great contest between the Reich and the Anglo-Americans has begun."[2] This last statement was unquestionably true, even though many members of the German High Command failed to see it. Sertorius also mentioned that the feeling among the German panzer forces was simply "They are coming."

SHAEF announced that several feints had been launched on June 6 to confuse the Germans. Apparently, at the end of the day, some, such as Hitler, were still confused and looking in the wrong direction, believing the actual invasion was the feint. It was not, and Allied troops would soon be fighting their way inland.

2. Sertorius may have only been this commentator's sobriquet.

GLOSSARY

Aldis Lamp. A signal lamp used on ships for sending Morse Code.

Axis. The alliance of Germany, Italy, Japan, and other countries.

Bailey Bridge. A British designed sectional panel bridge used by American army engineers. The panels were put together to make the desired length of bridge and one of the proper capacity for the anticipated load and then pushed over the gap it was to span by the troops.

Bangalores. Bangalore torpedoes. Invented by the British shortly before World War I and adopted by the U.S. Army in World War II, this was an explosive attached to an expandable pole. The pole was made of five-foot rods screwed together and was used to push the explosive charge toward the area that had to be cleared—under barbed wire, in a minefield, or even in a bunker embrasure.

Barracks Bag. A fabric bag for personal items such as clothing. Troops were issued duffle bags after 1943 to replace the two barracks bags (A and B), one of which was used for dirty laundry.

Bigots. Those individuals with top-secret clearance for invasion planning.

Bocage. The hedgerows or the hedgerow country of Normandy more generally.

Bofors. A 40-millimeter antiaircraft artillery weapon developed by the Swedish Bofors armaments manufacturer, which also produced 20-millimeter and 25-millimeter weapons.

Bosun's Mate. Same as boatswain's mate; a petty officer in charge of deck duties on a ship.

Bunker. A defensive position that can be constructed of wood, earth, and/or concrete. It can include anything from a small defensive structure for small arms to larger gun casemates and submarine pens.

Casemate. A concrete bunker with a position or positions for weapons mounted in embrasures in the walls.

Cloche. A bell-shaped cupola that does not rotate or retract. Some German bunkers in Normandy used these for observation and machine guns.

Coaster. Small ship that could negotiate shallow water and serve smaller coastal ports.

Dragon's Teeth. Concrete pyramidal structures of varying heights placed in several lines to impede armored vehicles.

E-Boat. German torpedo boat properly identified as S-boat for "fast boat."

Gig. A military demerit.

Hards. Concrete ramps built in English harbors to aid in loading landing craft.

Hedgehogs. Obstacles varying in design and including such items as a concrete star with four legs that looks like a giant jack from a child's set of jacks. They can be made of steel or iron rails, logs, or concrete and have three legs.

Hedgerow. A hedge consisting of trees, bushes, and earth created to serve as fences for farmer's fields in Normandy and southern England.

Higgins Boat. An early assault landing craft without ramps. Later assault craft with ramps—such as LCP(R) and LCVP—were constructed by Andrew Higgins of New Orleans, and the name was often applied to them.

Lighters. Shallow draft vessels that could unload large ships that drew too much water to unload in a small harbor or on a beach.

Luftwaffe. The German Air Force.

Mae West. Name given to a life preserver invented by sixteen-year-old Andrew Toti and sold to the War Department in 1936. The sailors and soldiers gave it the nickname since it made them appear to have a large bosom like the movie star Mae West.

Moors. A large treeless area covered by coarse grasses, heather, and/or mosses.

Mulberry. The artificial harbors developed by the British.

Mussette Bag. A bag, usually of canvas, that had a shoulder strap or a set of straps that could make it into a backpack.

Nissan Hut. Developed by the British in World War I, this was a simple structure with walls and roof made from a corrugated steel sheet bent giving the structure its distinctive shape.

Panzer. German term for armor. Usually refers to German tanks or armored units.

Para-Packs. These were equipment packs attached to the bottom of an aircraft or pushed out the door by the crew chief. The packs could carry a variety of weapons components, ammunition, or other types of supplies.

Pathfinders. Specially trained paratroopers dropped before the main body of troops in order to mark the drop zones. Can also refer to aircraft flying in advance of a bomber group to locate or mark the target area.

Petty Officers. The navy's equivalent of NCOs.

PFF Bombing. Aircraft tactic in which a Pathfinder Force uses special radar equipment to guide the main bomber force to the target.

Pillbox. A small defensive structure for light weapons.

Pom Pom. A rapid-fire, twin-barrel antiaircraft weapon.

PT Boat. American "patrol torpedo" boat.

Quonset Hut. American version of the more easily constructed Nissan Hut.

Renault Tank. French tanks built by Renault before 1941. A number of the turrets from the older Renault FT 17 tanks were placed in Tobruk-like positions in the German Atlantic Wall and South Wall.

Rhino Ferry. Large motorized barge.

***Stars & Stripes*.** Newspaper published for the U.S. Armed Forces first appearing in the U.S. Civil War and then returning in World I.

Tac Officer. Refers to a "tactical" officer during training.

U-Boat. German submarine

Tetrahedrons. A four-faced obstacle that could be conrete pyramids or a set of rails bolted together to form a four-sided pyramid.

Tetrytol. A high explosive more powerful than TNT. It consists of about 30 percent TNT and 70 percent of the more sensitive tetryl.

Tobruk. A small defensive position the Germans copied from the Italians after seeing it in use in North Africa.

Toggalier. Enlisted man used as a bombardier without a bombsight when bomber formations dropped their bombs based on lead bombers in the formation.

V-Mail. A special single-page form that was photographed onto microfilm and reprinted at the destination to save shipping space.

V Weapons. V-1 flying bombs and V-2 rockets, the first in a series of German "Vengeance" weapons.

Wehrmacht. The German Armed Forces.

***Yank*.** The weekly army magazine published during Word War II. The last issue was December 28, 1945.

ACKNOWLEDGMENTS

It took the accounts of more than 200 veterans to put this project together. There are too many names to list here, but all are listed with their unit in the bibliography (found in volume 3). Here we would simply like to acknowledge some of those who provided additional materials, such as memoirs or books, and gave permission to quote from them. Some veterans, like Larry Knecht and Peter Trioli, even conducted interviews for us early in the 1990s. In addition, we would like to thank the staff at NARA for helping us locate records; J. R. Slaughter (veteran), who allowed us to use accounts from his early manuscript; John Votaw (former director of the 1st Division Museum), who provided us with written accounts from a number of veterans; and Humphreys Publishing for permission to use excerpts from *Semmes America* by Curt Guenther and Anderson Humphreys. Thanks to those listed below who gave permission to quote from their books or unpublished manuscripts. And thanks, as well, to Chris Evans and Dave Reisch of Stackpole Books for taking on this project.

Special thanks go to John "Slim" Stokes, our reader, who spent many hours correcting errors in the manuscript and helping locate veterans with whom we had lost contact during the past fifteen years. We apologize to anyone we may have forgotten to mention.

Sadly, since we began this project in 1989, many of the veterans who contributed their accounts have passed away. It took until 2007 to find a publisher interested in this book, and by that time, many of the contributors had either forgotten about us or assumed the book would never be done. Some, like Robert Dove and Ray Hood, remained in contact and waited patiently, but passed away in the last few years. We regret that they and many other contributors will never see the final product, but we hope that their families and descendants will take the time to read their accounts. This work is dedicated to all those veterans who took part in this project and all those who fought bravely for their country.

The following is a partial list of those who made contributions to this volume:

Lt. Col. John A. Allison (veteran), who provided a copy of his memoirs.

Steven E. Anders, PhD, Command Historian, U.S. Army Quartermaster Center at Fort Lee, who provided information on army rations

Mark Bando, who provided data on the 101st Airborne Division and gave us additional contacts

Sidney Berger (veteran), who provided copy of his manuscript.

Raus Blondo (veteran), who provided a copy of the 112th Engineer Combat Battalion history

Byron Cook (veteran), provided a copy of his manuscript, *Little Boy Blue*

X. B. Cox (veteran), who provided a copy of his memoirs

Gerard M. Devlin, who provided contacts and additional information on airborne operations not included in his books

Eugene E. Eckstam (veteran), who provided additional material on Operation Tiger

Ray B. Hood (veteran), who provided a copy of his memoirs and other material, including a piece of his parachute from Normandy.

Wardell Hopper (veteran), who provided a copy of the history of the 741st Tank Battalion

Jack Ilfrey (veteran), who provided a copy of part of his 20th Fighter Group Unit History and the unit's association newsletters

Larry Knecht (veteran), who provided additional material and contacts for the 4th Division

Allan L. Langdon (veteran), who provided a copy of his manuscript

Rev. Melvin Larson (veteran), who provided new details for this book and another project

William Lewis (veteran), who stayed in contact and provided additional information for this and other projects

Bernard Lowry, who helped locate sites in England referred to by veterans (who often could not spell place names properly) and clarified details related to American bases in England

Harold Martino (veteran), who provided a copy of his unpublished manuscript

Ray Merriam, who provided contacts with veterans and copies of what are now rare books

Col. Don Patton, who located former veterans

Robert Robinson, who provided a copy of the captain's secret report on the sinking of DD *Meredith*

Gordon Rottman, who provided details on various items of equipment and special units

Capt. Robert Rowe, USN, who provided copies of invasion maps from his study of the first wave in Normandy

Harold Schebeck (veteran), who provided a copy of his memoirs

Jack Schlegel (veteran), who provided a copy of an interview given by Lt. Malcolm Brannen at a reunion

J. R. Slaughter (veteran), who provided a copy of his early manuscript concerning veterans of the 29th Division

John Stokes, our main reader of the manuscript who also helped with research

Lee Unterborn, who helped with general research and loaned books

John Votaw, of the 1st Infantry Division Museum at Cantigny, Chicago, who provided veterans' accounts, contacts, and information on the 1st Division

Steve Zaloga, who provided various items from NARA on operations in Normandy

We also thank all the veterans who contributed their accounts (they are listed with the bibliography in volume 3). We apologize for omitting the names of anyone who helped us along the way.

INDEX